To Kay and Marlo and Erica and Henry

MARSHALL LEE BOOK

Technical consultant: Joseph Gannon

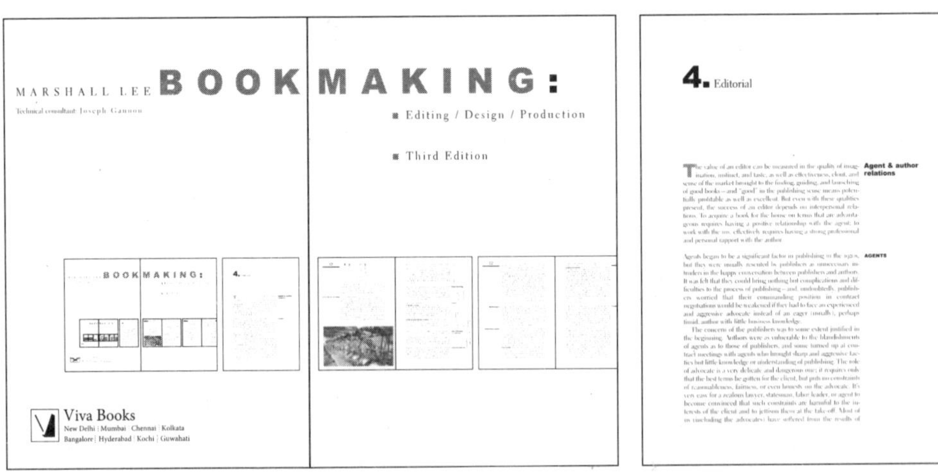

Viva Books
New Delhi | Mumbai | Chennai | Kolkata
Bangalore | Hyderabad | Kochi | Guwahati

MAKING:

Editing / Design / Production

Third Edition

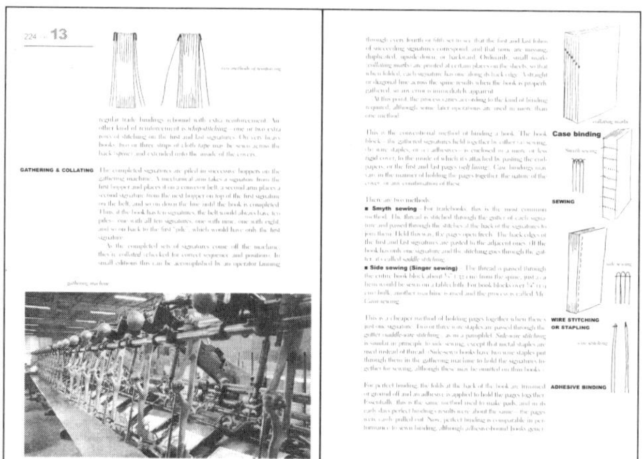

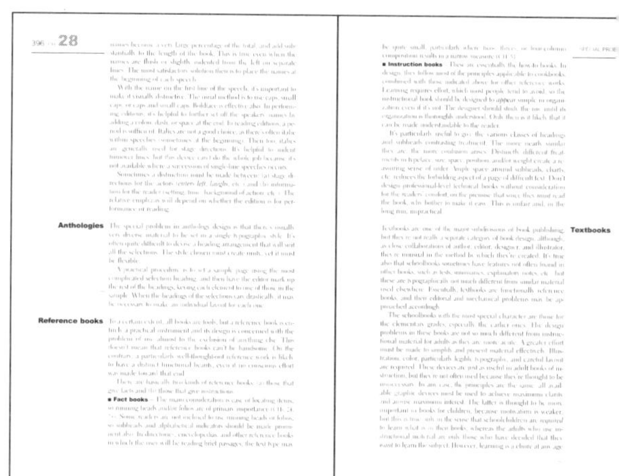

First Indian Edition 2010

VIVA BOOKS PRIVATE LIMITED

- 4737/23 Ansari Road, Daryaganj, New Delhi 110 002
  E-mail: vivadelhi@vivagroupindia.net, Tel. 42242200
- 76, Service Industries, Shirvane, Sector 1, Nerul, Navi Mumbai 400 706
  E-mail: vivamumbai@vivagroupindia.net, Tel. 27721273, 27721274
- Jamals Fazal Chambers, 26 Greams Road, Chennai 600 006
  E-mail: vivachennai@vivagroupindia.net, Tel. 28290304, 28294241
- B-103, Jindal Towers, 21/1A/3 Darga Road, Kolkata 700 017
  E-mail: vivakolkata@vivagroupindia.net, Tel. 22836381, 22816713
- 7, Sovereign Park Apartments, 56-58, K. R. Road, Basavanagudi, Bangalore 560 004
  E-mail: vivabangalore@vivagroupindia.net, Tel. 26607409, 26607410
- 101-102 Mughal Marc Apartments, 3-4-637 to 641, Narayanguda, Hyderabad 500 029
  E-mail: vivahyderabad@vivagroupindia.net, Tel. 27564481, 27564482
- Beevi Towers, First Floor, SRM Road, Kaloor, Kochi 682 018, Kerala
  E-mail: vivakochi@vivagroupindia.net, Tel: 0484-2403055, 2403056
- 232, GNB Road, Beside UCO Bank, Silpukhuri, Guwahati 781 003
  E-mail: vivaguwahati@vivagroupindia.net, Tel: 0361-2666386

www.vivagroupindia.com

Published by arrangement with

W. W. Norton & Company, Inc.
500 Fifth Avenue, New York
N. Y. 10110

ISBN: 978-81-309-1517-3

Published by Vinod Vasishtha for Viva Books Private Limited, 4737/23, Ansari Road, Daryaganj, New Delhi 110 002. Printed and bound by Swan Press, New Delhi.

ACKNOWLEDGMENTS

A major debt of gratitude and respect is owed to friend and colleague JOSEPH GANNON, whose profound knowledge of the technology and processes of bookmaking was indispensable in the writing of this book.

Many thanks to SUSAN LUSK for her technical advice and her significant contribution to this revision of the Second Edition. Thanks also to George P. Davidson for his early encouragement and his valuable comments on the final manuscript, and to Clive Giboire, Stephen Franzino, James Kelly, Jean Kunnold, Vicky Bijur, and the staff of W. W. Norton, who helped me bring *Bookmaking* up to date. And thanks to the many unnamed others who gave their time to answer my questions.

A special mention goes to Nancy Green, my editor at Norton, whose patient support and unyielding, but sorely tested, faith in my eventual completion of the work I hope and trust will be well rewarded.

It may be assumed that despite exhaustive efforts to get things right, some errors remain in the text. For these, and all opinions expressed, the author takes full responsibility.

ML

Read this first

The following paragraphs define the terms and explain the concepts and premises on which this book is based.

BOOK EDITING is the preparation of the content of a book, and sometimes its conception and planning, in cooperation with the author and designer.

BOOK DESIGN is the conception, planning, and specifying of the physical and visual attributes of a book.

BOOK PRODUCTION is the execution of the design, i.e., purchasing materials and services, scheduling and routing the work, coordinating the manufacture of the book with distribution requirements, and maintaining records.

Book editing, design, and production are all parts of a single function—*transmitting the author's message to the reader in the best possible way.* This means creating a product that can be profitably sold, as well as satisfying the requirements of author and reader. The term BOOKMAKING is used to express the whole function.

The word BOOK applies to many different kinds of products. As often as possible, the following text refers to a specific category of book (text, reference, paperback, juvenile, etc.), but when the term is used alone it may be taken to mean *tradebook,* the conventional hardcover book sold to the general public.

A WELL-DESIGNED BOOK means one that's (a) appropriate to its content and use, (b) economical, and (c) satisfying to the senses. It isn't a "pretty" book in the superficial sense and it's not necessarily more elaborate than usual.

ECONOMICAL means an efficient use of the graphic and material elements of the book and the money spent for its manufacture. This doesn't necessarily imply the smallest possible expenditure, but rather the smallest expenditure that will achieve the most successful result.

It's assumed that the importance of being PRACTICAL and ECONOMICAL at all times is understood, so reminders to this effect will remain implied rather than stated.

Each technical or special term is italicized the first time it occurs in a significant sense, and usually its meaning is given directly or by the context. At the back of the book is an Index, in which every italicized term is listed alphabetically. In the text there are references to other chapters (CH. 20, etc.) in which a term or subject is discussed.

Grammatical usage in the text defers to logic and efficiency more than custom. For example, space and reading time are saved by the use of contractions and abbreviations for some frequently used terms; in quotation punctuation, British practice (used throughout the English-speaking world) is followed; commas are used wherever they contribute to clarity.

This volume is *an outline of practical information and procedure* for those engaged in planning and producing books, and as such it's quite complete, but no book of this length—or many times this length—could describe in detail *all* the processes, equipment, and materials that go into bookmaking. "Sources of information" in the Appendix lists specialized books and other ways to find information on each subject.

Because of the current rapidity of technical development, even if everything known today about bookmaking were included in this book, there would be something lacking tomorrow. Although it seems that the technological principles on which bookmaking will be based for the next several years are in operation now, there'll undoubtedly be a constant flow of improvements and additions, so readers are advised to keep informed. Major changes in technology will be covered in future printings and editions.

Preface
TO THE THIRD EDITION

The need for the Second Edition was created by the advent of "cold type"—the various forms of photographically produced type that began to replace, and eventually make obsolete, the metal type that had been in use in the Western world for more than four centuries. At about the same time that photocomposition was introduced, computers began to change from room-size monsters into practical auxiliaries of the machinery of bookmaking. This transition was recognized in the Second Edition (1979), which also anticipated the extraordinary development of personally operated computers that has radically changed the nature of bookmaking. In the years since 1979, the computer-centered method of getting from the author's mind to completed book has come to dominate this part of bookmaking, and has made photocomposition as obsolete as *it* had made metal type—and created the need for this Third Edition.

Physically, the computer method isn't as dramatically different from photocomposition as the latter was from metal typesetting. But the computer much more profoundly changes the whole bookmaking process, because it involves not only the setting of type but the preparation of manuscripts, editing, illustration creation and processing, page-makeup, color separation, and preparation for printing. Even more significant than its use for these individual procedures is the computer's role in creating an integrated system that's greater than the sum of its parts.

Since the desktop computer has enabled the integration of all the bookmaking functions into a single interlocking process—an ideal that was envisioned before but not realizable until now—so have the functions been integrated in this edition of *Bookmaking*. The previous division into two parts—Design and Production in one and Editing in the other—has been eliminated and the editorial functions have been inserted into their natural places in the process. Now "bookmaking" refers to all of the publishing processes up to distribution.

The availability of a system for producing printed matter that can be operated by anyone with a computer, and enough knowledge to use it, has given us the term "desktop publishing". While the term may be applicable to the production of materials like newsletters or promotional brochures, it's a misnomer when used in connection with books—where "publishing" includes financing, production, and distribution. Of these functions, only production is involved in "desktop publishing", and then only the processes that precede printing and binding. I prefer the term "desktop production".

While the main impact of computers on bookmaking is in the editing, typesetting, page-makeup, and prepress functions, they're also an important element in all machine operations. In printing and binding, the operations are not changed so much as facilitated. The computers provide greater precision and automation. Formerly, squads of machine operators moved around the factory floor tinkering with and adjusting equipment; now one or two stand at a console pressing buttons to achieve even more precise and consistent control through computerization. In most cases, the controls are prearranged by loading programs into computers. Theoretically, no human operators are required, but in the real world even the most efficient machines break down or get out of adjustment, so human help is still needed. Maybe a day will come when machines are 100% reliable, but don't hold your breath.

Even if we see the advent of perfect machines, and the ultimate "thinking" computer, the need for conceiving, creating, planning, organizing, choosing, revising, foreseeing, and judging will prevent humans from becoming obsolete. Having said this, it must be understood that it *is* possible to formulate bookmaking plans that are sufficiently uniform to be executed automatically by computers. Perhaps this is bad for creativity in bookmaking, but it's inevitable and can be useful in some areas of publishing where bookmaking individuality isn't a primary concern.

In the revised text that follows, every significant aspect of the use of computers in bookmaking is covered to the extent that seems necessary to inform without overwhelming the reader, but two overarching points are worth mentioning here. One is the distinction between the early personal computers (PCs), which were quite difficult to use for visually oriented work like bookmaking, and the presently available Graphical User Interface machines, pioneered by Apple, which are well suited for graphic uses and made the computer feasible for primarily visual publishing applications. The second point is the distinction between doing the computer work yourself and having it done to your specifications by a composition house, service bureau, or freelance. It seems likely that all bookmaking computer work will eventually be done in-house, but in this edition both situations are addressed.

Books—or, at least, their contents—can now be delivered with technologies that differ fundamentally from the processes by which books have customarily been made and distributed. Electronic media make possible a movie-like presentation combining words, pictures—both static and moving—and sound, as well as links to other resources. These formats may be delivered to the reader on disks such as the CD or DVD, telecommunicated through a modem or wireless connection, or accessed (*streamed*) from the Internet. They may be read on a computer screen or an *e-book*—a portable reading device that displays the text and illustrations of digitized books on a small computer-like screen. Such electronic systems have expanded the range of content and the means of delivery beyond the limits of the conventional printed book, but before they can begin to function, the work of author, editor, and designer must still be performed as described in the following pages.

The electronic technologies mentioned—and those that haven't been thought of yet—offer advantages for certain publishing categories and fulfill some limited public needs. They will surely become more important in the future, but they're still peripheral to the overwhelming mainstream of bookmaking. Nevertheless, CH. 16 is devoted to explaining what they are and how they relate to the making and distribution of print-on-paper books.

What makes the writing of this edition different from the previous two is the present rapidity of technological change. In the past, change occurred incrementally over a span of years; now substantial developments in machines and their use come at intervals of months, or even weeks. A case was made for postponing the Third Edition because of the fast rate of change, but the situation seemed unlikely to be very different in the foreseeable future—and the need for updating the Second Edition was glaringly clear. Obviously, the difficulty of writing a book about a constantly evolving technology is formidable, and the reader is asked to overlook the unavoidable anachronisms that result when changes occur after publication, but the problem is mitigated by two factors: first, while new developments will occur during the coming years, they're unlikely to change the process of bookmaking fundamentally or in ways that are not foreseen; second, it's our intention to update the text in new printings as frequently as seems necessary and feasible.

But the Third Edition isn't about technological change only; all aspects of bookmaking have been reconsidered. The text has been changed where appropriate and kept intact where its facts and principles are still valid. However, even where the basic information is retained, the text has been editorially improved or completely rewritten to enhance clarity.

SOME SPECIAL NOTES

ON TERMINOLOGY

Much time (money) and energy are wasted, and countless practical and esthetic calamities are caused by misunderstandings due to our lack of a uniform terminology in bookmaking. The problem wouldn't exist if we had a central publishing school teaching one set of terms and signals; but, since there is none, perhaps this first comprehensive textbook of American bookmaking can help achieve the much-needed standardization.

So, it's urged that the terminology found here be adopted by, and disseminated to, all concerned with bookmaking. These terms are not necessarily better than others used elsewhere, but they're those most generally accepted. After all, it's not so important *which* term is used, but that the term used is understood by all.

ON METRIC MEASUREMENT

At the time of this writing, the metric system isn't in general use in the United States, but it *is* used in most, if not all, other places. Measurements are given in this book in inches and pounds, but metric equivalents follow (in parentheses) to prepare bookmakers to function in an increasingly international world. Conversion tables are included in the Appendix.

ABOUT PRICES

To make this book as useful as possible, actual prices, costs, fees, etc. are given wherever generalities would be inadequate. However, these amounts are approximate composite figures prevailing at the time of writing and are subject to variation according to time, locality, individual policies, and various special circumstances. The date for which the figures are valid is given on the copyright page. To update roughly, add the rate of inflation for each year as given on the website of the U.S. Bureau of Labor Statistics (www.BLS.gov).

Short contents

Contents

A. THE HISTORY

THE BEGINNING OF BOOKS

In its broadest sense, the story of bookmaking goes back to the beginning of graphic communication. The development of writing from the first picture-symbols scratched on bone or stone to the sophisticated alphabets of today is a fascinating study, but for our purposes, the story begins with the earliest codex, i.e., the first book in the form of bound leaves, as distinguished from the scrolls that preceded it.

No one knows when the first codices were made, but they came into general use in Europe during the 9th century. By that time, paper and printing were known in Asia, and some codices were used, but scrolls were still in favor there. A form of codex was developed by the Aztecs during this period, but only a few later ones survived the systematic destruction of the Spanish conquest.

2nd century Egyptian codex covers

Until the fall of Rome, papyrus had been the common material of books, and then it was vellum, the treated skin of animals. The Arabic art of papermaking came to the West in the 8th century and was ready to serve that voracious consumer, the printing press, which appeared in Central Europe in the mid-15th century. As far as we know, printing in Europe was invented without reference to the Asian craft that had been in use for hundreds of years—perhaps a thousand years—before Gutenberg.

a book printed in Mexico in 1544

Many of the conventions of bookmaking originated in the handwritten manuscript phase, and the general aspects of page form and binding were quite well established by the time printing began. Indeed, the first printed books were made to look as much like manuscripts as possible, largely in the hope that the difference wouldn't be noticed!

Whereas a complex alphabet and unfavorable social conditions discouraged a wide use of printing in China, its spread was relatively explosive in Europe. Within fifty years presses were established in every major country—and by 1535 printing issued from the first press in the New World in Mexico City. However, another century passed before printing came to the North American settlements.

The Book in America

From 1639, when the first printing was done in the American colonies, until the 19th century, the printer was publisher and bookseller as well. Working with presses little different from Gutenberg's, printers became increasingly involved in the complexities of publishing until it was impractical to operate these functions *and* the craft of printing from one office. Separation began with the advent of the steam-powered press (about 1815), when printing became a major business in itself.

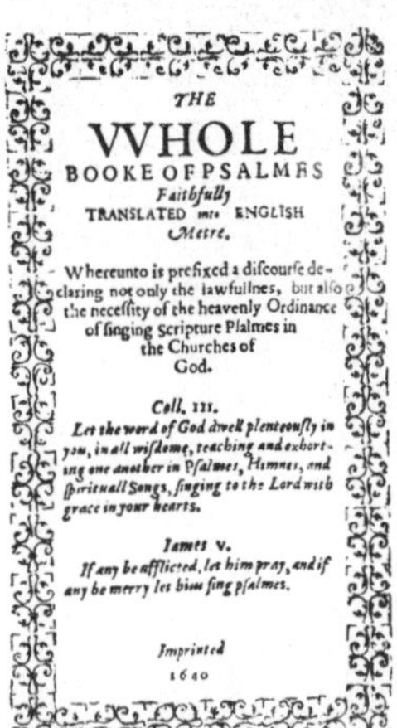
THE
VVHOLE
BOOKE OF PSALMES
Faithfully
TRANSLATED into ENGLISH
Metre.
Whereunto is prefixed a discourse declaring not only the lawfullnes, but also the necessity of the heavenly Ordinance of singing Scripture Psalmes in the Churches of God.
Coll. III.
Let the word of God dwell plenteously in you, in all wisdome, teaching and exhorting one another in Psalmes, Himnes, and spirituall Songs, singing to the Lord with grace in your hearts.
James V.
If any be afflicted, let him pray, and if any be merry let him sing psalmes.
Imprinted
1640

The Bay Psalm Book, the first book printed in the colonies

The power presses were capable of devouring all the handmade paper produced and more, but, fortunately, papermaking machines came along to meet the demand. Then, with the introduction of mechanical typecasting equipment around 1838, mass production of books became possible.

Rapid expansion had an unfortunate effect on typographic development. Where the hand printer was confined to a few basic typefaces (and therefore simple typography), the machine-age printer had types of every description—and many that defied description. The result, beginning at mid-century, was typographic chaos. About 1890, a reaction set in against the machine-made monstrosities. In England, William Morris revived the handcrafts of medieval bookmaking. In America, a few scholar-printers, notably Theodore DeVinne, Daniel Updike, and Bruce Rogers, restored the typography of the 17th and 18th centuries. Although no more inventive than was Morris's, this movement introduced the

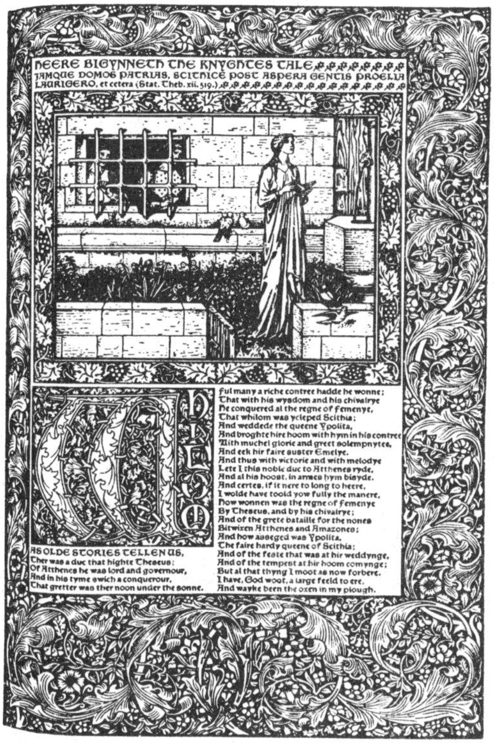

HEERE BIGYNNETH THE KNYGHTES TALE
IAMQUE DOMOS PATRIAS, SCITHICE POST ASPERA GENTIS PROELIA LAURIGERO, et cetera (Stat. Theb. xii. 519.)

WHILOM AS OLDE STORIES TELLEN US,
Ther was a duc that highte Theseus;
Of Atthenes he was lord and governour,
And in his tyme swich a conquerour,
That gretter was ther noon under the sonne.
Ful many a riche contree hadde he wonne;
That with his wysdom and his chivalrye
He conquered al the regne of Femenye,
That whilom was ycleped Scithia;
And weddede the queene Ypolita,
And broghte hire hoom with hym in his contree
With muchel glorie and greet solempnytee,
And eek hir faire suster Emelye.
And thus with victorie and with melodye
Lete I this noble duc to Atthenes ryde,
And al his hoost, in armes hym bisyde.
And certes, if it nere to long to heere,
I wolde have toold yow fully the manere,
How wonnen was the regne of Femenye
By Theseus, and by his chivalrye;
And of the grete bataille for the nones
Bitwixen Atthenes and Amazones;
And how asseged was Ypolita,
The faire hardy queene of Scithia;
And of the feste that was at hir weddynge,
And of the tempest at hir hoom comynge;
But al that thyng I moot as now forbere.
I have, God woot, a large feeld to ere,
And wayke been the oxen in my plough.

William Morris page

Bruce Rogers page

THE CENTAUR. WRITTEN BY MAURICE DE GUÉRIN AND NOW TRANSLATED FROM THE FRENCH BY GEORGE B. IVES.

I Was born in a cavern of these mountains. Like the river in yonder valley, whose first drops flow from some cliff that weeps in a deep grotto, the first moments of my life sped amidst the shadows of a secluded re-treat, nor vexed its silence. As our mothers draw near their term, they retire to the cav-erns, and in the innermost recesses of the wildest of them all, where the darkness is most dense, they bring forth, uncomplaining, offspring as silent as themselves. Their strength-giving milk enables us to endure with-out weakness or dubious struggles the first difficulties of life; yet we leave our caverns later than you your cradles. The reason is that there is a tradition amongst us that the early days of life must be secluded and guarded, as days engrossed by the gods.

My growth ran almost its entire course in the darkness where I was born. The innermost depths of my home were so far within the bowels of the mountain, that I should not have known in which direction the opening lay, had it not been that the winds at times blew in and caused a sudden coolness and confusion. Some-times, too, my mother returned, bringing with her the perfume of the valleys, or dripping wet from the streams to which she resorted. Now, these her home-comings, although they told me naught of the valleys or the streams, yet, being attended by emanations there-from, disturbed my thoughts, and I wandered about, all agitated, amidst my darkness. 'What,' I would say to myself, 'are these places to which my mother goes and what power reigns there which sum-mons her so frequently? To what influences is one there exposed,

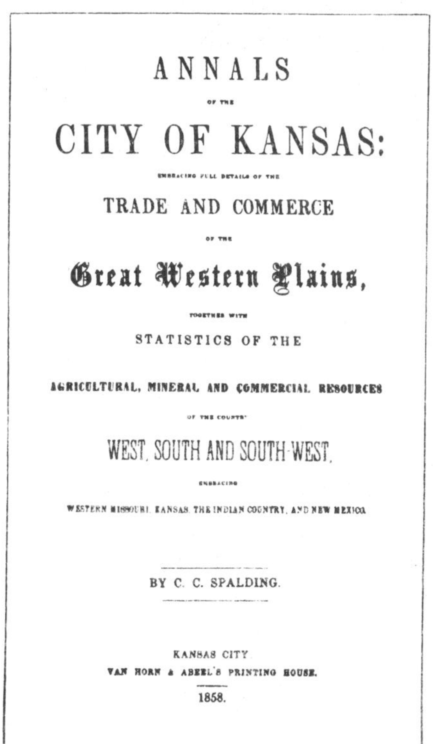

ANNALS
OF THE
CITY OF KANSAS:
EMBRACING FULL DETAILS OF THE
TRADE AND COMMERCE
OF THE
Great Western Plains,
TOGETHER WITH
STATISTICS OF THE
AGRICULTURAL, MINERAL AND COMMERCIAL RESOURCES
OF THE COUNTRY
WEST, SOUTH AND SOUTH-WEST,
EMBRACING
WESTERN MISSOURI, KANSAS, THE INDIAN COUNTRY, AND NEW MEXICO.

BY C. C. SPALDING.

KANSAS CITY
VAN HORN & ABEEL'S PRINTING HOUSE.
1858.

Victorian title page

mature traditions of printing to machine technology—and had a far greater effect.

The last basic bottleneck in printing was eliminated by the perfection of typesetting machinery in 1886. By this time, machinery had been introduced into the bindery, although some operations have only recently been mechanized.

The separation of printer and publisher that had begun at the start of the 19th century was far advanced at its end. Where an association remained, it was generally a publisher who owned a printing plant; rarely a printer who published books.

New distribution methods created the need for protective wrappers, which developed rapidly from plain paper to the modern full-color jacket. While books changed little in four hundred years, jackets evolved entirely during the first quarter of the 20th century.

At the beginning of the second quarter, a distinction between printer and typographer/designer took form. By then, technical developments permitted a wide enough range of expression in book design to attract some full-time designers. The names of T. M. Cleland, W. A. Dwiggins, Merle Armitage, Ernst Reichl, P. J. Conkwright, and others became known in the next decades. This was the period that saw book design emerge as a recognized department of publishing. Book design courses, the Fifty Books shows, clinics, and other activities of the American Institute of Graphic Arts (AIGA) grew in influence, and the publishing trade journal, *Publishers Weekly*, began a monthly department devoted to design and production.

World War II interrupted the progress of bookmaking, but one important development did come out of military needs: the technique of high-speed production of paperbacks, which paved the way for the postwar expansion of paperback publishing. The technology was ready when paperbacks began to be distributed through magazine outlets. This made possible very large printings, thus enabling greatly reduced costs and low retail prices. At first, these books were handled like magazines and, like the pulp magazines they soon drove off the stands, they tended toward Westerns and mysteries—with maximum pictorial appeal on the outside and relatively little attention to design inside. Gradually, the publishers and magazine distributors began to treat titles of more enduring interest as if they were books, and the better lines began to find their way into bookstores. An important breakthrough occurred when the Anchor books, a line of higher-priced paperback reprints of serious titles, demonstrated that the college market could absorb enough books of this kind to justify their publication. Similar lines followed, thereby creating a whole new segment of publishing. The design of these "quality", or "*trade*", *paperbacks* got off to a good start and has been in the main excellent.

By the 1950s, many publishers recognized the challenge posed

mass-market paperback covers of the 1940s

Design: Brenda McManus

Design: Abby Weintraub

trade paperbacks of 2003

by a generation accustomed to the dynamic graphics of advertising, magazines, and television—and books showed definite signs of responding to the visual esthetics of the 20th century. The design of jackets and paperback covers led the way, chiefly because they're closer to advertising and are often the work of designers whose training and experience were in that field. By the 1990s, the quality of jacket and paperback cover design had improved enormously. (A critical survey of individual designers and their work is outside the scope of this book—see "Sources of information" in the Appendix for further reading.)

The most marked development was in textbooks and children's books, where rapidly expanding markets and keen competition drove publishers to heavy use of color and illustration. At first, the competition was mainly in the amount of graphic effects used, but gradually the quality of design became the selling point.

Meanwhile, technical advances in color printing encouraged an already growing interest in art and illustrated books, with many publishers using foreign as well as American color-printing facilities. At the beginning of the fourth quarter of the 20th century these trends had created a responsive audience for many books of graphic interest. A major new category of trade paperbacks—large format and extensively illustrated—were published and sold in large numbers in regular bookstores.

There is still considerable adherence to convention in American book design, but it's becoming weaker. The change is good where meaningless and impractical conventions are dropped, but the blessing isn't unmixed. Too many young designers have cast themselves loose from conventional forms without having developed better alternatives, and there have been examples of typographic fads in which bad design, such as the use of hard-to-read tiny type, is imposed on readers by self-indulgent designers concerned more with patterns and faux-elegance than reading. Some publishers, too, have cast off concern with reading in order to achieve lively effects, directing designers to use distracting graphic elements and color backgrounds that attract attention but discourage reading (particularly when combined with too small type). On the whole, however, it seems preferable to open the possibility of creative design than to remain locked within rigid and outworn rules.

THE BEGINNING OF EDITING

In the sense that editing means selection and discrimination it can be said to have existed almost from the beginning of man's civilized life. Even before there was writing, editorial judgment shaped the oral literature. Each successive teller of a story related it a little differently, perhaps omitting the duller parts and rephrasing others to make the whole more effective. No doubt there were some embellishments and probably some substantial additions from time to time. Once writing began, it can be safely assumed that some persons other than the writers decided what writings would be cut into clay or stone and accepted into the official record. Further, it's reasonable to suppose that someone with authority asked for or made changes in the work submitted. The point is that in all such cases the "published" work was the product of not only its originator but also another person whose judgment affected either the work itself or its publication or both. Although such persons wouldn't have been called "editors", they performed editorial functions.

It's probable that some professional editing was done on the ancient Greek plays by their producers, and it's known that people were hired to assist in producing the vast amounts of Roman literature. These antecedents of the modern editor were followed by the scribes who made the medieval manuscripts. They applied not only selection and discrimination but a certain amount of the corrective work that we call "copyediting". Certainly there was "proofreading" in the sense that the work was not considered finished until it had been read and the errors corrected. If this editorial work was not up to the standards we set for ourselves today, neither was there the authority of an established dictionary to consult. Without accepted rules of grammar and spelling, the "editors" were left to make their own choices—but choose they did and languages developed through this process. Presumably, the works that showed better clarity, consistency, and logic were admired and imitated—leading to the eventual adoption of their style by the lexicographers to come.

Once printing began, the editing of books became institutionalized in the sense that it was then done as a professional routine. In the first decades after Gutenberg, printer-publishers generally did their own editing, although proofreading was given to an employee or family member. As printing-publishing houses grew larger, scholars were engaged to evaluate and sometimes correct or modify projected works in their discipline. Many printers were themselves considerable scholars, and several, like Aldus Manutius and Christophe Plantin, were honored as much for the editorial distinction of their books as for the quality of their typography.

By the 18th century, the full-time editorial employee was an established feature of publishing houses—which by that time were often separate from the printing offices where they began. Even then, the main editorial judgments were probably made by the head of the house and the editorial employees were primarily proofreaders. It was not until well into the 19th century that the size of publishing houses exceeded the capacity of the owners to handle all the editorial decision-making. They still made the primary decisions to publish or not, but even these were delegated in part to editors when the companies grew very large and began to departmentalize.

The professional editor as a qualified specialist has existed for not much more than one century. Since World War II, the profession has been dividing into specialties that form a chain linking management to the various departments of publishing. Where our image of an editor before 1950 was the Maxwell Perkins type who worked with authors and manuscripts (mss.) from concept to printed book, we now sometimes have as many as four editors involved with a single book, each concerned with a different part of the process. As book publishing companies become larger and their domination by professional managers increases, this tendency toward fragmentation and specialization of the editorial function will probably continue. Unfortunately, the trend also has seemed to diminish the concern for careful ms. editing.

THE BEGINNING OF PRODUCTION

While virtually all processes in bookmaking are now done by computer or with computer-generated materials, all bookmakers should have at least a rudimentary knowledge of how the basic processes were accomplished B.C.—Before Computers—in some cases for more than four centuries. Not only is this the history of your profession, it's the source from which came most of the present practices. So, be sure to read carefully the Typography and Composition chapters (CHs.5, 6) in particular, because these are the areas that have been changed most by the computer, and where it's most important to be well grounded. All other parts of bookmaking have been changed also in varying degrees, but in discussing each of them some attention has been given to what *was*, along with an explanation of what *is*.

B. OVERVIEW

The bookmaking process begins when the idea of the book is conceived by the author or in the publishing company, because this conception includes consideration of the physical and visual, as well as the verbal, characteristics of the book-to-be. After the decision is made to publish the book, a writer starts creating a text. This may be done with a quill pen and ink on paper, on a typewriter, with a voice recorder, or on a computer, but unless the work is done on a computer, the next stage is conversion to a computer text format. However, even if the original was done on a computer, it may be necessary to convert the computer *file* to make it compatible with the *software program* used in the next stage: editing. In turn, the editor's copy of the file might have to be converted for use on the designer's computer, and so on. Eventually, all computers and programs will be compatible with each other, but until that happy day, compatibility will be a factor to always keep in mind.

Although the bookmaking process has radically changed since the Second Edition of *Bookmaking*, the basic steps involved are the same. Simplified, they are:

(1) conception of an idea
(2) acquisition or creation of a ms., i.e., text and illustration, if any
(3) editing of the ms. materials
(4) design of the book
(5) setting of the ms. into type
(6) marking the illustrations (if any) for size
(7) color separation and color correction (if applicable)
(8) composition of the ms. materials into pages
(9) checking of the pages and correction
(10) merging text and illustrations (if applicable)
(11) preparation of final pages for the printer
(12) production of printing and binding

The ability of the computer to perform so many of these functions has transformed not only the process but also the roles of those performing these tasks. Traditionally, editors, designers, and production people have had separate professional identities, usually working in separate departments in a company. Roles were clearly delineated by training in a specific field. Work on a project moved sequentially from one expert to the next. But, as computer operations have become more and more multifunctional, the formerly distinct phases have blended into one another. Keyboarding of text no longer needs to be a separate task from typesetting. Typesetting can be combined with page layout and makeup. Editing can be done during typesetting or page composition. Final composed pages can be produced in the computer without having to create physical paste-up mechanicals. Production can be taken to prepress stages in the desktop computer where formerly outside services were required. It's now actually possible for one person to conceive of a book and, with one computer and the right assortment of equipment, write, edit, illustrate, design, typeset, scan illustrations, make color separations, compose all the elements to a disk, and send it to the printer completely ready for manufacture!

C. THE PROFESSION

1. Editing

Function

Whether performed entirely by one person or divided among several, the editorial function is the same: (a) book projects must be brought to the house (through the initiative of author, agent, editor, or publisher); (b) contracts between authors and publisher must be negotiated—although the complexity of contracts today requires the attention of specialists familiar with movie, television, reprint, foreign, electronic, and other rights; (c) mss. must be developed editorially to satisfy both author and publisher; (d) the mss. must be corrected and styled to prepare them for composition; and (e) the editorial work must be organized.

Where the functions are divided, there may be an acquiring or sponsoring editor (a) and (b), a working or manuscript editor (c), a copyeditor (d), and a managing editor (e). Another category is "production editor"—a link between the editorial and production departments, found mainly in textbook houses, sometimes overlapping (c) and (d). The preparation of contracts is often done by a "contracts manager".

RELATIONSHIPS

■ **Editorial to management**—The acquiring editor has the power to reject books, but doesn't usually have the authority to accept a book. Sometimes, when the editor is very senior in the company, or has a strong reputation, this authority is actually or practically in his or her hands. Under these circumstances, the editor is, in effect, part of management, since the decision concerning what is to be published is a business function as well as an editorial one. Some editors are given substantial autonomy, financial backing, and their own *imprint* within the company, i.e., their name appears on the title page of their books. In cases where the final decision is made by management—i.e., the publisher, rather than an editor, an editor-in-chief, or editorial director—the editorial department's role is professional advisor.

Editorial advice to publish is likely to be accepted by management when it's given with enthusiasm, supporting facts (such as market research or the author's previous successes), and the concurrence of the sales department. In the case of complex or illustrated books, the management's decision may be affected by cost factors that outweigh editorial judgment.

Most publishing houses have policies concerning the kinds of books they want to publish. Editors must observe these rules in general, but occasionally a book comes along that's so attractive it's accepted by management even though it doesn't fit into the program. Imprint editors generally set their own policies—with the approval of house management.

In all respects, an editor is the link between author and publisher, protecting the interests of both. However, the editor is primarily the publisher's representative, and in contract negotiations must try to make the best terms possible for the company.

■ **Editorial to design and production**—See CH. 2, "Design and production".

■ **Editorial to sales**—This section refers to "sales", "advertising and promotion", and "subsidiary rights" as separate departments, and so they are, but in the larger houses it's usual to have a marketing director who coordinates and controls the activities of these departments and any other activities related to selling the books.

The economics of publishing and the factors that influence sales of a book are discussed in CH. 2 under "Bookmaking to sales". This material is equally relevant to editors.

The first point at which editorial and sales intersect is when a project is offered to the house for consideration. The decision to publish or not is based on two considerations: the intrinsic quality of the book and its profit potential. Sometimes one aspect greatly outweighs the other and a mediocre book is taken because it's expected to sell very well, or a superb book is accepted even though it's not likely to make money, but generally it's necessary for both factors to be positive.

When both editorial and sales departments are enthusiastic about a project, there's no problem—except where an expensive production makes publication impractical because the retail price would have to be too high at the quantity the book is likely to sell. There may, however, be conflict between editor and sales department over the question of market. Generally, the sales department is accepted as the authority on the sales prospects of a book, but sometimes the author, the editor, or both have special knowledge of the audience for a particular book and the editor must press for acceptance against the reluctance of sales people (for example, the author may know of a strong collector interest in beer cans, but lacking that knowledge the sales manager might be expected to consider a book on the subject unpublishable).

Just as the special qualifications of the sales people are respected in matters of sales, the judgment of the editor is usually accepted in considering the merits of the book. But such judgments are subjective and differences of opinion sometimes occur. The sales manager may defer to the editor's judgment, but editors and publishers are usually wary about publishing a book that doesn't have the wholehearted support of the sales department. Most companies, especially the larger ones, publish more books than can be effectively sold anyway, and only those that are most enthusiastically marketed have much chance of success.

Once a book has been accepted, the editorial and sales departments join again to consider jacket and cover designs submitted by the art director. The editor is concerned that the jacket properly represents the book, and both editor and sales manager are anxious that the jacket be effective in sales. The most common disagreement is when the sales department prefers a design that the editor feels misrepresents the book. In some houses the editorial department has the last word, but in others sales is given the power to decide. In deadlocks, the publisher usually settles the question.

The sales department normally doesn't get involved with the design of the book, but on large illustrated books there's sometimes an exchange of ideas with the design and editorial departments.

After publication, editorial personnel keep in touch with sales staff to make decisions on revised editions, reprints, etc.

■ **Editorial to subsidiary rights**—While the main responsibility for *subsidiary rights* (sub-rights) sales—book clubs, translations, movies, television, radio, serial rights, condensations, e-books, etc.—rests with the sub-rights manager, the editor is interested in promoting these because they add to the success of the book, and therefore of the editorial department. An editor can contribute by making useful contacts or speaking up for the book, but must be sure to coordinate such activities with the sub-rights department.

Terms for the author's share of sub-rights sales are specified in the contract, but sometimes sales possibilities arise that are not covered by the contract or that require the author's approval. The editor must see that the author (or the agent) is brought into the negotiations. However, the sub-rights department usually is responsible for arranging terms between the house and the buyer of rights. The editor is notified of the terms but rarely consulted on them, unless a very important deal is involved.

■ **Editorial to advertising/promotion**—Editors always want more advertising and promotion for their books than is available, but the controlling factor is the budget. The amount allocated for each book is determined mainly by its sales prospects—a book that doesn't have exceptionally good prospects is, alas, not likely to get *any* advertising budget at all. This means that the sales manager has an important voice in the decision. In some houses, the editorial department is involved in determining the budgeting for advertising and promotion, but in others the decision is entirely up to marketing management. (The advertising and promotion people who spend the money rarely have much to say about how much is to be spent on each book.) Strong editorial support for a book can sometimes boost the initial advertising budget, but once the book is published, its sales performance determines how much advertising is done. It's generally believed that advertising alone can't make a tradebook sell, it can only boost the sales of a book that's already selling. (This publishing axiom is rarely accepted by authors, who are usually certain that their books would sell wonderfully if well advertised.)

APPROACHES TO EDITING In the layperson's vision of publishing, an editor reads mss. sent in by hopeful writers, selects a promising one, and calls in the ecstatic author to sign a contract. The editor then asks the author to make a few changes—which is done willingly—and the ms. is sent off to the printer.

This picture is true for only a tiny percentage of publishing. It was never *generally* accurate, but was much more the case three generations ago. Now, few publishers will look at unsolicited mss. from writers. To a large extent, publishers depend on agents to screen the mss., and in some cases to edit them. The only projects they consider are: (a) those offered by agents or by the few established authors who have no agent, (b) those conceived by editors inside the house, (c) those offered by someone known to a person in the firm, and (d) those offered by outside *packagers* who develop book projects that are sold to publishers as completed or partially produced books. Publishers also buy rights to books that originate with foreign publishers, and sometimes enter into agreements to co-publish books with groups of foreign publishers. This may involve a co-production, in which all editions are manufactured together for economy (CH. 36).

The tendency of especially the larger publishers to distance themselves from the so-called mid-list books—those that are publishable but considered not sufficiently profitable—has been criticized for its possible exclusion of valuable work written by the as-yet-unpublished who have no agent. As the flood of unsolicited mss. gets turned away by publishers, much of it finds its way to the agents—who are even less able to deal with it, since they have more limited resources than the publishers. However, most agents and some publishers are somewhat open to new writers in the hope that a literary masterpiece (and potential best-seller) will be discovered.

Under the circumstances, for editors there's obviously a premium on good contacts with agents, and many editors function mainly as conduits to these sources of "product", systematically meeting with them and talking about projects. While any editor worthy of the name is able to, and does, assist authors in developing their books, an editor who does no more than bring in an important writer is considered—and is—a valuable asset to the house.

The contribution of a manuscript editor can be anything from conceptual to mechanical. Some editors are concerned only with seeing that the main outline of a book is right and will leave the detailed give-and-take with the author to another. Some insist on seeing the work through to the final product themselves. In any case, there's always a going-over by a copyeditor (CHs. 4, 19, 30) before the ms. goes to design.

A substantial percentage of books published are not "accepted" but rather are originated by in-house editors who either hire or contract with writers to carry out an idea. This is discussed under "Concept" in CH. 17.

Requirements

TALENT

The innate abilities required by an editor depend on the kind of editor being considered. Acquiring or sponsoring editors need a natural rapport with the kind of person who produces the kind of books desired. An editor interested in how-to books should enjoy dealing with authors who are likely to be relatively down-to-earth but enthusiastic amateurs or no-nonsense professionals. Pursuing bestsellers means being comfortable with the high-powered agents and lawyers who handle the big-name writers. In all cases, the editor must have an instinct for sensing the real thing—the idea that's *really* sound, the book that will *really* get written, the agent who is *really* serious about getting together, the movie that will *really* get made. Acquiring editors must also have good business heads, as they're primarily responsible for the terms made with the author. They must have an innate sense of quality—not so much the ability to discern high art as the ability to recognize what is excellent of its kind. Finally, an acquiring editor needs to be good at persuading the company to accept the projects brought in.

The manuscript editor also should be effective in dealing with people. Working closely with writers, particularly creative ones, is often a trying experience. Writers have a strong emotional attachment to their books and no matter how mild tempered they may normally be, they tend to guard their work with a passion ranging from intense to ferocious. Even professional hacks can be difficult if their personalities don't jibe with the editor's or if they feel that their work is being mistreated. Diplomatic talent is even more necessary in a working editor than in an acquiring one, because the strain is usually sustained much longer and the matters dealt with are more emotionally charged.

Working with a ms. also requires a sense of what is good and true, but there must be in addition an ability to know what will correct deficiencies. Sometimes it's enough to be able to point out a flaw for the author to correct, but often it's necessary to show the author how to correct it. Theoretically, an editor need not be a good writer—but in fact every working editor does a considerable amount of writing in the course of making mss. work, and the editor's success depends to a large extent on the quality of this writing. Even some first-rate writers are inclined to let stand a sentence well rewritten by a respected editor.

The role of the copyeditor varies from house to house. In some, copyeditors are actually the manuscript editors and work directly with the authors. In most, they have very little latitude in changing the text and rarely deal with the author directly. A person in this situation doesn't need the personality traits of the acquiring or manuscript editors, but does require the ability to spot and correct awkward or badly constructed sentences. Beyond this, the copyeditor should have a natural inclination to be precise and meticulous and have the patience to examine very closely sizable amounts of material that may not be personally interesting. The worst fault of a copyeditor is a tendency toward lapses of close attention. A good copyeditor has the ability to sustain intense concentration over long periods, even when dealing with boring material, and also can avoid becoming so involved in interesting material as to lose sight of the details. Proofreading requires much the same set of talents as copyediting, but writing ability isn't necessary.

A managing editor needs to have the kind of personality that enables remaining calm at the center of a swirling storm of complex activity. This job requires: (a) a talent for judging people, since it usually involves hiring the administrative personnel of the department and, sometimes, the freelancers; (b) a natural ability to organize the traffic of editorial work efficiently (it's no small matter to control the comings and goings of dozens of mss. and proofs to a large number of authors, editors, artists, designers, sales people, promotion people, production people, sub-rights people, and others); and (c) a nonabrasive personality that keeps relations smooth and effective between the editorial and other departments. In some companies the managing editor is responsible for preparation of the department budget, so a mathematical talent is desirable. In sum, this job calls for a good administrator. In small companies, the managing editor often does some copyediting and ms. editing also.

BACKGROUND & TRAINING

The *ideal* background for any editor is to have: (a) an MA in English or comparative literature from a first-class university, with many courses in languages, psychology, and business administration; (b) been an insatiable reader since childhood of everything from newspapers and magazines to literary classics, as well as to have been a movie and television fan; (c) had a two-year postgraduate course in publishing—including editing, design, production, sales, and management; (d) spent at least one year working in bookstores and another year in typesetting, printing, and binding plants; (e) put in a few months' apprenticeship in every department in a publishing house; and (f) spent at least a year as a *book traveller* (a salesperson on the road servicing bookstores, wholesalers, libraries, and schools). It wouldn't hurt at all to have (g) spent a few months as a librarian. To be the child of a major publisher or editor and know personally a large number of important agents and writers would also be useful.

Few can afford to prepare themselves as fully as described above—or be so fortunate in their birth—but a considerable part of this education and experience is quite possible, and a substantial part of it is really essential. (At one time there were publishers heading large houses who had practically all of this ideal background.) Many publishing companies are willing to give promising young people apprenticeship opportunities and to finance some professional training as well.

CH. 2 includes information on professional courses available.

Opportunities

KINDS OF JOBS

Editors actually function in different ways, but these distinctions are not as structured as the different functions in design and production (CH. 2). Although some publishers hire people specifically as acquiring or sponsoring editors, an editor is usually hired as an editor without any other designation than, perhaps, "junior", "senior", or "associate". The way an editor operates tends to define the position more clearly than does a title.

One exception to this rule is the copyeditor, who is almost always hired as such and is limited to the specific functions of a copyeditor in that house. As discussed above, however, the definition of the copyeditor's functions varies from one company to another. It usually includes fact checking, and in some houses, copyeditors are also manuscript editors (CH. 4).

Another exception is the production editor, who also has specific functions. There is some variation in the duties of production editors, but they rarely extend into ms. editing or even copyediting.

The managing editor has a very definite job which does not, except perhaps in the smaller companies, overlap the other editorial functions. The work can be, and often is, done by an administrator with no editorial ability.

The contract-writing function may be included in the duties of the editors or assigned to specially qualified people who are designated "contract managers" rather than editors.

The general category "editor" is subject to the same hierarchical structure as other professions, with an editor-in-chief at the top, a managing editor below and a little to the side, then senior editor, editor, junior editor, associate editor, assistant editor, editorial assistant. The actual meanings of these titles in terms of responsibilities are far from exact. They represent different levels of pay and perquisites, but the work each does depends on the house. In one company, an assistant editor may be doing little more than secretarial work, in another, ms. editing. The titles tend to proliferate in the larger companies and drop away in the smaller ones. This is because in the latter each editor is likely to do a wide range of work so that the distinctions between the editors are very small.

At the bottom of the pyramid—but not to be ignored—are the editorial secretaries (like secretaries in general, they tend to be called "assistants"—blurring the distinction between them and editorial assistants, or even assistant editors). While they often do the same work as others with more exalted titles and feel undervalued, the important fact is that they're in the editorial department. This is the first rung of the ladder, and it leads to the second just as the second leads to the third and so on.

The number of staff editors a publishing company employs usually varies according to the size of the house; the number can range from one or two in the smallest to dozens in the largest, where they're usually organized in separate departments. Textbook publishers are likely to employ more editors than trade houses, but these are mostly copyeditors and production editors, whereas the tradebook publishers will have a large proportion of acquiring editors.

An editor-in-chief usually does some acquisition and even some ms. editing, but the job is essentially executive, with primary responsibility for the success of the firm's list. In very small houses, the title "editor-in-chief" may exist without the function, as the publisher personally supervises the work of the editors. The larger packaging houses also have staff editors, but relatively few compared with big publishing companies.

A word about proofreading is in order. Proofreading is as much a part of the editorial function as anything else, but it's not normally treated as a separate function in publishing houses. Sometimes proofreading is done in the house within the copyediting department, but more often it's given out to freelancers (some of whom also do copyediting). Proofreading is done also in typesetting houses and, in fact, was once left entirely to the printshop. Most publishers have all proofs read at least once in addition to the author's readings, and many have their nonfiction proofread by two readers (CHs. 4, 20).

Because proofreading, copyediting, and manuscript editing require days or weeks of uninterrupted work, they lend themselves well to freelancing. A large percentage of the proofreading and copyediting, and a smaller, but substantial, part of the manuscript editing done for publishers goes to freelancers.

FUTURES Ambition for a career in the editorial field can mean three different things, depending on one's interests:

(a) For those with a taste for high-living and an appetite for glamour, excitement, and recognition, the goal might be senior acquisitions editor in a major trade house—buying multimillion-dollar books by big-name authors, making newsworthy movie and television deals, and having an unlimited expense account to entertain important agents and writers. This is a real enough possibility for someone with the right kind of ability. The route to such positions could be a step-by-step climb from editorial assistant ($18,500 to $30,000) to junior editor ($35,000 to $50,000) to senior editor ($50,000 to $70,000) or, for the exceptionally gifted, a jump from assistant to the top of the ladder without stopping at the intermediate rungs.

(b) For those who crave position and executive authority, editor-in-chief in a major firm is the goal. Pay for such a job can range from $90,000 to $115,000 or more. Smaller houses may pay an editor-in-chief about the same as a senior editor—with the title in lieu of more money. Advancement to editor-in-chief is likely to be step-by-step, but a strong show of talent can result in a jump to the top in some cases. Sometimes a stint as managing editor ($60,000 to $75,000) leads to the top executive post.

(c) If you are more interested in making books than making deals, and have no love for administration, you would strive to become a senior editor in a good "literary" house (one that shows an interest in serious books and is less avid for hot commercial properties than most, but where profit is high enough to pay good salaries). You'd probably be near the lower end of the salary scale for senior editors, but you would have the pleasure of doing what you enjoy. Here the route to the top is most likely from the editorial assistant level upward in fairly slow steps through the intermediate positions.

Copyediting is a specialty that has its own reward for those who enjoy the nitty-gritty of ms. work and are not really interested in acquisition. Some people move from copyediting to acquisition, but most regard it as a profession that calls for the best they can give, and derive satisfaction from doing it well. Salaries range from $35,000 to $55,000. Freelance copyediting is paid for by the hour at rates from $20 to $30. While acquiring and manuscript editors rarely get credit lines in their books, copyeditors almost never do. However, many authors acknowledge the help they got from their editors.

Proofreaders can make $15 to $20 per hour for freelance work. These rates, as well as those for copyeditors, are for normal work. Prices for exceptionally difficult or specialized books can be higher.

HOW TO GET A JOB

As noted in CH. 2, jobs in book publishing have often gone to someone who happens to be around rather than to a qualified person from outside. This is probably more true of editorial jobs than any other, despite the fact that these jobs are the most sought after in publishing. Other industries systematically recruit for their more attractive entry-level positions from the top graduates of the best schools in the country; publishers often give these jobs to someone's friend or relative, an ambitious employee from the lower ranks, or someone who replies to a want ad and seems better than the other applicants.

There are some fairly good reasons for this state of affairs, but the most significant factor is probably the difficulty of knowing who will turn out to be a successful editor. A publisher who picks a bright English major from a top college knows that intelligence and some knowledge of literature will be brought to the job, but whether this person will have the ability to pick profitable books can't be predicted.

It would, of course, make a difference if publishers could recruit from a college-level publishing school, but unfortunately none such exists in America. Perhaps the closest to this that we have is the four-year program at Hofstra University on Long Island, New York, which offers a BA in English with a specialization in book publishing. There are several other excellent publishing courses being offered (CH. 2 and "Sources of information"), and this is all to the good, but there's no substitute for a broad, dedicated, four-year curriculum. Publishers do, however, hire the graduates of the better courses or offer internships that often become staff positions.

How then does the aspiring editor get a job? There's almost no way to show competence in the necessary skills except to submit writing that demonstrates a knowledge of grammar, structure, and style. The character of the presentation will also suggest personal qualities such as neatness, taste, and perhaps flair. Any publication experience—even the editorship of a high school newspaper—might indicate talent, knowledge, and competence. A good academic record is helpful and recommendations by school authorities or former employers are positive elements—and every little bit helps. Certainly a good personal appearance indicative of cleanliness, orderliness, and taste is essential.

Suppose you have all the good qualities described above; how do you reach a person who can give you an editorial job? There are eight routes: (a) take a good course in publishing and/or editing and make your desires known to the instructors, who are often asked for recommendations; (b) sign up with a personnel agency specializing in publishing jobs; (c) get a letter of recommendation to an editor or publisher from a mutual friend or associate; (d) send a very well-written, interesting, exceptionally well-typed letter with a resumé to many editors and publishers; (e) reply to want ads in *Publishers Weekly* and the major newspapers; (f) leave your resumé and appropriate forms with the personnel departments of many publishers; (g) go to bars, restaurants, resorts, and publishing events—particularly writers' conferences—where editors go, and (h) try to meet them, and check the job boards on the Internet, such as publishers' websites, monster.com, and The Publisher's Lunch.

For your first job you may be competing against people who are already visible and/or known to the hiring editor—a secretary in the department, a freelance copyeditor, a cousin who has the same background as you. However, there isn't *always* a suitable applicant nearby, so the outsider has a chance. If you take all eight routes listed above, or even some of them, you have a good chance of getting a job in a reasonable time.

Obviously, being known to editors makes it unnecessary to take *any* of the eight steps (although courses should be taken for their own value), so the best thing to do is to get a job inside a publishing house in *any* capacity, if you can. All other things being equal, you have a much better chance for the first editorial opening if you are on the spot. Being on the spot can also mean working in an agent's office, where you have frequent contact with editors. Editors hire people with agency experience because agents today often perform editorial functions. (And editors often become agents.)

FREELANCING

See CH. 2 for comments on the pros and cons of freelancing. In most publishing houses, the relatively routine jobs of copyediting and proofreading are often given to freelancers. But it's likely also that the exceptionally complicated and/or difficult editorial tasks will go to freelancers, although for different reasons. For one, it's simply impractical to tie up a staff editor for long periods on one book. For another, except in specialized publishing companies, there's usually no one in the house as qualified to do certain jobs as the freelance specialists available.

Just as it's convenient for publishers to give editorial work to freelancers, it's comfortable for editors to work on a freelance basis. There's relatively little running back and forth, and the work can (usually) be done alone. The pay isn't high compared with the amounts paid for some less demanding work, but it's adequate—if there's a steady flow of work. The key question is: Can you expect to find enough work to earn a living? There's no certain answer, but you may be willing to take the chance in order to enjoy the freedom of freelancing.

Along with the risk involved in finding work, you'll also have the problem of cash flow. A freelance professional is, in effect, running a business, and this means making sure that the money you earn comes in quickly and steadily enough to enable you to pay your bills (in this case, living costs) on time. The terms of your agreement to work for a publisher should include an understanding on the schedule of payment—and large companies can be just as slow in making payments as small ones.

2. Design and production

Function

RELATIONSHIPS

Design to production—Ideally, responsibility for the design and production of books is vested in one person who is well qualified in both aspects. Generally, however, the functions are divided. Because of its economic role, the production department almost invariably has a superior relationship to design. Planning usually originates in the production department, and often the designer is brought in only after the main decisions have been made. This arrangement doesn't tend to produce the best results, although a great deal depends on the particular production manager.

The larger publishers have an "art director" on their staffs. This can be effective where the art directors have some authority, but often they're simply heads of the design department, with about the same relationship to the production manager as the designer had before.

The logical relationship of designer to production manager is comparable to that of architect to builder. The architect (designer) plans the practical and esthetic aspects of the structure and the builder (production manager) carries out the plans. However, no matter how good the builder, the result won't be successful unless the architect has a thorough mastery of the materials and techniques of construction. From this it's apparent that the designer must be an expert in production or become merely a layout artist. Production people should, of course, learn as much as they can about design, but their role is primarily planning and executing the purchasing and scheduling functions to support the publisher's business objective.

■ **Design and production to editorial**—In practice, some of the principal decisions affecting design and production are made by editors, which is inevitable and proper because the editor represents the interests of publisher and author. But the weakness of this arrangement is that the editor often doesn't know production or understand design well enough to be able to make good decisions.

Publishing books is a complex and deeply interrelated operation, in which specialization can easily be carried too far. All participants must know their jobs extremely well, but each should have a working knowledge of all the other operations. The editor functions somewhat like the director of a play, supervising and coordinating the various elements. But, where the theater director is expected to be qualified to supervise acting, staging, scenery, costumes, lighting, and music, few editors are educated or experienced in the design and production of books. An encouraging development is the increase in publishing courses noted later in this chapter.

■ **Bookmaking to sales**—The bookmaker has two basic tasks:

(a) to facilitate communication between author and reader, and
(b) to make the book a successful commercial product.

This book will deal directly with both functions, but for a proper understanding of their background, it's necessary to know something of the economics of publishing and the way books are sold and distributed.

There are many kinds of publishing—direct mail, textbook, technical, medical, law, music, paperback, electronic, etc.—and each kind has its own economics, with unique problems requiring special considerations of design and production. It's obviously impossible to explain every kind of operation here, so this discussion will deal only with *tradebooks* (books published for sale primarily through bookstores and for circulation by public libraries). The particular problems of other kinds will be taken up in later chapters.

Publishers often have cultural or personal objectives when they accept a book for publication, but the object of publishing as a business is to sell books. However, it's only in the profit motive that book publishing resembles any other business. It's much more informal, unpredictable, complicated, and hazardous than most.

Toothpaste manufacturers, for example, hire people to create a few products to their desire (after considerable market research), standardize their manufacture, and turn them out in large quantities year after year. They can advertise and promote their products as much as they like, knowing that their campaign will take effect sooner or later. They can concentrate their money and effort on a single campaign that may be good for years. Their products are sold in stores accessible to virtually everyone and their production can be geared to their sales—or at least to an estimate of sales based on thorough research and experience. Most important, a satisfied customer is likely to continue buying the same product more or less indefinitely.

The publisher, on the other hand, must sell fifty, a hundred, or a thousand entirely different products in one year, each one a unique creation by an independent individual who has determined the nature of the product. There is no way of knowing how many buyers there'll be, so (except in rare cases) the product must be made in an uneconomically small quantity—the use of *POD (print-on-demand) xerographic printing* (CHs. 10, 12, 16) may be a help here. The amount of money and effort spent on promoting the book will be disproportionately high if there's only one printing (as usually there is), and the campaign must be immediately effective, because most books are highly perishable, like vegetables, and become almost worthless if not sold quickly. To sell the books, the publishing company has only a few thousand outlets plus the online booksellers, such as Amazon.com and BarnesandNoble.com. Even when the publisher sells its products to the booksellers it's not necessarily ahead, because booksellers can return the books if they don't sell them. Worst of all, the sale of a book to a reader doesn't mean that the same person will remain a customer of the publisher's, except perhaps for another similar book by the same author—which may not come in for years, if at all, and when it does, it may be from another publisher. To survive, the publisher must have other kinds of outlets—libraries, book clubs, e-books, etc.—each of which requires special handling and attention.

The sales and distribution problems of publishing are discouraging enough, but the economics are positively forbidding. Of the book's list (retail) price, about 47% is the average (combined) wholesaler's and retailer's discount, and at least 10%, and more often 12% or 15%, is the author's royalty. Of the 43% retained by the publisher, about 20% goes for making the book, about 5% might go into advertising, and 2% for storing and shipping. A share of the cost of salaries, rent, electric bills, and other items of overhead must be carried by each title—16% of the retail price is a realistic figure. With a little arithmetic you'll see that at least 100% of the book's price is accounted for and no profit has been mentioned. The picture is *this* bright only because we are assuming that all the books printed will be sold—which rarely happens. Further, there are numerous free copies—sometimes hundreds—given away for review and promotion. Some of the expenditures mentioned above are incurred even on books not sold.

From this it can be seen that cost must be held down, and that one of the most important decisions the publishing company makes is the size of the first printing. If it makes too few books, the unit price will be too high; if it makes too many—to keep the unit cost down—it will be left with many unsold books.

There are two factors that can lighten this otherwise bleak picture of publishing as a business: (a) a sellout of the first printing with the necessity of a second (and more) to meet the demand and (b) a sale of subsidiary rights to the book. Second printings mean profits, since some initial production costs are not repeated. Also, publishers seldom spend the whole advertising budget.

(The economics of e-books are not at all clear at this time. Without printing, paper, and binding costs, the picture would seem to be very different from conventional publishing, and this has been recognized in a willingness to increase royalty rates, but it also suggests that retail prices should come down, thus reducing the value of higher royalties. Add the complications of licensing fees, conversion costs, and author contract questions—i.e., does the publisher or the author own electronic rights—and the eventual resolution of this new economic model seems a long way off.)

What then is the relationship of book design to the book's sale? It's to be found buried in the complex of elements affecting the public's reaction to a particular title. This reaction isn't only unpredictable but also usually impossible to rationalize even after it's known.

There are at least a dozen factors that influence sales of a book:

intrinsic quality or interest,
reputation of author,
reviews,
advertising,
promotion and publicity,
current events,
efficiency of distribution,
price,
jacket design,
local interest,
competition,
availability, and
size and weight.

A commercial success may be attributed almost entirely to one of these elements, or it may be due to two or more of them. Except where the cause of success is truly obvious—such as the extraordinary content appeal that makes some books bestsellers despite an almost total lack of initial promotion, favorable review, or author fame; or a sensational news break; or the name of a superstar author—the reasons for any book's sale are almost impossible to identify.

The first factor listed—intrinsic quality or interest—includes the qualities of the book that generate enthusiasm in the reader or browser. This is believed by many to be the most influential single factor in sales, because it results in the "word-of-mouth" advertising that begins with "You *must* read . . ." and ends with a sale. It's in this area that the book's design operates as a cause of sales.

The importance of design can range from vital—for the "coffee table" books meant to sell as impressive gifts—to insignificant—for books with an appeal of a special, and nonvisual, kind (lurid novels, for example). Between these extremes lies a vast area in which design has an unmeasurable but definite effect on sales.

The public's reaction to book design is generally subconscious. Except where the visual aspect is spectacular, the nonprofessional browser is aware of only a vague sense of pleasure or satisfaction in the presence of a well-designed book and a vague feeling of irritation when confronted by a badly designed one.

While it's impossible to isolate the reaction to design from the other elements of a book's appeal, it's probably safe to say that good design is in many cases influential and, where a buyer is undecided, this influence, small as it may be, can tip the balance in favor of a purchase. This is particularly true in the case of expensive gift books and nonfiction that compete with similar titles. It's also effective in the sale of schoolbooks, where competition among several titles of almost identical content is common.

There are two psychological ways in which good book design aids sales: (a) it gives the buyer an impression that the book is highly regarded by the publisher and (b) it tends to make the book look more expensive than it is.

The importance of design in book publishing has much increased in the past decades as movies, magazines, television, and the Internet have heightened the competition for public attention, sharpened the public's appetite for visual excitement, and conditioned its taste. During this period it's become apparent that the public tends to follow leadership in matters of taste rather than insist on its own preferences. The soundest policy then—both esthetic and practical—is to do what seems best, without trying to guess what the public will like.

■ **Bookmaking to management**—Books are created by the combined efforts of editors, production managers, designers, and sales managers, but in many cases each of these knows little of the work of the others. In the early days of book publishing, this problem never arose. The publisher was editor, printer, and designer. Today, the publisher functions more like the producer of a play, hiring the principal members of the staff and making the major policy decisions. However, publishers are usually not equipped (by time, talent, or training) to direct the work of staff specialists. Most of the directing functions of management have been shifted to editors.

Most publishers now regard book designers as industrial designers who can help create salable products, and they regard production managers as experts who can help them operate economically and profitably. This is a great advance over the days when the "manufacturing man" was little more than a clerk who sent mss. to the printer, and the designer was a luxury to be used only for fancy editions.

This attitude toward professional staff has positive effects on morale and performance, but the emphasis on short-term financial goals brought to publishing by the business managers who increasingly dominate conglomerate-owned companies also imposes on publishing professionals unaccustomed financial disciplines and criteria. These sometimes adversely affect decisions that would otherwise be guided by the entrepreneurial judgment and instinct that are the essence of good publishing.

SCHOOLS OF DESIGN

There are two conflicting points of view on the purpose of book design:

(a) Book design should be concerned only with making an economical, tasteful choice and disposition of the book's material and visual ingredients.

(b) Book design is a communications problem, of which (a) is only a part.

The proponents of (a) contend that designers shouldn't interpret the content of the book. They should keep their work as neutral as possible, so that it won't "interfere" between author and reader. The other school (to which this writer belongs) feels that such neutrality, even if it were desirable, is impossible. A book inevitably has graphic and tactile characteristics, and these should be organized to the advantage of author and reader—don't ignore the reader's senses when the author's thoughts are being transmitted through a physical book that can and does affect those senses. The power of visual design is as properly applied to a book as it is to a play or a building.

The books of the "neutral" school are often poorly done but they're rarely offensive. On the other hand, a clumsy or tasteless attempt to use the full range of graphic effects in a book can be monstrous. This isn't an insignificant point, but the more important point is that a book produced by a skillful and sensitive designer can rise far above a work that aspires only to be neutral.

Requirements

TALENT

■ **Production**—"Talent" refers to innate capacities rather than acquired skills. The talent required by a production worker is primarily a sense of organization and secondly a superior ability to learn and retain facts. The successful production manager is one who knows the technical data, material specifications, prices, sources, processes, and equipment that go into the manufacture of books and who can organize this knowledge in a smooth and efficient operation. Also needed is a knack for getting cooperation from a variety of people. As a coordinator, the production manager must extract copy from editors, specifications from designers, materials and production from suppliers—always in good time and in competition with their conflicting demands. Patience and calm under pressure may not properly be called talents, but whatever they are, the production worker needs them.

■ **Design**—Failure in production is revealed by late schedules, broken budgets, and faulty manufacture, but a poorly designed book generally goes unnoticed. This doesn't mean that it's easier to design books than to produce them, it's simply easier to get away with incompetence.

Eighty years ago the limited technical possibilities of book design made few demands on the designer. Today, the graphic and technical resources available require a high level of designer competence. Designers must: (a) be definitely talented in the disposition of form, space, color, and texture; (b) be especially perceptive and analytical; (c) have some natural ability to assimilate technical knowledge; and (d) be able to master the important computer programs.

The designer is a partner (albeit a minor one) of the author and must be capable of analyzing and interpreting the author's intentions. This is most apparent in the creation of textbooks and other books in which the graphic part of the presentation is vital, if not equal to the verbal part. While this relationship isn't as well understood in connection with general tradebooks, it's no less valid.

A talent for graphic representation and mastery of graphic techniques are not absolutely necessary for book designers, because they either specify work that others carry out, or execute their own designs on the computer, but it helps to be able to draw well. One can design books without even a talent in visual art, but the possibilities are definitely limited. Book design without art is like building without architecture. However, don't give up if you have never thought of yourself as an "artist". Talent exists in many persons, unknown to themselves or to others.

BACKGROUND & TRAINING

The ideal background for a production manager is to have worked for at least some time in shops doing composition, color separation, printing, and paper sales or manufacturing. It would help also to have had a stint in an art studio as well as in the sales, editorial, shipping, promotion, and accounting departments of a publishing company. College courses in engineering, math, physics, chemistry, and statistics would come in handy. It isn't necessary to have this work experience and education to run a production department successfully, but the equivalent of a large part of it is very desirable. Most of it can be picked up on the job by reading books and trade publications, taking courses, visiting plants, and asking questions. A good production manager aims to know almost as much about the work of the suppliers as they know themselves.

The perfect background for a designer would include all of the above, plus a liberal arts education heavy on English and literature, a couple of years at a good art school, and at least a year's apprenticeship to a first-class designer. An extremely valuable experience for anyone in publishing is selling in a bookstore. This can provide insights not obtainable any other way.

An ideal four-year college program to prepare for either production or design work might begin with two years of liberal arts, with English as the major subject and the fundamentals of graphic arts and publishing as minors. The second half might concentrate on technical theory and practice, business administration, and design. During the last year, production students would stress administration and science, while the design students would emphasize design and literature. Such a curriculum, larded with field trips to plants and summer work in publishing houses, could radically improve the quality of American publishing.

A number of schools offer courses along these lines. These range from intensive graduate-level courses in book publishing offered at colleges and universities to seminars and workshops in design, production, editing, selling, and other publishing functions provided by a variety of schools and, in addition, by book industry groups such as the American Institute of Graphic Arts, Bookbuilders of Boston, Bookbuilders West, and Women's National Book Association chapters. (See "Sources of information" in the Appendix.)

The Association of American Publishers, One Park Avenue, New York, N.Y. 10017, maintains a current list of book industry–related courses in the United States. Information about many courses is available in the *Literary Market Place (LMP)*, an annual directory of publishing.

Opportunities

KINDS OF JOBS

The nature of each kind of job varies according to the size and organization of the company. In the smaller houses, usually one person does all the production work and directs, or actually does, the design. In the very smallest operations, the proprietor may handle these functions, although this is possible only when the list is small (a dozen books or fewer per year), and freelancers, as well as the service departments of other publishers or of manufacturers, are used.

In medium-sized houses (30 to 100 titles per year) there's usually one or two production managers and from one to three assistants. In such situations, a manager or one of the assistants may do most of the design—giving out only the complicated and "special" books to freelance designers. Some employ a full-time designer. In the larger companies (100 to 250 titles), the production department may consist of a half-dozen persons, or more, and four or eight designers. The largest houses (250 titles and up) may employ more than fifty people in design and production. In some, there's a separate design department under an art director or chief designer; in others, the designers work within the production department. There's often considerable specialization in the large production departments.

The nature of the company's operation is as significant as its size. Textbook and reference book publishers require more help in their art departments than tradebook publishers of comparable size. The same is true of children's book publishers, although some books for small children are created by author, illustrator, and editor, without the use of a designer. In mass-appeal paperback houses, design is emphasized less than direction of the cover art, which, because of the major impact it has on sales, is handled by (usually) well-paid art directors.

The design of jackets and trade paperback covers is usually given to freelancers in the smaller and medium-sized companies—unless the production manager is also a designer. In the largest houses, many of the jackets are designed by the staff.

Another source of jobs is the book manufacturer who employs customer service representatives to coordinate production problems of the publishers with those of the plant. This work is excellent preparation for a good production job in publishing. Finally, there are a handful of independent production and design services that employ assistants.

FUTURES Evaluating the ultimate rewards of each kind of job is a personal matter. The most money can be made by working through smaller production jobs to becoming head of production in a giant company. In large firms, such jobs may pay, roughly, from $75,000 to $100,000 a year and may include a vice-presidency with stock options and other financial benefits.

The production manager in a small company may have a salary in the $40,000 range, but will usually have, also, the satisfaction of intimate participation in company affairs. How satisfying such an arrangement will be depends to a large extent on the personalities involved. There is relatively little difference in pace and pressure whether 30 or 300 books are produced each year. Much more depends on the efficiency of the operation than on its size.

A production assistant with some experience may start at about $30,000 a year and work up to nearly twice that much. The scale for a production trainee—who will keep records, file, and so on while learning—will start at a much lower point than an assistant. Large, conglomerate-owned houses pay more than small independents.

For a designer, the ultimate—financially and, for some, in terms of satisfaction—is to become design head of a big firm. The same position in a medium-sized company brings less money, but usually more creative opportunity. For the art director of a small company, the salary may range from $50,000 to $75,000. It may run up to $100,000+ in a large firm. The satisfaction will depend on the compatibility of the management. For a head of both design and production the pay will probably be about the same as for a production manager. A senior designer's salary may be in the $40,000 to $45,000 range in small companies and up to $75,000 in some of the larger ones.

HOW TO GET A JOB

Book publishing being what it is, a large number of its positions are filled in accidental ways. (In fact, an Association of American Publishers report on education for book publishing is entitled "The Accidental Profession".) Although there are several intensive summer teaching programs, there's no central publishing school from which candidates can be drawn and there's no organized pool of applicants. People drift into jobs by knowing someone or being in the right place at the right time. Paradoxically, book publishing is one of the most desired (glamorous) fields, but many of its jobs go to those willing to take comparatively low pay.

Experience with a printer or book manufacturer is highly regarded as preparation for a production job in a publishing company. A period spent working in the plants where books are made will pay big dividends in better jobs and higher pay later. To get a first job in production, unless you have worked in a supplier's shop or know someone willing to hire you in spite of your lack of experience (to save money or to train you), you'll probably have to start in a relatively subordinate position in the company. As a wrapper, clerk, or even messenger, you have a better chance at a production job than someone outside. In a small firm it doesn't matter much where you work, because you can be noticed, but in a large one, try to get *any* position in the production department, because it's sometimes harder to move from one department to another than to get in at all. If you show yourself to be intelligent, diligent, and interested, there's a good chance that you'll be given a production job in time.

If you live outside the main publishing areas, look around for a nearby university press before rushing to the city. The university presses have few jobs and may not pay much, but they give good experience and are no harder to crack than any other. The same is true of local printers. You should also check the listings of publishers in *Literary Market Place* for companies in your area. There are thousands of specialized and small general publishers in the smaller cities and towns of America.

The first design job is in some ways easier and in some ways more difficult to get. You can show tangible evidence of your ability, but there are fewer design than production jobs. Also, it's essential that you have some bookmaking knowledge if you are to be given any responsibility.

It's a good idea to start by working at any job you can get in a production or design department, with the hope that you can move over into design work later (as suggested for getting into production). Whether you do this or attack a job directly, unless you can show some books you have already designed, the best thing you can do, after studying this book, is assemble a portfolio of computer-created layouts that show: (a) that you know what you are doing and (b) that you have real talent. You won't be given work as a designer unless you've mastered at least one computer layout program such as QuarkXPress or InDesign (CH. 3). Show the specifications for all the parts of at least one book, and preferably three or four. In your designs, be realistic in terms of commercial production, but let your imagination have a bit of play too. A truly impressive portfolio of this kind will be almost as effective as a bagful of printed books. If you have previously done any graphic work that could conceivably be related to practical book work—such as illustrations in woodcut, pen and ink, etc., or your own printing—put in some of this, provided that it shows an ability of specific value. Don't show the lovely but unprofessional collages and figure sketches from art school.

Buy or borrow a current copy of *Literary Market Place*—it's quite expensive, but you'll find it in almost any large library—and look up the names and addresses of the publishers. It's much more likely that you'll get started in a large house than a small one, so try them first. The listings show the number of books published by each company. Start with those that produce over 150. It may do you some good to get in to see the top person, but it really isn't necessary. If the firm is looking for someone, they're just as anxious to find you as you are to find them. They will probably have a human resources (personnel) department that does the hiring. In the smaller companies, look for the names of the production managers or art directors in *LMP* and call or write for appointments.

When you get an interview, the rules are the same as for getting any job. Be prompt, neat, reserved, but pleasant—and don't stay too long. There are employment agencies that specialize in publishing, but they're more likely to help you find your second job than your first.

FREELANCING Freedom, like peace, is wonderful. The idea of coming and going as you please with no grouchy old boss to be nice to is very attractive. But before you decide to freelance, remember that a lot of others like freedom just as much as you do—and the grouchy old boss comes through with a paycheck every week.

Generally, the routine design jobs are done in the house, while the more demanding and special ones may go to freelancers. These are given, of course, to the designers with experience and a reputation. It's not easy to start as a freelance designer.

In freelance production work, there's no room for any but the expert. If the large publishers send out production work at all, they will do so only for books that require more attention than they can give or that involve a special circumstance. In either case they want an experienced hand. The small publishers, who have production work done outside to avoid hiring someone on a salary, don't feel safe unless they deal with a competent and reputable person. They tend to use established production service companies.

Generally, it's best to have a number of years of experience before freelancing. For those who want to try this way of working, the following scale of prices will be useful.

- **Book design**—The range is from about $500 for an unillustrated book with uncomplicated narrative text, to thousands of dollars for a large picture-and-text book. The prices paid vary considerably according to the publisher and the standing of the designer. For illustrated books a layout fee is charged—about $15 to $25 per page.
- **Jacket and paperback cover design**—Prices run from about $800 to $1500, again depending on the publisher and designer involved. A few stars get much more.
- **Production work**—This is done on either a brokerage basis, in which the publisher pays a certain amount (about 10 to 20%) over the cost of manufacture for the service, or on a fee basis, whereby a flat sum is paid for the service, either for a period of time or for a specific number of books. Either way, the amount paid by the publishers should equal a proportionate share of what their production departments cost, or would cost if they had one.

D. BASIC KNOWLEDGE

3. The computer

Bookmaking with computers requires far more knowledge than the precomputer way. Before, the designer simply told technicians what was wanted and the technicians did the rest; now, the designer who uses a computer is also the technician. And computer technology is far more complex than the mechanical processes of the metal-type days, and substantially more difficult to operate than even the photocomposition-plus-paste-up system.

This book makes no attempt to explain how to operate a computer or how to use the many software programs available—there are shelves of fat volumes that supply such information. Here you'll find only the operating principles of computer technology and information on how computers are used in bookmaking. Unfortunately, it isn't possible to impart this quite large body of information in plain English because it has its own language and terminology. Worse yet, almost every computer term has one, two, or three different forms—all of which are used by some people (see "Computer terminology" below).

Those who are already experienced and technically advanced computer users will find the following explanations easy to follow, and they may pass over them entirely. But, technicians who work in the companies that provide prepress and printshop services to designers and publishers find that many of their clients know only enough about computers to do their work, and haven't gone further into the technology than absolutely necessary. However, there's a lot to be learned beyond the minimum, and this knowledge can greatly enhance the designer's capability. So it seems best to give a thorough account of the technology, even if some of it is elementary, because most readers (if not all) will find in these pages some useful information they lack.

Here's an encouraging word. The mind-numbing mass of information you read will begin to make more sense as you apply it at your computer. But there's bad news too. Computers are, or seem to be, neurotic. The unimaginable complexity that enables them to perform amazing feats also makes them vulnerable to a vast array of perplexing ailments. Computer enthusiasts will say that these are only machines and will do nothing but follow the operator's instructions. This seems logical but it isn't true, because the machine already contains a huge number of instructions put in by the devisers of all the programs it holds, and these often get snarled with each other as well as with the user's instructions. All computer users have shed tears of frustration—even after we think we've mastered the damn thing.

What is it?

The computer has become the publishing industry's undisputed engine. This incredible but modest-looking device, amazingly efficient at organizing information and solving complex problems, has made us quite dependent upon it. In bookmaking, every phase of the process is affected by it. Because it's so integral to our professional lives, we should know the basic history of its technology.

THE EMERGENCE OF "DESKTOP PRODUCTION"

Computers were being widely used in publishing during the 1970s and early 1980s for writing, editing, keyboarding data, and typesetting, with each of these functions performed by different people at different locations. Connecting one function to the next was time-consuming and cumbersome. The elements were sent by messenger or mail to the participants, often taking hours, days, or even weeks.

Then, in 1985, the confluence of four independent inventions suddenly made it possible to perform all these different tasks on one computer, and thus to revolutionize not only the publishing world but all print (and ultimately all other modes of) communication. First, Apple Computer introduced the Macintosh computer—the *Mac*—whose screen displayed graphic images that could be manipulated with a handheld pointing device (*mouse*) instead of the complicated keyboarding codes then needed for other computers. Apple also created the LaserWriter, a laser printer compatible with the Macintosh. Second, Adobe Systems invented *PostScript*, a page-description computer language that could convert a computer into a typesetting machine. Third, Allied Linotype Company, which owned the original Linotype typeface library, licensed it to Adobe for use with PostScript. And fourth, Aldus Corporation created *PageMaker*, a page-layout program designed for the Macintosh (Aldus was later bought by Adobe). This juxtaposition of technological wizardry paved the way for "desktop production"(inaccurately called "desktop publishing"—see Preface).

THE USER-FRIENDLY COMPUTER

Before the Mac came along, the IBM *microcomputer*, which came to be known generically as the *PC* (*personal computer*), was the standard in the industry. Several companies developed PCs to compete with the IBM models. All PCs used a common *operating system* (*system, platform, environment*), referred to as *DOS* (*Disk Operating System*). *MS-DOS* and *PC-DOS* are the same thing. The operating system enables the computer to recognize and execute commands given by the user. Computers using a DOS system not made by IBM are called *IBM-compatibles* or *IBM-clones*.

Until the arrival of the Mac, the only way to *interface* with (give instructions to) a computer's operating system was by using the complex typed codes that had to be memorized or looked up in a manual. The Macintosh was a radical improvement: appearing on the screen were symbols, called *icons*, representing instructions which could be selected by the use of the mouse—a lovely alternative to the cumbersome keyboard code commands. The interaction between user and computer became much simpler, more *user-friendly*.

This system, using graphic images on the screen to represent information, is called a *GUI* (pronounced "gooey"), an acronym for *Graphical User Interface*. It was so successful for Macintosh that Microsoft later created a program (*application, software*) called *Windows* to enable PCs to emulate the Mac's ease of operation. Windows eventually graduated from a program to an operating system that has superceded DOS. The Mac's graphic qualities made it instantly appealing to the developing desktop bookmaking market. The Mac became the platform (the equipment basis) of choice for designers, illustrators, and others involved in creating visual materials by computer. A flood of new programs was developed for word-processing, page layout, typography, drawing and painting, image-editing, scanning, and other visual art functions for use on the Mac. Most of the same programs were adapted to PCs after the arrival of Windows. However, because of its early edge in the book-publishing market, the Mac became more widely used than PCs for graphics-based work.

The two platforms are approaching a common ground. There is a program (SoftWindows) to make a Mac function like a PC with Windows (which was created to make a PC act like a Mac), which enables Mac users to run programs that were designed for PCs. In various ways, incompatibility between the two platforms has been lessened and probably will eventually disappear. Other operating systems, such as Linux and Unix, are used on some PCs instead of Windows.

Computer terminology

Some computer systems use terms particular to themselves, but there's a more or less universal terminology referring to computer equipment and functions. The terms defined or explained below appear frequently in the text, so, even though they're familiar to all computer users, it seems important to include them in this section just in case one has slipped by your notice.

A great deal of confusion arises from the use of different words or phrases for the same items or functions. Sometimes these have very subtle nuances in meaning, but not enough to justify the confusion. Because computer use has developed so quickly over such a large area with so many unconnected people involved, terms are being concocted, applied, adopted, adapted, and replaced constantly. Standardization of computer terminology seems almost hopeless, but in an effort to minimize the chaos, the text of this book uses only the terms generally used, and, at the first appearance of a term, follows it with the alternative usage(s) or definition in parentheses. When it's first used, a term is italicized and appears alphabetically in the Glossary-Index, with its definition if necessary.

To begin, *boot up* (start, turn on, power up) the machine. The image appearing on the *monitor* (*screen, display*) depends on which operating system you're using. The work area on screen is called the *desktop*, and traditional office terms are used to describe certain computer functions (e.g., *copy, cut, paste, delete*) and items for organizing data (e.g., *file, folder, trash*). *Desk accessories* are small programs available from the desktop, like a clock and a calculator. A *toolbar* (list of command options—as words or symbols) appears across the top or down the side of the desktop. *Commands* are instructions you give to the computer. When the computer has or needs information for or from you, a *dialog box* (a rectangle containing queries or messages from computer to user) appears on the screen. Items are *selected* (*highlighted, activated, swiped*), causing them to be set off by a color or contrasting tone with the use of the mouse, which is attached to the keyboard by a cable. A *click* (quick press and release) or *double-click* (two clicks in rapid succession) of the mouse button activates the user's command. The position of the mouse is indicated on the screen by a *cursor* (*pointer, arrow, marker*). The cursor can be *navigated* (moved) around by the mouse.

A program is a set of instructions to the computer designed to perform particular tasks. A *version* (*edition*) of a program gets *loaded* (transferred to active memory from a storage place) into the computer. You *launch* (start) the program to perform a particular function, such as *word-processing* (text typing) or layout. The program's *defaults* (preset specifications) are built in by the manufacturer. If alterable by the user, they're *editable*. *Data* are pieces of information. *Supports* (as in "Suitcase supports OS X") means "is compatible with".

Memory refers to the area in the computer for storing data that's in active use. *Storage* is the area for storing programs or data for future use. (See "Memory" below.) A file (electronic document) is a complete set of data entered in memory under a particular heading. When files or programs are transferred to a computer from another one, or from a remote site via *modem* (a computer attachment that enables transmission of data from one computer to another over telephone lines), the data are *downloaded*. When data are transferred to a computer from a scanner or a disk, they're *uploaded*.

The work you do is *input* (entered) into a file, which has been assigned a name so it can be used, stored, and retrieved. A group of related files are placed in a folder, a computer function for organizing files that are in the same category. You *open* a file to gain access to its contents, to read it or work on it with the editorial *tools* available within a program. *Trash* is the term for data you want to discard, which you do by dragging it to an icon on the desktop that looks like a garbage can and is labeled "Trash" on Macs, but on PCs it's called "*Recycle Bin*".

An open (active) file displays information inside *windows* (framed panels displaying data). You *scroll* (navigate) through the contents of a file by clicking the mouse on vertical and horizontal *scroll bars* that move the data up or down in an open window.

A *menu* is a list of the items found within a category, such as "Tools", "Insert", etc. Typically, a menu is accessed by clicking on the category name.

WYSIWYG (pronounced "wizzywig")—the acronym for "What You See Is What You Get"—refers to the system's presumed ability to replicate in the *output* (printed page, *hard copy*) exactly what appears on the screen. This usually works.

Save is a command used to "fix" the data input, including changes, by moving it from memory to storage. *Crash* refers to the computer's nasty habit of occasionally coming to a complete stop and refusing to do any more work without, seemingly, any reason. You *close* the file, *put away* a disk, *quit* (*exit*) the program, *shut down* (turn off) the computer.

In this book, the term "*printshop*" is used instead of "printer" to refer to a company that prints books, to distinguish this from "printer"—which refers to—the familiar desktop *peripheral* (an external device connected to a computer) that *prints out* data from a computer.

The computer system

Some components of a computer system are essential at various stages; others are optional enhancements. Some essential services can be bought from outside sources, like *service bureaus*, which saves the expense of buying equipment or software, but may not be the most economical course in the long run. Without a good grasp of the fundamental components, it will be impossible to make good decisions about the many choices from the vast assortment of equipment and programs available.

A computer system consists of both *hardware* and software. Hardware is the physical apparatus: computer, keyboard, printer, scanner, modem, etc. Software refers to the programs written to instruct the computer and its peripherals.

BITS & BYTES *Bits* and *bytes* are units of information. It may be hard to believe, but the fantastically complex feats of the computer are accomplished by the operation of a simple on-off switch—multiplied, of course, millions of times. The mathematical basis for all computer data transactions is the *binary system*. This is the two-way switch: expressed as 0 (zero) or 1. Either 0 or 1 forms a bit (contraction of *binary digit*). A bit is the smallest unit of data, but by itself it contains no information—it must be in a combination of at least two bits: 00, 01, 10, or 11. A byte is 8 bits grouped together. For example: 01100001. It takes one byte to form one text character (the example above forms the lowercase "a"). A computer's capacity for memory storage is expressed in bytes, which may have any one of 256 possible combinations of bits.

Below are the terms used for multiples of bytes:
1 kilobyte (K) = 1024 bytes
1 megabyte (MB or meg) = 1024 kilobytes = 1,048,576 bytes
1 gigabyte (gig) = 1024 megabytes = 1,073,741,824 bytes

Though actually only approximations, in computer jargon a *K* is a thousand, a *meg* is a million, and a *gig* is a billion bytes.

HARDWARE

Given the lightning speed of changes in computer technology, in the time between the publication of this text and your reading of it much of the specific information about products—like speed, power, memory, capacity, model features, and enhancements—will undoubtedly become outdated. Such data are provided here with the understanding that they may be useful only for their value in clarifying relative standards.

The computer components

The core elements—the *CPU*, its *motherboard* (main circuit board) and memory, internally mounted expansion cards, the internal hard disk, and other internal drives—are The Computer. On some models, the monitor may be incorporated into the basic computer, but it's generally attached as an external device.

THE CPU Until the early 1980s, computers were room-sized, climate-controlled behemoths called *mainframes*. Then they were miniaturized to desktop size for home and office, using the *microprocessor* as their *central processing unit* (CPU).

The microprocessor, the computer's brain, is an integrated circuit called a *silicon chip*. The chip determines which software can be run and it performs all information-processing functions. It also determines the *speed* of the computer—how fast it processes and displays information and performs functions. Its speed is measured in megahertz (MHz). In 1996 microprocessor speeds were over 166 MHz. Only a year earlier they had half the speed. By 2001 their speed hit a gigahertz (GHz) and by 2003 a whopping 3 GHz and counting. Speed is affected also by the CPU's *architecture*. Architecture refers to the size, in bits, of each instruction that the CPU can process. Early personal computers were built with an 8-bit architecture; later this was increased to 16-bit, then 32-bit, and then 64-bit. The larger the chunk of data that can be handled in each instruction, the more that it can accomplish. Further, the practical speed of a processor is affected also by the amount and type of its *cache memory*. Cache memory is within the silicon chip of the CPU and can be accessed at much higher speed than memory, which is separate from it on the motherboard.

MEMORY

In human terms, "memory" is defined as the ability to recall knowledge and experience. In computer terms, it refers to the machine's store of data and its instructions for using its data to solve problems. These instructions are called *programming*. So, while the computer doesn't actually "remember", it can summon its data resources to know how to respond to a given task.

The definition of computer memory can be confusing because the term is often applied interchangeably to two distinct, though related, functions. One is short-term or temporary memory—which refers to the work you are doing now. The other is long-term or permanent memory—the record of that work which you keep for the future. To keep the distinction clear, the short-term use of data, called *RAM* (*Random Access Memory*), will be referred to as "memory". The long-term preservation of data will be referred to as "storage".

The CPU gets the instructions it needs from the programs and does the work you command, showing it to you on the monitor. But until the work is saved—put into storage on the hard disk—it's not permanent. When the computer is shut down, the data in RAM or in temporary files on the hard disk that hasn't been saved *is instantly erased*. There are many other ways your work in progress can get erased. There is no protection other than *frequent* saving. Anything you didn't save is lost!

Another kind of memory in the CPU is *ROM* (*Read-Only Memory*). This is installed by the manufacturer and, unlike RAM, is never erased. It runs the basic operations of the computer (*BIOS—Basic Input/Output System*) and generally can't be altered. The exception is a special kind of ROM called *EPROM (Erasable/Pro-*

grammable Read-Only Memory). These chips are used to allow the BIOS to be upgraded when necessary.

In a computer ad you might see these arcane specifications: 64 MB (expandable to 256 MB)/6 GB. This means that the machine comes with 64 megabytes of RAM, which can be expanded to 256 (by adding memory chips), and 6 gigabytes of hard disk space. Both RAM and disk space can be expressed in megabytes or gigabytes. How much of each you need depends entirely on which programs you expect to be using and how much data you plan to keep stored in the computer. Be aware that programs become more sophisticated—and more memory-intensive—with each new version. What was ample memory and storage space before may be inadequate for a new program.

For general bookmaking use in 2003, 128 MB of RAM (with room to expand) is the minimum. A 20 GB hard disk for storage would do the job. For added graphics functions—layout, illustration, photo scanning, etc.—256 MB of memory and 40 GB for storage are better. But requirements change rapidly, so it's really impossible to forecast a system's needs even a year or two ahead. A safe policy is this: Buy a system with the most storage space that you can afford—you can never have too much.

Fortunately, it's easy to install more RAM. Computers are designed with built-in expansion slots for installing these printed circuit boards with memory chips attached. The expansion slots determine how much additional RAM you can add, depending on the model of the computer.

THE HARD DISK The computer stores its information on the *hard disk*—a memory storage space housed either in the same case as the CPU (*internal*) or in a separate case (*external*) connected to it by a cable.

THE DRIVE The mechanism used to read information from a disk and write information to a disk is the *drive*. All computers have a hard drive and many are equipped also with a recording removable media drive (see "Peripherals") such as a *floppy disk* (*diskette, disk, floppy*—so called because the first ones were a flexible material) drive, *Zip* drive, *CD-R (CD-Recordable)*, or *CD-RW (CD-Rewritable)* drive. Virtually all computer models also have a CD-ROM drive, but CDs, which hold up to 650 MB of data, are being superseded by *DVD* drives, which can hold about 4.5 GB. Some Macs are equipped with drives capable of reading CDs and DVDs and writing both CD-RW and DVD-R. Macs made after 1999 have no internal floppy drive. (See "Storage media" below.)

Peripherals

There are two categories of external devices (peripherals) that supplement the operations of the computer: input devices and output devices.

Input devices are the hardware for feeding data to the computer. Examples are keyboards, mouses, *digital graphic tablets*, *scanners*, and microphones. The process of electronically converting data into a form the computer recognizes is *digitizing*. A software program tells the computer how to interpret and process the data.

Output devices take the processed data and present them in some form to the user. Examples are monitors, speakers, printers, and *imagesetters*.

Some devices have both input and output functions. Hard disk storage, floppy disk storage, and modems are examples. They feed data to the CPU and extract data from it. Floppy disk devices and modems may be either external or internal.

STORAGE MEDIA

In addition to saving your work on the hard disk, it's necessary to store it elsewhere too, for these important reasons:

(a) To prevent the loss of programs and work in the event of a big disaster—total system failure. This happens, and your only insurance is to *back up*, i.e., copy everything you do onto another *storage medium*. DO IT!—periodically! regularly! frequently! absolutely!

(b) To make more room on your hard disk. Just as with a closet, stuff accumulates. Unclutter by putting files that don't need to be instantly accessible on other disks.

(c) To transport data from one computer to another. For instance, taking work home from the office or sending a job to the printshop.

There are two basic kinds of storage devices—disks and tapes. Most disks can be both read (data retrieved from) and written to (data added or changed); some can only be read. There are two basic types of disk: fixed (nonremovable) disks such as the hard disk, and removable disks such as floppy disks, Zip disks, and CDs.

■ **Removable magnetic disks**—Removable disks may be used not only to supplement the hard disk's storage capacity but also for transferring data into and out of the computer—for example, to make backup copies of files or to install new software. Until recently, the floppy was the most generally used magnetic removable disk, but it has been largely replaced by the CD.

Floppy disks used by both the PC and Mac platforms may be physically the same, but are *formatted* (specifically coded) differently for each. The Mac operating system allows disks formatted for the PC to be read in a Mac drive, but PCs require special software to read Mac disks. The file formats written by the two platforms are also different and often incompatible. On either platform file, translation utilities may be needed to make the files from the other usable. The success of these translations is often limited. Floppy disks vary in memory storage capacity. The kind used most are *HD* (*high density*), which hold 1.4 MB of data.

Although becoming obsolete, floppies are hard to beat for convenient and economical transfer of data between systems. Unfortunately, many computers no longer have built-in floppy drives, so it's necessary to attach an external drive. A floppy drive is still desirable, if not indispensable.

- **Removable drive cartridges**—Running out of hard disk memory space is always a problem, especially for those, like graphic artists, whose work creates large files. When a file is too large to transfer from a computer onto relatively low-capacity floppies—for example, when sending illustrations to a color separator—something with much greater memory capacity is needed. Removable drive cartridges, such as Zip, Superdisk, and Jaz, were designed for this. The storage capacity of these cartridges ranges from 44 MB to over a gigabyte, depending on the drive model. Each of the cartridges requires a different type of drive to read or write it. Be sure to check for compatibility if you plan to use removable media.
- **Optical removable media**—The first optical medium to achieve widespread use is the *CD*. Full font libraries, photographs, and artwork are all available on CDs. The familiar audio CD was the first practical application of optical disk technology. Audio CDs and *CD-ROMs* (*Compact Disk Read-Only Memory*) are read-only disks—their content can't be altered, deleted, or re-recorded. CD-ROMs also have multimedia capability—they can combine audio, video, and text on one disk played from a CD drive. Their enormous capacity for storing illustrative and textual data in a small, light, easy-to-carry, cheap-to-mail disk makes them ideal for many uses. Recordable CDs—CD-R (blank disks on which data can be recorded) and rewritable CDs—CD-RW (blank disks that can be recorded on and also altered) are the new standard for storing or transferring large volumes of data. Almost all new computers have CD disk drives, and most come with CD-RW drives.

  DVDs are essentially a higher-capacity CD (4.5 GB). A DVD drive is supplied as standard equipment in many computers, and some have DVD-RW drives.
- **Magnetic tapes**—Tape drives are another option for backup and storage. They can be installed internally if the computer is so equipped, or attached externally as a peripheral device. Generally, magnetic tape is cheaper than disks, but retrieving material is slower and testing the data is less convenient than it is with disks. Tapes are more practical for companies than for individuals.
- **Internet storage services**—There are several Internet services that will store your files online for a fee and protect them with a password, but we have seen that nothing on the Internet is safe from hackers—password, encryption, or not. However, Internet storage is easy and cheap, if not entirely secure. For storing large volumes of data over the Internet a high-speed connection is strongly recommended.

■ The modem—The modem (MOdulator/DEModulator) is a device to encode computer information in a form transmittable over telephone, cable, or fiber-optic lines, and other electronic channels. Modems may be internal (built into the computer housing) or external devices. Data files are sent from one computer to another along these channels at speeds that depend on their *bandwidth* (copper telephone wires are a relatively slow low-bandwidth channel; high-bandwidth fiber-optic cable lines are hundreds of thousands times faster). Other speed factors are the size of the file and the speed of the modems at each end. A small file can take seconds, a huge file hours to travel the line. Files can be *compressed* to save transmission time and storage space (CH. 8).

The speed of a modem is expressed in *bits-per-second* (*bps*) or *bauds*. The fastest modems in 2003 delivered 56,000 bps over the copper telephone wires. With the use of modems and special software, computers can send faxes to remote fax machines or to another computer. A high-bandwidth connection such as cable modem, DSL (Digital Subscriber Line), T1 line, etc. can provide much higher data transmission speeds.

INPUT DEVICES

■ The keyboard—The computer keyboard is like a typewriter's, plus extra keys for computer-specific commands. PC keyboards have an additional row of *function keys* (*F-keys*) that enable you to assign single keys to frequently used commands. The Mac has an extended keyboard for the F-keys and an additional cluster of six dedicated keys for instant access to certain navigating functions. Some keyboards have a built-in *trackball* (see below). For those who spend all day at the computer, there are ergonomically designed keyboards to reduce fatigue while typing.

■ The mouse—This handheld pointing device, used to convey information to the computer (see "Computer terminology"), controls the movements of the cursor either by moving a rolling ball under its belly (*mechanical mouse*) over a flat surface or by light sensors (*optical mouse*). The mouse is needed to operate Graphical User Interface systems, like for Macintosh or Windows for PC. A variation on the mouse is a trackball, a spherical sensor that's rotated within a stationary base.

■ The graphics tablet—This is an electronic drawing pad on which you can draw or write with a stylus—a pen-like instrument—as though working on paper. The tablet digitally converts the marks put on it into information that can be read by the computer. With graphics (or digital) tablets it's possible to experience the feel of traditional painting and drawing tools and create a broad range of visual effects.

■ The scanner—A scanner is an optical image-reading device that translates type or graphics into digital form and relays them to the computer, where they can be manipulated—altered, resized, positioned, screened, etc. Photographic prints, film negatives or positives (transparencies), paintings, drawings, diagrams, typewritten text, even three-dimensional objects, can be converted into electronic images by a scanner.

Monochrome scanners exist, but *color scanners* can make black & white and grayscale (black & white tonal) scans also—and they're so inexpensive that almost all scanners sold have color. Color scanners theoretically yield 16,777,216 different colors (256 shades of each of three colors—red, green, and blue—multiplied by their 256 possible combinations).

An extremely useful function that can save time and money is text scanning, known as *OCR* (*Optical Character Recognition*). Typed or printed pages are fed into the scanner to create image files of the text. Special software in the computer analyzes the images of the pages, reading each character and converting it into digital form. The digitized text can be transferred to a word-processing program or page-layout program for editing, eliminating the tedious work of typing page after page on the computer. The cost can be substantially lower than typing, provided the copy is clean. Even though the software has been improved to handle fuzzy faxes and uneven photocopies, OCR scans must be carefully proofread, as there's a tendency for them to confuse some characters with others (the numeral 0 with the capital O, for example).

SCANNER RESOLUTION: A *pixel* (contraction of *picture element*) is the smallest visual unit on a computer screen. Every image on the screen is made up of pixels, which are dots too small to be seen with the unaided eye. Scanner resolution is the measure of pixel density expressed in *dots-per-inch* (*dpi*). The more dots per inch, the sharper the image and the larger the size of the file (the more memory used). A detailed discussion of resolution is included in "Scanning" in CH. 8.

TYPES OF SCANNERS: Scanners operate in two different ways: those using *CCDs* (*Charge-Coupled Devices*) move the scan head across the stationary document; those with *PMTs* (*Photo Multiplier Tubes*) move the document across the stationary scan head. Except for the drum type, all the scanners described below use CCDs.

Handheld scanners are practical for making for-position-only scans but not for quality reproduction. They are small, inexpensive, very portable, and, with the appropriate software, can also read text. However, there are two drawbacks: (a) because the scan is controlled by the erratic motion of the hand, it's prone to distortion, and (b) the narrow width of the scanner (about 4") limits the scan swipe to that dimension.

Flatbed scanners are similar in operation to photocopiers. The original is placed face down on a glass screen and the scan head passes under it. Some models can be fitted with a transparency

Creo professional model flatbed scanner

adapter which moves a scanning arm above the glass, reading light through the transparency (see "Film scanners" below).

Sheetfed scanners take only individual pages, which are fed into a slot and carried through on rollers, so they can't scan anything bulky like magazines or books. Some do color while others are only for black & white text or line graphics.

Film scanners digitize slides, film negatives, and transparencies by passing light through the film into a slow-moving scanning arm. Some do only 35-mm slides, some can handle all transparency sizes from 35-mm up. Film scanners typically have higher resolution than flatbeds or sheetfeds.

Rotating drum scanners are the most expensive and are generally found only at graphic services suppliers and large companies with high-volume use. These precision machines produce superlative color quality, but they cost tens to hundreds of thousands of dollars and require specialized technicians.

OTHER SCANNING OPTIONS: *Video frame-grabbers* capture still images from video sources. These circuit boards that plug into the computer are not scanners but interpreters of electronic information. They convert video signals into digital data to be *bitmapped* (each computer type-character or graphic element is made up of multiple bits, or dots, arranged to create the image; the arrangement is a *bitmap*). The source can be a TV, camcorder, video disk,

Creo drum scanner

or a still video camera. The process is fast and cheap, but quality is limited by the video resolution.

Photo CDs contain color images scanned and saved onto a CD by a photo-processing lab. From 35-mm transparencies and film negatives, or from prints, a series of five scans is made in a range of resolutions from very low, for positioning, to very high, for making quality color separations. The pro version (at about ten times the price) adds two more scans for each image at even higher resolutions. The CD can store up to 100 images (with five scan resolutions each) on one disk in the standard photo CD format. Not all photo-processing labs make photo CDs.

Digital cameras are operated much like conventional cameras but differ in the way they capture and store the photographic image. Most record the picture using a CCD array similar to a scanner's and store the image in the camera's electronic memory instead of on film. To view or print the image, the camera is hooked up to the computer. The great advantage is instant gratification; unlike film, there's no developing process, and the picture can be immediately viewed, manipulated, or edited. There is no waste of time or materials, no additional expense for film and processing, and there should never be a need to go back and reshoot, since every image can be checked and approved as it's made. As the quality achievable with digital cameras continues to rise while their price falls, they're fast becoming the preferred alternative for professional photographers. *CMOS* (*complementary metal-oxide semiconductor*) sensor designs may bring the prices of high-quality digital cameras down to popular levels.

OUTPUT DEVICES

■ **The monitor**—The monitor enables you to view work done on the computer, from which it receives video signals. These appear on the screen as pixels, the invisibly small dots. Most graphics-related work requires a color monitor, and almost all monitors sold have color. Several factors determine the level of quality and comfort of a monitor:

SIZE: Monitor screens range in size from about 13 to 22", measured diagonally. At least 17" is recommended for working on page layouts and a minimum of 19" is preferred. Smaller screens may show only a portion of the page, so you must either reduce it to see the entire image, or scroll to view it in full size, a section at a time.

SCREEN RESOLUTION: Most monitors conform to *VGA* (*Video Graphics Array*) standards and are capable of resolving an image of 640 x 480 pixels. Some meet the *SVGA* (*Super VGA*) standard of 1024 x 768 pixels and many exceed even that standard, with resolutions ranging up to 2048 x 1536 pixels.

DOT PITCH: This is the spacing of dots on a color monitor. The smaller the distance between dots, the crisper the image. Dot pitches range from .008"(0.22 mm) to .015"(0.39 mm).

COLOR DEPTH: To meet VGA standards a monitor need be capable of reproducing only sixteen colors, but most monitors far exceed this. SVGA standards require a capability of more than sixty thousand colors and many monitors are designed for "True Color" reproduction, which is capable of creating more than sixteen *million* colors.

REFRESH RATE (VERTICAL SCAN FREQUENCY): This controls the screen flicker.

Remember that the monitor must be compatible with the computer's *video card* (this interprets the video commands from the CPU to control the monitor's output) and will be limited by the card's capabilities and available video memory. The two work together as a subsystem of the computer and their selection must always be considered together. Obviously, this isn't a problem if the monitor is built into the computer.

■ **The Printer**—Regardless of the type of printer, the more dpi the better the print quality. The level of quality needed depends on what the printer is used for. For text, 300 dpi is plenty. This is sufficient also for in-house proofs, which don't need to be as impressive as those for presentation. Proofs going to the service bureau or printshop as a guide for production should approximate the resolution of the final work as closely as possible (1200 dpi or even 600 should do). Top reproduction quality output by imagesetters and platesetters is 2540 dpi.

To relay data from computer to printer, they must be in a form both computer and printer understand. For this, data are bitmapped, i.e., organized by a *printer driver* into patterns of individual dots that appear as pixels on the paper to create an image. Without a driver, information sent by the computer could not be understood by the printer. The multitude of drivers needed to interface all of the software systems with all of the printers available posed a huge problem. Fortunately, there's PostScript to bridge the gap between what the computer knows and the printer shows. PostScript works with any combination of computer and PostScript-compatible printer. In theory, a PostScript file will print exactly the same on any PostScript printer. In practice, however, different PostScript *RIPs* (*Raster Image Processors*) can create subtly different output. For example, line spacing or even the size of the printed image may vary.

In general, a page printed without PostScript won't look as good as one printed with it. When buying a printer, be sure it's equipped with the most recent version of PostScript. If a printer isn't PostScript-based, it may be able to be modified (at additional cost) later. PostScript clones not made by Adobe can serve as well (CH. 5).

Adobe's *Acrobat* software, which creates *Portable Document Format* (*PDF*) files, is in some ways superior to PostScript. PDF includes most of the PostScript features and is faster and less subject to performance variations (CH. 10).

BLACK & WHITE DESKTOP PRINTERS: *Dot matrix printers* form letters with patterns of dots made by 9 to 24 tiny pins which strike an inked ribbon over a roll of paper. Printouts are rough looking, so these printers can be useful only where sharp image quality isn't required. Their continuous-feed paper tends to jam more often than individual sheets. Dot matrix printers aren't used in bookmaking.

Inkjet printers produce images by shooting ink dots at paper through nozzles. They are faster, quieter, and have better resolution than dot matrix printers. An inkjet's speed depends on how much built-in memory and how many jet nozzles it has. The image produced by lower-quality inkjet printers may not be as smooth and refined as a laser printer's (see below)—there may be a discernible dot pattern—but it can be an adequate proofing device. Some models can print a page up to 11 x 17". Higher-priced models may have PostScript or a PostScript clone built in. The cost of most inkjet printers is between that of a dot matrix and a laser. Almost all inkjet printers sold have color capability.

Laser printers work on the same principle as photocopiers. The computer sends a page to the printer, where a pulsating laser beam reads and "draws" it, dot by dot, onto a cylindrical photoconductive drum. The electrically charged dots on the drum attract toner (a fine black magnetic powder), which is fused by heat to the paper (xerography). Desktop laser printers have resolutions of 600 dpi and higher, which produces good-quality proofs and, where high resolution isn't required, can be used as *repro* (*reproduction proofs, camera copy*). More expensive models print up to 1200 dpi, and the difference is visible. Laser printers vary in output speed from 4 to over 40 pages per minute (*ppm*). However, the advertised speed is usually idealized, like gas mileage on cars. The real rate of output depends on the amount of data in a page, how they're processed by the computer, and other variables. Pages with many fonts, graphics, etc. take longer than simple text.

It's important to have sufficient RAM installed in the printer to cope with your needs. If you often print out pages with scanned images, you'll need more RAM than if you print only straight text. If needed, RAM can be added to the printer.

The standard printer paper size is *letter* (8½ x 11"). Some models can print *legal* (8½ x 14") and more expensive ones *ledger* (*tabloid*) (11 x 17") or even 12 x 20". Ledger size is very useful for printing two-page spreads and can be worth the cost if you often do large-format books. Laser printers don't print to the paper's edge (even those that claim edge-to-edge printing). If your layout exceeds the paper size, the printer can *tile* the pages, i.e., print them in sections which may be taped, waxed, or glued together.

Laser and inkjet printers can print most papers of normal letterpaper thickness, and many can be adjusted to take thicker stock and envelopes. As in any kind of printing, quality is affected by the type of paper. Inexpensive photocopy paper is serviceable for everyday use, but when making a great impression is important, it's worth the small extra expense to use the smoother, less absorbent laser papers.

Some points to consider when buying a printer:

(a) Not all printers are both PC- and Mac-compatible. Some may be adaptable to your platform with special software, but it's best to get a printer made to run with your computer.

(b) Not all printers can be connected to a *network* (a group of linked computers that share software, files, and peripheral devices like printers, scanners, etc.).

(c) Ink for inkjet printers comes in a disposable cartridge and can be relatively expensive to keep replacing as the ink runs out.

COLOR DESKTOP PRINTERS: Laser color printers are substantially more expensive than inkjet color printers but are faster. However, the resolution on some inkjet models can be 1440 dpi or more and their quality of reproduction for continuous-tone (halftone) images can rival that of conventional photographic prints. Most models have one cartridge containing three colored inks—*cyan*, *magenta*, *and yellow*—and a separate cartridge containing black. This allows them to print true *CMYK* (cyan, magenta, yellow, black) images. Some high-end models have separate cartridges for each of the four colors. Others have six ink colors. Inkjet technology is being used in some economical prepress proofers and there are a few specialized color printers made for producing graphic images.

Thermal wax transfer printers use three or four colored wax layers applied one at a time. The colored wax is heat-embossed to the paper. These printers produce extremely vibrant and saturated color, creating a poster-like appearance.

Dye sublimation printers use a specially coated paper that makes three or four separate passes through colored dye-imbued ribbons which, when heated, layer the dyes into the paper. The blending of the dyes eliminates the pattern of dots, creating a continuous-tone effect. Some hardware combines both thermal wax and dye sublimation technologies in one unit.

Inkjet thermal printers (also called *phase change printers*) combine thermal wax and inkjet technologies. Instead of firing ink onto paper as an inkjet does, colored wax is melted and sprayed through the nozzles.

- **High-resolution output**—Service bureaus (or *imaging centers*) have high-end versions of some of the output equipment described, and can provide the high resolution required for quality presentations and prepress production. Some large publishing houses find it economical to acquire this level of hardware for their in-house production.

SOFTWARE

There are two types of software: system and program. *System software* runs the general internal functions of the computer. *Program software* manipulates data to perform specific tasks, like word-processing or page layout.

A program enables you to instruct the computer how to accomplish work. It provides a set of tools with which to work, which is fine, but mastering them can be a challenge. If your needs are simple, you may never get into all the intricacies of the program, learning only what you have to know. But bear in mind that the capabilities of programs vary greatly, from low end, which can do the basics but not much more, to the high-end programs with very sophisticated tools for advanced-level work. To avoid frustration, it's important to choose a program that fits your needs and knowledge.

Program software can't think or make decisions for you, but it will instantly carry out your orders efficiently, provided you give it the proper instructions and the equipment you are using has the capability (a paint program can't show you color on a grayscale screen, no matter what you tell it). For design work, some kinds of software offer standard formats from which to choose. These are useful to start with until you get comfortable with a program, but the programs also provide the option of creating your own formats, and the creative designer will want to do this as soon as possible.

New software is constantly coming on the market. Established programs are constantly being changed and improved. Some, which have become standards for certain uses, like *Microsoft Word* and *WordPerfect* in word-processing, or *QuarkXPress, Adobe PageMaker,* and *Adobe InDesign* in page layout, tend to leapfrog each other with a succession of relatively minor innovations, called "tweaks" by the cynical.

There are two reasons to update software: new features are added and bugs (problems) in the program are fixed. New versions are identified by the number after the program name. For instance, if the current version is 3.3, the next minor upgrade will show a change in the number *after* the decimal, to 3.4. For major revisions (rewrites), the number *before* the decimal point changes, e.g., to 4.0. (Be wary of first versions—1.0—they are likely to have bugs in them.) When you buy a program, the registration card inside often entitles you to free upgrades and reduced prices for major rewrites. Returning the card puts you on a mailing list that will help you keep up with new developments.

Plug-ins are accessory programs that add functions to a main program. Sometimes they're produced by the main program's developer, but more often by third-party vendors that specialize in making accessories. Here it's important to say a word about copyrights: Program developers are publishers. Program packages have a seal stating that the terms of your purchase prohibit copying the program except for your own back-up purposes. By breaking the seal you agree to these terms. Illegally duplicating and distributing copies of programs to others, like pirate printing of books, is copyright infringement subject to prosecution.

Choosing the best program for the kind of work you do calls for careful investigation. Read computer magazine reviews. Talk to others who have used the program you're considering. (It's always useful to know someone you can call when you run into problems with your new program.) Some software companies offer free demo programs on floppy disks or CDs that contain the major features of the program, allowing you to "test-drive" it.

For bookmaking, there are four broad categories of programs available:

(a) word-processing,
(b) page layout (page-makeup),

(c) drawing and illustration, and
(d) painting and image-editing (photo manipulation).

There are other specialty programs that are not generally used in book design but could be, such as type design and manipulation programs that allow you to invent or modify type fonts, and 3-D programs like *CAD* (*Computer Aided Design*) that are used by architects and product designers to create, modify, and even animate three-dimensional images. In addition, there are accessory programs to add features, boost power, smooth operations, and generally improve the main programs.

INTEGRATED PROGRAMS Computer software developers produce some combined-function programs, such as ClarisWorks, PerfectWorks, and Microsoft Works. They do a modestly good job but can't replace dedicated single-function programs for demanding work. Using one program to perform all functions risks problems. For example, layout programs have some drawing capabilities, but using a layout program's meticulous page geometries to create a logo may use much more memory than would a drawing program. Some word-processing programs can lay out pages and some layout programs can process text. So then, why use separate programs? Because dedicated programs are designed to excel in their particular area of work. A book of pictures or graphics with few words can be efficiently done entirely in a page-layout program. A book consisting mostly of text with few one-color pictures or graphics can be set up in a word-processing program, but it can't then go into the prepress stage. A layout program is needed to go from page-makeup into film for platemaking and presswork.

WORD-PROCESSING PROGRAMS Dedicated word-processing programs are best equipped to prepare text. They make it possible to type, edit, and rearrange text, check spelling and grammar, key footnotes, create and access database information, set multiple columns, tables, extract, indexes, and more. To a limited extent, they can perform layout program functions: manipulate typography, handle color and scanned images, and manage master pages.

Text is input to a word-processing file either by keyboarding, *importing* it (transferring it by one of several methods described in CH. 6) from another file or program, or reading an OCR scan. It's edited and formatted and then *exported* to a page-layout program for typesetting, where it can still be edited. There are many word-processing programs. The most widely used are Microsoft Word and WordPerfect.

PAGE-LAYOUT PROGRAMS Page-layout (page-makeup) programs take type and illustration elements from other kinds of programs—word-processing, drawing and painting, image-editing, etc.—and organize them into pages. The final output can be low-res (low-resolution) printed proofs, imagesetter repros (high-resolution printouts), transparencies, film negatives and color separations from which printing plates can be made, platesetter output of the printing plates themselves, or even directly digitally printed matter.

All professional-level page-makeup programs perform the following major functions:

- **Type manipulation**—Layout programs make it possible to create refined typography on the computer. They enable fine-tuning of type size, letterspacing, wordspacing, and line spacing in tiny increments.
- **Text and picture handling**—Repositioning, resizing, reproportioning, and rotation of images are enabled by these programs. There are horizontal and vertical guides for measuring and alignment. With *drag and drop*, the cursor is used to pick up and relocate elements.
- **Master pages**—Standard formats can be set up for different types of pages in a book—chapter openings, text body, index, bibliography, etc.—to achieve consistency and efficiency in replicating design elements.
- **Management of illustrated and scanned images**—Limited control is possible over imported scans from image manipulation programs and art from draw or paint programs.
- **Prepress production**—The final stage in page-makeup is generally transmitting data to output film for platemaking. Color preparation for this step can be done only by layout programs. And it's important to use programs that are familiar to the service bureau and/or printshop that will produce the final product. Strictly speaking, "prepress" begins after page-makeup is completed, but the dividing line is somewhat blurred, because some prepress functions are sometimes performed by makeup programs.

The page-makeup programs developed by the various manufacturers are generally similar. The major competitors keep somewhat level with each other by adding features to new versions. They all strive for cross-platform compatibility (being usable on both PCs and Macs), more technical publishing features, and better prepress features.

Most people become proficient in only one layout program because mastering one takes a serious amount of time. So how do you choose which to learn? Obviously, some programs will be better for you than others because of their technical capabilities for the kind of work you do. Another good reason to choose a particular program is that it's used by the people with whom you are working. It's very helpful to be able to tap the knowledge of more experienced associates when you're learning a complex new program. Following is a brief review of the most popular programs.

PageMaker (Adobe) was the first layout program introduced and early desktop computer users learned on it. Its ease of use for relatively simple work gave it an early lead in the market and it's the most widely used layout program on PCs. But, since the Macintosh dominated the graphics field, the introduction of QuarkXPress for the Mac a short time later won over the bookmaking market. PageMaker has been relegated to the "office publishing" market and has been replaced by InDesign for professional users.

QuarkXPress (Quark) proved more facile with typography, layout, and handling of color than PageMaker. Its precision typographic and graphics controls and its powerful prepress capabilities gained it a reputation for providing substantial freedom and fluidity for creative designers. Its features were designed specially for the Mac, and an array of hundreds of add-on customizing features (called *XTensions* by Quark) made its flexibility even more appealing. Although the Macintosh is still the platform of choice in the graphics field, the introduction of Windows software by Microsoft has enabled PCs to perform similarly to Macs, with Quark available in both Mac and Windows versions.

InDesign (Adobe) is a major alternative to Quark. Adobe has designed it with features that rival, and in some cases surpass, those of QuarkXPress. It has similar capabilities overall and isn't troubled by some of the inconvenient Quark quirks. Adobe dominates the market for drawing and photo-editing software with their Illustrator and Photoshop software, and InDesign takes advantage of this common lineage by enabling closer integration of the three programs than is possible with its competitors.

FrameMaker (Adobe) works well for long and complex books with technical, mathematical, or scientific material. It has extensive word-processing features, drawing tools for charts and illustrations, and database capabilities. It's particularly useful for textbook publishing.

Corel Ventura is exclusively a PC program. It comes with Ventura Database Publisher built in for producing documents from database information. There has been an effort to enhance its graphics functions.

DRAWING PROGRAMS For computer layout, it's very useful to have a working knowledge of a drawing program. Also called illustration, or draw, programs, they're used to create decorative and technical drawings, maps, diagrams, and charts, and to customize (modify) type. Happily, once you've learned one illustration program you'll be able to navigate around others as well—the basic tools and methods are similar, though specific features vary.

Draw programs create *vector* images. The term refers to the way information about the image is perceived by the computer and communicated to the screen or printer. Lines, curves, and filled-in shapes are described mathematically as a set of instructions on how to draw the picture. This is one of two systems, the other being paint program bitmapping (see "Painting & image-editing programs" below).

There are major advantages to the vector drawing approach: Regardless of the size or resolution of the output device (screen, printer, etc.), the image always appears crisp and sharp. Also, since the description of the image usually requires much less information, vector art files are smaller for the size of the picture. More important is the difference in the way vector graphics look and act. They are images that layer atop one another. When one layer is moved or altered, others beneath it remain unchanged, whereas pixels moved in a bitmapped graphic leave a blank hole in their place.

Essentially, a draw program enables you to:

(a) create any line or shape with great precision;

(b) color in and around forms with an assortment of textures, blends, fills, and patterns;

(c) transform images; and

(d) customize type.

There are two major dedicated draw programs available for both the Mac and PC platforms—*Adobe Illustrator* and *Adobe Freehand*—but most layout and word-processing programs include limited versions of draw programs. *CorelDRAW* is very popular on PCs.

PAINTING & IMAGE-EDITING PROGRAMS

Paint programs create original art or manipulate scans of photos and illustrations as bitmapped graphics. These gridded, mosaic-like maps contain detailed information about every dot (pixel) in the image—its exact size, color, and position in relation to all the others. The larger the size and finer the resolution of an image, the more information its file contains. As noted above, when a part of a bitmapped image is moved, a blank space is left in the place where it was.

An image-editing program does photo manipulation—scanning, editing, and adjustment of picture images—but it also has some painting program features built in. For most book designers, a basic knowledge of such a program adequately satisfies the need for paint program capabilities like low-res scanning, retouching, and manipulation of artwork. Technically more difficult jobs can be farmed out to photo retouchers, digital imager and computer artists, or other specialists. Very complex and high-res graphics use an enormous amount of memory and storage space, so are not really practical for book designers, except those in large companies that can afford the necessary equipment. However, with the rapid increase in computing power and decrease in memory and storage costs, more and more designers are taking on the complex tasks enabled by these programs.

Image-editing programs provide the designer with:

(a) tools that imitate pen and pencil, oil, watercolor, pastel, charcoal, airbrush, and other art mediums, and enable variations of each;

(b) tools for editing directly scanned images, including color and light correction, sharpening and softening, size and shape distortion, isolation, integration with other images, and creating special effects; and

(c) color separation capabilities.

The leading image-editing program is Adobe's *Photoshop*. There are several less expensive programs with more limited features, and some have features of both draw and paint programs.

LEARNING THE PROGRAM

The best way to get familiar with a program is by learning it from an expert. Teaching yourself is an option, but it's like feeling around in the dark—eventually you'll find your way, but it's slow going and there are always bumps along the way. However, once you know the basics, working alone becomes a fascinating adventure instead of a nightmare. Here are some ways to get help:

Software companies host half- or full-day free seminars every couple of months in many parts of the country. You can't really *learn* the program this way, but you'll get a sense of it. Check local newspapers or call local dealers or the manufacturer to inquire about seminar schedules.

Training institutes, community colleges, computer dealers, workstation rental sites, and service bureaus are sources of expert instruction. Depending on your level of computer skills, a half- or full-day intensive workshop may be all you need, or longer courses may be necessary.

Tutorials that come with the program can guide you through its features. These sometimes come with CDs to install on your computer. Manuals published by others are useful also.

Instructional videos, computer magazines, newsletters, and trade association bulletins are sources for additional information.

User groups, mostly formed on the Internet, provide the support of people experienced in various programs. Local groups hold regular meetings, and phone support, newsletters, tutoring services, and specialized discussions are generally available.

Software companies provide telephone support lines (usually for a fee, sometimes toll-free). Frequently there's a long wait to talk with a technician, and the quality of assistance is uneven. Have your list of questions ready before you call and take notes during the talk.

You won't become a violinist by reading instructions, nor will reading all the above make you computer-proficient. It takes practice.

4. Editorial

Agent & author relations

The value of an editor can be measured in the quality of imagination, instinct, and taste, as well as effectiveness, clout, and sense of the market brought to the finding, guiding, and launching of good books—and "good" in the publishing sense means potentially profitable as well as excellent. But even with these qualities present, the success of an editor depends on interpersonal relations. To acquire a book for the house on terms that are advantageous requires having a positive relationship with the agent; to work with the ms. effectively requires having a strong professional and personal rapport with the author.

AGENTS

Agents began to be a significant factor in publishing in the 1920s, but they were usually resented by publishers as unnecessary intruders in the happy conversation between publishers and authors. It was felt that they could bring nothing but complications and difficulties to the process of publishing—and, undoubtedly, publishers worried that their commanding position in contract negotiations would be weakened if they had to face an experienced and aggressive advocate instead of an eager (usually), perhaps timid, author with little business knowledge.

The concern of the publishers was to some extent justified in the beginning. Authors were as vulnerable to the blandishments of agents as to those of publishers, and some turned up at contract meetings with agents who brought sharp and aggressive tactics but little knowledge or understanding of publishing. The role of advocate is a very delicate and dangerous one; it requires only that the best terms be gotten for the client, but puts no constraints of reasonableness, fairness, or even honesty on the advocate. It's very easy for a zealous lawyer, statesman, labor leader, or agent to become convinced that such constraints are harmful to the interests of the client and to jettison them at the take-off. Most of us (including the advocates) have suffered from the results of such advocacy. The aggravation and frustration endured by those who have had to deal with these situations is extreme. Advocacy excess has led to many an unwanted result—closed businesses, dropped deals, ended marriages, wars.

This negative aspect of the agent's role prevalent in the early days had largely (though not entirely) disappeared by the 1950s. This was due, perhaps, to the fact that author-publisher contracts had become much more complex than they were before and required a higher level of professionalism. While it's still possible for an author to choose a negotiator without experience, it soon becomes apparent that the person doesn't know enough to handle the matter effectively and it's likely that a professional will be brought in. (Such a logical outcome is less likely if a lawyer inexperienced in publishing represents the author. Lawyers are accustomed to dealing in subjects about which they have little knowledge, since those who know the subject usually don't know the law. However, in publishing contracts the questions are more likely to be matters of custom or business than law, so there are usually many that even the best lawyer can't handle without a lot of publishing experience. There are, of course, lawyers who regularly represent authors and know publishing well.)

Another bar to obdurate agents is the size and activity of publishing today. The sheer number of authors, publishers, books, and opportunities gives both sides enough alternatives to discourage intolerable behavior (by either party).

Indeed, publishers now welcome the agent as a knowledgeable, experienced business person who is usually a more reasonable and efficient negotiator than an author who knows little about the business of publishing and is often so emotionally involved with the book as to be unable to deal objectively with publishing considerations. Also, authors read about large advances and often have unrealistic expectations. This isn't to say that difficult and incompetent agents no longer exist—they do, and some are not very ethical, but now these tend to be the exception rather than the rule. An author (or editor) in search of a respected agent can easily find one by inquiring of the Association of Authors' Representatives in New York or by asking any experienced editor or writer. Agents may be found in *Literary Market Place*, on www.bookwire.com/agents, in writers' magazines, and in various books, some of them listed in "Sources of information" in the Appendix.

Just as there are different kinds of editors, there are agents who emphasize different aspects of their business. Some are concerned mainly with signing up profitable writers, others specialize in making complicated deals, others like to work with authors in developing their books. However, all agents must do all of these things to some extent. In the larger agencies, it's possible for an agent to get specialized help in areas such as movie contracts, translation rights, electronic publishing, etc.

The social aspects of dealing with agents are the same as in any other business. Even the most professional of agents are more inclined to do business with those with whom they're friendly than with others. It's doubtful that many agents will consciously take a book to the wrong editor because of lunches enjoyed, but all other things being equal, some judicious wining and dining can swing things your way. In any case, for an editor, maximum social contact with agents is desirable.

The usual means of establishing such contacts include taking selected agents to lunch, attending parties and other functions where agents are likely to appear, and attending writers' conferences. Usually, editors find agents who are particularly sympathetic and develop these relationships in depth. Of course, agents are also anxious to establish good relationships with editors, since most mss. are not so easily sold. However, an agent is the sole means of access to certain writers, while the agent has a wide choice of editors.

Entering contract negotiations with agents requires appraisal of the nature and knowledge of the agent. You may face an agent who is relatively inexperienced and tries to hide behind bluster and intransigence, or one who knows more about the intricacies of movie, serialization, and *co-edition* deals (publishers in two or more countries share the editorial costs of a book) than you do. Your approach should be determined by the personal characteristics of that person. And remember that the agent is sizing you up also. Contract negotiations usually involve a little formal dance at the beginning but then settle down to point-by-point bargaining that quickly reveals the qualities of each party.

AUTHORS

The history and function of agents were discussed at length because agents are the editor's main point of contact with writers. Far from being a handicap, this situation is a boon to the editor. Instead of having to wade through countless unpublishable mss. passed through by readers unsure of their own judgment, the editor now need consider only projects offered by qualified agents who haven't only screened them to eliminate the unsalable, but in many cases have worked with the writers to improve the books before they're presented. However, while this makes life easier for the editor in some ways, it also makes editors, as well as writers, dependent on a comparatively few agents for whose favor they must compete. From the writer's standpoint, there's also the very real danger that this system will result in screening out (their) excellent books that are not financially interesting to agents. Some such books may have little chance of being sold to large publishers, but might be taken by small ones. However, the latter generally pay very small advances, so the agents' commissions are often too small to justify spending the time required to earn them. Indeed, many agents, like many publishers, won't read unsolicited mss.

Writers now have the option of paying to have their texts printed xerographically (print-on-demand) in small numbers of copies—from one to hundreds—at low cost, without any need for agent *or* publisher. This differs from "vanity" publishing in the much smaller amount of money required, but it still doesn't provide much, if anything, in the way of marketing the books. Nevertheless, it's a way for rejected but worthy books to be made available—and occasionally one of these finds an enthusiastic audience and gets bought by a major publisher.

Since editors generally obtain their mss. and proposals from agents, there's comparatively little to say about editor-author relations in the acquisition stage. However: (a) editors do come into contact with writers through friends, etc.; (b) some writers with published books prefer to deal directly with editors; (c) editors will often go directly to a writer who can execute an idea; and (d) editors sometimes approach promising writers whose work they have read in a book or periodical. In many of these cases, after an initial contact an agent is called in, but sometimes the contract is arranged directly with the author. This is much less frequent with fiction than with nonfiction.

Some writers have had a lot of experience with contracts and know as much as any agent, but this is unusual. Most have little knowledge of the publishing business, and many have strongly held misconceptions. Book publishing is a subtle business full of contradictions which are not readily accepted by writers emotionally involved in their work and suspicious of the entrepreneur.

There is no best way to negotiate with an author. Much depends on the way the personalities of author and editor combine. An editor faced with an especially difficult author is advised to suggest that he or she get an agent. Reluctance to give an agent the standard 15% commission can be met by pointing out that the author is likely to get at least 15% more income with an agent than without. This isn't always true, but it's true often enough to justify the statement. If the author comes into negotiations with an inexperienced lawyer or friend, you can only hope that reason will prevail.

Editing the author's ms. can be rewarding or trying. Four elements are involved: the personality of the author, the personality of the editor, the editor's conceptual and literary skill, and the author's understanding of publishing. If the personalities clash badly, there's little hope of a happy outcome; even if there's no complete break, the final result is likely to be not as good as it could have been. If the author is difficult but nevertheless comes to respect the editor's ability, there's an excellent chance of producing a good book, and even developing a good relationship. If the author isn't able to appreciate a good editor's work, the prospects are very poor; a tolerant author will give the editor the benefit of any doubt and keep the relationship going, but authors who are both ignorant of publishing *and* difficult personalities usually break off the relationship or make life hell for the editor. A breakup can be caused also by an author getting bad advice from inexperienced friends.

An impressive display of editorial talent is probably the best single guarantor of a successful author-editor relationship. With a really good match of author and editor, the work can reach heights that could probably not be attained by the author alone. The editor's satisfaction in such a result can be worth whatever agony is suffered along the way.

So far it has been assumed that the author is the proprietor and creator of the work, but there's also the increasingly ubiquitous "*ghost*"—the writer hired to write for an "author" unable or unwilling to write the book satisfactorily. Ghosts are professionals who are usually, but not always, easy to work with. If the author is able to contribute substantially to the work but doesn't write well enough, the solution is a professional co-author. The distinction between ghost and co-author is sometimes fuzzy.

PACKAGERS

Sometimes the editor acquires a book from a *packager*. The packager is an individual or company combining the functions of agent and author—being both the proprietor (author) of the work *and* the party (agent) with whom the business arrangements are made. One way a packager differs from an author is that a packager may also be a producer selling materials to the publisher. The packager may deliver: (a) only a "manuscript" (generally in the form of a disk), (b) a disk with everything ready for producing printing film or electronic books, (c) the printing film ready for making plates, or (d) finished books. The two aspects of packaging, authorship and production, are separate functions and may be covered by separate contracts. Indeed, packagers often deal with both an editor and the production manager. In the package deal, the publisher gets whatever is delivered complete and ready for the next step.

The editor should think of a packager as an agent in the sense of being a source of projects, and as an agent-headed author in contract negotiations. Once a contract is made, the editor shouldn't deal directly with the writer—who is under contract to the packager—but should have the opportunity to see and approve the text, illustrations, layout, and proofs. If the editor spends substantial time doing text editing that the packager is supposed to have done, the financial value of the package deal isn't fully realized by the publisher.

Business dealings with packagers are usually easy, since the packager is an experienced professional with a proprietary interest in the deal—and won't kill it by being unreasonable. If there *is* trouble with a packager, it usually comes in the delivery phase, when results fail to match promises. Such failures may be beyond the packager's control, but the best way to avoid disasters due to incompetence or unrealistic promises of packagers is to deal with only those known to be experienced and reliable.

Contracts Most publishers use printed contracts known as "boilerplate". These, like insurance policies and real estate leases, used to be printed in very small type to discourage careful reading. Today, publishers have reset their contracts in readable type—often with useful subheads and marginal notes.

Like leases, publishers' contracts contain terms favorable to the house. By printing these terms, the other (inexperienced) party is led to believe that they're customary, and is more likely to accept them. Actually, the terms in publishers' contracts usually *are* customary. If ever they were not, the pressure of agents and competition have brought them into line. However, what is customary in one situation may not be in another, so it's often necessary to modify the printed terms to fit a particular deal. This is particularly true since the advent of electronic publishing greatly complicated contract negotiations.

The editor is expected to try for terms at least as good for the house as those in the printed contract, and can't very well ask for more, so any initiative to change the terms is likely to come from the author or agent. (Since most contracts are negotiated by agents, for brevity this discussion will refer only to agents.)

Publishers hope that the standard form will be usable for all contracts, so it contains provision for almost every kind of circumstance, but in each case there are usually some inapplicable clauses. Following are brief comments on the various parts of a typical contract:

■ **Preamble**—This legally identifies the parties to the contract and the work involved.

■ **Specifications**—These define the nature and extent of the work to be delivered, i.e., number of words and illustrations, bibliographies, indexes, other material to be included, etc.

■ **Warranty**—The authors give legal assurance that the delivered work will be their own property, won't contain libelous or obscene material, and won't violate the rights of others. Most contract forms include a provision that the authors will fully indemnify the publisher for all costs in connection with any lawsuit. Agents and authors' lawyers usually put up a strong fight against this clause. Editors can avoid a confrontation by referring the question to the company's legal department. The outcome is a fairly accurate indication of the relative strength of publisher and authors in a particular deal.

■ **Territory**—This defines the geographical area in which the publishers will have publication and distribution rights. American publishers ordinarily get the United States, Canada, and U.S. territories, sometimes world English-language rights, and less often world rights in all languages. Even in the first instance, the U.S. publisher usually gets "open market" English-language rights, which means that both the U.S. and British publisher may sell their books outside of their exclusive territories. These conventions hark back to the days before the breakup of the British Empire and the creation of the European common market, and new conventions are slow in being adopted. It's best to check with foreign rights, foreign sales, and contract departments. Agents usually (and packagers almost always) want to retain foreign-language rights, especially if a co-production is involved (CH. 36).

■ **Delivery**—This clause specifies the date on which the work is to be delivered. There is usually a grace period after which a penalty is sometimes levied. However, any experienced publisher knows that creative work can't be turned out on order, like sausages, so this clause is enforced only when there's evidence of bad faith or some extraordinary circumstance.

■ **Approval**—This provides that the publisher can reject the work if it's judged not publishable. There is often a provision for return of part, or all, of the author's *advance* (see "Royalty" below) if the work is later sold to another publisher, or even if it's not. The judgment of unpublishability is too subjective to be easily foisted on an author who has worked a year or more on a book (and already spent the advance) so this clause usually causes much anguish and contention when put into effect. These cases are dealt with on a high executive level.

■ **Publishing**—The publisher warrants that the book will be published within a limited time (usually one to two years) after (and if) the ms. is approved. The publisher's penalty for failure to meet this schedule may be forfeit of the advance and dissolution of the contract. The authors agree that the publisher has the sole right to make all publishing decisions, such as price, format, timing, advertising, etc., although a powerful agent may sometimes get some control, and it's customary for authors to get consultation, if not approval, in jacket and cover design. Titles are usually subject to mutual agreement.

■ **Royalty**—For unillustrated hardcover books there's usually a sliding scale, depending on the quantity sold, starting at 10% of the list price, going to 12½% and finally 15%. For established authors, some publishers pay 15% to start. The quantities at which these breaks come is a matter for negotiation, since the sales prospects of individual titles vary greatly. An advance against *royalties* is paid, ranging from a modest sum—usually about two-thirds of the royalty on the first printing—to very large, even huge, sums for brand-name authors. Sometimes advances amount to more than is likely to be earned in royalties because the publisher hopes that subsidiary sales income (CH. 1) will justify the payment, or simply to keep a hot author out of the hands of another publisher. However, since it's understood that advances are not expected to be returned (except as noted in "Approval" above) even if unearned by sales (although this is rarely written in contracts), such large grants are extremely hazardous and are usually made only under the pressure of competition (a net loss on the deal isn't unheard of). Royalties on illustrated books are generally lower, because a large part of the retail price—on which royalties are based—is the result of high production costs. Sometimes royalties are based on the publisher's net income from the book rather than the list price. No royalties are paid on books remaindered (see "Remaindering" below) or sold at cost or below.

■ **Subsidiary sales**—This clause defines the various kinds of *subsidiary rights* and other sales that are possible, and assigns the share that author and publisher will get from each sale. Printed contracts usually provide for a 50/50 share of the net proceeds of most sales of rights. These provisions come under strong pressure from agents, and the author's share of movie and some other rights sometimes goes well above 50%. Translation rights generally split 75/25 in favor of the author. British rights sales usually provide for 80% to the author, who often gets 90% of first serial rights (excerpts printed in periodicals prior to book publication). To hold top authors, publishers often give up major subsidiary right shares entirely. As in all other contract matters, it's author clout and agent know-how that make the difference. Such negotiations can involve large sums and should be handled only by experienced people on both sides. Always bear in mind that the income from subsidiary sales often supplies the profit in trade publishing (CHs. 1, 2).

Sub-rights has been enlarged and greatly complicated by the various kinds of electronic publishing—e-books and Internet distribution. Terms for these new areas of rights vary greatly, so it's very important for agents to be experienced.

■ **Payment**—The advance against royalties is usually paid in installments—sometimes half on signing and the remainder on acceptance of the text or part of it; sometimes it's divided into three parts, with one paid on signing, one on delivery of the text, and the last on publication. The payment terms for advances, like their size, vary greatly and are subject to bargaining. Royalty payment schedules—usually semiannual—are also covered in this clause.

■ **Reversion**—There is usually a provision for rights to be returned to the author if all editions of the book have been out of print for a certain period—usually between six and eight months—and the publisher refuses to reprint. However, the ability of print-on-demand technology to produce small numbers of copies economically means that titles need never go out of print, which makes *reversion* clauses irrelevant in the absence of some special agreement between author and publisher.

■ **Copyright**—The publisher agrees to take out copyright in the name of the author. In some situations, such as when the author works "for hire", copyright may be taken in the publisher's name.

■ **Remaindering**—Some contracts provide that the publisher won't *remainder* (sell remaining books for resale at a greatly reduced price) within a certain time—usually a year—after publication, but many publishers insist that this is a decision reserved by them. The author customarily gets an option to buy part or all of the remaining stock before it's remaindered.

■ **Free copies**—The publisher agrees to give the author a number of free copies and to sell additional copies at a discount (usually 40 to 50%).

■ **Continuity**—Both parties agree that the terms of the contract will be binding on their heirs and assigns, i.e., on anyone who acquires their property.

■ **Bankruptcy**—This usually provides that the rights will automatically revert to the author if the publisher declares bankruptcy.

■ **Option**—The author grants the publisher an option to publish the author's next book, which the publisher must exercise within a certain time (usually a month or so) after submission of the ms. Options are granted less and less often as publishing becomes more competitive.

The foregoing comments touch on only the main points in the average contract. Many details are omitted, and some contracts contain other provisions and lack some of those included above. Contracts often have paragraphs that limit liability, fix responsibility, define jurisdiction, or otherwise try to nail down the possible legal hazards. The Authors League has a model contract that's used extensively by agents. It's a good effort, but is biased toward the authors' interests just as much as the publishers' boilerplate represents theirs. Experience shows that it's hopeless to try to cover every possible contingency in a contract, and any serious attempt to do so results in endless leapfrogging of modifications that does nothing but make work for lawyers. In the end, the best insurance against trouble is to sign contracts only with people you feel are honest and reliable—and make the contracts simple and clear. Generally, a contract that only a lawyer can understand is a bad one.

Ghost writers sometimes have agreements with the author that give them a share of royalties. In such cases they are, in effect, coauthors and are often included in the author's contract with the publisher. In other cases, there's a separate agreement between ghost and author that provides for the ghost's compensation—a share of the author's income, a flat fee, or both.

Contracts with packagers vary considerably from the provisions discussed above. In the specifications clause, the manufacturing specifications of the book as well as the content are given. If only part of the book is to be delivered by the packager, the part is defined and described. The delivery clause provides dates for delivery of the books as well as for the text and illustrations. The royalty clause is sometimes omitted; a package deal may involve a single (*all-in*) price that includes both the book and the royalty. When a royalty is provided separately, it's often less than 10%, especially for illustrated books. Some publishers feel that the combined cost of books and royalty shouldn't exceed 50% of the *net receipts* (usually 53 to 54% of the retail price—see CH. 2), so the higher the book cost, the less there is for royalty. However, the whole matter is largely a question of how the publisher's overhead is calculated. (See "Acquisition" in CH. 17.) In package contracts, payment terms are based on the production schedule of the book, with a series of payments made at various stages of the work. Payment is made on the number of books delivered to, rather than sold by, the publisher.

Package contracts also contain the number of copies ordered by the publisher. There is always a provision for overruns or underruns of 5 to 10% or more. The smaller the quantity the more difficult it is to produce the exact number ordered, so the allowance is larger. The packager usually agrees to provide about 10% more jackets than books (to allow for replacement of damaged jackets and for promotional use). Sometimes a package contract provides for books to be supplied for book clubs at the *run-on price* (the cost of manufacturing without plant or makeready costs) (CHs. 10, 12) to enable them to sell at a lower price.

Printed contracts for college textbooks, reference books, and technical books usually give the publisher the right to decide if a revised edition is needed, and to have one written by someone other than the author if the author is unwilling or unable to do the revision. This is a controversial clause when the book represents a personal approach to the subject by a writer who is understandably reluctant to have someone else revise the work. At the same time, the publisher has a considerable investment in the book and isn't happy to see its sales stop for lack of needed revision. A possible solution is to ask the author to designate an acceptable person to do a revision if necessary. It's best for this point to be settled in the early stages of negotiation, as neither party may be willing to yield.

Elementary and high school (*el-hi*) textbooks are often written neither by their authors—who may be expert teachers or scholars but not writers—nor by ghosts, but by editors working for the publisher. The authors provide a master plan and guidance for editors who are proficient and experienced in the highly specialized technique of writing team-produced textbooks. The contracts with authors in such cases provide for this special circumstance. They also sometimes provide for the production of *ancillaries* (other works) based on the material used in the book—tapes, CDs, workbooks, audiovisual presentations, etc.

Copyediting & style

COPYEDITING

As remarked in CH. 1, the nature and extent of *copyediting* are somewhat indefinite, but for the purposes of this chapter it will be considered to be the finishing of a text—i.e., after the author and editor have done their work, the copyeditor will do whatever else is needed to make the text ready for production.

Finishing a text involves five functions:
(a) correcting errors of typing,
(b) correcting errors of fact,
(c) correcting errors of grammar,
(d) improving awkward sentences and paragraphs, and
(e) styling and marking.

Copyeditors often go well beyond these limits, revising the structure and even the sequence of chapters, rewriting large passages, and generally performing the function of editor. There is nothing wrong with this provided that the author and editor are willing, and the copyeditor is competent. However, when such extensive work is done, it can't properly be called copyediting. This chapter will deal only with the five functions listed above. (Some publishers require copyeditors to check for anything that might need permission or could be libelous, and it's certainly helpful to bring attention to such cases, but generally these matters are the responsibility of permissions and legal departments.)

■ **Correcting errors of typing**—This is self-explanatory.

■ **Correcting errors of fact**—The problem here is deciding how far to go in finding errors. It isn't obvious errors (Napoleon died in 1914) that cause trouble but those that *seem* correct. The copyeditor will properly check and correct a date if it seems wrong, but should it be checked if it seems reasonable (Napoleon died in 1813)? Such checking is feasible in a book containing only a few such facts, but in a fact-filled text, particularly with technical material, checking is no longer copyediting and is properly the author's responsibility.

■ **Correcting errors of grammar**—Here too, the question is how far to go. In fiction, memoirs, poetry, and other nontechnical writing, there's the author's style to consider. "Cleaning up" the grammar could mean robbing the book of its personal character or altering its tone. The rule should be: Use a light touch unless a clear understanding is reached with author or editor. Also, the copyeditor must be careful to distinguish between what are clear, undisputed errors of grammar and the optional usages that define style in the grammatical sense. (See "Style" below.)

■ **Improving awkward sentences and paragraphs**—This is a most dangerous area, threatening to the author's prerogatives. If "go lightly" is the rule for grammatical corrections that could damage the author's style, then the rule here should be *proceed with caution*. However, not every author is a stylist and many times the structure of a sentence or paragraph is unintentionally awkward. In a book where such bad locutions are few, they will be obvious and cry out for correction. Most authors will appreciate changes that improve clarity, provided their style is preserved. In books where sentence problems are numerous, or the rule, it's best for the copyeditor to consult with the editor before undertaking the necessary large-scale revision.

The copyeditor sometimes finds problems that only the author can solve, and often forms opinions about the writing that shouldn't be imposed on the text without the author's approval. In such cases, it's customary to write queries to the author or editor on slips of colored paper (*flags*) pasted or clipped onto the appropriate page. Such notes should be phrased carefully to avoid causing irritation. Sarcasm, condescension, or peevishness are unprofessional and can ruin your standing with the author.

■ **Styling and marking**—An author may provide one of two different kinds of copy—a typescript made on a typewriter (now rare) or a computer disk with a hard copy. In either case, the copyeditor generally works on a paper copy (for exceptions, see "Markup" below), which is submitted to the editor/author for approval or change and then to the designer for *markup*. The difference in copy becomes significant only after the paper copy is final. A typescript must then be *keyboarded* on the computer or passed through a scanner to create a disk; where a disk already exists, it's corrected according to the markings on the hard copy.

■ **Styling**—This term isn't to be confused with "style" as used in connection with a writer's manner of expression or with that quality of sophistication we call style, and certainly not with style as fashion. Here we're concerned with bringing grammatical and typographical order to a text.

In *styling*, the copyeditor adopts a consistent system of grammatical usage. If every writer and editor knew, and consistently used, a universally accepted body of grammatical rules, styling in the sense of establishing a pattern of usage (or style) in each text wouldn't be needed. But style exists as a problem because there's disagreement on certain points. The copyeditor's job is to resolve these differences in each text and to make the usage consistent throughout. The differences are resolved for a particular book by reconciling the preferences of the author, the editor, and the copyeditor. Some publishers have a house style that must be followed; others use a *style sheet* or allow the editor and/or the author to create their own. Occasionally, the matter is left to the copyeditor's judgment. The various considerations are discussed under "Style". As the copyeditor proceeds, style decisions are noted and are then compiled on a style sheet, which is sent to the author with the copyedited text. This tells the author what reference books were used, what general style rules were applied (serial comma, spelling out numbers, etc.), and whether there are any special treatments of words or terms.

Styling also means establishing a consistent, logical arrangement of the headings, subheads, extracts, listings, etc. to clarify the organization of the book for the reader and for the designer. The first step is putting its subdivisions in order. There should be a clear hierarchy of headings, descending in importance from part-titles through chapter titles and the various subheads, if any. The heads should reflect the importance of the texts they precede. Any material other than straight text should be similarly identified.

■ **Markup**—After the text has been styled (in the sense of arranging its parts in a logical order), each occurrence of each component throughout the text must be identified and marked with a code (color, number, letter, or symbol) to make its designated status clear to the designer and typesetter. If there are many listings, be sure that the same style is used for all; if each item in one list is preceded by a lowercase letter, be sure that capitals are not used in another. If there are many quotations, see that they're *either* run in with the text with quotation marks *or* set off as extract. If you want short quotations to be within the text and only the longer ones set as extract, fine, but establish a consistent rule. It's helpful to use vertical lines in colored pencil alongside extracts, listings, poetry, etc. to bring these to the designer's attention. Write "extract", "poetry", etc. as appropriate, or a code in the margin to identify the material. In complicated books it helps to use different colors to make distinctions (*color coding*).

When the designer receives the copyeditor's marked paper copy, it will be possible to do the *breakdown* (CH. 21). Once a typographic style for each kind of head and special material has been specified by the designer (CH. 24), the markings on the paper copy will tell the typesetter which elements of the text are to be set in each style. Observe the division of function: the copyeditor provides clearly identified copy; the designer specifies its typographic style. Do not confuse matters by making typographic markings on the text, i.e., don't write "center", "flush", or other positional instructions, and don't underscore words for italics, caps, small caps, or boldface unless the author has done so for emphasis or you are following a house style.

Text corrections on paper are made on the line or between lines. Only on proofs are corrections made in the margins. Everyone who marks a text should be considerate of those who must read their markings. Write legibly—print unless you have a super-clear script—in a reasonable size with a sharpened pencil that won't smudge. And copyeditors should consider that both designer and typesetter may need space for *their* markings. If there are any pencil markings already on the text, be sure to use a different color for yours.

There may be situations where no review by editor or author is required, and the copyeditor may work directly on an electronic file without marking a paper copy. It's possible also to work directly on the file even if there is to be editor/author review, using one of the word-processing programs that enables displaying the corrections, so they may be checked against the uncorrected version. This is a compromise solution, and the result is usually hard to read. Also, it's not a good idea for authors to work on edited files.

STYLE Style in the editorial sense is the guardian of three values: (a) clarity, (b) grace, and (c) structure—it has no independent value. It must be consistent, but consistency isn't its purpose.

The relationship of style to tradition is subtle. Automatic perpetuation of usage isn't valid, but style-as-rule is justified if it protects clear and logical usages from debasement through repeated error. Certainly, language should be enriched by the infusion of new words and expressions, but style should be a bulwark against the weakening, through misuse, of a language's efficiency—its ability to express thought clearly, precisely, and subtly.

For both the expository and the creative writer the ability to make fine distinctions is vital—which isn't possible with words and usages that have no clear, universally understood meaning. Nevertheless, while it's essential that style rules are consistently applied for explanatory or descriptive writing, they must be used with great care in editing creative writing. The work of a novelist or literary stylist stands on the writer's choice of words and how these are arranged. The choice and/or arrangement may appear to be bad, but they can't be judged wrong by any criteria of style; they're bad only if they fail their purpose.

If it's important to have rules to protect the integrity of the language—and guide the copyeditor—then it's necessary to have a rule book to which the writer and editor can look for authority and guidance. Unfortunately, at this writing there isn't one that's universally accepted.

Matters of style are covered by two kinds of authorities: (a) the stylebook and (b) the dictionary. If there were only one of each there would be no questions about style, but this isn't the case. (See "Sources of information" in the Appendix.)

■ **Stylebooks**—There are a dozen reference books that give style rules, but only three that are widely used: *The Chicago Manual of Style*, *The New York Times Manual of Style and Usage*, and the *United States Government Printing Office Style Manual*. The latter is useful in many ways, particularly for its foreign-language material, but it's primarily for government publications and is limited in value for other books. The other two are the main references for style questions, although each of them is somewhat specialized; the *Chicago Manual* was planned for a university press and the *Times Manual* for a newspaper. Each is excellent, but they don't agree in every respect. Most editors use the *Chicago Manual*, and, until a better one comes along, it would be best if everyone would adopt it so that some uniformity could be achieved in the treatment of the basic style features such as punctuation, abbreviation, capitalization, and hyphenation. There are also style manuals for specialized publishing, such as medical, scientific, etc. For the meaning of words, a dictionary is the authority to which we look.

■ **Dictionaries**—For many years, *Webster's New International Dictionary of the English Language* (unabridged; Merriam, 1934) was almost universally accepted as the authority. But with many new terms coming into use, in 1969 Merriam issued *Webster's Third New International Dictionary* (known as W3, while the 1934 work came to be dubbed W2). This was valuable for its thousands of new words, but it contained fewer entries in all than W2 and, more important, was assailed by many for being only a compendium of usage with too little guidance as to what is standard, nonstandard, substandard, slang, or erroneous. Indeed, it called many common errors "acceptable" or "alternative" meanings, thus hastening the deterioration of the language and confounding writers who had searched diligently for the exactly right word, only to find that it now had a different meaning. This view of lexicography has, unfortunately, become usual to one extent or another in all major "dictionaries" published since then. For these and other reasons, W2, though out of print, is still in demand and is consulted, along with the admittedly indispensable later publications that include more recent words, by careful editors.

Random House, American Heritage (Houghton Mifflin), Merriam-Webster, and a few other companies published many new wordbooks and revised editions in the last quarter of the 20th century. Most were excellent in some respects and all attempted to be up-to-date and inclusive—but all were swept along by the prevailing notion that a dictionary should reflect the current use of words rather than define their meaning. This destructive practice is defended on the grounds that "the language is living", and so must be its dictionaries. This is valid to the extent that it justifies including new words, but it surely doesn't justify elevating ignorant mistakes to the status of "new" meanings—especially when the "new meaning" of a word is the opposite of its correct meaning (e.g., "imply" and "infer").

At the turn of the 21st century, ambitious new wordbooks were introduced by both the established publishers and some new companies. In some cases, printed editions were published, with or without a CD-ROM version, but all rushed to make their definitions available on the Internet on one basis or another. There are new editions of the American Heritage, Random House, and Merriam-Webster wordbooks that are licensed in various ways to be accessible online (a particularly useful one is Merriam-Webster's at www.m-w.com). In 1999, Microsoft co-published *Encarta*, which was prepared by the British publisher Bloomsbury and is distributed in the U.S. book trade by St. Martin's Press. Of course, it's accessible through Microsoft software and on its own website. The American edition of a complete revision of the twenty-volume *Oxford English Dictionary* is available only online by subscription. When completed by 2010, it will have forty volumes. There may or may not be a print version. But the new *Oxford*'s claim that it includes "new definitions for some old words" rings alarm bells. The implications are unsettling. The two-volume *Shorter Oxford English Dictionary* appeared in 2002. It's said to include over 33% of the complete edition.

All the new dictionaries claim to be authoritative but, obviously, when there are several "authorities" that differ, there is *no* authority. This is the situation with which we must live until some publisher comes along with a dictionary that keeps the definitions of W2, but is up-to-date and achieves universal acceptance. When and if that happens, the work should be certified by the Library of Congress and the Bureau of Standards, and be declared as inviolable as the Constitution, to be amended only by the addition of new words.

■ **Questions of style**—For most of editorial style there's a universally accepted form: "cat" is spelled *cat*, the first word of a sentence is capitalized, declarative sentences end with periods, and so on. But there are many points on which there's no agreement, and options must be chosen.

Many questions of style divide into two schools: "British (or English) style" and "American style". While the latter has been generally accepted in the United States, American editors are increasingly leaning toward the British practices, which are usually more logical and are used by most English-speaking countries.

Some of the main questions of style on which choices must be made are listed below. Omitted are questions ordinarily left to the designer, such as the choice between *old style* or *lining figures*. British style is indicated by (B), American style by (A).

CAPITALIZATION: In chapter and subheadings, are all words except articles and prepositions to be capitalized, as in book titles, or only the first word and proper nouns? This question is discussed in CH. 25 under "Chapter titles", but in any event, authors should type *all copy* in *lowercase*, with caps only at the beginning of sentences, titles, and proper nouns. If the designer decides to capitalize all words in certain heads, it's easy to *add* caps, but changing from caps to lowercase involves editorial choices that should be made by the copyeditor. This causes delays that can be avoided by the author's proper typing of copy.

DIVISION OF WORDS: Are words at the ends of lines to be divided according to pronunciation, as in democ-racy (A), or according to etymological derivation as in demo-cracy (B)?

COMPOUND WORDS: Which words are to be hyphenated (as in "self-control") and which combined (as in "everything")?

NUMBERS: Which are to be spelled out and which set as figures?

NAMES: Which proper names are to be italicized and which not? (The question arises usually in the case of the titles of minor publications, aircraft, television shows, etc.)

PUNCTUATION: When is italic punctuation to be used? Are dashes to be one em (A) or two em (B)? Are double quotes to be used first and single used for quotes within quoted matter (A) or vice versa (B)? Is punctuation not belonging to quoted matter to be placed inside the quotes (A) or outside (B)?

REFERENCE MARKS: Are figures or symbols to be used for reference?

SPELLING: Presuming that American spelling is to be used rather than British ("-or" rather than "-our", "-er" rather than "-re", etc.), which dictionary is to be followed in doubtful cases?

CONTINUED LINES: In an index and similar copy, when breaking an entry from one page to another, is the heading to be repeated at the top of the new page with the word "continued" after it?

There are many other minor questions of style, as well as variations of those listed above. See "Read this first" for a discussion of the style used in this book, and see also CHs. 6, 9, 25.

When decisions have been made on all the questions, the editor or copyeditor includes them on the style sheet, which is a vital reference and checklist for the copyeditor and the proofreaders.

Proofreading

In book publishing, jobs such as writing, designing, editing, and *proofreading*, which don't require manual skill, are often undertaken by unqualified people in the belief that such work can be done by *anyone*, at least adequately. Not true. Anyone *can* write, design, edit, or read proofs, but without natural and learned skills they're not likely to do it well enough to be "adequate". Proofreading in particular is often considered unskilled work that may be assigned to unskilled office workers.

In fact, good proofreading means accurate proofreading, and it requires experience, knowledge, and skill. Readers must not only find and correct errors, they must be able to understand copyeditors' markings and mark corrections properly. Besides having a sharp eye and good powers of concentration, they must have enough knowledge of style (and, if possible, fact) to be able to spot errors that escaped the copyeditor. This isn't a proofreader's responsibility, but many whopping mistakes have been discovered by good proofreaders, and editors are wise to look to them as another, and sometimes final, chance to perfect the text. Few books are published without some errors getting into print, so no means of detecting and exposing them should be overlooked.

For a serious text, experienced professional proofreaders should be employed. There is no harm having amateurs read *also*, but don't depend on them. For reference or instructional books it's best to have the proofs read twice—by two professional proofreaders. It's practically certain that each will find errors not found by the other. (A third reader will find still other mistakes, and so on to infinity.)

The best way to catch errors is to have one person (the *copy-holder*) read the ms. copy (CH. 6) aloud while another (the *reader*) simultaneously reads the proofs. This enables the reader to check the text without having to look away from the proof, which sometimes results in catching errors that are so reasonable they might otherwise go unnoticed. Obviously, having two people read is more expensive than having just one, so the practice is becoming increasingly rare. However, in books with many proper names, technical terms, and/or foreign words, it can be slower (more expensive) for a single reader to check the copy for the spelling of these names and words than if a copy-holder spelled them out loud.

With a single reader, a common practice is to read the proof with the copy at hand to check whatever seems to be wrong. The weakness here, of course, is that errors that don't *seem* wrong won't be checked and corrected. Since "errors" in proofreading terms are simply disparities between proof and copy, the proofreader using this method must know the author's and copyeditor's preferences in optional matters of style. For example, the lack of a serial comma in the proof is an error if the editor's style is to use serial commas, but isn't otherwise. It's essential that proofreaders get the copyeditor's style sheet (see "Style" above).

Careful proofreaders read the copy first and then the proof, alternately line by line, sentence by sentence, or, ideally, phrase by phrase, or even, occasionally, word by word. Probably the best practice is to put the copy page on top of the proof, covering everything above the line being read, then follow the copy with a finger of one hand while following the proof with a pencil in the other.

MARKING PROOFS Unlike many matters of style, the proofreaders' marks are standard and universally accepted (although they differ for each language). The problem here isn't lack of a commonly understood system, but the failure of some authors, and even some editors, to learn and use the system correctly.

As previously noted, corrections in proofs are made in the margins (with a mark at the place in the line where the correction goes) rather than on or between the lines as in copy. This is mainly because the typesetter must be able to find the corrections easily, but also because there's normally not enough room within typeset text to write most corrections. On the other hand, in setting copy, the typesetter has less trouble reading the corrections if they're in their proper place. There is ordinarily enough room in double-spaced typescript for the kind of correction needed in the copy-editing stage.

Some of the principles of marking proofs are discussed in CH. 20. Following is a chart showing the standard *proofreaders' marks*, with demonstrations of their use. Every person working *in any part* of bookmaking should learn these marks and how to use them correctly.

proofreaders' marks

Marginal sign	*Mark in text*	*Meaning*	*Corrected text*
℘	Proofreadings	Delete, take out letter or word	Proofreading
℘ (closed up)	Legibillity is	Delete and close up	Legibility is
first	the requirement	Insert marginal addition	the first requirement
⁀	of a proof reader's marks.	Close up entirely	of a proofreader's marks.
‿	Symbols should be	Less space	Symbols should be
#	inline with	Add space	in line with
eq.#	the text to which	Space evenly	the text to which
¶	they refer. Place	New paragraph	they refer.
	marks carefully.	No new paragraph	Place marks
no ¶	Paragraphs may be		carefully. Paragraphs
			may be
□	□ indented one em	Indent one em	indented one em
□□	□□ two ems or (rarely)	Indent two ems	two ems or (rarely)
□□□	□□□ three ems. Head-	Indent three ems	three ems.
[	[ings are flush left	Move to the left	Headings are flush left
]	or flush right]	Move to the right	or flush right
] [	] or centered [	Center	or centered
⊔	Marginal marks	Lower to proper position	Marginal marks
⊓	are separated	Raise to proper position	are separated
x	by vertical	Replace defective letter	by vertical
w.f.	in a line of type	Wrong font; change to proper face	in a line of type
tr.	is beside noted the	Transpose	is noted beside the
?	nearest bend of the line.	Is this correct?	nearest end of the line
Sp.	and the 2nd next.	Spell out	and the second, next.
	in this way both margins	Transfer to position	both margins are used in
	are used	shown by arrow.	this way

Marginal sign	Mark in text	Meaning	Corrected text
b.f.	English Finish	Change to boldface type	**English Finish**
b.f. ital	English Finish	Change to boldface italics	***English Finish***
rom.	*galley* proof	Set in roman type	galley proof
ital.	is laid paper	Set in italics	is *laid* paper
u.c.	Book of type	Set in upper case, or capital	Book of Type
Caps	Book Papers	Set in large capitals	BOOK PAPERS
s.c.	BOOK PAPERS	Change to small capitals	BOOK PAPERS
c.s.c.	Book Papers	Initial large capitals; other letters, small capitals	BOOK PAPERS
l.c.	the first Type	Change to lower case or small letter	the first type
×	baseball player	Broken type	baseball player
Stet	to ~~the~~ editors	Retain crossed out word	to the editors
2	Water, HO	Insert inferior figure	Water, H_2O
2	$X^2 \div Y^2 = Z$	Insert superior figure	$X^2 \div Y^2 = Z^2$
‖	The paper The ink The type	Align type	The paper The ink The type
ld	prepare copy and submit it	Insert lead between lines	prepare copy and submit it
hr. #	P/A/P/E/R	Hair space between letters	P A P E R
⊙	to the printer‸	Insert period	to the printer.
,‸	the proof‸but	Insert comma	the proof, but
; or ;/	excellent‸it is	Insert semicolon	excellent; it is
: or :⊙	to the following‸	Insert colon	to the following:
’	authors notes	Insert apostrophe	author's notes
“/”	called‸caps‸	Insert quotation marks	called "caps"
-/or =	halftone	Insert hyphen	half-tone
1/em	‸Robert Henderson	Insert em dash	—Robert Henderson
1/en	1939‸1940	Insert en dash	1939–1940
?	"Where‸" she asked.	Insert question mark	"Where?" she asked.
!	"Stop‸" he cried.	Insert exclamation mark	"Stop!" he cried.
(/)	author‸see page 2‸	Insert parentheses	author (see page 2)
[/]	‸To be continued‸	Insert brackets	[To be continued]

5. Typography

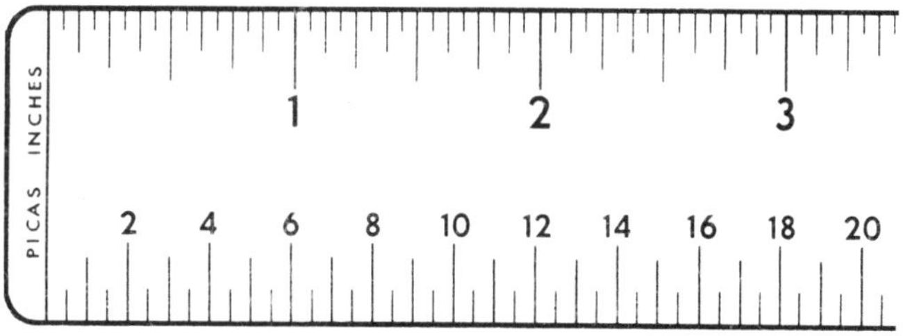

Introduction

This chapter deals with typography in the sense that it's the art of arranging *printed* type. We say "printed" because the term typography refers also to the physical setting of the type (CH. 6). Firms that set type are called *typographers* (or *compositors*), although now computer typesetting is subsumed in the operations of the service bureaus. Designers who arrange printed type also are called typographers. With a computer anybody can be a typographer, but to be a designer—a good typographer—requires exceptional judgment and visual skills.

In typography, as in other aspects of bookmaking, it's necessary to reconcile esthetic and practical demands. In metal typesetting (CH. 6) it was physically *possible* for a compositor to do almost anything a designer requested—even though the request may have been extremely impractical and expensive to execute. For economy's sake, responsible designers generally avoided making such demands. Those practical limitations tended to impose an esthetic rigor that's beneficial for design.

Such practical and economic limitations scarcely exist in computer composition, so there's no impulse on those accounts for esthetic restraint. Previously, typographers were guided by the best examples of work done by their predecessors and by the traditions of the craft. While this often resulted in uncreative repetition, it also provided a framework on which designers of all levels of competence built excellent work. Since desktop typesetting became prevalent, the traditions of typography have lost their influence, with some chaos as the result. Without tradition, the only insurance against visual excess is *taste*, which is basically innate, but can be trained and sharpened. However, before talking about the art of type, it's necessary to explain the system of type measurement and introduce its terminology.

Measurement & terminology

While computers provide the options of using points, inches, or centimeters to measure all parts of type composition, in metal type everything is measured by *points*. One point is .01384", and 72 pts.

equals almost exactly 1" (2.54 cm). (Many European countries use the *Didot* point, which is slightly larger than the U.S. point. For example, 30 pt. U.S. is the equivalent of 28 pt. Didot. See equivalent table in the Appendix.) Twelve points U.S. equals 1 *pica*, so there are approximately 6 picas to 1". Twelve Didot points equals 1 *cicero*. In a move toward simplification, in 1985 "PostScript points" were introduced as a new standard by Adobe Systems, maker of the PostScript page description language (CHs. 3, 6). There are exactly 12 PostScript points per pica, and exactly 6 picas or 72 PostScript points per inch.

Type size and *leading* (pronounced "ledding"—the vertical space between lines) should always be specified in points. Picas and half-picas are used to measure the width and depth of pages or columns, and other distances of 1 pica or more. Dimensions are given in multiples of picas plus a half-pica, or plus the appropriate number of points, e.g., 24½ picas; 17 picas 4 pts. Dimensions up to 6 picas may be expressed in points, e.g., 24 pts., 28 pts., 42 pts., etc.

Paper, illustration, and margin measurements are traditionally given in inches or centimeters. In general, measurements within the type area are given in points and picas, those outside in inches or centimeters.

Another unit of type measurement is the *em*, which is theoretically the square of the type size; i.e., the em of a 10 pt. type is 10 pts., of a 12 pt. type 12 pts., etc., although this varies somewhat according to the typeface. An *en* is half an em. Ems and ens are used as units of horizontal measurement, such as indentions, sentence spacing, wordspacing, letterspacing, and dashes. In writing, the em may be expressed as M or □. The en is either N or $\boxed{\text{N}}$. In speech, compositors call an en a "nut" to avoid confusing it with the similar-sounding em.

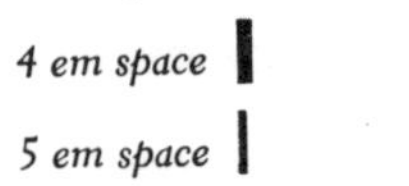

Horizontal spacing is further divided into multiples and fractions of the em. The multiples are called *quads*. The fractions are called *spaces*. One-fifth of an em is called a 5-em space, one-fourth a 4-em, and one-third a 3-em. This terminology has largely fallen into disuse, and when it's used it's almost always misused. For example, if a 4-em space in 12 pt. type is specified, what is most likely meant isn't a 3 pt. but a 48 pt. space, even though that's an incorrect use of the term "4-em space".

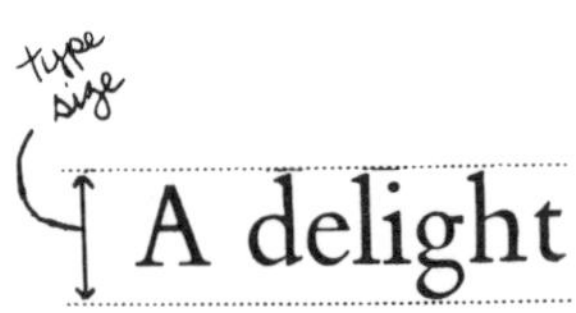

The *type size* refers to the distance from top to bottom that includes the highest and the lowest points in the alphabet. For example, in a 10 pt. type there'll be a distance of 10 pts. from the top of, say, the lowercase "f" to the bottom of the "y". In another 10 pt. face, the highest point may be the top of the capitals or the lowest may be the bottom of the "g". (In large sizes, the face of the type is sometimes a little less than the nominal type size. In small sizes there's occasionally a minute variation.)

The apparent size of the characters may vary considerably

among faces of the same type size. The height of the *lowercase* letters exclusive of *ascenders* or *descenders* is called the *x-height*. While this isn't used as a unit of measurement itself, it's often referred to in the specification of distances. The x-height of two 10 pt. typefaces may be quite different (see "Leading" below).

nylon nylon

10 pt. Granjon 10 pt. Electra (enlarged)

Alphabet length is the measurement in points of a complete lowercase alphabet in any type face and size. This in itself isn't a particularly useful figure, except in comparing the relative width of various typefaces, but it's the basis for determining the average *characters per pica*—an important unit of measurement in typography (CHs. 6, 21).

In metal type, *body size* refers to the three dimensions of the metal on which the type is cast. A 10 pt. type is usually cast on a 10 pt. body, but it may be cast on one 11 pts., or even 9 pts. high. Type may be cast on a larger body in order to provide extra space, or leading, between the lines. Type set in 10 pt. on a 13 pt. body (the additional 3 pts. is at the bottom of the line), is expressed as 10 on 13, or 10/13. If there's no extra lead added to the body, it would be *solid*—10/10.

The body width of a piece of individual metal type is usually the width of the character itself—i.e., a "w" is cast on a wider body than an "i", although some types are designed with a slightly wider body on some characters to provide more space between them and others.

The third dimension of metal type is its height from the surface on which it stands to the printing surface. This distance, called *type-high*, is .918 of an inch in the United States, but is slightly different in some countries. Metal or plastic *plates* (CH. 12) that print with type are mounted on wood or metal blocks to make their printing surfaces type-high.

In metal type, 1, 2, and 3 pt. leading spaces are made of metal strips called *leads*. Spaces of 6 and 12 pts. are made with *slugs*. All spacing between lines is made with combinations of these five sizes, except for spaces of less than 1 pt., for which strips of cardboard are used. Leading, like horizontal spaces, is less than type-high so it won't print.

1 Point

2 Point

3 Point

6 Point

12 Point

The *measure* of a line is its width in picas. This is expressed as, for example, 11 pt. Electra on 13 by 24 picas, or as Electra 11/13 x 24. *Full measure* means the line is set the full width of the type page, without any indention.

A *font* is a collection of all the *characters* (items) in one *typeface* (a distinctive design of lettering) and size, including not only the alphabet in capitals (*uppercase*) and lowercase, but *figures* (numbers), punctuation, symbols (dollar sign, ampersand), and sometimes decorative ornaments. Fonts can be also collections of symbols or ornaments. A typeface may have variations such as bold, italic, bold italic, *condensed* (narrow), *expanded* or *extended*

EXPANDED

CONDENSED

(wide), *outline*, and/or *small caps* (capitals of x-height). The variations may be included in the normal font or be a separate font.

N.B. In computer terminology the term "font" is used to mean typeface or face. This is one of the unfortunate errors that came with the transition from metal/photographic typesetting. As explained in CH. 6, "font" has a different meaning. While this error is too entrenched to correct, since "typeface", "type", and "face" are generally understood, they're used as the preferred terms in this book. "Font" is used where it's correct.

ABCDEFGHIJKLMNOPQR
STUVWXYZ&
abcdefghijklmnopqrstuvwxyz
1234567890$ Qu ct
. , : ; - ' ' ! ? [ ] fi fl ff ffi ffl Æ Œ

ABCDEFGHIJKLMNOPQRS
TUVWXYZ&
abcdefghijklmnopqrstuvwxyz
A B C D E G J K L M N P Q
R T U W Y & *h k v w z*
1234567890$ *. , : ; - ' ! ? fi fl ff ffi ffl st*

Font proof of 24 pt. Caslon 337 and italic. Note the swash *(decorative) characters in the italic.*

ornamental brackets

rules

Hairline

¼ Point

½ Point

¾ Point

1 Point

1½ Point

2 Point

3 Point

4 Point

6 Point

8 Point

10 Point

12 Point

18 Point

24 Point

30 Point

straight rules

ornaments

Type classification

In the era of metal type, founders were few in number and they had their own designs—although most had also their own versions of the best classical faces. Creating a new design in metal type was a big undertaking, and that limited the number of faces available.

Today there are many companies producing a huge number of computer typefaces—some of these are radically new, but most are slightly modified versions of the metal-type faces with different names. For this discussion, rather than getting involved with all the alternative names, it was decided to use as examples the metal typefaces, even though some are no longer available, and to retain their original names. It would be a good idea for designers to become familiar with the faces shown in this chapter, and then compare them to the substitutes and imitations.

Traditional systems of type classification are based on relatively insignificant variations of historical, rather than visual, concern. They classify type according to the time and place of their design, factors that may have little to do with the appearance of the face. Worse yet, because of the burgeoning of printing during the first three hundred years after Gutenberg, much is made of minor design differences in typefaces created during that time, while quite dissimilar groups of later faces are either lumped together in catchall categories or ignored entirely. The variations of type design *are* very complicated, so, in order to ease comfortably into their classification, it's necessary to make a simple division at first, and get into the complications later.

Ba

Roman

Ba

abstract

Ba

cursive

Ba

decorative

Visually, there are four broad classes of type:

- **Roman**—The classical letter with serifs and graduated thick and thin strokes.
- **Abstract**—Letters with more or less straight edges and lines of uniform thickness, having no serifs (*sans serif*) or square serifs of the same weight as the letter (*block serif*).
- **Cursive**—Letters based on slanted writing with a more or less continuous line, including script and the italic forms of Roman.
- **Decorative**—All the faces that have exaggerated characteristics of the other three classes, or distinctive features that place them outside the other classes.

Ultimately, type design details and subtleties are important if first-rate typography is to be produced, but first the major characteristics of the typeface must be considered. For broad design purposes, when combining faces of different classes it hardly matters which typeface within each class is used. Graphic design is concerned with combining lines, forms, and spaces; the details are less important than the general visual characteristics.

ROMAN

Variations in Roman type consist largely of the shapes of serifs, and to some extent the relative weight of thick and thin strokes. Groups within the class are named for their historical or geographical origin, but it's their visual characteristics that concern us. The most significant subdivisions are:

■ **Old Style**—Based on freely drawn manuscript writing, there's a flowing passage from thicks to thins and strong brackets on slanted serifs. The types of Jenson, Garamond, and Caslon are typical. This style was widely used for the first three centuries of printing.

■ **Transitional**—The mid-18th century types of Baskerville and Bulmer were designed to be printed on smoother papers. The faces are generally more angular, with stronger contrast between thick and thin strokes. Serifs are straighter, brackets less pronounced.

■ **Modern**—These faces are a development of the Transitional types, but are no more "modern" than they are, having originated shortly afterward with Bodoni and Didot. They further accentuate the contrast between thick and thin and eliminate entirely the brackets on serifs. Serifs and the other square strokes are perfectly straight, as though mechanically drawn.

■ **Egyptian**—A 19th-century development, this group has particularly heavy serifs with brackets. There is little contrast between thicks and thins; the serifs are usually at least as heavy as the thins and are squared off at the ends. Examples are Fortune, Clarendon, and Consort.

■ **Miscellaneous**—In the ever-expanding catalog of typefaces, there are many that don't fall into one of the above groups. Examples are given in the discussions of both text and display types.

Garamond
Caslon
old style

Baskerville
Bulmer
transitional

Bodoni
modern

Fortune
Consort
Egyptian

The main subdivisions of Abstract faces are (a) serifed and (b) nonserifed. The serifs in this class are simply short strokes of about the same thickness as the main parts of the face and have no brackets at all, or only a slight rounding at the junctures. If the bracket becomes pronounced, and a variation of thickness occurs within the curved lines, the face is more properly classified Egyptian than Abstract.

■ **Sans serif**—These may have strokes of uniform or varying thickness, with edges perfectly straight, as in Futura, or slightly curved, often with a slight swelling at the ends of straight strokes and the middle of curved ones. Examples are Lydian and Optima. Almost

Futura Light
Futura Medium
Futura Bold
Futura Ex Bold

Lydian
Optima

sans serif

all the sans-serif faces come in several weights—some varying from spidery fine to heavy black.

Beton
Memphis
block serif

■ **Block serif**—The variations in this group are somewhat smaller than within the sans serif. Typical are Beton, Memphis, Karnak, and Cairo. Each has numerous weights. This group borders on Egyptian, and is considered Egyptian (note the names) in most systems. However, there's an important visual distinction between the faces of almost purely mechanical design (Abstract) and those whose designs are strongly in the direction of Roman. There are borderline cases, but the extremes are far enough apart to justify the distinction, as the examples show.

CURSIVE

The primary visual characteristics of these faces are their slanted and generally continuous feeling. They vary mostly in the character of their line.

Garamond Italic
Bulmer Italic
Bodoni Italic
italics

■ **Italics**—This slanted form of Roman faces is based on the handwritten books that preceded printing. Early types designed by Aldus Manutius were italic, resembling writing done with a narrow square-tipped pen. Almost all italics are variations of this "Aldine" type. (A few italic types that are slanted but lack the cursive feeling of handwriting are called *obliques*.)

Typo Script
Kaufmann Script
Brush Script
scripts

■ **Scripts**—These are faces drawn to look as though they were handwritten. They have no serifs or other resemblance to Roman type. They vary from formal 18th-century pointed-pen scripts (Typo Script or Bank Script), through round-pointed pencil or pen scripts (Kaufman Script or Mistral), to informal brushwriting, such as Brush Script.

DECORATIVE

There is no way to subdivide these faces. They are usually exaggerated or embellished forms of the other classes (Ornata, Profil, Saphir, etc.), but they can be treated as graphic elements without reference to their antecedents. Some, such as Rustic and Astur, are so bizarre as to be unique. *Black Letter*, also known as *"Text"* or *"Old English"*, was the common form of writing in northern Europe through the Middle Ages, and persists in some German printing today. In American typography it's used mainly to suggest antiquity.

PROFIL
Ornata
RUSTIC
decorative

Old English

Type characteristics

Text types are used for the body of a book and are no larger than 18 pt. *Display types* are used for headings, titles, initials, etc. and are usually from 12 to 96 pt., or occasionally larger. The sizes may be modified on computers, but too much magnification often results in heavier and clumsier type than the smaller sizes. Theoretically, the only difference between text types and display types of the same name is size. In metal type, it was often true that a name was all they had in common, since they were usually made by different manufacturers and created by different designers. It's logical that they should be studied separately.

TEXT TYPE

The text typefaces discussed here were designed for, and produced as, metal type by three typesetting machines: Linotype, Intertype, and Monotype. To distinguish the faces from others of similar name, their names are sometimes preceded by the name of the machine for which they were created.

The problems of *copyfitting* (CHs. 23, 24) tend to divide text faces into groups according to width (characters-per-pica, see CHs. 6, 24). Some are exceptionally narrow for their height (Linotype Granjon, Electra, Times Roman, Bodoni Book, Garamond, Weiss), some are normal in width (Linotype Baskerville, Caledonia, Caslon, Janson), and some are particularly wide (Intertype Waverley, Linotype Primer). The difference in width of individual characters is minute, but multiplied by a half-million or so this difference will seriously affect the length of a book. For example, in a book of 500,000 characters with an average page size, a shift from 11 pt. Caledonia to 11 pt. Granjon will save twenty-four pages. The various computer faces based on these designs vary differently in their widths, so it's best to check the width for each face you want to set. The computer does enable condensing and expanding type (CH. 6), but use this capability with caution, since you are altering the design of the face and can easily spoil it.

Bookmaking
Bookmaking
Bookmaking

top to bottom: 14 pt. Granjon, Caledonia, Waverley

Text types vary in visual character just as much as display types, but the differences are not as noticeable because of the smaller size. So, while readers may not consciously perceive the distinctive nature of a text face, they're affected by it and it should be chosen for its harmony with the text.

One of the most discernible differences in types is their degree of strength or delicacy. Some are definitely strong and rugged, some are clearly light and delicate, some are in-between. Although here, as in other classifications by character, there'll be differences of opinion, it's reasonably safe to say that almost everyone would find Caledonia, Times Roman, and Monticello relatively strong; Granjon, Weiss, and Bodoni Book relatively delicate. But in all cases, the feeling conveyed by the type depends partly on the way it's used.

Times Roman
Weiss Roman

Type faces—like people's faces—have distinctive features indicating aspects of character beyond just strength and delicacy. Some features are quite pronounced, some are very subtle and more subject to personal interpretation. Here are some text faces with capsule character analyses:

Baskerville—Classical and elegant
Janson—Round and warm

Baskerville
Janson

Granjon
Caledonia
Times Roman
Electra
Fairfield
Bodoni
Waverley

Granjon—Round, warm, and graceful
Caledonia—Clean, firm, business-like
Times Roman—Stiff, cold, formal
Electra—Light, cool, efficient
Fairfield—Fussy
Bodoni—Dramatic
Waverley—Round and cool

In choosing type, it's better to consider these characteristics than to follow historical or conventional rules. It's the type's character, not its history, that affects the reader.

Electra Italic
[Oblique]
Electra Cursive

No primarily cursive faces are in regular use for book texts. There is a general reluctance to use italics for large amounts of text because it's believed that italic is harder to read than *roman* ("roman" as the opposite of "italic" is spelled with lowercase "r". "Roman" as a type classification has a capital "R".) If this is true it's only because people are less accustomed to reading italic. Like most theories about readability of type, this is hard to prove. The only valid study would be one that neutralizes the factor of experience, which would require an experiment with some subjects who had always been exposed to italic and others brought up on roman, but in reverse of the present proportion—a practical impossibility (see "Readability" below).

Janson *Janson*
Baskerville *Baskerville*
Caslon *Caslon*
Granjon *Granjon*

italics

An attempt to deal with the problem of reading italic was made by W. A. Dwiggins in 1935, when he introduced Electra with an italic that's slanted but lacks the cursive feeling. Because it made too little contrast with the roman, Electra Italic (or "Oblique", as it's generally called) was not accepted as an italic, and Electra Cursive was issued later. Among the other text faces, the italics vary somewhat in their cursiveness and style; probably the most distinctive is Janson. Some italics, such as Baskerville, Caslon, and Granjon, contrast with the roman particularly well. This is a factor in choosing type for books in which italic is much used.

Spartan
Metro
Erbar Light Condensed
Optima
News Gothic
Helvetica
Gothic Condensed No. 2
GOTHIC NO. 31

Memphis
Cairo

Spartan Heavy
Spartan Heavy Italic

abstract

There are a number of Abstract text types widely used. Among sans serifs are Spartan, Metro, Erbar, Optima, Helvetica, and Standard. Of the block-serif faces Memphis and Cairo are typical. Each of the Abstract faces has variations of weight in both roman and italic. The italics of these types are actually "obliques", having no cursive feeling. They don't contrast well with the romans.

The block-serif faces are quite similar to each other, but the sans serifs vary considerably. The contrast between Roman and Abstract type is so striking that people tend to miss the differences among individual sans-serif faces (the way that people tend to think that those of another race "all look alike"). But there's at least as much difference among sans-serif types as among Romans. For example, Spartan, Metro, and Helvetica are more uniform in thickness and straight of line than others; Optima, in contrast, has varied line thicknesses and curves that make it almost a serifless Roman.

DISPLAY TYPE

There is a much larger variety of display types than of text types, but many are infrequently used in books. On the computer, much of the display used is enlarged text type.

The rarely used faces tend to be in the Decorative class. Most of them are created for advertising typography and are not generally suitable for books. Advertising display types are designed to attract attention, which isn't the purpose of book typography (except on jackets and paperback covers). However, many of these faces are well designed and can be effectively used in books when appropriate. A skilled designer can use such types in a way that exploits their dramatic qualities yet avoids a blaring effect. The idea is to use them as an accent rather than as the dominant element of the page. Their impact can be controlled by reduction in size, by letterspacing, and by counterbalancing blocks of space or type. Even where a Decorative type is the only element on the page—on a part-title, for example—it can be restrained in its relationships to the space around it.

Roman display types are often not very close in design to the text faces of the same name. Many text faces don't have a display type of their name, but there are display faces of sympathetic character for any of them. For example:

Caledonia—Scotch, Bulmer
Electra—Corvinus, Bodoni Book
Fairfield—Garamond, Deepdene
Granjon—Garamond
Waverley—Scotch

Some confusion is caused by the practice of naming typefaces after the designers of earlier models. So, when choosing display faces named after early designers, consider each face on its visual merits, not its celebrity name.

The Cursive display types most used in books, besides the italics of the Roman faces, are those based on Spencerian script (Typo Script, Bank Script, Royal Script, Excelsior Script, etc.). In general, the other Cursive types are too informal for most books. However, not all books are classical works, so even the least formal face may find an appropriate use. Below are some Cursive display types:

Stationers Semiscript
Slogan
Constanze
Commercial Script
Legend
Excelsior Script

Maxime
Scritta a Lapis
Lydian
Charme
Bernhard Tango
Reiner Script

Stradivarius
Salto
Virtuosa No 1. and 2
Ondine
Champion

OUTLINE

LINED

SHADOW

Extra Condensed

Extended

abstract display faces

There are large numbers and a great variety of Abstract display faces. The variations of weight and style are about the same as for text types, plus open, shadowed, extended, and condensed forms. Sans-serif faces range from the relatively hand-lettered feeling of Lydian or Post Title to the mechanically drawn regularity of the numerous Gothics—Franklin, Airport, News, Alternate, etc.—and the more carefully designed Helvetica, Venus, Microgramma, and Standard series. The block-serif faces are less numerous and range less widely in style, as they tend to run into the Egyptian group once they acquire brackets. Below are some examples:

Stymie Medium Condensed

BETON OPEN

Tower

Girder

Memphis Medium

block-serif display faces

BOLDFACES The desire for contrast in type weight, to make distinctions in style or just to create graphic interest, led to a demand for "boldface". With rare exceptions, bold forms of Roman faces are unsuccessful designs and are best avoided. The reason is that they're not new faces at all, but simply thickened versions of the regular face. The overall dimensions of the type are altered hardly at all, but the relationships of weight, form, and line—so carefully balanced in the original design—are distorted far from the ideal in order to achieve the desired "color". If type designers made no attempt to retain the character of the regular weight, it would be possible to produce a boldface of good design, but the need to combine the new proportions and the old characteristics dooms Roman boldfaces to ugliness.

The Abstract faces seem to withstand fattening much better. Some of them range from wire thin to heavy black—with each weight as successful as any other. This is in part because there are no distinctive details, such as brackets, serifs, etc., that need to be modified as the weight of the face changes. Also, where the Roman faces have a special character related to their origin in writing, and can't be modified too far before they lose that character, the Abstract faces are original constructions that can be modified almost indefinitely with success—provided each variation is individually designed.

The modern *"fat faces"* (Ultra Bodoni, etc.) succeed because the original design is based on a sharp contrast in weight between thicks and thins, so the extreme contrast creates a different and

Garamond

Garamond Bo

Venus Light Extende

Venus Medium Exter

Venus Bold Exten

Venus Extrabolc

Bodoni

Bodoni Bold

Ultra

boldface

interesting form while retaining the basic features of the regular design. On the other hand, Bodoni Bold simply disturbs the happy proportions of the regular face and fails to create a valid new design.

It's almost impossible to achieve a successful page using a poorly designed display face, even though the type may be appropriate and is skillfully used. One poor element in a design tends to spoil the whole as the rotten apple spoils the whole barrel. Fortunately, the computer enables designers to modify typefaces, or even invent new ones—but, of course, the result will be only as good as the designer is talented. Be warned.

Typographic design

While it's true that the vast majority of readers are neither aware of nor informed about typefaces, it's wrong to assume that they will fail to respond to good typography—even in its more refined state. Their reactions are subconscious, but are no less definite for being so. Indeed, the conscious choices of readers frequently differ from the presumably subconscious responses they give in psychological tests. This casts some doubt on the importance of habituation in responses to typography and suggests that designers should strive for maximum excellence by their own visual standards and make the minimum compromise with what is thought to be popular taste.

COMBINING TYPE

In combining type it's better to use very close harmony or definite contrast than to mix faces that are only slightly dissimilar. The near-miss relationship creates a sense of uneasiness, even among those who are not familiar with type. They sense a difference and get a feeling that something is wrong because they're not consciously aware of the difference. For example, the use of a Roman Old Style face like Janson with a Transitional like Baskerville in text sizes would tend to create this effect.

Baskerville
Janson

The use of an Abstract face with a Roman, or any other combination of types of distinctly different classifications, provides a contrast that has a settling effect because it leaves no doubt as to the designer's intentions.

Univers
Janson

The surest and safest procedure is to use only one face throughout, but it's possible to mix faces of the same category successfully if they're very close in appearance (Granjon with Garamond, Bulmer with Baskerville, etc.).

Garamond
Granjon

A judicious use of both contrast and harmony is usually the best solution. The cardinal sin in design is to be equivocal and vague. Relationships may be subtle, but there must never be any doubt that the relationship was *intended*. Design *is* intention, the deliberate creation of order.

Variety is essential in design, but not necessarily in large amounts. As indicated above, an entire book can be printed in one

Bulmer
Baskerville

typeface—or even one size of one face—with great success. On the other hand, it's possible to make a mess using many different faces, or using too many variations with few faces. There is no one "right" way to use variety. The degree of activity or restraint that's proper depends on two factors: (a) the nature of the book's content (CH. 21), and (b) the visual requirements of the design. In both cases, the only guides are intelligence and intuition.

EMPHASIS To establish an order of relative importance, or to direct attention to an element of text, it's necessary to give type various degrees of emphasis. There are many ways to do this. Emphasis can be achieved by the choice of:

- **Typeface (font)**—A decorated or cursive face will get more attention than another, all other things being equal.
- **Type weight**—A boldface is more prominent than a lighter one. A strong face will dominate a thin, weak one.
- **Type size**—Large size is, of course, more emphatic than small.
- **Italics**—In most cases, italics imply emphasis.
- **Capitals**—Size for size, capitals have more emphasis than lowercase.
- **Position**—This is a difficult point about which to generalize, but there are a few broad principles. Emphasis can be achieved by isolating an element, placing it at the top of the page, placing it adjacent to the most important element, or placing it in any unique situation, e.g., at right angles to the rest of the type, on a slant, upside-down, etc.
- **Color**—The ability of certain colors to advance may be utilized (CHs. 8, 22).
- **Spacing**—Letterspacing is effective. It's used in Europe sometimes to emphasize proper names. A block of type can be emphasized by increasing or decreasing leading.

The attention-getting power of *contrast* is a key factor in achieving emphasis. Any element will become conspicuous (and therefore emphasized) if it's unlike any other. A word in 8 pt. type is emphasized if it's in a page of 30 pt. type. A line of lowercase will stand out if every other line is in caps. Roman stands out among italics. Even a gray-blue can outshine bright red if it's the only other color on the page.

KINDS OF ARRANGEMENT No general style of typographic layout is better than another. The only criterion is success. It's possible to do a bad job with a centered arrangement or with an asymmetrical one.

Symmetrical arrangements, however, are relatively simple, and the centered style has the fewest problems. The moment that dependable center axis is left behind, designers find themselves in a structureless expanse, without guidelines or conventions. It's the difference between traveling on roads and navigating the open sea.

The asymmetrical arrangement permits a far greater range of expression, but it also requires much more design skill. The problem isn't only to make a visually pleasing arrangement of type and space, but to achieve a solid structure with unequal balance. With a centered fulcrum you know that each side must have the same weight. When you move the fulcrum off center, you must be able to determine how much weight is needed on each end to prevent collapse. In graphics there's no way of computing this. Everything depends on the designer's sense of balance. The difficulty of creating such a structure with complex copy isn't to be taken lightly.

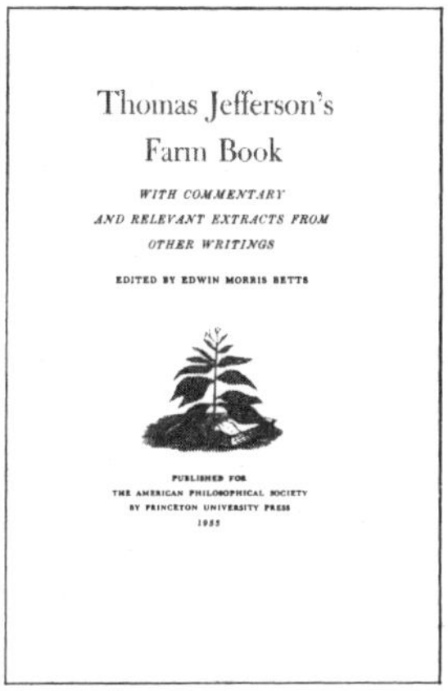
Thomas Jefferson's
Farm Book
WITH COMMENTARY
AND RELEVANT EXTRACTS FROM
OTHER WRITINGS
EDITED BY EDWIN MORRIS BETTS
PUBLISHED FOR
THE AMERICAN PHILOSOPHICAL SOCIETY
BY PRINCETON UNIVERSITY PRESS
1953

symmetrical

While the centered arrangement is easier because a structural framework exists, the use of this style by no means guarantees success. The *worst* disasters (common in asymmetrical layout) will be avoided, but the achievement of an excellent page still depends on a superior choice and disposition of the various elements of design.

It's possible for a combination of symmetrical and asymmetrical elements to be used successfully in a book, but this requires such mastery of design that it's very improbable. Since there's rarely any need to have such a combination, there's really no reason to attempt it. This isn't a "rule" (there is only one rule in design: *If it works, it's good*); it's a logical conclusion. As soon as an unsymmetrical element is introduced into a symmetrical arrangement, the design ceases to be symmetrical. A centered element in an asymmetrical layout doesn't of itself make the design symmetrical, but it does introduce an ambivalence that's just as unsettling and out of character. A single centered line in an asymmetrical layout is usually absorbed by the overall plan and doesn't seem to be centered at all. When there are two or more centered lines together, they create a sense of conflict that's death to design. This is true even if the centered lines appear on a facing page.

THE COMPLETE WORKS OF O. HENRY
FOREWORD BY HARRY HANSEN
VOLUME I
1953
DOUBLEDAY & COMPANY, INC. GARDEN CITY, N.Y.

asymmetrical

A formal arrangement doesn't need to be centered; it may be aligned to one side or the other. "Formal" implies a certain regularity of arrangement, rather than any particular one. An informal style results from the placement of elements according to caprice rather than a rigid structure, and from the use of elements, including typefaces and illustrations, that have a light, fresh touch—even a bit of eccentricity—rather than classical forms.

There are many ways to convey dynamism in graphic design. Strong contrast is dynamic, and so is strong movement. Sharp curves are more dynamic than gradual ones, diagonals are generally more dynamic than horizontals, short lines more than long ones, and an informal arrangement is more dynamic than a formal one. The converse of these axioms is applicable to placidity. The choice of elements isn't as significant in this respect as their interaction—the result of their combination and arrangement. Any kind of design—symmetrical or asymmetrical, formal or informal, dynamic or placid, etc.—can be either strong or delicate in feeling.

formal

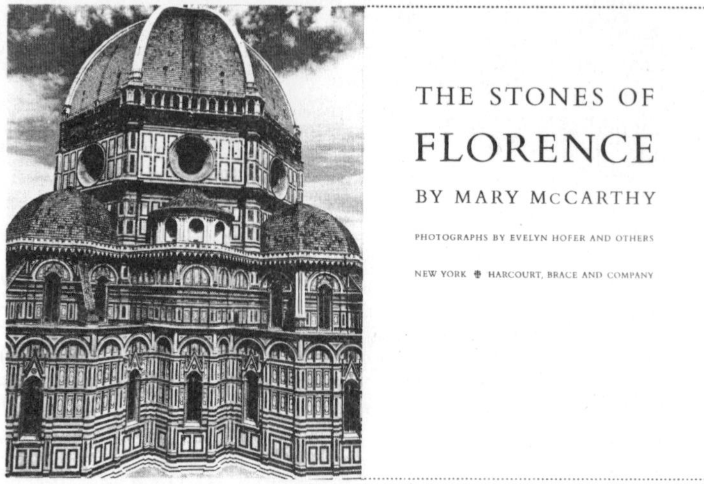

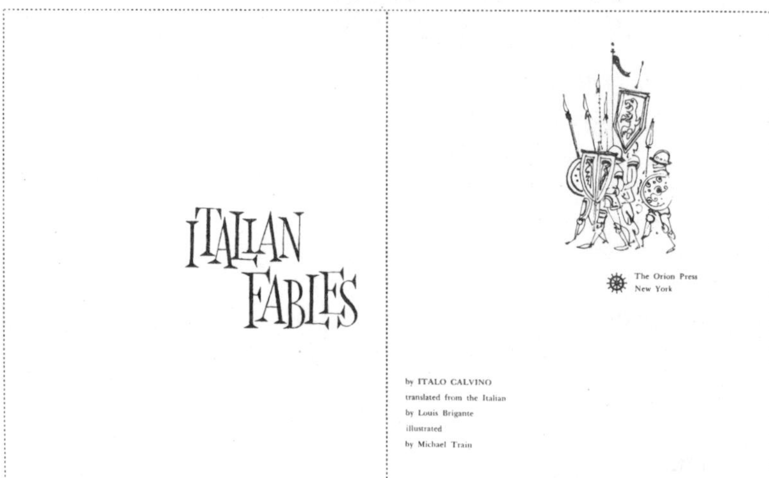

informal

CHANGES There are many elements in a typographic design, and their interaction is complex. No element can be introduced, deleted, or changed without affecting all the others. The successful design is a perfectly balanced construction of type, illustration (if any), and space. Sometimes a change can be countered successfully with a comparable modification in another part of the design, but in a simple and delicately balanced composition, any change may require a new start. Among a designer's frustrations is to have a title page come back from the editor marked "OK as corrected" when a subtitle or an author's middle name has been added or deleted, as though the change didn't affect the design.

THE SHAPES OF WORDS One of the least understood principles of typography is that the visual features of the copy are a vital factor. For example, some beginning designers are fond of arranging the words in a title one above the other. This has been done with great success and will be again, but only when the words in the particular title lend themselves to such a scheme. The words must be of such length as to form an interesting pattern when disposed vertically—either aligned to one side or centered on each other. (They may sometimes be staggered with satisfactory results.) Also, if a large size of lowercase display type is used, a great deal depends on what letters make up the words, as the occurrence of ascenders or descenders in the wrong place can be ruinous.

Any combination of words and letters can be beautifully and effectively arranged, but they must be arranged to suit their own form—not squeezed into a designer's arbitrary scheme. The decision to use (a) all caps; (b) upper and lower case (*ulc*), i.e., cap initial letter of all major words; or (c) cap and lowercase (*clc*), i.e., cap initial letter of first word only, and the choice of size, placement,

HOLIDAYS
IN
THE
SUN

awkward

THE
OLD
LIDO
SUN

less awkward

IN
SUNNY
SOUTHERN
ITALY

pleasant

Thy
Only
Myth
of
Logic
Holy

awkward

Thy Only Myth of
Logic Holy

less awkward

THY
ONLY MYTH
OF LOGIC
HOLY

better

or style of type must all be based on the nature of the copy, as this is unchangeable. It isn't a bad idea to begin by trying the display words in both caps and ulc or clc. Often, the words will naturally make a shape that suggests the best arrangement.

USING SPACE The design of any flat surface consists of two parts—the covered and the uncovered areas. In a sense, one is no more important than the other. When we print a word in black ink on a rectangle of white paper, we are creating a composition in black and white. While the type's primary value is its symbolic and graphic (black) pattern, it's also delineating areas of space around and within itself. In a well-designed page, the white areas effectively interact with the black—the page is alive. In poor typography, the type seems printed on top of a white background—the page is dead.

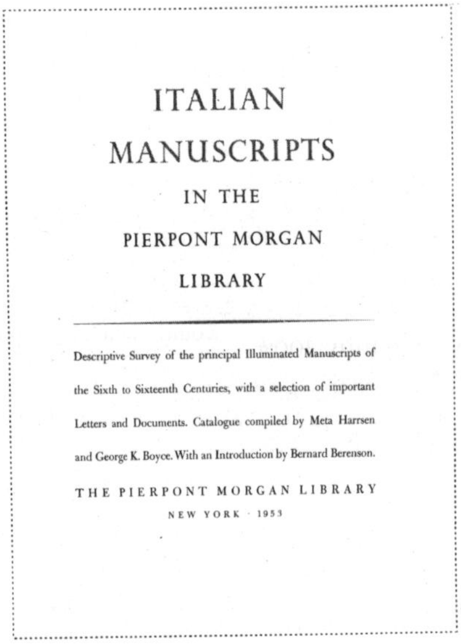

ITALIAN
MANUSCRIPTS
IN THE
PIERPONT MORGAN
LIBRARY

Descriptive Survey of the principal Illuminated Manuscripts of the Sixth to Sixteenth Centuries, with a selection of important Letters and Documents. Catalogue compiled by Meta Harrsen and George K. Boyce. With an Introduction by Bernard Berenson.

THE PIERPONT MORGAN LIBRARY
NEW YORK · 1953

live page

GUNS
of
ARIZONA

Originally published as
BREED OF THE CHAPARRAL

NELSON C. NYE

KLEY PUBLISHING CO
• New York

dead page

LETTERSPACING Both capital and lowercase letters in our alphabet vary so much in shape that a nasty visual problem can arise from an unlucky sequence. For example, the capitals IN together create an entirely different spatial pattern than the combination LAT. But these combinations make one word—LATIN—which is by nature uneven in "color". It's difficult to reduce the space between LAT, but we can *add* space between IN to make an evenly spaced LATIN. This word is perhaps an extreme case, but a problem arises to some degree in any line of caps (or small caps). If the amount of copy is small and the size of type large, spacing between letters can be adjusted as shown. Where optically adjusted *letterspacing*

LATIN

LATIN

is impractical, some uniform spacing should be added, and as much as possible. The addition of 10 pt. letterspace to L A T I N doesn't eliminate the irregularity of space, but the latter becomes proportionately less significant.

The problem is even more acute in the lowercase alphabet and grows with the size of type. The word "billowy" in 60 pt. type is almost hopeless, but it can be saved with substantial letterspacing.

billowy b i l l o w y

There is a prejudice among some American typographers against letterspacing lowercase, directed mainly against using letterspacing as a means of filling out a line of text, a practice common in newspapers and magazines where narrow columns often create awkward problems. If a line starts with two long words and the next one is an unbreakable word that doesn't fit, the alternatives are: (a) leave a giant space between the first two words or (b) letterspace them. Of the choices, letterspacing is the least objectionable, but it would be better to reset a few lines to get a better break, or ask the editor to make a change in the copy. A sequence of lines with excessive word space results in unpleasantly loose composition and noticeable *rivers* (jagged vertical white lines caused by a series of wide spaces in about the same place on successive lines).

The best solution is to use the computer's refined *tracking* (letterspacing) and *justification* functions to make minute letter and word space adjustments throughout the text or in a part of it. This avoids offensively wide spaces by spreading the space changes imperceptibly over a large section of text.

enlarged word spaces

seemed so irrelevant at the time, had been eliminated! Unquestionably, Germany would then have conquered all Europe, and would still have been ruling it today. From the

letterspaced

seemed so irrelevant at the time, had been eliminated Unquestionably, Germany would then have conquered all Europe, and would still have been ruling it today. From the

reset

seemed so irrelevant at the time, had been eliminated! Unquestionably, Germany would then have conquered all Europe, and would still have been ruling it today. From the Atlan-

ALLUSION

The relationship of typography to content is discussed in CHs. 24, 25, 28. Avoid allusive typography that's only an imitation of the style of a period or place. It's okay to *suggest* another time or place, but imitation is neither honest nor effective. Actually, typographic imitation becomes more unsettling the better it's done. The reader begins to wonder whether it's an imitation or the real thing. The best practice is to express the spirit of the period or subject, rather than to reproduce its typography.

Readability

Readability and *legibility* are sometimes considered synonyms; they're not. There is a tendency (hastened by permissive dictionaries) for the distinctions among words of similar meaning to blur and disappear, but in an increasingly technological society we need all the precision of language possible. The terms "readability" and "legibility" describe two quite distinct qualities.

Legibility is the quality of type (or writing) that makes it *possible* to read. Readability is the characteristic of a body of type that makes it *comfortable* to read. Both are relative terms. For example, 4 pt. type used for a credit line under an illustration may be legible because it *can* be read at the normal reading distance for a book. To read a billboard atop a building, the smallest legible size of letter may be 6" (15.24 cm) high. Similarly, 8 pt. type with no leading may be readable for an encyclopedia in which the text for each item is only a paragraph or two, but it wouldn't be readable for a 320-page novel—although it would be legible in both cases.

Both readability and legibility are so fundamental to the design of books that there's no more need to praise them here than to praise structural strength in discussing architecture. The desirability of these qualities may be taken for granted. Our concern with them isn't *should* they be achieved, but *how*.

In all aspects of readability, habit and experience are larger factors than is generally conceded. Psychologists who test reading tend to draw conclusions from the performance of their subjects without giving much weight to the influence of training. Peoples of other cultures learn to read easily in alphabets very different from our own, so it's reasonable to assume that we would respond very differently to reading tests if we had been otherwise trained. Thus, the testers' conclusions are not empirical facts so much as observations of conditioned behavior. (If it's true that more than 3 or 4 pts. of leading hampers reading—as many psychologists claim—why do editors and typesetters prefer double-spaced typescript having about 12 pts. of leading?)

There has been a considerable amount of research in readability, but the problem has too many subtleties to ever yield to rational study alone. Nevertheless, where many tests are in agreement with each other *and* with the observations of experienced designers, it's fair to assume that some truth has been found. The opinions expressed in this section, while those of the author, relate to the scientific data available.

The readability of a page is affected by no fewer than nine factors:

typeface,
size of type,
length of line,
leading,
page pattern (which includes "margins"),
contrast of type and paper (which includes color),
texture of paper,
typographic relationships (heads, folios, etc.), and
suitability to content.

Some factors are more significant than others, but it's their combined effect that gives the page its character, and it's only when all are in perfect balance that a truly readable page results.

Paper is covered in CH. 11. Typographic relationships and suitability to content are referred to in CHs. 24, 25, and elsewhere throughout the book. The following discussion deals with the remaining factors of readability.

TYPEFACE (FONT)

We have seen that typefaces—even text types—have individual characteristics that can be matched with corresponding characteristics of the text. The choice of typeface should be made initially on this basis. If it becomes apparent that the face chosen can't produce the required number of characters per page (CHs. 23, 24), a compromise may be necessary. As always, begin with that which seems best and give up only what you must.

SIZE OF TYPE

It's the apparent, or *visual*, size of type with which we are concerned first. The *actual* type size, i.e., the point size (see "Measurement & terminology" at the beginning of this chapter), will affect the book's length, but it's the appearance of the face that affects readability.

Readability is relative to the reading ability of the book's user. For normal book use—that is, for a general audience of adult readers—minor differences in type size are not significant. When the anticipated readers are either very old or very young, type size becomes an important factor.

It's generally accepted that larger sizes are desirable for children learning to read, but many children's book editors in America favor extremely large type in comparison to the sizes ordinarily used for the same age group in England and other countries. In the five-to-seven age group, 18 pt. faces are probably not excessive, as the children are still having some difficulty recognizing letters. From ages seven to about ten, there's probably no need for anything larger than an average 12 pt. face, although 14 pt. type is often used. Between ten and twelve, a good reader needs no more than a large 11 pt., and over twelve years old an average child shouldn't have any difficulty reading the 11 pt. faces commonly used for adult books, as long as the other elements of the text page are selected for particularly good readability (plenty of leading, fairly short lines, etc.). Some editors and teachers feel, however, that larger sizes are necessary to make reading seem easier. This may be justified in view of the poor reading scores of many schoolchildren in these times.

While the use of large type for children is based more on (somewhat debatable) psychological than optical reasons, for elderly readers larger sizes may be needed because failing sight requires them. Unfortunately, little attention is given to this consideration in regular trade editions. There are, of course, books published in large type sizes especially for the elderly and those with poor vision, but here we are discussing books for the general reader that are expected to have an audience of older people with average vision for their age. (It may be true that proper eyeglasses would eliminate some of the problem, but the book designer's function is to accommodate the readers, not to drive them to the optometrist.)

In books intended primarily for people over sixty, the text type should be not smaller than a large 11 pt. Where space permits, 12 pt. is preferable. The other elements of the page should be chosen, as they are for small children, for maximum readability. For adults whose sight can be presumed to be normal, the larger 10 pt. faces are adequate, if the other elements of readability are favorable. Most hardcover books are set in 11 pt., although paperbacks have sold in large numbers with 10 and 9 pt. text types, and sometimes 8 pt.

Readability is relative also to the kind of reading. Normal sizes of type are needed for sustained texts such as novels, etc., while brief texts, as in encyclopedias, can be set smaller without impairing readability.

By the 1990s the concern of many designers—and editors and publishers—for readability diminished almost to the vanishing point. It isn't uncommon to see the entire text of a book set in a size previously reserved for footnotes. Small blocks of copy are often set in even smaller sizes, which are not only not readable but practically illegible. Too small type is sometimes used with lines of excessive length—with disastrous effects on readability. It seems that the public must love reading very much to tolerate the difficulties created by designers/publishers.

This unfortunate disregard for readability developed at a time when the level of design quality was rising. Somehow, designers were released from the constraints of readability—presumably with the tacit permission of editors and publishers—and used this freedom to create excellent graphics in which type is used primarily as a design device. If a better effect can be achieved by making the type tiny, so be it; little or no consideration seems to be given to the difficulty of reading that size. This is a trend that should be stopped. Perhaps it will have to die slowly as the public reacts against it. It's hoped that the readers of this book will resist the temptation to make nice patterns at the expense of the reader.

In 2001 an exhibition called "Size Matters" was mounted in the New York City headquarters of Lighthouse International, an organization that helps people with vision problems. The exhibition promoted the idea that too small type and other deficiencies of typographic design, such as inappropriate typeface, poor contrast, and insufficient leading, make reading more or less impossibly difficult. The show was concerned with the problems of visually impaired people and the readability of ads, but its findings applied equally to readers with normal sight and all kinds of printed matter, including books. The basis for the show's conclusions was research by the Arline R. Gordon Research Institute. The exhibition was an important indictment of designers who fail to give sufficient attention to readability.

LENGTH OF LINE

There are few aspects of readability that are truly measurable, but length of line is one. In view of this, it's insupportable that the most frequent destroyer of readability, after tiny type, is excessive length of line. The reason is quite obvious. Long lines of type, especially when well leaded, look graceful—just as tall, long-legged models do. But most models are too skinny for anything but modeling, and very long lines of type are not efficient for reading.

rooms (when the normal day ending at 10 p.m. would be much prolonged) girls have asserted . . . that they enjoy the excitement of such nights, unless too often repeated; the furious haste with which the work is pushed on, the speculation as to whether it will be finished in time, and the additional refreshments provided on such occasions,

too long lines

Tests have shown many disadvantages in long lines: (a) The eye must blink at intervals during reading—after each blink, an optical adjustment and refocus of vision takes place. The longer the line, the more frequently blinks occur within, rather than at the end of lines. (b) There is time and visual effort lost in traveling back to the beginning of the next line. (c) At the end of each line there's momentary difficulty in determining which is the next line (sometimes the wrong one is selected). These interruptions—the blink, the trip back, the search for the right line—cause loss of reading efficiency and reader fatigue.

Another optical factor that affects reading comfort is the span of vision. Without moving your eyes or head you can see clearly straight ahead and about 2" to each side. Naturally, the less movement necessary, the less fatigue. For comfort, there's a maximum line width for each distance from eye to object, the ideal width becoming greater as the distance increases. At normal book-reading distance—about 16" (40 cm)—the maximum comfortable width is about 5" (12.7 cm/30 picas). At billboard-reading distance, a line of 20' in length can be read with no more muscular effort than required by a 5" line in a book.

All the factors of visual comfort tend to suggest a maximum of about 70 characters per line in a page of average size. Fewer characters is better—down to about 50, where it becomes difficult to set justified lines without excessive hyphenation of words and irregular wordspacing. The ideal is probably between 55 and 60 characters per line, at a length of about 4" (10.2 cm/24 picas) for justified text. For unjustified lines, 45 characters is about optimum. It may be necessary to vary from the ideal for economic reasons, but then it's better to make a radical change in the specifications than to exceed by very much the maximum and minimum limits. However, the limits relate to the reading capabilities of each audience. For children, the elderly, and the visually or mentally handicapped, the lower limits are appropriate. For the experienced reader and the mentally gifted, the upper limits may be used.

LEADING Neither size of type nor length of line should be selected without considering leading. The larger the type, the more leading is needed to avoid confusion. If the space between lines isn't sufficient in relation to the space between words, the horizontal movement of the eye is disturbed. The longer the line, the more leading is needed to distinguish the lines and facilitate finding the beginning of the next one (see "Length of line" above).

every page
at full width

too little leading

Up to a point, the more leading the better. Beyond this point, additional leading may detract from readability. The optimum amount depends on the typeface, its size, and the measure. Where wordspacing is unusually large, as in books for young children, the amount of leading should be in proportion. With so many variables involved, the choice of leading is more a matter of visual judgment than mathematics.

In general, 10 pt. and 11 pt. faces on measures up to 22 picas can do with 1 pt. of leading; from 22 to 25 picas with 2 pts.; over 25 with 3. Twelve and 14 pt. types generally need a minimum of 2 pts., require 3 when set wider than 25 picas, and read better with 4 pts. on 28 picas or over. Small sizes, such as 8 and 9 pt., need proportionately more leading than the larger sizes, to compensate for their lower readability. When set in narrow measures, this need diminishes. For example, 8 pt. type set 12 picas wide can be read quite comfortably with 1 pt. leading. On a 20-pica measure it might need 2 pts., on 23 picas, 3 pts. But remember that the x-height (the height of the lowercase letters without ascenders or descenders) of each face greatly affects the leading needed. A face with a small x-height needs less leading than one with a large x-height. For this reason, a table indicating the proper leading for each size and measure wouldn't be practical.

When I wrote the following pages, or rather the bulk of them, I lived alone, in the woods, a mile from any neighbor, in a house which I had built myself, on

8/9 x 12

When I wrote the following pages, or rather the bulk of them, I lived alone, in the woods, a mile from any neighbor, in a house which I had built myself, on the shore of Walden Pond, in Concord, Massachusetts, and earned my living by the labor of my

8/10 x 20

When I wrote the following pages, or rather the bulk of them, I lived alone, in the woods, a mile from any neighbor, in a house which I had built myself, on the shore of Walden Pond, in Concord, Massachusetts, and earned my living by the labor of my hands only. I lived there two

8/11 x 23

width and leading

PAGE PATTERN

The term "*page pattern*" may seem unfamiliar in this context, but it's used deliberately to avoid the word "*margins*". The concept of a page as a block of type surrounded by a frame of "margins" is a vestige of early printing. Then the text was a rectangular block of metal arranged on the page so as to leave enough paper on each side to meet the printing and binding requirements of the time. The proportions of these margins were determined largely by the need to minimize the size of the 4-page forms generally used on hand presses in those days. This meant reducing the *head* (top) and *inside* (*gutter*) *margins* to get the pages as close together as possible, so that a good impression could be obtained with a minimum of effort. This left plenty of paper on the outside and bottom edges of the printed page. That practical necessity soon became an esthetic dogma, and the conventional, but obsolete, margin proportions have been taught to designers ever since (CHs. 9, 12, 25).

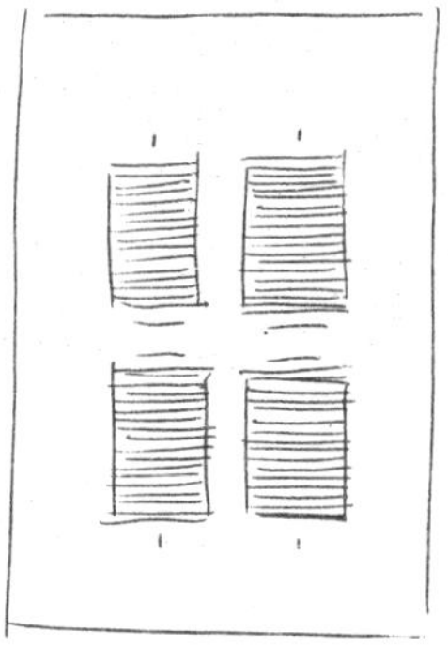

four-page form for handpress

If you want to see what designers would do free of the mechanical constraints of printing, look at the medieval manuscripts. In these, the pages were regarded as areas to be filled in the most beautiful and effective way, with words, pictures, and space arranged over the entire *spread*, rather than the individual page. The manuscript maker's criteria were visual and functional, not conventional and mechanical—at least in the beginning.

The graphic freedom of the manuscript books is available again. In any method of printing in which photomechanically or digitally created film is used, the mechanical limitations of the hand press no longer apply. There is no significant reason—esthetic, practical, or economic—to remain bound by the obsolete conventions of "margins".

Millions of paperbacks are sold and read with outside margins of minimal size. In defense of the conventional arrangement it has even been claimed that a large foot margin is necessary to provide room for the reader's thumb! Aside from the obvious fact that anyone able to read would have sense enough to move his

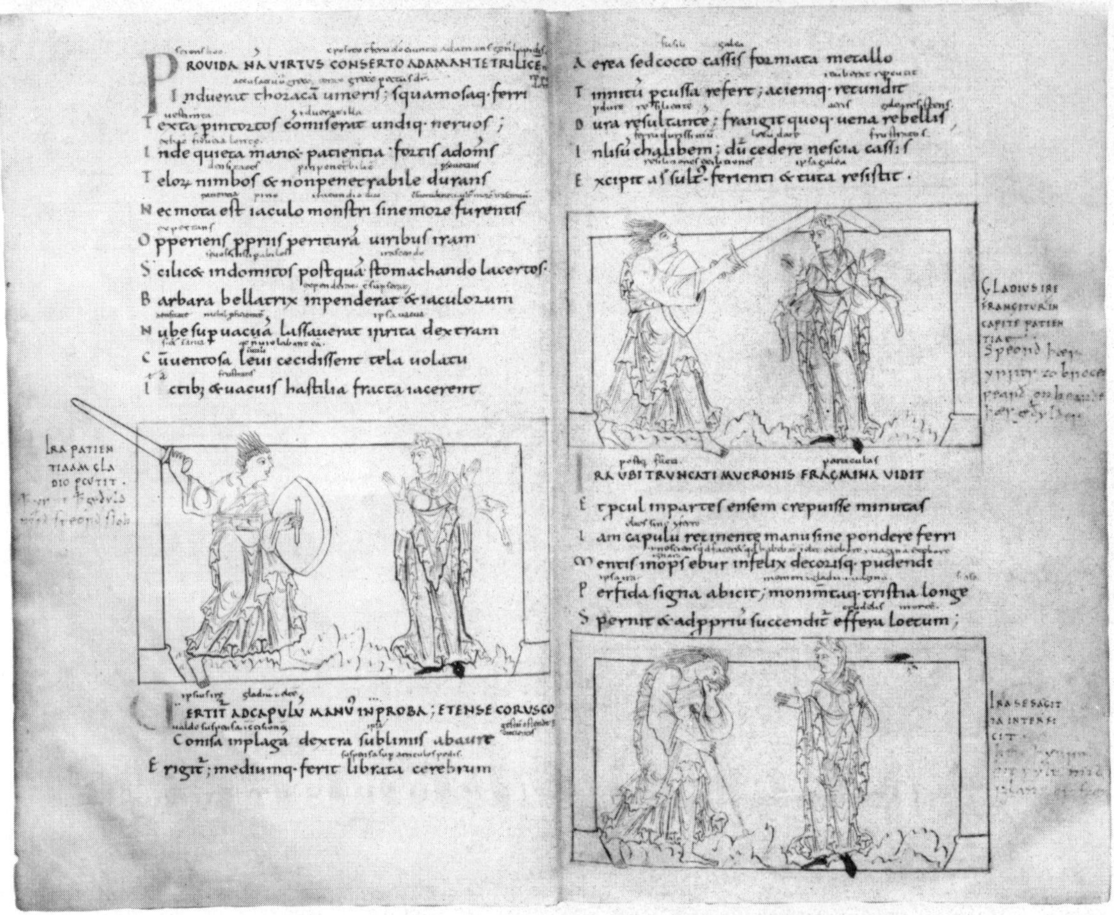

8th century manuscript

thumb if it happened to cover the next word, no one is likely to hold a book at the bottom unless reading while walking—an uncommon and risky practice.

This isn't to say that a conventional page pattern is bad. It may very well be the best. The point is that the size, shape, and position of the type areas and other elements on the page should be determined by the visual, practical, and economic requirements of the individual problem, not by the application of a rigid formula. For example, if the book has a tight adhesive binding, the text should be placed farther from the gutter than with a sewn binding. If the problem is well analyzed and solved, any arrangement can be justified.

In conclusion A truly personal style in typography takes many years to develop. There are some who feel that in book typography the designer's personality should be completely submerged. It's doubtful, however, that the personality of a designer, as it's revealed in a well-done book, is any more detrimental to the content than the personality of an actor is to a play or that of a conductor to a symphony. As long as the interpreter's personality doesn't dominate or alter the work, it can enliven and enrich it.

The heights attainable in typography are limited by talent and experience. In the beginning, simplicity is best because it's necessary for success. Later, it becomes an essential part of the designer's outlook. In between, experiment has its place.

This chapter has dealt with typography in general—later chapters will discuss typography in relation to particular phases of bookmaking.

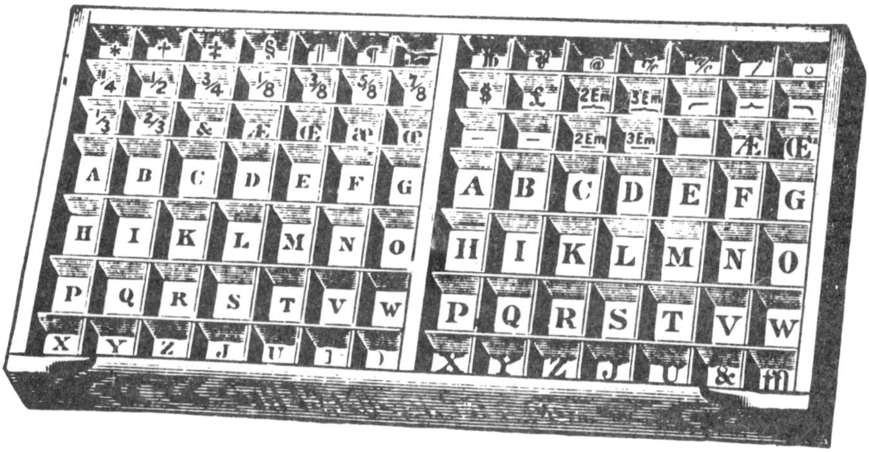

upper case

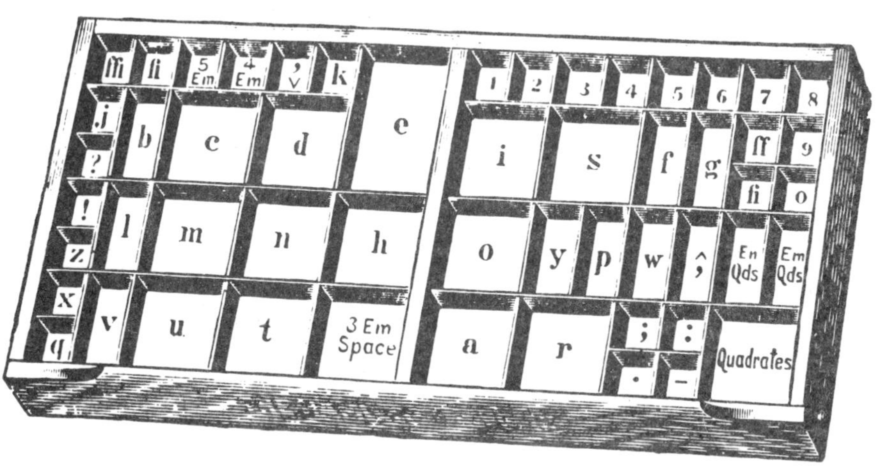

lower case

6. Composition

From the middle of the 15th century, when hand-set movable type began to be used in Europe, until the 1880s, when type began to be set by machines like the Linotype, which produced a solid bar of metal for each line of text, "composition" could be defined as *the assembly of individual metal-type characters into words, lines, and pages.*

In the 1960s, metal type was being nudged aside by photocomposition, a process in which an image of the type was created by exposing photographic paper through a negative film. At first, each character had to be positioned and exposed individually, a tedious process not suited to producing large amounts of text. However, once computer systems began to control the process quickly and automatically, photocomposition became the dominant typesetting technology. Within a few years, new systems could form the character images digitally, and by the 1980s *digital typesetting* took over the world of composition. Advances in composition software now enable pages, including their illustrations, to be made up and assembled for printing without ever having taken physical form. Today we might define "composition" as *the transformation of original content into a form suitable for printing or making printing plates.*

Although digital composition is now universal, it must be emphasized that the basics of typesetting originated in metal type—and particularly hand-set type—composition, and these basics are essential knowledge for digital typesetters. The terms and specifications of typesetting were established when type was hand set, and it's necessary to learn them, even though some of them have undergone change in computer terminology (CH. 5).

Type specification The original material that's to be set (or otherwise converted for reproduction) is the *copy,* which may be pages from a typewriter or printout from a computer. In order to have type set as it's wanted, specifications of a certain kind must be given for every line or character. Here is the information required for each item:

(a) typeface;
(b) type size;
(c) whether caps, small caps, lowercase, cap and lowercase, upper and lower case, or cap and small caps;
(d) whether italic or roman;
(e) letterspacing, if any;
(f) vertical position (1. *sinkage*—the distance down from the topmost element on the typepage, or 2. the distance to the next item above or below);

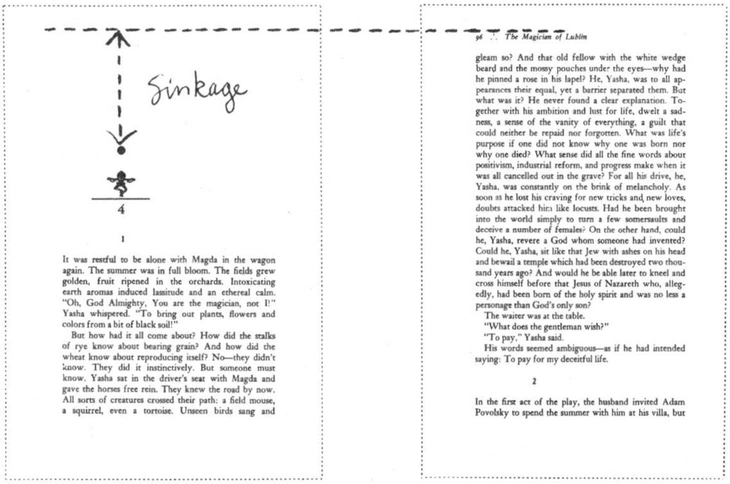

4

1

It was restful to be alone with Magda in the wagon again. The summer was in full bloom. The fields grew golden, fruit ripened in the orchards. Intoxicating earth aromas induced lassitude and an ethereal calm. "Oh, God Almighty, You are the magician, not I!" Yasha whispered. "To bring out plants, flowers and colors from a bit of black soil!"

But how had it all come about? How did the stalks of rye know about bearing grain? And how did the wheat know about reproducing itself? No—they didn't know. They did it instinctively. But someone must know. Yasha sat in the driver's seat with Magda and gave the horses free rein. They knew the road by now. All sorts of creatures crossed their path: a field mouse, a squirrel, even a tortoise. Unseen birds sang and

96 ∴ *The Magician of Lublin*

gleam so? And that old fellow with the white wedge beard and the mossy pouches under the eyes—why had he pinned a rose in his lapel? He, Yasha, was to all appearances their equal, yet a barrier separated them. But what was it? He never found a clear explanation. Together with his ambition and lust for life, dwelt a sadness, a sense of the vanity of everything, a guilt that could neither be repaid nor forgotten. What was life's purpose if one did not know why one was born nor why one died? What sense did all the fine words about positivism, industrial reform, and progress make when it was all cancelled out in the grave? For all his drive, he, Yasha, was constantly on the brink of melancholy. As soon as he lost his craving for new tricks and new loves, doubts attacked him like locusts. Had he been brought into the world simply to turn a few somersaults and deceive a number of females? On the other hand, could he, Yasha, revere a God whom someone had invented? Could he, Yasha, sit like that Jew with ashes on his head and bewail a temple which had been destroyed two thousand years ago? And would he be able later to kneel and cross himself before that Jesus of Nazareth who, allegedly, had been born of the holy spirit and was no less a personage than God's only son?

The waiter was at the table.

"What does the gentleman wish?"

"To pay," Yasha said.

His words seemed ambiguous—as if he had intended saying: To pay for my deceitful life.

2

In the first act of the play, the husband invited Adam Povolsky to spend the summer with him at his villa, but

(g) leading (if more than one line);
(h) measure (if set on justified lines or to a particular width);
(i) horizontal position (flush left or right, indented, centered, etc.);
(j) *wordspacing* (tight or wide, if other than normal); and
(k) weight (if the typeface is available in more than one weight, e.g., bold, semibold, etc.).

Note that the introduction of *scalable* fonts (which can be scaled to any size from the same font file) has led to the practice of referring to typeface and style without specifying size.

Specification markup on hard copy should be written legibly in the margin with a sharp pencil of a different color than used elsewhere, and according to the sequence indicated by the layout software being used. For typographic markup it's best to label the elements in the copy with simple, unique, style names, such as "extract", "table", etc. These can then be defined for translation to the appropriate format. If the copy is in a word-processing format, the style names can be applied to the elements within that format, so the translations will be done automatically when the copy is converted into type.

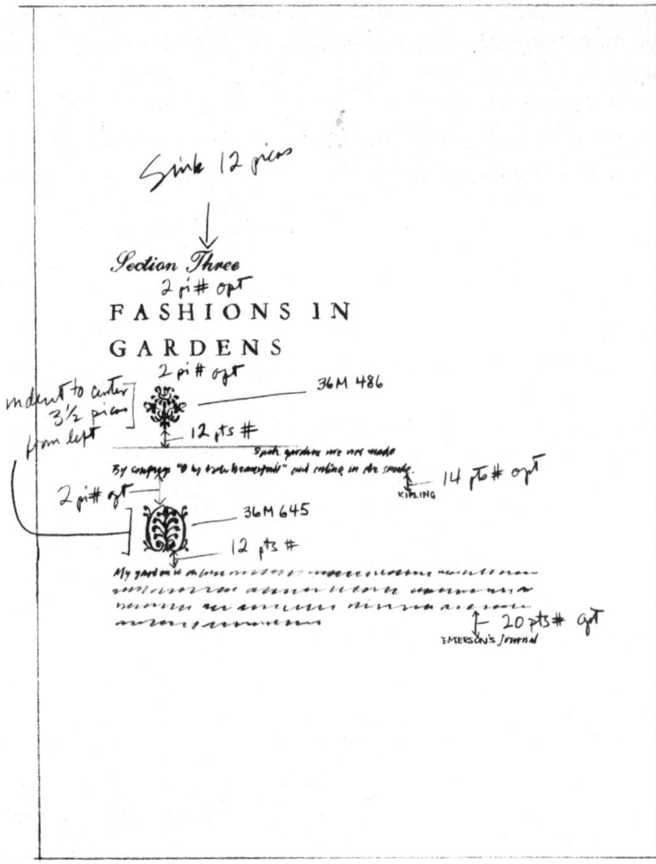

layout marked for position of elements

For some kinds of digitized production, the copy may have to be marked up with *HTML (Hypertext Markup Language)* or *XML (Extensible Markup Language)* coding. In HTML, the codes (*tags*) specifically indicate how the text is to appear. So, copy to be in boldface may be preceded by a code that means *begin boldface* and followed by a code that means *end boldface* (for example: <b> copy </b>). A change to italic or any other change in the copy may be handled in this way. Alternatively, the codes may simply refer to each element. Then the typographic information for each element's appearance is defined in a "style sheet". This coding is usually done in the word-processing stage. The codes don't appear in the printout, but the type has been set as directed by them.

XML, which is similar to but more flexible than HTML, defines a document's structure rather than its appearance. XML codes not only name the elements in a document, they define their content. Where HTML codes are specific (boldface is always b), you can make up XML codes to suit a particular document. This makes XML able to function with highly specialized subjects—neuroscience, astrophysics, philology, etc. Style sheets then format each element's appearance. Once a document has been coded in XML it can be distributed in any medium by simply changing the style sheet definitions. The document itself remains the same. (See "Sources of information" in Appendix for materials that explain these markup languages, or check with your service bureau.)

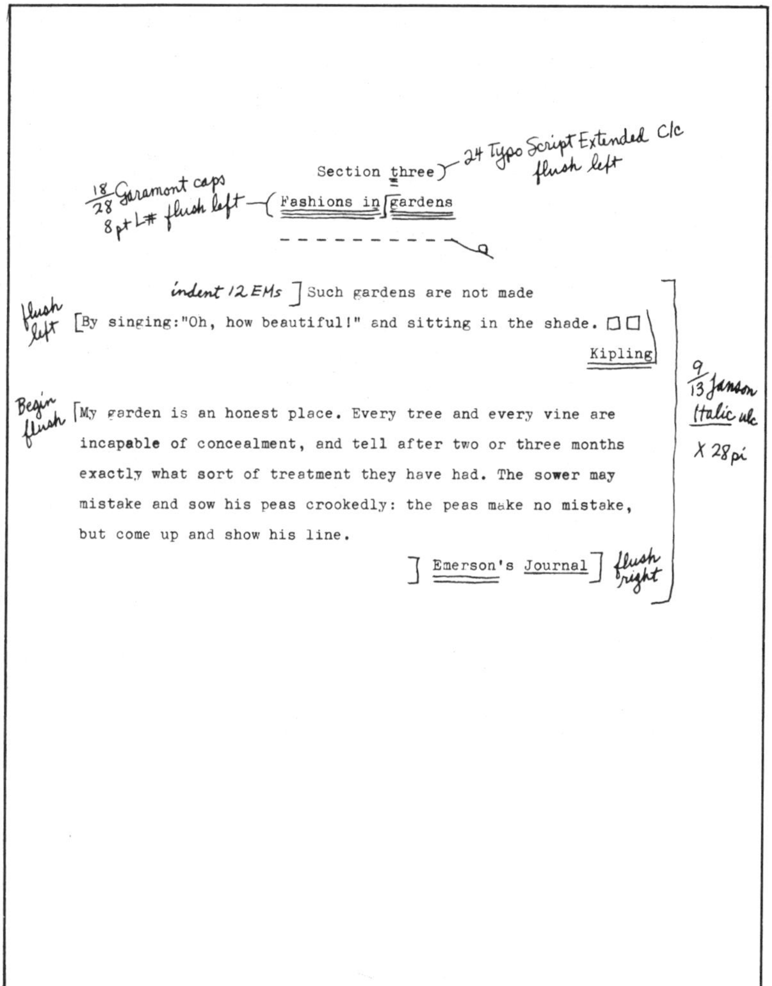

copy marked for type specifications and position

Computer composition

Desktop composition by computer has become the mainstay of book production, with the typesetting integrated into page-layout programs like QuarkXPress and Adobe InDesign. The ability of a designer to make subtle adjustments and manipulations that used to be possible only for professional typesetters is now built into these programs—only the user's skill limits the degree of refinement. And because the desktop typesetter may now be the designer/editor/layout artist/production manager rolled into one, the job of composition is much more complex than merely setting words into type.

For designers who set their own type, the ability to modify a design until they're satisfied makes the process a work-in-progress, like painting a picture. Acting as editor, the typesetter can make changes and corrections in text while retaining or modifying design elements. Acting as the layout artist with the power to make design changes, the typesetter meshes text and graphic elements in the best way. Being in control of production, the typesetter formats the text for prepress. The boundaries between these functions are not always sharp; often one role will overlap another. Nor will every job require the typesetter to take on all roles, but the possibility is there.

Following are the main features found in sophisticated composition programs.

COMPUTER FONTS Both the PostScript and PDF (Portable Document Format) page-description languages created by Adobe Systems use *outline fonts*. These require only a mathematical description for creating the characters, rather than dot-by-dot bitmap details (each character in a *bitmap font* is made up of tiny dots coded in a particular relationship to the other dots in the character) to produce a smooth image. Outline fonts are scalable; until they were developed, an entire set of bitmap codes had to be installed in the computer for every size in a typeface.

PostScript Type 1 has been the standard in the industry, and Adobe licenses many other typeface makers to produce it. *TrueType* is Apple's version of an outline font. Though the two versions produce the same results, their technology is somewhat different. PostScript Type 1 fonts contain two files: the screen (bitmapped) font, and the printer (outline) font. TrueType requires only one file for both screen and printer rendering. The versions are generally compatible and can be used together in the same document, although some compatibility problems may arise when using TrueType fonts. These can generally be resolved by converting the document to the PDF format with the fonts embedded. Avoid PostScript Type 3 fonts, which often cause compatibility problems in processing. When using *any* fonts other than PostScript Type 1, run a test file through prepress or ask your printshop to run a test.

Adobe has a newer standard for fonts called *OpenType*. These fonts have several advantages over PostScript Type 1 fonts. Being compatible with both Macs and PCs they can eliminate the headaches in moving files across platforms. Also, they have a much larger character set, which allows all the ancillary characters (small caps, swash caps, special symbols, etc.) to be available within the font.

PDF has become the standard for the distribution and exchange of electronic documents. It preserves the fonts, images, graphics, and layout of any document, regardless of the application and platform used to create it. Any document can be converted to PDF using Adobe Acrobat software or any of several alternative PDF writers. PDF files are perfect for the e-mail delivery of *soft proofs* (proofs viewed on the computer rather than printed out). The recipient can add annotations of any corrections directly to the PDF document, or print the pages out for marking up. While it is possible to make some corrections in the PDF document itself, it is generally best to make them in the originating software and remake the PDF for the corrected pages. Also, a "prepress PDF" can be created to deliver the actual production files to the printshop's prep department. When preparing a PDF for prepress use, be sure to ask the prep department for their PDF file preparation requirements (CH. 10).

Computers and printers come with a limited assortment of typefaces called *resident fonts*. These are usually the most widely used faces, like Helvetica, Courier, Times Roman, Geneva, Palatino, etc. To have more diversity of styles, you must buy individual fonts or font packages from *type foundries*. (Metal type is made by actual foundries, but the word is used now for makers of computer types.)

An almost limitless number of design permutations from individual fonts is available from Adobe's *Multiple Masters* series. Accompanied by special software, these unique master fonts enable you to create a vast number of type design variations in weight, width, style, and optical size.

Font sources are aplenty. In addition to the classic typefaces digitized for the computer from the libraries of metal-type founders ITC, Mergenthaler, and others, there are many catalogs filled with newly designed or adapted styles. The largest of the computer type foundries are Adobe, Bitstream, Linotype-Hell, Monotype, and URW. There are many small vendors of interesting and unique fonts. Check *The PrecisionType Font Reference Guide*, a comprehensive catalog of over thirteen thousand fonts from more than sixty sources.

Fonts are supplied on floppy disks or CD-ROMs, or they can be downloaded via modem directly to your computer. You can buy an entire font library on CD-ROM, which can be very expensive, or you can make individual or group selections from it. CD-ROM typeface collections contain encrypted fonts, to which you get the access code from the vendor in exchange for your credit card number.

When having a document output by a service bureau, check to be sure they carry the font you want. With thousands on hand they're likely to have it, but if they don't, either they must buy it or you must provide them with a copy of both the screen and printer fonts. If you use one of the most widely used outline font formats (today, PostScript Type 1 and TrueType) you'll have the fewest problems working with outside output sources.

FONT ACCESSORY SOFTWARE

Some software makes it possible to invent your own typeface, alter an existing one, or copy and digitize typefaces from nondigital sources (an ancient manuscript, for example). *Fontographer* (Macromedia) is one of several such programs. Font files you create or edit must be sent to a service bureau to be output correctly.

Having several font management and utility programs is essential to successful type handling. Without these, fonts installed in your system can create confusion and inefficiency, not to mention frustration. A few of the most useful programs are briefly described below.

Suitcase (Extensis) unclutters the system folder, in which actively used fonts are stored. Inactive fonts stored there can slow down a computer. Suitcase organizes fonts by project or function so they're easily accessible.

Adobe Type Manager (ATM) automatically generates high-quality screen fonts from outline font data. It lets you scale, rotate, and skew fonts without getting jagged edges. ATM Deluxe incorporates features similar to Suitcase, but it's being, or has been, discontinued.

Font Reserve, a popular font managment package, has been purchased by Extensis and its powerful features are being combined with those of Suitcase.

Adobe Type Reunion sorts and displays font families alphabetically and shows submenus of styles and weights. Font names are coded to indicate style. In the Futura family, for instance, the following partial list appears:

Futura
B Futura Bold
O Futura Oblique
H Futura Heavy
HO Futura Heavy Oblique
XB Futura Extra Bold

Being alphabetized by first letters, the fonts in any family would get scattered all over a listing, but Font Reunion neatly re-sorts them into the family listing.

TYPESETTING FEATURES

Learning to set type without a program manual or two at hand is a doomed exercise. Layout programs have many intricate details which can be used to your advantage, but discovering them is possible only by careful reading of word-processing and typography sections in the manuals—unless you're lucky enough to have an expert at your call. Reading the manual will help you get comfortable with the terminology and facile with the process. Pick up additional tips and tricks from computer magazines and books.

The essential elements for typesetting are described below. Because QuarkXPress is the industry standard at this writing, its features are used to illustrate the various functions. However, general information about features and procedures is usually applicable to all major layout programs. Consult the appropriate manual for specific details.

All the elements described here are bound by preset defaults. Since defaults vary somewhat from one program to another, it's important to learn the details in each program you use. Nearly all default settings can be changed (if they're editable), so check the program manual on how to adjust them and the advantages of making changes.

■ **Typeface (Font)**—Apart from the virtue of simplicity in design, limiting the number of faces used in a document is more efficient. For each one, the printer must download the full font in order to print. Using several faces slows the process considerably; too many faces may cripple the printer if it doesn't have enough RAM.

■ **Key Caps**—This is a built-in accessory that shows all the characters in a particular font. By pressing either the Shift or Option key, or both together, the full character set is displayed.

■ **Size**—Type can be set in any size between 2 and 720 pts. in .001 pt. increments. With scalable faces, any size in this range can be rendered accurately and smoothly on the screen and by the printer.

■ **Style**—The name of the type appears in the font menu, which can be accessed through the toolbar. ("Style" is used also in Microsoft programs to mean a specification for setting a type element. Why a unique word was not chosen for this meaning is a mystery.) The following options are available:

Plain: This is the style you initially select. It could be italic, bold, or something else, but whatever it is, *any* change you make is a modification of it. For example, if you select Helvetica Bold from the font menu rather than Helvetica, then "plain" is Helvetica Bold, not Helvetica.

Bold and *Italic*: These are versions of the selected, i.e., plain, face. If, say, Helvetica Bold is designated as the plain style, calling for bold will make it extra bold. (In a display of computer obstinacy, an order for italic or bold styles will sometimes be ignored or processed incorrectly by the RIP [Raster Image Processor]—see CH. 3). While styles are the most convenient way to achieve italic or bold, it's best to replace the styled versions with their actual fonts before sending the job for output. This can be easily accomplished with the Font Usage utility in QuarkXPress. More importantly, when applying an italic or bold style to a font that has no italic or bold, it's essential to run a test file through prepress to find out if the styled font will RIP properly. Very often such styled fonts will revert to plain when RIPed. If so, the problem can generally be solved by creating a true italic and/or bold font using a font editing program like Fontographer.

Outline and **Shadow**: Self-explanatory.

Underline: This underscores both characters and spaces. "Word underline" underscores only characters, not the space between words. The default weight of the line can be altered.

SMALL CAPS: These are usually created 75% of the full cap height (although this default can be altered), but a few fonts have custom-designed small caps. To get "CAPS & SMALL CAPS" (c/sc) in some programs, type upper- and lowercase, then apply "small caps" in the style menu to the whole selection.

ALL CAPS: This command sets all the characters as capitals regardless of how they were originally typed. (If you set all caps by setting the Caps Lock key, you may not be able to change to lowercase in the style menu.)

^{Superscript} and $_{\text{Subscript}}$ These are characters positioned above or below the baseline and reduced according to a default percentage (usually 50%) of the full cap height.

Dropout type: In Quark, this is accomplished by indicating a light shade or white as the type color and black (or dark) for the background of a text box. In some layout programs the setting for this is "Reverse Type".

Leading (see also "Measurement & terminology" in CH. 5): Leading can be set from 1 to 1080 pts. and adjusted in .001 pt. increments. "Auto" spacing is 120% (editable) of the font size. Thus, a 10 pt. type in auto mode would be on 12 pts., i.e., with 2 pt. leading.

Kerning: This refers to closing up the space between certain pairs of characters to improve the visual fit, e.g., fi, Ta, etc. For this, one unit of space is .005 (1/200) of an em space, and space can be changed in .001 (1/1000) increments, so spacing between characters can be fine-tuned by .000005 (1/200,000) of an em!

Fonts have preset spaces between every pair of characters when the automatic kerning function is on. This spacing may not please you, especially in larger type, but individual character pairs can be kerned to reduce the space. It's best to magnify the screen image to its maximum when you make adjustments. By editing the *kerning tables*, which show all the pairs and their settings, you can adjust any character combination *globally* (throughout a document).

Tracking: This is the addition of letterspacing (why isn't it just called letterspacing?!) to a selected group of characters or words, generally only headings or small selections of text, to either improve appearance or space out short lines in justified setting. As in kerning, units of space are .005 em and can be adjusted in .001-em increments.

Alignment: There are five alignment options: flush left, flush right, centered, justified, and force justified.

When type is flush on only one edge, the other is said to be *ragged* (e.g., flush left/*rag* right). Good-looking "rags" can be achieved by manipulating hyphenation or adjusting tracking (letterspacing) to make lines rebreak.

Justified text (flush left & right): This can be modified by adjusting wordspacing and character spacing in the *hyphenation and justification (H&J)* specifications to achieve the desired "color" of text. Open, airy text looks lighter than tightly set, dense type.

Force justified: Space is added between characters to expand a line out to full width in justified setting.

Hyphenation settings: These can determine the maximum number of consecutive hyphens, the size of the smallest hyphenated word, the minimum/maximum number of letters to precede and follow a hyphen, whether capitalized words may be hyphenated, where the hyphens may occur on a ragged edge. The program has a hyphenation dictionary, but you may not always agree with its choices. You can make your own exceptions.

Justification settings: These determine the amount of space between characters and between words. You could have tight letterspacing with widely spaced words, for example, or almost any other variation.

Baseline shift: This moves type above or below the baseline as much as 72 pts. in 1 pt. increments. It's useful for adjusting alignment of text elements—like initial caps or making captions line up with adjacent graphics.

Horizontal/vertical scaling: This function enlarges or reduces fonts on either their horizontal or vertical axis, rather than universally, thus expanding or condensing the typeface.

Stickup and *drop* (or *hanging*) *initials* (CH. 25): These can be created in several ways. Automatic settings can achieve some of these effects, but there are limitations. Learning the program's nuances, you'll find ways to overcome these obstacles. (The tricks you learn—or invent—to impose your will on the stubborn default settings are called *workarounds*.)

Runaround: This is text that follows the contours of an adjacent graphic by varying the width of lines. By manipulating the runaround specifications and the *polygon* tool, it's possible to create elaborately sculpted blocks of type.

Rules (*lines*) (CH. 5): There is an almost infinite number of styles—plain, decorative, solid, dotted, dashed, multiweight combinations—in widths up to 864 pts. Everything prints somewhat heavier on a low-resolution device like a 300 or 600 dpi printer than on a high-resolution imagesetter, but the difference isn't usually significant for proofs. But for fine rules, like hairlines, it's important to have a high-res printout made.

Frames or borders: These can be placed around text or graphics automatically from a menu of design options in widths up to 864 pts. Customized borders can be made by drawing lines, then rotating them at right angles and joining corners. (Use maximum magnification to do this cleanly.)

Rotation: You can turn an item up to 360° in either direction.

Color and shade: Type, rules, borders, pictures—anything—can be assigned any color in the palette of a document. Shades of colors are percentages of the solid color in 1% increments. (Printed output of shades doesn't always represent screen values accurately. Get a sample high-res printout of the page to make final color judgments) (CH. 8).

Ligatures: These are combinations of individual letters formed into a single character, like "ff" or "æ". Text can be specified to automatically substitute ligatures for certain character combinations if the font comes with them. Not all fonts contain ligature characters.

Style sheets Terms are at their most confusing when they have more than one meaning. "Style" is probably the champ in the field. In CH. 4 we spoke of: (1) *style* as the author's manner of expression, (2) *styling* as the marking of text to create grammatical and typographic order, and (3) *style* to mean the choices in matters of usage. We said that the decisions made in the styling and usage should be compiled on a *style* sheet to be used by author, editor, designer, and proofreader to ensure universal understanding. In this chapter we have defined "style" as (4) the design of a typeface in its various permutations—italic, bold, etc., and, in its inscrutable wisdom, Microsoft has used "style" to mean (5) the specifications for setting an element of type.

Now we are speaking of another kind of style sheet, one that compiles the items of "style" in the Microsoft meaning. This style "sheet" is in the computer and ensures consistency of typographic style throughout a document. To create it, each type element—body text, heads, captions, etc.—is defined and may be assigned a *keypad* number (a one-key code) which applies a described typographic style to that element. The style sheet description can contain, in addition to the principal attributes like typeface, size, and color, the nuances of style, including rules, indentions, and spacing. If an element is redefined, changing it in the style sheet ensures that the change will be made globally (throughout the document).

Text input Text is delivered to publishers in several forms. The most efficient is a file created by word-processing. This requires the fewest interim steps in production. Word-processed copy can be delivered on disk or as an attachment via e-mail. Text that hasn't been word-processed, whether a typewritten ms. or printed pages, can often be converted to disk form by *OCR scanning* (see "OCR scanning" below). Ms. that has been heavily marked with handwritten corrections or printed pages with poorly defined type can't be successfully read by an OCR scanner and will need to be typed into a word-processing program.

TEXT ON DISK

A file on disk should be submitted with a hard copy (printout). This makes it easier for the editor to work, even though the text is edited and styled in the word-processing program. Sometimes conversion from one format to another may be necessary—PC to Mac, for example—but software is available to do this. If necessary, the disk submitted can be sent to a service bureau for conversion.

OCR SCANNING

Scanning pages directly into word-processing programs sidesteps the tedious and expensive keyboarding process, but no matter how accurate the OCR program claims to be, it's essential to check the scanned text carefully. These programs have a tendency to misread characters. For instance, the numeral one (1) or lowercase "l", or both, in some typewriter styles may be misread as a right bracket ( ]). If that happens, run a search in the word-processing program to find all right brackets and replace them with 1s or ls (and put back the brackets you want).

MODEM

Text that has been word-processed and sent to the publisher by e-mail can be handled in the usual manner in a word-processing program. If there's a conflict because the sender uses a PC and the receiver a Mac, or vice versa, the text may need to be transmitted in *ASCII*, the "text-only" format, which any computer can read (see CH. 8, "File formats"). However, ASCII doesn't retain style formats (like italics or bold), so these may be lost. Another option is to save the file in *Rich Text Format* (*RTF*), an enhanced ASCII transfer format that retains styles by embedding codes in the document. Most word-processing and layout programs can read and write RTF files, albeit with occasional lapses in accuracy. However, if there's such incompatibility, it's really better for the sender to create a disk that can be converted.

WORD-PROCESSING

Typing on a computer, rather than a typewriter, makes it possible to accomplish much more than simply getting words onto paper. A word-processing program offers you the great luxury of being able to change your mind as much as you like before committing text to paper. The computer allows you to easily change or move a single character or a word or a whole page, erase what you choose not to keep, and save in its memory what you have done. When you're finally happy with what you see on the screen, you can give a print command and make a hard copy. Or you can very easily make one or more variations of the same thing—changing typeface or size, for example—print out the variations and then decide which version you think is the best one.

The basic functions of word-processing software are keyboarding, editing, and formatting of text, although some programs have limited layout and drawing capabilities as well.

KEYBOARDING

■ **Macros**—Most word-processing programs allow assigning commands or frequently used groups of characters—a company name or book title, for example—to function keys or other key combinations. The modifier keys, such as Shift, Alt, Control, Option, and Command, can, in combination with other keys, either create alternative characters or execute other preset macros to access commands or functions. You can string together a group of commands and have them all executed at once with a single keystroke or combination. For example, a logo in one type style with an address in another, both in a ruled box, can appear with the execution of a single macro. When assigning macros, be careful not to override an existing one by using the same key combination.

■ **Word count**—Word-processing programs keep a running count of characters (keystrokes), words, lines, and paragraphs for an entire file or a selected portion. This can be useful in calculating the number of pages in a book, but it's a good idea to cross-check with counts arrived at by another method (CHs. 23, 24).

EDITING

■ **Drag-and-drop**—The cut, copy, and paste functions allow you to delete, duplicate, and rearrange portions of text with keyboard commands or with a mouse. The drag-and-drop feature is another, often easier, way of moving text: using the mouse, highlight a section of text, drag it to where you want it, and drop it there. It's like having an editorial crane.

■ **Hyphenation**—Using the program defaults, lines are automatically broken to maintain even wordspacing. The hyphenation dictionaries in these programs are generally reliable, but occasionally a word is broken according to the program's formula that really shouldn't be broken that way (for example, the-rapist).

■ **Spell checker**—Spell checking is useful for catching typing errors, like transposed letters, and for checking words of whose spelling you are unsure. Some programs alert you to double words ("the the") or will automatically correct commonly mistyped words ("teh"). However, don't expect it to alert you to a correctly spelled but improperly used word (like "too" instead of "two").

■ **Grammar checker**—There's no substitute for a good editor. The grammar checker tool will correct some errors, but its constant querying can make it more trouble than it's worth.

■ **Dictionary and thesaurus**—Depending on the program and the user's needs, these reference tools also may prove to be of only limited value.

■ **Find and replace**—This search feature enables finding particular characters, words, symbols, or styles in a text. It also allows you to change them in content, format, or style globally.

FORMATTING

■ **Style sheets**—With the style sheet feature all the styles used in a document are collected, which allows you to automate the formatting to ensure consistency. Carrying over a document's style sheet from the word-processing to the layout program simplifies the page-makeup procedure (CH. 9).

■ **Repagination**—As text is added, deleted, or moved anywhere in a document, the program automatically corrects the numbering of the pages. Selected sections of text can be numbered separately.

■ **Headers and footers**—The repeated elements—page number (*folio*), book title, chapter title, part title, or author—that may appear at the top and/or bottom of book pages, are called *running heads*, but are called headers and footers in some word-processing programs, e.g., Microsoft Word.

ORGANIZATIONAL FEATURES

■ **Outline**—Word-processing programs can help organize material logically with the outline function. The various levels of heads in a book can be arranged in order of importance to view the text in outline form.

■ **Table of contents**—To automatically generate a table of contents from the text, add codes to the headings that are to appear in the contents page. The program is then instructed to collect the coded heads, grouping them in correct order and showing their page numbers in the text.

■ **Index**—After page-makeup has been completed, words or phrases in the text may be coded to compile an alphabetical index of any degree of complexity, with page references for each entry.

■ **Footnotes**—Footnote entries can be inserted automatically in pages, with their numbering, placement, format, and style done according to your instructions. If notes are added or deleted in the text, the listing is automatically renumbered. Footnotes can be specified to appear on the same page as the reference in the text or in a separate listing at the end of the chapter or end of the text.

7. Illustration

Relation to design

Far from simply "laying out" pictures supplied with the text, the designer may initiate the idea of illustrations and suggest their character. Book designers function as graphic engineers, using the science and art of visual presentation to enhance communication, so the conception, inclusion, and selection of illustrations—as well as their placement and reproduction—are parts of book design. Properly, illustration matters are discussed jointly by author, editor, designer, and production manager.

In tradebooks, the use of illustration is considered less often than it should be, because of the common assumption that it involves great expense. This isn't necessarily so.

Kinds of illustration

Illustration includes a wide range of visual material, which becomes clear when the kinds of illustration are divided by function. There are four kinds:
(a) *Informative*, (b) *Suggestive*, (c) *Decorative*, and (d) *Representative*.

■ **Informative**—Illustrations whose purpose is to explain or depict facts, circumstances, characters, things, or places. Examples are the realistic drawings commonly used in teenage fiction and the photographs, drawings, diagrams, etc. found in many technical and other nonfiction books.

■ **Suggestive**—All graphic elements designed to establish or enhance mood or atmosphere.

■ **Decorative**—Graphic elements whose purpose is simply to ornament the page.

■ **Representative**—Pictures being shown as works of art for the purpose of approximating the pleasure of seeing the original, such as the reproductions in art books.

Some illustrations fall into more than one category, but a dominant purpose can usually be identified. For example, some "realistic" illustrations may have enough evocative power to put them in the "suggestive" category. They may be used as such if they seem more valuable for the moods they induce than for the information they impart. Some "decorative" material may be particularly allusive and thus be treated as "suggestive". (Hardly anything less abstract than type rules and some stock ornaments can fail to suggest subject matter.)

An illustration may be used for several purposes, falling into a different category in each case. The distinction is in the intent, which determines how the illustration is used and reproduced. For example, a fine photograph of Wall Street used in a guidebook would be "informative". In a book of poems about cities the same picture would create atmosphere ("suggestive"). In a book of photographs, it would be reproduced to give the reader pleasure and so would be "representative".

Ways of introducing illustration

INFORMATIVE

It's sometimes helpful to use a map or diagram to clarify a point in the text. The simplest sketch can do the trick. It need be no more elaborate than the kind you would make to show someone the way to your house. Drawn directly and simply, such a sketch can be very effective. In some cases, it may be possible to use an old map.

author's sketch

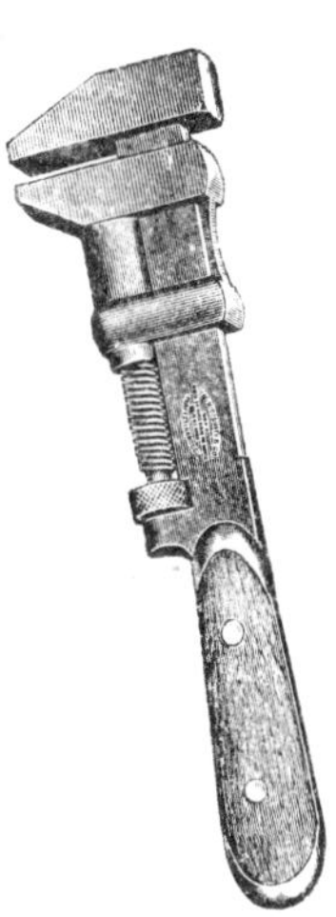

Illustrations of objects, characters, and places can be useful and interesting. These too can be rough sketches by the designer (or the author) or they can be taken from existing pictorial material. For example, some charming and accurate engravings of carpenter's tools were taken from an old hardware catalog and used in a new book on finishing cellars and attics. Many travel books of the 19th century had pen-and-ink drawings of various places. These could be used in travel books, biographies, fiction, etc.

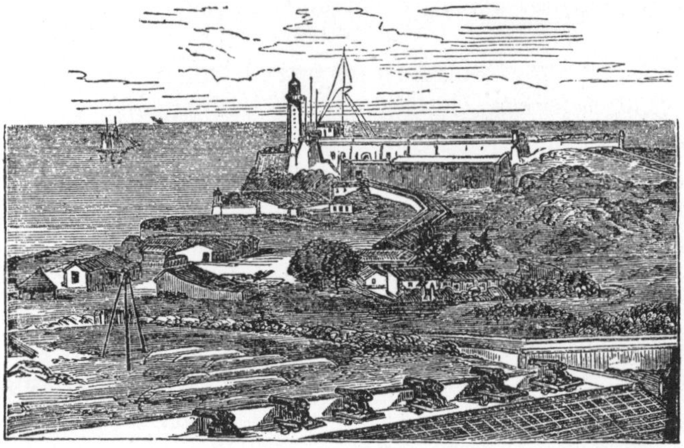

SUGGESTIVE Here the opportunity for illustration is truly unlimited. The whole range of symbolism, from literal to abstract, is at the designer's disposal.

Of literal symbols there are all the insignia, emblems, and devices of organizations, nations, families, societies, companies, etc. A book about submarines can use the submarine officer's insigne, a book with England as its subject can have a British lion or even a royal coat of arms, and so on. Other symbols can be created from type ornaments and rules. Anything that establishes or enhances a mood or atmosphere can be used. The most abstract device can have suggestive power. A classic example is the black border that effectively creates a funereal mood.

Pictures can be used to enhance atmosphere. Among the thousands of works by artists, many by great masters, there are some expressing virtually every state of feeling—happy, sad, tragic, bucolic, orgiastic, tender, terrible—pictures abound. These can be your background music. Old Chinese drawings of bare trees were used to create a wintry feeling. Bacchanalian scenes from Greek pottery have been used to set a party mood. The possibilities are endless.

DECORATIVE

An excess of decoration in the late 19th century was followed by a clean functional style in the early 20th. It can be argued that pure decoration, without informative or suggestive value, is meaningless and superfluous. Yet, the total absence of decoration in architecture brought about a "postmodern" revival of decorated surfaces, and a recognition that decoration need not be at odds with function. (Louis Sullivan, one of the prophets of the "form follows function" school of architecture, used decoration extensively—as did his follower, Frank Lloyd Wright.) It is, however, quite difficult to use decoration functionally—and very easy to use it as pointless gaud. In any case, decoration shouldn't take precedence over other aspects of the book.

When decoration is used to suggest the style of a period related to the text or is otherwise allusive, it isn't "decorative" but "suggestive" illustration. It hardly seems worth using decoration that has no suggestive value, but it can be done. There is a great deal of typographic ornament available, ranging from abstract rules, dots, squares, etc. to the most elaborate florets. These may be combined in infinite ways to create a pattern covering a whole page—one of the more interesting uses of decoration—or a spot on a chapter-opening or title page.

REPRESENTATIVE This kind of illustration is an integral part of art and photography books, but a reproduction of a picture can enhance the visual value of almost any kind of book. A single reproduction may be used as part of the frontmatter or several may be scattered throughout the text, either at random or at specific places, such as on part-titles (CH. 27).

When a picture's subject is related to the text, the illustration has suggestive value, but if its main purpose is representative, it should be treated as such. An abstract or nonobjective picture presents no such problem.

Sources of illustration

There is a huge store of graphic material available to the designer who has the imagination and knowledge to use it. Illustration can be obtained in four ways: (a) by commissioning an illustrator, (b) by paying for reproduction rights to existing pictures, (c) by using graphic material in the public domain or available without charge, and (d) by doing it yourself. The cost of illustrations, if any, is usually borne by the author, but sometimes by the publisher, depending on the nature of the project and the contract.

ILLUSTRATORS

Keep a file of illustrators and folders with examples of their work. Such a file can be developed by interviewing artists and by clipping interesting illustrations from magazines and newspapers or making photocopies of illustrations in books. Useful sources of illustrators are the *Illustrators' Annual*, published by the Society of Illustrators, and *American Showcase* annual. Agents who specialize in representing illustrators are listed in *Literary Market Place*.

In general, younger artists charge lower prices and sometimes do work that's fresher and less commercial-looking than the more experienced illustrators. It's possible to get attractive work at even lower prices from art school students, but the results are comparatively uncertain. It takes a long time to develop a reliable technique and to be able to deliver a good job in a very high percentage of tries under the pressures of time and stringent requirements.

The question of how much to pay an illustrator involves many factors: the artist's experience, talent, and reputation; the job's difficulty, complexity, magnitude, and end use; the prices asked by comparable artists; whether the job is a one-shot or one of many the artist will get; whether it's a rush; etc. There's no easy way to get to the right answer. It must be worked out with goodwill on both sides.

Book illustration is artistically satisfying work, so some first-rate artists prefer this occasionally to the better-paying advertising or magazine work—and they may sometimes be persuaded to accept little or no more than what a mediocre professional illustrator would be paid.

It's good to support and encourage living artists, and a lot more could be done in this respect than is being done, but sometimes it becomes necessary to look to other, less costly means of finding illustration.

REPRODUCTION RIGHTS

If the illustration needs of the book can be met with pictures that already exist, the rights to use such material can usually be obtained for much less than it would cost to commission the work (and the uncertainties of made-to-order illustrations are avoided).

The amount of the fee must be worked out for each case. It can be very little, or the artist/photographer/owner may ask for a lot. If the asking price is too high, there's no need to accept it, although sometimes a picture is so desirable or important it becomes necessary to pay a high price for it. Photographs by contemporary photographers are usually available from them directly or through a picture agency. Prices asked often are based on the fee schedules of the American Society of Magazine Photographers (ASMP). However, the economics of magazines and advertising are much different from book publishing's, so these prices are painfully high, although they're somewhat adjusted for books. Generally, fees vary according to use—more for jackets or covers than inside pages—with a sliding scale according to size: full-page, half-page, quarter-page. Color is usually more expensive than black & white (although the photographer's cost may be less). Some agencies relate fees to the quantity of books printed. The fee is generally for one-time use in one edition, with additional fees for reprint and foreign-language editions—unless a fee is set for all editions.

"Fine" artists are not as organized as photographers. Their work isn't done for reproduction, and it's relatively rarely reproduced outside of art books or textbooks, so they're less dependent upon reproduction fees. Some of the less famous see a book reproduction as a valuable advertisement for their work and ask no fee. Before the boom in the contemporary art market in the 1960s, even major living artists generally were delighted to have their work published and asked for nothing, but now well-known artists usually ask for substantial reproduction fees. Many artists are represented by agencies such as *ARS* and *VAGA* in the United States, which set reproduction fees and collect them on behalf of the artists and their estates as well as agencies abroad. In some cases it's necessary to deal directly with foreign agencies who have no representation in America.

The cost of the fees set by artists' and photographers' agencies, plus the administrative cost of getting permissions, negotiating fees, etc. and paying museums and other picture sources for photographs of the works for reproduction, can make it economically unfeasible to publish a book with many pictures. Fortunately, there are often less expensive alternatives.

There are two kinds of material for which reproduction fees are paid: that which is in copyright and that which is not.

■ **Copyrighted material**—The old U.S. copyright law replaced in 1976 was in many ways inadequate, but it was quite simple as to duration of copyright. The period was 28 years, with one renewal for another 28 (extended during wartime and the gestating years of the new law). Unpublished works were protected indefinitely by common law. The 1976 law is more fair to authors, but it's more complex. Following is a simplified outline of some relevant features:

For works created

1. before September 19, 1906, all U.S. copyrights of published works are expired, unpublished works are protected as in 2(c) below,
2. from September 19, 1906 through December 31, 1977,
   (a) copyrights not renewed by the end of the 28th year after publication are expired.
   (b) if renewed, add 47 years (instead of 28) for a total of 75.
   (c) works that are unpublished and unregistered have the same protection as works created after 1977, but are protected at least through 2002. If they're published before 2003, protection extends 25 years more (through 2027). If unpublished but registered, (a) and (b) above apply. Their status once their registration expires isn't clearly defined.
3. For works created after December 31, 1977, a 1998 amendment to the 1976 law provides that:
   (a) most works have copyright protection for the life of the author plus 70 years, except,
   (b) works by anonymous or pseudonymous authors and "works made for hire", i.e., made by someone employed or commissioned by the copyright owner, are protected for either 95 years from first publication or 120 years from creation, whichever occurs first.

(The term "author", as used in the copyright law, refers to all creators of original copyrightable works, including painters, sculptors, photographers, etc.)

When the maximum term of "old law" copyright was extended from 56 to 75 years, a provision was made for authors to get the benefit of the extra 19 years. If a work had been licensed for the full term before 1976, authors can (by complying with some complex formalities) get the rights back when the 56 years expires, even though the term is now 75 years.

Another new provision in favor of authors allows them (again, with considerable effort) to get most of their rights back after 35 years, even though they have granted them under the new law (after 1977) for their own lifetime plus 70 years.

Under the present law, all copyrights expire on the last day of the calendar year. Formerly, the expiration was on a particular day, so it's not possible to tell from the notice—which gives only the year of copyright—exactly when the renewal began, since there was more than a year during which renewal was possible. The Copyright Office will search its records and report on the copyright status of a particular work on request and payment of a modest hourly charge.

Under the old law, a work that was published in the United States without a proper copyright notice ordinarily lost its copyright forever. The new law still requires the notice, but allows for some curative steps in case it's omitted—provided they're taken within 5 years after publication. Thus, a work published without a notice under the new law isn't in the public domain as long as it's subject to the remedies allowed. Note that once a work has passed into the U.S. public domain, for whatever reason, it can never be restored to copyright status.

The copyright notice in a book covers the illustrations within it. However, since the notice is usually in the name of the author or publisher, it's best to include a separate notice for the illustrations to avoid complications if an artist or illustrator wants to defend a picture right.

Registration of a work with the U.S. Copyright Office isn't essential to protection so long as a notice appears on the work, but with registration the legal protection is better.

The law provides that the author, as the initial copyright owner, has the exclusive right to grant reproduction rights. If a work is sold—a painting, for example—in 1976 or later, the rights of the buyer to authorize reproduction are nil unless the painter specifically grants some. Nonexclusive reproduction rights can be conveyed verbally (a shaky basis), but if the buyer is to get exclusive rights, the artist must grant them in writing. With the exclusive right to reproduce the work goes copyright ownership to the extent necessary to protect that right.

Under the old law, some courts assumed that copyright was transferred along with physical ownership of a painting in the absence of anything specific to the contrary, while some took other positions. The 1976 law is clear enough, but applies only to transfers taking place after 1977. Since transfers of ownership before 1976 are not covered by federal law, they're subject to the individual laws of the fifty states. Add to this the ambiguities of situations involving long-deceased artists and it becomes apparent that the question of reproduction rights is murky indeed. Even under the present law, when a living artist assigns exclusive rights to a purchaser, and the new owner gives authorization to a publisher, it's customary for the latter to ask the artist's permission out of respect for artistic integrity. Whether this courtesy extends to the estate of a recently deceased artist is a matter for personal decision.

Whatever the actual legal rights of a museum to grant, or withhold, reproduction permission in a particular case, as a practical matter one must either respect their requirements or risk being denied access to their collections thereafter.

The foregoing applies only to U.S. law and publication in the United States. To the complexities of domestic copyright law must be added the international dimension. Under the 1886 Berne Convention, works protected in one contracting nation are protected in each, according to its own laws. Most Western countries signed this agreement, but the United States held out until 1988. Under the UNESCO Universal Copyright Convention, of which the United States is a signatory, protection in all participating nations usually is obtained by publication in any one, provided the proper notice is used (a "c" in a circle ©, the year, and the name of the copyright owner) in the proper place. Again, the protection given in each country is the same as given to works published under that country's laws.

The copyright owner has a right to demand a fee for reproduction or to refuse permission altogether—and violation of copyright is punishable by law. When there's genuine doubt about the copyright status of a particular work, inquiries should be made on the assumption that there *is* copyright protection.

Copyright law—both domestic and international—is not only often imprecise, it's riddled with exceptions and special conditions. The foregoing outline is meant to provide a general view of the subject, not a legal definition. The information above was true at the time of this writing, but may be changed later by act of Congress. It's a good idea to become familiar with current copyright requirements and to check the website of the Copyright Office (www.copyright.gov) whenever in doubt.

The existing copyright laws were written when their enforcement, at least in countries with concern for law, was relatively easy. The widespread use of high-quality photocopying complicated enforcement for some kinds of material, but with the introduction of the Internet the problem became critical. Internet technology makes it possible for anyone to acquire any copyrighted material—text, pictures, music—without getting permission or paying a fee. This situation attacks the fundamental premise of copyright protection and at this writing there is much concern about the problem but no apparent solution. It may be that the only way to protect copyrighted material is to keep it off the Internet, and that may not always be possible.

■ **Noncopyright material in private ownership**—A vast amount of graphic material not protected by copyright is yours to use—if you can get it. There are several kinds of agencies that collect such material for the purpose of charging reproduction fees. These include picture agencies and photography agencies, many of them available on the Internet, some private museums, libraries, etc. Most of these will search their files for pictures you request, and then charge a fee for supplying them for reproduction, usually for one use only. Fees are determined according to the difficulty of finding the material, its rarity, the use, etc. The owners of the pictures can charge whatever they want. This can be a relatively expensive way to illustrate a book, but it usually costs less than hiring an illustrator, and sometimes the material is unobtainable otherwise.

FREE MATERIAL

By far the greatest quantity of picture material in existence is available without charge. People have been creating pictures for thousands of years, much of it of excellent quality; there's no reason why it shouldn't be effectively used. The problem is simply to find it. Free graphic material can be found: (a) in the public domain and (b) in private ownership.

■ **Material in the public domain**—This includes all uncopyrighted material usable without permission. But be careful about determining what is in the public domain. For example, nonmechanical (handmade) reproductions of works in public domain may be protected by copyright.

The most extensive, available, and inexpensive source of free illustration is undoubtedly electronic *clip art*. Many companies sell CD-ROMs containing a staggering variety and number of graphic images which are free for unlimited use by the buyer, although in some instances images may be restricted to noncommercial use. Where all these images come from and whether they're entirely without some ambiguities of ownership are questions you don't have to ask, because the sellers of the disks relieve the buyer of responsibility. The images range from simple diagrams to elaborate pictures, maps, designs, textures, etc. in both black & white and color. These images are editable, so they may be modified by the user (a basis for ethical qualms, see "Do-it-yourself" below). Photographs available on disks are another matter. Some vendors give you free use of the images, but most allow free use for layout purposes only. Reproduction in a book requires payment of a fee.

A major source of free illustration is old books. The great libraries are treasure houses of such material, but you need a special key. Except for some specialized collections, books are cataloged according to their literary content, and a great deal of searching is required to discover pictures among them unless you know specific titles containing the pictures you want. Librarians can be very helpful, but most are not trained to think in terms of illustration, and their time is limited. It's best to go first to a specialized source or to someone familiar with the subject.

The print collections of libraries, historical societies, and museums are excellent sources of pictures. In almost all cases, a few dollars are charged for photocopies, but this is so small compared to the value of the pictures that they may be considered free. However, many institutions now charge reproduction fees also. Curators are usually able to guide you to material by subject, although most collections are cataloged by artist, title, number, etc. Some very old and rare prints and books may be unavailable for reproduction because of their delicate condition.

There are several public picture collections that arrange material by subject and lend pictures for reproduction or other use at no charge. The best of these are at the New York Public Library and the Library of Congress in Washington. The latter combines the features of a print collection and a picture collection, while the former confines itself mainly to clippings, movie stills, and some magazines. There is a good collection at the Philadelphia Free Library and others of varying size elsewhere. The use of pictures from these collections usually requires no fee to the lender, but the borrower is responsible for getting permission from copyright owners where necessary.

Old books, magazines, catalogs, prints, etc. can be bought in used-book stores cheaply—if you count the value of the pictures they contain. With luck, and time, you can pick up good picture material at country auctions. A few cents will sometimes buy a boxful of old publications of no value to anyone but a picture user. Old postcards are also a valuable source, although some may still be in copyright.

One publisher, Dover Publications, has made a business of selling books of reprints of old, out-of-copyright pictures. Their printing is excellent, and the pictures are available for reproduction. But Dover has only scratched the surface—they could never reprint more than a cupful from the oceans of picture material that exists.

A very valuable (and extensive) source of public domain material is the U.S. government. This includes any work prepared by an officer or employee of the U.S. government as part of that person's official duties. Among other items, there are thousands of photographs taken for the departments and agencies of the government, which may be used freely (except those that are classified) and without charge.

■ **Privately owned material**—Thanks to the desire of many business and other organizations to publicize themselves, there's a tremendous amount of free picture material available to anyone who can provide a credit line. Almost any medium-sized or large company will gladly supply pictures of their products, and some of the largest corporations maintain picture libraries of considerable scope. The public relations department is the place to ask. Another good source is the promotion department of a country, state, city, or resort anxious for publicity to attract visitors.

Movie stills can be purchased for small amounts (rare ones are not cheap) at shops in the larger cities or directly from the movie companies. Most picture agencies, and some museums and libraries, will supply them for a fee. The question of copyright for movie stills is quite complicated. Many of the older ones are out of copyright, but most movie companies ask reproduction fees for their use. Even trickier is the question of the right of actors in the photos to require permission, and sometimes a fee, to reproduce their likeness in a book. It's best to check with an expert.

It's possible to obtain *color-separation films* or electronic files

(CH. 8) of illustration material under certain circumstances. Museums, art galleries, book, calendar, and magazine publishers all have separation films of pictures which they have used, and will sometimes supply these at cost plus a fee, which varies according to the owner. Usually, the fee is a fraction of the cost of making a new set of color separations. Be aware, however, that reproduction permissions and fees are not affected by such arrangements. If films are obtained from someone other than the owner of the reproduction rights, the latter must still be approached for permission.

Some museums require you to submit color proofs for their approval and reserve the right to deny permission if they believe the quality of your reproduction fails to meet their standards. Some have strict regulations concerning the use of images they own, and require that you sign an agreement that you won't alter the image by cropping, bleeding, surprinting, enhancing, or putting it on the Internet. Again, there may be no legal right involved, but it's unwise to cross a great museum whose facilities may be denied in the future.

It's worth repeating that the real problem in getting illustration material is finding it. No one who hasn't done picture research personally has any idea how much time it can consume. To make the use of existing pictures feasible, you must be able to go to the proper source without too much trial and error. Study the history and development of illustration to become familiar with the sources. When looking for pictures, keep in mind the possibility of future use. Some excellent material may be discovered in the course of a search for something else. It's a good idea to build up a picture collection of your own. Cut out usable or unusually interesting graphic material from your old magazines, catalogs, etc. File your pictures by subject and you'll sometimes save yourself a trip and some money. Always remember that the picture you want to use may be someone else's property, and that the copyright laws are to be observed.

It's important to consider getting written releases (model releases) from anyone identifiable who appears in a photograph you want to reproduce (note the previous reference to this in connection with movie stills). The right of privacy is very strongly protected by the courts, even where no apparent injury is involved. Professional models, as well as others, should be asked to give their signatures to a simple form you can prepare. This is sometimes difficult to arrange (even someone in a crowd scene can claim invasion of privacy under some circumstances), but every effort should be made. If you rent a picture, the owner should provide releases. It isn't easy to know exactly when releases are needed, so unless you are very experienced in this matter it's best to get legal advice before deciding that a release isn't necessary.

DO-IT-YOURSELF

A certain amount of illustration may properly be considered part of the design. If designers introduce minor pictorial elements into a title page, they should, under most circumstances, execute or provide the drawing as part of their function. If the illustration is at all extensive, and the designer is capable of producing it, he or she should be considered an illustrator and paid accordingly.

Even designers who are not trained or experienced in illustration can execute simple drawings and diagrams, but there's a minimum of talent required. If you are in doubt, get some competent outside opinion before you include your own drawing in a book.

Modified clip art may be considered illustration of your making provided the amount of change is sufficient. This raises some real questions. How much change is sufficient to allow you to claim credit for the work? And no matter how much you modify another's work, there's probably reason to have some ethical, if not legal, uneasiness about the original artist's rights. There are no pat answers to these questions; your own moral and ethical instincts must be your guide. This problem is aggravated by the ease with which any image found anywhere can be scanned into a computer and included in a book. While it isn't likely that such images would be lifted in their original form, the temptation to use one with computer image-editing modifications may be hard for some to resist. A strong case can be made for avoiding such use of *any* copyrighted image, no matter what changes might be made to it.

Treatment of illustrations

Illustrations must be treated according to their nature and purpose and to their physical relationship to the text. The factors involved are:

editorial requirements for position (CH. 23),
methods of binding (CH. 13),
the processes of platemaking and printing (CH. 8),
the paper (CH. 11),
layout (CH. 26), and
preparing the illustrations for reproduction (CH. 12).

8. Illustration production

Scaling

Scaling (calculating the final size and shape of reduced or enlarged copy) is a technique that has been made almost obsolete by the ability of computers, scanners, and copying machines to perform its functions easily, quickly, and accurately. This parallels the virtual abandonment of pencil-and-paper mathematics to the calculator. You may never have much need to know how to multiply or scale without machines, but in both cases it's unhealthy to become totally dependent on them. Learn the nonelectronic methods of scaling.

There are three methods of scaling—mechanical, proportional, and calculated.

mechanical scaling

■ **Mechanical scaling**—This is based on the fact that all rectangles of the same proportions have the same diagonal, i.e., a rectangle 8 x 10" (20.3 x 25.4 cm) will have the same diagonal as one 4 x 5" (10 x 12.7 cm.), 6 x 7½" (15.2 x 19 cm), etc.

To reduce a horizontal 8 x 10" photograph to a width of 5⁹⁄₁₆" (14 cm), lay a sheet of tracing paper over the copy and draw a line between diagonally opposite corners. Then measure 5⁹⁄₁₆" along the 10" side and draw a line from this point parallel to the 8" side. When this line touches the diagonal you'll have the height of the reduced picture.

There are available transparent plastic devices that eliminate the need for drawing lines and measuring and are more accurate.

■ **Proportional scaling**—You don't have to be good at mathematics to use this method. The basic principle is mathematical proportion, but with the use of a *proportional scale,* or slide rule, it's simply a matter of aligning two dimensions and then finding a fourth by reading it on the scale opposite the third. So, to find the height of an 8 x 10" picture being reduced from 10" to 5⁹⁄₁₆" wide, align 5⁹⁄₁₆ with 10, then find 8 on the same line as 10. The number opposite 8 will be the answer: 4⁷⁄₁₆ (11.3 cm). You will have not only the dimensions, but the percentage of the copy's original (linear) size after reduction (55+%) and the fractional proportion (9 to 5). These are extremely useful for *ganging* (economical gathering of subjects with the same focus for scanning). The principles of proportion are, of course, the same for inch or metric measure.

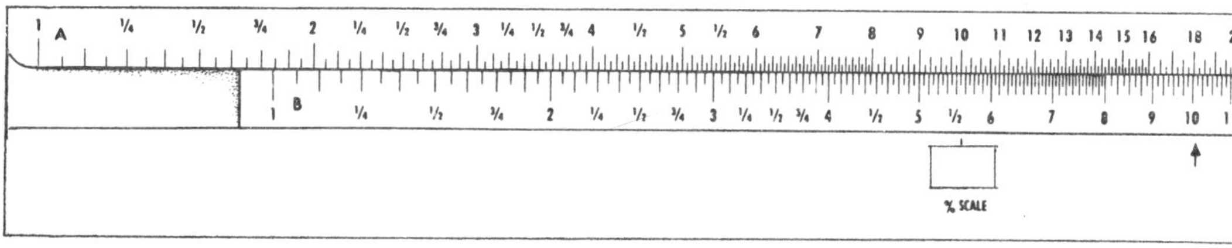

slide rule

Another type of proportional scale is the *proportion wheel,* which has two disks with calibrated circumferences revolving independently on the same center. A small window cut out of the top disk enables reading percentages on the bottom one. The principle of operation is the same as for the slide rule.

■ **Calculated scaling**—Proportions can be worked out also by using a calculator. This method beats the others for ease of reading, accuracy, and speed. For example, to reduce an 8 x 10" picture to 5⁹⁄₁₆" wide, just divide 5⁹⁄₁₆ by 10 and then multiply the result by 8. The only drawback here is that calculators use decimals rather than fractions. This is easily overcome by making a list of decimal equivalents for each ¹⁄₁₆" (.16 cm) and keeping it handy for quick conversion. Easier yet is to make all your measurements for scaling in the metric system, which is based on decimals.

Scanning

A scan translates an illustration into digital information that enables it to be reproduced on an output device such as a monitor screen, a printer, or an imagesetter, and ultimately on a printing press, including a xerographic press. In the print-on-paper process, halftone (one-color continuous tone) and color images are reproduced from a plate on which versions of the picture composed of tiny dots are transferred to the paper. The dots may be created electronically by software that determines the dot values by analyzing the relative values of adjacent pixels from the scan data. These dots may be generated by an imagesetter on the film from which plates will be made, or they may be generated directly onto the plates by a *platesetter.*

The fineness of dot screens is expressed in *lines-per-inch* (*lpi*). Screens range from 65 lpi for newspaper use to 600 lpi for fine art and photography reproduction. Most illustrated books are

halftone screens

60 85 100 120 133 150

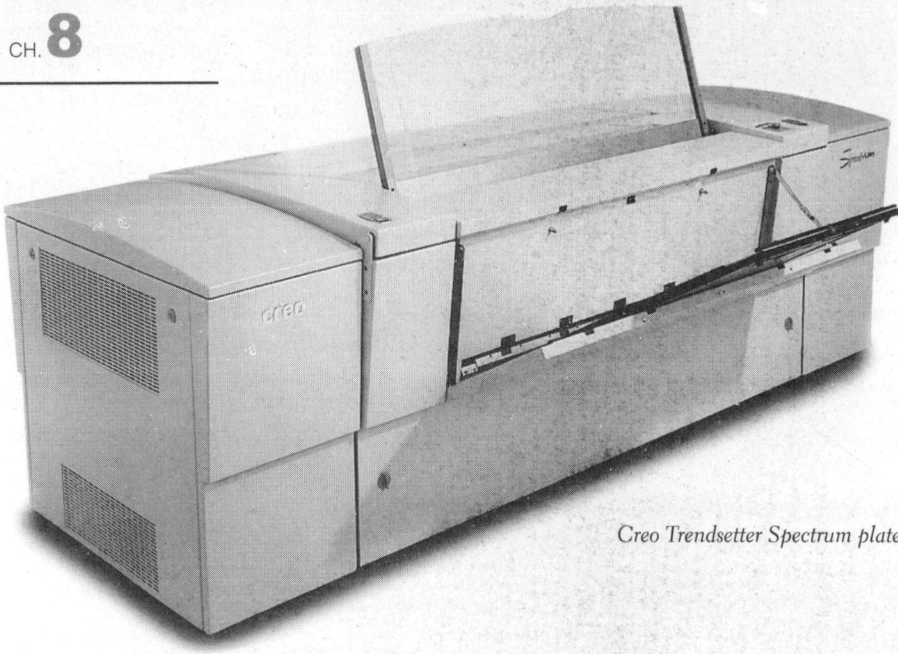

Creo Trendsetter Spectrum platesetter

printed with 133- or 150-line screen. For xerographic printing, the scanner image is sent electronically to a computer that puts it into position and the pages are sent directly to the press (CHs. 9, 10, 12). Print-on-demand xerographic presses are generally limited to about 75-line screens.

The scanner comes with software that enables it to interface with your computer. This may be stand-alone software that acts independently of the other software on your computer or it may be plug-in software that can be used from within an image-processing program like Photoshop. Usually, both kinds are supplied.

Obviously, the better the original, the better the resulting scan. The magic of image-editing can repair many imperfections in a scan, but that requires skill, time, and expense. It's worth the effort needed to start with the best possible original image.

■ **Image-editing**—The manipulation of images isn't limited to correcting imperfections. It's possible to make many variations in the way images are presented: a halftone or color image can be combined with a line illustration (*combination*); the background of an image can be eliminated, leaving only an object or a figure (*silhouette*); the background can be made to fade away at the edges in any shape desired (*vignette*); the screen can be dropped out in highlight areas, leaving pure white (*highlight* or *dropout*); halftones can be made with straight, wavy, or circular screens instead of dots; halftones can be scanned with such great contrast that they become line copy, or line copy can be scanned to look like a halftone; and flat screen patterns (*bendays*) can be added to an image (CH. 10).

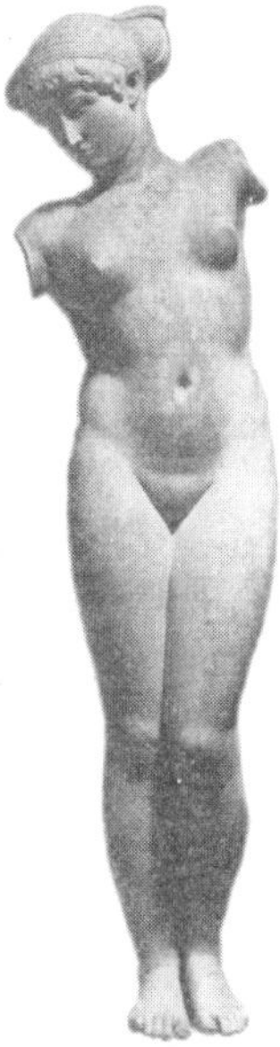

silhouette

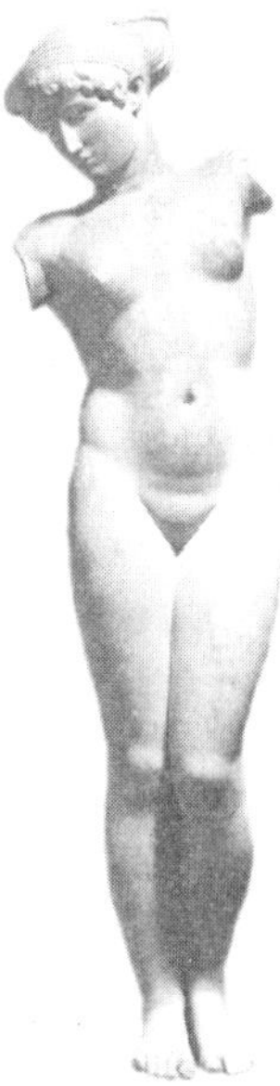

dropout

vignette

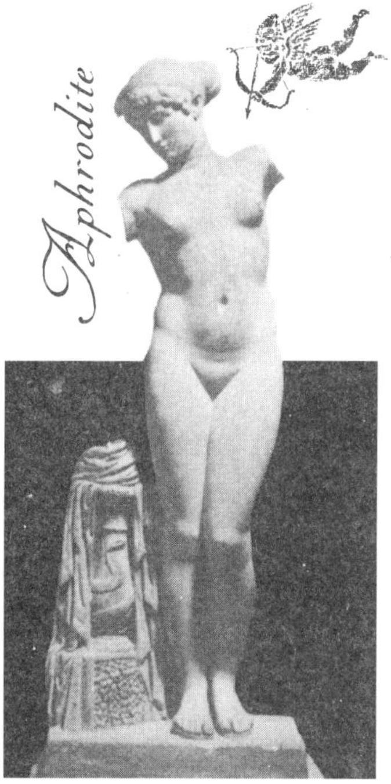

combination

circular screen

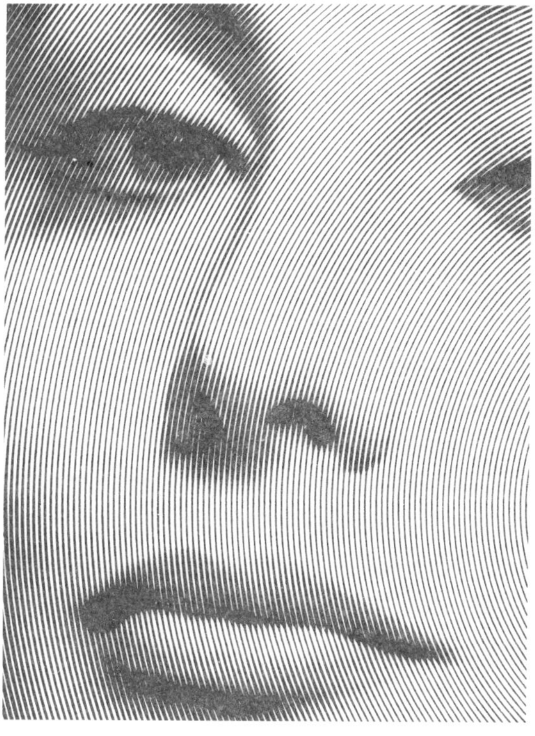

benday

Benday or *tint screens* are measured according to their lpi and the size of their dots. So they're specified by both their screen size—lpi (120, 150, etc.)—and their tint, which is a percentage of solid black.

Another important variation is the *duotone*. Traditionally, the halftone original was photographed twice, once with high contrast, once with low. Now, the original is scanned once and the two images with different contrasts are created in a program like Photoshop. Separate plates are made for each, requiring two passes through the press. The high-contrast image is printed in black ink, the other is printed in a gray or color ink. The result is a reproduction with richer tones than is possible with only one plate. The problem in making successful duotones is finding just the right combination of contrasts, which often requires several tries, even by skilled technicians. This isn't something to be attempted by the inexperienced.

Making scans It isn't necessary to make a *high-resolution (hi-res) scan* for design or layout purposes. If your output will be to a monitor with a resolution of 72 dpi or to a 300 dpi printer, making a high-res scan will be a waste of the considerable extra time and memory it takes. If you plan to print a color photograph in a book, you'll need a very high-resolution scan of superior quality produced by experienced professionals. For preliminary procedures, scan for a resolution no finer than your output device can handle.

tints

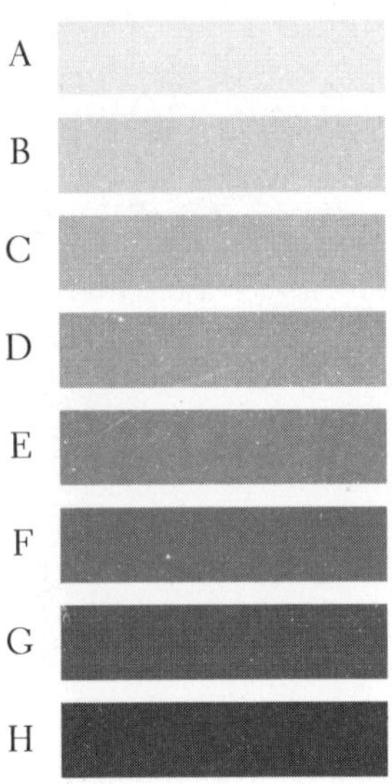

Not every operation can or should be done on a desktop computer. Whether you do the critical work of quality graphic reproduction yourself or send some of it to specialists will depend on your equipment, your skill in using it, and the particular situation. Here are a few typical scenarios:

(a) You need a rough rendition of an image to show its size, position, and cropping. A *low-res scan* is quick, it can be done with a minimum of technical skill, and it produces data files small enough to be manageable on your hard disk. A desktop scanner can do the job.

(b) You want to manipulate the image—retouch and alter it—into its final form, a high-res scan. If you are not skilled in this work, and your equipment doesn't have the large memory required for such scans, the solution is to send the job to a service bureau or the printshop. Their high-resolution scan can be reworked and edited to your satisfaction by a computer retoucher or digital artist with professional equipment. If you are able to edit the image but can't make a high-quality scan, send it to the service bureau for scanning and then manipulate the result yourself.

(c) You need both a low-res scan for viewing (*viewfile, proxy*) and a high-res scan for final reproduction. A service bureau will make both, sending you the low-res for your layout and retaining (*archiv-*

ing) the high-res scan to use later as separations to be integrated with the final films—which avoids your storing large files that serve no purpose. There are several standard systems for automatically substituting the archived high-res images for the *FPO* (*for position only*) low-res images: *OPI* (*Open Prepress Interface*), *APR* (*Automatic Picture Replacement*), and *DCS* (*Desktop Color System*).

To summarize, unless you are going to make the major investment in equipment, software, and training necessary to achieve professional results, do low-resolution FPO scans in the layout on your desktop scanner and leave the high-res scans to an imaging house or the prep department of the printshop. Their sophisticated scanners and skilled technicians can achieve more accurate color, fuller tonality, greater range of brightness and contrast, and better shadow density and highlights than most designers can achieve on office equipment. Improvements in scanner technology are bringing desktop quality to an acceptable level for book publishing, but high-quality image reproduction is usually best left to experts.

To get the best scan results there are three factors to consider:

- **Type of output**—An image will be handled differently for printing on a desktop printer than for printing to a high-resolution imagesetter or viewing on a monitor.
- **Scanner mode**—There are three basic choices: line art, *grayscale*, and color. There may be several kinds of color formats from which to select: RGB, CMYK, LAB, etc. (see "Color models" below). Any of these will suffice for FPO scanning, but if you're scanning for actual production use, the decision requires considering many factors. (To make a black & white image of a color original for, say, layout purposes, choose grayscale.)
- **Scanner resolution**—This is expressed as *dots-per-inch* (*dpi*), or sometimes *pixels-per-inch* (*ppi*), which are equivalent measures. In choosing the resolution for a scan, four factors must be considered:

  (a) size of original art (35 mm slide, 8 x 10" print, etc.),
  (b) type of original (continuous tone or line art),
  (c) size of final image, and
  (d) screen size (lpi) required for output.

HALFTONE

The rule of thumb for a 1:1 size ratio (the scanned size being the same as the original picture), is:

scan resolution = 2 times screen lpi

For example, a 4 x 5" original to be reproduced as 4 x 5" and printed at 133 lpi screen should be scanned at a resolution of about 266 dpi. If the size of the scanned image will be larger or smaller than the original, the formula changes proportionately. So, if the scanned size will be twice the size of the original, the resolution should be 4 x screen lpi (532 dpi in the example above). If it will be half the size, use 1 x screen lpi (133 dpi), and so on.

Using this formula may give you more resolution than needed. You may get acceptable quality with somewhat less. Start with the formula, then reduce resolution 25% at a time until you begin to see an unacceptable loss of quality in the output. The minimum resolution is 1½ x screen lpi.

Most scanner software allows you to specify line screen and final size so that scan resolution is determined automatically, making it unnecessary to use the above calculations. However, it's important to understand the basis for determining the needed resolution, particularly when the scans have been produced by an outside source and you want to change the scale.

LINE ART

To achieve optimum quality with line art, scan at the same resolution as the output device—if that's a 600 dpi printer, scan at 600 dpi; if it's an imagesetter printing at 1200 dpi, use 1200 dpi. If you are getting jagged lines, increase the resolution until the lines are smooth.

Good-quality line art scans don't require the equipment sensitivity or skill needed for continuous tones, so they can be done on desktop hardware.

Color

While all color originates in light, the light source determines how color is perceived. Generally, we see color as light *reflected* off solid surfaces—flowers, pages, walls. But color seen on a TV or computer monitor or in a transparency is the result of light *transmitted through* the screen or film directly to the eye.

COLOR MODELS

Computer output shows color in these two very different ways: on the computer screen and on the printed page. In the transition from screen color to printed page, the luminous color of the transmitted light can't quite be achieved by inks on paper; the transition is by nature imperfect and the printed result will always be an approximation. To describe color, the computer uses several methods, called *color models*. Graphics programs give color model options for translating colors into data. The model used depends on where the color is to be output.

- **RGB**—The colors seen on screen are created by tiny radiated points of light, either in combinations of three colors—red, green, and blue (RGB)—or as single colors. Just as a prism refracts white light into all colors of the spectrum, the RGB screen colors are produced by transmitted light; when all three colors are added together, pure white light results. The absence of all three results in black. The RGB system is called an *additive* color model.
- **CMYK**—On printed pages, light bounces off the surface, which absorbs (or subtracts) all light frequencies except the color we see. The absence of colors in this model is white. In light, the primary colors are blue, red, and yellow. In printers' inks, the complements

are cyan (a green-blue), magenta (a violet-red), and yellow—CMY. When the three primary colors are mixed in paint, the result is black, but mixing CMY together produces a murky brown, so black ink (K) is added to the mix to get a good black. The CMYK system is a *subtractive* color model.

CMYK is known as *process color*. Artwork is *color separated* into the four color components using a scanner, and the resultant film is screened to make a printing plate for each color. When run through a press, the combined dot patterns of the four plates create the impression of full color. CMYK is almost always used for color printing on paper.

- **HSB (hue-saturation-brightness)**—This is based on the way the human eye perceives colors. "*Hue*" describes the color, "*saturation*" refers to the intensity of the color, and "*brightness*" is the measure of how much black the color contains. In some programs this is called *LAB*, in others *LCH* or *LAB* (*CH*) or *HSV*.
- **HiFi color**—Standard four-color process is limited in the range of colors that can be reproduced. Reproducing bright oranges and greens, and differentiating subtle variations between similar colors are very difficult. To make up for these shortcomings, several extensions to the CMYK ink set, using six or more inks, have appeared. Among these extensions, collectively known as HiFi color, *Hexachrome* (Pantone), which adds orange and green inks, has come to be accepted as the standard for high-quality color reproduction. The use of HiFi color by book publishers has been limited by its higher prep cost and the expense of running on six-color presses.
- **Spot color**—Unlike process color, which uses combinations of the four ink colors (cyan, magenta, yellow, black) to create the entire spectrum, *spot color* is ink premixed to a specified color. Spot colors, either solid or shades of a color, are generally chosen from a standard matching system such as the *Pantone Matching System* (*PMS*) or other color-matching libraries that provide spectrums of standardized colors achievable with ink formulas universally available from printshops. Graphics and layout programs support several different color-matching systems. Since colors appearing on screen can't be accurately represented with inks, it's vital to specify colors for print from a printed sample. Use numbered swatches or color chips printed on both coated and uncoated papers to specify colors. Remember that the paper to be printed on will affect the perceived color of the ink. When an exact color match is critical, request a *draw down* (printed sample) on the production stock.

CALIBRATION

To ensure rendering the printed image as closely as possible to the color image on the screen, all hardware and software involved need to be speaking the same language. Scanner, monitor, imagesetter, and software must be adjusted, or calibrated, to uniform standards via a color management system like *ColorSync* or *Kodak Precision*. Many programs automatically calibrate the monitor, but sometimes it's best to work backwards in calibration: i.e., starting with a sample color proof from a file and adjusting the monitor to match the proof. Truly accurate calibration of all devices involved requires the use of spectrophotometers to measure the color's output by monitors and printers or proofers and sophisticated software to create ICC (*International Color Consortium*) profiles for each device.

DOTS Halftone (black & white) and color pictures printed on a press are actually made up of very closely spaced tiny dots that the eye combines to form an image. The density of the dots in each case results from the fineness or coarseness of the screen (measured in lines-per-inch) used to break up the picture into a dot pattern. The finer the screen, the better detail can be captured. But it's not just the number of dots that affects the look of an image, it's also their shape and the pattern in which they're arranged. The angle of the lines of dots in each plate must be set so as to put each of the four colored dots in correct relationship to the others, forming a pattern in which the dots are separate and avoiding undesirable *moiré* patterns. Occasionally, patterns within an image, such as lattices or lace, will interfere with the normal dot pattern. This can be avoided by using *stochastic screening*, in which the dots are arranged in an irregular rather than a linear pattern. In any case, the dots must be sharp—in perfect focus—to achieve accurate color balance. Where the color in an image is most intense, as in shadows, the dots are their maximum size. In light areas, the dots are smaller. When the dots are extremely small, it's important that they're not dropped out entirely by imperfect exposure of film or plates, as their loss can seriously harm the appearance of a printed image. At the same time, thought must be given to *dot gain*—enlargement of dots due to faulty exposure or to the spreading of the ink in printing, which is affected by both the type of paper and the presswork.

TRAPPING & REGISTRATION Each of the process-color plates printing on a press must be positioned precisely in relation to the others to get perfect registration. When they aren't, minute white spaces appear where colors don't meet. The problem is most apparent in drawn images, in which distinct areas of color abut one another, but it's just as serious, if less apparent to the untrained eye, in continuous-tone images where colors blend into one another. Printing an element of one color on a background of a contrasting color is an especially difficult problem.

The technique used to deal with this problem is *trapping*—a process performed with software when preparing color separations for printing. Trapping involves creating a slight overlap in two abutting colors to eliminate the possibility of gaps. This is done by either *spreading* or *choking* colored objects (type, drawings, shapes). Spreading enlarges a foreground object to slightly overlap its background or *knockout* (white) area. Choking shrinks a background object so the foreground object will slightly overlap it. Whether to spread or choke depends on the nature of the colors. Generally, the lighter color dictates the trap. A light color is spread over a dark one. A light background is choked under a dark foreground. This avoids a dark outline along the edge of the overlap.

File size & compression

Scan files are much larger than text files and can quickly exhaust a computer's storage space, so it's important that they're made no bigger than necessary. The problem can be seen in this comparison: A 1-square-inch 1-bit line art file at a resolution of 300 dpi is 10 K; an 8-bit grayscale is 90 K; and a 24-bit color file is 270 K. Doubling the size of the image to 2 square inches increases the file size by a factor of four—to 40 K, 360 K, and 1080 K (1.1 MB). It's worth your time to study the literature that accompanies the scanner to learn how to maximize resolution while minimizing file size.

File compression alleviates the problem of storing, transporting, and transmitting large bitmap images created by scans. There are many programs that compress files. By condensing or even discarding data, compression programs reduce file size, sometimes very radically. Some compression programs lose data (*lossy*) in the process, others don't (*lossless*). *JPEG* (*Joint Photographic Experts Group*) was developed specifically for use with photographs and, although it's a lossy method, it's become the standard international high-compression method. If JPEG compression is used it is essential that the level of compression is kept low enough to maintain the quality of the image. Choosing the appropriate method in each situation should take account of the nature of the file, the document, and the output. Get advice from a service bureau on which one, if any, to use. JPEGs will usually have to be converted to TIFF or EPS for prepress use.

Getting huge files from a hard drive to the service bureau can be done on removable drive disks (like Zips, optical disks, or CD-Rs) or via telecommunication systems such as modems, the Internet, or intranet. Temporarily compressing the files makes the transfer easier and faster. Compressing has drawbacks, however, like slowing down the Save operation to wait for compression, or some loss of image integrity (data in the file).

File formats

Whether artwork is created in a paint or draw program or is scanned in through an image-editing program, the digital information it contains is stored in a coded structure called a *file format*. The file format organizes the data, enabling it to be read by the various programs and devices it will encounter on its way to becoming a printed (or electronic) page.

Different programs use different formats. Not all graphics programs can read each other's formats, so a few formats have been standardized and are used more frequently than the rest. Many programs have proprietary formats that can't be read by other programs without installing special filters. To transfer work to other programs it's best to use a format common to most. Page-layout programs, which are designed to unite text with illustration, can accept many formats, enabling the transfer—or import—of artwork from graphics programs. Image-editing programs also can import a variety of formats.

Many generic file formats can be transferred—imported and exported—by most graphics programs. They fall into two broad categories: text and graphics.

■ **Text**—ASCII (American Standard Code for Information Interchange)—pronounced "askee"—is the main file format for text. It's a basic code for letters, numbers, and symbols and is understood by most computers.

■ **Graphics**—These file formats are much more numerous and complex. To decide in which format to save a graphic, the question is: Can it be supported—that is, read and saved—by the destination software (e.g., a layout program) as well as the output device and its software? Other determining factors are:

(a) Is the image created in and/or destined for a PC, Mac, or other platform? Some formats accommodate multiple platforms, while others are designed for only one system.

(b) Is the image *vector* or *raster*? Vector images are described by curves and lines and are created by draw (or illustration) programs. Raster graphics are described in pixels and are made by paint and image-editing programs (CH. 3). Some formats are confined to either vector or raster images; others, such as *EPS* (*Encapsulated PostScript*), which is based on the PostScript page-description language (see below), can contain both. Images can be converted from vector to raster (and vice versa) to achieve different effects or for purposes of storage or transmittal.

(c) Where is the image going and for what purpose? Some formats are unique to a particular program, and while they can be read in others, they may not be editable there.

(d) How large a file will the format create? Vector files may be smaller than raster files because they don't contain the intricate dot-by-dot information of a bitmap. A vector format can be scaled to any size using the mathematical formula it contains. Bitmapped images are resolution dependent and should be saved at approximately the same size in which they will appear. If they're enlarged too much, the image breaks up into a visible pixel pattern. If reduced too much, the pixels are too condensed, obscuring detail and darkening the image.

(e) Does the destination software support the format? If not, it's easy to convert to a different one within a program that handles both the present and the intended format. RTF (Rich Text Format) is a method of encoding formatted text and graphics for easy transfer of documents between different operating systems and programs. Most word-processing software can write and read RTF files, so it provides a means to move documents back and forth between systems without losing the formatting and graphics. Save as RTF on one system then open the RTF on the other. Quark doesn't directly import RTF format.

The most commonly used file formats are described below. There are many others, some used for specialized purposes by digital imaging and prepress technicians. It's best to check with the technicians handling your job to be sure that the formats you plan to use are the most suitable for the intended output.

PS (PostScript) is a text file containing the PostScript language instructions that describe the vector and raster components, both text and graphics, of a page. It contains no screen preview image and so must be rasterized (RIPed) to produce a screen image if needed.

PDF is a file for which *Acrobat Distiller* "distills" the complex instructions in a PostScript file into a database of the objects that appear on each page, including all the fonts and images needed to produce them. PDFs for print production must use prepress optimized Distiller settings and high-res images. There's no simple answer for "How do I create a PDF file?" There are many ways, depending on what software you start from and what the file is to be used for. Ask your prepress shop or printshop to tell you how to prepare the PDF file for their particular needs (CH. 6).

EPS is the most widely used format for layout programs. It combines a PostScript text file with a *PICT* (black & white picture) or *PICT2* (color picture) (see below) component. It's used mostly to store vector images but can accommodate bitmaps as well (though the resulting files may be very large). It's supported by various computer systems, printers, and software, providing a common denominator for file exchange between desktop programs.

PICT and *PICT2* are Mac formats which can compactly store both vector and bitmapped images. They can also be exported to PC systems with a *PCT* extension. PICT formats are useful for on-screen display but not for creating color separations or printing. They are widely used for transferring documents between programs.

TIFF (Tagged Image File Format) is the most popular format used for bitmapped images. Scanned images are usually saved in

TIFF, and all draw, paint, image-editing, and layout programs support it. There are versions to handle a variety of images, including line art, grayscale, RGB (screen color), and CMYK (printed color). A TIFF may also contain a *clipping path*, which defines the outlines of silhouettes. This format easily converts from Mac to PC. While TIFF files are large because they contain detailed pixel data, various compression utilities can reduce their size for storage.

Other widely used formats are BMP, PCX, WMF, TGA, and DCS.

Proofs See CH. 10

9. Page-makeup

Page-makeup is the assembly of all the elements of a book and their arrangement on its pages in their proper position. There may be many sources of these elements: word-processing, illustration, paint or image-editing programs, CD images, illustration or photo scans. The primary device for accomplishing page-makeup is a layout program. Although these programs are capable of originating some of the material to be assembled, there are usually more efficient ways to do that. For example, you *can* enter text into a layout program, but keyboarding and formatting it in a word-processing program is much faster and simpler. Layout programs are designed specifically to gather and organize elements and prepare them for the next step in the process.

The predominant *page-layout programs* used in publishing are QuarkXPress, PageMaker, and InDesign. They are called *frame-based programs* because the pages are constructed by a series of text and graphics boxes—or frames—which may be linked together and/or layered to compose the layout. The relationships these frames have to one another depend on their properties. They can be grouped and anchored together, locked for security, and layered to build images for different effects.

Page-makeup doesn't have to be done entirely by computer. Some, or all, of the work can be done with paper, as it was done before there were computers. You can order repro proofs of the type (ideally with all elements in their correct relative position) and prints or proofs of illustrations to size, then paste (rubber cement or wax) these into position on boards prepared with outlines of the pages. These *mechanicals* (CH. 10) can then be sent to the printshop to be photographed onto film. The artwork is scanned (if it hasn't been already) and screened on film, then stripped into place on the films with text.

Although most designers have moved entirely to electronic methods, some prefer to combine these with paste-up. They do the typesetting and page layout on computer and send a disk to the prepress or print shop. Reproduction of artwork is done by the printshop or imaging houses. A paste-up of low-resolution scans of illustrations in position onto page proofs provides an accurate dummy (CH. 10) to be sent with the disk. Text and graphics are then assembled, either on film, as with mechanicals, or electronically, to complete the page-makeup.

Maximum efficiency is achieved by providing all elements of a book on computer disk. This is commonly done where all elements are simple enough to create on available equipment or where the equipment is sophisticated enough to handle all the technical problems. As technology has advanced, more and more is being accomplished on desktop machines.

Before beginning computer layout of a book, it's a good idea to sketch out preliminary designs on a pad. This is still the fastest way to determine whether a design is going to work or not. Making roughs on the computer takes a lot of time, and there's always the temptation to get into trivial details, like carefully letterspacing a headline you may not even use. (If you do make roughs on the computer, it's a good idea to print them out. Images on the screen can be deceiving.) It's better to use pencil and paper to narrow the choices for a final design. When you have a rough that looks good, that's the time to start computer-generated sample pages (CH. 25).

Components of a layout program

Knowing the components of a layout program will help you understand how they interact to make up the pages of a book. Function and option names vary among programs, but the terms and specs used here are those of QuarkXPress, which are widely used and apply generally to the professional-level makeup programs.

THE ELECTRONIC PASTEBOARD

In a layout program, the screen is designed to represent an artist's drawing board. When you create a new file, you are asked to indicate page specifications—width and height, number of text columns, and margin dimensions. Then a window opens with a page set up to your specs (you can change them later if you wish). Surrounding the page is an area called the *pasteboard*, which can be used to experiment with type and/or graphic ideas that may be moved onto the page or discarded.

The *clipboard* is a holding area where items to be copied or cut and pasted are temporarily stored. Only one item can be kept there at a time—the last to be copied or cut. Previous such items are automatically discarded and replaced by the current one.

THE MENU BAR

Above the pasteboard is a row of pull-down menus. This *menu bar* lists the categories that contain controls (commands) for both the general functions—like saving, copying, moving, printing—as well as the specific functions affecting the disposition of individual elements in the document.

By holding the mouse button down or by clicking on a menu category, its full list of commands appears. Those in black type are accessible, those in gray are not. The program allows access to options only under certain circumstances—for instance if the cursor is inside a type box in order to change a font style.

Some menu selections lead to a dialog box asking you for information. For example, if you give an improper type measurement, the dialog box asks for clarification. When you fill in the correct measurement, the box disappears and the correction is applied. Other menu selections have keyboard commands (shortcuts) listed next to them. A particular combination of keystrokes will have the same effect as choosing the command from the menu. A third option for executing commands is through *palettes* (see below).

Many of the options have built-in defaults based on the programmers' judgment of what most users will prefer in particular situations. Examples of defaults are the size and style of typeface a program uses if no others are specified. Defaults can usually be changed by adjustments made in the preferences, sometimes for an entire program, sometimes only for aspects of the active document.

Familiarity with the location of each menu and its contents is very important in navigating around a program effectively.

SCROLL BARS

Along the right and bottom edges of the pasteboard are scroll bars: movable white boxes in shaded panels which can change the view—up/down, right/left—in that window. The larger the computer's monitor, the less scrolling necessary, because more image fits in the window.

RULERS & GUIDELINES

Along the left and top of the pasteboard are vertical and horizontal rulers calibrated in the unit of measure you choose for display. The default is inches, but other options are available, like metric, picas, and ciceros (a European unit). The starting point of either ruler or both can be changed to measure particular elements. From both rulers you can pull out guidelines to position on the page or the pasteboard to accurately align type or other elements. Alignment accuracy is best achieved by enlarging the page area to its maximum (in QuarkXPress 4.1 or 5 that's 800%).

MARGINS & COLUMNS

The basic text structure is created by specifying the number of columns on a page and the size of spaces between and margins around them. When importing text from a word-processing source, using the automatic text box feature will make it flow continuously through all the columns on all the pages of the document. The book's length can be easily adjusted by changing the type specs, the sizes of the columns, and/or the margins. Other ways of affecting the total page count are discussed in CHs. 23, 24.

Columns consist of blocks of text. Introducing another item, either a text or picture box, into a text area will force the type to flow around it unless you instruct it otherwise. Items in a text area can be made to *runaround* or overlap.

PALETTES Palettes are movable windows which may be used to control some of the features of a program rather than accessing them through the menus. They are often more convenient to use than menus and can be repositioned on the screen or hidden from view. There are several kinds of palettes, and they differ somewhat in each program. The most frequently used are described below:

■ *Tool palette*—A collection of artist's tools represented by icons on the pasteboard. This tool kit is the electronic equivalent of the layout artist's X-Acto knife, pens, rubber cement, T-square, triangle, protractor, burnisher, etc. There are different categories of tools—item-creation tools, linking tools, editing tools—and each group performs specialized tasks.

Some item-creation tools form frames, or boxes, others rule lines. To import an element into a layout program from another program, it must be placed in an active box drawn by an item-creation tool.

Linking tools connect the flow of text between text boxes in any sequence designated. Links can be broken and resequenced.

Editing tools can select, move, rearrange, resize, rotate, skew, and magnify text or picture boxes and the material inside them.

■ **Measurements palette**—Enables editing of items such as dimensions, angles, and other attributes. In QuarkXPress this handy control panel also enables editing typographic features like font style, size, alignment, leading, tracking, and kerning.

■ **Color palette**—Displays the current color selections of the document and enables editing or application of colors and blends.

■ **Document layout palette**—A graphical method of inserting, deleting, moving, rearranging, and repaginating, and for manipulating and applying master pages (see below).

■ **Style sheets palette**—Displays the typographic styles and formats of the document and enables them to be applied, edited, created, and deleted.

■ **Library palette**—Used to store layout items for future use, including text, pictures, lines, decorative elements, or combinations of items.

Formatting ■ **Master pages**—Once the design format—the basic grid and its variations—has been determined, and sample pages have been approved, the specifications can be locked in by making *master pages*. This is one of the most useful computer options in designing a book. You set up customized defaults with preset specifications for text, columns, margins, headers and footers, even recurring rules and borders. Facing pages can be given different attributes, like variations in running heads. Page numbers can be automatically inserted in sequence. Different master pages can be created for parts of a book that differ from the body—the index, for example. By creating master pages you avoid the repetitious, time-consuming work of styling each page.

■ **Style sheets**—Set up a style sheet to ensure consistency in typography throughout a document. Using this feature, with a single keystroke or key combination you can assign to type a whole group of attributes—size, style, color, and format (including spacing, indents, rules, initial caps, etc.). Assigning keyboard commands to the standard elements in a design greatly simplifies the typesetting process.

■ **Templates**—Any document can be saved as a template, which retains all page, paragraph, and text characteristics, including master page and style sheet specifications, if any. Templates are used for making repeated copies of a format.

■ **Registration and crop marks**—These are applied in the layout program through the Print command. In a multicolor job, registration marks are guides that the printshop uses to accurately superimpose the different color plates for perfect alignment. Crop marks are short lines outside the corners of each page to indicate its trim-size and are used by the bindery as a guide for trimming the book. If the design includes areas of color or illustrations that *bleed* (extend to the edge of the page), they must extend an additional ⅛" beyond the crop marks to ensure that there'll be no white showing when the book is trimmed. In the layout program, crop marks can be automatically set to appear in the proper positions.

Editing text

Minor editing of text in a layout program is easily done. Small changes of copy can be handled by either adjustments in layout or manipulating text. Extensive changes to the text, however, should be done in word-processing rather than in the layout program, where long edits are slower and clumsier.

Inserting text & graphics

There are several ways to transport text and graphics to a document in a layout program from another program or from a different document in the same program.

■ **Cut and paste**—Use the commands in the Edit menu to cut or copy an item in the originating document, then paste it into the layout document. Both documents must be open to do this.

■ **Importing text**—You must have an open text box on a page in the layout document, and the file which is being imported must be in a format compatible with the layout program. All the major word-processing programs are compatible with professional layout programs, but if there's a problem with incompatible files, a service bureau can generally solve it.

■ **Importing graphics**—A picture box must be drawn by one of the creation tools, and the source file—a scan, illustration, or paint file—must be in a format compatible with the layout program. There are dozens of graphics file formats, but layout programs support only the most popular ones, such as EPS and TIFF (CH. 8). The source program doesn't need to be open to be imported. Some computers have difficulty reading cross-platform—for example, Mac files on PCs and vice versa—but there's conversion software that can usually remedy this. Service bureaus are able to convert files between formats if necessary.

■ **Publish and subscribe** (called *object linking* and *embedding* in Windows)—This is particularly useful when more than one person is working on a file (say, an editor and a designer). It's like importing but with one big difference: even if the original item (the "publisher") has been recently altered, it always appears in its current version when opened in the master or layout document (the "subscriber"). Linking automatically updates the item as long as the paths connecting the documents are maintained. Instead of adding all the data of a linked file to a layout document, only its location and path to the site are stored in memory.

Working with graphics

Graphics can be changed within the layout program. They may be resized, recropped, repositioned, or reframed, but it may not be possible to edit the content of a graphic inside the layout document in some programs. Changes might have to be done in the originating or an image-editing program.

It's possible in most programs to *suppress* images in order to speed up slow progress of screen redraws and proof printing in memory-intensive graphics files. Screen redraws can be speeded up also by *greeking* the image, i.e., by marking its position on screen with a gray area, but this won't speed its printing.

As noted in "Margins & columns" above, introducing a graphic into a text area can force the type to flow around it. The spaces between text and runarounds—or *text wraps*—can be controlled.

Picture boxes can be altered in size, shape, position, angle, background color, and shade. In some file formats, the picture itself (apart from the box background) can be altered in color, shade, line screen, and contrast.

Makeup problems

Makeup shouldn't begin until all text has been corrected and the *castoff* (CH. 31) has been made to determine how many lines should be on the text page. This, with the *sample page* specifications (CH. 25), will provide the information on which master pages and style sheet will be based.

Theoretically, every page has the same number of lines of text (except the beginnings and ends of chapters), so the makeup should be simple. Actually, there are several complications.

WIDOWS

The most common cause of difficulty is the *widow* (a line of less than full width occurring at the top of a page). In a page of justified lines, widows give a ragged appearance and it's desirable to eliminate them by one means or another. A short line of conversation isn't usually considered a widow, but the end of a paragraph is. Some designers will allow a widow of four-fifths of a line, others will tolerate three-fourths, and purists insist on a full line. However, it's doubtful that the not-quite-full line warrants the effort required to remove it.

The simplest way to correct a widow is for the editor or author to add words to fill out the line or delete words to eliminate it. If these options are not available, the usual procedure is to take the last line from the bottom of the preceding page and make *it* the first line of the new page, instead of the widow. But this creates a short page. The solution then is to make the facing page one line short also. Here the plot thickens. If the offending widow occurs on a right-hand page (*recto*), all that's needed is to leave that page one line short and it will match the preceding left-hand page (*verso*) from which the rescue line was taken. If, however, a left-hand page widow occurs, the two preceding facing pages must be made a line short, thus providing two full lines over the widow—that is, *if* the two preceding lines are full width. If not, the complications extend farther back. And, if making the adjustments necessary to eliminate the widow creates a widow on another page, a half-dozen or more pages may become involved. (This can make one more tolerant of widows.)

Facing short pages may be left that way, or they may be filled out to full depth by adding small amounts of leading (called *carding* in metal-type makeup, see CH. 5). This practice is frowned upon by some because the lines don't then back up those on the other side of the page. But, since the amount of added leading is likely to be only a fraction of a point, the misalignment on backup is unlikely to be perceived.

An even naughtier practice is to lead out only the one short page so as to leave the facing page undisturbed. Here the misalignment *may* be detected by an expert, but considering that this much or more misalignment frequently results from inaccurate folding, the imperfection isn't likely to be noticed at all.

These remarks may sound like incitement to the lowering of standards, and strictly speaking they are, but the relatively imperceptible refinements insisted upon by some, at the cost of considerable efficiency, seem a waste of good intentions when there's so much improvement needed in areas where the faults are glaring and only a little care is required for relief.

When the text fits very tightly into the desired number of pages, the solution is to make facing pages a line long instead of short to avoid widows. If this is done, be sure there's enough margin space below the last line of text.

The widow problem—and makeup problems in general—are eased when the book contains many subheads, illustrations, and other opportunities to adjust space. When the "opportunities" are so numerous that they create their own problems, a *dummy* may be made, either on the computer (*electronic dummy*) or by pasting up rough proofs on pages of correct size and number (CH. 10). This gives designer and editor a chance to experiment with the arrangement. Once the dummy is completed with the problems worked out, the makeup is a purely mechanical process.

Another possible solution to the widow problem is to use the computer's ability to add small amounts of letterspacing ("tracking") to affect the number of characters in a line—and then in a paragraph, and ultimately in a page. This procedure can alter the text sufficiently to eliminate a widow, but it also destroys the integrity of the type design. Not recommended.

RUN-IN BREAKS Another problem inherent in page makeup is what to do when subheads, *spacebreaks* (one- or two-line spaces in text), or *run-in chapters* (chapter-openings that occur on the same page as the end of the preceding chapter) (CHs. 24, 25) fall at the bottom of the page, with insufficient room for a minimum number of text lines underneath. It's best to settle these questions in advance and have the solutions incorporated in the style sheet.

ODD-DEPTH SPACES When all pages must be made up to the same depth, problems may arise when spaces other than full lines are used. For example, the use of half-line spaces above and below poetry or extract causes trouble when the item begins on one page and ends on another. Each half-line space must be increased to a full line or eliminated entirely, unless some text is leaded out to take up the other half-line of space. The problem is complicated by the odd space resulting when the poetry or extract is set on a body size different from that of the text. The solution is usually to add leading as necessary.

10. Prepress

The term *prepress* refers to the production processes between the completion of page-makeup and the preparation of printing plates. Traditional prepress includes the preparation of a dummy and/or mechanicals, imaging the type, photographing line and halftone illustrations, making color separations, proofing and correction as needed, assembly of the text and art films into the press imposition, and final proofing and correction of the imposed film. This process has been largely replaced by digital prepress, which has blurred the lines between prepress and page-makeup. Now, illustration prepress is usually carried out before the completion of page-makeup and includes scanning the art to produce high-resolution files, adjusting those files to prepare them for printing, and making proofs of the images. The image files are returned to page-makeup for merging the text and images. Files with the complete pages are then sent to prepress for final processing, proofing, and the generation of film or plate-ready files.

Some of this procedure is covered in CH. 32, but there's some technically complex information involved which would be good for you to know—although your suppliers have technicians able to make the decisions if you prefer to let them do so (which is usually a good idea). Enough of that information is provided in this chapter to make you familiar with the terminology and give you a basic understanding of the processes, so that communication between you and your suppliers—service bureau and printshop—will be more successful. It's important to remember that errors made in preparing material will be reflected in either a poorly executed job or the expense of having the errors corrected by technicians.

Preparing for prepress

DISKS TO PREPRESS

When page-makeup has been completed, proofread, and corrected, the file for the entire book is sent in electronic form to whoever will be doing the prepress work. This will probably be a service bureau specializing in these functions or a printshop.

There are many different storage media on the market, so be sure that the type you are submitting is compatible with the service bureau's or printshop's systems.

There are several ways to submit electronic files. One is in the form of *layout document files* (e.g., QuarkXPress, PageMaker, or Adobe InDesign files). The other common formats are PostScript and PDF files. The practical difference is less in the content of the files than in the way they can be handled in production.

Layout document files (sometimes called *native files*) can be altered by the computer operator if problems arise during prepress or last-minute changes are needed. This is a great advantage, but there's also the danger of new errors creeping in.

PostScript and PDF files can't be easily altered. What you put in is what you get out—errors and all. If such files have been perfectly prepared, there should be no unpleasant surprises, but unless you're absolutely confident in their accuracy, it's best to submit document files. If you do supply PostScript or PDF files, prepare test files in advance to be sure that fonts are compatible and that all the file preparation settings are correct (preflighting—see CH. 32). And send the document files as well, so the printshop will be able to make any last-minute corrections (CHs. 6, 32).

DUMMY However you submit files or artwork for prepress production, you should send also a full-size dummy or printout showing what items belong on each page and their positions. For this purpose, black & white printouts of page proofs are sufficient, even for color material. If the page size is larger than your printer can handle, use the tiling function in the Print command of your program. This automatically prints partial pages that can be pieced together to make up complete pages. Wherever graphics are indicated, either low-res scans or photocopies of artwork, in final size, should be placed in position.

The procedure for preparing a dummy for use by a prepress shop is the same as that described in CH. 9 for preparing a dummy for makeup, except that only final (fully corrected) proofs may be used.

Margins should be given for any graphic elements not in the page-makeup file. When you are giving margins, one must be to the top or bottom of the page, the other to the inside or outside. When giving distances between elements on a page, you should leave out at least one vertical and one horizontal measurement to allow minor inaccuracies to be absorbed. Shown on the facing page are two examples.

Since everything in the file you are sending is in correct position, the dummy is meant as a general guide and reference, so it's appropriate to write on it any notes that might be useful in helping the prepress technicians understand the work to be done.

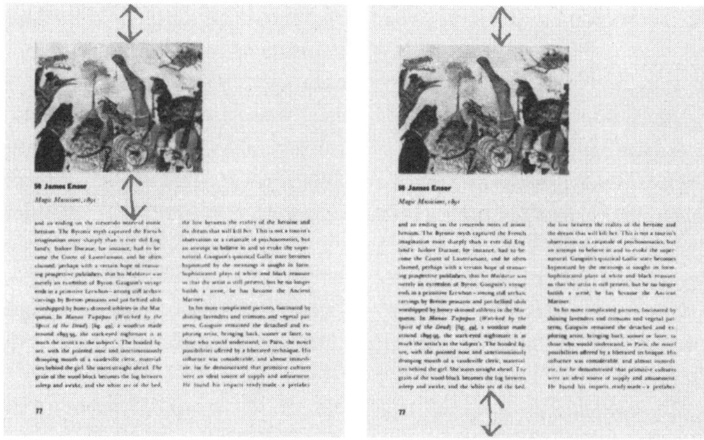

two ways of indicating vertical position

MECHANICALS

As noted in CH. 9, an alternative to making up pages by computer is to make mechanicals. This, like other hand processes mentioned, is rarely used, but there are times when it's the most efficient way to go (for example, in some complex picture books with informal layouts), so it's important to know how it's done. (The term "mechanical" is used also for computer-created pages.)

A mechanical is a piece of final copy consisting of one or more elements, accurately positioned and marked. When mechanicals for a whole book are being prepared, it's worth having boards—about 50 lb. (136 gsm) cover weight—printed in nonphotographing light blue ink with the outlines of a two-page spread and whatever

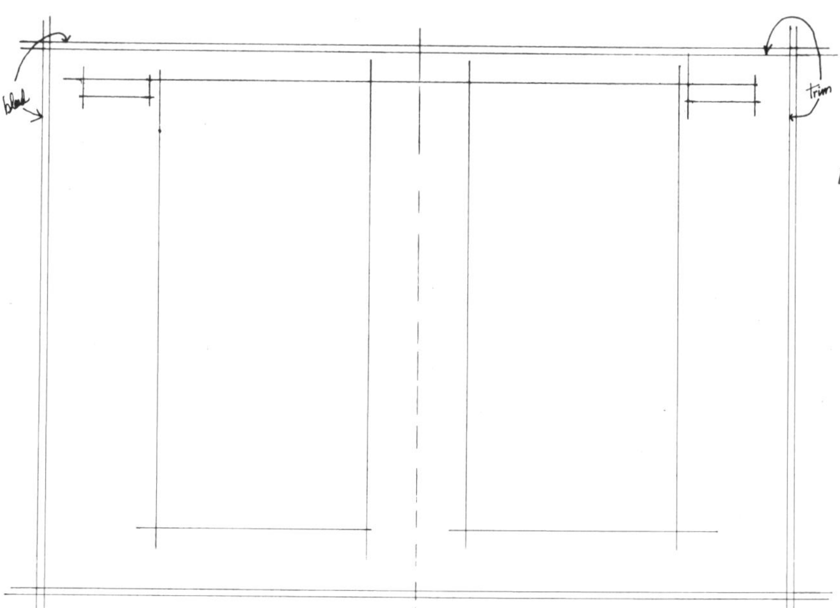

layout of mechanical board

guidelines, corners, etc. would be useful in speeding the pasteup and increasing accuracy. For small numbers of mechanicals, printing can be avoided by drawing the page outlines in light blue pencil on a board, or working on a light-table with a transparent *guide sheet* (a sheet with guide lines drawn in black) taped to the glass. In any case, *trimming guides* (lines that indicate where the printed sheets are to be trimmed) outside the page area should be printed or drawn in black or red so they will be picked up by the camera or scanner.

Maximum economy in mechanicals means minimizing the amount of shooting and stripping work required. It would be best to combine *all* the elements of each page on one board to be scanned or shot in a single pass. This isn't always possible, but the closer you can come to the ideal the better. There are three requirements for single-shot copy:

(a) each part of the copy must be in the same scale,
(b) the parts must be in the proper position in relation to each other, and
(c) there must be no part that requires a different screen or exposure than any other.

In practice, original artwork (photographs, drawings, etc.) is usually larger than the finished size, and can't be combined on a mechanical with type, so the artwork is scanned separately and the film combined with the films of the type in a position indicated on the mechanical by an outline, or a photocopy or low-res scan, in the correct size.

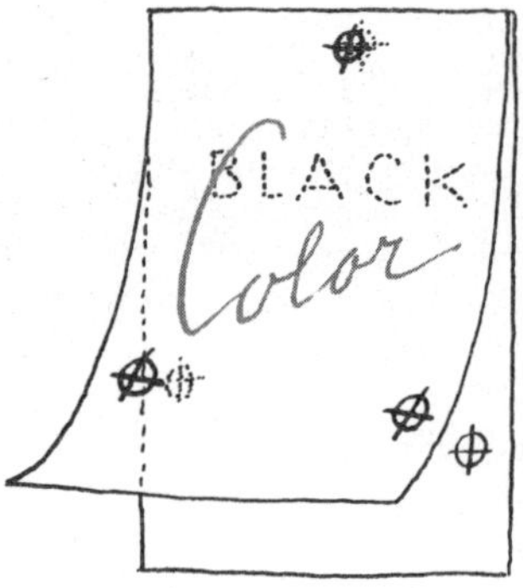

overlay

If one part of the copy overlaps another, it can be pasted on a transparent *overlay* in the correct relative position. Copy that overlaps (*overprints*) may be black & white—a tint, a halftone, or a line drawing—or color, either simple (CH. 12) or process (CH. 8).

If more than one color is involved but none overlaps, all the copy may be pasted into position on the board or on an overlay. If the colors overlap, separate black & white copy is prepared for each. The dominant color is pasted on the board as the *key plate* and the copy for the other colors is pasted on overlays to register with the key plate. This is called *pre-separated copy*. There should be at least three widely separated register marks on the base copy, and corresponding marks on the overlays.

Copy can be "pasted" with rubber cement—(regular or one-coat), tape, a melted (wax) adhesive (*dry mounted*), or by use of pressure-sensitive adhesive-backed paper. Squaring can be done with a T-square or with a transparent grid device on a light-table. Each method has advantages and disadvantages; the only important thing is the result—which should be accurate, secure, and clean copy. Remember that paper edges, cuts, cement excess, dirt, or anything else that's visible but not part of the copy may be picked up by the camera or scanner.

mechanical—all line copy

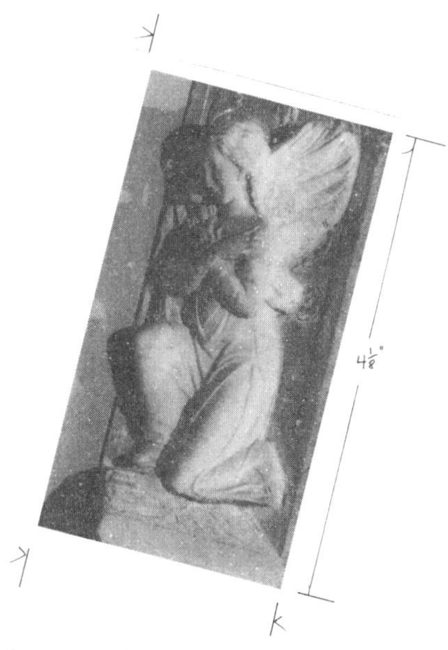

mechanical—line copy, with halftone to be sized and merged

MARKUP

Even perfect copy won't bring a good result if it's not marked properly. Instructions must be clear and complete. And remember, what may seem clear to you may not be clear to others—particularly if they're being rushed. There is a tendency to omit things that seem obvious, forgetting that they're not obvious to someone unfamiliar with your intentions. To compensate for this tendency, write your instructions as if they were directed to an idiot. You might be surprised to find that your instructions are no longer getting confused—and no one will complain.

Here are some of the markings that should appear on copy when appropriate:

(a) *Register marks*—Place them outside the copy.
(b) *Indication of bleeds*—Write "Bleed" wherever one occurs. (Extend bleed copy ⅛" outside trim.)
(c) *Indication of whether line or halftone.*
(d) *Size of halftone screen*—Indicate only if screen wanted differs from the standard screen used by the printshop.
(e) *Trimming guides*—Make clean, fine lines *outside* copy in black or red.
(f) *Folding guides*—Same as (e).
(g) *Dimensions*—Indicate if sizes and distances are before or after trim.

jacket proof marked for printing

(h) *Scale* (how reduced or enlarged). Scale can be confusing. Cameras and scanners use the relative percentage in *linear* size of the finished work to the copy, i.e., if 8 x 10" copy is to be made 4 x 5", that's 50%. If 8 x 10" is to be 12 x 15", that's 150%. *Same-size* (S/S) is 100%, etc. The marking should be: *Focus* 50, Focus 150, etc. (or F50, F150, etc.). Ideally, everyone would use this system and there would be no trouble. However, some say "reduce 50%" in the first instance and "enlarge 50%" in the second. Others say "reduce ½" and "enlarge 1½ times" (1½ x). Still another method—and probably the safest in view of the confusion possible with percentages—is to use proportions. The first example would be expressed as "reduce 2 to 1", the second is "enlarge 1 to 1½". Whatever system you use, it's best to let the printshop know about it in advance. With work coming in marked in several ways, it's understandable that there might be confusion.

It's possible also to give the actual dimensions to which the copy is being reduced or enlarged. A dimension with arrows pointing outward on each side (←5 9/16"→) indicates that the entire copy is to be made that size in that direction. If the copy is to be reduced so that a part of it is to become 5 9/16", a mark should be made in the margin opposite each end of the part concerned, and the indication 5 9/16" *BM* (*between marks*) written between them.

In no case should more than one dimension be given, unless you give permission to *crop* (cut away part of the picture) as necessary (as when illustrations must align). In general, it's best to indicate one dimension and scale the subject so that the other dimension will be correct after reduction or enlargement.

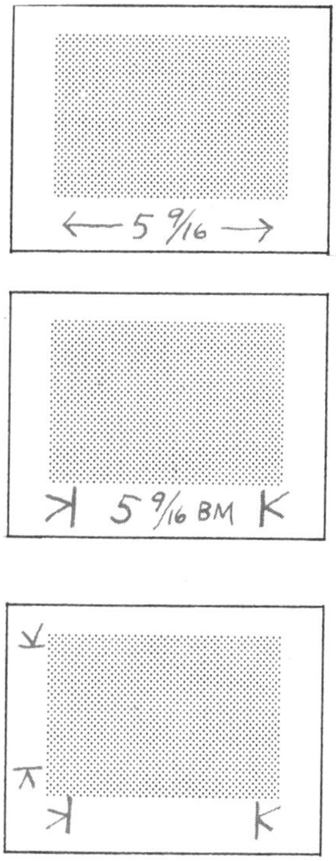

three ways of indicating size and cropping

■ **Cropmarks**—These should be clean lines in the margin of a photo indicating the places for cutting. An arrow should point to the mark in the direction of the portion of the picture being retained. If there's no margin, attach a slip of paper to the edge. Cropmarks within the image area or on the back of a picture are a source of trouble.

■ **Color**—Indicate the color wanted for each part of the copy. Supply a sizable (at least 1 x 2") swatch of flat, even color to be matched, or refer by number to a color system such as PMS (CH. 8).

■ **Silhouetting**—Unless the outlines are obvious, make a tissue overlay to indicate how the silhouetting is to be done.

■ **Indication of picture position**—On prints or photocopies used to indicate position of illustrations to be stripped in, write FPO (for position only).

All instructions, except register, trim, and fold marks—which must be black—should be marked in color so that they won't be confused with copy. On photographs, mark with a removable grease pencil or tempera paint. Ballpoint pens make permanent marks. Printshops sometimes provide adhesive tags or labels with spaces for entering instructions. These can be attached to art or photos to prevent disfiguring markings on copy.

Prepress operations

Some of the operations described here are sometimes performed by the designer or typesetter as part of page-makeup and sometimes by a service bureau or printshop as part of prepress. This flexibility is consistent with the integrated nature of contemporary bookmaking, in which the process is a continuous, almost seamless flow of functions with blurred demarcation of departments. The function is more significant than who performs it.

IMAGE DIGITIZING

For illustration images—photographs, drawings, paintings, diagrams, etc. (CH. 7)—to be included in the page-makeup, and all the bookmaking processes, they must be digitized. This can be done by putting the original art into a scanner (CHs. 3, 8), which converts its tones and lines into a pattern of dots and separates color copy into its component colors (CH. 8). Photographs can be digitized directly by using a digital camera, as is being done by many professional photographers. Art also can be created in digital form, using programs such as Adobe Illustrator or Adobe Photoshop. The major stock-art suppliers have digitized their collections, supplying image files on disks or the Internet.

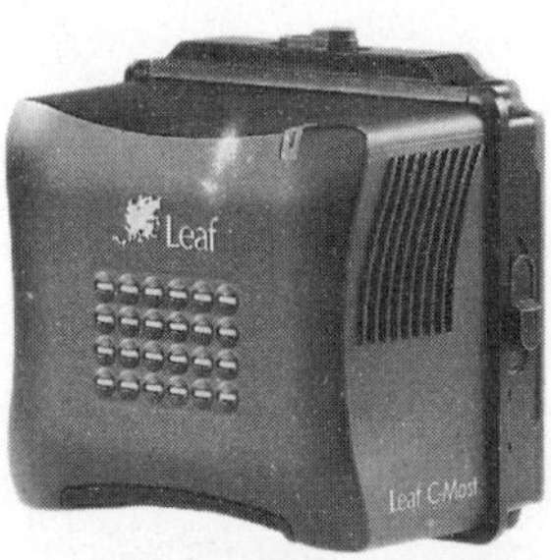

digital camera back used by professional photographers

Be sure that the file format and specifications of your digital illustrations are compatible with the requirements of your prepress house or printshop. Beware of digitized images coming from nonprofessional sources. In particular, authors who expect to supply such images often require technical guidance. A collection of incompatible digitized illustrations can spell disaster, especially if they come in at the last minute. Text is automatically digitized when keyboarded on a computer or word-processor.

IMAGE MANIPULATION

After an image is digitized, it may be necessary or desirable to alter it in some way—cropping, silhouetting, sizing, modifying color or the image itself (by deletion, distortion, or moving its parts), or adjusting the image to make it more suitable for the press, paper, and/or inks that will be used in the printing. These procedures are accomplished on a computer with appropriate software. The simpler jobs can be done on desktop computers, but such work usually calls for the skills of experts and professional equipment (CH. 8).

MERGING TEXT & GRAPHICS

When the text has been made up into pages, with the exact size and position of the illustrations indicated by either an FPO image such as a low-res scan or photocopy, or by an outline, the high-res scans to be used in printing are merged with the text by placing them in the positions indicated. This is done by computer using the page-makeup and illustration files with appropriate programs such as QuarkXPress or InDesign (CH. 20). The result is a single file containing the complete pages ready for *imposition* (see "Imposition" below).

Merging may be done also using traditional methods by converting the page-makeup (with the FPO images or outlines) and the high-res images into film separately and assembling them on a single sheet of plastic (or several sheets, if many colors are to be printed), which holds together all the elements of the pages. This operation may be performed by hand by *strippers* (yes, there are women who do this work and they get tired of the jokes very quickly) who tape the various pieces of film into position. The stripped-up film may be prepared as single pages to be imposed later at the printshop (see "Making imposed film" below). The assembled pieces of film are then usually exposed onto single sheets of film (*compositing*) to avoid problems with small pieces of film moving or coming off. These composited films are generally referred to as "one-piece-per-page-per-color".

IMPOSITION

Books are designed as facing pairs of pages—spreads (CHs. 24, 25). For printing, the pages are arranged on the sheet to be in the correct order when it's folded. This is the imposition (CH. 12). A specific number of pages will be printed at one time, the number being determined partly by press size and binding requirements (CH. 13). The imposition (which involves also placing the pages so that the margins will be correct) is determined by the binder according to the folding equipment to be used. When merging is completed, the pages are placed in position for printing, either electronically or by stripping, in the appropriate imposition.

A large page printed on a small press may have only 6 pages on each side of the sheet (i.e., a 6-page *form*); a small page on a large press may be printed with 64 on each side. Both printing and binding require a multiple of 4 pages, and preferably no fewer than 8 per sheet. Most books are printed in forms of 16, 32, or 64 pages, but some have 6-, 8-, 12-, 20-, 24-, or 36-page forms.

Properly, the term "form" refers to the pages on one side of a sheet, but don't be surprised if you hear both sides called a form. This is one of those errors that gets started through ignorance and then gets picked uo and perpetuated by those who should know better. There's a good chance you'll hear the term misused by your suppliers. Be careful. You may also hear a sheet called a signature—which is also wrong. A sheet becomes a signature after it's folded—and a sheet may be made into two or more signatures (CH. 13). The correct terminology, which has been used for centuries, is very simple and logical. Use it yourself and correct those who misuse it.

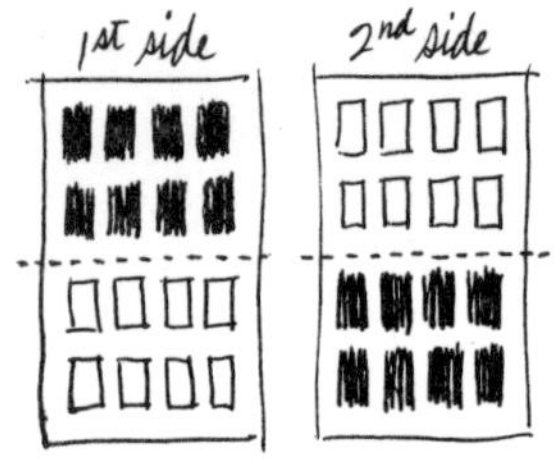

work-and-turn imposition

sheetwise imposition

The designer should have an imposition diagram (CH. 13) while making illustration page layouts (CH. 26). In cylinder press printing (CH. 12), one edge of the sheet is held to the cylinder by *grippers* requiring about ½" (1.27 cm) space, so there can be no bleeds on the gripper edge, unless a larger sheet is provided.

Sometimes two small forms are printed together on one side of a sheet and the plates kept on the press while the pile of sheets is turned over lengthwise and the other side is printed. Thus, form 1 backs up form 2 on one end of the sheet, and 2 backs 1 on the other, so that two complete units are printed with the number of impressions required for one, and with only one form to make ready (CH. 12) instead of two. This is called a *work-and-turn* imposition. A normal imposition, in which a single form is backed by another, is called *sheetwise*.

When small units, such as endpapers, are printed in large quantities, they may be imposed with 4, 8, 12, or more units in one form (*4-up*, *8-up*, *12-up*, etc.), provided the smaller number of impressions required justifies the increased plate cost and the larger press. Sometimes books are imposed for printing 2-up in order to facilitate 2-up binding. This is a very economical practice, provided that large quantities are involved; however, 2-up binding sometimes results in cross-grain binding, i.e., the spine edge folding is against the paper grain, which causes problems (CH. 11).

The imposition requirements of *webfed presses* are in principle the same as for *sheetfed* presses, differing only in detail. Since most webs have *in-line* folding—a machine is in-line when it's attached to the machine that performs the preceding work, so that no handling of the material between machine operations is required (CHs. 12, 13)—there's no problem of coordination between printshop and bindery.

MAKING IMPOSED FILM

In traditional prepress, all of the single-page films that will appear on an individual printing plate may be stripped up manually on a large plastic sheet called a *flat*. Each flat is then composited onto a single sheet of film as described in "Merging text & graphics" above. These single sheets are called *one-piece flats*. One-piece flats may be prepared also by large automated camera imposition systems such as *Opticopy*. In such systems, single-page repro or film is photographed and the image is projected into imposition on the one-piece film flat.

If single-page files have been prepared digitally, the page files are arranged in the proper imposition in the computer with a program such as *Impostrip* or *Print Express*. The resulting data are sent electronically to a Raster Image Processor (RIP), which creates a bitmap pattern for the imagesetter's laser to expose on the film. The imagesetter produces single pieces of film for each form, with separate films for each color. If the press form is too large for the imagesetter, the film may be output in parts (*assemblies*) and joined by stripping and compositing.

COMPUTER-TO-PLATE (CTP)

When the imposition has been created digitally, it's possible to do away with the need for film entirely. Instead of outputting film on an imagesetter, plates are output directly from the imposed files using a platesetter.

ThermoFlex CTP device

Proofs

Unless you order press proofs (see below), your last opportunity to see what will go to press—and to make corrections if necessary—is a proof of the final imposed film or plate-ready files. By this time there should be no corrections on the pages (although there are always errors that get by even the most careful readers), but this will be your first chance to check the position and sequence of pages (CH. 20).

BLUEPRINTS

The most direct method of obtaining a proof from film is to make a *blueprint*, or one of its variations. A blueprint is actually a contact print of the film. Blueprint paper is treated chemically so that when a strong light strikes it through the transparent (or translucent) part of the film, the blue color becomes fixed. The paper is then passed through a chemical bath and the blue is washed away where no light came through. This gives a negative image of the film. When a negative film is used, the blueprint is, of course, a positive.

Blueprints shouldn't be taken as a certain indication of the quality of a film. A spot or other unwanted mark on a blueprint should be brought to the printshop's attention, as the defect might be in the film, but such marks are usually in the print only. An illustration may appear too light or too dark on the print, but this doesn't mean that it's so in the film.

Blueprints shrink irregularly when washed, which makes them unreliable for checking register, and they can't be used for precise measurements, but they're adequate for most proofreading purposes. On *square* (rectangular) *halftones*, check size and squareness. On silhouettes, check silhouetting to be sure that it follows the edges of the subject exactly, and that the edges are soft and natural. Watch out for inside silhouetting (such as the space between arm and body) where the background should be dropped out.

The *whiteprint* is an improvement in that it makes a positive from a positive (the unexposed parts are fixed) and it's developed by ammonia fumes instead of a liquid wash, so it doesn't shrink or warp. The most-used brand is Ozalid, which has become the generic name for whiteprints. There are other brands with various trade names, such as Dylux, all generally called "*ozalids*".

There are several forms of *digital blues*, most using some variety of laser printing. To qualify as digital blues, they must be made from final bitmap files output by the same RIP that will be used to create the imposed plates or film. Bitmap proofs are an accurate indication of what will be printed, except for color. Final color proofs must be provided with the bitmap proofs to give the printshop something to match.

Blueprints are usually delivered folded into *signatures* and *gathered* in proper sequence (CH. 13). In this form they're called *book blues* and are obviously a great convenience for checking. Digital blues may or may not be folded as book blues and may include additional markings to show margins and trim.

BLACK & WHITE PROOFS The printing cost to make press proofs of black & white pages on the production press is very high. They can be printed on a smaller proof press, but then the plates used for proofing must be discarded. Not only is this expensive, but the value of the procedure is dubious, since the results with the final production plates may be quite different. However, where top halftone quality is required, production press proofs are worth the cost. Another, less expensive, way to check halftone quality is to request *T-prints* (high-resolution printouts on photographic paper) of the digital files before blues.

In halftone proofs, look for a good range of tones. There should be definition of form in the lights and shadows, and a nice spread of middle values between. Watch out for either a flat, lifeless proof of all middle tones or an excessively contrasty one with washed-out highlights, solid shadows, and few middle tones. Remember that the halftone reproduction can't (normally) be expected to be better than the original, and don't assume that it will be as good.

COLOR PROOFS

Service bureaus and color imaging shops can provide many kinds of proofs, ranging in cost from cheap color-copier prints to expensive dye sublimations. The kind you order should depend on how they're to be used. There are two reasons for ordering a color proof: to display it in a dummy or presentation and to check the accuracy of a color separation. For display purposes, a copier color print would be adequate for a rough dummy; the expense of a dye sublimation print might be justified for a trade show promotion display.

When the purpose of a proof is to evaluate color separations, there are a number of options: The one traditionally considered best is the *press proof* pulled on the actual stock being used for the book, but be warned that these are expensive and not necessarily accurate. Faults in platemaking, inking, or presswork can give misleading results. If multiple images are printed on the sheet, problems can occur unless the imposition is the same as in the actual press run. Also, be sure that the *color rotation* (the order in which the colors are printed) used for the proofs is the same as will be used in the actual printing. The proofs should be accompanied by *progressives* (*progs*) (proofs of the individual colors and combinations of two and three colors). These help in determining what corrections are needed.

Nonpress proofs can be broken down into two general categories: (1) *Pre-proofs*, which are often made on inkjet and laser printers and are not usually accurate for color but can be useful for preliminary assessments of quality. They're sometimes used for matching on press when cost is a primary concern and color accuracy isn't critical. (2) *Contract proofs* are significantly more expensive and are produced in carefully managed conditions with extremely accurate controls. Three popular kinds at this time are

Veris desktop digital proofer

Matchprints, Chromalins, and Kodak Approvals, but there are others that work just as well. New and better proofs are constantly being developed, so it's best to check with your printshop or service bureau before deciding which to use. Be careful when using proofs made directly from digital files rather than from films to be used for platemaking. Frequently, the RIP used to make the proofs is different from the RIP that will be used to make the film or plates. In that case, subtle (and sometimes not so subtle) variations from the proof can occur when the job is printed. Warn the printshop to carefully read the plates against the proofs to be sure that no errors are introduced.

With all the limitations of press proofs, it's important to understand that the final printed result is strongly affected by the interaction between inks and paper, which even the best contract proofs can't take into account.

If press proofs are ordered, the prepress shop usually furnishes one set of progressives, which must go to the printshop for matching. Additional progs and/or proofs may be ordered as needed; one complete proof goes in the file and another may be sent to an artist or photographer for checking. Normally, only one copy of contract proofs is provided. Additional copies are an extra cost.

PRINT-ON-DEMAND (POD) It's possible to go directly from paged files to a xerographic or inkjet "print-on-demand" press (which is essentially a large version of a desktop printer combined with a copier) (CHs. 12, 16), but be aware that when this tempting shortcut eliminates a stage of the proofing process, it can lead to disaster. For example, your page proofs may seem perfect, but blueprints of films might, and sometimes do, reveal an error created by the final processing of the files for printing. If you don't see blues or an equivalent proof, those faults will probably appear in all copies of your book. However, the unique capability of print-on-demand presses to produce a single copy of a book economically enables them to provide a final copy for proofreading before making copies for sale. Don't fail to take advantage of this final check.

Plates

Platemaking is covered in CH. 12. This may be treated as the final process in prepress or the first part of printing, depending on circumstances. It's usually a function of the printshop, which is really best, since the plates must be made to the specifications of the press. It's also worth considering film-making as part of the printshop function because it's frequently necessary to remake plates while the job is on press, and the printshop should have full control of the means to do this quickly and properly.

11. Paper

From the time paper was invented (probably in China in the 2nd century A.D.) until the introduction of papermaking machinery in the early 1800s, there were comparatively few varieties. The technique of making paper from rags by hand determined its character, and there was so little paper produced that it barely met the needs of bookmaking in the first four hundred years of printing. There was then neither the demand nor the supply of this precious commodity to support the fantastic variety of uses that exist today, from fish wrapping to computer printout. The book uses alone are too numerous to be covered here. Of these, many items (such as shipping cartons) are purchased as finished products; others—proof papers, the paper used to reinforce bindings, etc.—are purchased by printers and binders according to their needs. This chapter will deal with only the uses of paper in which the bookmaker exercises a choice.

A knowledge of paper is important for two reasons: (a) paper has properties that affect the success of a design and (b) a large part (usually more than 20%) of the production cost of a book is in its paper.

Printing paper is generally bought from paper brokers (merchants) rather than from mills (some very large publishers buy directly from mills). The broker takes a small profit in return for providing service—stocking and delivering the paper, giving advice, and supplying samples as needed. The paper merchants' advice should be sought, not only because it's being paid for but to take advantage of their special market knowledge and product familiarity.

The process

Each kind of paper is made a little differently, but the basic process of papermaking is common to all. Variations are more in the ingredients and finishing than in the method of manufacture. The essentials of this method are described below.

INGREDIENTS

The chief ingredient of most papers is wood. Some papers may contain cotton fiber (*rag paper*) and the best are made entirely of cotton (100% rag). The character of a paper depends to a large extent on the kind of wood used, but the major distinction is between the long-fibered woods used for strength (*kraft* paper) and the shorter-fibered woods used in quality printing papers. The cotton fibers used are taken from waste in fabric manufacture and discarded fabric articles such as mail bags, uniforms, work clothes, etc.

Water is another main ingredient, and a few other chemicals are added as required: dyes and pigments for coloring, rosin and alum for *sizing* to resist penetration of ink and water, titanium and clay *fillers* for opacity and surface improvement.

PREPARING THE STOCK

Stock is the term for fiber when it's processed. The wood pulp and/or the rags are chopped up, soaked, cooked, bleached, beaten, and mixed with the appropriate chemical ingredients until they're a slushy mass. In this process, the fibers are reduced to the proper size and shape for the kind of paper being made. Cheaper papers, called *groundwoods*, are made with finely ground, uncooked wood pulp. These fibers deteriorate relatively quickly. The better papers are made with wood chips cooked to remove impurities. A paper free of groundwood is called a *free sheet*, or *wood-free*. Acid-free papers became popular in the 1980s as libraries urged publishers to use more durable paper.

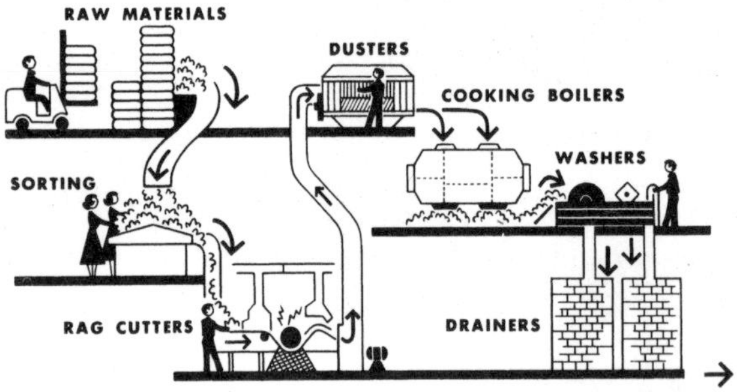

1. processing the raw materials

THE PAPER MACHINE

Around 1800, the Fourdrinier brothers in England invented a papermaking machine, whose principles are still in use. The stock (or *furnish*, as it's called when all ingredients have been added) is introduced at the *wet end*, where it's poured onto a wide—as much as 25' (7.6 m)—endless belt of fine-mesh wire screen. The *wire* carries it over a long—up to 300' (91.4 m)—distance, constantly vibrating so that the pulp fibers interweave and the water drains away. Despite the vibration, the fibers tend to lie in the direction of flow, and this is the way the *grain* of the paper runs. The top side of the paper is laid down by the *dandy roll* (a cylinder of finely

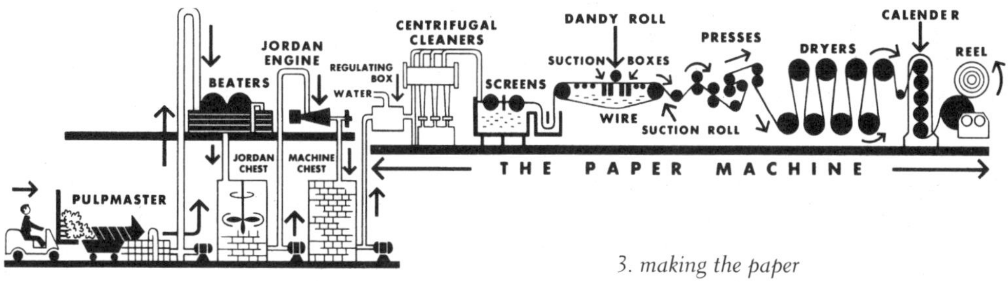

3. *making the paper*

2. *preparing the stock*

woven wire cloth that revolves over the wire and affects the surface characteristics). By the time the end of the wire is reached, the stock has dried enough to become a sheet of very soggy paper, still about 90% water. The sheet passes over a felt blanket onto a series of rollers that squeeze out a large part of the water, then it passes over heated drums that reduce the moisture content to the proper level. The paper then goes through a *calender*, where it's pressed between a series of steel rollers to give it the desired degree of smoothness. The side of the paper that ran over the wire (*wire side*) is usually a bit rougher than the other, or *felt side*. Considering that the furnish is 99% water and the paper that comes out has only 5% water, it's clear that the paper machine is basically a moisture-removing device.

FINISHING

Some finishes are applied during the manufacturing process, either by pressure from a dandy roll or by the texture of felt blankets on which the paper is pressed. Other finishes are applied by separate machines after the paper is made. Textures are made by pressing the paper between special rollers; coatings are generally flowed on. Sizing is applied to papers in two ways. It may be mixed with the stock (*internal sizing*), in which case it becomes part of the paper itself, or it may be applied to the surface. Surface sizing is applied by running the paper through a vat of sizing material. All plain lithographic papers are *surface-sized* to prevent penetration of water and to increase surface strength, as the tacky offset inks tend to pick the surface from the paper.

4. *finishing and packing*

Papers intended for use on webfed machines are, of course, shipped in rolls, but other paper is cut into sheets. Large orders are shipped on *skids* (wooden platforms) that hold about 3000 lbs. (1360 kg). Most printing paper is stocked in *cartons* of about 150 lbs. (68 kg), and some of the better papers are wrapped in *packages* of 250, 500, or more sheets, depending on their weight and size. Some papers are stocked with a *deckle* edge (the feathery, untrimmed edge) on two sides.

Kinds of paper

The varieties, finishes, qualities, weights, etc. of papers seem almost unlimited, but there are three main kinds manufactured, of which all others are variations.

ANTIQUE These are relatively soft-finish, "toothy" papers. In the antique category, *eggshell* is a fine-textured finish and *vellum* is even smoother. Some antique papers have a *laid* finish, which is a pattern of close parallel lines crossed by a series of widely spaced lines pressed into the paper by the dandy roll. Paper without *laid marks* is called *wove* finish.

MACHINE FINISH Most papers are made more compact by calendering on the paper machine. Some are given a little extra calendering to achieve a smoother surface, called *machine finish.* Papers intended for this finish have very short fibers and a heavy mineral content, which produce a rather shiny smoothness when calendered.

COATED Finishes of still greater smoothness require coating with fine clays that are flowed onto the surface of the paper with adhesives and then supercalendered with extremely smooth rollers. These are called *gloss coated.* Paper made with clays that finish dull and are less calendered are *dull coated,* or *matte coated.* Some papers are coated on one side only, others on both sides. A group called *film* or *wash coated* are lightly coated papers—quite smooth and with better ink holdout than uncoated sheets, but less expensive than fully coated.

USE CLASSIFICATIONS Since the same kind of paper may be used for different purposes—for example, coated paper may be used for the illustrations in a book or the cover of a paperback—the sale and distribution of paper is organized according to use rather than kind, although with some exceptions. Thus, the papers commonly used for the pages of books are classified as book papers. The more expensive book papers are often made in colors (for use in promotion pieces, pamphlets, etc.) and are designated *text papers.* A category of thicker papers of all kinds and finishes called *cover paper* is used for pamphlet and paperback covers. Some papers are made with the characteristics required for *endpapers.* These and others are sometimes stocked in rolls and are designated *binding papers.*

Any of these categories can be and are used for purposes other than the one named, but this is how they're generally listed in catalogs and price lists, and this is the basis for some of the standards used in paper distribution.

Weight, bulk, size, & grain

WEIGHT

The term "weight" is sometimes used to refer to paper thickness, but this is misleading because paper is sold (mostly) by its actual weight in pounds or grams, and this doesn't always correspond to its thickness. Obviously, a coated paper will be much thinner than an antique eggshell weighing the same amount. Pick up a book of coated paper and notice how heavy it feels compared to a book of the same thickness with antique stock.

The weight of paper is determined and specified in the United States by a *basis weight* system that's fairly complicated. (The rest of the world uses a simpler metric system.) You can leave the matter in the hands of the paper merchant, but if you buy paper you should understand the weight system so that you can make your own calculations.

When a paper is called "60 lb." (60# basis or, properly, *substance* 60), it means that 500 sheets (a ream) of it in a certain size (*basic size*) weigh 60 lbs. (basis weight). The basic size of book papers is 25 x 38" (63.5 x 96.5 cm), but for cover papers it's 20 x 26" (50.8 x 66 cm). Since paper isn't always sold in its basic size, it's sometimes necessary to know the *actual* weight of the paper being used or shipped. The actual weight (*finished weight*) per ream for a particular sheet size can be calculated using the formula:

finished weight per ream = basis weight × actual sheet area (sq. in.) ÷ basic size area

Example: 60 lb. basis weight × 1900 sq. in. (38 x 50") = 114,000 ÷ 950 sq. in. (25 x 38") = 120 lbs. finished weight

The billing and shipment of book paper may refer to reams or sheets, but prices are based on weight, usually using 1000 sheets as the unit. The weight of 1000 sheets is referred to as *M weight.* To find this, use the above formula and multiply the ream weight by 2, or calculate using this formula:

M weight = basis weight × actual sheet area ÷ half of basic size area.

Example: 60 lb. basis weight × 1900 sq. in. (38 x 50") = 114,000 ÷ 475 = 240 lb. (240 M)

With these formulas, one can always find basis or ream weight if M weight is known, and vice versa.

Paper prices are quoted in dollars-per-pound or dollars-per-hundredweight (abbreviated as cwt.: 1 cwt. = 100 lbs.). Deliveries of paper (and other materials used in book manufacturing) are usually subject to customary allowances for variation from the quantity ordered, due to the imprecision of high-speed machine operations. These allowances may be as much as 10%. Paper orders are subject also to minimum quantities and to fixed weight increments dependent upon standard roll sizes or skid (shipping pallet) weights. Paper is billed based on the actual weight delivered.

The weight of a particular paper may be expressed in terms of its basis weight—44 x 66" basis 50—or, much less frequently, its M weight—44 x 66", 306M—or both—44 x 66", 306M, basis 50. (The term "basi<u>s</u>" is used generally for weight and "basi<u>c</u>" is used with size, but sometimes the words are erroneously interchanged.) When paper is shipped in rolls, reference is made usually to the basis weight, the roll width, the total weight, and sometimes the length in feet.

The weight of European papers measured in *gsm* (*grams-per-square-meter*) relates to a basic size—a square meter—different from that used in the United States, so don't try to convert pounds mathematically to grams for basis weight. For example, the Italian equivalent of 60 lb. text paper (25 x 38" basis 60) is (approximately) 89 gsm, but the mathematical conversion of 60 lbs. to grams is 27,220. The gsm weight refers to the weight of one square meter of paper. To get an accurate gsm equivalent, multiply a U.S. book paper basis weight by 1.48. Conversely, divide gsm by 1.48 to get basis weight (see table of equivalents in Appendix).

BULK The proper term for thickness in paper is *caliper*, but the term used in book publishing is "*bulk*", although the word has come to suggest an artificial, blown-up character. Paper is improved in printing qualities when compressed to be harder and smoother, but many book papers are made in the least compressed state possible to satisfy publishers' demand for fatter books (CH. 23).

Paper bulk is usually expressed in *ppi* (*pages-per-inch*). Caliper is expressed in *points* (thousandths of an inch) or in decimal inches. Groundwood papers and cover papers are most often specified in points or decimal inches. Calculate conversion between decimal inches and ppi using the following formulas:

bulk (ppi) = 2 ÷ caliper (decimal inches)
caliper (decimal inches) = 2 ÷ bulk (ppi)

Bulk depends on fibers as well as the manufacturing process; the more fiber there is, the thicker the paper. "More fiber" may mean bulkier or additional fibers. The latter results in heavier paper (100 lb. paper has about twice as much fiber as 50 lb. of the same finish) while bulky fiber may add thickness without weight. This is because the fillers are heavier for their mass than the fibers.

Paper manufacturers and distributors print bulk tables showing the number of pages per inch for each weight and finish in almost all grades of paper. Obviously, the more calendered sheets will have less bulk than others of the same weight, but there's also considerable variation among different makes of paper in each category. The table shows the approximate range in the most common grades and weights.

GRADE	50 lb.	55 lb.	60 lb.	65 lb.	70 lb.	75 lb.	80 lb.
Antique	380–400	350–370	320–340	290–310	270–290	250–270	220–250
Eggshell	430–450	390–410	350–380	330–350	300–320	280–300	260–280
Vellum	440–480	410–450	370–420	350–400	330–370	310–350	290–320
Machine finish	490–560	440–510	410–470	380–440	355–400	330–370	300–350
Matte coated	620–700	570–630	520–560	480–520	440–470	400–430	370–390
Coated	800–850	730–790	640–740	590–680	530–620	490–580	440–530

bulk table

SIZE

The paper merchant keeps hundreds of items in stock—different brands, kinds, qualities, finishes, colors, weights, and sizes. The printshop has presses of various sizes, but comparatively few. Since bookmakers generally want to utilize the full size of the presses, they need mainly the paper sizes that fit the presses available, and, obviously, the paper merchant wants to reduce the number of items carried. Consequently, paper is made in a few standard sizes and any others must be made to order (*making-order*). Each paper mill has its own minimum quantity requirements for making special sizes in each grade of paper, but the average for book papers is 5000 lbs., and for text and cover papers 2000 lbs. These minimums may sometimes be cut in half, but this usually requires payment of a penalty.

In book papers, the common stock sheet sizes and the page size (trim-size) to which they fold are:

35 x 45" (88.9 x 114.3 cm)—5½ x 8½" (14 x 21.6 cm)
37 x 49" (94 x 124.5 cm)—6 x 9" (15.2 x 22.9 cm)
38 x 50" (96.5 x 127 cm)—6⅛ x 9¼" (15.6 x 23.5 cm)
41 x 61" (104.1 x 154.9 cm)—5 x 7⅜" (12.7 x 18.7 cm)
44 x 66" (111.8 x 167.6 cm)—5⅜ x 8" (13.7 x 20.3 cm)
45 x 68" (114.3 x 172.7 cm)—5½ x 8¼" (14 x 21 cm)
46 x 69" (116.8 x 175.3 cm)—5⅝ x 8⅜" (14.3 x 21.3 cm)
50 x 76" (127 x 193 cm)—6⅛ x 9¼" (15.6 x 23.5 cm)

The first two sheet sizes listed would take 32-page forms, the others, 64s (CH. 12). The underlined number in each size indicates that the grain runs in that dimension. If a book is perfect-bound (CH. 13), the folds are trimmed off, reducing the trim width by 1/8 to 3/16". For a book with many bleeds (CH. 10), the trim size must be reduced slightly (about 1/32") to allow for 1/8" of unprinted paper on all edges of the sheet, so that bleeds can't print off the end of the sheet onto the cylinder.

Text and cover papers are stocked in generally smaller sizes:

13 x 20" (33 x 50.8 cm)
20 x 26" (50.8 x 66 cm)
23 x 35" (58.4 x 88.9 cm)
25 x 38" (63.5 x 96.5 cm)
26 x 40" (66. x 101.6 cm)

and sometimes in:

35 x 45" (88.9 x 114.3 cm)
38 x 50" (96.5 x 127 cm)

Paper in rolls may be stocked in the following widths:

22½" (57.2 cm)
23¼" (59 cm)
23½" (59.7 cm)
24½" (62.2 cm)
25" (63.5 cm)
33" (83.8 cm)
34" (86.4 cm)
44" (111.8 cm)
45" (114.3 cm)
50" (127 cm)

Most xerographic (print-on-demand) presses (CHs. 10, 12, 16) print one page at a time, either singly or 2-up on sheets. While they incorporate trimmers, their economy is increased if they use paper exactly the trim-size of the book. To accommodate this need, paper mills and merchants stock a few standard sheet sizes, such as 6 x 9" and 8½ x 11", and double these for 2-up printing. Some machines are web fed and use roll widths specially stocked for them.

GRAIN When paper is folded against the grain, the fibers break, the surface cracks, the fold is ragged, and the pages won't lie properly. These effects are more pronounced in some papers than others, but it's always desirable to fold with the grain. For this reason it's important to know how the sheet is to be folded when ordering paper.

Book papers are frequently stocked with a choice of grain directions, while the more expensive text papers are usually available only one way. For making-orders, it's usually possible to get the grain in either direction. In rolls, the grain always runs with the length of the paper—around, not across the width, of the roll.

12. Plates & printing

Successful bookmaking requires a knowledge of both the principles of printing and the equipment. Either a design must be matched to the press available or a press must be found that's suited to the design. Just an eighth of an inch added to a book's page size could add a lot to the cost of printing—planning a book for one press instead of another might save 20% or more in printing, paper, and binding cost. A printshop isn't likely to let you put a job on an unsuitable press, but it's best to know enough about printing yourself to ensure against a costly mistake.

There are four principal printing techniques:

- **Relief printing (letterpress)**—The printing parts are raised above the nonprinting parts and are inked. The ink is transferred to the paper by pressure.
- **Planographic printing (lithography)**—The printing parts are virtually level with the rest of the plate, but they're treated to accept a greasy ink. The nonprinting parts accept water and repel ink. The ink is transferred to the paper by contact.
- **Intaglio printing (gravure)**—The printing parts are etched into the plate and are lower than the surface. They are filled with ink, which is transferred to the paper by pressure and suction.
- **Xerographic printing**—Electrostatically charged toner powder (ink) is transferred to oppositely charged paper (CHs. 10, 16).

Another technique is of interest. Although it's not used in printing the text of books, it's used in some bookmaking operations:

Kinds of printing

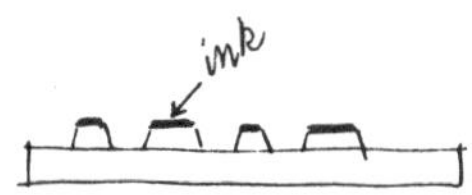

relief

planographic

intaglio

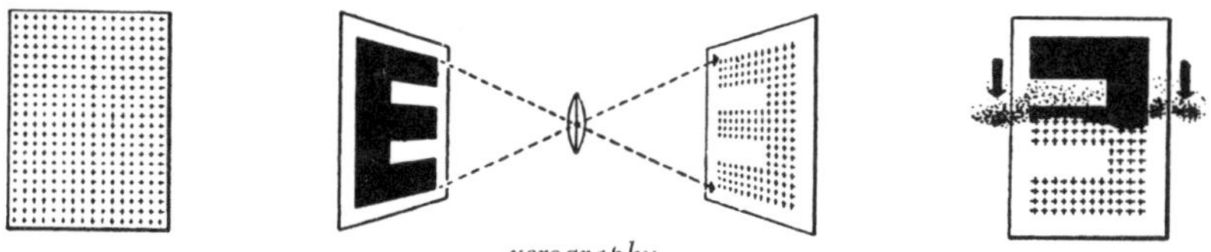

xerography

1. The paper is given a positive charge. 2. The image is projected onto the paper. Where there is no image, light strikes the paper and removes positive charge. 3. Negatively charged powdered ink is applied to the paper and sticks only where there is positive charge.

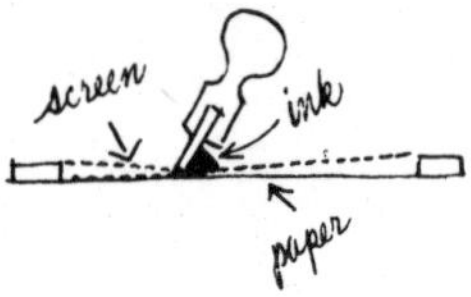

silkscreen

- **Screen printing (silk screen)**—A fine-mesh screen is stretched taut and the nonprinting areas are blocked out. The screen is placed over the paper and ink is squeezed through the open parts.

Gravure isn't used now except for special applications outside of commercial book printing. Letterpress is still used for printing mass-market paperbacks with *photopolymer plates*. Xerographic printing is practical for very short runs (print-on-demand) and has many uses. Otherwise, all commercial book printing today is done by *offset lithography* (usually referred to as "offset"), a modified form of lithography. In offset printing, the plate transfers its ink not to the paper but to a rubber-covered cylinder which in turn "offsets" the ink to the paper.

Offset lithography

While lithography has been used in some form since 1798 when it was invented by Alois Senefelder in Bavaria, its application to mass production is comparatively recent. The offset technique was developed in the early part of the 20th century, but it was not until the 1920s that any considerable commercial printing was done by this method, and it was not until after World War II that it became a major book-printing industry.

The method would have had more use in its early days had it been able to deliver a better result, but the technology was not advanced enough to avoid the gray, flat quality that marked offset lithography as a "cheap" process. Good lithography depends on achieving a perfect balance of water and ink, and it was not until the 1950s that this technology was perfected to the point where it became possible to produce the best quality of printing—in both black & white and color—by offset lithography.

THE PROCESS

Lithography means "stone-writing" in Greek, and it was originally a method of printing by: (1) processing the surface of a flat, smooth stone into grease-receptive (printing) and water-receptive (nonprinting) areas, (2) wetting the stone with water (*dampening*) so that the nonprinting areas would repel a greasy ink which (3) was spread over it, and (4) pressing paper to the stone to transfer the ink from the printing areas.

Stones were used until the end of the 19th century. By that time, lithography was a popular medium for artists because it was much easier than engraving in wood or metal and permitted a wider range of graphic techniques and effects. Many lithographed posters and magazine illustrations were produced by leading artists. The stone is still used by artists (on flat-bed presses), but for commercial printing it has been replaced by metal sheets treated to imitate the stone grain.

Another important change in the technique of lithographic printing is the use of the rotary offset method. Several advantages are gained by printing first on a rubber blanket instead of directly on paper: (a) the plates last longer, (b) less water comes in contact with the paper, (c) the resilient rubber cylinder permits printing finer copy on rougher paper, and (d) speed is increased.

For books of text only, there's relatively little makeready needed in offset lithography. Quality of plate and correct adjustment of inking and dampening are the main factors in the result. In process-color printing however, the makeready time on a large press can take several hours, as it includes adjustment for perfect register and matching color.

Two related factors that affect quality are screen size and paper. Because of the light impression (*kiss impression*) of the rubber blanket, 133- and 150-line screens can be printed well on comparatively rough-surfaced papers; on very smooth papers, 300-line screens can be used. A finer screen will produce better results provided that the paper and all other factors are right.

Paper characteristics tend to affect lithographic printing quality very strongly. Because of the use of water in the process, excess moisture may enter the paper and gray the ink or cause distortion resulting in register problems. Another factor is the tendency toward *picking* (pulling fibers or pieces of coating from the paper surface), due to the tacky inks used.

PLATES

Unless printing is done by xerography (CHs. 10, 16) directly from digital files, it involves plates. For offset lithography they're made photomechanically. A film negative or positive is made by either: (a) photographing mechanicals or (b) outputting from electronic files. The film is contacted against a photosensitized metal plate

An offset plate room. In foreground: light-table and tools for stripping film. At far corner: film being exposed onto plate.

and exposed to light. The plate is then treated with chemicals that affect the exposed parts differently from the rest. Depending on whether the film is positive or negative, the exposed parts are printing or nonprinting.

In computer-to-plate systems, the plates are exposed directly on a platesetter; no film is required.

There are many kinds of lithographic plates. However, these divide roughly into three groups: (a) *surface plates*, (b) *deep-etch plates*, and (c) *multimetal plates*.

▪ **Surface plates**—A metal sheet is coated with a light-sensitive, ink-receptive substance. When this is exposed to light through a negative film, the coating hardens in the (printing) areas where the light hits it and remains soft in the other (nonprinting) parts. The soft parts are then washed out and a coating of water-receptive material is applied. This adheres only to the bare metal, so the plate is divided into ink-receptive (printing) parts and water-receptive (nonprinting) parts. Surface plates differ in materials and, to some extent, processes. The main varieties are *albumen*, *presensitized*, and *wipe-on*.

▪ **Deep-etch plates**—While surface plates leave the printing areas on the surface (thus subject to wear), deep-etch plates are made in reverse with positive film, leaving the printing areas slightly *below* the nonprinting areas (somewhat like an intaglio plate). These plates are used for longer runs and for especially fine work in process-color printing. They cost more than surface plates.

▪ **Multimetal plates**—For even longer runs and better quality, there are bimetal plates. These have a light-sensitive protective coating on an ink-receptive metal base. After exposure, development removes the coating from the nonprinting parts, which then receive a plating of water-receptive metal in an electrolytic bath. Another bath washes away the remaining coating, exposing the ink-receptive base metal in the printing areas. On some plates, the metals are reversed, i.e., the plating is ink-receptive while the base is water-receptive. Bimetal plates are rarely used for runs under 100,000 because of their high cost. On trimetal plates, the base metal is given a plating also. Such plates appear to be virtually indestructible.

PRESSES

Offset lithography presses are basically the same, whether large or small. Except for the difference between webfed and sheetfed, the main distinction between the smallest and the largest sheetfed press is the control mechanism.

An offset lithography press has five kinds of cylinders or rollers:

(a) *the plate cylinder* around which the plate is wrapped;
(b) *the blanket cylinder* around which the rubber blanket is attached;
(c) *the impression cylinder*, which carries the paper;

(d) *ink rollers*; and

(e) *water rollers*.

As the plate revolves, it comes in contact first with the water rollers, then the ink rollers, then the blanket cylinder. The impression cylinder presses the paper against the blanket from which the inked image is offset (printed). There are several water and ink rollers for better distribution and control. Most modern presses

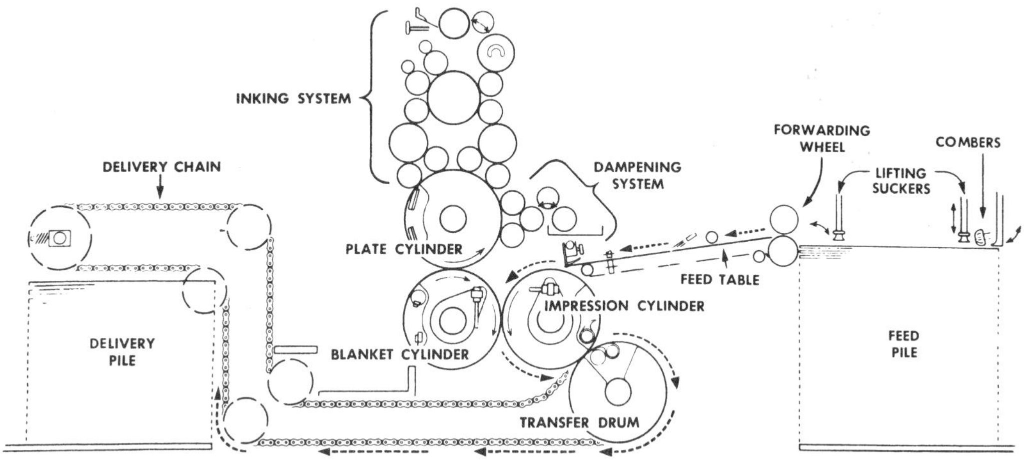

diagram of a one-color offset press

have computer-monitored devices to control register and inking and more water and ink rollers. Multicolor presses have the same set of cylinders and rollers as single-color presses, but have as many sets as the number of colors they can print (either 2, 4, 5, 6, or more). There are also *perfector presses*, both sheetfed and webfed, that print both sides of the sheet in one pass.

Sheetfed presses usually run at 7500 to 9000 impressions per hour. The larger web presses can run high-quality process-color work at 16,000 to 40,000 impressions per hour.

Speed is a major consideration in choosing presses, but size is paramount. The size of a press refers to the maximum size sheet or roll it can take. For large orders, paper can be made in special sizes, but in most cases it's best to use one of the standard sizes carried in stock (CH. 11). When a stock size of paper is used, there will probably be a press to fit it, and this is almost certainly the press to use. A smaller press would require cutting (and wasting some of) the paper and printing a smaller form—which means more forms and more impressions. A larger press may mean paying a higher rate than necessary because the hourly cost of running a press generally increases with its size.

a two-color sheetfed offset press

The cost of presswork is the charge for use of a press for a period of time, so the running speed isn't as significant as the amount of work the press can perform per hour. Press A may not run any faster than Press B, but it may be printing four colors, or both sides of the sheet in one color, while B is printing only one color on one side, or it may deliver folded sheets while B delivers them flat. However, it doesn't necessarily follow that Press A is the one to use, because the more a press can do, the higher the cost of using it. Not only is it a more expensive piece of equipment, but being more complex it may require more makeready time and more help to run.

The speed at which a press is run will depend to some extent on the kind or quality of work it's performing. Halftones on coated paper or very detailed illustrations on any paper will be run more slowly than type on regular book stock. In general, the higher the quality desired, the slower the press is run. Also, quality printing requires frequent examination of printed sheets so that adjustments, plate cleaning, etc. can be done before problems go too far.

Small work, such as jackets, endpapers, illustrations, etc., is generally printed on 17½ x 22½" (44.5 x 57.2 cm), 19 x 25" (48.3 x 63.5 cm), or 20 x 28" (50.8 x 71 cm) presses. Unless the run is short, say under 10,000, a duplicate set of films will probably be made and the work printed 2-up. For example, the sizes mentioned will accommodate two jackets for average-sized books. If the run is long, say 25,000, three or four sets of films may be made, or the image of the form will be repeated on the plate, and the job run on a 22½ x 35" (57.2 x 88.9 cm) or 25 x 38" (63.5 x 96.5 cm) or larger sheet.

sheetfed press for small work

a four-color webfed offset press with control console in foreground

The text of a normal-size tradebook is most likely to be imposed in 32- or 64-page forms and be printed on a narrow-web press or, for short runs, on a sheetfed press ranging from 38 x 50" (96.5 x 127 cm) to 50 x 76" (127 x 193 cm). The commonly used sizes are discussed in CHs. 11, 23. For economical printing of simple black & white books, sheetfed perfector presses may be the best choice.

Substantial savings are possible with high-speed, webfed rotary presses, provided the job is suited to the equipment. Most book printing consists of runs too short to effectively utilize wide-web presses, some of which can turn out 30,000 impressions of a 64-page form in one hour. A first printing of 5000 copies (very common for tradebooks) would thus be completed in ten minutes of running time—with the time needed to make the press ready fifteen times as long. Paper spoilage on web presses tends to be higher than on sheetfed, although computer controls hold web spoilage to as little as 7 to 10%. As a result, runs as short as 1500 are feasible if the number of forms is large enough to effectively utilize the roll of paper. In many cases, however, such short runs are uneconomical, especially for multicolor books. Even when the first printing is large enough to economically use a wide-web press, consider the possibility that a much smaller reprint may be needed later and it may be necessary to reimpose the film to run it on a sheetfed machine.

Narrow-webs or *mini-webs* using narrow-width rolls provide an answer to the problem of printing fairly short-run books by web offset and have to a considerable extent displaced sheetfed perfectors for this purpose. These rolls have widths of 22½ to 33" (57.2 cm to 83.8 cm) as compared with widths of up to about 61" (55 cm) on the wide-web presses.

Webfed rotary presses usually have folders and slitters built in. This means that a wide-web can print 64-page forms on both sides and deliver four completely folded 32-page signatures ready for the next bindery operation (CH. 13). One limitation to keep in mind is the thickness (caliper or bulk) of the paper. Most web presses have trouble handling paper that has a thickness of more than 6 pts.—.006" (.15 mm)—or 330 ppi (CH. 11).

Another aspect of web printing that's crucial is the *cutoff* (the length of sheets cut from the roll), which is determined by the circumference of the impression cylinder, and in turn determines the final trim-size. One dimension of the page size must be divisible into the cutoff size or there'll be wasted paper. For example, with an 8½ x 11" page, the 11"—which is 11¼" including trim—will fit two times into a 23" cutoff. It wouldn't fit into a 40" cutoff except by wasting about 6"—some 15%—of the paper. When choosing a trim-size for a web, remember that the grain of the paper runs the length of the web, i.e., around, not across the roll (CH. 11).

On all presses, there's a maximum printing area, which is somewhat smaller than the maximum sheet size. This is due to the space required for guides, grippers, and other mechanical features of the machine.

COLOR PRINTING

■ **Simple color**—In simple (nonprocess) color printing, the only extra cost is the ink *washup*. The previous color must be completely washed out of the press before the new color is used. On short runs, there may be a small charge if a color is specially mixed. Otherwise, the presswork is about the same as printing black. Thus, a two-color job costs about twice as much as one color, three colors cost three times as much as one, etc., provided, of course, that the printing problems in each color are otherwise equal, and each color is run separately. However, most multicolor work is run on two-color, four-color, or five-color presses and the cost per color is much less than if each color is run separately.

On any press run, more care is required when halftones or very fine line copy are involved, but printing with two or more colors brings in the problem of *register* (alignment of colors to each other). The register may be very simple or extremely fine. Assuming that the copy and plates were properly aligned, there are still several obstacles to perfect register. Poor paper feeding, faulty plate mounting, and irregular trimming of paper are causes of trouble, but the most difficult problem is distortion of the sheets due to moisture. This may result from excess water in lithographic printing or from a change in general humidity between impressions. Because the paper is likely to expand or shrink more in one direction than the other, a serious problem in register may occur, especially in large sheets. Preventive measures include sizing the paper to resist moisture (CH. 11) and storeroom and pressroom air conditioning, but these are sometimes not enough. Moisture causes the least amount of trouble when all colors are printed in one run through a multicolor press. Many web presses have electronic controls that automatically adjust register every few seconds so that sheets can be brought up to acceptable printing quality very quickly. (If excellent results are wanted, a trained eye is necessary from this point on.) Of course, register problems are reduced when the computer-to-plate (CTP) system eliminates the film step and plates are made directly from final files (CH. 10).

A method by which colors may be used at less than the usual cost is *split fountain*. On cylinder and rotary presses, ink is picked up by the roller from a trough called a *fountain*. The fountain can be divided into sections of any width and a different color ink put in each section. The roller is then inked with the different colors along its length and transfers the colored inks to the corresponding parts of the plates or type. Thus, if the fountain were divided into three parts, with black on the left, red in the middle, and blue on the right, everything on the left side of the sheet would be printed black, everything in the middle red, and the right blue. If a printing job is designed to take advantage of this arrangement, a quite spectacular multicolor effect may be obtained at very little more than the cost of one color. Theoretically, there's no limit to the number of colors possible with split fountain, but there are some practical limitations. Unless the ink roller is actually cut into sections so that the colors can't meet, there's bound to be some mixing of color where the inks come together. The vibrating of the ink rollers normally spreads the mixed area to about 2½" (6.4 cm), although it's possible to reduce the vibration. The mixing of color can be avoided entirely if there's no printing in the border areas. This may cause the designer some difficulty, but the cost of cutting a roller is quite high, unless a long run is involved.

■ **Process color**—In process-color printing, to achieve the truest color it's essential to have nearly perfect register, because the dot pattern of each color must be related exactly to the others (CH. 8). Also, the proper inks must be chosen and the inking well done. Assuming that the causes of misregister discussed above are avoided, the main problem is color correction of the films (CHs. 8, 10). If the separation films are right, and the inks are held to a narrow tolerance of *density* (black: 155 to 160, cyan: 135 to 140, magenta: 130 to 135, yellow: 100 to 105), there should be little trouble getting accurate color on press, particularly if the color plates are built from electronic files without a negative stage so that register problems are virtually eliminated. It's possible to compensate for some inadequacies in the films or plates by controlling the amount of ink in the makeready, by using modified inks, by using specially selected paper, or by changing the color sequence, but the effectiveness of such measures is limited and they usually can't fully overcome the handicap of poor films or plates. Even with electronic separation, it's well worth insisting on seeing proofs, as other problems can and do occur.

If the bookmaker wants to have control of the printing result, there's no good alternative to going to the pressroom and checking printed sheets against okayed proofs (preferably press proofs with progressives for high-quality color printing) as the job is made ready (it's rarely feasible to let a press stand idle while sheets are sent out for approval). A weak or too strong color in one part of the sheet can be corrected by increasing or decreasing the amount of ink flowing into the fountain at that point, but then there may be another illustration in the same row of pages that needs the opposite treatment. On large presses there may be six or eight illustrations in each row, so it's often necessary to compromise, or to improve one subject at the expense of another. If possible, have the originals also at the press, to help in making good decisions when compromises are necessary.

Compromise may be necessary in register also. If one subject on the form is slightly out of register, it can usually be corrected by an adjustment of the plate positions on the press. However, this will introduce a certain amount of misregister in other subjects. If this isn't acceptable, it may be necessary to take the plates off, then re-register the films, and make new plates. Before such a drastic measure is taken, it should be determined whether the problem is paper distortion. If so, compromise will be necessary unless other paper can be obtained and time is available to wait for the change.

Quality process-color printing is rarely easy to achieve.

Xerographic printing

As noted in CH. 10, a xerographic (print-on-demand) press is essentially a superior version of the desktop laser printer in which the printing process is the one used in most office copying machines. The advantage of a xerographic press—and it's a considerable one—is that it requires almost no set-up time, no makeready, no film, and no plates, so it can produce very short runs, even single copies, of paperback books very quickly and at much lower cost than is possible on a conventional press.

Like your desktop printer, the xerographic press gets its data from the digital files of a computer, either directly or from a disk. The file sent to it contains the final page-makeup with illustrations included (CH. 10). A built-in computer programs the machine with the data from the file and any special instructions for the printing or binding of the book. The data are transmitted electronically to a laser which projects the page image onto an electrostatically charged plastic drum. Where the light touches

Xerox DocuTech POD machine

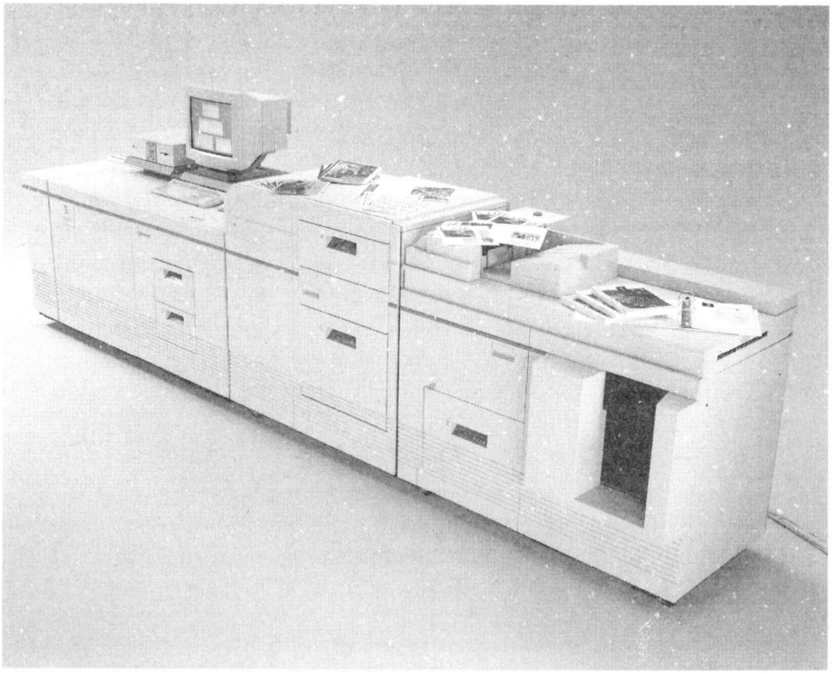

the drum, the charge is cancelled. Oppositely charged *toner* powder (ink) is attracted to the charged parts of the drum. The paper is given a charge opposite to that of the toner, and when it's passed close to the drum, it attracts the toner, which transfers the image. The toner is fixed to the paper by heat and pressure. Resolution is generally 1200 dpi. The pages are printed on both sides as single sheets up to 115 pages per minute. It's possible to print 2-up, and sometimes 4-up, on larger sheets.

A scanner can be hooked up to a xerographic press to transmit the data on printed copy digitally to the printer. This enables, for example, the printing of books without retypesetting.

In line with the press is a *perfect-binding* (CH. 13) machine, which has folding and cutting functions, glues the back edge of the assembled pages of a complete book (*book block*), then adds a paper cover—which may be printed in color by a separate but similar press—and trims the pages and cover together to make a finished paperback book. Hardbound copies can be produced by forwarding the book block with endpapers to a bindery that makes a cover, *cases-in* (CH. 13), and, if required, applies a jacket.

With a print-on-demand (POD) machine, a single copy of a book with 300 black & white pages and a four-color paper cover can be printed and bound in about four minutes. This is a dramatic performance, and improvements are certain, but the technology isn't suited to large-scale production. Runs of 20 to 500 copies are the most frequent, and the maximum is about 1500 before it begins to be cheaper to print by offset.

Xerographic printing is a short-run system that admirably serves several publishing needs. It makes feasible publishing books for very small audiences, keeping worthy titles in print when it no longer pays to reprint by offset, producing advance copies of bound books for review or comment, and instantly producing copies "on demand" for individual bookstore customers—which means that books may be produced in response to orders rather than printing and warehousing large numbers of copies, some of which won't be sold or will be returned. Xerographic printing makes possible also sales-testing titles in small quantities before committing to a large printing and promotion expense, thus taking some of the risk out of publishing and potentially saving enough cost to lower book prices (CH. 16).

While some xerographic presses do process-color printing, the plant cost of color prepress can't be avoided, and this, plus slower running speed, makes short runs of color-illustrated books relatively expensive. The primary use of these machines is to print paperback covers.

Even with its several advantages, xerographic printing as presently designed is likely to complement rather than supplant offset printing for trade editions in the foreseeable future.

Two leading xerographic presses are Infoprint 4000 (IBM) and DocuTech (Xerox). These operate on the same general principles but Infoprint prints on a roll of paper rather than sheets. The paper is cut into sheets in the machine. Some other xerographic presses are Océ and BookMachine. Paper suppliers stock sheets and rolls in sizes specifically for such presses (CH. 11).

For xerographic printing, the bookmaking processes are unchanged through page-makeup.

Silk screen

Silk screen was originally a process for producing fairly simple designs in small quantities. It then developed into a handcraft used to make complex posters and prints (called *serigraphs*) in many colors, usually in runs of no more than a few hundred. With the introduction of machinery capable of relatively high-speed production, silk screen became feasible for long-run commercial work.

Silk screen is much more expensive than the other methods of printing, but it has certain unique advantages which make it worth the price when its special qualities are needed. Two features are outstanding: (a) any kind of surface—including rough cloth—can be printed, and (b) the ink may be completely opaque "paint" which can be built up to a thickness comparable to embossing. These attributes are obviously of interest in relation to covers, and will be discussed further in CH. 29, but there's also use for them in printing endpapers, jackets, and illustrations.

THE PROCESS

The nonprinting parts of the screen may be blocked out by application of a liquid filler, but the most common method is to use a sheet mask or *stencil.* Simple masks can be cut by hand, but for most work, film is used and the image is cut photomechanically. The mask is applied to a very fine screen (it may be silk or metal mesh) which is stretched tightly on a frame. This is then mounted horizontally on a press and the paper is fed underneath, where it receives ink squeezed through the screen by a *squeegee* (a rubber-edged bar). A separate mask is made for each color, although it's possible to print more than one color at a time if the design is properly prepared. Inks may be bright metallics or rich, flat finishes. They may be applied very thin or thick enough to cast a distinct shadow. The process is well suited to printing areas of flat color, but it's possible to reproduce small type, and even halftones, provided conditions are suitable.

13. Binding

Binding is a complex process. Hardcover binding involves about eighteen different operations and uses a dozen materials, most of which are chosen individually for each edition, so there are many possibilities for variation—with both esthetic and economic significance. Such possibilities are discussed in CH. 29. This chapter describes the mechanics and materials themselves.

There has been little radical innovation in binding compared with composition, prepress operations, and printing. The hand operations were converted to mechanical processes in the 19th century, and since then there have been very few changes in the principles of their performance.

The main area of improvement is in reducing handling between steps. Machines perform several operations instead of only one, and binderies are laid out as a continuous line of machines, with the product of one feeding automatically into the next. Also, computers have improved the efficiency of binding machinery and enabled a considerable degree of automation.

If any change can be called major, it's the swing toward adhesive rather than sewn binding. This is due less to technological development than to a desire for economy.

The above comments generally refer to conventional hardcover book binding. There are, however, some departures in technology when other kinds of binding are considered.

Kinds of binding

There are basically three kinds of binding—(a) *case* (*hard binding* or *hardcover*), (b) *paper* (*paperback, softcover*), and (c) *mechanical* (*wire, ring* binding, etc.)—with many variations of each. The distinctions will be discussed later in this chapter. Up to a point, however, the binding process described below is the same for all kinds.

The basic operation

FOLDING

The method of folding printed sheets is determined for each job before the pages are imposed for printing (CH. 10). There are many methods, each one based on: (a) the number of pages on the sheet,

(b) the arrangement of signatures (folded sections) desired, and (c) the characteristics of the paper. The imposition is selected by the binder with the concurrence of the printer.

The fewer signatures there are in a book, the less its cost. This would suggest making signatures with as many pages as possible, but the number is limited by the bulk and flexibility of the paper. Too many pages in a signature cause wrinkling, buckling, and a tendency to spring open. Generally, antique stock up to 70 lb. (103.5 gsm) is folded in 32-page signatures, from 70 through 80 lb. (118.3 gsm) in 16s, and over 80 lb. in 8s. Very lightweight papers may be folded in 64s, up to about 30 lb. (44.4 gsm). Coated papers of comparable weights are less bulky, so it's possible to have more pages per signature. For example, with 80 lb. it's usually safe to have 24 pages, for 100 lb. (147.9 gsm) 16 pages, etc.

Given a particular number of pages per signature, the sheet may be folded in different ways. The more pages on the sheet, the more variations possible. Successive folds may be parallel or at right angles to each other; the sheet may be cut into two, four, or eight sections on the folding machine; the sections may each be folded in a variety of ways; and, finally, the sections may be inserted into, or wrapped around, others to become part of larger signatures.

The chief reason for choosing one imposition over another is binding efficiency, but the choice may also facilitate distributing color throughout the book more effectively. For example, if a second color is printed on only some forms, the imposition can be arranged so that signatures with color will be in various parts of the book rather than all together.

It would take too much space to describe all the standard impositions, and there are innumerable special impositions used in unusual circumstances. A simple 16-page imposition is described below to illustrate the principle.

To make a 16-page signature from a sheet with eight pages on each side using three right-angle folds, each form would have two rows of four pages each printed head to head, i.e., one row would be upside-down. The arrangement looks like this:

imposition for 16-page sheet

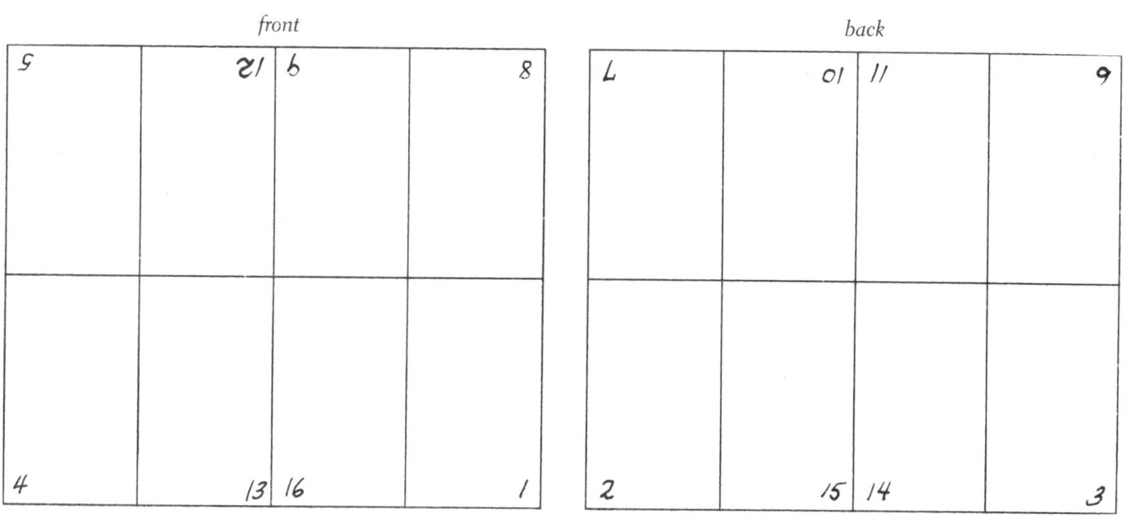

To see how this works, take a sheet of paper and mark it as in the diagram. You will see that page 1 backs 2, 3 backs 4, and so on. Fold the sheet in half, then again in half at right angles to the first fold, then again at right angles to the previous one, and you'll have a signature in which the 16 pages are in consecutive order.

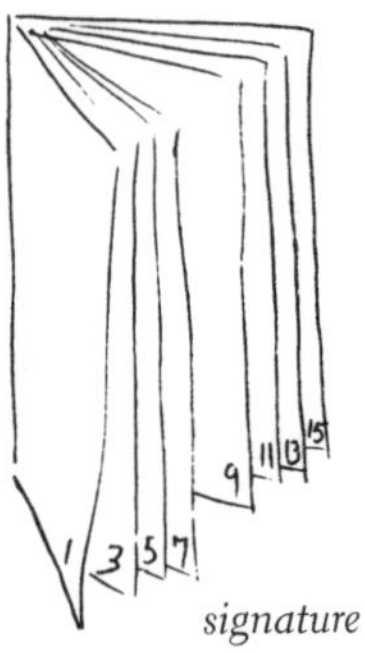

signature

Folding machines vary according to the kind of folding done, the size of sheet handled, and the principle of operation. Most book folding is done by the *tape-and-knife* method. The sheet is carried on a set of narrow endless belts or *tapes* until it's in position for a dull blade to drive it between rollers that press the fold to a sharp crease. This operation is repeated until the sheet is finished. The machine slits or perforates certain folds to prevent *gussets* and wrinkles and to allow trapped air to escape. On the larger machines, a sheet can be cut into sections (*slit*), each of which is folded separately but simultaneously. Thus, a 128-page sheet may come off the folder as eight 16-page signatures, four 32s, etc. The machine may deliver a 32-page signature folded from a single sheet (*straight* 32) or it may produce two 16s, with one inserted in the other (*double* 16 *insert*), or with the two 16s in consecutive order (*double* 16 *straight*).

tape-and-knife fold

Small units, such as endpapers, are folded on a *buckle* or *loop folder.* The sheet is passed between two plates until it hits a stop which causes it to buckle at the proper place. Two rollers grab the buckle and press it to a sharp fold.

buckle fold

Most web presses have coordinated folders at the end of the press so that the printing of the paper (both sides) and its folding are virtually simultaneous. This may mean folding at a speed of about 25,000 sheets per hour instead of the usual 3000 to 4000. The tape-and-knife method can't work fast enough, so a different principle is used. It's too complex to be explained here, but it's based on high-precision manipulation of the sheets by grippers and cutting the sheet into small units to reduce the number of right-angle folds needed.

TIPPING, WRAPPING, & INSERTING

The signatures delivered by a folding machine are *bundled* (subjected to pressure and tied tightly between boards) and sent to the *gathering* department, where they're assembled in consecutive

bundled signatures

order into books. Before they're gathered, the endpapers, if any, are *tipped* onto the first and last signatures, and any illustrations not comprising a separate signature are tipped, *inserted*, or *wrapped* at the proper place.

■ **Tip**—Tipping means pasting onto a page with about ⅛" (.32 cm) of paste along the inside, or *gutter*, edge. Tips may be a single leaf or a 4-page fold (as are the endpapers). Pasting tips onto the outsides of signatures is simplest; in the middle of signatures is more difficult; and most difficult is tipping within a signature—which usually requires slitting open a fold by hand. Outside tips are done by machine, but the others are hand operations.

■ **Insert**—Inserting into a signature means placing four or more pages in the middle or elsewhere, thereby enlarging it by that many pages.

■ **Wrap**—Wrapping is the reverse of inserting; here the pages go around the *outside* of the signature. A wrap can be placed around certain of the pages within a signature (for example, around pages 5 and 12 in the 16-page signature diagrammed above), but this is a hand operation.

In sewn books (except side-sewn), tips are much weaker than inserts or wraps because no stitching goes through them. To avoid tips, it's possible to make 2-page (single leaf) wraps by leaving an extra ½" (1.27 cm) *stub* on the inside edge of the leaf to wrap around the signature, but this isn't very practical for large-edition binding, and the stubs are unsightly where they protrude between pages.

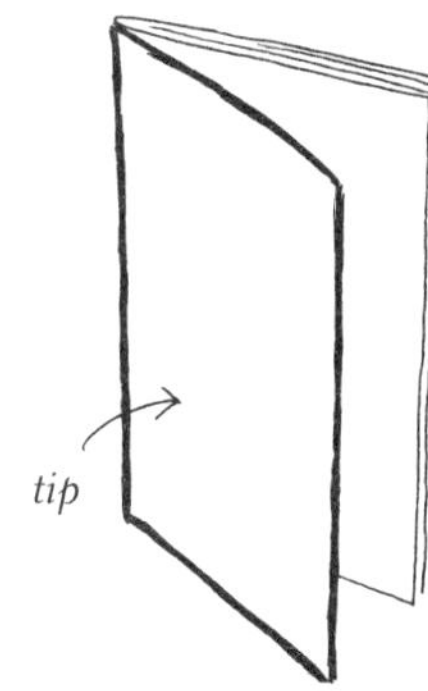

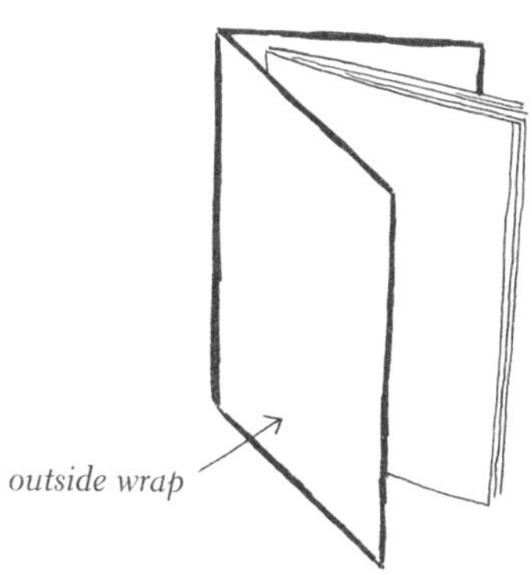

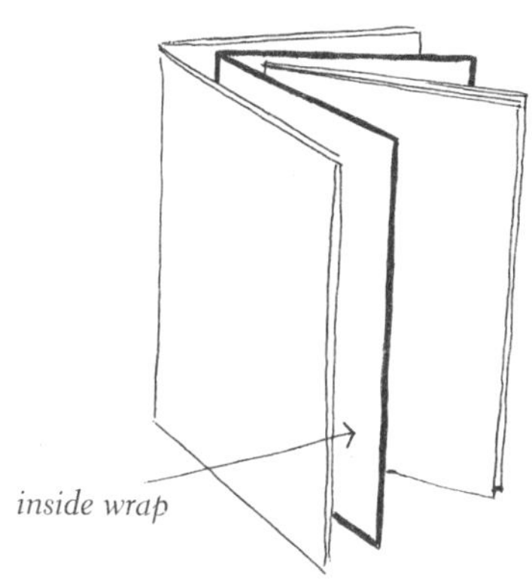

REINFORCING

Reinforcing the binding, when required, is usually done at this stage. There are several methods. Generally, these consist of pasting a 1" (2.54 cm) strip of cambric cloth along the back folds of the first and last signature after the endpapers are on, or pasting it on the outside of the endpapers only, without going around the signatures—depending on the kind of sewing used. Sometimes books are specially reinforced when bound for library use (*prebinding*) separately from the regular edition. Libraries also have

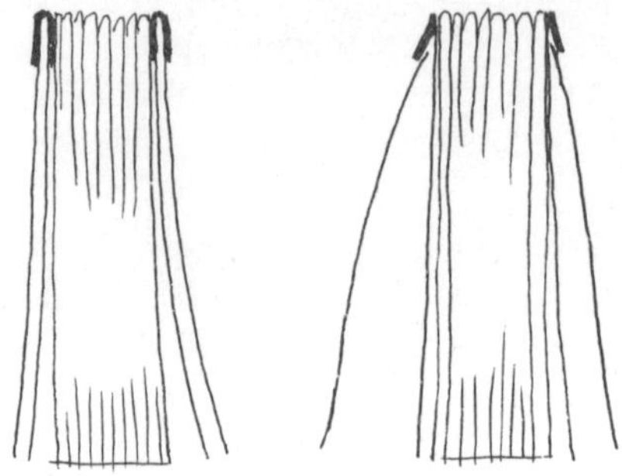

two methods of reinforcing

regular trade bindings rebound with extra reinforcement. Another kind of reinforcement is *whip-stitching*—one or two extra rows of stitching on the first and last signatures. On very heavy books, two or three strips of cloth *tape* may be sewn across the back (*spine*) and extended onto the inside of the covers.

GATHERING & COLLATING The completed signatures are piled in successive hoppers on the gathering machine. A mechanical arm takes a signature from the first hopper and places it on a conveyor belt, a second arm places a second signature from the next hopper on top of the first signature on the belt, and so on down the line until the book is completed. Thus, if the book has ten signatures, the belt would always have ten piles—one with all ten signatures, one with nine, one with eight, and so on back to the first "pile", which would have only the first signature.

As the completed sets of signatures come off the machine, they're *collated* (checked for correct sequence and position). In small editions this can be accomplished by an operator fanning

gathering machine

through every fourth or fifth set to see that the first and last folios of succeeding signatures correspond, and that none are missing, duplicated, upside-down, or backward. Ordinarily, small marks (*collating marks*) are printed at certain places on the sheets, so that when folded, each signature has one along its back edge. A straight or diagonal line across the spine results when the book is properly gathered, so any error is immediately apparent.

At this point, the process varies according to the kind of binding required, although some later operations are used in more than one method.

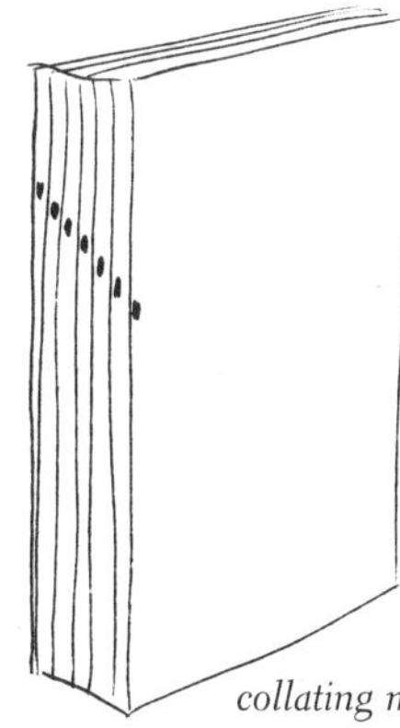

collating marks

Case binding

This is the conventional method of binding a book. The book block—the gathered signatures held together by either (a) sewing, (b) wire staples, or (c) adhesives—is enclosed in a more or less rigid cover, to the inside of which it's attached by pasting the endpapers, or the first and last pages (*self-lining*). Case bindings may vary in the manner of holding the pages together, the nature of the cover, or any combination of these.

Smyth sewing

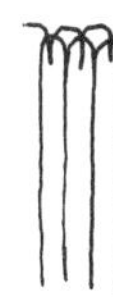

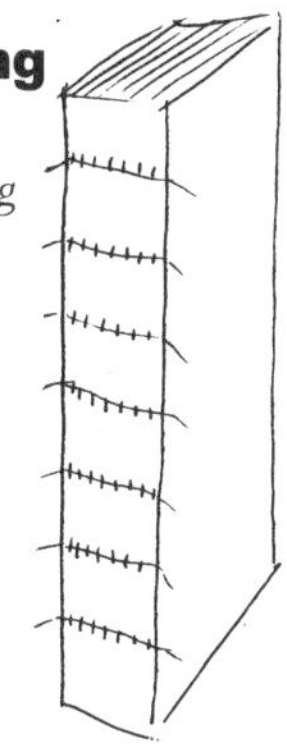

SEWING

There are two methods:

■ **Smyth sewing**—For tradebooks, this is the most common method. The thread is stitched through the gutter of each signature and passed through the stitches at the back of the signatures to join them. Held this way, the pages open freely. The back edges of the first and last signatures are pasted to the adjacent ones. (If the book has only one signature and the stitching goes through the gutter, it's called *saddle stitching.*)

■ **Side sewing (Singer sewing)**—The thread is passed through the entire book block about ⅛" (.32 cm) from the spine, just as a hem would be sewn on a tablecloth. For book blocks over ¾" (1.9 cm) bulk, another machine is used and the process is called *McCain sewing.*

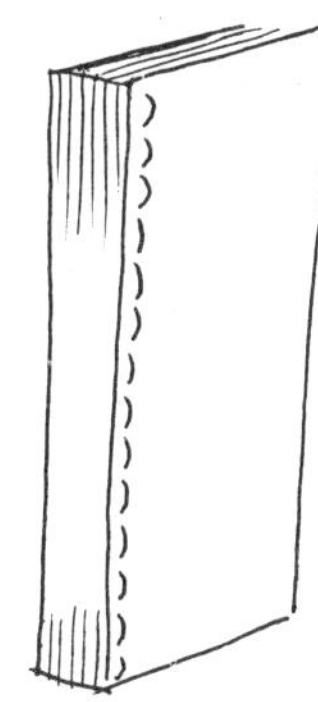

side sewing

WIRE STITCHING OR STAPLING

This is a cheaper method of holding pages together when there's just one signature. Two or three wire staples are passed through the gutter (*saddle-wire stitching*), as in a pamphlet. *Side-wire stitching* is similar in principle to side sewing, except that metal staples are used instead of thread. (Side-sewn books have two wire staples put through them in the gathering machine to hold the signatures together for sewing, although these may be omitted on thin books.)

wire stitching

ADHESIVE BINDING

For perfect binding, the folds at the back of the book are trimmed or ground off and an adhesive is applied to hold the pages together. Essentially, this is the same method used to make pads, and in its early days perfect binding's results were about the same—the pages were easily pulled out. Now, perfect binding is comparable in performance to sewn binding, although adhesive-bound books generally don't open easily or lie flat when open. There are several kinds of adhesive binding, but all involve increasing the amount of paper surface to which the adhesive can be applied. In *notch binding* the folds are notched; in *burst binding* the adhesive is forced into holes punched in the folds.

adhesive-bound book

A more sophisticated type of nonsewn binding is done by electronically welding together the molecules of specially made paper. The book is then not so much a series of pages adhered or sewn together as it's a single piece of paper in the form of a book. This process is, so far, too expensive to be a practical option.

NIPPING

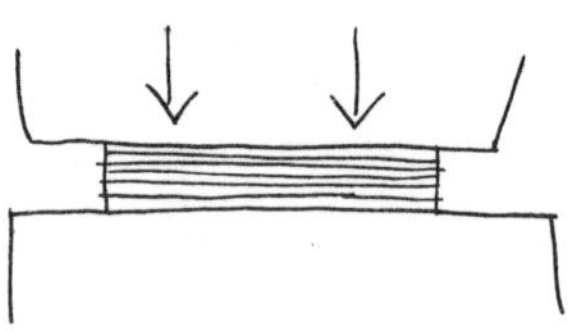

To produce a compact unit, sewn books must be given a strong, rapid squeeze to eject air from the folds and compress the paper. This process is called *nipping* (or *smashing*) and is applied at the end of the sewing machine, where the sewn signatures are pressed between two metal plates. In the perfect-binding operation, only enough pressure is applied to compress the pages firmly. No more is necessary because there are no folds to hold air.

GLUING-OFF

gluing-off

This is the first operation in *forwarding*. Even though sewn tightly, the spine of the book block tends to loosen a little after nipping, so a thin coat of flexible glue is applied to hold the signatures in place. This is done by running the books, spines down, over a series of glue-carrying rollers, and then over a heating element that dries the glue so that it's hard enough to make the book firm in time for the next operation. Perfect-bound hardcover books are glued-off after the back folds are cut off and before the other three sides are trimmed. A cloth strip is applied to the spine. Other adhesive-bound books are glued-off in the same way.

TRIMMING

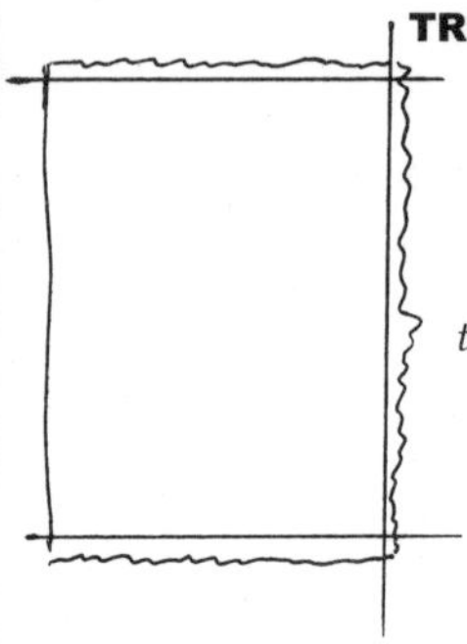

trimming

After being glued-off, the book block is trimmed. Heavy knives chop off approximately ⅛" (.32 cm) at the *head* (top), *front* (*fore-edge*), and *foot* (bottom), thus opening all folds (or *bolts*) except those at the spine. This is called a *smooth* (or *full*) *trim*. If a *rough trim* is desired at the foot, the knife takes off only enough to open the bolts, which are made to protrude slightly beyond the slit edges during folding. For a rough front, all folds are slit on the folder and there's no trim. The result is a more or less ragged edge somewhat resembling that of a book printed on handmade or deckle-edged paper. This adds about ⅛" to the trim-size of the page.

EDGE COLOR

edge coloring

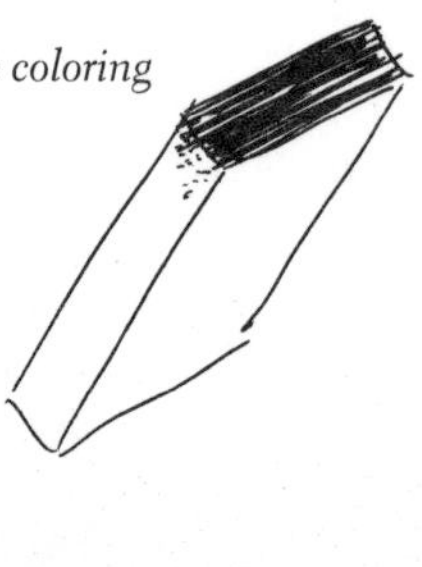

On case-bound books, edge color is applied ordinarily only to the top. The color is an aniline dye and is sprayed on stacks of books about 1 foot high. The spray is directed at an angle from the spine so that no excess color will get on the front. It may be applied by hand or by machine. Genuine gold edges are applied by hand using gold leaf (*gilding*), although it's possible to have an imitation gold applied by machine at much lower cost.

ROUNDING & BACKING

Sewn books, and some adhesive-bound books, are put through a machine which: (a) nips the back (spine); (b) rounds the back with a set of knurled rollers (producing a concave fore-edge); (c) clamps the book sharply *except* at the very back, thus allowing the back to flare out slightly; and (d) curves the back with curved backing irons.

The ridge created by the flaring of the back is called the *joint* (or *hinge*) and is very important structurally. It's at this point that the (hard) cover hinges and the pages bend when turned. The joint is also a locking device that tends to keep the book block from slipping out of its cover. Books can be made with *flat backs*, but they're not as strong as those with round backs, particularly when the bulk is large and the paper heavy. Very thin books are usually made flat-backed because there isn't enough bulk for rounding and backing.

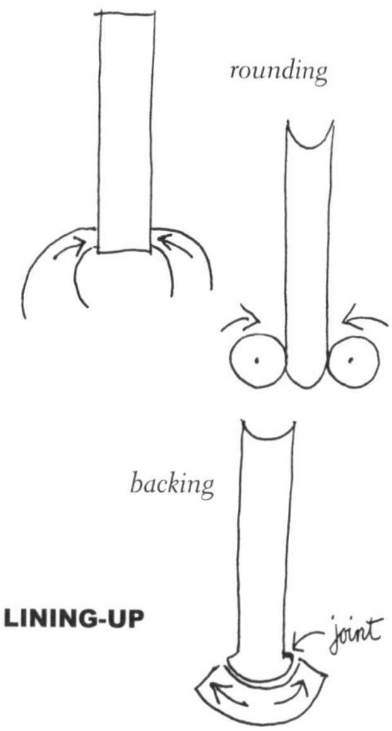

LINING-UP

This is the major reinforcing process. First, a coat of glue is applied to the spine. On top of this is placed a strip of *crash* or *super* (a gauze) extending almost the length of the spine and about 1" (2.54 cm) over each side. Rollers press the crash into the wet glue and then apply another coat of glue on top of it. On this is applied a strip of tough paper cut to the length and width of the spine. The crash is very important, being the only link between cover and book other than the endpaper. On books requiring unusual strength, an extra-heavy crash (*legal crash*) or a double layer may be used. (In a bound book, the crash can be detected underneath the endpaper.) These operations are usually performed on the rounding and backing machine.

Headbands are the decorative strips of colored cloth that protrude slightly at top and bottom of the spine. They are applied during lining-up, being glued to the spine between the crash and paper.

After lining-up, the book block is ready to be inserted into its cover, which is made while the folding, gathering, and forwarding are in progress.

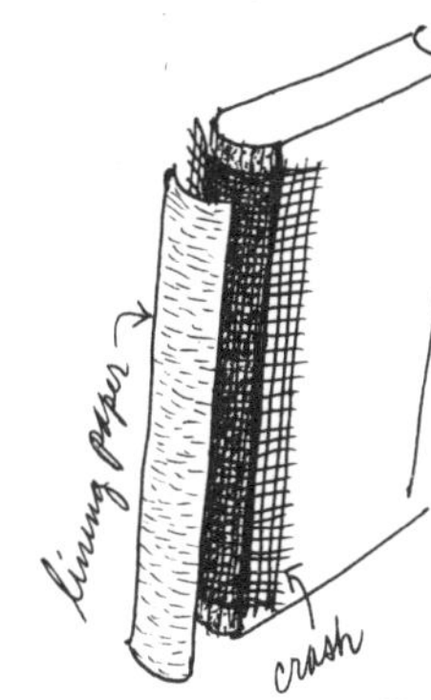

lining-up

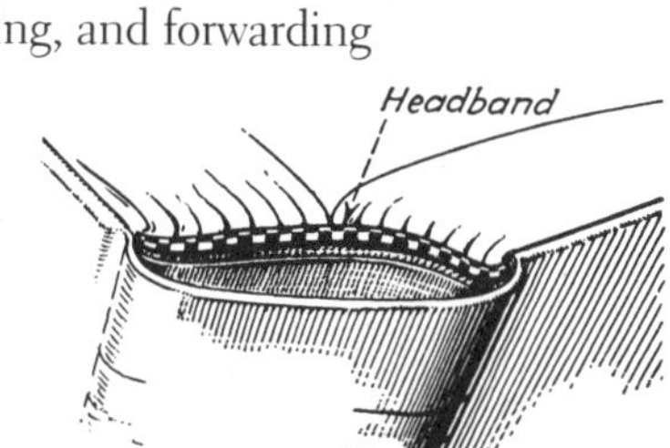

CASEMAKING

The conventional *case* (cover) of a hardbound book consists of a more or less rigid board on each side and a strip of paper or board

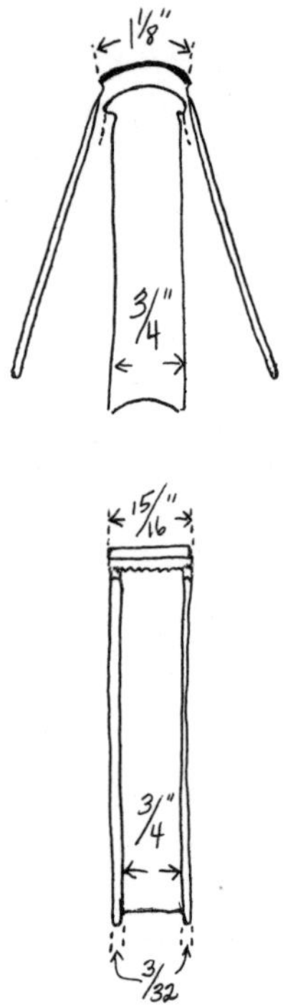

casemaking dimensions

at the spine, all covered with a decorative/protective material. The characteristics and varieties of these materials are discussed later in this chapter. The process of putting them together is *casemaking.*

The boards and the backstrip are cut to the height of the trim-size of the book *plus* ¼" (.64 cm)—which provides for an overhang of ⅛" (.32 cm) at head and foot—but the boards are made ⅛" *less* than the width of the trim-size to allow for the hinge. The backstrip for a round-backed book of normal bulk is made about ⅜" (.95 cm) wider than the bulk of the pages (*paper bulk*) to allow for the flare of the joint. For very thick or very thin books the additional width may be more or less than ⅜". A useful formula is to make the backstrip 1.33 times the bulk. For flat backs, the backstrip will equal the paper bulk plus the thickness of the boards. In a flat back, the backstrip is generally a rigid board rather than paper. This partly compensates for the lack of strength at the spine and gives a neater appearance.

The cover material is cut to the height of the boards plus 1¼" (3.17 cm)—which allows ⅝" (1.59 cm) at the head and foot for *turn-in,* i.e., for the material to wrap around the edge of the boards. In width, the material is made the width of both boards plus the backstrip, plus 1¼" turn-in, plus ¼" (.64 cm) for the joints on front and back. At the joint, a space of ¼" is left between the boards and the backstrip. Each corner of the material is cut off to prevent excessive bunching of the turn-in. Laid out in position for casemaking, the boards and cover material for a round-backed 7 x 10" (17.78 x 25.4 cm) book bulking ¾" (1.91 cm) would appear as follows:

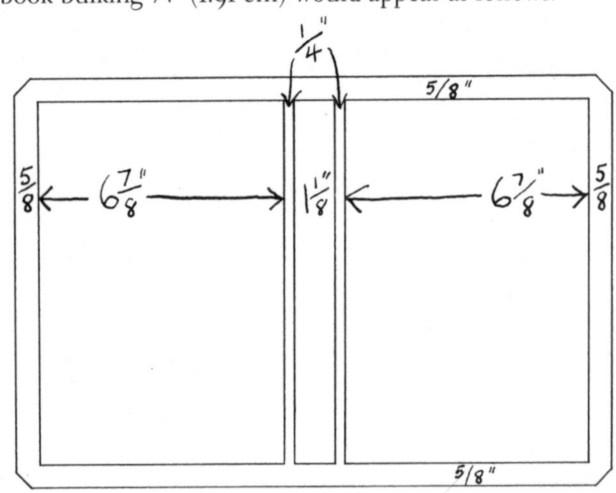

layout of materials for a case

A cover like this could be made in two ways: (a) with precut pieces on a *sheetfed casemaker,* or (b) on a *webfed casemaker* with only the boards precut, the cover material and backstrip paper being in rolls. On the sheetfed machine, the material is glued on its inside surface and the boards and backstrip are dropped onto the wet glue in the proper position. To complete the cover, small rollers push the turn-ins over the edges of the boards and press them down. In webfed casemaking, the material passes over a glue roller and then, glue side up, under a hopper that holds the boards, which are dropped into position. At the same time, pieces of back-strip paper are automatically chopped off a roll to the proper length and dropped into place on the glued material. As the web moves along, the material is cut off to the proper length, the corners are cut, and the edges are turned in.

On some webfed machines, the width of the web is the height of the material, so that front board, backstrip, and back board fall successively (*side feed*); on others, the web is the width of the material, so the three pieces drop simultaneously alongside each other (*end feed*).

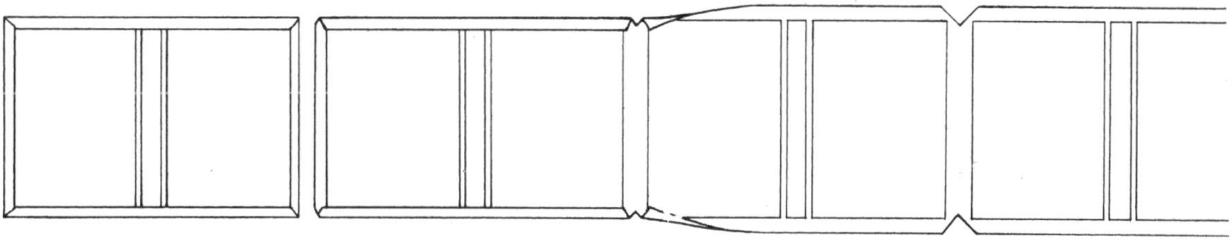

side-feed casemaking

end-feed casemaking

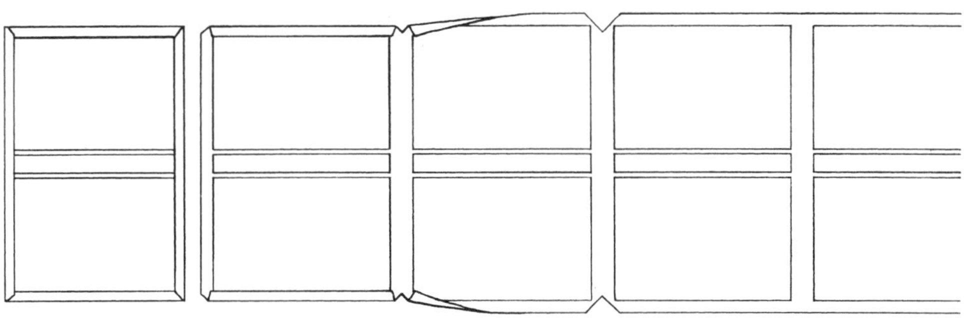

This distinction is of no significance when a cover is made with a single piece of material, but it's of primary importance if a cover is to be made with two or more pieces. When such covers are made by running material simultaneously from two or more rolls, it's obvious that on a side-feed machine the strips of material would run across the cover and on an end-feed one they would run up the cover.

The most common use of this technique is the three-piece cover made on an end-feed machine, with one material for the

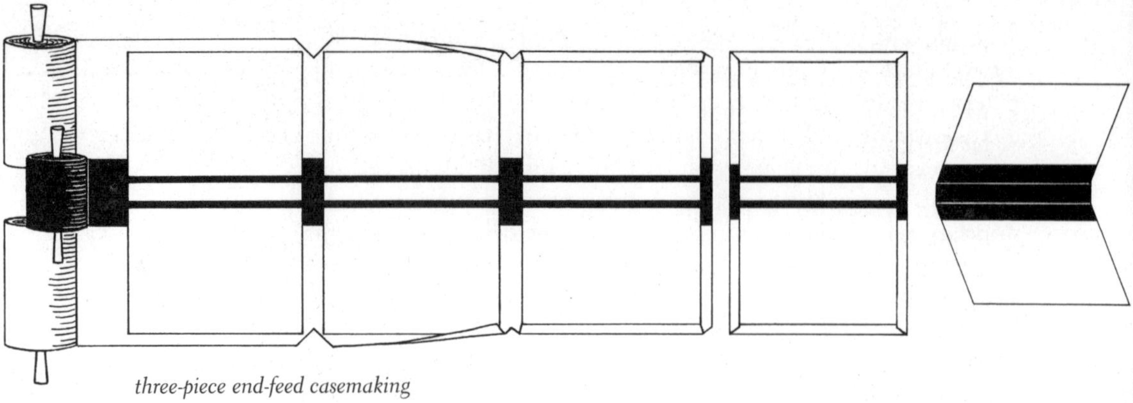

three-piece end-feed casemaking

sides and another for the spine (with some of the spine material extending onto the sides and overlapping the side material). Almost any combination of materials is possible in this method, but each strip must be wide and strong enough to withstand the tension of the almost 15-foot web, and to prevent difficulties caused by its length. For average materials, at least 2" (5.1 cm) width is usually required, but more may be needed in some cases. Regardless of how much of the spine material is supposed to show on the sides, at least ⅜" (.95 cm) should extend onto the boards to ensure sufficient strength. It's the spine material that holds the cover together and provides the structurally vital joint. The side materials, which have virtually no structural importance, may overlap the spine material by any amount, with ⅛" (.32 cm) the minimum, to allow for inaccuracies in the casemaking. The same method may be used on the side-feed casemaker, but here each piece forms part of the hinge and must have the requisite strength.

Multipiece covers can be made on sheetfed machines, but ordinarily not in one operation. The standard three-piece case is made by putting the spine material on first, then putting the two side pieces on in a second run. However, some binderies assemble three pieces of material to make a unit, which is then used to make a three-piece case in one operation.

Covers can be made by molding them from a single piece of plastic. The problem here is the need to have flexibility in the joint and rigidity in the sides. This can be accomplished by molding a sheet of plastic with the necessary variations in thickness. "One-piece" plastic covers are made also by laminating pieces together instead of molding, often with a piece of board between the layers. The edges are then *heat-sealed* (melted together). Such covers are not often used in trade books because the economy in the casemaking is likely to be offset by the relatively high cost of the plastic.

STAMPING There are three methods used to apply lettering and other designs to covers: (a) printing the material before the cover is made, (b) printing on the cover by silk screen, and (c) *stamping* on the cover. The techniques of the first two methods are explained in CH. 12 where the printing processes are discussed. It's the third—and by far the most common—method which is described here.

There are two kinds of stamping: *cold* and *hot.*

■ **Cold stamping (ink stamping)**—This involves the application of ink by impression from a raised surface. The stamping press drives the raised image into the material hard enough to place the ink below the surface. This is necessary to prevent the ink from being rubbed away too quickly as the book is handled. The hard impression is needed also to flatten the relatively rough-surfaced materials used for bookbinding. A light impression on a natural finish cloth, for example, would place ink on top of the threads only and not make a solid mark.

Ink stamping is done on a platen press. The stamping plate (*die*) must be of hard enough material to withstand the heavy wear. It's made of ¼" (.64 cm) thick metal and is deeply etched. Dies are discussed later in this chapter and in CH. 29.

Because of the hard impression and frequently rough material, ink stamping can't give the fine results possible in printing on paper. When the cover material is comparatively smooth, however, small type, fairly fine line drawings, and even coarse-screen halftones may be stamped satisfactorily. Stamping light inks on dark materials isn't usually satisfactory unless two or more impressions are used.

■ **Hot stamping**—This is used: (a) to apply *foil* (or *leaf*), (b) for making *blank* impressions (*blind stamping*), and (c) for *embossing.* The process is substantially the same as ink stamping, except that the metal die is heated by the press. Heat is necessary to transfer the leaf from its carrier (see "Binding materials" below) to the cover material, and, in blind stamping or embossing, to help mold the material and boards. The amount of heat used varies from 200° to 275° F (93.3° to 113° C) according to the kind of leaf, the cover materials, and the kind of stamping.

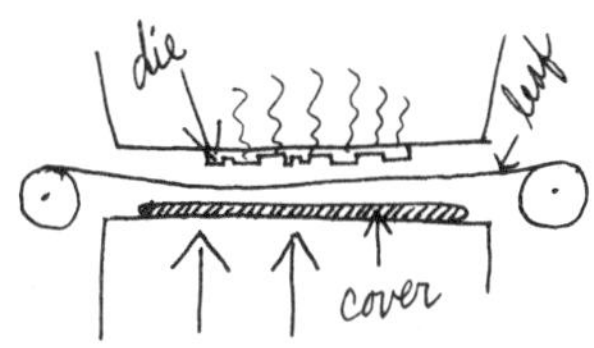

hot stamping

Leaf stamping once meant the application of genuine gold from small sheets ("leaves"), and this is still the method used in making cover designs with hand tools. On a stamping press, a roll of leaf (metallic or flat color) just wide enough to cover the die is mounted on one side, and the leaf ribbon is drawn across the die by an arm on the other side, with the pigment side facing away from the die. The leaf is pressed against the cover by the heated die and the pigment is transferred. The pressure not only impresses the leaf below the surface, but forces the pigment into the weave or grain of the cover material. After each impression, the arm pulls the leaf just enough to move the stamped part past the die.

multiple-color leaf stamping

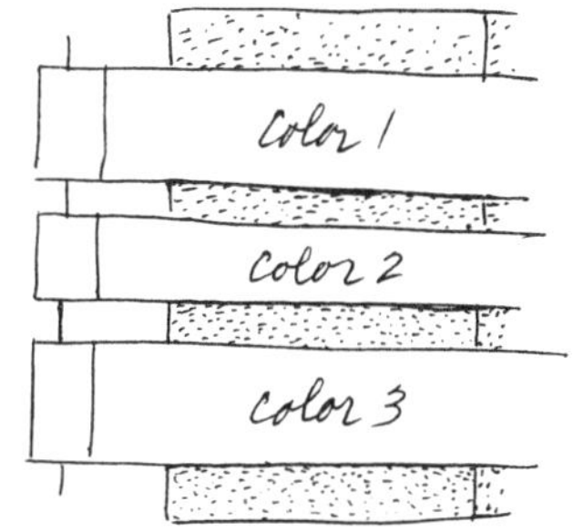

It's possible to mount several rolls of leaf of different colors on the press simultaneously and stamp from all of them at each impression. (Some presses have side feeds also, enabling them to run rolls at right angles to each other.) In making designs using multiple leaf colors in one impression, be sure that the printing image of each color is at least 5⁄16" (.79 cm) from that of any other color, since each ribbon must extend 1⁄8" (.32 cm) on both sides of the die to ensure that all of it is covered and another 1⁄16" (.16 cm) is needed for a divider to keep the ribbons apart. These paper-thin ribbons being pulled over a span of about 3 feet are not very stable—particularly if they're narrow.

Blank (or blind) stamping is done by the same process as leaf stamping except that no leaf is used. The visual effect results from changes in color and texture of the material due to heat and the heavy impression, as well as the shadows created by the impression. To be effective, blind stamping must be impressed into the board as well as the cover material. Blank stamping and leaf stamping can be done in the same impression but, because heat is required, can't be done together with an impression of ink.

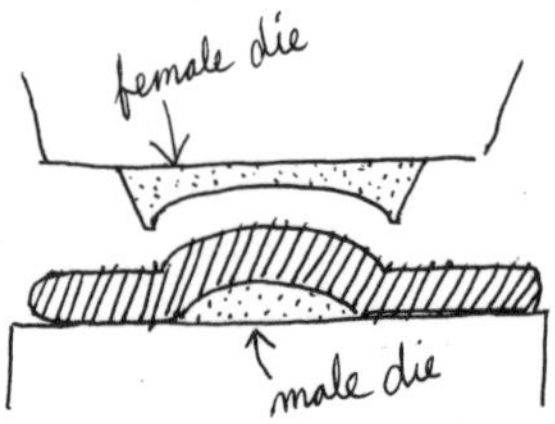

embossing

Embossing is similar to the other hot-stamping operations, but the image produced is raised *above* the surface instead of pressed *into* it. This usually requires use of male and female dies. The latter is stamped on top of the cover while the male die is positioned underneath to press a negative image into the inside of the cover. (If this is too large and/or deep, it can interfere with pasting the endleaf onto the board.) When the image is fairly simple, the male die may be omitted, using in its place a piece of cardboard cut to the proper shape. This saves the cost of a die (embossing dies are very expensive) and reduces the height of the embossing. An effect similar to embossing can be obtained without embossing dies by making a reverse die, i.e., a background is stamped, leaving the image raised on it.

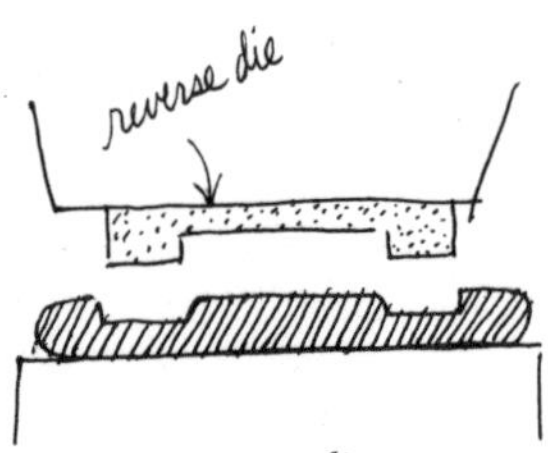

reverse die

After leaf has been stamped, each cover is given a light brushing with fine steel wool to wipe off the excess leaf. (This can cause smears if a dark-colored leaf is used on a very light-colored material.)

CASING-IN

With book blocks and covers made, the next operation is *casing-in* (putting the book block into its case or cover). The book blocks are fed into the machine, spines up, astride vertical metal vanes. The endleaves are given a coat of paste just before the books pass under a hopper of covers. As each book block goes through, a cover drops over it and is clamped from both sides, pasting the endleaves to the inside of the cover. (For round-backed books, before the covers are dropped into place, a heated bar forms their spines to correspond to the round backs.)

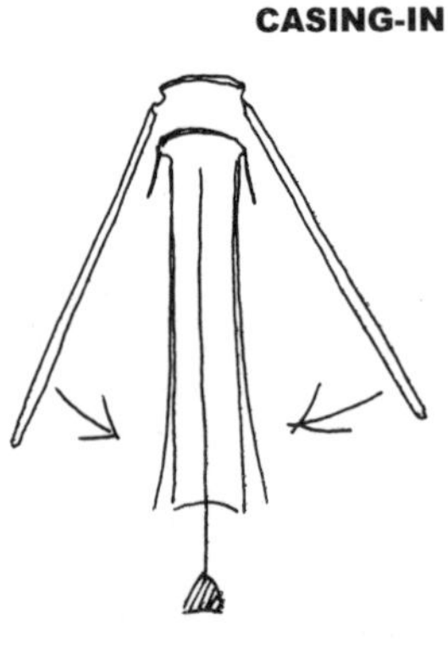
casing-in

Casing-in a self-lining book is the same, except that in the absence of endpapers, the paste is applied to the first and last pages, and these are pasted to the cover. Some books are made *tight-*

backed, i.e., the spine of the cover is glued to the spine of the book block.

BUILDING-IN

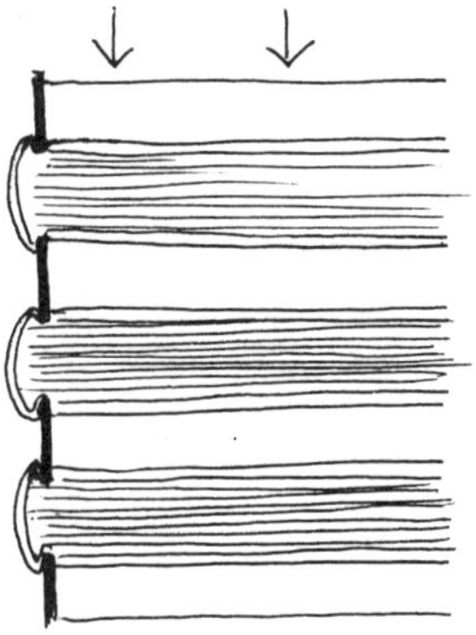

building-in between boards

The cover would warp badly if the endleaf paste was permitted to dry by itself. To prevent this, the books are *built-in*. The old method—still used for oversized books—was to put the books between wooden boards which were then piled on other layers of books and boards. A projecting metal rim around the edges of the boards pressed into the joint to hold the shape. The pile was then kept under pressure for 6 to 24 hours while the paste dried.

Now, building-in machines apply pressure and heat from both sides of the books, accomplishing in seconds what formerly required a day. The basic principle of all building-in machines is the same, but they vary in the heat, pressure, and *dwell* (the amount of time that pressure is applied) used. This is important to know because cover materials have different thermal properties.

INSPECTION

Some inspection is done at each step in the binding process, but in spite of this, imperfections remain undetected, so a final check is made just before the books are wrapped. This inspection covers the entire range of possible faults—even those created by composition and printing. Composition errors will, of course, appear in all copies, and if serious enough (e.g., omission of the author's name from the title page) may necessitate remaking the entire edition. Printing faults are also likely to affect many copies. In binding, a great many things may go wrong but, because of the relatively slower speeds of binding machines and the numerous occasions for inspection and rejection, the faults at this stage are likely to be limited to a few copies. The most common problems are: sheets folded on a bias, corners folded in, inverted signatures, endpapers stuck together (due to oozing of excess paste), books cased-in upside-down, and endpapers not centered or square in covers. Occasionally, imperfections in paper are discovered (holes, tears, stains, etc.).

Imperfect books are sent to the *repair department* where they're made acceptable, if possible. Skillful repair work restores a remarkably high percentage.

JACKETING, SLIPCASING, & PACKING

Almost all books are given some kind of individual wrapping. Tradebooks customarily have a printed paper or clear *plastic jacket* (a removable wrapper, as distinguished from the *cover*, which is attached to the book). Technical and school books usually have a jacket of plain paper or *glassine* (a rather brittle, translucent paper). All jackets were once put on by hand. Now jacketing machines are used, but hand jacketing is still used for very short runs and some oversized books.

It's important to provide instructions for positioning printed jackets on books, because it's not always obvious how they should

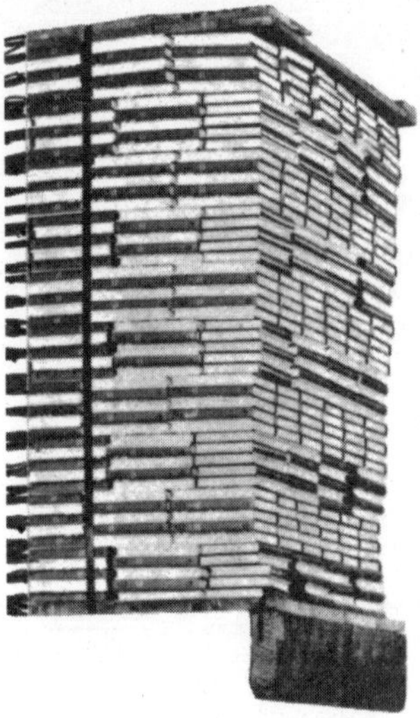

fit. This is particularly necessary with off-centered spine designs, for there's a tendency to center the type on the spine of the book when wrapping.

Insertion of books in *slipcases* (open-ended boxes) or individual mailing cartons is usually done by hand, although very large editions may be cartoned by machine. Relatively expensive books are usually cartoned individually, but most books are packed in bulk cartons containing 35 to 40 lbs. (15.9 to 18.1 kg) of books. The cartons are then loaded on skids (*pallets*). Sometimes books are loaded individually on skids. A wooden cover is placed on top and metal bands are wrapped around from top to bottom to keep the books under pressure to prevent warping and to keep them from slipping out. Skids, particularly those shipped by sea, are usually then shrinkwrapped in plastic to protect the books from dirt and moisture.

Paperbacks

Paperbacks divide into two categories significant to their manufacture: (a) trade paperbacks, which are sold through regular book outlets in quantities roughly comparable to hardbound tradebooks, and (b) *mass-market paperbacks*, distributed mainly through magazine outlets, drugstores, and airport shops and printed in quantities of 10,000 to 50,000. Major titles may have runs from 100,000 up to millions. The retail prices of these categories differ considerably, reflecting different production values, which relate to the different quantities involved.

TRADE PAPERBACKS

These are sometimes the same trim-sizes as hardcover books—often being printed from the same plates as, and sometimes simultaneously with, a hardbound edition. The basic binding operations for trade paperbacks are performed in the usual way. Most of these are adhesive-bound, although some are sewn—particularly when the run is small. The sewn book blocks are fed into a machine which applies an adhesive to the spine, drops a preprinted paper cover into place, then trims book and cover together. Sometimes the books are nipped first. If an edge stain is used, this is sprayed on after trimming.

paperback cover drop-on

When trade paperbacks are adhesive-bound, they go directly from collating to the binding machine, which trims off the back, applies an adhesive, and then completes the operations described above for sewn books.

MASS-MARKET PAPERBACKS

The web offset press that does the printing of mass-market paperbacks has a folder built in, which produces signatures that are sent to the binding machine, which gathers them and completes the books as described for adhesive-bound trade paperbacks. The books are almost always bound 2-up at a rate of 200 to 400 per minute.

Mechanical binding

The term "mechanical binding" refers to a binding that uses a mechanical device to hold pages together, not to a binding process. In fact, mechanical binding is much less automatic or mechanical than case binding.

There are many kinds of mechanical bindings. All of them involve a metal or plastic device that joins single sheets by passing through holes on one edge. Some snap on, some wind through the holes, some have posts or rods, others have rings, etc.

Although the mechanical devices differ considerably, the binding process varies only in the way that each device is attached. The basic operations of folding and gathering are the same as in all binding. The gathered books are then trimmed on all four sides, holes are punched through the pages, and the metal or plastic binding apparatus is attached. There are no endpapers needed on mechanically bound books, but the front and back covers are gathered with the signatures and hole-punched together with the pages.

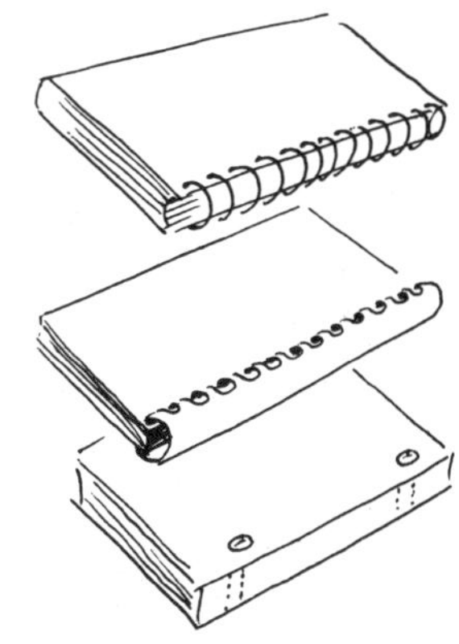

three kinds of mechanical binding

Slipcases, plastic jackets, & cartons

SLIPCASES

When books are sold in slipcases, they're referred to as *boxed*. Usually, two volumes are boxed together, but sometimes a slipcase contains only one book; occasionally, three or four may be in a single box. The construction of a slipcase varies according to the number and weight of the books.

Slipcases are made of boards similar to those used in covers on hard bindings. The boards are covered usually with paper of about the weight and strength of a good text. The box is made of two pieces of board, *scored* (blank stamped along the folding line), folded, and held together with paper tape. For extra-heavy books, some panels may be reinforced with another layer of board. The cover material may be preprinted or plain. In the latter case, there's usually a printed label pasted on the side(s) and/or edge. Sometimes the covering is put on in several pieces, with the printed label constituting one or more of them. The material is turned-in about ½" (1.3 cm) on the edges of the boards at the open end.

It's customary to die-cut half-moon finger openings on the front edges to facilitate removing the book, although this isn't as necessary with heavy books, which are inclined to slip out by their own weight.

slipcases

PLASTIC JACKETS

Clear plastic jackets are made of acetate, polyester film, or vinyl in several thicknesses. The one most used is 5 pt.—.005, or five-thousandths of an inch (.01 mm), but 7½ pt. (.02 mm) and even 10 pt. (.025 mm) are used for very heavy and/or very expensive books. In all cases, the folds must be pre-formed with heat. The material is too resilient to fold cold without springing open, and if a cold fold is pressed too hard it's likely to crack. This is true to a lesser extent of 3 pt. (.008 mm), but this weight is too thin to be heat-formed.

Because of the forming, it's necessary to give the supplier a bound dummy of the book on which to base the jacket measurements.

CARTONS Mailing cartons for individual books must be able to protect their contents well enough to bring them to their destinations in perfect condition. Particularly when the books are expensive, they will be returned if damaged due to inadequate packing. The rigors of going through the mail or a delivery service are severe enough for average-sized books, but very large and heavy ones are subject to considerable stress. (Mechanically bound books are a special problem.)

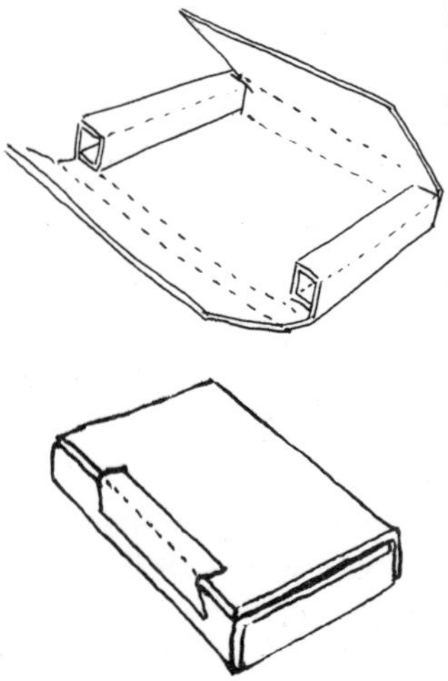

bumper-end carton

Many attempts have been made to achieve maximum protection at minimum cost. One of the most successful is the *bumper end carton*, made from a single piece of die-cut corrugated board. The ends are folded over four times to make bumpers that effectively protect the corners of the book—and it's the corners that take the most abuse in mailing or shipping. The sides are turned over on top, so that only one edge need be taped closed. One flap is the full width of the carton and overlaps the other, so when the tape is cut, the blade won't harm the book.

There are two weights of corrugated board in general use for cartons, 200 lb. (90.72 kg) test and, for heavy duty, 275 lb. (124.74 kg) test. These are made in the standard brown color or sometimes in white. Printing is done on the cartons when flat, using soft rubber plates. The results are fairly crude.

Binding materials

In cooperation with the state agencies that buy books for public elementary and high school use, several industrial and educational groups, including the Book Manufacturers' Institute (*BMI*), established minimum standards, known as *NASTA* (National Association of State Textbook Administrators) specifications, for making books to be used in schools. The NASTA standards cover almost all aspects of production, but particularly binding materials. In general, these requirements exceed what is necessary for satisfactory performance in tradebooks, but they are, nevertheless, often met in making tradebooks that are of interest to libraries. Library books are not ordinarily treated as strenuously as schoolbooks, but they're used continually over long periods, and the librarians, understandably, want them to last as long as possible. The NASTA specifications are revised as conditions change.

COVER MATERIALS—LEATHER For hundreds of years, animal skins—vellum and leather—were almost the only cover materials used for bookbinding. In the 19th century, some decorative papers were used on sides to make *quarter-bound* (three-piece binding) and *half-bound* (three-piece plus corner pieces) books. It wasn't until the latter part of the century, when mass production of books by machinery came about, that leather was replaced by cloth, which not only is relatively uniform, but also may be produced in rolls for use on webfed casemaking machinery.

Today, leather is used for covers mainly on bibles and on special editions. Modern tanning methods, as well as polluted air and dry heat, tend to shorten the life of leather, so most fine-quality leather-bound books use skins from England, where the old tanning method is still in use. However, the large-scale use of leather generated by the mail-order sales of leather-bound classics in the 1970s created a market sufficient for the development of a domestic industry producing book-binding leather of good commercial quality.

There is also *bonded leather*, which consists of small leather particles compressed and bonded with a resin. This material looks, feels, and smells like leather (which it is). Made in rolls, bonded leather can be used on casemakers just like cloth or paper. While economical from a labor standpoint, and much less costly than using whole skins, this material costs about three times as much as the most expensive cloth.

COVER MATERIALS—CLOTH

The cloth used for book binding is mostly cotton or rayon, despite the use of such terms as "linen" and "buckram". Before any processing, the material is called *greige* (pronounced "gray") *goods* and comes in various grades. These are measured mainly in terms of the weight of thread and *thread count* (the number of threads per square inch). In 1936, the U.S. Department of Commerce established specifications for grades of cloth from A to E. However, the demand for cheaper cloth and the competition of paper substitutes inspired the book-cloth manufacturers to produce a lower grade—and later, a still lower grade.

The way that the greige goods are processed varies also. The main distinction is in the *filler* used. Some cloth is filled with a composition consisting chiefly of starch, while others have some plastic—usually pyroxylin or vinyl—in them. The *starch-filled cloth* is easily damaged by moisture, while the *plastic- impregnated* material has enough water resistance to take wiping with a damp cloth. NASTA standards for schoolbooks call for at least a C-grade plastic-impregnated cloth. Some cloth is *plastic coated* rather than impregnated. These materials are just as water resistant as the others, as long as the coating lasts.

Book-cloth finishing is done by running the material through various vats and rollers that apply color and surface characteristics. The chief distinctions are between *natural finish*, *vellum finish*, and *linen finish*.

In vellum-finish cloth, the goods are dyed first, then the filler is applied to both sides of the material. The face is given a coating that includes the coloring, while the back is sized to take the adhesives used in casemaking. To make a linen finish, the goods are undyed and the face coating is scraped so that the white threads show partly through. Steel rollers smooth the surface and emboss if required. Natural-finish cloth is dyed, then is filled and sized from the back only, leaving the face in its soft, natural state. Increasingly, book cloths are laminated to paper backings to prevent glue penetration on high-speed casemakers.

Rolls are put up in widths of 38" (96.5 cm) to 53" (134.6 cm), which makes it possible to economically cut out covers for most books. The usual length of a roll is 250 yards (229 m).

Cloth prices are quite uniform from one supplier to another. In 42" width they range from about $1.75 per yard (.91 m) for the poorest grade to approximately $5.60 per yard for the best. In A grades and better, most materials may be obtained plastic impregnated, at about 7¢ per yard more than starch filled. The price per yard varies with the size of the order, going down as the quantity increases.

Cloth manufacturers stock a large number of colors and finishes of several grades of material and can usually deliver an order within a few days. They will make special colors and finishes for orders of reasonable size. All companies stock white cloth specially prepared for offset printing. Sample sheets 12 x 18" (30.5 x 45.7 cm) and swatch books are available from the principal manufacturers—of which there are only a few. The larger binders stock quantities of the more popular cloth items for sale to their customers.

COVER MATERIALS—NONWOVEN

Under the pressure of escalating cloth prices, affected by the fluctuations of a cotton market over which book-cloth manufacturers had almost no control, the standards for textbook covering material were revised by NASTA in 1965 to allow the use of substitutes for cloth—generically called *nonwoven materials.* The pressure for this change existed for decades, but it took the development of an acceptable material to bring it about. The breakthrough was made by DuPont's Tyvek, a 100% synthetic fiber material that met the requirements for a C-grade pyroxylin cloth—the minimum standard for textbook use. It was not until 1976 that NASTA approved another class of nonwovens, made of acrylic-reinforced cellulose and known as "Type II" material. (Tyvek is actually a Type *III* material. Type I is coated paper, which isn't acceptable for textbooks.) The nonwovens are about two-thirds the price of equivalent cloth.

COVER MATERIALS—PLASTIC

The plastic materials available are mostly *vinyls* of 4 to 7 pt. (.1 to .18 mm) thickness with paper backings. The backing provides rigidity to enable working the material on bindery machines, and it facilitates gluing. Vinyl isn't without problems. While it *can* be fabricated with almost any qualities desired, it's difficult to achieve desirable qualities without creating undesirable features. For example, if the material is made to resist the heat used in stamping and building-in, it may lose too much cold resistance (*cold-crack*) and shatter when a carton of books is dropped onto a loading platform in midwinter. Other problems sometimes encountered are stretching, sticking together, repelling ink or leaf, etc. These can be and have been overcome, but not without some difficulty. Pyroxylin and other plastics also are being used as binding materials, usually in combination with paper backing.

COVER MATERIALS—PAPER

When cloth was scarce during World War II, paper was widely used as a cover material. It was found to be adequate for one-piece covers on tradebooks of small to average size, and where no hard use was involved. Libraries strenuously objected. However, when cloth became available again, the use of these papers continued because of their economy. Even when the lowest grades of cloth were introduced, their price was still much more than that of the paper substitutes. The best of the papers are still below the price of the cheapest cloth.

There are two kinds of paper used on covers. One is the kind that's strong enough to be used for one-piece cases, the other is used only for the sides of three-piece cases. Of the former, one grade, selling at about $1 to $2.85 per yard (the range of prices relates to the amount ordered; large quantity = low price, small quantity = high price) is made of kraft paper with resin impregnation and a coating of lacquer or pyroxylin (sold as Duroid, Kivar, Sturdetan, Permacote, etc.). These are strong enough for most tradebook purposes.

Several lines of cheaper *binding papers* sell for around 19¢ to 27¢ per yard. These are dyed-through kraft papers with some resin impregnation but without coatings and are adequate only for small books with light handling probability. The papers in this group (Permalin, Rainbow, etc.) represent the minimum quality acceptable for one-piece cases. For this purpose, no stock less than 80 lb. is adequate.

There are some paper materials with special formulations that make them unique. One is Elephant Hide, which has a marble-like appearance, considerable strength, and, without any coating, surface resistance to moisture, soiling, and scuffing. This material is manufactured in Germany by a secret process. It comes in a large number of colors and patterns of unusual appearance, is strong enough for most tradebook uses, and sells for around $1.10 to $4 per yard. Another unique material is Linson, made in Scotland of especially tough impregnated fibers. It too requires no coating to perform satisfactorily and comes in colors with or without embossing. It's in the same price range as Elephant Hide. A lower-priced version is Econolin, at $1 to $1.40. In addition to the lines mentioned, there are a number of others with special finishes and patterns, some with a variety of printed and embossed effects available.

All the products mentioned are sold in rolls—generally 40" (102 cm) or 42" (107 cm) wide—or in sheets. While they're intended primarily for one-piece covers, they can be, and are, used as sides of three-piece cases.

Any paper of at least 70 lb. basis weight and reasonable strength may be used on sides, as there's no structural requirement, but only the lines available in rolls are classified as binding papers. This includes several of the better 80 lb. text papers. These are papers of superior printing qualities and appearance, but their price is low in comparison with even the cheapest papers made for one-piece bindings. Also available in rolls are Multicolor and Colortext, two lines of colored stock developed primarily for endpapers, but very satisfactory for sides, and even usable as one-piece bindings in some circumstances. These are slightly lower in price than the text papers mentioned above. Both the text paper and endpaper lines are colored through. Neither has any coating.

There are lines of European—particularly Italian—and Japanese papers that are more or less equivalents of the American ones described.

COVER MATERIALS—PAPERBACKS Most mass-market paperback covers use an 8 pt (.2 mm) or 10 pt. (.25 mm) *coated-one-side* (*C1S*) stock. For larger-format trade paperbacks, 10 pt. or even 18 pt. (.46 mm) stock is used. Such papers are flexible enough to fold, yet provide protection for the pages. Less expensive, although not as scuff resistant, are uncoated stocks of the same thickness. They cost less, not only because they have no coating, but because they require no protective finish over the printing. However, they're not as sturdy as coated papers with plastic finishes.

There are several papers that are tougher and thicker than the regular stocks and are intended to provide longer life for the book (Kivar No. 3, Lexotone, etc.). They cost several cents more per copy on an average trade paperback edition.

New cover material lines and modifications of existing lines are in almost constant development. Contact with suppliers and regular reading of trade periodicals are necessary to keep abreast of these changes.

ENDPAPERS Endpapers have distinctive and significant strength requirements, since they're the main agent in holding the hard cover and book block together. All material sold as endpaper stock is made to specifications required by the NASTA standards for schoolbooks, which call for an 80 lb. kraft. For a discussion of endpaper use, see CH. 29.

DIES The best dies for leaf or ink stamping are made of brass. They're hand-finished, cut to more-than-adequate depth, and have excellent resistance to long-run pounding. However, as handcraftsmanship became an increasingly expensive (and rare) commodity, it was necessary to find a cheaper way of producing dies of satisfactory quality. The fully etched *copper alloy die* provided the answer. The metal is claimed to be harder than brass and it etches very well. For most work it's entirely satisfactory, and the cost is far less than that of brass dies. An even less expensive etched die is made of magnesium, but this is satisfactory only for relatively small runs on fairly smooth cover materials. The performance of etched dies is controlled by the limited depth of acid etching. For simple embossing, etched dies can be used, but *brass dies* are needed for intricate embossing, where it's necessary to sculpt the subject in bas relief with beveled edges—both positive and negative—and this must be done by hand.

It's impossible to rate dies in terms of impressions, because there are a number of variables involved. One kind of die may give 10,000 satisfactory impressions on one job but only 6000 on another. The die's performance can be affected by the material being stamped, the nature of the subject, the heat required, and the speed of stamping. A more elusive variable is the amount of wear inflicted during the setting-up process. An initial miscalculation of the pressure needed may give the die a pounding equivalent to a thousand impressions with the pressure properly adjusted. Accidental feeding of two covers at once can have the same effect.

LEAF & INK

The ink used for stamping is similar to printing ink, but is thicker. More ink is deposited than in printing and there's proportionately less absorption by the material, so more dryer is used to hasten air-drying. This gives the ink a shiny look. A flatter look is possible, but this requires running at slower speed. Special inks are required for printing on plastic or plastic-coated materials.

Leaf is a paper-thin (or thinner) layer of colored mineral powder or metallic powder laid on a gum and wax base, which holds it to a plastic carrier (acetate or Mylar). Over the layer of powder (pigment) is a layer of resin, which bonds it to the material on which it's stamped. Leaf is made up in master rolls 24" (61 cm) wide and 400 to 600' (121.9 to 182.9 m) in length. These are cut into narrower rolls as needed by the stamper.

Metallic leaf includes not only (imitation) gold in several shades, but aluminum, bronze, and a number of metallic colors. These were subject to rather rapid deterioration (tarnishing, fading, or darkening) until *anodyzing* was introduced. The anodyzed imitation gold is supposed to keep its appearance almost indefinitely.

Colored pigment leafs vary considerably in their stamping qualities. There are chemical differences that prevent some leaf from "taking" on certain materials. The amount of pigment needed to cover varies with the color; the degree of heat needed varies with color, backing, and lot; and the colors vary greatly in their light-fastness. On top of this, the performance of leaf varies according to the manufacturer. It's advisable to make sample covers whenever possible (CH. 29).

The variation in heat required is particularly significant when covers are being stamped with more than one color per impression. Since the colors may differ in their heat requirements, the quality of one part of the stamping must be sacrificed for another.

Each leaf supplier has a card showing samples of the colors carried in stock. The cards, the names, and the numbers vary, but the colors are about the same from one to another. Special colors can be made, but only for large orders. Special *panel leaf* is available with an extra thickness of pigment.

COATINGS & LAMINATIONS

It's usually necessary to apply a finish to protect a printed surface on cover materials. Some materials, such as natural-finish cloth and uncoated paper, absorb so much of the ink that they need no protection because the normal abrasion of use wouldn't penetrate below the ink. Also, there are special inks of such hardness when dry that they resist scuffing to a considerable extent. Whether these inks are adequate protection or not depends on the amount of wear to which the book will be subjected.

There are basically two kinds of protective finish. One is a transparent liquid coating, of which there are many kinds; the other is *lamination*, i.e., adhering a sheet of clear plastic to the surface of the base material. There is also *liquid lamination*, which consists of applying a layer of plastic in liquid form, but this is really more a coating than lamination. *UV coatings* have replaced the older liquid laminations, but a warning is in order. If a UV coating isn't properly cured, and is applied over foil, the foil may disintegrate.

Coatings may be applied by spraying, by roller, or by a printing plate. The least expensive coating is the *press varnish* (a coat of varnish applied on a printing press just like an impression of ink). There are specialized shops called *finishers* that can apply a large variety of varnishes, lacquers, liquid plastics, aqueous coatings, and other concoctions designed to provide protection for various materials in varying degrees. It's always best to ask the finisher to recommend a coating for a particular job.

Sheet lamination with polypropylene or Mylar is relatively expensive—several times the cost of press varnish—but it gives the maximum protection and a glossy finish matched only by a clear plastic jacket. The hazard in lamination is a possibility that the plastic sheet will come loose. It's not advisable to laminate on a rough material. The smoother the base, the firmer the adhesion.

Make allowance for the slight discoloration protective finishes cause, particularly on process-color printing. This varies from almost none with lamination to a distinct yellowing with varnish. Consider also the possibility of using a press varnish as an overall film of color, at no additional cost. Any color may be used. It's possible also to have a *spot varnish* on selected areas.

Inform the printer of the finish to be used, as special inks are required in some cases.

BOARD

There are four kinds of board used for hard covers:

- **Binder's board**—This is the best and the most expensive. It's made much like paper, as a solid sheet of fibers, and is less likely to warp or crack than any other. NASTA standards require binder's board for textbooks.
- **Chipboard**—This is made somewhat like binder's board but it's not as dense and is made not more than about 65 pts. (1.65 mm) in thickness. It's the cheapest board, but it's relatively weak and is little used for tradebooks.
- **Pasted board**—It can be made in any thickness, being two or more layers of chipboard or oaktag pasted together. This is used for most tradebooks.
- **Red board**—This is a thin, tough, flexible board used for "limp" or flexible covers, mainly on books meant to be carried in pockets and some bibles.

The boards used in most books are between 70 and 90 pts. (1.8 and 2.3 mm) in thickness, with 80 to 88 pts. (2 to 2.2 mm) the most popular. Large, heavy books may use 110 or 120 pts. (2.8 or 3 mm). Red board is usually 36 pts. (.91 mm).

THREAD, CRASH, & LINING

These three items are selected and purchased by the binder, but it's useful to know that extra-strong grades of each are available when their use is indicated. The decision to use heavy grades should be made in consultation with the binder. An alternative to the use of crash plus paper is to double the amount of crash. Sometimes nylon thread is used rather than the heavier cotton thread, to avoid excessive bulking at the back. There are, however, some technical problems connected with nylon thread that tend to limit its use.

ADHESIVES

This, too, is a technical matter best left to the binder. Production people should be aware, however, of the very large range of adhesives available and the need to fit the adhesive to the job. Obviously, for adhesive-bound books the adhesive is all-important.

Adhesives fall into several categories: the *pastes* (similar to library paste) used to adhere endleaves to the cover, the *glues* used to adhere cover material to the boards, and the *flexible glues* used in backing (gluing-off) and adhesive-binding. There was considerable experimentation to find the ideal adhesive for adhesive-binding. The range extended from the animal glues originally used in bookbinding to "hot-melt" glues made of plastic compounds. The problem was to find an adhesive that's fluid enough to penetrate the interstices of the paper fibers, that dries fast enough to match the speed of the machines, that's very strong and flexible when dry, and that won't become brittle and crack with the passage of time.

HEADBANDS Headbands are made in long strips of cotton cloth about ⅝" (1.59 cm) wide. The cloth is like a good canvas and has a rolled edge that's sometimes woven with colored threads, making a pattern of alternating stripes. Some headbands are solid colors. About a dozen choices are usually available. Headbands may be regular or *mercerized* (having a silky gloss) (CH. 26).

14. Estimating cost

A basic knowledge of the subjects covered so far should be sufficient for most readers now. You *should* know more, but this knowledge will come only in time as you gain experience. Estimating, however, can't be done properly without a *deep* knowledge of the subject and a thorough knowledge of the art of estimating. It's simple enough to use a table or chart to arrive at the cost of basic operations, and sometimes this information is very useful, but once details, complexities, and variations enter the picture, nothing less than an intimate acquaintance with all aspects of the problem will keep you out of trouble.

Approximations are extremely dangerous in cost estimating. The profit margins in book manufacturing and publishing are very small, so a slight error or miscalculation can easily doom your company to a loss. A seemingly minor deviation from the usual procedure in any operation may turn out to be a major cost problem, involving the use of a larger machine, a hand operation, or a time-consuming adjustment.

Because estimating requires more knowledge than can be gotten from this (or any one) book, and the consequences of even a small error can be disastrous, this chapter makes no attempt to enable you to perform the function yourself. The information provided here is meant simply to give you enough familiarity with estimating to make it possible to deal effectively with those engaged in it. No reliance should be placed on your own estimates until you have had much practical experience in book production and in estimating itself.

Finding the probable cost of materials is relatively easy, but even this has booby traps. Price increases, penalties, extra charges, spoilage allowances, taxes, shipping charges, overruns and underruns—any or all of these can cause trouble for the inexperienced estimator. But it's in estimating the cost of manufacturing processes that the real dangers lie. The time required to perform a routine operation is known—but how long will it take to make up that special running head, or to do the makeready to print those unusual illustrations, or to insert books in that special carton? Not even the technician in the shop knows exactly how much time these things will take, and your guess is likely to be less accurate.

A rough guess about cost is usually worse than no figure at all. No important decisions should be based on such guesses because they could be, and usually are, wrong. There is a tendency to guess under the actual cost—which will lead to certain disaster—and rough figures obtained from a professional estimator are likely to be high—which may discourage a perfectly sound project. Professional estimators usually decline to give rough estimates at all, but if pressed they generally add a substantial percentage to their own guess in order to cover themselves. Even when a figure is thoroughly understood by both parties to be only a guess and not a contract, bad feeling often ensues when the bill comes to more than the guess. Moral: Don't operate on *anything* but a formal estimate in writing.

Having given this warning, it must be admitted that publishers often want and use rough estimates in the early stages of planning a project. These are frequently made by comparison with the cost of previously published books, and sometimes they're prices based on dummy specifications, but in either case they're based on actual costs, not guesses. However, the danger remains, because the new book will rarely come out exactly like either the previous one *or* the dummy specs. Such preliminary figures can be helpful, provided they're used with caution and are replaced by detailed estimates before final decisions are made.

Some of the estimating problems and practices encountered in each area of bookmaking are discussed in this chapter. Additional information on costs may be found in the chapters dealing with each subject.

Composition

Most book designers do their own typesetting and page-makeup on the computer, using appropriate programs such as QuarkXPress and Adobe InDesign (CHs. 6, 9), but some prefer to create designs on paper and send specifications for their execution to a typesetting shop or service bureau. In either case, the cost of the work is estimated on the basis of the number of pages of each kind of material, taking into account the trim-size of the book.

A price-per-page is quoted for pages of text only, pages with text and illustrations, pages with illustrations only, and special pages such as title page, copyright page, contents page, index pages, bibliographies, etc. For each kind of page, consideration is given to the nature of the material; a page with four illustrations costs more than a page with one, three-column text costs more than one- or two-column text, an illustration with a caption costs more than one without, etc. Ultimately, cost is based on time, and obviously it takes more time to produce a complex page than a simple one.

Typesetters charge according to their estimation of the value of their time plus their overhead (rent, utilities, salaries, taxes, etc.), so it's not surprising that prices vary from one to another. Also, some average out the different amounts of work on the pages and give a single price for all pages in each category, while others give prices for the various subcategories according to complexity of the material. Because of these differences in pricing practice it's unwise to evaluate the quality of typesetters' work by their price. It's best to ask for samples of their work and references to their customers. Even then, it takes a trial job to really know. Quoted prices are useful for comparison only when you are sure the bidders do comparable work.

Because they're based on volume production, the rates of book compositors are lower than those charged by typesetters doing advertising and other commercial work. The latter can deliver high-quality work on short notice, but the staff and facilities needed to supply such service (customarily required by ad agencies) call for higher prices.

Of course, it's assumed that the typesetter—whether designer or service bureau—is working from a fully edited and corrected disk containing the text. If the text comes in as a typewritten ms., there's the additional cost (and time) of having it either keyboarded using a computer word-processing program or scanned into a computer (CH. 6). Either way the charge is per page, although some "*inputters*" (keyboarders) will charge by the hour. The least expensive way is probably buying an inexpensive scanner and scanning the pages yourself.

The price of composition includes the cost of a minimum number of proofs—one set of page proofs and one set of corrected page proofs (CHs. 6, 9, 10). Additional proofs are charged at a price per proof. Copies of proofs can be made by a copy service or your own copier. For dummying a complicated illustrated book, a *galley proof* (running text without breaks for pages) may be ordered (CH. 26).

Composition prices, regardless of the method of pricing, are for the initial setting and makeup only. *Author's alterations (AAs)* (changes, not corrections of typesetter's errors) are charged separately (CH. 6). These are usually charged by the hour and can add up to major costs, so it's worth taking the time to make the editing, word-processing, and specifications as good as possible.

Prepress

Assuming that you supply the prepress house, service bureau, or printshop with a disk containing made-up pages with either outlines or FPO images indicating the size, shape, and position of illustrations, if any, the items of cost will be: (a) scanning and color-separating illustrations; (b) making and correcting random color proofs; (c) merging illustrations with text in the pages; (d) placing pages in imposition; (e) making final film or CTP files (CH. 10); (f) making blueprints or composed color proofs; (g) making corrections, if any; and (h) making plates, unless that's included in the printing price. Items (e) and (f) won't be included if you're using a computer-to-plate (CTP) system.

Prepress charges are generally per page, so the price depends on the size and number of pages affected, and the number and kind of illustrations, if any. Plates, if quoted separately, are charged according to the size and number of plates.

The prices for prepress work are usually quoted with (a), (b), and (c) as one item, (d), (e), and (f) as one item, and (h) as a separate item. Some suppliers quote the prices in other combinations, and some lump them all into one number. Later trouble can be avoided by insisting on the quote being broken down into individual items. Corrections of supplier's errors are, of course, not charged, and usually an allowance for some customer corrections is built into the quoted prices, but over that amount charges (g) are added. At this stage such corrections can be very costly. The charge for color separation usually includes one set of chemical proofs (Matchprint, Chromalin, etc.), digital color proofs (Kodak Approvals, Dupont Digital Waterproof, etc.), or several sets of press proofs, and one or two rounds of corrected reproofs. More than that means additional charges.

Plates & printing Plates may be made by a service bureau, which will quote a price for them based on their kind, size, and number, or, more likely, the printshop will make the plates and the cost may or may not be included in the printing price.

The price of printing consists of the charge for the estimated makeready time plus a price per thousand impressions, which is based on the cost of operating the press, i.e., the pay of the operators, amortizing the cost of the machine, the rent or taxes on the space it occupies, and general overhead (electricity, bookkeeping, maintenance, etc.) during the time required to print the book. Except for some overhead items, the cost increases with the size of the press.

The ink cost is relatively minor and is included in the printing price. Occasionally, when an unusual amount of ink is required, a separate charge is made. When a color other than black is used on a one-color press, there's a charge for washup each time, but this is a minor amount on a normal run and is usually not noted separately.

The relative cost of makeready and impressions varies according to the specifications of the job. For example, a form of straight text can be made ready and can run faster than one containing color process; a form of 32 pages can be made ready faster than one of 64 pages; high-speed presses and perfectors reduce the importance of impressions in relation to makeready time; in general, the shorter the run, the larger the makeready looms in the price.

Although the printshop's cost per thousand impressions is the same for each thousand, the price per thousand usually decreases somewhat with larger quantities. The main economic benefit of long runs, however, is in reduction of the unit cost of makeready.

There's also a cost advantage in larger forms, up to a point. It doesn't take nearly twice as long to make a 64-page form ready as a 32-page form, so it's usually cheaper to have fewer, larger forms. This isn't always true, however, since the time charge on a larger press is usually more than that of a smaller one. With a short run on a large, fast press, the high cost of makeready time may make it more economical to run on a smaller press, even with more forms, as there's little advantage in the speed.

Almost all web presses have built-in folders, so the prices quoted generally include the folding. In both webfed and sheetfed printing the paper is sometimes supplied by the printshop. In this case, the paper may be quoted as a separate item or as part of the printing price. It's important to be clear about what is included when comparing bids from two or more printshops.

Xerographic printing requires no plates or makeready, so the cost consists of the running time and paper. Since these presses are used essentially for print-on-demand production of bound books, the prices quoted are usually a single figure for each bound copy, including the cover—and, of course, overhead and profit. There's almost always a small charge for setting up and handling the job.

Paper (See CH. 11)

Binding

Estimating binding costs is much more complex than figuring printing prices, as there are many more operations and materials. The price quoted by a binder is a unit price (per copy) according to the size of the run, usually without any itemization. While there are a great many items involved, no one of them accounts for a major part of the cost. Usually, about 80% of the total is materials, and these costs don't vary much per unit in the normal range of quantities. The cost of operations is, as in printing, a combination of makeready, or setting-up, and running, but due to the much slower speeds of binding equipment, the setting-up costs are relatively small compared to running time. Consequently, there isn't much difference in the unit cost of binding a small edition or a large one. Only in extremely small quantities is there a really appreciable difference. Editions under, say, 2000 become quite expensive because the setting-up cost is spread over so few copies. For example, it might cost 70¢ per copy to bind

5000 copies, 69¢ for 10,000, and 68½¢ for 50,000—a spread of only 1½¢ over 45,000—but the price for 1500 copies would be 78¢—a spread of 8¢ over 3500.

The only material items large enough to be worth calculating with a view to saving money are the cover material—which may account for about 10% of the total price—and the endpapers—which may amount to about 5%. For one-piece covers on a 6⅛ x 9¼" (15.6 x 23.5 cm) trim-size book, ten covers can be cut out of a running yard of material, including spoilage. Thus, with a $2 material, the cost per book is about 20¢, a $3.50 material means 35¢ per book, etc. Using this rule of thumb it's quite easy to estimate the effect on unit cost of any change of material for a one-piece cover.

In estimating three-piece covers, each material is figured separately. To find the cost of a material used on part of a cover, divide the width of the piece into the width of the roll, then divide the height of the piece into 36", multiply the two answers and you have the number of pieces that will cut out of a running yard. Divide this number into the price per yard to get the price per piece. Thus, a 5 x 7½" trim-size book with a 2½"-wide strip of cloth showing on the spine and sides would require a piece 3" wide—to allow each side to overlap ¼"—and 9" high (CH. 13). The 3" would cut fourteen times out of a 42"-wide roll and the 9" cuts four times out of a yard of length. This gives fifty-six pieces (four times fourteen) per yard. So, if the material costs $2.24 per yard, each piece costs 4¢. If the spine were 1" wide, the side pieces would each be 5" wide x 9" high. If the sides were a paper from a 25"-wide roll, the 5" would cut out five times and there would be four pieces 9" high out of the yard length. This would provide twenty pieces, or ten books (two sides per book), out of a running yard. At 20¢ per yard, the sides would cost 2¢ per book. The total cost of cover material is then 6¢.

The cost of a one-piece cover of the same cloth as that used for the spine in the example above would be 18⅔¢—the width of the piece is 12½", which cuts out three times from a 38" roll (with ½" waste) and the 9" height comes four times out of the yard, making twelve pieces per yard. Dividing twelve into $2.24 comes to $.1866 (18⅔¢).

Each endpaper is twice the untrimmed page width. Thus, on a trim-size of 5 x 7½" the untrimmed page is 5⅛ x 7¾", so the endpaper is 10¼ x 7¾". Endpapers are usually cut from sheets, not rolls. Remembering that the grain should run with the fold (7¼"), this size would cut out of a 26 x 40" grain-long sheet ten times (two times 10¼" out of 26" and five times 7¾" out of 40") with some waste. From here, the cost would be calculated as for any other paper (CH. 11).

The labor costs in binding divide roughly into: (a) sheetwork—

folding, gathering, sewing; (b) forwarding—trimming, backing, etc.; (c) casemaking; (d) stamping; (e) casing-in; and (f) wrapping. The costs of the items vary in their proportion of the total binding cost according to each book's characteristics and the length of the run. Some of the alternatives are discussed in CHs. 13, 29, but in general, you won't get involved in the cost of the individual items.

Assume a total cost of 69½¢ for labor, with about 10½¢ added for materials other than the text paper and the cover material. If the latter were 7¢, the total binding cost would be about 87¢. The prices would vary also according to the individual binder, the kind of equipment used, and when the work is done.

A figure for packing and shipping should be added, as these are customarily in the binder's price. Where packing is on skids and delivery is local in bulk, 4¢ should be enough. For packing in bulk cartons, add about 7¢, including the cartons. For individual carton packing, figure at least 13¢ for labor and between 12¢ and $1.50 each for the cartons, depending on the size of the book, the number of copies, and the design of the carton. Where individual carton labeling is to be done by the binder, there's an additional charge of about 8¢, including delivery in bulk to the post office. There is no charge for skids if they're returned.

CAUTION! See "A Special Note on Prices" on page 4 and "Some Special Notes" on page 13.

15. Schedules & records

Schedules

In making books for publishing, it's essential to get the books made not only well and economically, but efficiently. This means getting books finished in time to be published as scheduled. The financial success or failure of a title may hinge as much upon when it's published as any other factor.

There are two main problems in choosing a publication date: (a) deciding when the book is likely to be best received by reviewers, booksellers, and the public, and (b) relating publication time to the financial needs of the house. The latter is a relatively minor consideration for all but the smallest publishers, but once the decision is taken, the apparatus of distribution is set in motion—a catalog is printed, advertising is prepared, salespeople are briefed and begin selling, orders are taken—and any change in schedule can have serious consequences.

THE HAZARDS

Even if only one title is being produced, the problem of keeping a publication date is formidable—but when a hundred, or five hundred, are in work simultaneously, nothing short of high efficiency (and a generous helping of luck) will succeed. The causes of schedule-breaking delay are many: If the publication date (*pub date*) is set before the ms. is completed, as is often the case, there's a good chance that the ms. will be late. The author may become ill, be distracted by pressing personal matters, run into an unexpected difficulty in writing, go abroad on a windfall fellowship, or decide that the ms. is no good and rewrite it. Once it's turned in, it may require considerable editing, checking, or examination for libelous material. When released by the editorial department, the ms. goes to the designer—who may find it badly organized, incomplete, or economically impractical. With the problems solved and design worked out, the text goes into composition. If it's sent out for typesetting, it may be delayed by a busy compositor or set incorrectly by mistake. Then proofs go to the author and editor, either of whom may delay their return for one or more of the reasons mentioned. These hazards exist for page-makeup as well. In the prepress stage any one of a number of calamities may strike—loss of proofs in the mail, loss or damage of plates in transit, late delivery of illustrations or films, receipt of new material from the author, etc. Delays caused by a busy printshop are to be expected, and there could be late delivery of paper, faulty paper, plate injuries on press, or press breakdown. In the bindery, another delay is possible as the binders try to fit the job into *their* schedule; the possibilities for small and large disasters during binding are multiple. At every stage there's the possibility of delays caused by labor disputes. These are some of the reasons for missing a publication date even *if* the production department operates efficiently.

Another production scheduling problem is the concentration of publishing in two or three seasons. Publishers deplore this, but the distribution of books in such a large country as the U.S. makes it difficult to do otherwise. It's more convenient to have a sales conference at which all the salespeople are briefed on the season's list than to brief them individually on a few titles at a time, and, since they're scattered from Maine to California, it isn't feasible to bring them together more than two or three times a year. All this, combined with the massive emphasis on the Christmas gift market, tends to perpetuate the practice of producing books in batches.

THE TIME REQUIRED

Normally, tradebooks should be manufactured in time for delivery at the warehouse about six weeks prior to pub date. This allows time to ship books to all parts of the country, and to send them to reviewers far enough in advance to enable appearance of reviews at or about publication date. (The use of bound galleys or xerographic, i.e., on-demand, printing of books can relieve the review copy problem.)

A book of average size with no problems *can* be produced in about three weeks if everyone concerned puts all else aside, but the actual time needed is about five months. Complicated texts, illustrations, high-quality production, and thorough proofreading require still more time. An average book should go into production six months before publication to allow for unforeseen problems.

A realistic production schedule for a book of about 320 pages of straight text and few or no illustrations in an edition of 7500 might run as follows:

	weeks required
analysis, design, & sample pages	2
typesetting & 1st page proofs	3
reading 1st page proofs	4
revised page proofs	1
reading revised pages	1
correction & making final page files.	1

making film or CTP files & checking blues or proofs	2	
platemaking & printing	2	
binding	(hardcover) 3	(pbk.) 2
total weeks	19	18

It's possible to make a book in less time by omitting a pass of proofs (although some of the reading and correction time then gets added to the next proofs) or working faster, but it would be dangerous to allow less unless the suppliers were to give firm promises of an earlier completion date—and even then there are too many possibilities for unexpected delays (as noted above, plus indexing, shipping, etc.) to depend on the date.

For a book with many halftone illustrations, in which all pages must have individual layouts, the following schedule would be typical:

	weeks required
analysis, design, & sample pages	2
scanning FPOs	1
typesetting & layout	3
reading 1st page proofs and checking illustrations	4
correcting 1st proofs & illustrations	2
reading revised pages	1
correcting page proofs.	2
making film or CTP files & checking blues or proofs	2
platemaking & printing	2
binding	3
total weeks	22

If process-color illustrations are involved, more time might be needed to make separations, proofs, and corrections, unless this can be accomplished while other work is being done—which may be quite possible if the color requires little correction.

PROMISES & PRESSURES Generally, suppliers of services won't give definite schedules until a job is in their hands for production, for they have no way of knowing in advance what work will be in their plant when the job does come in. For a very big or important job they may give a firm date in advance, but this obviously means that some other work will be pushed aside if necessary. Since you may at some time be on the pushed as well as the pushing end, it's best to avoid asking for such promises. The hard truth remains, however, that with the best of intentions and the most efficient planning, circumstances beyond your control sometimes make a crash program necessary. The object in bookmaking is to see that such cases are the exception rather than the rule.

With many jobs in work at the same time, and conflicting pressures from all sides, suppliers may easily fall behind. While it isn't wise to push too hard too often, a gentle reminder at proper intervals is quite necessary. Knowing just when and how to do this is vital for a production manager. It's best to prod when there's still time to get the job done on schedule even if the supplier has been delinquent. On a long-term job, occasional, well-timed reminders are in order. Written reminders are effective and not as distracting as phone calls.

Records

The number of details involved in producing even one book is astonishing; keeping track of many books in various stages of production can be overwhelming unless systematic records are maintained.

It would be nice to be able to say that a simple chart is sufficient, but it isn't. To be effective, a record system must cover every detail, and this means that a progress chart should provide a place for each item of production. Anything not carried on the chart is likely to be overlooked at some point.

There are as many ways of arranging production records as there are people keeping them—and any system is good if it works. The basic idea is to provide a space to be filled when a particular operation is completed, so that the blank spaces are reminders of what isn't yet done. This would be relatively simple if all operations were successive, but there are many things to be done concurrently, and the problem is to get them all done *when they're needed* (like cooking a four-course meal). For example, all of the following may be in progress on one title at one particular moment:

text in composition,
frontmatter copy coming from author,
foreword and/or preface being written,
Library of Congress number applied for,
illustration scans being made,
a missing illustration being made,
paper for text being made,
paper for illustrations ordered,
binding design out for approval,
bulking dummy being made,
jacket separations being made, and
jacket *flap copy* being written.

The extent of this list isn't an exaggeration, but a common occurrence. And if ordering something were sufficient to get it done, the problem would be complex enough, but each item must be followed up or it may be late and hold up the entire job.

It isn't possible to record the progress of *every* detail of production, yet every detail must be somehow covered. The more records kept, the better for accuracy, but keeping up records takes time too, and a small staff is usually not able to make all the entries needed. Each office must find its own compromise.

On the following page is a typical record form. Note that spaces are provided for the dates when various items are *due*, as well as the dates they *actually* (ACT) arrive. A considerable amount of work is needed to maintain such records, but it's better to use a form and fail to keep it perfectly than to use an inadequate form.

In addition to keeping a chart on which the progress of each title is recorded in detail, it's desirable to keep a chart showing the progress of all titles in work, so you can see at a glance how the whole list stands in terms of the season's publication schedule.

Each title should, of course, have its own folder containing a copy of every proof or document relevant to its production. Although there's a good chance that the world will collapse under the weight of all the records being accumulated, it's better to keep anything that might be useful than to throw it away and need it later. (The paperless office promised by the computer turned out to be a mirage.) A system of periodic destruction of old files will keep the accumulation from getting out of hand. For items that exist as computer files, storage on disks or tape is the answer to permanent filing of important documents.

Many filing systems in production offices are based on letter-size folders, but it's a good idea to use the larger legal-size files, which are very handy for keeping large proofs, sketches, illustrations, etc.

The most important records in book production, besides those needed to keep schedules, concern expenditures of money. Sometimes an order is placed in the course of a conversation, and this may be sufficient for the supplier, but to keep the records straight, a confirming order on a numbered order form should be executed. Besides the copy or copies required by the bookkeeping department, at least one copy of all orders should be made for the records of the production office.

It's customary for book manufacturers, printshops, and binders to file jobs by title, so, even though books are referred to by author in publishing houses, confusion is minimized by using the title outside the house. The chances of a publisher having two authors of the same name on one list are small, but suppliers may deal with dozens of publishers, and the chance of a duplication of authors' names is substantial.

For a discussion of preparing composition orders, see CH. 30. Printing orders are covered in CH. 34 and binding orders in CH. 35.

PRODUCTION SCHEDULE

Title________________________Author________________ISBN____________

Editor__________________Designer__________________ Trim size_____ x _____"

No. Pages________Quantity___________Est. book date__________Est. pub date_________

Compositor______________________Prepress ______________________

Printer: book________________jacket/cover________________Binder________________

COMPOSITION:	DUE	ACT
Ms to design		
Sample pp IN		
Estimate OK		
Ms to copyed		
Copyed ms to comp		
Galleys IN		
Castoff OK		
Frontmatter to comp		
" pfs IN		
" " OK		
1st pass pages IN		
" " " ret		
2nd pass pages IN		
" " " ret		
Final pages IN		
" " OK		
Index ms IN		
" to comp		
" 1st pass pp IN		
" " " " ret		
" 2nd " " IN		
" " " " ret		

ILLUSTRATION:	DUE	ACT
Art IN		
Sized art to scan		
Scans OK		
Captions to comp		
Captions pfs IN		
1st pass insert pp IN		
2nd " " " IN		
Final insert files IN		
Insert proofs OK		

PREPRESS/PRINTING	DUE	ACT
Final text files to prep		
Text PDF proof IN		
" PDF files to prtr		
Final index files to prep		
Index PDF files to prtr		
Final proofs/blues IN		
Dummy/order to prtr		
On press		
Sheets to bindery		

JACKET/COV PTG :	DUE	ACT
Design ordered		
" IN		
" OK		
Flap copy IN		
" " to comp		
" " prfs OK		
Jacket/cov pfs IN		
" " " OK		
PDF proof to prtr		
On press		
Sheets to bindery		

BINDING:	DUE	ACT
Binding design IN		
" " OK		
Dies ordered		
" IN		
Printed cover art IN		
" " " to prtr		
" " Blues OK		
Sheets to finisher		
" " bindery		
Sample covers ordered		
" " IN		
Order to bindery		
Bound books		

MATERIALS:	DUE	ACT
Text paper ordered		
" " IN		
Insert paper ordered		
" " IN		
Endpaper ordered		
" IN		
Jacket paper ordered		
" " IN		
Binding mat'l ordered		
" " IN		

MISC:	DUE	ACT

16. Electronic publishing

The electronic systems of publishing are in their infancy, and, given the dynamic growth potential of electronics, they're very likely to change, so the following discussion should be read with that probability in mind. Indeed, for those reading this printing of *Bookmaking* long after publication, changes not mentioned may already have arrived.

There are several electronic ways of bringing the content of books to readers. These are subsumed under the term "*e-books*"—for which the two main means of distribution are handheld reading devices (readers) and Internet dissemination. All together, this activity may be referred to as "*electronic publishing*". This will probably become a significant factor in book publishing some day, but it doesn't seem likely to supplant the traditional printed book entirely, and perhaps not even to a major extent. Nevertheless, it's important for all in bookmaking to be familiar with it.

An element of confusion has entered the subject of e-books by the misleading use of the term "electronic printing" to describe machines that print by the process of xerography (CHs. 10, 12) and are also known as "print-on-demand" presses. While the content printed by these machines is digital files delivered electronically to the press, the same is, or can be, true for other kinds of printing machines. "Print-on-demand" machines are xerographic presses—their electronic features are only incidental.

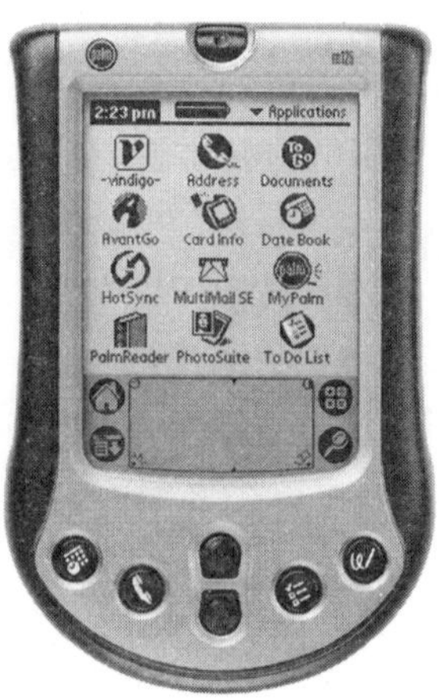

Palm IIIc

E-books

READERS

There are many *electronic readers* on the market, each with its particular design features, but the principle is the same for all. A flat metal or plastic device, small and light enough to be carried, contains what is essentially a tiny computer capable of being loaded with the digital content of one or more books and displaying lines of type on a small glass or plastic screen. The lines of type can be scrolled for continuous reading or whole pages can be displayed in succession.

E-book readers got off to a slow start because of their high cost—several hundred dollars each—and the relatively small number of titles available. Both obstacles were functions of the comparatively few machines in use; as the number of users grew, prices declined and availability of titles multiplied. Efforts were made to improve the readability of the type.

Some of these reading devices have also some of the convenient features of a computer, such as e-mail access, reference capability, etc. The cost of reading a book on one isn't very different from buying a printed copy, and there remains the question: How many people will find it satisfying to read lengthy texts on a small screen in comparison with reading—and owning—a printed-on-paper book? The number may eventually be quite large for books of only text, but isn't likely to be substantial for illustrated books in general, or for art books. Among illustrated books, only reference titles seem likely to go into e-book format.

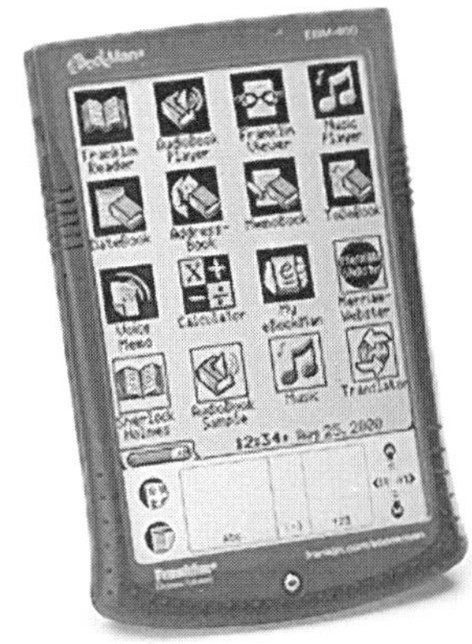

Franklin EBM-900

In terms of bookmaking, to the extent that the page-makeup is digitized for exact transmission to the e-book reader, there would be no change in the process through makeup. It's possible that there might be some modification of the specifications in the conversion—in which case corrected galleys would be the last stage of the process. At the same time, if e-book reader conversion is in the initial plan, designers will need to keep in mind the relatively small size of the screens in making their basic decisions (CH. 23). And note that in most readers it's possible for the owner to modify type size and/or face.

INTERNET DISSEMINATION

Variety is greater on the Internet than in e-book readers. Whole books may be made available for reading on screen or for downloading and printing, or only chapters or small parts of the text may be offered. The title offered might be an original from a conventional publisher or a specialized electronic publisher, or it could be a traditionally published title being offered on the Internet as a supplemental form of distribution. In any case, this is an area full of unanswered—or only partially answered—questions.

Here again it remains to be seen if a significant number of people will be happy sitting in front of a computer for hours reading on the screen, or printing out the text and reading from hundreds of loose sheets. Obviously, a key element is the number of pages in the book. Where a 60-page novella might be acceptable, a 400-page book might not be. Even more of a problem is protecting the publisher's—and author's—financial interests in the intellectual property. The open nature of the Internet makes it relatively easy for unauthorized users to obtain the work, making copyright a frail, almost useless, form of protection, although there are systems available that claim to fully protect the content. Then there's the problem of finding "buyers" of electronic publications. The number will undoubtedly increase in time, but the starting numbers, with a few exceptions, tended to be small. It may turn out that the best use of the Internet in publishing will be as a means of promoting the sale of printed books by making available free samples of the texts and showing favorable reviews, although publishing customized college text materials seems a promising use. A likely practice is making some titles available in both of the electronic publishing formats.

Bookmaking relates to Internet dissemination much the same as to e-book readers. Page design isn't necessarily a factor, but short of that, the bookmaking process is unchanged.

"Electronic paper"

A development on the periphery of electronic publishing that's potentially a major factor, but isn't yet (at this writing) in use for books, is "*electronic paper*". Quotation marks are used because this extraordinary material isn't really paper, although it can be used like paper. There are two competing products, invented more-or-less simultaneously in the 1970s, but only recently brought into commercial use. One, developed at Xerox laboratories, is called Smart Paper; the other, originating at MIT, is named E Ink.

Smart Paper is a clear plastic sheet, with about the thickness and flexibility of a transparency, which contains millions of tiny particles. The particles are bichromal, i.e., half are one color, say, black, the other half another color, say, white. When an electrical charge is applied to the sheet, the particles rotate to show one of their colors. The charge can be applied so as to create images of text and pictures. This can be done by feeding the sheet into a small printer-like device. The exciting feature of this technology is that the material is reusable; images can be erased and new images created thousands of times. E Ink uses a similar technology, but its particles can be applied to any surface.

Electronic paper (it's not likely to be carried by paper merchants) lies somewhere between conventional printing and computer screen images. It has a great number of possible applications, particulary for displays, but eventually also in books and other publications.

E. PROCEDURE

Editorial

17. Concept & acquisition

The title of this chapter reflects the two basic sources of book properties: (a) the house-conceived project and (b) the project or manuscript (ms.) brought in from outside. The percentage of published titles from each of these sources varies greatly from company to company. In some trade houses, perhaps half the list originates outside; in others—usually the more "literary" publishers—few books are done in this way. In elementary and high school textbook publishing almost all titles are planned in the house to meet competition or a need reported by educators. Proposals for college texts generally come from professors, from college travelers, i.e., salespeople who sell to college bookstores, and sometimes from the acquisition editors, who, in any case, drive the development of the projects.

Concept

House-conceived books tend to be scorned by some editors and publishers for being commercial concoctions. They usually are just that and that's indeed usually the intention. Sometimes an editor will plan a book to meet an intellectual or cultural need, but most house books are conceived as objects of desire, with a definite market in mind. Either the editor observes a widespread interest in a particular subject and develops a book intended to satisfy that interest, or a book is created out of a particularly intriguing idea that's expected to arouse the buying interest of a part of the public. For the editor, this isn't the same as being the instrument by which a writer-artist reaches an appreciative audience, but it's a valid part of publishing, and is probably the part that makes it economically possible to be also an instrument of literature and art.

Editors in publishing offices are not the only ones who conceive book ideas. Projects come in various states of development from agents, writers, illustrators, photographers, freelance editors, and packagers. Except for packagers, who come to publishers with fully planned proposals, the outside sources usually approach editors with projects that are in the form of written descriptions or outlines, or are simply verbal suggestions. If the idea seems interesting, the originator may be asked to proceed with its realization, or at least to carry it further and submit a detailed outline, some sample text, and perhaps a dummy. In other cases, the editor takes the raw idea and develops it within the house—hiring writers and illustrators as necessary.

The question of compensation for ideas is one of the most difficult an editor faces. There is no copyright or patent protection for ideas that don't have a tangible form, so an idea itself has no legal standing. This is an upsetting concept to people who are creative and have good ideas that they can't execute themselves, but it's rooted in the understandable difficulty of establishing value in the absence of a concrete work. If the creator of an idea had a copyright and failed to produce or publish, this would prevent anyone else who got the same idea from producing it, and the idea would be lost to the world. This would be contrary to the purpose of copyright laws, which is to encourage bringing creative works to the public.

At the same time, ideas can have enormous commercial value, and the use of them should be compensated accordingly. The problem is determining what percentage of the profit from a product is due to the idea, the realization, and the marketing. The proportion varies in each case, and even a Solomon would lack the wisdom to make an accurate judgment. In the end, the various contributors must negotiate and arrive at a division that reflects their actual strength. Unfortunately, the person with the idea is usually in the weakest position and often gets less than is deserved.

In fairness, it must be said that many people who have ideas undervalue the realization and marketing contributions. They see their idea as a unique element that causes sales, and the other elements as replaceable mechanical functions. They often fail to appreciate that the idea could succeed or fail according to the skill and imagination with which it's produced and sold. There is also a tendency to underestimate the element of risk in publishing, and the compensation due to it.

When an editor has an idea for a book, the next step is usually to write a proposal comprising: (a) a description of the project; (b) a statement of the sales prospects in terms of potential audience, propitious circumstances (if any), previous successes in the same field (if any), and the competition (if any); (c) a note about the proposed author and illustrator (if any); and (d) a suggested format, retail price, and publication date. The proposal is generally accompanied by cost estimates obtained from the production department—particularly if the project involves color illustrations or other costly production elements—with a projection of the financial prospects. Assuming that the editor needs the approval of higher authority to undertake the project, the proposal is submitted to the editor-in-chief for consideration. Approval of the head of the editorial department may be sufficient, but in some companies all proposals are submitted to an editorial board, usually including the heads of editing and marketing, one or two officers of the company, and sometimes the senior editors. In some houses, a majority vote decides, in others the votes are advisory and the publisher makes the final decision.

In most cases, the editor has discussed the idea in the proposal stage with a suitable writer, but if the project is approved and no author is already involved, the editor will either try to interest a particular writer or writers—directly or through their agents—or ask one or more agents to suggest writers they represent.

The terms for the writer of commissioned books may be a flat fee or a fee plus a small royalty, particularly when the writer makes a relatively small creative contribution and doesn't have a selling name. If the writer's name is likely to generate large sales and/or if the text is large and there's little or no illustration, the full royalty may be paid to the writer, even though the idea is the editor's. Should negotiations with the writer break off, it's understood by custom that the idea remains with the house and can't be used by the writer for a book with another publisher.

If the project requires illustration, the editor will consult with the art director or designer. (For a full discussion of illustration planning and acquisition see CH. 7.) If existing pictures are used, the terms of the owners prevail—usually payment of a reproduction fee. If new illustrations are to be made, the terms usually correspond to the magnitude and sales value of the work: as with the author, a fee with or without a small royalty if the contribution is relatively minor, a substantial royalty if the illustrations constitute a major part of the book and/or the illustrator's name can be expected to attract buyers. For a book in which both author and illustrator are major contributors—as in a juvenile *flat* (a large-format picture-and-text book for preschool children)—they may share the royalty equally. (See CH. 4 for a discussion of contracts.)

Acquisition

Here the project is originated outside the house and submitted by an author, agent, or packager.

In the case of a packager, the submission will be in the form of a proposal such as described above, but usually including a specific author and illustrations, with a dummy or sample spreads showing some of the pages as they will appear in the finished book, and a jacket or cover design. These will be accompanied by either complete specifications for the production of the book and a proposed price, or a price for only disks or films with a proposed royalty (CH. 4).

The acquisition of packaged books may be very advantageous for a publishing company as it provides products ready to be sold; not only is a negligible amount of effort required of the house staff, but very often the books acquired are of a nature which the staff would find difficult or impossible to produce. For the editor, no further work is needed once the contract is signed except to approve the materials submitted by the packager (CHs. 4, 36).

Packaged books are also financially attractive for the publisher. Since they're bought for the packager's cost plus a small royalty, the publisher can charge to these books the same overhead as house books without having the editorial, design, and production expenses. However, the packager gets paid the royalty on all books delivered, whether sold by the publisher or not, so the publisher's risk is higher than usual. But then, the royalty built into the all-in package price is relatively small—and advances given authors by publishers are frequently equal or nearly equal to the royalty on the entire first printing, and sometimes much more. Finally, the packager has the financial risk of the production; a mistake in specifications, the failure of a supplier, or an uninsured accident can cost more than the whole royalty is worth. For this reason, some packagers prefer to deliver only disks or films and let the publisher print and bind the books.

Packaged books are often illustrated, so they cost more than most and their acquisition involves relatively large sums, the expenditure of which usually requires management approval.

When a book is proposed by an author or agent, it may be in any state ranging from just an idea to a finished ms. with a dummy. The more successful the writer, the less is likely to be required before contract. Top-selling writers can get a contract for their next book (or their next three) without even knowing what it (or they) will be about. At the other end of the scale, a first book of fiction is usually submitted in the form of a completed ms. For authors in between those extremes, an agent can usually get a contract for nonfiction on the basis of an outline and sample chapter. Fiction almost always requires submission of a complete text.

There was a time when submitting a ms. simultaneously to more than one publisher (*multiple submission*) was considered bad form, and few editors would consider a book they knew was being read by others. Today, the practice is widespread and accepted as the norm, although agents generally inform editors that others are reading the ms.

In multiple submissions, each editor informs the agent of his or her interest or noninterest in the proposal. If more than one editor is interested, the agent either chooses one on the basis of preference and/or judgment, or takes the one that offers the best terms. Sometimes low bidders are given an opportunity to top the highest offer and an auction ensues. If no one expresses an interest, the proposal is sometimes sent to another group of publishers. With an exceptionally desirable project, the agent may go directly into an auction, sending the proposal to several publishers with a list of minimum acceptable (*floor*) terms and a date and hour by which offers are to be received. The period allowed may range from forty-eight hours to a few weeks, depending on the nature of the material submitted. Provision may be made for two or more rounds of bidding to give low bidders a chance to up their offers. A publisher may preempt bidding with a big offer.

Publishers often allow editors to offer advances under a certain amount, requiring management approval of only bigger deals. Auctions generally involve the larger sums, so it's usually necessary for acquiring editors who want to bid to go to higher authority for approval of the project and the amount to be offered. Bids may include details of the terms, such as *escalator clauses* (increases in the royalty rate as sales increase), subsidiary income splits, or advertising guarantees, but the basic element is the royalty guarantee (advance). Advances may exceed the estimated royalty earnings for the book if the publisher can count on large subsidiary rights income (book clubs, foreign sales, reprint editions, movies, television, e-publishing, etc.). Indeed, as the owners of major publishing houses demand higher profits, sub-rights possibilities are an increasingly important element in considering a book for publication.

Materials accepted for consideration by an editor and then rejected should be returned within a reasonable time. The length of time varies according to the nature of the material and other circumstances, but the agent or author should be given some word within a month and preferably sooner. With specialized nonfiction, the ms. is usually sent to experts for appraisal, which takes an amount of time determined by the experts, not the editor. An agent will understand this if kept informed. Some publishers won't return unsolicited rejected materials unless a self-addressed, stamped envelope (SASE) is provided by the author. This is the policy of most agents also.

Mss. that come into the house should be logged in with a record of the time and date of arrival and the means of delivery. The wrapping should be kept if there's a postmark or messenger service label on it. The main purpose of this is to avoid loss of the ms., but these records are useful also in disputes about the length of time a ms. is held, particularly if it's rejected. A record should be kept of the movement of each ms. from person to person, and signed receipts obtained. In all cases, the author should be told that it's expected that a duplicate ms. exists. Some publishers ask that a computer disk for the text accompany the hard copy submitted, but this isn't usually required unless and until the book is accepted. Similar, but even more detailed, records should be made of the arrival and movements of original illustrations. In many cases there can be no duplicates of these and their loss—or claimed loss—can result in high-cost lawsuits.

Some mss. from highly respected agents will be read immediately by the editor, but otherwise at least one prior reading is done and a report submitted to the editor with a recommendation. At one time, all the larger houses had staff readers and some still do, but now that unsolicited mss. are rarely accepted and mss. are already screened by the agent, this practice has declined. Now, reading is done mostly by freelancers or by junior editors. In borderline cases, a ms. may go from the first reader to a second, more experienced one, whose recommendation will help the editor decide to read it or not.

After the editor has decided that a proposed book should be published, the procedure is the same as when an editor has a house project. A proposal is prepared for consideration by the editor-in-chief and/or the editorial board, or, in a small house, the publisher. In houses with large editorial boards, it's common for acquiring editors to lobby board members in favor of a project days before the next board meeting.

When a decision has been made to accept a book, unless there's an auction, the process of negotiating a contract begins.

The procedure for acquiring books from foreign publishers is similar to acquiring other mss. if the text is in English. If the text is in a language the editor doesn't read, then it must be screened through a reader of the original language and a judgment made on the basis of a summary in English and a report. Such books most often come through agents or scouts abroad who are paid a fee to find suitable properties. The contract terms for foreign books usually take into account the U.S. publisher's cost of translation, if any.

If the text of a foreign book hasn't yet been completed, the terms may be based on a co-edition, whereby the participating publishers share the editorial costs. This is most practical with large projects in which the editorial cost is very high. If the project involves much color illustration, then the participating publishers may enter into a *co-production*, whereby certain plant and manufacturing costs are shared (CH. 36).

Some publishers and packagers offer proposals for projects that are not economically feasible *unless* a co-edition and/or co-production is arranged. Such arrangements are usually initiated at international book fairs, such as the ones held each year in Frankfurt, London, and Bologna, at the annual Book Expo in the U.S., and at somewhat smaller annual fairs in Canada, Israel, Mexico, and Spain. Many purchases of rights to foreign books are made at these fairs also, usually by the heads of small firms and/or top editors of large ones.

18. Working with marketing

Publishing is a business and the object of a business is to make profit. Occasionally, a large trade publishing house will publish a book because it's exceptionally important even if it's expected to lose money. This happens rarely in small companies. Such books have customarily been taken up by university presses, but now that's less likely than before. Even when a publisher does take a book that has no profit potential but brings prestige to the house, there's usually a long-range commercial purpose behind the decision. Prestige attracts good writers and good writers can bring profits. In the past, some books with poor commercial prospects were published because it was believed that the author would produce profitable books later and it was considered important to establish a relationship. This hardly ever happens in large houses anymore, and it's a difficult practice for small publishers with limited financial resources. Almost without exception, the decision to publish is based on an expectation of, or at least a hope for, profit in the short term.

Yet, book publishing is one of a few industries that are intermediaries between the public and its culture, so there's an implicit responsibility to act in the public interest. Publishers, more than other businesspeople, are expected to allow considerations of quality to influence their decisions. While these considerations will rarely persuade a publisher to issue a book that's a sure loser, they sometimes cause the rejection of a potentially profitable book that's deemed substandard, and borderline commercial decisions are sometimes nudged into the affirmative column by the exceptional quality of a project.

The decision to publish a book, then, is based on two factors: (a) its sales potential and (b) its quality. The meaning of this in terms of *marketing* (the sum of all the activities that advance the commercial success of a book—selling, promotion, advertising) is that the editor must consider sales importantly in planning the publication of a book, but must also be guardian of its intellectual and artistic integrity. Respect for the work should be, and usually is, present in sales and promotion people, but their specific responsibility is to sell the book, and their zeal sometimes obscures concern for its cultural values. This most often finds expression in significant—if unconscious—misrepresentations of the nature of the book in the advertising, jacket design, flap copy, salespeoples' presentations, or all of these. The editor's duty is to defend the book against inaccurate representation, if that should occur.

The editor starts working with marketing when a project is first proposed. Since the commercial prospect is primary, whatever the editor's opinion of a project, it must have the support of marketing. The first question to ask about a proposal is: Will it sell? If the editor believes the answer is yes, then the next question—which should be asked in the same breath—is: Is it good enough? If that answer is also affirmative, a third, less important but nevertheless significant, question is: Is the project consistent with our publishing program? The editor who believes the answer to all three questions is yes will then ask the marketing department for an opinion on the first one: Will it sell?

If the editor is negative on the first point but very positive on the other two, a check with marketing is still in order. If marketing *also* is dubious of the sales prospects, the editor will ordinarily drop the project unless there's a very compelling consideration besides profit—such as prestige or author relations. However, going ahead with a project for such policy reasons would be a decision for management rather than the editorial department.

Although the editor looks for a yes or no opinion from marketing at this stage, the marketing people are likely to do some specific thinking about how to market the book in the course of forming an opinion of its salability. It's usual for the editor to have input in such thinking, partly to persuade but mainly to provide information about the project and its presumed audience, particularly concerning what the author can bring to sales in the way of a famous name, a following based on previous books, or a "*platform*"—a regular TV or radio show, a string of shops or galleries, etc.

Once a contract has been signed for a project acquired from outside, or the decision has been made to go ahead with a house project, the editor meets with marketing people to consider the marketing approach that will be taken, and the scope of the marketing effort that will be made—which is determined largely by the amount of money budgeted for the book. These plans will often affect the way in which the editor develops the project.

Sales concepts

Before a marketing approach can be formed, the marketing people must listen to the editor carefully to learn the exact nature of the book, i.e., what they will be selling. A misunderstanding at this point is likely to lead to a mistaken approach to selling, and the project will suffer.

For a "literary" book—a work of fiction or poetry—written and published on what might be called an as-is basis (i.e., there's no way that the book can be modified for sales purposes) a simple exchange of information between editor and marketing is sufficient. The editor must be careful to make clear the exact nature, content, and quality of the book, and tell as much as is known about the audience the author is trying to reach and has reached with previous books—including their sales histories. Marketing tells the editor what the sales possibilities appear to be, and gives some indication of the advertising and promotion program that's planned; at this point, it must be decided how much, if any, advertising will be done, and whether or not a promotion tour by the author is feasible. Some thoughts about the advertising approach (if there's to be any—it isn't likely unless the book either has big sales potential or begins to sell well after publication) will probably be conveyed to the editor in this meeting. There will also be a discussion of the general approach to the jacket or cover (in the case of a paperback) design (see below). If the editor disagrees strongly with the marketing plan—either its extent or nature—an argument will develop that may have to be resolved by management. Otherwise, the editor begins working with the author to ready the ms. for production, and marketing begins to develop a program.

In some companies, a request to the art director for a jacket or cover design is initiated by the editor, in others it comes from the marketing department. In either case, all three discuss the approach to be taken, with the object of achieving a result that will be a good combination of editorial, marketing, and design ideas.

When the project is conceptual—i.e., it can be shaped by the publisher's staff and/or the author to produce a desired result—the meeting of editor and marketing is more in the nature of a creative thinking session than an exchange of information. A give and take between a creative editor and creative marketing people can, and often does, improve the original concept of a project. The editor's role here isn't to defend the project but to be open to constructive criticism and ideas. This isn't to say that the editor should abandon the original concept to the opinions of marketing, but with conceptual projects there can be more flexibility than with works involving art or scholarship. From this point, the procedure is similar to what happens in the case of a "literary" work once the editor and marketing people have formulated their own ideas and shared them with the others.

Jacket & book design

JACKET DESIGN

The jacket design ("jacket" here should be taken to mean "cover" when a paperback is involved), like the design of the book itself, is determined partly by editorial and partly by sales considerations. Neither concern should be served at the expense of the other, but the jacket is primarily a selling device so here sales considerations are dominant. (See CH. 29 for a discussion of jacket design.) This, however, is where the editor must be alert to any tendency to misrepresent the nature of the book. Because the sales function is primary in jackets, the art director and designer may be more concerned with sales-effectiveness than with editorial accuracy, and the marketing department isn't inclined to complain if a small distortion of the book's character is present in a strong selling design.

This isn't to suggest that a deliberate distortion would be made or encouraged. It's simply that zeal to produce a sales-effective design sometimes overwhelms concern about the correctness of the representation. Also, under the pressure of deadlines, designers sometimes don't have time to read enough to get a true sense of the book, or they get a mistaken impression of it from the information they're given. While it's the art director's job to get a correct understanding of the book and convey this accurately to the designer, it's ultimately the editor's responsibility to see that the jacket does present the true nature of the book.

The editor must convey a clear idea of the book to the art director, either directly or through the marketing department, if that's the custom of the house. Then, the editor must check the submitted design to be sure that it does accurately reflect the book.

This is the point at which conflict between editor, art director, and marketing manager often arises. It can be minimized if the editor takes a stand on the element of editorial integrity only and leaves the art director and marketing manager to battle over the question of effectiveness. The editor is properly concerned with the esthetics of the design only when its style may be at odds with the style of the book. The art director was hired as an expert in esthetics, so the editor shouldn't try to impose a judgment of taste on the design unless it relates to appropriateness. The editor usually has final approval of the jacket, but it's important that this decision be made on the basis of specialized professional judgments rather than personal taste.

BOOK DESIGN

The editor's role in the design of the book follows roughly the same procedure as for jacket design. (See CH. 21, "Editorial analysis", and CHs. 22, 23, 24 on the designer's approach to editorial considerations in book design.) However, the editor's emphasis in considering the book design is generally more on editorial than sales aspects—not because sales is less important but because the way to help sales is to make the best book possible.

The extent to which the editor becomes involved in the book's design depends on the nature of the book. Where there are no illustrations or other visual elements, the editor meets with the art director and/or designer primarily to describe the text. At this meeting, the designer may suggest a design approach and ask the editor's opinion. Again, this would be not for esthetic reasons as much as to check the correctness of the designer's interpretation.

When a design is conceived, the design department will present it to the editor in the form of layouts and sketches or a printed sample. Here too, as with the jacket design, the editor must balance editorial and sales considerations; but here the editorial side will carry more weight. Nevertheless, the design is expected to help sell the book (CH. 2), so the editor must give appropriate weight to that aspect.

If the book is extensively illustrated and its visual element is an important part of its interest, the editor becomes more deeply involved in the design. In some houses, the marketing people will also participate in the planning stage of design.

With books of this kind, the editor and designer should join in developing a design concept that will most effectively and accurately convey the content of the book to the reader. In such efforts, the designer should control the results, but the editor should contribute an understanding of the author's intentions and needs, ideas for expressing these intentions, and constructive reactions to the designer's proposals. The design result should be the sum of what both editor and designer can bring to the problem. If marketing can suggest directions that will be effective in reaching the audience or arousing interest, so much the better. This is particularly likely if Internet publishing is involved.

It's tempting for editors to take command of the design of their books (and the jackets) and order changes to suit their ideas. In one sense, this would be appropriate, as editors are the ones whose role corresponds to that of the director of a play or movie (CH. 2), and it seems logical for them to control all of the elements to ensure unity and a high level of quality in every aspect of the work. But editors don't ordinarily bring design talents or background to their jobs, and are not expected to be competent in any but editorial functions—although they're expected to have a developed sense of fitness. Similarly, designers are assumed to be talented and trained specialists in their area. The reality is that editors exercise the coordination and executive functions of a theater director in the absence of such a position in publishing, but it's wise for them to exercise a restraint appropriate to their professional limitations and in observance of the professional qualifications of the designers. There are, presumably, occasional situations in which an editor has better taste, imagination, and design sense than the designer, but this is an anomaly that the editor must handle with utmost subtlety in order to achieve the maximum input while preserving the illusion of role integrity. The danger, of course, is that some editors may *believe* they have superior design abilities when they do not.

Editors should read *all* the text in this book to gain as full a knowledge and understanding of the design and production of books as they can, in order to exercise their directorial power with the maximum wisdom and judgment.

Advertising & promotion

Marketing departments want to get from the editor as much knowledge of the book as possible in order to write correct advertising and promotion copy. They are obliged to respect the editor's definition of the book's nature, but the extent to which the obligation is observed varies, depending on the positions and personalities of the marketing manager and the editor.

The editor should supply marketing (and design) with an information sheet describing the book in detail, giving a biographical note about the author (including sales facts about previous books) and presenting whatever is known or believed by author or editor about the prospective audience. On the basis of this, and a verbal presentation by the editor (usually made at a regular editorial meeting or at a *launch* meeting), the jacket flap copy and ads (if any) are prepared.

In some companies, flap copy is written in the editorial department—by an assistant to the editor of the book or even the editor—and sent to marketing for review. In others, the advertising department prepares the copy and sends it to the editor for review. Who has the final word usually depends on the relative strength of the editorial and marketing chiefs or the custom of the house.

The preparation of ads is initiated by marketing and the results are shown to the editor and, ordinarily, to management. Sometimes everyone is pleased by the first layouts and there's no problem. More often, someone disagrees with the approach, layout, or copy and a more or less polite battle ensues. Here, too, the outcome of the battle typically depends on power. Usually, a compromise is reached.

Book advertising divides into two categories: (a) trade (aimed primarily at booksellers and librarians), and (b) consumer (leveled at the general public and special interest markets). There are differences in approach and content between the two, but these are of little concern to the editor. The editor's concern with ads is, as always, that the book is properly represented. A certain amount of hyperbole is tolerable, but too much is embarrassing. A serious work of history shouldn't be promoted as a now-it-can-be-told exposé. The more sensational aspects of a biography or a novel can be mentioned but an ad shouldn't give the impression that the whole book is like that. A reasonably sophisticated public reads between the lines of advertising copy and discounts much of the excess, but the editor must speak up when the book is presented as something substantially different from what it is.

The editor should keep a close watch on all promotional and

publicity copy. The latter particularly is a problem, since it usually gets rewritten by newspaper, magazine, and TV writers who, in their haste and relative ignorance of the book, generally make some mistakes and distortions. Since the editor has no control over such rewrites, the copy sent out should be as clear and accurate as possible.

If the book has strong sales potential and the author is attractive and articulate, the promotion department might want to arrange a *tour* of cities where TV or radio appearances could be booked. In this event, the editor is asked if the author would be willing to make such a tour (at the publisher's expense). If the author is willing—and few are not—then the editor brings author and promotion manager together and from there on the editor isn't involved, except to comfort outraged authors who complain (as almost all do—with justification) of no books in the stores of a city where a smashing TV appearance aroused great demand, failure to be met at one or more airports, expenses beyond the amount paid by the publisher, no customers at a bookshop autographing party due to lack of publicity, etc. The editor must protest the deficiencies, but the problems mentioned, and others, are endemic to promotion tours and there's little hope for improvement. However, large sales will have a soothing effect.

Author tours are arranged mostly for nonfiction books. Tours for fiction are arranged mainly when the author is well known or the book has a timely interest. Tours are becoming less frequent due to the rising cost and questions about their effectiveness. "*Satellite tours*" are a way of getting the benefit of a multicity tour with relatively low cost. The author is interviewed in one location and the interview is telecommunicated to many radio and TV stations around the country. Some authors go on tours at their own expense.

In *el-hi* (elementary-high school) textbook publishing, the editor's relation to marketing is somewhat different. The purchasers of the book are not individual consumers but are usually professional buyers with a committee of educators and bureaucrats to convince. In this case, the selling material is a factual prospectus that makes the book sound as good as possible, but without the generalized hype used for tradebook jacket flaps and newspaper ads. In all textbook marketing there's a complex web of academic purchasers, administrators, and influential teachers to reach and persuade. This often involves use of the editor's personal contacts.

19. Working with manuscripts

Theoretically, there exist times when an author delivers a ms. ready to be turned over to production with nothing needed but a transmittal memo. In real life this doesn't happen. All mss. need *some* editorial work.

The work needed to make a ms. ready for typesetting is divided into two categories: (a) *manuscript editing*—substantive revision of the text, and (b) *copyediting*—finishing the ms. as described in CH. 4 and marking it for composition.

No ms., no matter how well written, should be sent to production without copyediting. The copyediting might produce very little change, but it's doubtful that any book-length ms. has been delivered by an author entirely free of the kinds of errors and inconsistencies that copyediting is meant to correct. In any case, the ms. must be marked with coded instructions that enable the designer and typesetter to do their work.

While copyediting is unavoidable, ms. editing may or may not be required. It's very unlikely that none will be needed, but some mss. require very little revision. In many cases, however, substantial revision is needed, and in some, the revision is extensive.

The obvious question is: Who determines whether extensive revision is needed? Answer: The editor. Next question: Does the author agree with this judgment? Sometimes yes, sometimes no, often both. This is the most critical point in the relationship of author and publisher. If the author has confidence in the editor's judgment, matters can go quite well. If the author doesn't accept the call for revision, matters will go poorly or not at all, i.e., the editor will refuse to accept the ms. or the author will ask to be released from the contract or to have another editor assigned (rarely done). None of these alternatives is pleasant, and, in practice, if a complete ms. has been submitted, this point is usually raised before a contract is signed. If there's no agreement then, it's easy to break off before a contract is made. The real trouble arises if the ms. is delivered after there's a contract in effect and author and editor strongly disagree.

Considering the emotional attachment that writers, quite naturally, have to their works, it's surprising that so much author revision is done at the request of editors. It seems really unlikely that an author—who may have a string of successful books—after spending perhaps two years writing and polishing a text, will accept a request to substantially, sometimes drastically, change it, particularly if the request comes from someone with no author's credits or other evidence of superior perception. Yet, such changes are frequently made under such circumstances. The answer lies, probably, in the intense desire of the author to have the book succeed, and the hope that a good editor can help that happen; self-interest overrides the hurt pride, subjective judgment, stubbornness, and plain weariness that would otherwise cause a flat rejection of such requests, even those coming from respected editors.

This doesn't mean that authors change their books even though they disagree with the editor's opinion. When they do make important changes, it's because they see merit in the editor's suggestion. Of course, the editor isn't always right, so the author may refuse to make the changes requested or may make only some of them. There are probably even some (rare) cases where an author has made changes despite strong doubts that the editor was right in requesting them; this *can* happen where there's a strong-willed editor and a compliant author. Major changes at an editor's request are made much more frequently in nonfiction than in fiction. Editors very rarely make important changes in fiction themselves.

MANUSCRIPT EDITING

What is the nature of the changes that an author might be asked to make, and by what process are they made? The process is somewhat different for each editor, but here is a typical scenario:

The ms. under discussion might be complete or only partially finished. In any case, it's read carefully by the editor in the way preferred. This might mean a first reading for pleasure to get a general impression, followed by a more critical reading to locate areas of weakness, and then intense study of the parts that seem to need change. Other editors might pick out the trouble spots on the first reading and go directly to work isolating and analyzing them. However the latter stage is reached, it's the prerequisite for a valid recommendation for change.

Once the editor has a clear idea of what needs to be done to bring the ms. to optimum quality, the question becomes: Who should do the work? There are three possible answers: (a) the author (or *ghost*), (b) the editor, or (c) the copyeditor. In most cases, the work is divided, but the real question is: Who does what? The copyeditor's function is usually well defined, but this leaves the problem of agreeing on who will do the remaining work—the author or the editor. There is no easy answer, and the solution varies according to the nature of the author-editor relationship (CH. 4).

Ideally, the editor presents recommendations to the author, who then makes the changes—and does them well. In practice, the author may be unable or unwilling, for a variety of reasons, to do the work and may ask the editor to do it. Where the author is unwilling to delegate the changing but isn't able to do it alone, it's usual for author and editor to work together. This generally means that the editor gives detailed guidance and then critically reads the author's changes in relatively short passages. (This isn't very different from the ideal situation, in which the author takes the ms. away and returns it later with all changes made.) The editor then goes over all the changes in one reading and gives the author a critical judgment. Obviously, working together is likely to bring a result closer to the editor's ideas, but it is, of course, much harder work for the editor and takes much more time than when the author makes the changes. If the editor alone were to make the changes, the result would probably be most satisfactory, but the time required would probably be more than the editor has available, and there's always the risk of having the editor's work rejected by the author.

This raises the extremely difficult matter of resolving unreconciled editorial differences between author and editor—i.e., publisher, in this context. Publishers shouldn't have to publish books that contain substandard writing or errors of fact, but it's equally wrong to expect authors to let their names be put on books containing material to which they object. In some such cases, publishers must choose between accepting whatever the author demands or rejecting the ms.—which is usually a very hard choice.

It isn't uncommon for an author to make the major changes and leave the less important ones to the editor—who in turn delegates some of the work to a freelance editor or copyeditor. The way this work is divided depends largely on the author's confidence in the editor, and to some extent on the author's ego, workload, and professional interest in writing.

However the work is accomplished, the editor must examine the revision as carefully as the original version. The revision may not work; it may be insufficient, or it may create problems that were not there before. If necessary, a second editorial critique and another round of changes will have to be undertaken. At this point, nerves and patience may be strained, but a good editor will keep a cool head and convince the author of the need for more work. It helps to emphasize how embarrassing it is to have flaws in a published book, how the author would later regret not having taken the opportunity to make changes when there was still time.

Now we look at the kinds of changes that might be needed, and the kinds of problems that make them necessary. There are two categories of problems: writing and substance.

Writing

The basic features of writing are: (a) *structure*—the plot or architecture of the book, and (b) *style*—all the characteristics of writing other than structure, but including the construction of sentences and paragraphs.

PROBLEMS OF STRUCTURE

Structural faults are frequently errors of sequence. Writers sometimes organize their book in an order that works well enough for them because they have the whole picture in mind, but confuses the reader, who must get the information in a different sequence in order to understand or use it properly.

One of the most important and difficult parts of writing is maintaining constant awareness of the reader, and particularly of the reader's ignorance relative to the author. Whether it's fiction or nonfiction, by definition the author knows more than the reader (except for peers reading critically rather than for learning or pleasure). The constant danger is forgetting this and writing on the basis of the author's knowledge rather than the reader's. When this happens, it leaves the reader confused and irritated, e.g., because fact C, which followed fact A, can't be easily understood without fact B—which the author omitted because it seemed obvious. Of course B was obvious to the author—who had many years of experience in the subject or, in the case of fiction, had knowledge of the whole plot and a clear picture of the scene—but B was not obvious to the reader, who needed it to make sense of the information that followed it.

The tendency of writers to overlook the reader's relative lack of knowledge is a major justification for the editor's role. And just as it's important for writers to understand what happens when their work is read by someone less informed, it's important for an editor who has specialized knowledge to develop an objective point of view when editing works in that subject.

Another major structural problem is balance. Sometimes a writer will give one aspect of the work too much or too little space in proportion to its value relative to the other aspects. The editor approaches this area with caution, since these are value judgments and (presumably) the author is more qualified than the editor to make them. But here too is the problem of an author's subjective viewpoint. Has the author given a topic space in proportion to its actual importance or to a personal interest in it? This isn't to say that a writer isn't entitled to emphasize what seems to be important; it *is* to suggest that an editor must be alert to situations where an author has let enthusiasm or emotion elevate a point far beyond its proper place in the whole work. In didactic works such exaggerations can damage the reader's confidence in the author's judgment and reliability; in fiction, these imbalances can spoil symmetry and break the delicate thread that joins the reader to a story that inspires belief and involvement.

The most difficult structural defect to correct is *lack* of structure. This usually results from a lack of planning—when a writer begins writing without a clear idea of how to reach a goal. Some writers can produce a well-designed text without making an outline, but most have to work out the sequence, flow, and balance of the whole book and its parts in advance of writing. If this isn't done well, the result is likely to be a disorderly mass of material—all the parts of which may be very good—that fails to hang together.

Major structural faults are often easier to correct than some style problems. On a computer an author (or editor) can easily revise the sequence of materials while hardly changing a word. Imbalances due to *too much* writing in one part can frequently be corrected by simply lopping off unnecessary sections. Even lack of structure can be corrected on the computer by moving parts of the text around to create a well-planned order, adding transitional passages where needed.

PROBLEMS OF STYLE

Style problems fall into six main categories:

(a) poor *syntax*,
(b) poor paragraph structure,
(c) overwriting,
(d) clichés,
(e) repetition, and
(f) weak logic.

(Another style problem is lack of grace or "style" in the sense of quality. This fault is likely to be too pervasive and basic to be corrected by anything short of rewriting, so it's not treated here as an editorial problem.)

■ **Poor syntax**—This includes both grammatically incorrect and awkward sentence structure. Correction of these faults is normally left to the copyeditor (CH. 4), but when they're too frequent, the editor may discuss the problem with the author and ask for improvements. If the editor believes that the author can't do much better (often true when an expert who isn't a professional writer is asked to write a book) or the author is too busy and important to be bothered (which happens with books by big-time statesmen, industrialists, scientists, etc.), then the work is given to a copyeditor. If the author is a professional writer, it's proper to send the ms. back with a request that more work be done, although this is usually avoided if the author is a big-selling writer who must not be offended.

- **Poor paragraph structure**—Awkward arrangement of the sentences in a paragraph can be corrected by a copyeditor also, but if this is extensive it begins to look like rewriting. The considerations involved here are the same as with bad sentence structure, only in greater degree. If too many paragraphs have sentences in the wrong sequence, the author should be asked to revise. If necessary, a very good copyeditor can be given the job, but must take great care, since such extensive revision can easily distort the sense and character of the book.
- **Overwriting**—The most common style fault is the use of too many words to express a thought. Even good professional writers tend to write too much, but the best ones cut and pare until their expression is economical. This means that it usually takes more time to write less, which partly explains why there's so much excess verbiage.

Some cutting can be done by the deletion of sentences, paragraphs, parts of, or even whole chapters, but sometimes this isn't possible because the problem is in the way of writing itself—the use of roundabout constructions and unnecessary words and phrases, e.g., "it is probable that" instead of "probably", or "due to the fact that" instead of "because", etc. (If the reader should happen to find any such faults of that kind in this book, it's probable that this is due to the fact that the author didn't have enough time to do better.)

Another kind of overwriting is the use of fancy instead of plain words. Beginners often believe their writing will be more impressive if they use long words or uncommon or scholarly words. The opposite is true. Excessive use of fancy words marks the writer as insecure, pretentious, or inexperienced. Don't confuse this with the use of fresh and unexpected words—which is good. Readers are less aware of words than the concepts they convey, and concepts are conveyed more effectively if expressed in a new way.

Overwriting also means using elaborate language instead of simple expressions, and exaggerating qualities, feelings, and activities by the use of adjectives that overstate. A particularly offensive form of overwriting is the use of professional jargon to make the simple appear complex.

For examples, read *The Elements of Style* by William Strunk Jr. and E. B. White, where this and other aspects of writing are explained briefly but very well. Indeed, if all writers did no more than memorize the "List of Reminders" on the contents page under Chapter 5 of that book, the need for ms. editing would nearly disappear. Two other useful books are *Woe Is I* and *Words Fail Me* by journalist Patricia T. O'Conner, which deal with most common grammatical and style questions.

Overuse of fancy or elaborate language can be corrected by a good copyeditor, but if it's too pervasive it may be better to send the ms. back to the author with an explanation of the problem. If the author is unwilling or unable to do what is necessary, it might be best to reject the book. This decision would depend on the importance of the content and/or the author. It's always possible to hire someone to do the work, no matter how extensive, if the book is worth the cost. Of course, the author should be charged for such work if possible.

- **Clichés**—These are the worn-out and overworked words, expressions, and rhetorical devices that inexperienced (and some experienced) writers like to use. Two reasons clichés are so common in writing are: (a) they're so familiar they come easily to (a lazy) mind, and (b) they're usually excellent expressions, which is why they became so popular and overused. It's unfortunate that such useful words and phrases have to be discarded, but their overuse gives writing a stale, hackneyed sound that's intolerable after a while. Vigorous, effective writing calls for fresh, vital ways of expression that keep the reader alert. Fixing clichés is copyeditors' work.
- **Repetition**—Carelessness is the main cause of repetitive writing. Unintentional restatement of thoughts or reuse of expressions often results from the writer's inability to remember what was written a day or a week or a month before. Sometimes excessive repetition is due to a writer being overanxious to make a point. The temptation to restate a strongly felt idea is resisted by only the most experienced writers. There are, of course, times when reiteration is effective, but too much weakens the impact—just as beating makes lovely whipped cream, but a few too many beats makes the cream separate into liquid and butter. Cutting repetitions should be discussed with the author, especially where strong feelings are involved.
- **Weak logic**—This includes faults such as the use of poor analogies and metaphors, non sequiturs, and failures to present arguments fully or effectively. These are matters of style, but are a short step from faults of logic like inconsistencies and contradictions that are matters of substance. Here the editor must be careful not to unintentionally change meaning when only changes of style are intended. Logic flaws are best discussed with the author before any editing is done.

Substance

An editor must be careful to respect the author's writing ability, even when the author isn't a professional writer. While some nonprofessionals are quite protective of their writing, many recognize their limitations and will gladly take direction and criticism from a respected editor. But this compliant attitude rarely extends to subject matter. Unless the editor's knowledge of the subject equals the author's, the latter is likely to resist any attempts to change the facts or the ideas in the ms.—or even the way that they're presented.

Nevertheless, it's customary to have nonfiction mss. read by experts other than the author, and differences of opinion often arise. Differences that are entirely matters of opinion are usually resolved in favor of the author, unless the expert reader is very much more qualified than the author by experience and professional standing. In such cases, the author can sometimes be persuaded to modify, or at least soften, the opinion in question. There are, however, differences of opinion about matters of fact where no authority can be cited to settle the matter, and both author and expert reader insist they're right. Such disputes can sometimes be settled by reference to a third expert, but the author is usually granted the point unless it seems clear to the editor that the others are right. When the latter occurs, the publisher again faces the unhappy alternatives of printing what are believed to be errors or rejecting the book.

Inconsistencies and contradictions are usually easier to handle. Some authors resist such criticism, but with persistence and diplomacy the editor can usually get the author to agree to the necessary changes. It's best to let the author make them to be sure that no misinterpretation or wording error alters the author's intended meaning.

The worst problems of substance are the absence of essential values—plot, tension, drama, information, advice, facts. These problems are sometimes insoluble because of the author's limitations. It's important to recognize such basic faults at an early stage so the project can be rejected before it becomes a terrible burden.

MANUSCRIPT PREPARATION

Having gone as far as is considered necessary to ensure the adequacy, if not the excellence, of the ms., the editor turns it over to the copyeditor for finishing. As explained earlier, the extent of this work varies from house to house, and even among editors in the same company. The nature of the work is discussed in CH. 4.

Where there's a staff copyeditor, close coordination with the editor is customary. Freelance copyeditors are less likely to communicate with the editor, but do so when questions of policy arise. In cases where the ms. is very complicated and needs a lot of work, a freelance copyeditor may temporarily move into the publisher's offices, where the editor is more accessible.

The editor gives the copyedited ms. a once-over to be sure the job was properly done. If the copyediting was extensive, the editor may refer some questions to the author. After editor and author settle any questions, the changes are entered in the master electronic file—usually by the author, although minor changes may be inserted by the publisher's staff—and the disk, with a hard copy printout, goes to the proofreader and then, after final correction, to the design department for page-makeup (or the production department, if that's the channel in the house—in some companies, it goes through the managing editor for traffic control, both from copyeditor to editor and from editor to design). Since the text normally goes directly into pages, the author's disk should be worked on until it's as error-free as possible. Extensive revision of page-makeup is costly and inefficient. Even when galleys are used for layout, the text must be corrected to avoid problems in paging.

Most professional writers, particularly in fiction, don't like any tampering with their work and frequently complain about the copyediting. However, copyediting is a professional procedure that's the province of the publisher, so the author is expected to accept the publisher's judgment of its quality. It's the editor's responsibility to see that the copyediting is held to a high standard—which includes maintaining respect for the integrity of the author's work while making it conform to the editorial style of the house.

20. Working with design & production

In a general way, the progress of a book through a publishing house is from: (a) editorial to (b) design to (c) production to (d) sales. This is true in the sense that these four departments carry the ball in that sequence, but in practice, all four are actively involved throughout the process. The editor continues work on a book after the ms. has been delivered to design, and sometimes even after the books are being sold (CH. 18). This chapter deals with the editor's participation in design and production, but with the assumption that the editor understands those functions as they're explained in other parts of this book.

Editors are involved with the design/production process in two ways: (a) imparting knowledge of the book to design, and (b) checking the preparation of the book for accuracy.

Contributing to design

The editor's role in developing a design concept for the book as it relates to acquisition and marketing plans was discussed in CHs. 17, 18. Once the final ms. has been turned over to design, the editor resumes the earlier dialog with the designer or design director, but in more specific terms. By this time, the character and content of the book have been determined and the house's perception of the quality and sales potential of the book has been crystallized.

The editor sends the copyedited file and marked hard copy to the designer with an information sheet giving: (a) the basic publishing facts—list price, quantity to be printed and bound, marketing plans for all editions, subsidiary sales if any, descriptions of competing books, and any previously determined specifications such as trim-size, number of pages, etc., and (b) a summary of the content.

By this time the illustrations, if any, and permissions for their use, have been obtained (CH. 7). These should be accompanied by a list or log of illustrations numbered according to identification numbers on the pictures. If there's no such log, whoever receives the original illustrations, editor or designer, should count them, make a numbered list, and sign a dated receipt for them. The loss of original pictures, particularly color transparencies, can be catastrophic in terms of time as well as money. Receipts may not enable lost pictures to be found, but they do make the signers more careful and help establish responsibility for the loss. If the illustrations are related to specific passages in the text, the editor should indicate on the hard copy of the ms. exactly where each one belongs, by writing the illustration number in the margin next to the most relevant line of text. The illustrations, list, and marked hard copy are then delivered to the designer.

The interaction of editor and designer is described in CH. 18. The design concept formulated in the acquisition or marketing-plan stage is checked and refined by the designer at this point. With the final ms. in, the editor's thoughts on the design problems and any special editorial problems that require a design solution are discussed with the designer, who then proceeds to create sample pages (CH. 25). If the design in the sample pages fails to solve the editorial problem (CH. 21), the editor should discuss the matter with the designer and, if a radical revision is needed, and there's enough time, ask for revised samples.

If no design concept was formed previously, the editor-designer conferences described in CH. 18 take place after the designer has studied the ms. and the information sheet; the subsequent procedure is the same as described above.

Unless the book is strongly visual in nature, only rarely, and then only as a courtesy, are sample pages shown to the author. If they're shown, any constructive comments should be passed to the designer, but the design of the book is a publisher's prerogative and the author should be expected to observe this. Alfred Knopf firmly put down authors' incursions into design because he respected his designers and their special qualifications, but many publishers and editors are inclined to cave in when an author, especially an important one, takes a strong position on design. Be as firm as you can, especially if the author's demands involve extra expense.

When the design of an unillustrated book is approved, the editor has no further work in this area until first (rough) page proofs are received. If a book is illustrated, and particularly if the illustrations are within the text (as opposed to being in a separate section), the editor and the author check the page layouts for editorial flaws and illustration problems.

Checking for accuracy

The editor may have as many as ten opportunities to check the production for errors, or only a few. The number depends on the kind of book and the method of production. The largest number occurs when the book is illustrated with full-color illustrations within the text. The possible checking opportunities are as follows, in their approximate sequence:

galley proofs (if a book is dummied for layout)
first page proofs
layouts (if a dummy was made)
random color proofs (sometimes)
second (revised) page proofs
mechanicals (rarely)
final file proofs
prepress proofs or other final proofs

This number might increase if the volume of corrections, and available time, warrant revised proofs. The other extreme occurs when a book has no illustrations. In this case, once sample pages are approved, the editor gets to check first page proofs. After corrections are made, final page proofs are checked and the final file goes to the prepress or printshop where films are made. Then blueprints are checked, plates are made, and the books are printed. With computer-to-plate (CTP) production, the editor's last opportunity for checking may be the final page proof, but most manufacturers will supply digital proofs before making plates.

Since an index can't be made until the final page proof is corrected, copyediting and checking index proofs are separate operations that must be accomplished between the final page proofs and platemaking, while causing as little delay in the printing schedule as possible.

Following is a discussion of the editorial procedures and practices involved in handling the various kinds of materials to be checked.

GALLEY PROOFS Galleys are normally bypassed and the first proofs are page proofs. This is feasible when all editorial changes, including copyediting, have been incorporated in the ms. If changes that affect the number of lines are made in page proofs rather than in ms. or galleys, they can cause serious problems and should be discouraged. If a book has many illustrations in the text, especially if the text is complicated with subheads, tables, charts, etc., it may be better to get galley proofs, have them read and corrected, and then send them to be dummied by the designer, laying out the galleys and illustrations into pages (CH. 26). This allows layout problems to be solved for the approval of all concerned before the page-makeup is done on the computer. Some designers are comfortable with this procedure, but most prefer to do the layout and paging directly on the computer. The decision is the designer's.

All readers of the text should initial every proof they have read. Readers should be asked to use different colored pencils if any set is marked by more than one person. Generally, all who read the proofs finish at about the same time, but often the author takes longer. (Contracts frequently provide that proofs will be considered approved if not returned in a specified time—usually three weeks—but this provision isn't likely to be enforced against a valued author.) In any case, once all copies are returned, the editor goes over them to resolve all important questions. Then the editor or copyeditor collates the corrections on all sets and the net result is marked on the master set and incorporated in the computer file.

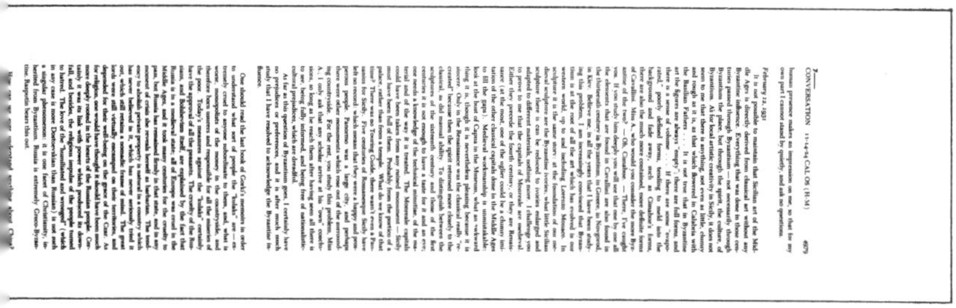

galley proof

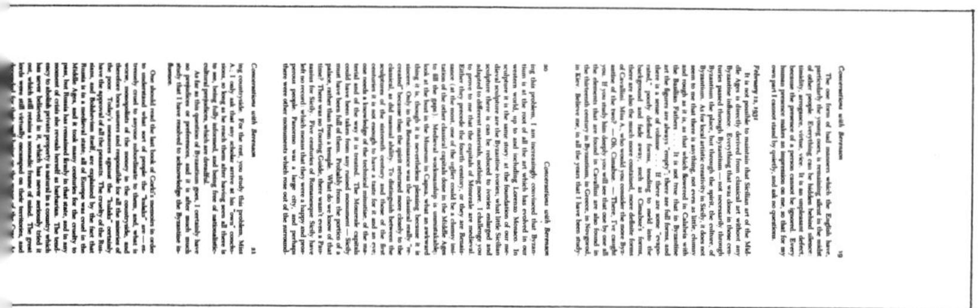

page proof

FIRST (ROUGH) PAGE PROOFS

Page proofs should be checked to find PEs (*printers' errors*) made in page-makeup. Checking for PEs is done by the proofreader and the designer, and sometimes the copyeditor, who look also for widows (CH. 9), missing or duplicated lines, or pages that are too long or too short. Page proofs are sent to the author to check for errors, but with the caution that there are to be no author's changes. Any changes at this point, even the length of a line, can disrupt the makeup from there on.

LAYOUT

When the pages of the book—or a section—contain illustrations (CHs. 9, 26), the editor should check the layouts for editorial errors. This is normally done from printouts of the rough page-makeup. In cases where the layout is done by dummying, layouts are brought to the editor's office by the designer, who goes over them with the editor, answering questions and making corrections in the process. Sometimes, particularly when it's important to have the original illustrations at hand and they're too fragile or bulky to be moved easily, it's more practical for the editor to go to the designer's desk, or even to the studio of a freelance designer.

There are two kinds of editorial flaws to be checked: (a) factual errors, such as the wrong caption on a picture, a *flopped* (inverted) picture, or two pictures confused with each other, and (b) faults of editorial judgment by the designer, such as an unimportant picture made too large, a picture out of sequence, or an editorially significant element cropped off a photograph. Here, as with the other aspects of design, the editor should refrain from imposing esthetic, as distinct from editorial, opinions on the designer.

After the layouts in a dummy have been checked, the designer makes the changes required if they involve only space adjustments or very minor changes in the type, but any substantial type changes are made by the editor in the computer file and the layouts are revised, using proofs with the changes. The designer or compositor then makes up pages on the computer according to the layouts in the dummy. From that point on, the work proceeds in the same way as when the layouts are made on the computer directly.

It's sometimes necessary, because of schedule constraints, to begin page-makeup with an uncorrected ms. and/or without scans or other graphic representations of the illustrations. This is feasible only if the editor can give the designer assurance that the amount of copyediting correction will be minor and if the layout isn't too complicated. Then the designer can insert boxes to represent the illustrations, if any, and the makeup can be adjusted for the editorial corrections in a second proof. However, if the adjustments are too extensive it may be necessary to have a third proof (thus losing the time saved by beginning without final copy).

When ordering page-makeup, state the number of proofs required. Page proofs always go to author, editor, and designer, and generally go to other departments, such as sub-rights and marketing, according to the practice of the house.

COLOR PROOFS The first proofs of color illustrations seen by the editor may be included in the page proofs, or they may come as *random proofs*—the images alone without text. In either case, the editor can check to see: (a) if they're all present, (b) that no errors were made in the cropping or silhouetting (CH. 8), and (c) that no flopping has occurred. The latter is fairly common, since transparencies can easily be turned over at the wrong time and left that way if the picture doesn't look wrong. (Where abstract paintings are involved, a check must be made to be sure they're not upside-down or on their side.) If the color proofs are included in the page-makeup, they should be checked also to see that the correct caption is with each picture and that the pictures are correctly placed in the text, if that's appropriate to the layout.

Checking process-color proofs for accuracy of color reproduction is a special skill—perhaps "art" is a better word—best left to specialists (CHs. 8, 10) unless the editor happens to be very experienced in the field.

SECOND (REVISED) PAGE PROOFS

Don't assume that only corrected lines in page proofs need to be checked. Although it's theoretically impossible for accidents to occur in computer composition, they do happen—a dropped character isn't uncommon, and dropped lines or even paragraphs are possible—and errors can be created in the course of making corrections, so the entire second page proofs should be read, or at least carefully scanned. Unless there are enough corrections to require an additional proof (see above), the second is the final page proof. A copy of this may be used to make an index.

If there are illustrations, they should, if possible, be inserted in the final pages in their final form—with high resolution and all cropping, silhouetting, retouching, color correction, etc. Checking the technical accuracy and quality of these features is done by the designer and production department, but the editor should check them also for the kinds of editorial flaws mentioned above. If the final illustrations have been inserted to replace proxy (FPO) images checked in the first page proof, there should be no need to check them again, but errors are possible, if unlikely, so another lookover is recommended.

FINAL FILES

When the final page-makeup has been fully corrected, and all illustration images in their final form have been inserted, a printout of this final file should be carefully checked by editor, designer, and production department for errors of any kind, particularly to be sure that all proxy images have been correctly replaced by the final high-res and fully corrected versions. If the final page proofs were complete and nearly error-free, there should be little or nothing to correct in the final file printout. It's assumed that high-quality random proofs (CH. 10) of the halftones and color illustrations were previously checked and corrected. Replacing the proxy images with high-res versions can be done by the designer with good equipment and lots of computer memory, but it's much more practical to have the prepress technicians do it. Ideally, the index will be included in the final file, but if it can't be, the file is sent with the printout to the prepress house or printshop for the next step without it. The edited and corrected index sometimes arrives just before plates are made.

If the computer-to-plate process is used, the printout of the final file is the last opportunity to find errors before the books are printed. Where corrections in final page proofs were extensive, it might be a good idea to have the author check final file proofs. Otherwise, it's not considered necessary.

Final file proofs may be printed on high-quality copy paper by the desktop printer. In the (rare) event when it has been decided to make mechanicals of the pages for all or part of the book, and have the mechanicals photographed to create film for making printing plates, the final proofs must be repro (reproduction) proofs made by a very high-resolution printer on very smooth paper. As with other final proofs, the corrected lines in repros, if any, are to be checked for new errors. When books are to be printed on a xerographic press, there's no step between final files and printed books, but because it's possible to print a single copy of a book in this process, one or a few copies can be produced as proofs to be checked before the whole edition is printed.

MECHANICALS If it has been decided to make the film for the book, or part of it, by photographing pasted-up repro proofs (mechanicals) (CH. 10) rather than making up the pages by computer and creating the film (or plates) electronically, checking for errors is done just as it would be with page proofs. The difference is that it's much more difficult to make changes in mechanicals than on the computer. The purpose of editorial checking of mechanicals is to see that no errors were made in the placement of the various pieces of text or illustrations. As the arrangement itself was settled in the layout, no position changes are to be made. Once the mechanicals are completed, there's no question of textual changes except to correct errors that might have been missed in previous readings of the proofs. This is the last chance to catch serious errors and faults of content or arrangement, particularly in the contents page and the pagination, so if there's anything found that shouldn't be in the printed book, and the deficiency is correctable by moving pieces on the mechanical, this is the time to speak up.

PREPRESS PROOFS There are several kind of proofs that can come between final files or mechanicals and printing. These are essentially proofs-of-last-resort.

■ **Blueprints**—These are generally proofs of films (CH. 10), but they can also be made digitally (digital blues) directly from final files. Ordinarily, each one contains all the pages on one side of a printed sheet (a form) and they're customarily folded and trimmed so that they look much like a printed book (they are then called book blues). Blueprints are not to be criticized for printing quality. They are relatively crude photoprints that can't be controlled past a certain point. They may be too light or too dark in part or whole or have spots, but these are not indications of the printed result to come.

Blueprints made from computer-produced film or files are used mainly to check the position of pages and any corrections that might have been made in the final file. Editorial checking of blueprints made from film produced from mechanicals is more complicated. It involves the search for errors in the sequence of pages, the dropping of elements, such as folios or running heads—which happens frequently due to the masking that's used—accidental cutting of a piece of film, flopping of film, misplacement or transposition of illustrations, etc. The type and line illustrations (CH. 10) are pasted in place on mechanicals, but the halftones and color illustrations are stripped into position in the film, so the blueprint is the first opportunity to see that these have been placed properly.

■ **Press proofs**—These are proofs of the final pages made on a printing press with plates made for the purpose, usually including only a part of a form. It's very unusual to make press proofs of an entire form. To do so requires setting up the production press just as though the whole edition were going to be run, and then stopping it after a few hundred sheets in order to get a few good ones. This is an expensive procedure justified only if the book has very critical printing problems (usually in color illustrations) or to provide advance printed sheets for sales purposes. Press proofs would ordinarily be shown to the editor only for information, not for approval. Certainly, if some truly disastrous error were to be discovered in these proofs, it might still be possible to make a correction, but this decision probably should involve management, as the cost in time and money could jeopardize the publication (CH. 10).

■ **Composed color proofs**—These are proofs of color illustrations in their correct position in the form but without the page-makeup. They are made electronically without the use of plates or printing press, and are much less expensive than press proofs. As with press proofs, they're useful for checking some aspects of the illustrations, but corrections can be made with much less cost.

It's been said that the final file and the mechanical are the last chance to make vital corrections. This is true in the sense that editorial changes in prepress proofs are unthinkable. Such changes are very expensive, if possible at all, and usually involve upsetting the production schedule. Having said this, it would be wrong not to point out that really vital changes can sometimes be made at the prepress proof stage.

Once all the proofs have been checked and the book has gone to press, the editor can only pray that all will go well, and that the reviewers won't notice (and mention) the errors that will almost certainly remain.

Design

21. Analysis

The process of design has three steps:

(1) analysis of the problem,
(2) consideration of the possible solutions, and
(3) selection of the best solution.

Actually, this is the process of problem-solving. Design is the name given to problem-solving in certain fields, of which bookmaking is one. If the three-stage process isn't carried out, the result can't be called design.

The use of stock solutions for unexamined problems may produce adequate results at times, but over a long period there will be many more failures than successes. For that reason, this book offers guides to procedure, rather than rules. Rules can be found in style books, but they're primarily to help beginners produce usable work, or at least avoid the worst mistakes—they can't produce excellent design. The few rules given in this book are related to principles rather than procedure.

With experience, it's possible to shorten the distance between (1) analysis and (3) selection. Repeated encounters with one kind of problem enable a designer to instantly reject some solutions and move swiftly toward others. It may even appear at times that the middle stage of the design process has been omitted entirely, just as it may seem that the transmission process from nerve ending to brain has been omitted because one feels pain immediately upon touching a hot object. In both cases, the speed of the process makes it imperceptible, but the process nevertheless takes place.

Even intuition can be encompassed by the analytical process. Creative intuition won't produce answers of value unless preceded at some time (however far back) by logical thought. The intuitive process will be discussed in CH. 22; now we are concerned with analysis.

The problem in bookmaking

The characteristic of book publishing that makes it perpetually interesting—and confounds the conventional businessman—is its multiple purpose. A single book may be an object of commerce, a work of art, an act of faith, and an article of practical use, or a half-dozen other things. The problems of bookmaking reflect this diversity.

Every book presents three kinds of problems: (a) mechanical, (b) commercial, and (c) editorial.

- **The mechanical problem**—Turning the ms. into an efficient and economical book.
- **The commercial problem**—Producing a book that's suited to its market, aids sales, and can be sold profitably.
- **The editorial problem**—Creating a book that properly and effectively expresses the author's message.

Some dispute the legitimacy of a designer's concern with the editorial content of a ms., considering the analysis completed once the mechanical and commercial problems have been examined. Others hold that the design must do as much as it can for the author—that it must support visually what the author is saying verbally. (See "Schools of design" in CH 2.) This book is based in that assumption.

The esthetic element hasn't been omitted from consideration; it's implicit in the three factors named, but is subordinate to them. Esthetic success shouldn't be achieved at the expense of any of the three basic factors, although, paradoxically, a book is less likely to achieve its maximum mechanical, commercial, or editorial potential if it fails to succeed esthetically.

Mechanical analysis

The analysis of a ms.'s mechanical problem begins with a breakdown. A breakdown is a division of the ms. into its different kinds of material, with the amount of each kind counted by the most suitable method. The object of the count is to estimate the number of pages there will be in the book.

When mss. were produced by typewriters, making a breakdown of a typescript was a slow, tedious process. Some writers still stick to their typewriters, but this is no longer a factor in bookmaking, as publishers generally insist on getting computer disks with hard copy from authors.

It shouldn't be assumed that there's no value in making an estimate of the length of a book just because it's so easy to adjust the length by changing the type specifications on the computer. Those who never worked at bookmaking when metal typesetting was used can't imagine how important accurate estimates were then. A serious miscalculation could mean melting down hundreds of pounds of metal, completely resetting—rekeyboarding—the text, and making and reading new proofs. Although correcting a miscalculation is easier now, it's still a considerable problem in books with complex picture and text layouts. It's best to get it right the first time.

There are two ways of making a count for a breakdown: by hand, in the manner described below, or by using the counts provided by some word-processing programs. The latter display the number of characters typed and the number of lines, so a character count for straight text is readily obtained. However, heads, line-for-line items, tables, etc. remain to be counted separately. Also, some designers find that computer character counts are not always accurate, so it's probably safer to make a hand count.

Most counting can be avoided by actually setting the entire book according to the final design specifications—typeface, type size, leading, line length, and number of lines per page for each kind of material—in a layout program such as QuarkXPress or InDesign and noting the result. This may be done without including spaces for chapter openings, subheads, etc., and adding to the result a calculation for these as well as for frontmatter, backmatter, and illustrations, if any. Alternatively, the spaces may be included in the composition. In that case, the result is close to actual page-makeup for a book with no illustrations (keeping in mind the possibility of later changes by the author and/or editor). This is the method almost always used by designers to find the estimated number of pages in a book, but there are times when a hand count of all or part of a book is needed (for example, when an estimate of length is needed but it's too soon to decide on design specs), so it's important to know how to make one.

There are four ways of counting: (a) by characters, (b) by lines, (c) by units, and (d) by pages. Following are instructions for making these counts by hand.

CHARACTER COUNTS *Character counts* are used to determine the amount of material in continuous prose. Authors and editors use "*word counts*" in measuring the size of a ms., but this is an inaccurate method. Vocabularies vary according to the writer and the subject. One writer may average 5.5 characters per word while another may average 6.1. This is a difference of only 10%, but in a 320-page book the difference means 32 pages. A book on sociology will probably have a higher proportion of long words than a novel. There are also errors in making word counts. If the estimate is an average of 10 words per line and there are really 9.5, that's an error of 5%, or 16 pages in a 320-page book. There are other errors inherent in this method, such as the fact that there's often material that must be counted in other ways, so it would be best for editors to use character counts and encourage authors to do the same.

In a character count, each letter, number, punctuation mark, word space, and sentence space is counted as one unit.

■ **The text**—While the computer provides counts of text characters in new writing, breaking down a printed book (e.g., a British book or an old book being republished) is another story. To make a character count of printed text, the best way is to scan the pages into the computer and convert the text to a word-processing program, which will display the character count. If this isn't possible (perhaps because a very old book is too fragile to go through scanning), it will be necessary to make a hand count of the original text.

First determine the average number of characters per line. This figure is crucial because it's multiplied thousands of times and any error will carry to the final result in proportion. As we have seen, even a few percentage points of error mean a substantial number of pages in the book.

The width of line in justified printed copy is uniform, but the number of characters in the lines will vary (up to 10%) because of the justification process (CH. 6). However, if enough lines are counted, an accurate average can be found. A count of about 20% of the lines on a page can reasonably be projected to that page and all pages set like that one.

When an average character count per line has been determined, multiply this figure by the total number of lines of text. To find that number, multiply the number of lines per page by the number of full pages—note that some pages may be made a line short or long to avoid widows (CH. 9). Count several pages to be sure you know how many lines are on a normal one. Then add to this the number of lines on short pages—usually chapter openings and endings. If there are spaces in the text (around subheads, etc.), they're subtracted from the line count.

Any prose in the text—both new writing and printed copy—that might ultimately be set in a style different from that of the main text should be character-counted separately. If you count everything in with the text, you have no way of knowing how the length of the book would be affected if you should decide to set some part of it in a different size type, a narrower measure, or with different leading. The kinds of copy that usually require a separate character count are:

■ **Extract**—This is quoted material that isn't run in with the text.

■ **Appendix**—An appendix may be any kind of copy, but when it's prose it should be counted separately.

■ **Introductions**—A long introduction is usually set as part of the text, but to be safe, count it separately. Each short introduction to a part or chapter should be counted separately.

■ **Notes**—Whether positioned as footnotes or collected at the end of chapters or the book, notes are a separate item.

■ **Foreign language**—Whether treated as extract or part of the text, this is counted separately, if only for pricing purposes (CH. 14).

LINE-FOR-LINE COUNTS Any line of copy in the ms. that will definitely begin a new line on the printed page and will definitely not extend beyond one line may be counted as *line-for-line* copy. Obviously, it's necessary to know how many characters per line the printed page will have in order to make such a count, but an approximation is usually sufficient. Where the line of copy is clearly less than the probable number of characters, there's no problem. Where it's clearly more, but definitely not more than twice the number, count it as two lines. In borderline cases, guesses must be made—but these should average out. Subtract the number of line-for-line lines from the text line count.

There are several kinds of line-for-line material and these should be counted separately. Some of the most frequently encountered are:

■ **Conversation**—Short lines of conversation and other short lines in text, such as courtroom testimony, questions and answers, etc.

■ **Poetry**—Some poetry has a number of lines of about one-line width. Guess the number of characters per line there will be in the printed book, make a paper strip of that width, and measure the lines in the ms. Count all wider lines as two. Stanza breaks are counted as one line each.

■ **Tables**—Count tables in the text separately from those in an appendix, as you may want to set them differently.

■ **Glossary**—If the definitions are brief, this can be counted line-for-line, otherwise it's best to make a character count.

■ **Bibliography**—Make a separate character count for descriptive paragraphs under titles. Count the book titles as line-for-line.

■ **Lists**—If a list is typed double column, the line count should note this, in case you decide later to set it single column.

■ **Subheads in text**—Subheads long enough to take more than one line should be counted as lines, in addition to the heading count (see below).

UNIT COUNTS Sometimes you need to know only how many of a particular kind of material are in the ms. rather than how many characters or lines there are. This is true mainly of elements of space, or elements surrounded by space. Since the space that can be allocated in the printed book is variable, it's more important to know the *number* of elements than how much space they occupy in the ms.

■ **Subdivisions**—Count the number of part-titles, chapter titles, section titles, and subheads—giving each class of subhead a code number or letter and a separate count. Do not count lines or characters.

■ **Spacebreaks**—These are usually one line each. Count them and subtract the number from the total line count for the text.

■ **Units**—Count the number of occurrences (or units) of each kind of material in the text. It isn't enough to know that there are *x* number of characters of extract, or *y* number of lines of poetry, you must know how many times extract or poetry occur, because you may decide to put space before and after each quotation and/or poem, and you must be able to compute the amount of space involved. It's necessary to estimate the number of footnotes if they're to appear under the text, because you'll need some space in between. This is difficult to calculate accurately because you can't know how the notes will fall in the page-makeup. A reasonable way of figuring this is to count all the footnotes and, if there are fewer notes than pages of ms., assume that each footnote will fall on a separate page. If there are more notes than pages, assume that there will be footnotes on every page in the book. You may not be exactly right, but you probably won't be too far wrong.

PAGE-FOR-PAGE COUNTS

In the frontmatter and *backmatter* (CH. 27) there will probably be material that will obviously fit on one page in the book. The *half-title* (usually the book title set in small type on the first page), the title, the copyright notice, the dedication, a brief acknowledgment, a small contents page, part-titles, etc. need not be counted for characters and lines. Simply note their existence. The same is true for pages in the text, such as a full-page table or chart. Make a character or line count only where it's possible that the copy will run more than one page.

INDEX

If the ms. is a printed book, there's no problem. Simply count the number of lines in the printed index (counting the lines in each column, not per page). With a new ms., you can only guess. As a rule of thumb, allow one page of index for every forty pages of average-copy ms., one to thirty for a ms. with many names and/or technical terms. Check your guess with the editor's and use that figure if it differs from yours.

ILLUSTRATIONS

This is usually the most difficult part of a mechanical analysis. It's certainly the most difficult to discuss in general terms, because there are so many possible situations. It's also the most important to understand, since it often must be done even when the length of the text has been determined by a computer page-makeup. It can be avoided if all the illustrations are in hand and proxy images are included in the paging, but this requires that all decisions on illustration size, cropping, and position (and probably captions) have been made. It's usually necessary to have an estimate of length before all this information is available.

The first step is to divide the illustrations into: (a) process-color, (b) simple color, halftone, (c) simple color, line, (d) monochrome, halftone, and (e) monochrome, line—as each kind has its own technical requirements. Then make a tentative determination of the approximate amount of space to be occupied by each illustration, even if it's only a rough guess, somewhat as in the following example:

(a) process-color:
    8 full page
    6 half page
(b) simple color, halftone:
    2 half page
(c) simple color, line:
    3 full page
(d) monochrome, halftone:
    6 full page
    19 half page
    23 quarter page
(e) monochrome, line:
    52 half page
    67 quarter page

You may be surprised to find how naturally illustrations will fall into such size-groups at a glance. The space might not ultimately work out exactly as you guessed, but it's useful to have an estimate such as this from which to start.

TABULATION The information in the mechanical analysis (breakdown) should be tabulated in an orderly and useful form. Include all data that may be of some use. Nothing is lost if you don't use a particular figure, but it's very frustrating to need something that isn't there. For convenience, note the ms. page on which each kind of material first occurs.

Type all items at the left, leaving the right side of the sheet for inserting the calculated number of pages for each item. Make lines across the page under each item to prevent overlooking one. On the opposite page is a specimen breakdown sheet. Note that the tabulation is arranged according to the parts of the ms. or kinds of material, with the character, line, page, and unit counts for each listed together (c = characters, L = lines, pp = pages). This makes it easy to take all elements into consideration in deciding, for example, how many pages to allow for a bibliography containing material counted in several ways.

A *spreadsheet* program is a great tool for doing this sort of thing. You can create a table with specific relationships between the *cells* in the grid. When a change is made to one cell, the oth-

TITLE: DATE:
Ms pp: 339

FRONTMATTER
half title__pp, title__pp, cpyrt__pp, ded__pp
preface 2762 c
contents 44 L
introduction 5250 c
TEXT:
538,050 c
103 L
EXTRACT: (p.67)
5892 c
POETRY: (p.29)
129 L
14 units
PLAYSTYLE: (p.162)
1264 c
10 L
4 units
TABULAR: (p.212)
42 L
12 units
BIBLIOGRAPHY: (p.318)
4922 c
53 L
INDEX:
allow · pp
FOOTNOTES:
1640 c
14 units
ILLUSTRATIONS:
halftone:75
line:28
SUBDIVISIONS:
part titles:3
chapters:8
A heads:18
B heads:41
spacebreaks:19

specimen breakdown

ers change automatically, based on the formula that you write. For instance, you can define the cell at the bottom of a column of numbers to be the sum of the column. Whenever you change any number in the column, the sum at the bottom automatically changes accordingly.

COMMERCIAL ANALYSIS

There are many possible considerations to include in the commercial analysis, but the main ones are:

(a) the nature of the intended audience,
(b) the formats (electronic and/or print) to be used,
(c) the kind of distribution anticipated, and
(d) the quantities of the first printing and binding.

These, and whatever other commercial problems there may be, must be fully considered so that the design and production of the book will contribute to a financially successful publication. The sale of the book isn't the only commercial consideration. Even with the sale of a large number of copies, a title may not be profitable if it's not well planned in terms of its distribution.

THE NATURE OF THE AUDIENCE

Who are the potential buyers and readers of a book? They are not always the same person. The buyers of books read by young children are usually adults, as are the buyers of schoolbooks and most reference books for the young. Books for all kinds of readers are bought by libraries. A large proportion of the books purchased in America are not read by the buyers but are intended as gifts. So, any design features based on audience must consider two aspects: the buyer and the reader.

Examine the characteristics of both groups. What are their occupational backgrounds? What kinds of education have they? What is their social and economic status? What are their tastes and prejudices? What are their ages? What physical disabilities might they have? These are not impertinent questions. The answers will affect design decisions. Size and kind of type, shape and weight of the book, durability, dirt resistance, style of typography, quality of materials, number and kind of colors, number and kind of illustrations—these and other design factors are subject to audience requirements.

For example, take a title on retirement activities for the financially secure. The reader will be past middle age, so the type should be a bit larger than usual (CH. 5). Light weight would be appreciated by older readers, particularly those with ailments that limit manual powers. Presumably, good-quality materials and attractive colors would please the younger friends and relatives who might buy the book as a gift, as well as the potential readers. The economic status of the reader suggests a retail price that would make such an approach feasible.

FORMATS

There are three possible formats for traditional printed books: hardcover, trade paperback, and mass-market paperback. Electronic formats consist of the various types of e-books. "Print-on-demand" isn't actually another format, but simply a different manufacturing process for producing traditional printed books. It's distinguished from the other processes mainly by its ability to produce very small quantities economically (CHs. 10, 12, 16). Decisions as to format are made by editorial and marketing departments and management.

DISTRIBUTION

Most books are sold in several ways. Each method of distribution has its own needs and these must be known so that they can be met. Some of them are:

- **Bookstore sales**—These usually require striking jackets and are helped by illustrations and other attractive visual elements. In most cases, it helps to have as large and thick a book as possible, to enhance its "perceived value". (While these physical attributes have little or no relation to the content, they have a positive psychological effect on many book buyers.)
- **Mail-order sale**—Light weight is good to keep down postage, although some mail-order books must be large and lavish to succeed. In any case, control weight to avoid going just over a postage weight bracket. Damage in handling and transit is also a factor to consider.
- **Library sales**—A strong binding is important. Librarians have definite views on binding specifications. They do buy paperbacks, but reluctantly.
- **Textbook sales**—Elementary and high school books usually require a lot of color and illustrations. They must meet NASTA standards for materials and manufacture (CH. 13). College texts are less demanding. Books in subjects that are quickly changing (science, politics, etc.) need to be updated frequently.
- **Gift sales**—These suggest large size, extensive color and illustration, and high-quality materials.
- **Internet sales**—These are actually mail-order sales, so the same considerations apply.
- **E-books**—For these electronic methods of distribution the requirements are varied, so they should be checked in each case.

When several methods of distribution are used, their demands sometimes conflict and have to be reconciled. At other times, the commercial requirements may not be apparent from the ms. alone. For instance, an editor may anticipate future books by the author of a new ms. that might eventually be sold as a set or series. Knowing this, a designer will avoid an arrangement of the title that wouldn't be adaptable to another, will avoid the use of odd lots of material that can't be obtained for the subsequent volumes, etc. Ask the editorial and sales departments what plans they have that might affect the commercial analysis.

SIZE OF PRINTING & BINDING

The publisher's decisions as to how many copies to print and, of these, how many to bind, are based less on the cost of production than on an estimate of the book's sale. The unit cost can be held down through a large printing, but there will be no profit if many of the books remain unsold.

Most titles are printed in relatively small quantities, especially in a "*just-in-time*" program in which the idea is to reduce the likelihood of being stuck with unsold copies by avoiding large printings. Yet, it takes about the same amount of time to make a job ready to run, the same investment in machinery, the same amount of floor space, the same amount of editorial and administrative work, and the same cost in composition, prepress, film, and plates for a run of 5000 as for one of 50,000. Obviously then, the design and production plans for a short run must be quite different from those for a long one.

If the printing is small, economy in *plant cost* (items not affected by size of edition, i.e., composition, illustrations, plates, etc.) is required. If the printing is large, the expenditures for plant are less significant than the cost of materials and other items that remain about the same per unit regardless of the size of the edition. A small edition might make it possible to take advantage of a special lot of paper or cloth at a good price, but a large one will permit you to order a special color, size, or finish without penalty. (Remember that a later printing may be too small for a special order. Have a satisfactory substitute in mind.)

A decision to bind only part of the edition printed has limited effect on design or production planning. Usually, most of the edition is bound, so it's worth ordering materials for all at the same time. Also, it's common practice to do the sheetwork (CH. 13) for the whole edition and hold back only the remainder of the binding operations until sales justify completion.

Ideally, bookmaking departments participate in discussions on the size of the first printing. In any case, management's thoughts in this matter should be thoroughly considered as part of the commercial analysis.

Editorial analysis

Visual support of the author may be mostly practical—good organization and a clear presentation of the material. The support may be mostly esthetic—subtle suggestion of mood and atmosphere. In almost all cases there'll be a combination of both. A factual book, if well designed, will have a functional beauty that grows naturally from its sense of order and fitness, like a fine bridge or aircraft. But even a book of fiction or verse must be made to function satisfactorily. No amount of atmosphere or graphic beauty is sufficient if the practical problems are unsolved.

To make an accurate and effective visual presentation of the text, the designer must become deeply familiar with the ms. and must clearly understand the author's intentions. The designer's attitude toward the subject may be different from the author's, but the job is to present the writer's approach—not one's own. However much of the designer's personality and viewpoint is apparent in the published book should be no more than a residual, inadvertent by-product of an effort to express those of the author.

READING TECHNIQUE

A designer must develop techniques for quickly extracting the essence of a ms. and learning what must be known about it. No method is perfectly satisfactory without reading the entire ms., but this is usually impracticable, so a compromise must be made.

With fiction, an effective method is to read the first eighteen or twenty pages, then two or three pages at intervals of about thirty, and then the last six or eight. In this way, one can usually absorb the setting and atmosphere of the story, feel the style of the writing, catch the general development of the plot, and discover the ending. With practice, a fairly accurate reading of a 350-page ms. can be made in about an hour. This is a very unsatisfactory way to read for pleasure, but it's a sacrifice the designer must make. It's important, however, to be alert and flexible, as some stories are so constructed that a misleading impression might result from a strict adherence to this system.

Nonfiction in narrative form can be read in about the same way. A writer will usually explain the subject and premises in the beginning and state the conclusions at the end. A spot check through the body of the text will give the general drift of the story or argument, as well as a feel of the author's style. If the ms. has several parts by the same or different writers, each piece can be studied in somewhat the same way, reducing the number of pages read in proportion to its length.

Nonfiction of complicated organization or varied content should be examined page by page. The text will have to be read to the extent necessary to understand its organization, intent, and style, and each page must be looked at to ensure that every problem has been seen.

There are many kinds of mss. and no one study procedure can be effective for all. The principle is to sample where a sample is sufficiently revealing, and examine in detail where necessary. Read all prefaces, forewords, and introductions even if you can't read anything else. People are inclined to bypass these, but that's usually a mistake. By their nature, these are statements considered by the author too significant or special to put in the body of the text. In them, authors often explain their purpose and/or summarize the content of the text. There, other writers will throw light on the character or background of the authors and their work, providing insights that are often the equivalent of a chat with the author.

Whatever method is used, there must be enough study and

analysis of the ms. to determine, as closely as possible, the exact nature, feeling, and intention of the book. Designers should check their interpretations with the editor before making any decisions. Often, because of insufficient time, an editor's briefing will have to substitute for a thorough reading of the ms.

In conclusion It's a good idea to make a brief written summary of your commercial and editorial analyses. This will help clarify your thoughts and fix them in your mind. Remember, *in making an analysis you are not to draw any conclusions about the design.* At this stage you are only to learn about your problem. Before you decide on anything, you must go through a process of considering alternatives, in which you use your thought, intuition, and experience.

22. Creative solutions

The creative problem

In book design, the creative problem is to correctly interpret and indicate the nature of the content. The indication *must* be accurate; it *should be* interesting and pleasing. In an exceptionally successful job, the accuracy creates a profound sense of fitness, while the design is interesting to the point of being intriguing, and pleasing to the point of being beautiful.

Every ms. has a unique character which can be analyzed and interpreted. Whether simple or complicated, the character of the work can be expressed in more or less abstract visual terms. Some books are more easily expressed than others, some appear to be almost impossible to express. It's unreasonable to expect that the total aspect of any book can be rendered graphically, but it's probably better to tend deliberately in the right direction than to leave the tendency to chance.

The book designer's creative problem is somewhat like that of the abstract painter—to communicate with the viewer's subconscious mind, where the response will be an automatic reaction rather than conscious thought. The average readers may not be consciously aware of design in books, but they can't escape being affected by visual elements that establish character and mood. Scientific studies confirm the power of subconscious impressions to modify states of mind or attitudes. A striking, and frightening, demonstration of this principle is the use of subliminal communication to implant ideas. (During a movie or TV show, an unrelated message is repeatedly flashed on the screen so rapidly that the viewer is unaware of its existence, yet responds to its content.) The designer must exploit the psychological devices that can help create a receptive atmosphere for the author's work.

Any decision affecting the physical aspect of the book can have expressive value. Every physical attribute contributes to the total effect and helps establish its character and atmosphere. It makes a difference whether any part or the whole is delicate or strong, bright or somber, masculine or feminine, simple or complex. Even the format can be significant. For example, the reaction to the sight and feel of a book that's squarish and chunky will be different from one that's tall and slim, and the relation of weight to size has a definite effect.

No element of a book's appearance can fail to have *some* character, and therefore some effect, either positive or negative. It's the designer's job to mobilize all these elements so that each of them and their sum will contribute to a successful solution of the creative problem. At the same time, the creative solution must not only avoid conflict with the mechanical, commercial, or editorial requirements, but be in complete harmony with them.

The creative process To reconcile the divergent needs of the various aspects of bookmaking, decide first on what *should* be done creatively, then modify these decisions as necessary to accommodate the practical considerations. In other words, plan the ideal first and retain as much of it as you can as you face conflicting realities. This works better than any other procedure because the creative process functions best when it's free of practical considerations. The moment you accept mechanical or economic limitations, your imagination tends to freeze. Not that it merely restricts itself to the practicable—it tends to act as though the limiting walls were glass, so it swings in a cramped arc far short of those walls. This is a safe enough procedure, but one that precludes any chance of extending the possible. The history of civilization shows that most advances have resulted from expeditions well beyond the practicable. To remain always within the walls leads to stagnation and sterility.

To best conceive ideal creative solutions, you must tap the creative force within you. Merely recalling routine devices and standard arrangements won't produce anything but stock solutions. Rational mental effort unaided won't produce creative solutions. The automatic mechanisms of the mind will usually set the creative process in motion, and they will help to some extent—but it's much better to consciously invoke the creative force and utilize it fully. People who fall into deep water will automatically thrash their arms about in an effort to avoid drowning, and they may sometimes succeed, but they're much more likely to succeed if they know how to swim.

After studying the ms., put it down and relax. Let your mind create associations at random. From these, try to recall everything from your experience related to the subject—sights, sounds, smells, textures, people, places, pictures, words, colors—anything and everything. Then, if possible, let some time pass while you do other things. A few hours might be enough, but overnight is better. During this time, the conscious thoughts associated

道

with the subject will seep down into the lower layers of consciousness, arriving eventually at the region in which the creative forces originate. Subject matter meeting creative force produces ideas and imagination, which tend to rise to conscious awareness, and when they do, we speak of "inspiration" and "intuition". Sometimes these impulses burst into the open despite any obstacle. More often they must be given receptive conditions or they will remain unborn, or arrive in weakened and misshapen form.

The most propitious condition for creativity is an utterly blank mind. Such a state invites ideas just as a blank sheet of paper invites drawing or writing. Far from being simple, achieving a blank mind is quite difficult. Our minds are filled with a lifetime of impressions and thoughts. Eastern mystics, particularly Taoists, make tremendous efforts to develop an ability to wipe their minds clean at will. Some of the greatest works of Asian art are attributed to the creative powers invoked in such a state. The technique involves reducing mental activity by concentrating on a single point. Eventually the concentration is total, and the mind engaged with nothing but a single point of light, a distant mountain peak, or some other isolated focus. From here, the mind goes into a trance-like state in which even the point of concentration is eliminated. This is, obviously, the process of self-hypnosis. Masters can put themselves instantly into such a trance, even without a concentration point, but this takes years of effort and lots of self-discipline.

You may think this is Oriental mumbo-jumbo having nothing to do with you or your work. Not so. For one thing, what the Asians have known for thousands of years is now being "discovered" by modern science. The psychological studies of the past hundred-and-twenty years or so tend to confirm this understanding of creativity. Also, unless you intend to exclude creativity from your work (and this is your choice) it's essential to understand and enter into the creative process.

Of course, you can't safely sit in your office staring for hours at a distant mountain peak or anything else. You would be either fired or carried off in a padded wagon. Nor are you likely to find there the peace and quiet essential to total concentration. The fact is, the conditions of most modern businesses are unsuited to creative activity. Nevertheless, create we must, and there's really no substitute for the creative process, so an effort must be made to utilize that process whatever your conditions of work.

Not every ms. warrants, or can be given, a major creative effort. Also, the creative process isn't an either/or matter—it will operate to the degree in which you participate. So, if you can't put yourself into a deep trance, you can at least take a few deep breaths, shut your eyes, and try to concentrate on the darkness for a few minutes. If this fails to produce good enough results, you might get an inspiration in the middle of the night or while dozing on the train.

The point is, you must take positive action toward freeing your imagination if you want the best results. You simply have to recognize the limitations and work within them. True, not everyone has a fertile imagination and the seeds you plant may not sprout—but the evidence suggests that there's a lot more creativity in most people than they realize.

The object of this creative effort is achieving a clear visualization of the ideal finished book, in all its details. The actual result may not much resemble this ideal, but certainly the technical facilities available today make anything possible.

The creative means

With the desired result visualized, begin to assemble the devices with which to achieve that ideal. These devices include all the elements of visual art, used with the insights of psychology plus intuition. The most effective and accessible tools are: (a) symbolism, (b) color, and (c) texture. We access the reader's subconscious by suggestion, and these devices are rich in suggestive power.

SYMBOLISM

The use of symbols has vast possibilities for both suggestion and graphic effects. If the symbolism used is visually effective, effectiveness as symbol isn't essential. The first principle in the use of symbolism is: It must look good. A symbol will sometimes be obvious, sometimes subtle. If it looks good and is obvious, it will surely be effective to some degree—and it doesn't matter how much. If it looks good and is subtle, the worst that can happen is that it will be ineffective as symbol, but again, it doesn't matter. This isn't to imply that it's unimportant whether or not symbolism is effective. The point is that if it fails as symbol, it does no harm provided it's visually effective.

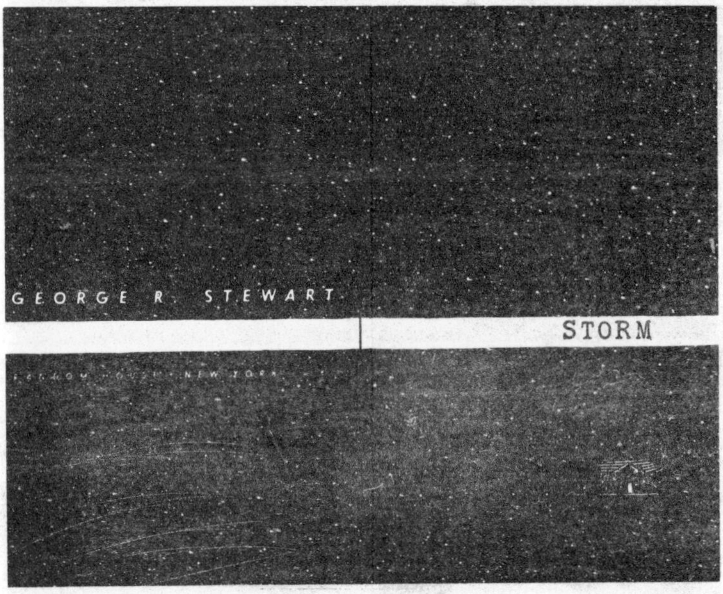

The telegraph tape, once a symbol of urgency associated with disaster, was used imaginatively by Ernst Reichl. The background tone was printed in color.

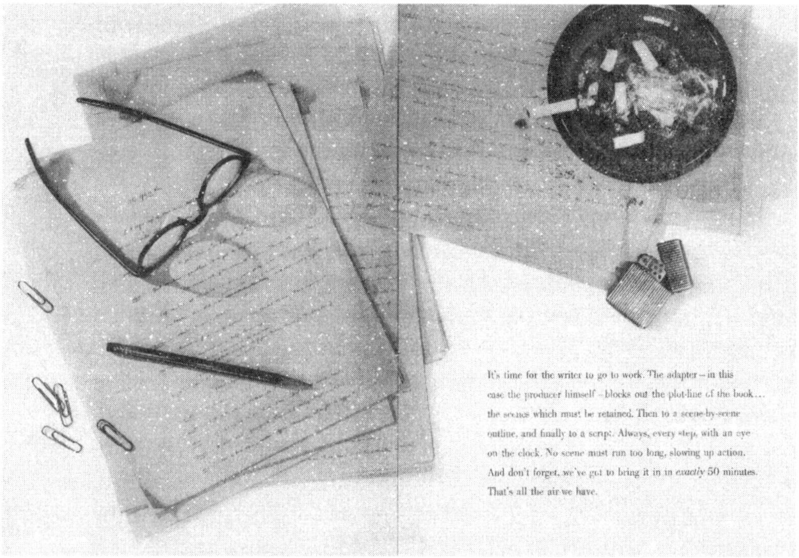

The artifacts of conference are suitable for this factual account of how a radio program is created. Design by William Golden.

Whether the symbol is obvious or subtle, it should be used imaginatively. By treating it in a creative way, you can make the symbol a meaningful part of the book. The degree of subtlety required of symbols depends on the nature of the ms. When the text is factual, a literal or representational symbolism is appropriate. Fiction, or any text with a romantic quality, shaded meanings, or indirect allusions, calls for a more subtly suggestive symbolism.

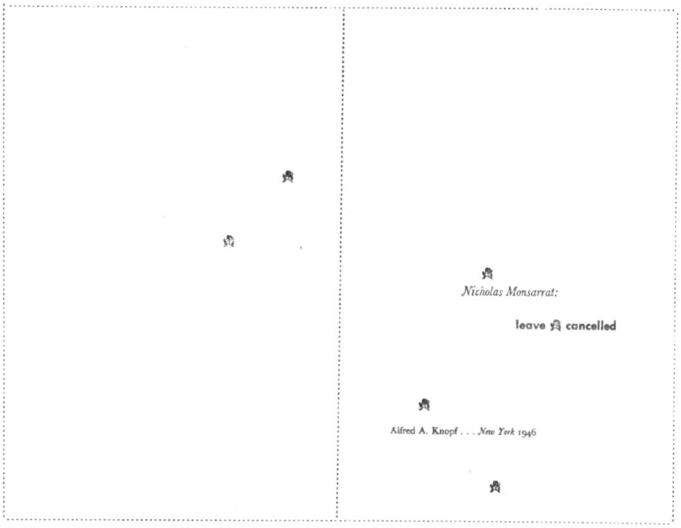

Scattered roses are appropriate symbols for this novel designed by Paul Rand.

The symbols used may represent any aspect of the book. They might be related to the subject or they might be associated with the mood, the atmosphere, a plot, a character, or even the author. Their purpose is to suggest salient features of the ms. in support of the designer's effort to create a book that accurately reflects and reinforces the author's message. If a symbol is dominant in the graphic arrangement, it should be related to the dominant characteristic of the book. The relationships of symbols to each other must reflect the relationships of the textual elements they represent. The total effect of the symbolism used must be a true indication of the basic character of the book.

The range of symbols is virtually unlimited. Graphic symbols

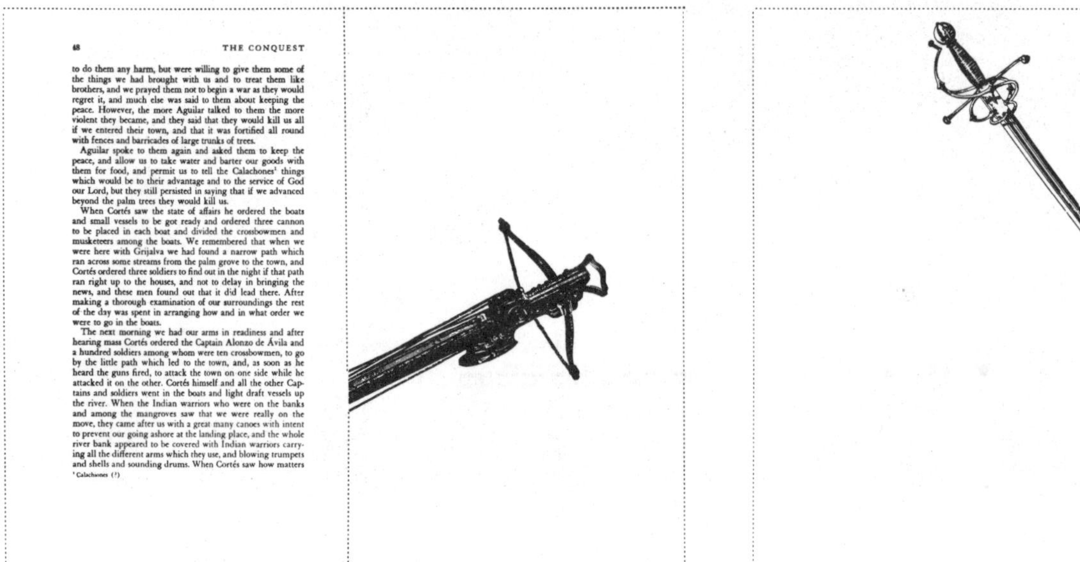

48 THE CONQUEST

to do them any harm, but were willing to give them some of the things we had brought with us and to treat them like brothers, and we prayed them not to begin a war as they would regret it, and much else was said to them about keeping the peace. However, the more Aguilar talked to them the more violent they became, and they said that they would kill us all if we entered their town, and that it was fortified all round with fences and barricades of large trunks of trees.

Aguilar spoke to them again and asked them to keep the peace, and allow us to take water and barter our goods with them for food, and permit us to tell the Calachones[1] things which would be to their advantage and to the service of God our Lord, but they still persisted in saying that if we advanced beyond the palm trees they would kill us.

When Cortés saw the state of affairs he ordered the boats and small vessels to be got ready and ordered three cannon to be placed in each boat and divided the crossbowmen and musketeers among the boats. We remembered that when we were here with Grijalva we had found a narrow path which ran across some streams from the palm grove to the town, and Cortés ordered three soldiers to find out in the night if that path ran right up to the houses, and not to delay in bringing the news, and these men found out that it did lead there. After making a thorough examination of our surroundings the rest of the day was spent in arranging how and in what order we were to go in the boats.

The next morning we had our arms in readiness and after hearing mass Cortés ordered the Captain Alonzo de Ávila and a hundred soldiers among whom were ten crossbowmen, to go by the little path which led to the town, and, as soon as he heard the guns fired, to attack the town on one side while he attacked it on the other. Cortés himself and all the other Captains and soldiers went in the boats and light draft vessels up the river. When the Indian warriors who were on the banks and among the mangroves saw that we were really on the move, they came after us with a great many canoes with intent to prevent our going ashore at the landing place, and the whole river bank appeared to be covered with Indian warriors carrying all the different arms which they use, and blowing trumpets and shells and sounding drums. When Cortés saw how matters

[1] Calachiones (?)

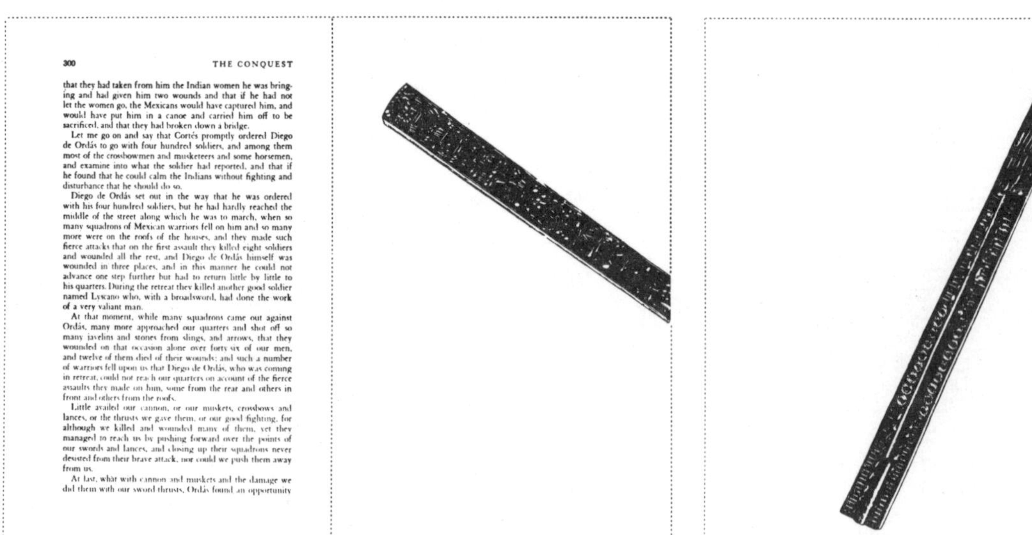

300 THE CONQUEST

that they had taken from him the Indian women he was bringing and had given him two wounds and that if he had not let the women go, the Mexicans would have captured him, and would have put him in a canoe and carried him off to be sacrificed, and that they had broken down a bridge.

Let me go on and say that Cortés promptly ordered Diego de Ordás to go with four hundred soldiers, and among them most of the crossbowmen and musketeers and some horsemen, and examine into what the soldier had reported, and that if he found that he could calm the Indians without fighting and disturbance that he should do so.

Diego de Ordás set out in the way that he was ordered with his four hundred soldiers, but he had hardly reached the middle of the street along which he was to march, when so many squadrons of Mexican warriors fell on him and so many more were on the roofs of the houses, and they made such fierce attacks that on the first assault they killed eight soldiers and wounded all the rest, and Diego de Ordás himself was wounded in three places, and in this manner he could not advance one step further but had to return little by little to his quarters. During the retreat they killed another good soldier named Lyscano who, with a broadsword, had done the work of a very valiant man.

At that moment, while many squadrons came out against Ordás, many more approached our quarters and shot off so many javelins and stones from slings, and arrows, that they wounded on that occasion alone over forty six of our men, and twelve of them died of their wounds; and such a number of warriors fell upon us that Diego de Ordás, who was coming in retreat, could not reach our quarters on account of the fierce assaults they made on him, some from the rear and others in front and others from the roofs.

Little availed our cannon, or our muskets, crossbows and lances, or the thrusts we gave them, or our good fighting, for although we killed and wounded many of them, yet they managed to reach us by pushing forward over the points of our swords and lances, and closing up their squadrons never desisted from their brave attack, nor could we push them away from us.

At last, what with cannon and muskets and the damage we did them with our sword thrusts, Ordás found an opportunity are illustration, and their broad graphic possibilities are suggested in CH. 7. The symbolic values of color and texture are discussed later in this chapter. A book's shape or the proportions of a text page can be symbolic. Even the sequence and placement of illustrations can have meaning. In an edition of Bernal Diaz's *Discovery and Conquest of Mexico* (Farrar Straus & Cudahy, 1956), some of the illustrations are drawings of Mexican and Spanish weapons of the period. Mexican weapons appear in the text where the Aztecs were ascendant, Spanish weapons where Cortez triumphed. Weapons are in profusion when the battle waxes and are few when it wanes. The effect is somewhat like the offstage clash of arms in a play.

design for Discovery *and* Conquest of Mexico *by the author*

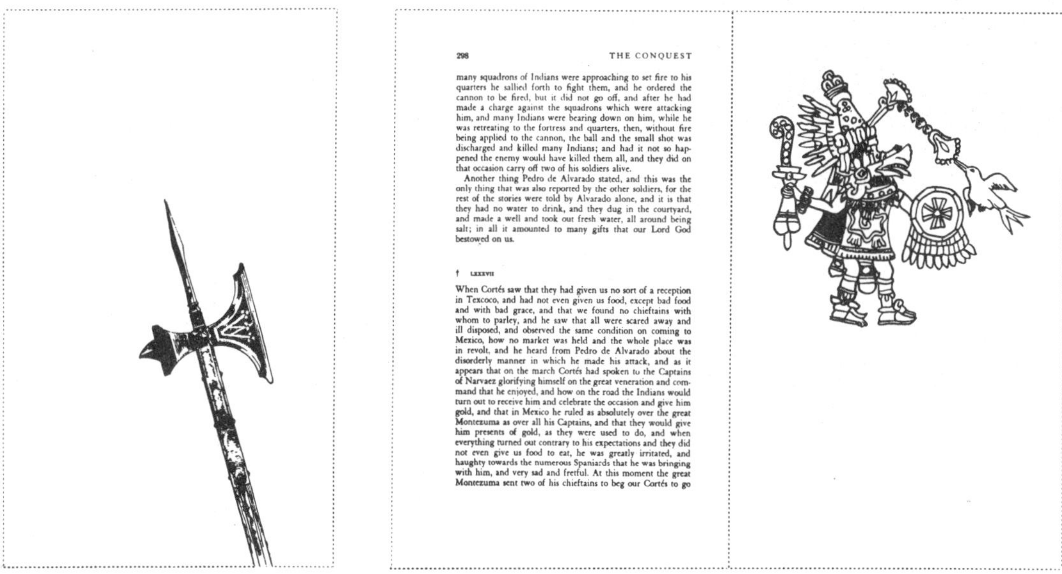

298 THE CONQUEST

many squadrons of Indians were approaching to set fire to his quarters he sallied forth to fight them, and he ordered the cannon to be fired, but it did not go off, and after he had made a charge against the squadrons which were attacking him, and many Indians were bearing down on him, while he was retreating to the fortress and quarters, then, without fire being applied to the cannon, the ball and the small shot was discharged and killed many Indians; and had it not so happened the enemy would have killed them all, and they did on that occasion carry off two of his soldiers alive.

Another thing Pedro de Alvarado stated, and this was the only thing that was also reported by the other soldiers, for the rest of the stories were told by Alvarado alone, and it is that they had no water to drink, and they dug in the courtyard, and made a well and took out fresh water, all around being salt; in all it amounted to many gifts that our Lord God bestowed on us.

† LXXXVII

When Cortés saw that they had given us no sort of a reception in Texcoco, and had not even given us food, except bad food and with bad grace, and that we found no chieftains with whom to parley, and he saw that all were scared away and ill disposed, and observed the same condition on coming to Mexico, how no market was held and the whole place was in revolt, and he heard from Pedro de Alvarado about the disorderly manner in which he made his attack, and as it appears that on the march Cortés had spoken to the Captains of Narvaez glorifying himself on the great veneration and command that he enjoyed, and how on the road the Indians would turn out to receive him and celebrate the occasion and give him gold, and that in Mexico he ruled as absolutely over the great Montezuma as over all his Captains, and that they would give him presents of gold, as they were used to do, and when everything turned out contrary to his expectations and they did not even give us food to eat, he was greatly irritated, and haughty towards the numerous Spaniards that he was bringing with him, and very sad and fretful. At this moment the great Montezuma sent two of his chieftains to beg our Cortés to go

THE CONQUEST

Plaza we placed a cannon and with
the enemy were so numerous that the
all. The Spaniards seeing that there
ch was our greatest danger) deter-
and when the enemy saw this carried
e multitude of our allies (although
unless they were in our company)
ter them until they were shut up in
which was enclosed with a masonry

e large enough to hold a town of
wever, a breach was made and the
ed it and remained there and on the
When the people of the city saw that
with us they turned again on the
from the towers and courts, and as
ger, for it was worse than a retreat,
rticoes of the courts; however, the
n so severely that they abandoned
Plaza whence they were driven out
liged to abandon the cannon which

withstand the onset of the enemy,
and would have suffered great loss
at at that moment three horsemen
the Plaza, and when the enemy
that there were more of them and
emen killed some of them and we
losure. On the most important and
ver a hundred steps to reach the
ian chieftains had sheltered them-
the Spaniards clambered up, and,
t bravely, they gained the summit

en had now arrived, and they and
buscade by which they killed over

got the men together and ordered a
uch a host of the enemy fell upon
the horsemen the Spaniards must
owever, as I had had all the bad

The use of type as symbol is discussed to some extent in CH. 5. This is a particularly difficult area of symbolism because type has not only its suggestive characteristic, but also communicates thoughts. Typographic symbolism can be valid, but it's inclined to be obvious and is easily overworked. Use it with care and moderation. On these pages are a few examples of type used symbolically with some success.

Alexey Brodovitch used very tall, dramatic letters to suggest a line of dancers, and a potpourri of decorative typefaces to evoke the romantic, varied world of ballet.

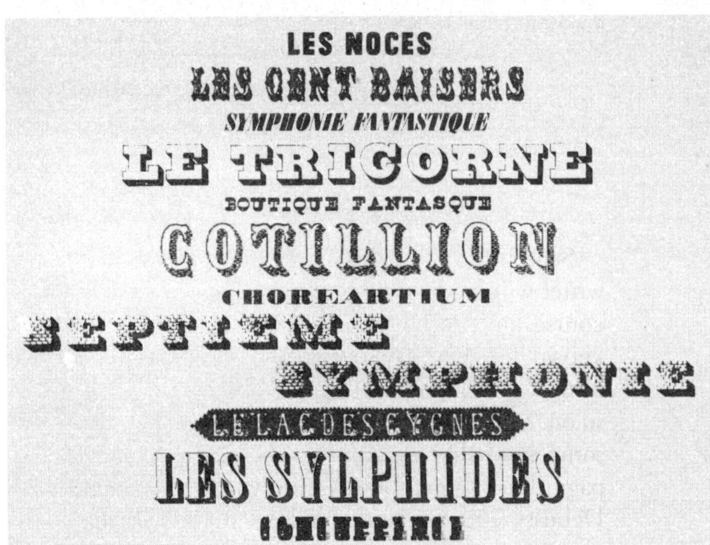

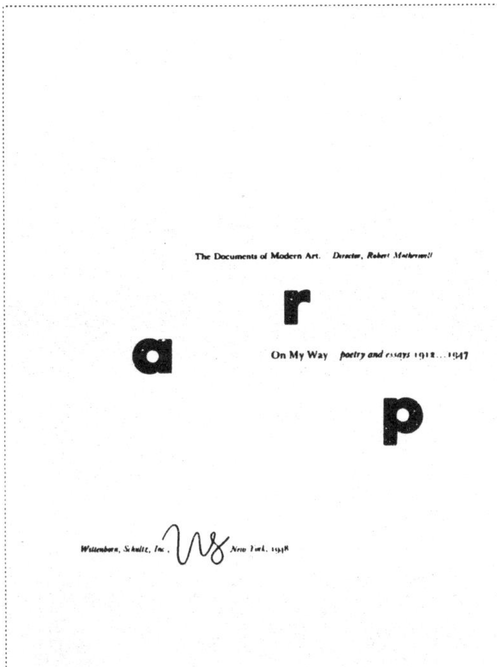
The Documents of Modern Art. *Director, Robert Motherwell*

r

a

On My Way *poetry and essays 1912 . . . 1947*

p

Wittenborn, Schultz, Inc. , *New York, 1948*

The form and feeling of Arp's work is reflected in Paul Rand's choice and arrangement of type for his name.

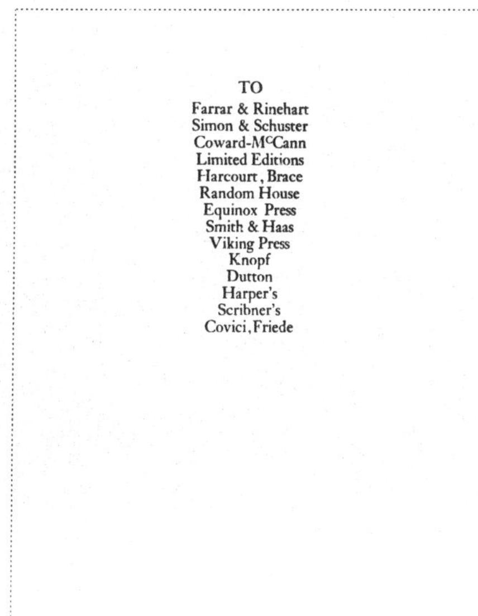
TO
Farrar & Rinehart
Simon & Schuster
Coward-McCann
Limited Editions
Harcourt, Brace
Random House
Equinox Press
Smith & Haas
Viking Press
Knopf
Dutton
Harper's
Scribner's
Covici, Friede

S. A. Jacobs used an ancient typographic technique to raise a cup in dedication.

Search the ms. for symbols used by the author. Sometimes a writer will inadvertently or consciously repeat a theme. Poets, of course, are entirely at home with visual images, and they're often known for their favored symbols—W. B. Yeats for his golden birds, towers, trees, etc.; Edith Sitwell for her roses, drums, and so on. Sometimes the book's subject will be a person with whom some symbol is associated. For example, see on the following page illustrations showing the use of characteristic symbols for Debussy and Stravinsky. Where no readily apparent symbol is present, the designer may have to create appropriate symbols from a study of the editorial analysis.

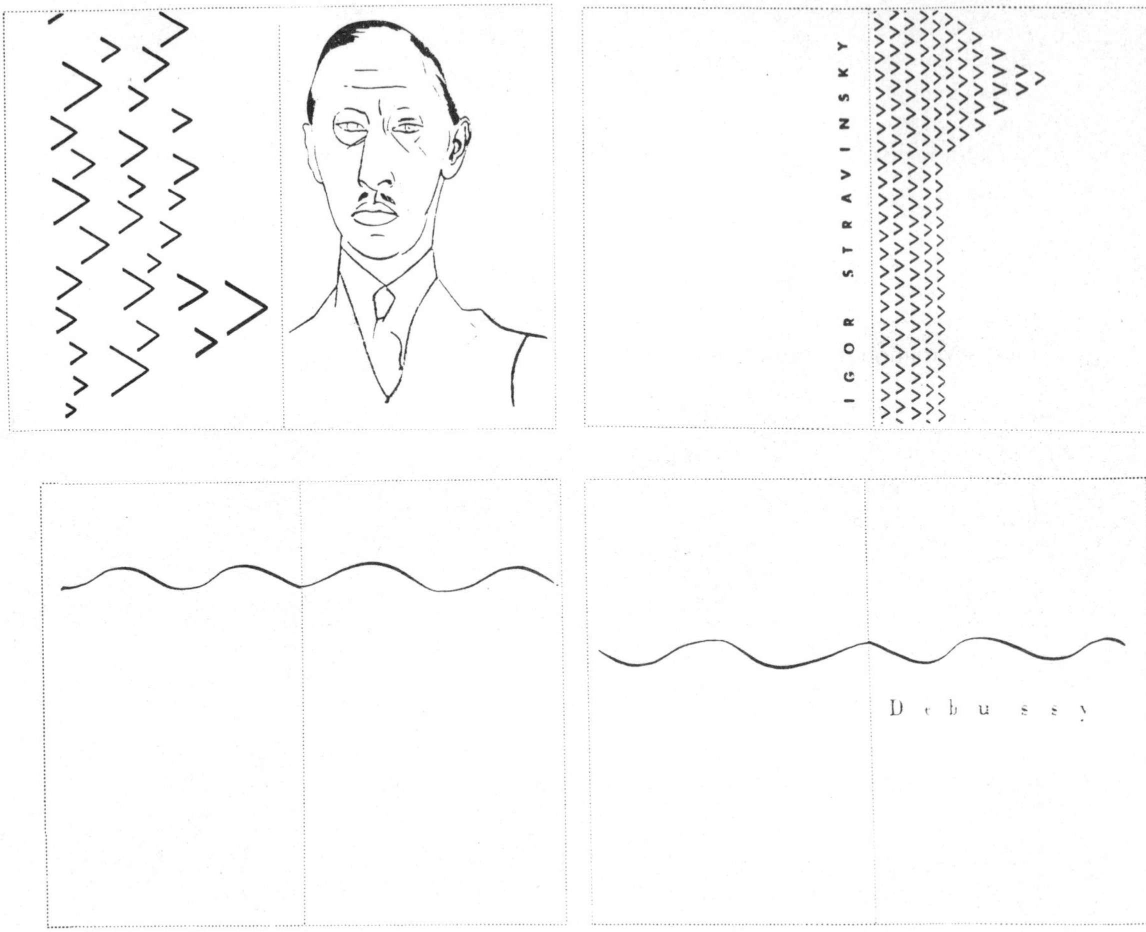

The sharp, staccato symbols of the Stravinsky book and the undulating line in the Debussy volume capture the characteristics of each composer's work. Both designs by Merle Armitage.

COLOR Of all the graphic elements, color surely has the most powerful psychological effect. Except for some specific associations discussed below, color is almost entirely without intellectual content and speaks directly to the subconscious. A connection between color and emotions is clearly established. As one of the most effective tools of communication, color should be used in book design even more than it is, but it must never be used in such a way as to hamper reading. Putting a block of color behind type is a poor idea, one which gets worse as the color becomes stronger. A knowledge of the use of color is as important to the book designer as a knowledge of typography.

Because of its psychological powers, color is particularly valuable in creating atmosphere and mood. Sometimes an author will be thinking in terms of a particular color while writing

(Flaubert said that he thought of *Madame Bovary* in terms of *puce*, which is the "rich" dark red characteristic of 19th century French bourgeois interiors), but, even if not, the ms. will have *some* character and this will suggest a color, kind of color, or combination of colors.

Color has three aspects: (a) hue, (b) intensity, and (c) value.

■ **Hue**—The "color" of the color (red, blue, yellow, green, orange-red, etc.).

■ **Intensity**—The purity of the color (intensity is lowered as the color is grayed).

■ **Value**—The darkness of the color (even in pure primary colors there's variation in value: yellow is lighter than blue, blue is lighter than red, etc.; however, an intense yellow may be darker than a blue whose intensity, and value, has been lowered by the addition of white).

The psychological effect of a color changes as it's modified in hue, value, and/or intensity. For example, a blue with a slight tinge of green and high intensity may be happy in effect. A blue on the violet side lowered in intensity by the addition of black can be quite somber, while the same violet-blue grayed with white might be soft and romantic. The variety of colors, considering the modifications possible, is infinite.

Not only is there an infinite number of colors, but these can be used in an infinite number of combinations—each of which has its own psychological properties entirely independent of the individual colors within it. For example, two colors, both of which are quite mild by themselves, may, when combined, create a clash that's anything but mild. Several intense colors can be combined to produce a feeling of subtle harmony if they're closely related in hue. A dark color of low intensity and a light color of low intensity can be combined to produce a dramatic effect of contrasting values.

Some colors and combinations of colors have very specific associations—school colors, national colors, company colors, club colors, etc. In an appropriate context, these colors convey meaning just as surely as do words. Don't scorn their use because they're obvious. As with graphic symbols, the questions are: Is it appropriate? Does it look good? If both answers are yes, final judgment will be based on how you used the colors, not why.

There are other, less specific associations that can be used symbolically. Certain greens are associated with vegetation and nature in general. Some browns are conventionally connected with masculine matters because of their association with wood and leather. Some exotic combinations of violets, pinks, and greens have a tropical look, blues are used to suggest water and sky, and so on. These nonspecific color symbols can be used very effectively where they're not required to convey the meaning alone. Again, while subtlety and freshness are very desirable in design, there's no need to avoid the use of an appropriate color just because it's obvious. A slightly odd shade or an interesting combination with other colors can easily save it from banality.

Color has the potentials of a symphony orchestra, but it's not a simple matter to use color masterfully any more than it's a simple matter to create great music with an orchestra. Much is to be learned, much experience is required—and it helps a lot to have talent.

TEXTURE As a device for communicating with the subconscious, texture is as effective as any. It can be apprehended through two senses—sight and touch—which gives it an additional entrance to the area of response.

While texture is particularly effective, it's also relatively limited in its range of expression. However, it's an inevitable element of book design and should be utilized for positive ends.

The textural possibilities in bookmaking are not as meager as one might suppose. Printing papers are made with surfaces ranging from glassy-smooth to pebbly. Endpapers are somewhat more limited in range, but stock cover materials are reasonably varied, and a wide variety of textures can be had on special orders. Vinyl can be obtained with a surface as slick as patent leather and some of the more expensive cloths come as rough-textured as tweed.

The possibilities are greatly enlarged by the use of embossing or blank stamping (CHs. 13, 29). Suppliers of binding materials have stock embossings that can be applied as ordered, but these are mostly imitation cloth and leather textures. Far more variety can be achieved by the application of texture in the stamping operation. With etched dies, this isn't unduly expensive. For example, on a book about the Florida swamp country, the cover was given a texture of alligator skin by blank stamping with a die made from an alligator-pattern wrapping paper.

Various subjects and moods suggest particular textures. A book about machinery would suggest a smooth texture, while a book on Irish farmers calls for a rough, tweedy feel. The atmosphere of a novel might be slick, soft, or bristly. One book may suggest contrasting textures, another similar ones. Or it may be desirable to use texture literally by using a rope-like or canvas-like material on a sailing book or binding a book about glass in glass-like plastic. These might be rather expensive bindings, but an affordable substitute can usually be found.

As in other forms of symbolism, the esthetic and suggestive functions of texture can be justified independently. Regardless of the psychological use of texture in the design, its graphic and tactile values should be well handled. However, it would be as much a mistake to make a handsome combination of textures that were inappropriate to the feeling of the book as it would be to use the wrong graphic symbol or unsuitable colors.

In conclusion

The most judicious use of symbolism alone isn't likely to reveal the nature of the book or establish the atmosphere. Nor is the expert handling of color or texture able to achieve the whole objective by itself. The typography can achieve just so much and illustration has its limitations. It may seem impractical to apply so much effort to achieve the relatively minor effect of a good textural scheme or color combination. It would indeed be a waste of time to carefully develop one aspect if the others were neglected. The point to remember is that each factor contributes something toward the desired end, and the combination of all of them is likely to have a positive effect worth the effort.

A perfect orchestration of superbly handled elements will result in a book that greatly enriches the work it conveys. If the result falls somewhat short of this ideal, it will have value in proportion to the success of its parts—and in design, the whole can't be any better than the poorest of its parts.

23. The basic decisions

Having analyzed the problem and visualized an ideal solution, you are ready to begin the decision-making process. This includes the second stage of design—consideration of alternatives—and the final stage—making choices. To some extent, you went through these stages in the creative visualization, but no firm decisions were made because only one aspect of the problem was involved. At this point, *all* aspects of the mechanical, commercial, and editorial problems will be brought into consideration, and the decisions made now must be practical and economical, as well as creatively sound.

It may appear that the middle stage gets little attention compared with the first and third. This is because each choice entails examination of the available possibilities, so consideration and decision seem almost simultaneous as the work progresses. Nevertheless, they're successive processes, even if they intermingle so closely it's sometimes difficult to see that.

There are seven basic decisions. These are made first because they affect all others. They relate to: (a) retail price, (b) size of first printing, (c) trim-size, (d) editorial arrangement of illustrations, (e) printing process, (f) paper, and (g) number of pages.

Retail price & first printing

Two decisions, the retail price of the book and the size of the first printing, are usually made by the editorial and sales departments before the ms. is released for design and production. These require estimating what the market will bear for a book of the kind and size. The procedure appears simple enough with a tradebook; it means basing price and quantity on experience with similar books. However, estimating correctly is far from simple.

What seemed to have been a similar book sold 10,000 copies two years ago, so presumably this one will do about the same. But there are several reasons why this may not work out. In two years (or two weeks!) the public's interest may have shifted away from the subject; the demand for that kind of book may have been satisfied by the earlier book and others like it; or, as is often the case, what seem to be similar books may differ just enough to make one a popular success and the other a failure.

The price is a somewhat less hazardous decision, but it too has uncertain elements. A general increase in retail prices may justify adding a dollar to the price of the earlier book for the new one, but a weaker demand for the new book may not support the higher price, or a general resistance to higher book prices may develop at the time of publication.

Variations in the cost of manufacture are a likely source of difficulty. Unless the second book was prepared as an exact duplicate of the first, chances are the production costs will differ. Editors are not usually familiar enough with production to be able to spot the seemingly small variations that make big differences in cost. Besides, there may have been price increases in composition, printing, binding, or materials since the other book was manufactured. Whenever the ms. is complicated or unusual in any way, one should get production estimates before the retail price of the book is determined. Such estimates are often the basis for deciding whether or not the book can be economically published.

Trim-size

CUSTOMARY SIZES

The page size of the book is generally an arbitrary decision based primarily on custom. Economy affects the decision, but in most cases custom has been shaped by economy, so there's little conflict. Once a press size has been standardized to accommodate a preferred trim-size, paper is made to fit that size.

In American tradebooks, there are seven sizes in common use:

5⅜ x 8" (13.7 x 20.32 cm)
5½ x 8¼" (14 x 21 cm)
6 x 9" (15.2 x 22.8 cm)
6⅛ x 9¼" (15.6 x 23.5 cm)
7½ x 9¼" (19 x 23.5 cm)
8 x 10" (20.3 x 25.4 cm)
8⅜ x 10⅞" (21.6 x 27.94 cm)

By custom, 5⅜ x 8" is used for fiction and for nonfiction of minor importance, usually unillustrated. Fiction by major authors (or of unusual length) and most nonfiction call for 5½ x 8¼". The 6 x 9" or 6⅛ x 9¼" size is used generally for nonfiction of major importance or for books in which illustrations suggest a larger page. The anticipated retail price is also often a factor in choosing a size. Higher-priced books of any kind may be put into the 6⅛ x 9¼" format. Picture books, i.e., books in which pictures are at least as important as text, are usually made 7½ x 9¼", 8 x 10", or 8⅜ x 10⅞". These customs are by no means invariable, but they do prevail in most cases. Picture books are often made in odd sizes—usually large—and shapes.

Since xerographic presses print only one or two pages at a time, rather than forms of multiple pages, there's considerable flexibility in page sizes. However, they have their own technical requirements and may be limited by the stock sheets and rolls of paper available from suppliers, so they sometimes offer only five or six sizes that are different from, but similar to, the standard sizes for offset printing. Before choosing a size, check with the printshop to see if it's available. Some shops will provide any size up to about 8½ x 11".

Mass-market paperbacks are 4³⁄16 x 6⅞" (10.6 x 17.5 cm), or 4³⁄16 x 6¾" (17.1 cm). Juveniles are 5 (12.7 cm) or 5½ x 7½" (14 x 19 cm). The (near) standardization here is quite rigid because of the need to fit retailers' racks, although a few lines have special racks for their own size. The higher-priced lines are, in many cases, produced in tradebook sizes because they're often printed simultaneously with hardbound editions. These are the "trade paperbacks"—so called because they're sold in bookstores rather than through the mass-distribution outlets where the mass-market lines are sold.

Textbooks in elementary and high school grades vary little in size—ranging from 6⅛ x 9¼" (15.9 x 23.5 cm) to 7 x 10" (17.8 x 25.4 cm). They are printed almost without exception on web offset presses with 38 to 41" (96.52 to 104.14 cm) cut-offs and web widths of either 41 or 61" (104.14 or 154.94 cm). College texts are more often made in common tradebook sizes, as they're sold in stores as tradebooks also. The most used size is 6⅛ x 9¼".

In children's books, particularly in picture-and-caption books for preschool children (usually called "*flats*"), page sizes vary considerably. Pages of 6⅝ x 10" (16.8 x 25.4 cm), 8½ x 11" (21.6 x 27.9 cm), and 9 x 12" (22.9 x 30.5 cm) are not uncommon. Teenage books are generally made in regular adult tradebook sizes. (Books for high-school-age children are called "young adult" books. This shameful deceit was concocted in the 1960s to pander to teenagers' supposed objection to being referred to as such.)

CHOICE FACTORS Deviations from the above usages are usually related to the availability of paper. With the price of paper being lower on larger quantities of one item or one size (CH. 11), publishers tend to buy as few sizes as possible. Consequently, their paper stock may not contain the customary size, and the book will be made in a size to fit the paper on hand. Another influence in the use of unconventional size is the desire to make a big "package" to appeal to the gift buyer.

Actually, books could vary in size by using less than the full dimension of standard sheets—for example, by taking 5 x 8¼" (12.7 x 21 cm) instead of 5½ x 8¼" (14 x 21 cm) out of 45 x 68" (114.3 x

172.7 cm). This would waste 4" of the sheet, or about 9%. On larger orders, the paper could be made to size.

Cost is a minor factor in choosing between 5⅜ x 8" and 5½ x 8¼". The only difference is in the amount of paper—about 5%—which usually means only a few cents per book. Going up to 6⅛ x 9¼" (15.6 x 23.5 cm) involves an increase of about 30% in paper, and probably an increase in press cost. Either a larger (more expensive) press must be used, or there must be fewer pages per form—and thus more forms. Generally, the larger the page size, the more costly the printing per page.

STANDARDIZATION

Complete, or nearly complete, standardization of book sizes would result in fairly substantial savings in the cost of production. At one time during the letterpress era, some printers tried to lower their costs by keeping certain presses set for one size of sheet, plates, and margins. Books that conformed to those specifications were then printed at lower prices. Efforts (particularly speeches) in the direction of large-scale standardization have been part of the book industry for decades. These efforts haven't generally been successful and are not likely to be, except in mass-market paperback publishing, in which price is the primary consideration.

A certain amount of de facto standardization has resulted from the manufacture of presses to fit the most popular trim-sizes, but there's still some room for varying sizes within the limits of each press. On web presses, the cut-off (CH. 12) imposes a definite limit, but it's possible to vary the roll width up to the maximum for the press. Yet, the decision to use a standard trim-size may arise from a concern about being able to quickly reprint a fast-selling title. The standard presses and paper sizes are most readily available.

The possible savings in complete standardization are not, however, sufficient to sacrifice flexibility in handling diverse editorial materials, to warrant the considerable extra work necessary to make all books fit one size, or to overcome the competitive urge to do the unusual, or the esthetic urge to see variety rather than uniformity prevail. Books are not, after all, purely utilitarian objects. They have an esthetic component that justifies some expenditure of money and effort. It would be more economical, also, to make all houses exactly alike, but whenever this is done there's an outcry against "look-alikes". It's true that the houses in many parts of the world were made alike before the industrial era—the thatched stone cottages of western Europe, the tile-roofed stuccoed houses of the Mediterranean regions, the igloos of the Arctic, the buffalo-skin teepees of the Plains Indians—and we admire these structures without deploring their uniformity, but there was an identity of function, material resources, and environment that justified the similarity. In books, almost every problem is unique, so the solutions can't properly be the same.

The basic decisions concerning illustrations are:

(a) where they're to occur in the book, i.e., what physical relationship they will have as a whole to the text; and
(b) how and on what they're to be printed, i.e., which printing process and which paper.

These decisions are so closely related they must be treated as one. The same considerations affect both, and each depends on the other. Where the illustrations are a major element in the book, these decisions will have a big part in determining the specifications for composition, printing, and binding, and will influence the other basic decisions. Variations in treatment of the text are relatively limited, but there are many ways to handle illustrations, and the way chosen will have an important effect on the character of the book.

The decisions on illustrations must consider two factors (besides time and cost):

(a) editorial requirements for the relationship of illustrations to text, and
(b) the nature and purpose of the individual illustrations.

EDITORIAL REQUIREMENTS

The question is: Must an illustration accompany the relevant text and, if so, how closely? Usually, the editor or author can answer this, but sometimes neither can and it's up to the designer to find the answer.

There is no system for deciding when to place illustrations in close proximity to the text. In principle, the arrangement that's most practical is best, and it's not necessarily better to have picture and text together. Unless there's a need for readers to see an illustration before proceeding (as in a step-by-step explanation), they might be better served by putting it elsewhere so they may read without interruption. Sometimes an illustration is referred to several times in the text, and it's better placed where it's accessible at any time. This is frequently true of maps, which are more accessible on the endpapers or at the front or back of the text than inside. Some books are written with text and pictures closely integrated, but in many cases the best relationship isn't so obvious—and must be carefully considered.

The ideal arrangement of illustrations isn't always possible within budget limits. For example, it might have been better to place the illustration of four-color process printing that's now on the front endpaper of this book opposite the explanation in CH. 8. However, an additional cost in paper and binding was saved by putting it on the endpaper, where it's so accessible that inconvenience to the reader is negligible. (Also, this illustration makes an attractive and appropriate endpaper design.)

There are several possible ways of placing illustrations in a book. They may be:

(a) printed on the text paper with the text,
(b) printed on different paper from the text and bound into the book in one of several ways (CHs. 13, 29),
(c) printed on the endpapers, or
(d) printed on the cover (CH. 29).

Any combination of these methods may be used in one book. Where there are many illustrations of various kinds and purposes, the best method or combination of methods should be found for each of them.

Desirability and cost should be considered simultaneously, but it's quite difficult to do this effectively because of the numerous variables involved. Any change in the plan is likely to affect several other factors. The final cost of an alternative might be higher, even though the alternative itself is cheaper. A printing decision may affect paper and binding, a paper decision may affect printing, which in turn may affect binding, and so on. Where alternative plans are being considered, it's usually necessary to have actual estimates made. Guesses are likely to be wrong.

Iin offset there's little or no extra cost involved in printing any black & white illustrations—line or halftone—in the text, so the decision for their placement can be made entirely on editorial and esthetic grounds.

If sales or esthetic considerations call for the use of color, particularly process-color illustrations, and if the illustrations may be editorially separated from the text, it's possible to save money by printing them separately. Then the higher cost of printing the illustrations will apply only to the pages on which they appear, rather than the entire book. It's even cheaper to put the color illustrations together and print only part of the book in color and part in black & white. If the color illustrations are printed separately and the highest quality is required, they can be printed on coated paper while the text is printed on less expensive stock. However, the economic advantage may be lost in the bindery, as the cost of tipping, inserting, and wrapping is high (CHs. 13, 29). That is why publishers tend to compress illustrations into one or two sections in the book, even though flexibility of editorial arrangement is sacrificed.

Printing the illustrations separately makes it possible to use the most suitable process and paper for both pictures and text. This factor has economic value in terms of the book's sale and must be weighed with the other factors in making the basic decisions. If the pictures are placed in the text, both can be printed at the same time, which is economically feasible when there's a relatively large amount of color illustration in relation to text.

The other primary consideration, the nature and purpose of the illustrations, is discussed in CH. 7, where it's explained that illustrations have various uses, and each use has its own requirements. It's these requirements that are taken into account in arriving at the basic decisions.

■ **Informative illustrations**—These must be given maximum size and clarity because their purpose is elucidation. They shouldn't therefore:

(a) be reduced too much,
(b) be printed on too rough a paper (this reduces sharpness),
(c) be bled or cropped if significant details are lost thereby,
(d) be printed in colored inks (black ink on near-white paper gives optimum clarity), or
(e) have too coarse a screen (sharpness in halftones increases as the screen becomes finer).

■ **Suggestive illustrations**—These are concerned with effect rather than accuracy, so any treatment or means of reproduction is acceptable if it achieves the desired end. Unless accuracy happens to be the effect wanted, any amount of reduction, enlargement, cropping, bleeding, silhouetting, etc. is justified. For example, it may be desirable to enlarge the screen of a halftone or gray it down until almost all definition is lost.

■ **Decorative illustrations**—These are distinctly secondary elements, so the decisions on printing, paper, and binding should be based on the needs of the text, with the illustrations made suitable for reproduction within the specifications chosen.

■ **Representative illustrations**—These are subject to the same general principles as informative illustrations. All decisions must lead to the most accurate reproduction—with even higher standards required in this group. Nothing should be allowed to prevail over decisions made for the representative purpose. Here, the situation is opposite to that of decorative illustrations—if necessary, the text must be treated in less than the best way. For example, if the illustrations call for coated paper, it should be used, even though the text on those pages may not then be as readable.

Printing process & paper

Many considerations that affect the choice of printing process and paper have been discussed already. Properly, these choices are made to accommodate the copy—text and pictures—with due respect for the commercial aspects of publishing. The sales department will certainly be happy with a book that's handsomely printed on the most suitable paper, but they will be especially anxious to have one that makes a big package. This refers not only to trim-size, but to bulk. More than once has a book been printed on an uncoated or matte-coated rather than a gloss-coated paper to obtain the benefit of larger bulk.

The primary considerations, however, are the requirements of illustrations, the choice of trim-size, and the cost elements in binding. All the basic decisions are interdependent, and each must be made in the light of the others.

Behind an intelligent and perceptive choice of printing processes and papers there must be a knowledge of their characteristics. These are discussed in CHs. 11, 12. The number of possible combinations of copy and circumstances in book problems is infinite, and it's obviously impossible to deal with every one here. We will, though, take a hypothetical situation and arrive at printing and paper decisions by the recommended procedure.

Suppose we have a nonfiction tradebook with an extensive text and a fairly large number of illustrations. The retail price will be quite high, and the sales prospects make possible a substantial first printing, so it won't be necessary to find the very cheapest way to produce the book. On the other hand, there's a lot of book to be produced, so the budget does have limits.

The mechanical analysis shows that there are 103 illustrations—of which 75 are color photographs that can be called informative, and the other 28 are line drawings having a primarily suggestive purpose. A study of the ms. indicates that the photographs need not appear in a specific place in the book, but they should be fairly close to the relevant text. The line drawings are simply to enhance the atmosphere of the text, so they may be scattered at random.

With these factors to consider, we might decide that printing the text and line illustrations together by offset on an antique stock (CH. 11) would be the most effective and least expensive method. The color illustrations we would print as 32 pages by offset on gloss-coated paper, to be inserted in the book as four 8-page wraps. The gloss-coated stock would give us maximum reproduction quality. The four wraps would spread the pictures fairly widely through the book, permitting us to place them reasonably close to their textual references without excessive cost. Most of the book's pages will be the antique stock, so the bulk will be adequate. The text paper need not be too smooth, as the line drawings don't present any difficult printing problems.

For the book you are now reading, it was decided to print the entire book on an off-white paper with a relatively soft surface. The illustrations should appear with the descriptive text, yet there are relatively few halftones, so it was not considered necessary to print the whole book on coated or heavily calendered paper. On an off-white stock without excessive smoothness or glare the text type is easier to read, the illustrations of book pages and type look better, and the halftone illustrations can be reproduced adequately for their purpose.

The decision to print a book on a xerographic press is made on the basis of the number of copies wanted. For text and black & white halftone illustrations, quality is comparable to commercial-standard offset, assuming comparable screens are used (offset produces higher quality when finer screens are used than are currently possible in xerography), and for quantities below about fifteen-hundred copies, the cost is lower than offset. Cost advantage is greater the smaller the run. It's possible to print books with four-color process xerography, but the cost can be as much as ten times that for black & white. It'll take new technologies to bring the cost down.

Number of pages

Given any ms., one can make a book of relatively few pages or many. Indeed, an effective demonstration of the role of book design is to place side by side two books of radically different appearance, pointing out that the mss. for both were almost identical.

The length of a book is determined to some extent by each of three factors:

(a) the size of the ms.,
(b) the retail price of the book, and
(c) the requirements of paper and presses.

The esthetic considerations of format—whether the book should be thick or thin—may have some influence, but this is rare and almost never decisive.

DETERMINANTS: THE MANUSCRIPT

In most cases, the size of the ms. is the dominant element in the decision, which is modified by the other factors only as necessary. A very small ms. is often padded out to justify a retail price, and a very large one is usually held in to reduce the cost, but the number of pages in the printed book is ordinarily related to the amount of material (text and illustrations) in the ms. In any case, start with the ms. to determine the approximate length of the book as it would be normally set.

There are several methods of approaching this answer, depending on the nature of the ms. and the nature of the problem, but the principle is always the same—you start with known elements and combine these with a hypothesis or supposition to arrive at tentative answers, which can then be used to find other answers. You work from the known to the unknown. The procedure used in each case depends on which elements are known. There are two main alternative situations: (a) a specific total number of pages is required and the problem is to make the ms. fit, or (b) no specific number is required and the ms. is estimated to determine how many pages it will make.

Suppose you are told that the book should make 352 pages (perhaps because that's the size of a competing book that sells for a higher price). The problem is to determine if the ms. can be fitted reasonably into 352 pages of the chosen trim-size.

The first step is to make an estimate of the number of pages that would be occupied by all the material other than straight text.

■ **Page-for-page material**—In the breakdown (CH. 21) is a list of the frontmatter copy, which can usually be counted in this way. A typical frontmatter sequence might run as follows:

1—half-title	8—preface
2—title	9—contents
3—title	10—contents
4—copyright	11—introduction
5—dedication	12—introduction
6—blank	13—introduction
7—preface	14—blank

A long introduction may be lumped in with the text for this purpose. A wrong guess of one or two pages on the shorter pieces won't be serious at this point. Count other page-for-page material in backmatter, full-page tables, etc. The allowance for part-titles is discussed under "Subdivisions and units" below.

■ **Character-count material**—As described in CH. 21, the number of pages that will be required by the straight text alone can be determined quickly and accurately in a layout program. However, before this can be done, it's necessary to decide on the basic design specs you'll use. You can choose some arbitrary specs and see how they come out, but to plan the book properly it's best to follow the procedures described below and in CHs. 24, 25.

First establish a tentative text-page size. This can be done in a page-makeup program or on a sheet of tracing paper. For the latter, rule a rectangle for the trim-size and place within it a rectangle for a text area (not including running heads or folios). The text area may have any size, shape, or position you want, provided it's far enough from the gutter to avoid the curving of the page in a bound book—at least ⅝" (1.6 cm)—and far enough from the outside edges to avoid being cut by the trim. Also, the folding and

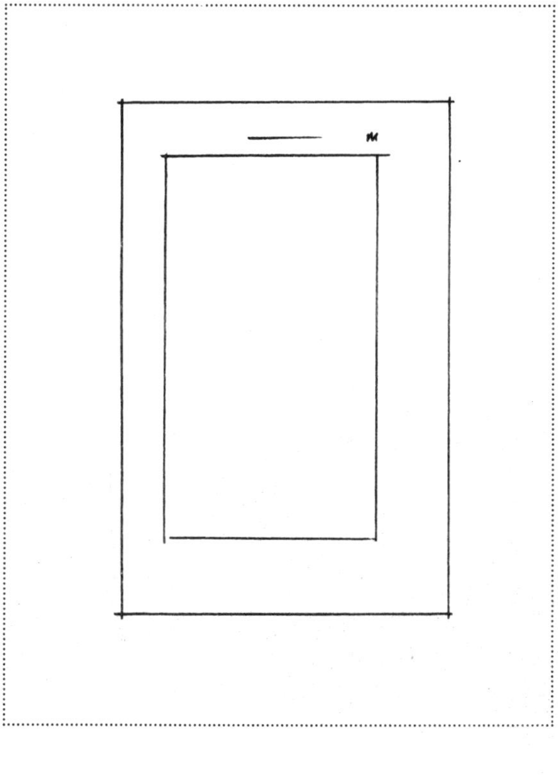

layout of text page

trimming may not be square, so stay at least ⁵⁄₁₆" (.8 cm) away from trimmed edges to avoid making irregularities too noticeable. Usually, an allowance should be made at the top or bottom of the text area for running heads and folios, although these may go at the side (as in this book). The most practical distance of these from the text is about one pica. The width of the text should be measured to an even pica or half-pica. On very large pages, it may be best to set the text in two columns. See CHs. 5, 23 for discussions of maximum text width.

The purpose of the tentative text-page size is to help determine an approximate number of characters per page for use in estimating the number of pages. A rough rule of thumb is: Multiply the width of the text area in picas (exclusive of running heads) by the depth and double this number. For example, if the text page is 23 x 39 picas, the product is 897, so the number of characters per page would be twice that—1794. While it's possible to have much less or much more text on a page of this size, 1794 would be a reasonable starting point.

An even quicker (but rougher) method is to use 2000 as an average number for medium-sized mss. and 3000 for large ones. While these figures are not likely to be as close to the final result, they're handy for mathematics and they obviate the need for drawing a text area, etc. Since the approximate number of characters per page is only a hypothetical figure that will be corrected anyway, it doesn't really matter how wrong it is, within reasonable limits. With experience, you'll be able to guess quite closely how many characters per page there'll be in each book.

With an approximate number of characters per page, you can calculate the number of pages of any item other than text, if it's been counted by characters (CH. 21). Simply divide the total number of characters by your approximate number per page. If any of this material should be set smaller than the text, add 20 or 25% to the per-page character number (1794 + 20% = 2152). For footnotes, which are ordinarily set much smaller than the text, add 50%.

■ **Line-for-line material**—To find the number of pages, divide the line counts by the text-page depth in picas if the ms. is large, or that number less 3 if the ms. is medium in size. For very small mss., use that number less 6. In the first instance, we assume that the text will be set on a 12 pt. body, in the second, on a 13 pt. body, and in the third, on a 14 pt. body. This assumes also that the text will be about 36 picas deep, so the addition of each point of leading will reduce the number of lines by 3 (1 pica = 12 pts., 1 line = 12 pts., 36 pts. = 3 picas, 3 picas = 3 lines). For example, if there are 363 lines of poetry in a medium-sized ms., they would take 11 pages if the depth of the page were 36 picas (33 lines of 13 pts.). This method may be used for almost any size page, as the error won't be very large if the depth is a few picas more or less.

For tabular matter and other line-for-line material which would probably be set smaller than the text, *add* 3 or 6 to the number of picas of depth, depending on how many points less than a pica the body might be. For example, if the tables were figured for 9 on 11, and the depth of the page is 36 picas, the total number of lines of tabular copy would be divided by 39 (36 picas plus 36 points or 3 picas).

■ **Subdivisions and units**—The space allowance is figured as follows:

(a) Allow 2½ pages for each part-title—one page for the title itself, one page for the blank backing it, and one page for blanks following preceding parts that end on right-hand pages. As the latter is likely to happen in 50% of the parts, the allowance is a half page.

(b) Allow one page for each chapter (a half page for chapter sinkage and a half page for the average chapter ending) if chapters begin on a new page. If the chapters are to start on right-hand pages only, allow 1½ pages (half will have preceding blanks, as with part-titles). If there are very many chapters and the ms. is large, it may be best to run in the chapters. In this case, allow part of a page (a third, a half, etc.) for each one, to account for the space from the end of one chapter to the first line of the next. (This space includes the chapter title, etc.)

(c) Allow a reasonable number of text-size lines of space for each class of subhead—the largest number of lines for the major subheads and progressively smaller numbers for the lesser subheads. (This allowance includes the space taken by the head itself, as well as the space above and below it.) Multiply the number of subheads of each class by the number of lines allowed for each. Then divide the product by the number of text lines per page to find how many pages each kind of subhead will occupy. Thus, if there are 150 subheads of a class for which 6 lines each are allowed, they will take 900 lines (150 x 6). If the page has 36 lines, this class of subhead will require 25 pages (900 ÷ 36).

(d) For each occurrence of extract, poetry, table, etc., allow some space to separate it from the text. (Make the allowance either a half-line or one full-line space above and below. A full line is best, as the half-line space often creates a problem when the unit starts on one page and ends on another.)

(e) Allow one line space for each occurrence of footnotes to separate it from the text. (CH. 21)

(f) Allow one line for each spacebreak.

■ **Illustrations**—If there are illustrations that print with the text, a rough space allowance may be made for them as explained in CH. 21. The space allowed should include space for captions also.

■ **Index**—Make allowance as explained in CH. 27.

When everything except the actual text has been estimated, subtract the number of pages allowed for that from the total number required—in this case, 352. The result will be the number of pages left for the text. Divide this into the text character count to find the number of characters per page required. For example, if everything other than text adds up to 74 pages, there'll be 278 pages for the text itself. Suppose that there are 538,050 characters of text. If you divide this by 278, you find that each page of text should have 1935 characters.

If this figure roughly equals the approximate number of characters per page used for your estimate, you may assume that the book will make 352 pages. If the figure varies substantially from your tentative number, you'll have to make some changes in your specifications, such as enlarging or reducing the text-page area, changing the space allowance for subheads, modifying the allocation of space for illustrations, etc. If this can't be done, abandon the idea of 352 pages and aim for another number, either more or fewer.

When there's no specific total number of pages required, the procedure is somewhat different. First, ideal specifications for text and illustrations are selected, and calculations are made to determine how long the book will run using these specs. The quickest method is to adopt a round number of characters per page as suggested previously and divide this into the character count for text and other character-counted matter, then divide the line-for-line counts by an estimated number of lines per page, and continue to estimate the length of each kind of material as described above. However, a more accurate result is obtained if the number of characters per page is determined by making a page layout and selecting type face, size, and leading (CH. 9). The result of this procedure will be the "normal" (or ideal) length of the book. This number of pages may be impractical for one reason or another, but you'll have, at least, a reasonable figure that can be modified as necessary.

Sometimes the designer begins with other definite factors that influence the number of pages. The illustrations may be planned for a specific size, the type page may be required to match that of another book, or the type size may be prescribed for editorial reasons. Again, the principle is: Work from the known to the unknown. Use whatever figures or decisions are given you to determine other answers. For example, if you are told that the illustrations must occupy 16 pages, this figure can be subtracted from a total number of pages at the start, or it can be used to arrive at a normal length.

When the second procedure is used, and a normal number of pages is established, a final decision on number of pages is reached by considering the two other main factors—retail price and the requirements of printing and paper.

DETERMINANTS: RETAIL PRICE

Let's say that the normal number of pages estimated from the ms. is 359. Presumably, it's possible to reduce or increase this by about

10% without serious effect. The retail price that seems to be right for the book's potential market is $24.95. In any case, this is what has been decided. It's determined that this price won't support a book of more than about 350 pages, considering the illustrations, length of run, etc., but there should be at least that many pages to make the book seem worth the price.

DETERMINANTS: PRINTING & PAPER

Now we know that the *normal* length is 359 pages, and the *optimum* length from the commercial standpoint is 350 pages. What about printing and paper?

The trim-size has been determined as 5½ x 8¼" (5⅝ x 8½" untrimmed). This prints 32-page signatures on a narrow web press, so there's obviously an advantage in a total number of pages that's a multiple of 32. The nearest multiple of 32 to 359 is 384, which isn't very close, but the nearest to 350 is 352, so eleven 32s for 352 pages would seem to be the best number. (A multiple of 16 can be used, but the printing and binding become progressively less economical as the units become smaller [CHs. 12, 13].) On a sheetfed press, 32-page forms would print on a 35 x 45" sheet, producing five 64-page and one 32-page signatures, or 64-page forms could be printed on a 45 x 68" sheet.

If it's been decided to print the book only on a xerographic press because relatively few copies are required, there's no need to think of the number of pages in terms of multiples of forms, since the pages are printed on single sheets, or at most as 2-page forms. Any total that's an even number is feasible. However, if the book is to be printed also by offset in large forms, the above considerations apply.

In conclusion

The book's problem has been analyzed and studied in its mechanical, commercial, and editorial aspects. The creative concept is established. The basic decisions have now been made. We know the trim-size, the arrangement of illustrations, the printing processes, the papers, and the number of pages—as well as the retail price and the size of the first run. At this point, it's possible to begin detailed planning of the various parts of the book, in accordance with our overall design.

24. The text plan

The text *is* the book. It's the source of the designers' inspiration and the object of their efforts. Except in some picture books in which the text is hardly more than captions for the illustrations, the text is the primary consideration in all bookmaking decisions. The object is to make it supremely readable—which means that it must be maximally legible, inviting, pleasing, appropriate to its subject, and suited to its audience (CH. 21).

Planning the text is a complex process, despite the often simple appearance of the result. Esthetic and practical factors must be kept in constant balance, so that conflicts may be resolved without vital damage to either. The demands of readability and economy are dealt with separately in the following discussion, but in practice they're considered simultaneously.

Copyfitting (I) In the previous chapter, rough calculations were made to determine the number of pages the book will have. Now refine the calculations to be certain that you do indeed get that number.

The example used gave us 359 pages as the "normal" number and we decided we would aim for 352. Even though the mathematics may be perfect, several factors could cause a miss: the character count might be inaccurate, the author might make changes in galleys, or there might be an unusual number of bad breaks in chapter endings, subheads, widows, etc. An error of 2% in either direction could easily result from any one of these factors. It wouldn't matter much if we came out 7 pages short, but it would be very awkward to run 7 pages over. So, instead of aiming directly for 352 pages, we'll aim for 344. This means coming down 15 pages from the normal length of 359.

If the space allowances for chapter openings, subheads, etc. were generous, it may be possible to pull in enough pages by reducing these. Usually (not always) chapters can begin on left *or* right rather than only right-hand pages, or even run in, without seriously hurting the design concept. If it's not possible to reduce these spaces, it's usually possible to save pages by combining frontmatter or reducing illustrations, but it's best to leave such measures for emergencies—even with the best planning it may be necessary to make a last-minute effort to save space (CH. 9). A sound policy at this point is to increase the number of characters in the text page—which may not be possible at a later stage.

To find out how much the number of characters per page must be increased, subtract from 344 the total number of pages of other-than-text material (74) as determined in the rough estimate. This will give the number of pages of text you must have (270), which, divided into the text character count, will give the number of characters per page required. Using 538,050 as the text count, the answer is 1992, which compares quite well with the 1935 of our preliminary estimate. Granted that this figure depends on some rough guesses in the calculation of other-than-text matter, it's not likely to be very far off, especially if there's a relatively small amount of other-than-text. In any case, it's subject to correction after all other calculations are made.

If the alternative method of computing the length was used, i.e., the copy was fitted into a required total number of pages (352), simply reduce the number of text pages (278) by about 2% of the total pages (8), to allow for error, and divide the reduced number (270) into the text character count (538,050). This will give the number of characters per page (1992) needed for 344 pages (the safer objective).

The basic arithmetic tentatively settled, typographic decisions are next.

The text

Decisions concerning the text should consider all the factors of readability. In CH. 5, these factors are listed and the principles of readability are discussed in detail. Since all decisions can't be made simultaneously, each of the presently required ones,

(a) text typeface,
(b) text type size,
(c) text measure,
(d) text leading, and
(e) number of text lines per page,

must be made in the context of earlier visualizations and general plans. Subsequent decisions are made in the light of the previous ones plus approximations based on the original conception.

While some of the text-page specs are not needed until later (CH. 25), some broad plans are necessary now to properly develop those required. With the basic decisions (trim-size, paper, etc.) made (CH. 23) and the editorial problem analyzed, what remains is to determine a tentative page pattern comprising the text and whatever other elements occur with it.

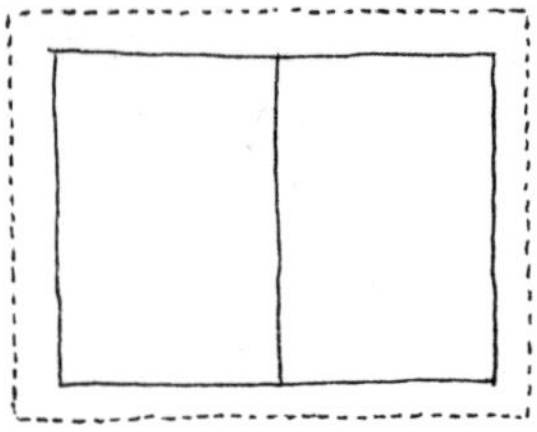

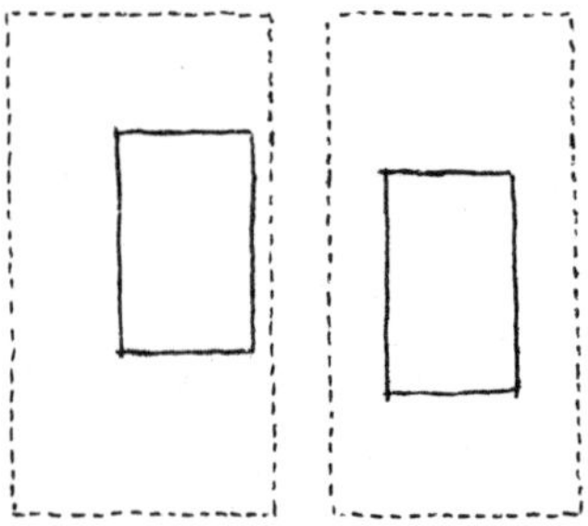

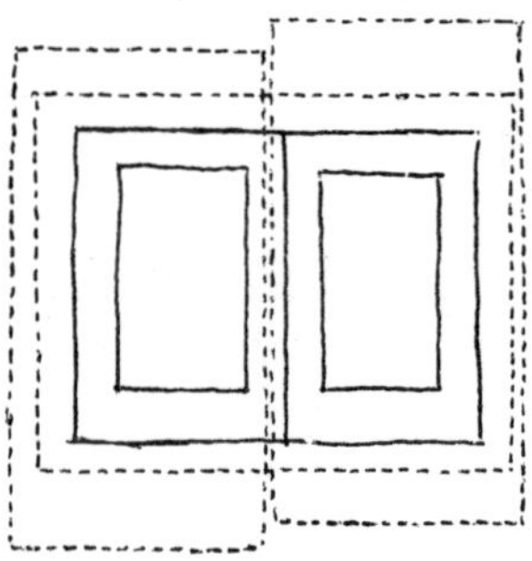

The unit used for copyfitting purposes is the single page, but in planning a page pattern, the double spread (facing pages) should be considered as a unit. If you are comfortable working with pencil and paper, an effective method of developing the visual arrangement is: (1) on tracing paper, rule the outlines of two facing pages in actual size; (2) on separate sheets, rule the outlines of two text areas as conceived; (3) move the two text areas around under the page outline until the positions seem best; and (4) sketch in a tentative indication of running heads and folios, moving the text areas again if necessary. When the arrangement is decided, draw all elements on one sheet. The pattern arrived at isn't necessarily final, but it represents thinking that should precede decisions on the text typography. A similar procedure can be followed in a computer page-makeup program to achieve a similar result.

In this book, the pattern was determined by the following rationale: (a) Standard paper and press dimensions suggested a height of 10" (25.4 cm). For economy of space, the text area utilizes as much of this height as is visually and practically desirable. (b) The reader would frequently want to find other parts of the text because there are many references and the factual and procedural discussions are separated; therefore, it would be useful to have easy-to-find heads on the outside margins. (c) The ideal width for 11 pt. type, considering both the need to fit as much text on the page as possible and readability, is 24 picas. (d) To have marginal subheads with this measure requires a page at least 6¾" wide; 7" (17.8 cm) was chosen to avoid cramping. (e) Since most of the margins wouldn't be occupied by subheads, it would be possible to put small illustrations there, saving space in the text. (f) The running heads and folios could also be placed in the outside margins, where they would be very accessible for reference, without using more space.

The text typeface, Electra, was chosen because its narrow width (CH. 5) is economical of space, it has a clean look suited to the didactic nature of the book, and its tall, narrow shape suits the shape of the text area. With its large x-height the 11 pt. size is satisfactory for general adult readers, and 2 pts. of leading seems optimum for the length of line.

For the example being used, suppose that all considerations led to a choice of 11/13 Baskerville x 23, with 36 lines per page.

Having made these decisions, you must calculate their effect on the number of pages. If the result is substantially different from the number needed (270), changes in the specifications must be made. These modifications will be final. Note that this concerns the basic text only—refinement of specifications for illustrations and other matter comes later—but in each case the procedure is the same: (1) preliminary calculation is followed by (2) detailed specifica-

layout of facing text pages

tions, which are then (3) modified to accord with decisions resulting from the preliminary calculation.

To calculate how many pages of text will result from the specs chosen: (a) find out the characters-per-pica (CHs. 5, 6) for the text typeface and size (11 pt. Baskerville = 2.4), (b) multiply this figure by the measure (23 picas) to get the number of characters per line (2.4 x 23 = 55.2), (c) multiply that by the number of lines per page to get the number of characters per page (55.2 x 36 = 1987), and (d) divide that into the total number of characters of text (538,050) to get the number of pages of text (271). This is close enough to the number needed (270) so that no changes in specs are required.

If the number of pages must be changed, and the difference can't be made up by manipulating illustrations or other-than-text matter, the text will have to be modified by changing one or more of the following:

(a) the typeface (to one that's narrower or wider),
(b) the type size,
(c) the measure, and/or
(d) the number of lines per page.

Changes in the number of lines per page of more than one or two lines usually require an addition or deletion of leading in order to maintain the page depth. However, if the preliminary calculations of length were done properly, there should be no need to make such extensive corrections. Addition or subtraction of a pica or half-pica in the measure, or a line on the page, should suffice. A change of type face or size is undesirable if these were carefully chosen for suitability. If a change is made in the dimensions of the text area, its position on the page should be reconsidered. In making any adjustments, all the considerations that went into the original choices should be reexamined.

Special matter All the kinds of matter other than text must now be specified in detail so that the amount of each can be calculated. There are many special problems involved in this material, but the principles of readability apply here as in text.

LINE-FOR-LINE There is usually no special treatment of line-for-line matter in text or within extract, appendixes, etc., unless it's one of the categories of copy that are counted entirely by lines, such as poetry. Sometimes there's miscellaneous line-for-line matter that's neither part of the text nor a separate category, such as e-mail messages, signs, newspaper headlines, etc., but each such case must be dealt with individually.

POETRY The most frequently encountered line-for-line matter is poetry. The treatment of poetry books is covered in detail in CH. 28. Verse that appears in prose text is a somewhat different problem, because it's usually in small amounts and is subordinate to the text.

Poetry in prose presents a distinct change in style of expression so it's appropriate to set it differently than the prose. Like all brief

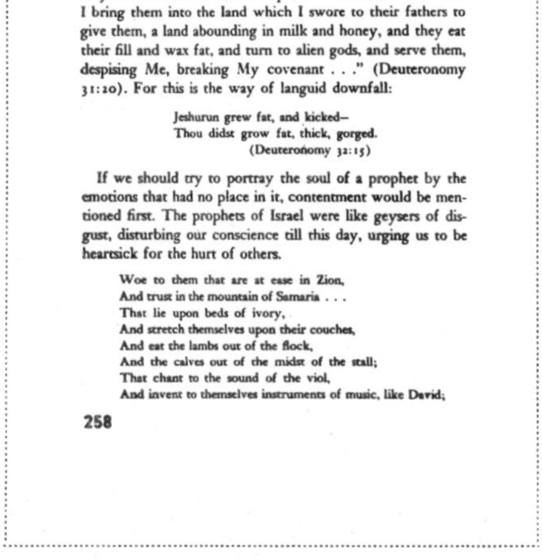
a seed of endless discontent. It is because of men's dissatisfaction with the customs, sanctions and modes of behavior of their age and race that moral progress is possible. New insight begins when satisfaction comes to an end, when all that has been seen or said looks like a distortion to him who sees the world for the first time.

Self-contentment is the brink of the abyss, from which the prophets try to keep us away. Even while the people of Israel were still in the desert, before entering the Promised Land, they were warned to brave the perils of contentment. "When I bring them into the land which I swore to their fathers to give them, a land abounding in milk and honey, and they eat their fill and wax fat, and turn to alien gods, and serve them, despising Me, breaking My covenant . . ." (Deuteronomy 31:20). For this is the way of languid downfall:

Jeshurun grew fat, and kicked–
Thou didst grow fat, thick, gorged.
(Deuteronomy 32:15)

If we should try to portray the soul of a prophet by the emotions that had no place in it, contentment would be mentioned first. The prophets of Israel were like geysers of disgust, disturbing our conscience till this day, urging us to be heartsick for the hurt of others.

Woe to them that are at ease in Zion,
And trust in the mountain of Samaria . . .
That lie upon beds of ivory,
And stretch themselves upon their couches,
And eat the lambs out of the flock,
And the calves out of the midst of the stall;
That chant to the sound of the viol,
And invent to themselves instruments of music, like David;

258

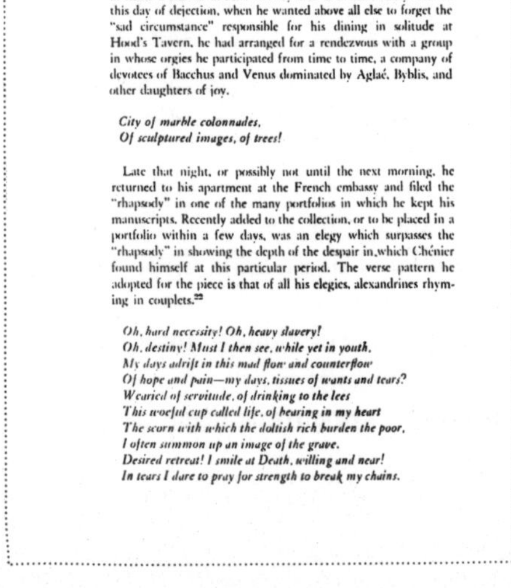
116) ANDRÉ CHÉNIER

familiar with as many words chosen from what I aspire to write for all the world!

With the "rhapsody" carefully folded and safe in his pocket, André Chénier met his appointment. It might have been with certain English acquaintances whom he occasionally joined at a club where men of such eminence as Richard Price and William Wilberforce were wont to lead discussions of social problems, or it could have been with a group of artists in Mrs. Cosway's drawing room. But Chénier's inability to converse with ease in the English language would have made him all the more depressed at either a club or at Mrs. Cosway's. So it is more likely that on this day of dejection, when he wanted above all else to forget the "sad circumstance" responsible for his dining in solitude at Hood's Tavern, he had arranged for a rendezvous with a group in whose orgies he participated from time to time, a company of devotees of Bacchus and Venus dominated by Aglaé, Byblis, and other daughters of joy.

City of marble colonnades,
Of sculptured images, of trees!

Late that night, or possibly not until the next morning, he returned to his apartment at the French embassy and filed the "rhapsody" in one of the many portfolios in which he kept his manuscripts. Recently added to the collection, or to be placed in a portfolio within a few days, was an elegy which surpasses the "rhapsody" in showing the depth of the despair in which Chénier found himself at this particular period. The verse pattern he adopted for the piece is that of all his elegies, alexandrines rhyming in couplets.[22]

Oh, hard necessity! Oh, heavy slavery!
Oh, destiny! Must I then see, while yet in youth,
My days adrift in this mad flow and counterflow
Of hope and pain—my days, tissues of wants and tears?
Wearied of servitude, of drinking to the lees
This woeful cup called life, of bearing in my heart
The scorn with which the doltish rich burden the poor,
I often summon up an image of the grave.
Desired retreat! I smile at Death, willing and near!
In tears I dare to pray for strength to break my chains.

examples of poetry in text; centered and indented

passages, it can be set smaller and still be readable. Indeed, it may be set entirely in italic, which has a somewhat more lyrical quality than roman.

It's conventional to center poetry in books having a centered plan, but this rarely works well. Poetry by nature is oriented to the left and ragged right, so it looks best when flush left or indented from the left.

TABLES

Tables vary greatly in their nature and their relationship to the text. In general, they're set two or three sizes smaller than the text. In simple tables, each column can be set on its own measure, with vertical rules between. Tables that require both horizontal and vertical rules are more complicated to set. If there are too many columns for the width of the page, it may be necessary to turn a table with the columns running across the page instead of up and down (*side turn*).

LISTINGS

Lists are usually set in the same size as the text, except where two or more columns are required and it becomes necessary to reduce the type. Ordinarily, lists can be reduced to 8 or 9 pt. without adversely affecting readability. Under some circumstances (such as a list of ingredients in a recipe) it may be desirable to use a larger size—or even a contrasting face—for emphasis or clarity.

OUTLINE

The outline form itself normally provides the distinctions required to clarify this kind of material, so there's seldom need to make any typographic change. Sometimes, however, the outline is so complex that the customary devices (indention, numbered paragraphs, etc.) are not sufficient. In such cases, italics, boldface, and/or variation of type size can help.

EXTRACT

Extract is quoted material in the text, but set apart from it, as opposed to that which runs within the text line, preceded and followed by quotation marks. It's important to make clear typographically that such material is from another source, especially if it's by another author. There are several ways to make distinctions. The use of one may suffice, but more likely two or more of these devices will be required:

- **Indention**—The extract may be indented one, two, or more ems from right or left, or both.
- **Size**—Extract may be set larger or smaller than text, although it's almost always smaller.
- **Leading**—An increase or decrease of leading is usual, particularly the latter.
- **Face**—Italic, boldface, or an entirely different classification of type may be used.
- **Space**—A line or half-line space above and below each item of

SPENCER, D. M. *Disease, Religion and Society in the Fiji Islands.* American Ethnological Society, Monograph 2, New York, 1941.

FIJIAN PHARMACOLOGICAL THERAPY

Plant Drug Employed as Abortifacients		*Part of Plant Used and Method of Preparation and Use*	*Source*	*Remarks*
SCIENTIFIC NAME	FIJI NAME			
Cerbera manglias Linn.	rewa	Inner bark of root is soaked in cold water; drink liquid until desired results are obtained	Field notes	This turns foetus to liquid which is passed out as blood, according to native theory
Hibiscus (Abelmoschus) diversifolius	kalani soni	Juice of leaves used	Seeman [1]	
Hibiscus (Abelmoschus) Abelmoschus	waki waki	Juice of leaves used	" "	

[1] Seemann, Berthold. *Flora Vitiensis.* London, 1865–73.

side turn

extract may be used to separate it from the text. These spaces may be increased or decreased as needed to align facing pages.

While making extract distinct from text, remember that it also must be readable. It can be reduced in size, leading, etc. without serious loss when it occurs in brief passages, but when it's extensive, the solution might be to use a different but equally readable type face and size. Note that when the extract occupies full pages, indention becomes ineffective, unless very pronounced, because there's no full-width text for contrast.

two ways of setting extract

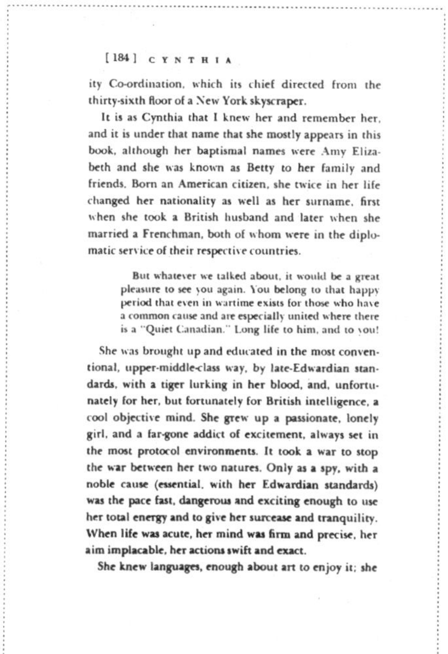

[184] CYNTHIA

ity Co-ordination, which its chief directed from the thirty-sixth floor of a New York skyscraper.

It is as Cynthia that I knew her and remember her, and it is under that name that she mostly appears in this book, although her baptismal names were Amy Elizabeth and she was known as Betty to her family and friends. Born an American citizen, she twice in her life changed her nationality as well as her surname, first when she took a British husband and later when she married a Frenchman, both of whom were in the diplomatic service of their respective countries.

> But whatever we talked about, it would be a great pleasure to see you again. You belong to that happy period that even in wartime exists for those who have a common cause and are especially united where there is a "Quiet Canadian." Long life to him, and to you!

She was brought up and educated in the most conventional, upper-middle-class way, by late-Edwardian standards, with a tiger lurking in her blood, and, unfortunately for her, but fortunately for British intelligence, a cool objective mind. She grew up a passionate, lonely girl, and a far-gone addict of excitement, always set in the most protocol environments. It took a war to stop the war between her two natures. Only as a spy, with a noble cause (essential, with her Edwardian standards) was the pace fast, dangerous and exciting enough to use her total energy and to give her surcease and tranquility. When life was acute, her mind was firm and precise, her aim implacable, her actions swift and exact.

She knew languages, enough about art to enjoy it; she

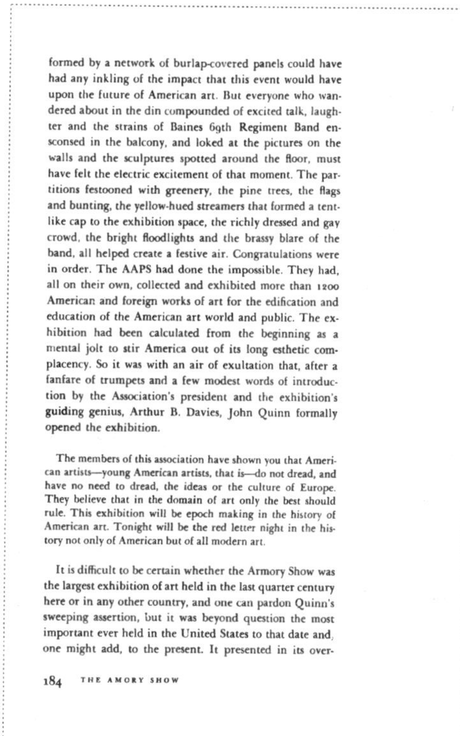

formed by a network of burlap-covered panels could have had any inkling of the impact that this event would have upon the future of American art. But everyone who wandered about in the din compounded of excited talk, laughter and the strains of Baines 69th Regiment Band ensconsed in the balcony, and loked at the pictures on the walls and the sculptures spotted around the floor, must have felt the electric excitement of that moment. The partitions festooned with greenery, the pine trees, the flags and bunting, the yellow-hued streamers that formed a tent-like cap to the exhibition space, the richly dressed and gay crowd, the bright floodlights and the brassy blare of the band, all helped create a festive air. Congratulations were in order. The AAPS had done the impossible. They had, all on their own, collected and exhibited more than 1200 American and foreign works of art for the edification and education of the American art world and public. The exhibition had been calculated from the beginning as a mental jolt to stir America out of its long esthetic complacency. So it was with an air of exultation that, after a fanfare of trumpets and a few modest words of introduction by the Association's president and the exhibition's guiding genius, Arthur B. Davies, John Quinn formally opened the exhibition.

> The members of this association have shown you that American artists—young American artists, that is—do not dread, and have no need to dread, the ideas or the culture of Europe. They believe that in the domain of art only the best should rule. This exhibition will be epoch making in the history of American art. Tonight will be the red letter night in the history not only of American but of all modern art.

It is difficult to be certain whether the Armory Show was the largest exhibition of art held in the last quarter century here or in any other country, and one can pardon Quinn's sweeping assertion, but it was beyond question the most important ever held in the United States to that date and, one might add, to the present. It presented in its over-

184 THE AMORY SHOW

PLAYSTYLE

Not all playstyle is dramatic script. Any material that's a succession of statements by identified speakers is playstyle, such as interviews, courtroom examinations, hearing records, etc.

The problem is mainly how to handle the speakers' names. This is discussed in detail for the design of plays in CH. 28, but the technique is the same for all playstyle. There is usually no reason to set playstyle within text in another size, unless it has the character of extract, but when there's no difference in size, it's a good idea to separate each passage of playstyle from the text with a line space before and after.

FOOTNOTES

There are two kinds of footnotes: (a) references and (b) explanations. Each is treated according to its nature.

■ **Reference notes**—These are references to sources and bibliographical information intended for the scholar and researcher rather than the general reader. They are a distraction at the bottom of the page and are comparatively difficult to reach at the end of each chapter. The most practical location for them is at the back of the book, where they're most accessible to scholars and out of the way of the reader. For the treatment of reference notes, see also CHs. 6, 27.

■ **Explanatory notes**—If they're to be useful at all, these notes must be read at the proper time and so should appear on the page where the reference occurs. It's an imposition to ask readers to search for explanatory notes at the back of the book (and a felony to make them find notes at the end of each chapter). Many, if not most, readers don't bother to read them under these conditions, so the notes are a waste of time and space for part of the audience and a source of irritation for the remainder, who do take the trouble to find them.

Some publishers, editors, reviewers, and a great many readers feel that the appearance of footnotes in a book is somehow repellent. The book that's "cluttered" with footnotes is disparaged as academic and a forbidding chore for the reader. This attitude is probably justified, but for the wrong reasons.

After all, if the text is interesting and well written, the addition of useful footnotes should increase, rather than lessen, the pleasure of reading, providing the notes are conveniently placed. But the mingling of bibliographical references with explanatory notes at the bottom of the page is a real nuisance. At each reference mark readers must go to the bottom of the page to find out whether the note is of interest or not. If not, they must travel back up the page and find their place—probably in the middle of a sentence that must be reread. Of course, where a footnote *is* pertinent to the text, readers may wonder why it wasn't incorporated in the narrative. (Very often they will be correct in assuming that it was an afterthought which the author found easier to insert as a footnote than to rewrite the text.) Yes, footnotes are to be avoided, but only when they're misplaced or unnecessary. Those that are necessary should be placed where they're most useful.

Footnotes may be set in very small sizes, but they too must be readable. Very brief notes—a line or two—can be readable in most 8 pt. type with one or two points of leading. Longer notes should be set larger. Sometimes, the footnotes are a major part of the book—perhaps 20 or 25%. If these notes are essential, they should be as readable as the text and probably the same size or slightly smaller. They can be distinguished from text by using a contrasting face or a particularly readable italic or oblique.

Footnotes can be separated from the text by a line space when there's a sharp contrast in size. Where sizes are closer, a small typographic device such as a dash, asterisk, colon, or suitable ornament may be set in the space. In some cases, a rule of full measure or nearly so may be required. This must be kept distinct, however, from the full-measure rule ordinarily used above footnote material that has run over from the previous page.

Reference marks may be handled in several ways. The most expensive is resetting lines (after page-makeup) to insert references that begin a new sequence of numbers on each page. This can be avoided by commencing a sequence in each chapter or, if there are not too many notes, continuing one sequence through the entire book.

The reference marks may be symbols, such as asterisks (*), daggers (†), section marks (§), etc., and the doubling and tripling of these. If numbers are used, they may be *superior figures* (small numerals above the x line[2]), or the regular text type figures enclosed in parentheses (2). The corresponding reference marks in the notes may be either regular or superior figures, although it's best to use the same kind as used in the text. In the notes, the use of parens around regular figures isn't essential, as these numbers occur only at the beginnings.

The first line of each note may be indented as a paragraph or it may be flush, with the turnovers indented (*hanging indent*); or all lines may be flush. In the latter case, it may be best to separate the notes from each other by some space. Whatever style is used, consider the probability that two or more one-line notes will occur successively on the same page. When there are many short footnotes, it's often possible to set two or three on each line with a few ems between, rather than wasting space by placing one beneath the other.

footnotes in four different styles

* This question is discussed on page 273, but in any event *all co*
be typed in lower case with caps only at the beginning of sentence
and on proper nouns. When setting type, if the specifications call for

* This question is discussed on page 273, but in any event *all copy*
be typed in lower case with caps only at the beginning of senten
and on proper nouns. When setting type, if the specifications call f

* This question is discussed on page 273, but in any event *all copy*
be typed in lower case with caps only at the beginning of sentence
and on proper nouns. When setting type, if the specifications call for

7 *Ps.* lxvii, 2. 8 *Titus* i, 10. 9 The Manichaeans. 10 *Ephes.* v
11 *Jo.* i, 9. 12 *Ps.* xxxiii, 6.

SUBDIVISIONS

It isn't necessary to decide on specifications for chapter heads or subheads at this time, as they will be contained within the spaces allowed for them. Their treatment is covered in the next chapter.

Copyfitting (III)

Each kind of special matter can now be calculated for length according to the specifications adopted.

To calculate the number of pages of line-for-line material being set on lines of the same depth as the text (13 pts.), divide the number of lines of such matter by the number of lines per page of text (36). To calculate copy which will be set on a line of a different depth, first multiply the number of text lines per page (36) by the size of the text plus leading (13 pts.) to find the depth of the text page in points (36 x 13 = 468). Then you can find the number of lines per page for any line depth by dividing 468 by that depth. So, if poetry is being set 9/11, divide 468 by 11 to get 42 lines. (Drop the odd points left over. These will be absorbed in the space around each item.) Dividing 42 into the total number of lines of poetry will give you the number of pages of poetry.

Prose copy (extract, outline, etc.) should be calculated as though each kind was the text of a separate book. The only figure carried over from the text is the depth of the page in points. For example, suppose the extract is set 10/12 Baskerville and is indented 2½ ems on the left in the 23-pica measure. This gives it a measure of 21 picas (approximately). If 10 pt. Baskerville has 2.6 characters per pica, multiply 2.6 by 21 and you get 54.6 characters per line. Divide 468 pts. by the 12 pt. line depth to get 39 lines per page. Thus, a full page of extract will have 2129 characters (54.6 x 39). Divide this into the total number of characters of extract to find out how many pages there will be.

The calculation of footnotes is always inexact, even knowing how they're to be set. It's almost impossible to determine how many pages will have footnotes, which, if any, will run over to another page, or how many short ones can be combined. Nevertheless, the best figures possible must be obtained. The usual procedures for calculating line-for-line and prose copy are followed, with some generous allowances made for combining, frequency of occurrence, runovers, etc.

On the appropriate lines on the breakdown sheet, enter in a column the number of pages calculated for text, each kind of special matter, space allowances, illustrations, page-for-page material, and, if there's one, the index. The total should come close to your objective (344 in the example). If not, carefully examine each item before deciding where to make the changes necessary.

In conclusion

In all estimating, it's better to figure a little on the high side rather than too low. If, after composition, the book should turn out to have fewer pages than estimated, there are usually some easy solutions available. Should the number of pages turn out to be *more* than estimated, there may be serious difficulty. There are several ways of shortening a book, but their use may not be possible in all circumstances (CHs. 9, 23).

TITLE: *Example* DATE: 12/2/82

Ms pp: 339

FRONTMATTER		
half title 1 pp, title 2 pp, cpyrt 1 pp, ded 1 pp	6	6
preface 2762 c	2	2
contents 44 L	2	2
introduction 5250 c	4	4
TEXT:		
538,050 c		271
103 L	3	3
EXTRACT: (p.67)		
5892 c	3	3
POETRY: (p.29)		
129 L	4	4
14 units	1	1
PLAYSTYLE: (p.162)		
1264 c	1	1
10 L	—	—
4 units	—	—
TABULAR: (p.212)		
42 L	1	1
12 units	1	1
BIBLIOGRAPHY: (p.318)		
4922 c	2	3
53 L	2	1
INDEX:		
allow 8 pp	8	8
FOOTNOTES:		
1640 c	1	1
14 units	—	—
ILLUSTRATIONS:		
halftone:75	—	—
line:28	10	10
SUBDIVISIONS:		
part titles:3	8	8
chapters:8	8	8
A heads:18 @ ~~6L~~ 4L	3	2
B heads:41 @ 3L	3	3
spacebreaks:19 @ 1L	1	1
	74	(344) / 352

352 − 74 = 278

278 ⟌ 538,050 = 1935

344 − 74 = 270

270 ⟌ 538,050 = 1992

2.4 ch/pica × 23 = 55.2 ch/line

55.2 × 36 = 1987.2 ch/page

1987 ⟌ 538,050 = 270+

The breakdown with final calculations. The left-hand column of figures is the first, rough, calculation of items other than text.

25. Sample pages

With basic decisions and text specifications settled, the design process goes into a largely graphic stage. The details of the book's visual aspect are considered one by one, but they're parts of the concept visualized earlier, and each choice—no matter how small—must be based on the analysis and a real consideration of alternatives.

Begin by setting and printing sample pages showing at least one example of each kind of material in the book. This gives everyone, including the designer, a chance to see how the problems have been solved and how the pages will look. Changes at this stage cost nothing—later on they can be expensive.

For an average book, two or three pages of sample are sufficient. To include all the problems in a complex work may require six or eight pages. The object is to make the sample pages as useful as possible in minimizing delays caused by unexpected problems in composition and page-makeup. This requires a careful selection of specimens with both typical and extra-difficult problems. You fool no one but yourself by using relatively easy material.

Minimally, sample pages should show the following:

(a) some text—preferably two full facing pages,
(b) an example of each kind of special matter (if any),
(c) running heads and folios on facing pages,
(d) a chapter opening, and
(e) subheads (if any).

It's useful to show a part-title, if there are any, but this isn't absolutely necessary. A careful sketch will usually suffice. To avoid overloading the sample, omit examples of material of which there's very little.

Since it's so easy to make even global changes on the computer, it's possible to bypass sample pages for books of straight text, particularly when the design is done in-house, where rough layouts and partial design can quickly be shown to editors for approval before going ahead with composition and page-makeup.

Chapter openings

With the text already planned, it would seem logical to complete the text page by designing next the running heads and folios. However, the chapter openings set the typographic style of the book, particularly in the choice of display type, so they should determine how the text page will look, rather than the other way around.

There are chapter openings throughout the book and their design should be very carefully considered so that *all* of them will look good, not just the one used for the sample. This is sometimes difficult because of wide variations in the copy. There seems to be a conspiracy among authors to make one chapter title so different from all the others as to frustrate any successful design. When most titles have one or two words, one will almost surely have twelve or fourteen, or vice versa. So, if small type is chosen to accommodate the very long title, the short ones look weak. If the short titles are set larger, the long one looks enormous.

Chapter openings need to be kept subordinate to the title page and part-titles. They shouldn't reach, or even approach, the limits of emphasis or graphic interest. Remember also that the impact of a single chapter opening in a sample page is one thing, but the effect of, say, fifty of the same may be too much. There's no harm in making a title-page design first and then the chapter opening, as long as the requirements of the latter are met. The title page can be changed if necessary to maintain a good relationship with the chapter opening.

The design of chapter openings depends to a considerable extent on two factors: (a) the number of chapters in the book and (b) the length of the run. The time needed to create a complex chapter opening isn't so important if there are only six chapters, but it *might* be important if there are sixty. Spending a lot of composition time on a chapter-opening design might seem justified if the print run is 20,000 copies, but not if the run is only 2000.

CHAPTER-OPENING SPACE

Before the choice and arrangement of display type are considered, decide on the exact amount of space in which it's to appear. If chapters run in, this space will have been allocated when the length of the book was calculated (CHs. 23, 31). For chapters beginning on a new page, an allowance of one page was made for each—assuming that the opening would take half. Some variation of this is usually possible; the space may be more or less than a half page if desired. If there are only a few chapters, the addition or subtraction of some lines of text on opening pages won't matter much. If the book has very many chapters, varying the number of lines may make a serious difference. To know what, if any, effect such changes will have, it's necessary to calculate the length of each chapter separately (this is fairly simple when there's no other-than-text material, but may be tedious otherwise). You must find out how many lines will be on the last page

554 CHINA IN THE SIXTEENTH CENTURY

stations in the smaller cities. Moreover, they were preparing to open a residence in Hancian, the metropolitan city of the Province of Cechian, which was only a three day journey from this mission at Scianhai, and it was thought that this new field could be taken care of from there. It was the opinion of the Fathers that they could accomplish more in the larger cities of the kingdom. And so, with the full consent of Ciu Paul, who had already returned to Pekin, the direction of this mission was transferred to Hancian, and the new converts, agreeing that the larger undertaking was more for the glory of God, had no objection to the departure of the Fathers.

Concerning this particular mission at Hancian, nothing further will be said in this diary, because it was begun after the death of Father Ricci, with which the first volume of Chinese history is closed. However, so that our readers may not be deprived of what was accomplished there, a separate work containing the annals of the two following years will be published, which may be added to the present diary to make a complete history.

19. A Weird Journey from Xaucea to Macao

ALTHOUGH IT MIGHT seem that the good will of the Magistrates and the honesty of the new Admiral, in judging the case of Father Cattaneo, had restored affairs at Xaucea to their former condition, the wound that was inflicted by wagging tongues was not as yet fully healed and probably never could be. The tumult of the so-called rebellion had just ceased, when another incident occurred that proved to be almost as troublesome.

One of the domestic servants was sent with letters from Xaucea to Macao, and on his return journey with the replies, he was apprehended by the military guards. Sending letters to foreigners outside of the realm is nothing less than treason. The servant was ordered to pay a

run-in chapter opening

of each chapter to know which will gain or lose a page when the number of lines on the first is changed.

There are several reasons for varying the number of chapter-opening text lines. You may want to reduce the number to make room for illustrations, or increase it just to reduce the total number of pages. Also, chapter openings are one of the few opportunities in most books—often the only one—to introduce some space (light and air) into the text.

STYLE & FEELING The chapter-opening pages, like all aspects of the design, should flow from the concept arrived at in developing the creative solution (CH. 22). If you didn't visualize the actual appearance of the chapter openings at that time, you at least conceived of their general feeling as being, like the design as a whole, formal or informal, dynamic or placid, strong or delicate, etc. Now you can interpret these characteristics in terms of the choice and arrangement of the type and illustrations on the chapter openings.

Thinking of a book's characteristics in terms of opposites doesn't mean that there are no gradations or subtle variations. On the contrary, most books won't fall into simple categories. The important thing is to impart to the chapter opening, as well as the rest of the design, the true essence of the book. While this must pervade every aspect of the design, the chapter opening is the first opportunity to create the proper feeling.

ROUGH LAYOUT With the chapter-opening space decided, make an outline on paper of two facing text pages. Indicate the text lines and roughly sketch in the approximate size and position of the heads. At this point there's no need to decide on typefaces. The general arrangement should be settled first, with two main purposes:

(a) to indicate the relative importance of each element, and
(b) to establish the basic style of the layout.

In books that have copy, such as an author's name, in addition to the title on the chapter-opening pages, the problem of creating a proper order of relationships is the same as in designing a title page (CH. 27). There are many ways to achieve emphasis (CHs. 5, 23), so the chosen order of importance among elements can be maintained without sacrificing esthetic or other values.

CHAPTER HEADS The *chapter head* (the *number* of the chapter is the head, not the title) is usually the least important element and is best subordinated unless: (a) the numerical sequence has a special significance (as it might in a suspense novel), or (b) the head is used as an important graphic element, either because there's no other copy or to emphasize a chapter title by contrast (as in this book). The word "chapter" usually serves no purpose at all unless it's used as a graphic device, and is best omitted.

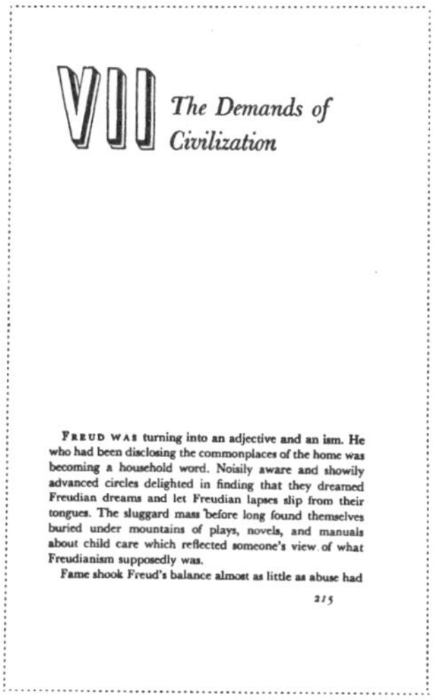

VII *The Demands of Civilization*

FREUD WAS turning into an adjective and an ism. He who had been disclosing the commonplaces of the home was becoming a household word. Noisily aware and showily advanced circles delighted in finding that they dreamed Freudian dreams and let Freudian lapses slip from their tongues. The sluggard mass before long found themselves buried under mountains of plays, novels, and manuals about child care which reflected someone's view of what Freudianism supposedly was.

Fame shook Freud's balance almost as little as abuse had

215

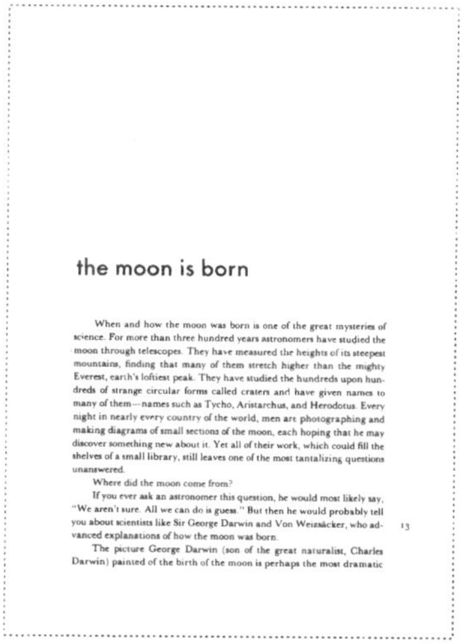

the moon is born

When and how the moon was born is one of the great mysteries of science. For more than three hundred years astronomers have studied the moon through telescopes. They have measured the heights of its steepest mountains, finding that many of them stretch higher than the mighty Everest, earth's loftiest peak. They have studied the hundreds upon hundreds of strange circular forms called craters and have given names to many of them—names such as Tycho, Aristarchus, and Herodotus. Every night in nearly every country of the world, men are photographing and making diagrams of small sections of the moon, each hoping that he may discover something new about it. Yet all of their work, which could fill the shelves of a small library, still leaves one of the most tantalizing questions unanswered.

Where did the moon come from?

If you ever ask an astronomer this question, he would most likely say, "We aren't sure. All we can do is guess." But then he would probably tell you about scientists like Sir George Darwin and Von Weizsäcker, who advanced explanations of how the moon was born.

The picture George Darwin (son of the great naturalist, Charles Darwin) painted of the birth of the moon is perhaps the most dramatic

13

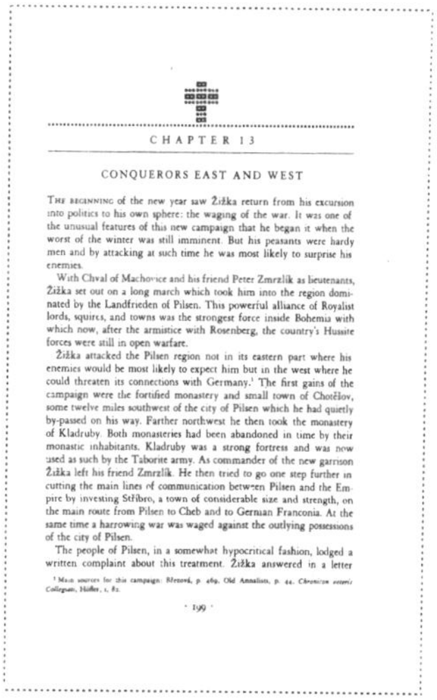

CHAPTER 13

CONQUERORS EAST AND WEST

THE BEGINNING of the new year saw Žižka return from his excursion into politics to his own sphere: the waging of the war. It was one of the unusual features of this new campaign that he began it when the worst of the winter was still imminent. But his peasants were hardy men and by attacking at such time he was most likely to surprise his enemies.

With Chval of Machovice and his friend Peter Zmrzlík as lieutenants, Žižka set out on a long march which took him into the region dominated by the Landfrieden of Pilsen. This powerful alliance of Royalist lords, squires, and towns was the strongest force inside Bohemia with which now, after the armistice with Rosenberg, the country's Hussite forces were still in open warfare.

Žižka attacked the Pilsen region not in its eastern part where his enemies would be most likely to expect him but in the west where he could threaten its connections with Germany.[1] The first gains of the campaign were the fortified monastery and small town of Chotělov, some twelve miles southwest of the city of Pilsen which he had quietly by-passed on his way. Farther northwest he then took the monastery of Kladruby. Both monasteries had been abandoned in time by their monastic inhabitants. Kladruby was a strong fortress and was now used as such by the Taborite army. As commander of the new garrison Žižka left his friend Zmrzlík. He then tried to go one step further in cutting the main lines of communication between Pilsen and the Empire by investing Stříbro, a town of considerable size and strength, on the main route from Pilsen to Cheb and to German Franconia. At the same time a harrowing war was waged against the outlying possessions of the city of Pilsen.

The people of Pilsen, in a somewhat hypocritical fashion, lodged a written complaint about this treatment. Žižka answered in a letter

[1] Main sources for this campaign: Březová, p. 469. Old Annalists, p. 44. *Chronicon veteris Collegiati*, Höfler, i, 82.

· 199 ·

three different chapter openings

first rough sketch of chapter opening

Roman numerals over thirteen should be avoided in any situation where the public is expected to read them. As the era of the Caesars recedes further into the past, fewer people are able to translate CXLVI or LXIV fast enough for practical use. This archaic form is useful for period flavor or when a decorative purpose is served, otherwise it adds nothing but confusion and irritation.

CHAPTER TITLES Very long titles are better set in lowercase than caps. Lowercase takes less space and is easier to read. (Large amounts of capitals are less readable mainly because we are unaccustomed to them.)

When breaking chapter titles into more than one line, break for sense, i.e., at logical places. Also, avoid excessive breaking. Don't make it difficult to read the title just to achieve a graphic effect.

Chapter titles shouldn't be set like book titles, with all words beginning with a cap except articles, conjunctions, etc. This deprives the author of the use of capitals for their proper functions—designating proper nouns and the beginnings of sentences. Sometimes, a lack of distinction between proper nouns and others creates confusion, so it's best to capitalize according to normal grammatical usage. There are adequate typographic means of indicating the special value of chapter titles without limiting their ability to communicate.

breaking long chapter titles

SHADOWS IN MODERN
PHOTOGRAPHY

poor sense

SHADOWS
IN MODERN PHOTOGRAPHY

better sense

INITIALS When the first letter of a chapter or part is set in large, decorative type it's called an *initial.* Initials originated as a means of marking the beginnings of new chapters in medieval manuscripts when space was too precious to waste on chapter breaks. This solution is still applicable to very crowded books in which there's little room for space around chapter openings. Initials are useful, too, to provide graphic interest where there are no chapter titles or heads for display.

When initials are used, they may be either: (a) set into the text two or more lines deep (*dropped*) or (b) projected above the text (*stickup*).

DROPPED INITIALS should align with the base of a text line at bottom, preferably with the top of the x line at the top if the following letters are lowercase or small caps, and with the top of the line if followed by caps. The alignment at the top isn't vital, but a sloppy appearance results at the bottom if the initial sinks below the baseline or fails to reach it. Be careful of "J"s and "Q"s that descend below the baseline.

STICKUP INITIALS should align with the base of the first text line. They, like the dropped initials, may be followed by lowercase, small caps, or full caps for the remainder of the first word, the first phrase, or the whole line. Either kind of initial may be indented or flush.

If no special initial is used, the text may begin in one of several ways: (a) the first word, phrase, or line may be set in small caps or caps with various amounts of letterspacing, or (b) it may start with a cap and continue in lowercase without any special treatment.

A variant of the display initial idea is to set the first word or phrase in display size, rather than just the first letter. This is effective graphically, but thought must be given to the editorial effect of so much emphasis on these words. There are probably some very special books in which such a device is appropriate, but generally it's unduly distracting.

To some extent, the same is true of the use of small caps or caps for the first few words. A fine writer carefully constructs each sentence, and the use of capitals where they were not intended does violence to this delicate balance. It can be argued that this affects only a few of the thousands of sentences in a book. It can also be argued that most books are not that well written nor that important. Some writers on book design tend to assume that every book is a classic, but among the tens of thousands of titles published each year, some are fine, some are mediocre, some are trash—and each should be designed according to its kind. A classical treatment for a frivolous text is just as wrong as the opposite. However, any typographic device that radically alters the emphasis of words must be carefully weighed.

Indentions of various amounts may be used with any initial style, but it's unwise to indent so far that there isn't enough width left to avoid bad breaks. Enough means about thirty-five characters, and even this may not be sufficient with a particularly awkward combination of words. When the first line consists of letterspaced caps or small caps, the problem is made worse.

It's possible to emphasize a chapter opening also by setting the first few lines or first paragraph in a different style than the text—with larger type, more leading, ragged right or left, a different face, etc., or a combination of such devices. Used sensitively, this sort of thing can work, but there's always the danger of distorting the author's intentions.

And chapter openings offer opportunities to use illustrations of various kinds (CHs. 7, 8), with or without initials or special typographic treatments.

CHOICE OF TYPE Now the choice of typefaces for display can be made. Again, this means actualizing a visualization that may or may not have included this detail. In any case, the choices should be based on the considerations discussed in CHs. 5, 23, 24.

The type size in each case is determined by your rough layout. Fortunately the computer enables the designer to make the size of the type exactly what is needed, even to a fraction of a point.

THE FINISHED LAYOUT When the type faces and sizes have been selected, the layout can be completed. This means going back to the layout program and inserting the display type in its exact position in relation to the text.

For convenience, we have spoken in terms of making all your type selections first, and then completing the layout. In practice, it's better to make the choice of each face and size after having set the one before. Thus you can see what the effect of a particular line of type will be, rather than just visualizing it. Actually, the processes of visualization, consideration, and choice are usually intermingled and will vary in relationship according to the particular problem and the individual designer.

Indicating illustrations is discussed in CH. 8.

Subheads

Subheads are like chapter openings on a lower scale of value, so problems of design are basically the same: (a) How much space shall each be allocated? (b) How is the first line of following text to be treated? (c) What type face and size? (d) What shall be the position? In each case, the decision should be related to the chapter opening, with a descending order of emphasis (chapter title, first order of subhead, second order, and so on).

■ **Space**—The allocation of space was decided in determining the length of the book (CH. 23). If a closer examination of the problem suggests a change in this allocation, compensating change must be made to retain the same total number of pages.

■ **First line**—The first line of text following subheads usually calls for some special treatment, but unless the subdivision is of major importance, beginning flush or setting the first word in small caps is the maximum distinction appropriate. For lesser subheads, the regular paragraph indent is sufficient. In no case should the treatment of a subhead be more distinctive than that of a superior subhead or a chapter opening, as the primary purpose is to clarify the book's organization by indicating the relative value of headings.

■ **Type face and size**—The typographic treatment of the headings themselves should reflect their relationship to each other. A number 2 subhead doesn't merely follow a number 1 head, it's a subdivision of it, and this should be made clear. Remember, though, the average reader isn't as sensitive to typographic distinctions as you are, so the differences among classes of headings must be quite pronounced or they may be overlooked.

One of the values of subheads is the graphic interest they add. Subheads are sometimes inserted in books simply to break up the large blocks of text that discourage some readers, especially children and those who don't ordinarily read books. But even where the subheads have a real textual function, they offer opportunities to add variety and visual interest. Contrast with the text is useful not only to enliven the page, but to help the reader find the subheads. The amount of contrast should be adjusted to the importance of the subhead and the frequency of its occurrence. A degree of visual excitement that's desirable in a few places can be irritating when repeated too often.

■ **Position**—The arrangement of subheads within the allowed spaces should be consistent with the style established for the chapter opening. (The need for consistency must be considered in every choice or decision.) Consistency in this sense doesn't mean necessarily the same in form, but it does mean the same in spirit. Achieving a finished book that has real unity—the visual integration that conveys a sense of "rightness"—is more difficult than it may seem. It's possible to have consistent outward forms, yet the total won't have the essential inner harmony. It's somewhat like trying to create a man by putting all the right parts together in the right way. You will get the form, but you won't get a living thing unless there's something more than that.

Subheads may be centered, set flush left or right, indented from left or right, or centered on some point other than the center of the measure. They may be set on a separate line or run in on the first text line. In a book with several classes of subheads, a combination of these positions will probably be necessary. Be sure to provide for those occasions where two or more classes of subhead occur together. The combination of centered and off-centered arrangements should be avoided as much as possible (CHs. 5, 23), but the needs of editorial sense must be met, even at the expense of harmonious design.

Run-in subheads should contrast sufficiently with the text type to stand out. The use of italics alone is usually inadequate, although the addition of a substantial space (at least one em) after the subhead may make enough difference. Attention can be drawn to a run-in subhead by using a strong typographic device at the beginning, such as a paragraph mark, bullet, star, etc., or a different color.

The style and position of subheads must be considered in relation to the running heads as well as to the text. Any subhead may fall just beneath a running head, so they shouldn't be too similar. If possible, no subheads should be set in the same size and face as any running head, unless one is italic and the other roman, or one is in small caps and the other italic, etc. Where running heads and subheads are only slightly dissimilar, it helps to set one flush left and the other flush right. Subheads that are numbered, or contain numbers, should avoid conflict with folios.

The subheads in this book that are alongside the text didn't require size to stand out. They're set small because of the narrow measure and in a contrasting class and weight of typeface (CH. 5) to make them distinct from the text and the running heads.

Running heads & folios

RUNNING HEADS

Running heads may serve as practical guides, as in reference books and textbooks, or they may have a purely decorative function. In books with no part or chapter titles, the book title may be used as a running head to add graphic interest to the spread, but it may also be used to heighten a psychological effect. (For example, in a book titled *Pressure*, about tunneling under a river, repetition of the word "pressure" would give an insistent quality to an ever-present menace in the text.) On the other hand, repetition of a title of no evocative value is pointless and irritating unless it can be justified typographically. There is almost never any excuse for repeating the book title twice on one spread (i.e., on both right and left pages).

Conventional practice is to use the left-hand page for a book or part-title and the right for the next smaller subdivision (left, book—right, part; or left, part—right, chapter; or left, chapter—right, subhead; etc.). However, the arrangement should be based on the usefulness of the various heads.

Sometimes book, part, and chapter titles are very similar in wording. It's particularly important in those cases, but useful in all books, to make a typographic distinction between the left- and right-hand running heads if they are different titles. This helps clarify the book's organization, permits distinctions in emphasis, and provides graphic interest. The typographic difference should be sufficiently pronounced to avoid confusion. A frequent combination is small caps on one side and italics on the other. Entirely different typefaces can be used effectively.

If the titles being used for sample page copy are very long, don't specify widely spaced caps or deep indentions. Sometimes the titles are so long they must be shortened, but don't pick a style that will just miss fitting in short or medium-length titles.

FOLIOS

Folios, like running heads, vary in importance. In some reference books they're vital and should be prominent in style and position. Other reference books, particularly those with alphabetical-order running heads (directories, etc.), need no folios at all. In any book with an index, the folios should be very accessible. In fiction, folios are helpful to some readers, but most use the jacket flap or a library card to mark their place.

The most effective position for folios is the upper outside corner of the right-hand page, the closer to the edge the better. The lower outside corner is only a little less practical. The folio becomes less readily found as it moves further in toward the gutter. For books in which the folio has no practical value to the reader, the inside corner, top or bottom, is a satisfactory position.

Opinions differ as to the need for folios on chapter-opening pages. They are not needed in locating the chapter, because the opening page is identified by the title or head. Indexes do refer to page numbers, but there's usually a folioed page facing the chapter opening. If chapter-opening folios are used, it's probably best to place them in the same position as on the other pages. If this isn't possible, they should still be treated as a respectable part of the page. They may be put at the bottom of the page even if the others are at the top, provided they're carefully made a part of the page design and not simply tacked onto the last line in reduced size without regard for their appearance.

From the reader's standpoint, a good case can be made for the elimination of left-hand folios on many books and the omission of all page numbers on some. Certainly, it should be sufficient in most cases to number the spread—not both halves of it. However, it's worth retaining folios if only because they're helpful to the compositor, printer, and binder.

RELATING RUNNING HEADS & FOLIOS

The relationship of folios to running heads isn't significant, except in cases where having them together enables the reader to use either one for reference. Otherwise, they may be: (a) on the same line, either close together or at opposite ends (if close, have at least a pica space or some typographic device to separate them); (b) on separate lines, one above the other; or (c) on separate lines with one at the top of the page and the other at the bottom.

POSITION & LAYOUT

Putting running head and folio on one line rather than two is simplest for typesetting, but, if the book is being stretched out to a larger number of pages by using a small text area, placing one at top and the other at bottom tends to fill the page more.

Except where the need for easy reference dictates a particular position, there's no reason why the running head or folio must be at top or bottom. The conventional position for running heads is at the top of the text area, but they might just as well be at the bot-

"It is a portion of a stag's antler. It was, when still fresh, exposed to fire and it was worked with a crude stone implement, probably not a flint; some sort of primitive chopping tool."

"But that's impossible. It comes from Choukoutien."

"I don't care where it comes from; it was fashioned by a man and by a man who knew the use of fire."

The bit of horn came, in fact, from a site in the Western Hills, some thirty-five miles southwest of Peking where had been found, during the preceding three years, portions of the skulls and other bones of a sort of Man that had not been quite satisfactorily classified, but who obviously lived a very long time ago. It was, in fact, some 400,000 years ago. No one in 1930 suspected that this "Peking Man" had used fire. Man's mastery of fire was thought to have been achieved much later on in our history. Indeed, until comparatively recently, some held that fire did not enter into men's lives—at least as a servant—until the time of pots and pans, earthenware; that is to say, in New Stone Age or neolithic cultures which even in the Near East did not begin until some 10,000 years ago at the most, and not until very much later (about 2500 B.C.) in Britain.

A fortunate meeting, then, between two priests in Paris, led to one of them radically changing our ideas about Man's past. Although it was known by some in 1930 that the Neanderthaloids used fire maybe a hundred centuries ago, no one had supposed that the much more primitive "Peking Man" had been a fire maker. Since learning to control fire was the first great step towards Man's mastery of his surroundings—for such control enabled him to see in the darkness and to penetrate into new areas—obviously men, a very long time ago, were more advanced in com-

ing to terms with their environment than had been thought probable. This identification of the Choukoutien implement as having been fired was but one of the many discoveries we owe to the Abbé Henri Breuil who, during his long lifetime, was to revolutionize prehistory—that is to say, mankind's history before the invention of writing—and consequently our views of Man's past.

On the matter of the Choukoutien bone, he was proved to be absolutely right. His deduction of a great fact from a tiny bit of bone was indeed one of his more spectacular achievements. For the proof he gave that hominids (a less question-begging term than "men") hundreds of thousands of years ago used fire gave us new concepts of the life of our remote ancestors and threw light on one of the most puzzling problems in our whole history.

There is evidence that men occupied caves from very early on in their careers. Yet it is fairly clear that man could not occupy caves until he knew the use of fire and could light a blaze to keep off prowling beasts attracted by those rattling grunts he makes while he sleeps (further proof of our kinship with gorillas, chimpanzees and orang-utans). The great apes and ourselves are the only mammals to snore, emitting a buzz-saw noise while sleeping.

In Europe, in fact, there is little evidence that our ancestors used caves as homes before possibly 150,000 years ago, during the last Interglacial, or warm, Period between two Ice Ages. But then, until the last Ice Age (or Würm, beginning some 70,000 years ago) men probably did not live in Europe at all during the great cold.

However, in other parts of the earth, sparks from flint chipping, lightning, volcanic eruptions, all offered Man flames very early on in his story. Maybe men played with

has contributed so much to the vocabulary and syntax of other modern western languages, particularly English, that it is almost impossible to gain an intelligent control of any of those languages without it. Greek, on the other hand, supplies major portions of our scientific and technical vocabulary. Often scientific terms which are puzzling in their English form become crystal-clear when they are analyzed into their Greek components. ("Microscope," for example, is "small-see," while "telescope" is "distance-see.") This situation is not at all peculiar to English but applies to all western languages. So widespread is Latin and Greek participation in the terminology of the more scientific, literary, and intellectual segment of European vocabularies that many people think this Graeco-Latin complex will form the nucleus of the international language of the future.

The Latin-Greek role in the formation of modern languages is not, however, merely a matter of vocabulary contributions. The civilization of the Greeks and Romans forms the basis of our common western culture. Views of life and habits of thought that Westerners today hold in common have been inherited from Greece and Rome, having been blended with a new religious element stemming from the Hebraic culture of the Jews and early Christians. Our philosophy of religion, government, human relations, science, and progress rests firmly upon this classical foundation, which has a continuous history extending from antiquity to our own day.

During the Middle Ages and the Renaissance, Latin was the common language of scholarship and international intercourse in western Europe, while Greek performed a similar function in the Balkans and Asia Minor. With the fall of Constantinople to the Turks in 1453, Greek was

reintroduced by refugee scholars to western Europe, and the two languages were used side by side until the final emergence of the modern tongues as languages of written and official as well as spoken communication relegated them to the position of cultural tongues.

Today, Latin is fully available in the American educational system, and it is the language selected by many as their first choice when they venture outside the field of their native English. Greek, once widespread, is now less generally available. The study of Hebrew, once the pursuit of Biblical scholars, has a new vogue in connection with the rebirth of a national Jewish state in Israel.

From the point of view of the individual seeking to expand his knowledge of languages, the claims of the classical tongues deserve serious consideration.

The practical, spoken-language use of Hebrew is limited to the relatively small population of Israel, which is less than two million. The classical Greek taught in the schools has strong points of contact with the modern Greek used by about eight million inhabitants of Greece, and a transfer from the one to the other is not too difficult. Latin, outside of its use in the Catholic Church, has no immediate speaking population.

There is, however, a powerful transfer value that attaches to each of these tongues. Hebrew unlocks the gates to the Semitic languages, and one who knows Hebrew finds Arabic relatively easy. A good foundation in Latin acts as a key to the entire Romance group of modern languages and gives us a sharper understanding of English. Both Latin and Greek give an insight into the basic structure and vocabulary of the entire Indo-European language family (see page 254), of which they are typical. Since some of the languages of the family, notably Russian and the other

text pages with running heads at top and at bottom

tom or the sides. When they're not being used for reference, they're actually less obtrusive at the bottom left corner than anywhere else. A running head that's flush left at the top has a tendency to read as the first line of the page, particularly if it's similar to the text type and when the space underneath isn't much more than the text leading. To avoid the latter, an optical space (CH. 5) of about a pica is the minimum needed with normal text sizes and leading. This space should be increased if there's more than 2 pts. of leading in the text.

When the running heads and folios have been designed, they should be set and placed on the sample pages. In this book, it was decided to put the chapter title at right, where it's most easily found when going through the book from front to back, and to place the chapter number on the left, where it's most accessible to a reader referring back from one of the many chapter references in the text. The running heads and folios are in the upper outside corners for maximum convenience. The line underneath prevents confusion if a subhead occurs directly underneath.

Margins

It's true that the designer should think in terms of relating graphic elements on a page (page pattern) rather than margins (CH. 9), but, having done so, one must specify margin dimensions to include in the pasteboard of the layout program (CH. 9) and for printing purposes (CH. 12).

The text margins are determined by measuring: (a) the distance from the top of the page down to the topmost element of the type area (*head margin*) and (b) the distance from the gutter to the nearest element of the type area (*inside margin*). No other margins should be given. Since the width and height of both text area and paper page are fixed, the head and inside margins automatically determine the foot and outside margins.

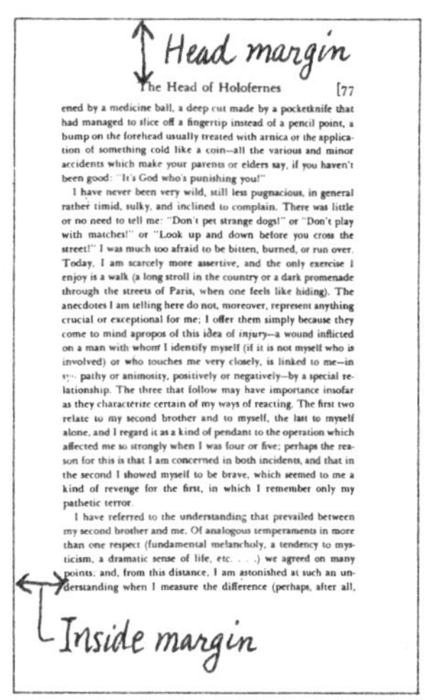

Be sure to allow for the requirements of perfect binding, side stitching, and mechanical binding when planning inside margins of books to be bound by one of these methods (CHs. 13, 29).

Margins are given in inches because they relate to paper dimensions, which are measured in inches. Measurements within the text area are given in picas and points, because they relate to type—which is measured that way (CH. 5).

Specifications

Type specification requirements are described in CH. 5. For the information of those who will see the printed sample pages, the full specifications, the book title, the trim-size, and the text margins should be printed on the last page.

If the text type has both lining and old-style figures, indicate which are to be used. The choice is purely esthetic. Old-style figures look well in text because they have more space around them, but for some kinds of tables they can be confusing.

26. Illustration layout

Illustrations were discussed in CH. 7 in terms of their origin, nature, and function. Their relationship to text, printing press, paper, and binding were covered in CH. 8. From the standpoint of layout, there are three basic situations, with several variations and combinations possible. The illustrations are:

(a) scattered through the text,
(b) accompanied by some text, and/or
(c) printed separately without text.

General principles

No matter how simple an illustration layout may be, it should be considered as a double spread. It will be seen as a spread, so it should be planned as one. All elements on the facing pages—text, illustrations, captions, space, and, if any, running heads and folios—must be in balance.

The principles of layout for picture-and-text books are not different from those for books with only occasional illustrations, but the practice is more complex. Pictures may be more flexible to arrange than lines of type, but they require more imagination and ability to organize. So the possibility of making a stunning layout with pictures is greater, but so is the possibility of making a botch. Each spread must be not only appropriate, interesting, and handsome, but it must remain an integral part of the book, with a well-balanced relationship to the other spreads and to the basic pattern and spirit of the design.

The elements

SIZE

The illustration sizes were determined roughly in calculating the length of the book. After the type is set, and the actual amount of space available for the illustrations in the text is determined by the castoff (a method of calculating the number of pages the text will occupy [CH. 31]), the rough sizes can be further refined. (When the illustrations are printed in a separate section, the castoff has no bearing.) In making layouts, there's no need to use the sizes originally chosen, but there should be compensatory changes whenever a size is drastically changed.

In crowded books, there's a tendency to make all the illustrations medium size to save space. A better solution, usually, is to make some large and some small. This has the editorial virtue of providing opportunities to reflect the relative importance of the pictures (they are rarely of equal interest), it gives the designer an opportunity to compensate for variations in the quality of the original pictures, and it introduces contrast and variety into the layout.

SHAPE

The sizes of pictures in the layout relate primarily to their importance and purpose, but their shape is largely an esthetic matter. Make an effort to create interesting and varied shapes, but without doing harm to the content of the pictures. A book full of similar rectangles can be very dull. Most photos can stand much more cropping than is generally done, so it's usually possible to vary the golden rectangles with some narrow ones and some squares. A sprinkling of silhouettes helps greatly.

CONTRAST & VARIETY

In general, contrast is preferable to insufficient variety. While a majestic effect can be achieved by skillful repetition of identical elements, a profusion of similar elements is likely to become boring, unless broken occasionally by a sharp change. Contrast is accentuated variety; it can be used to enliven the page and create a distinct rhythm.

There are many ways to achieve variety and contrast in illustration layout—not only in size and shape, but in value, pattern, style, scale, subject, period, atmosphere, etc. The problem is to orchestrate these elements into a unified whole.

Some of the ways of producing variety and contrast are to use:

(a) large pictures with small ones,
(b) square pictures with silhouettes,
(c) long oblongs with squarish oblongs,
(d) photographs with line drawings or engravings,
(e) dark pictures with light ones,
(f) close-ups with panoramas,
(g) curving subjects with angular subjects,
(h) crowded areas with blank areas,
(i) old subjects with new subjects,
(j) quiet pictures with active ones,
(k) color with monochrome, and
(l) formal with informal arrangements.

ORDER & CONSISTENCY

Sometimes order can be created even when there's a profusion of varied layouts by repeated use of a prominent element, such as a running head or folio, that recurs in the same position on all or most spreads. Another useful measure is to repeat the layout pat-

pages with uninteresting shapes

tern of a particular spread. If these devices are to be effective, they should be pronounced enough to make the reader aware of them.

In creating dynamic layouts, it's necessary not only to maintain a sense of unity and order, but to be consistent with the nature of the text. It's quite possible to have a beautiful and very dramatic illustration layout that's wrong for the book because the text is low in key or vice versa. The intensity of contrast and the extent of variety must be in harmony with the book's character.

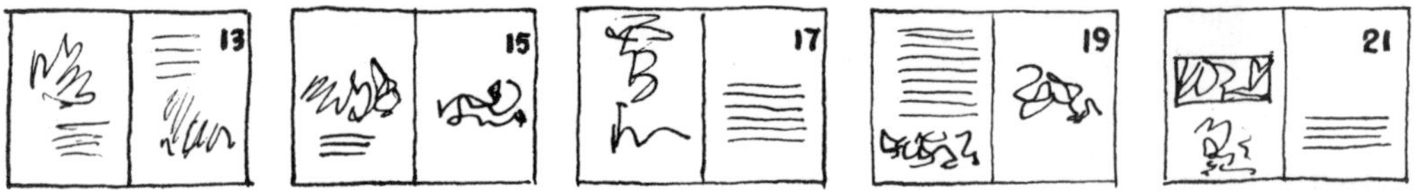

creating order and continuity with repeated prominent element

Procedure Illustration layouts are created as part of page-makeup using a computer layout program, with low-resolution scanned images representing the illustrations (CHs. 8, 9). Under some circumstances, particularly for books with many illustrations that must appear close to their related text, it can be useful to first make layout sketches on paper. Thumbnail sketches are useful for preliminary planning, but the effect of small layouts can be misleading, so such layouts should be made the actual size of the book in a dummy. Eventually, the layouts will be executed as computer page-makeup files, but first making a dummy has the advantage of enabling the designer to see the book as a whole, easily adjust the layouts to relate well to each other, and maintain the unity of the design. The value of a dummy is primarily esthetic, but it also

pages with contrast and variety

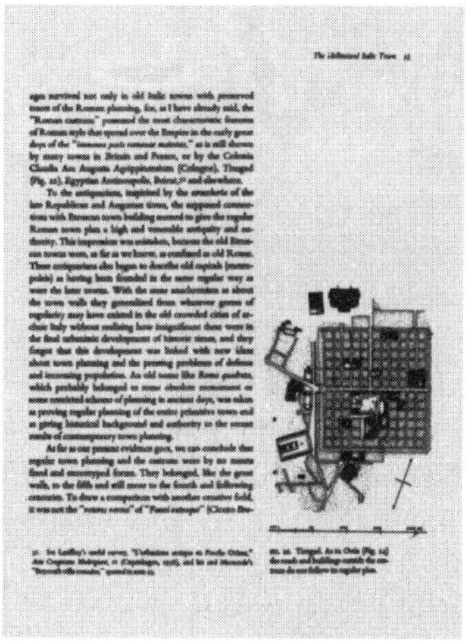

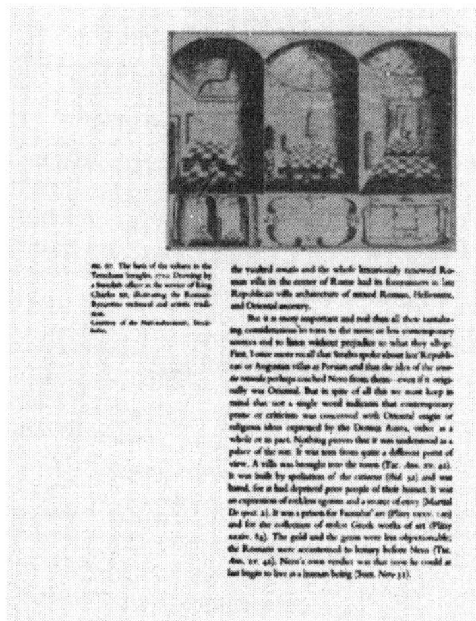

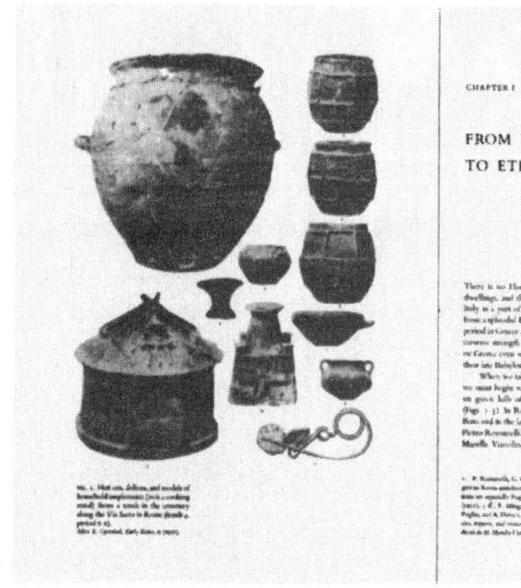

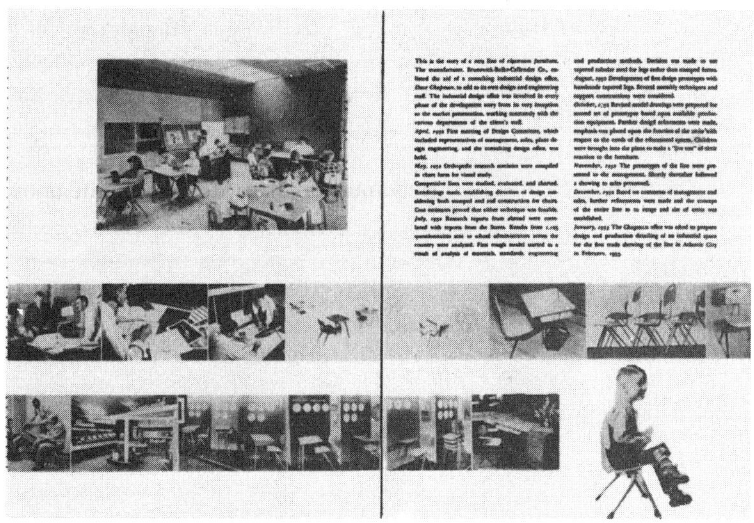

has the practical value of solving all the layout and makeup problems before the computer page-makeup is done. Whether this results in a shorter or longer makeup is hard to say. In any case, dummying is worth considering for some books (like this one), so an explanation of the procedure is given in this chapter.

Kinds of problems

ILLUSTRATIONS SCATTERED THROUGH TEXT

In books in which illustrations appear occasionally in the text, it's necessary to determine:

(a) their size and shape;

(b) their vertical position—whether they're to be at the top, bottom, or middle of the page;

(c) their horizontal position—centered, indented, flush left or right;
(d) how much space will separate them from the text; and
(e) the style and position of captions.

Thought must be given to the sequence of illustration position and size, as well as to the layout of each spread. Variety, rhythm, and order should be planned in terms of the whole book. For example, illustrations might be placed alternately at top and bottom, or they might repeat a sequence of bottom, middle, top, etc. Sizes and shapes should develop in an interesting pattern from first page to last. A haphazard sequence will result in confusion and lack of unity. This is one of the more subtle aspects of book design, but it's important. Books have a consecutive order more like a motion picture than a series of separate frames. They exist in time as well as space—which distinguishes them from other graphic forms.

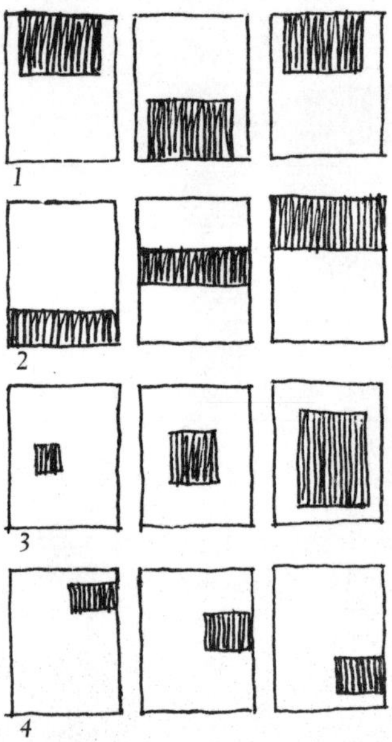

four kinds of development in sequence

Runarounds (illustrations with text alongside) are generally to be avoided; when the lines alongside are short, they usually look poor because of awkward wordspacing. If the book has just a few small pictures, it's better to place them in the full width of the text and avoid runarounds. When there are a great many, they may be combined so that two, three, or more fit on one page, or it might be possible to place them in the margins (as in this book).

When pictures occur at the tops of pages or occupy a full page, there may or may not be running heads and folios. If there are a great many such pages, the advisability of omitting that many folios must be considered. Otherwise, it's simply an esthetic matter. Illustrations usually look better without running heads above them.

ILLUSTRATIONS ACCOMPANIED BY TEXT

Where the proportion of pictures and text is heavily weighted toward pictures, the layout problem is complicated, particularly if the illustrations and related text must be close together. Not only is it more difficult to achieve a specific total number of pages, but very often the sizes of pictures must be changed in order to keep them on the same spread as the text to which they refer.

First the text is set according to the text plan (CH. 24). A castoff (CH. 31) will show whether the total space allowed for illustrations needs to be changed. If a drastic change is called for, the illustrations should be reviewed and resized. Small variations can be managed in the course of making the final layouts. For books of this kind, making a dummy is sometimes a good idea.

ILLUSTRATIONS SEPARATE FROM TEXT

When illustrations are to be printed separately from the text and inserted in the book as a tip, wrap, insert, or signature, the layout problems are somewhat simpler, although the principles remain the same. Everything said about illustration layout applies here, except for the comments on the relationship of pictures to text.

Since the first and last pages of such inserts will face pages of text, blanks, or perhaps the endpapers, these too must be treated as parts of spreads. Sometimes it's impossible to know what the facing page will be like, but try to find out as soon as possible, so the illustration page may be adjusted accordingly.

While the absence of text (except for captions) on these illustration pages relieves the designer of the need for editorial integration, it obliges the designer to make a sensible, as well as an esthetically satisfactory, arrangement of pictures. The sequence of pictures is usually decided by the editorial department, but there's often considerable leeway in how they may be combined and arranged. The designer must plan each spread so that it makes sense and must arrange the sequence of spreads so that the whole section tells a coherent story.

Sometimes the editor (or author) has no idea other than to include all the illustrations provided; sometimes a sequence is suggested which can be improved. Even when the editor's sequence is followed strictly, there's need for intelligent thought in layout. For example, if pictures 6, 7, 8, and 9 are related in subject, while 10 and 11 belong to another category, it would be more reasonable to place the first four on two facing pages and the other two on the next page together, than to put 6, 7, and 8 on one spread and 9 on the next page with 10. This seems obvious enough when put this way, but in practice it's easy to neglect consideration of the subject.

The problem is further complicated by the various kinds of subject relationships on which an arrangement could be based. A group of pictures might be arranged chronologically, geographically, or by subject development in a number of different ways. A perfectly good arrangement could be made on each basis, but one may be better than the others. Normally, this decision would be left to the designer, but it's subject to editorial judgment and approval.

from the perpendicular (its state of rest) and then set free, falls toward the perpendicular and goes the same distance beyond it—or only so much less as the cord, the resistance of the air, and other accidents impede it. The same thing is shown by water which, descending through a siphon, climbs back up as much as it went down.

23 *The First Day*

SALV. You argue very well. And I know that you will make no question of granting that the acquisition of impetus is measured by the departure of the movable body from the point of origin and its approach toward the center to which its motion tends. So will you not put an end to your difficulty by conceding that two equal movable bodies, descending by different lines and without any impediment, will have acquired equal impetus whenever their approaches to the center are equal?

SAGR. I do not quite understand the question.

SALV. I shall express it better by drawing a little sketch. Thus I take the line AB as parallel to the horizon, and at the point B I erect the perpendicular BC, and then I add this slanted line CA. Now the line CA is meant to be an inclined plane, exquisitely polished and hard, upon which descends a perfectly round ball of some very hard substance. Suppose another ball, quite similar, to fall freely along the perpendicular CB. I ask you to concede that the impetus of that which descends by the plane CA, upon arriving at the point A, would be equal to the impetus acquired by the other at point B after falling along the perpendicular CB.

FIG. 4

SAGR. I surely believe it would. In fact, they have both advanced equally toward the center; and by what I have already granted, the impetus of each should be equally sufficient to carry it back to the same height.

Equal impetus of two bodies which have fallen an equal distance toward the center

SALV. Now tell me what you believe the same ball would do if placed upon the horizontal plane AB?

SAGR. It would lie still, the said plane having no inclination.

SALV. But on the inclined plane CA it would descend, though with a slower motion than by the perpendicular CB?

The body stands still on a horizontal plane

SAGR. I was about to answer confidently in the affirmative, it seeming to me necessary that the motion by the perpendicular CB should be faster than by the inclined plane CA. Yet if that is

runaround

mortals have the power to destroy much of mankind. We may be used to the fear, but it does not go away. We may shrink from thinking about the unthinkable, but there is no topic that requires better thought. To make us think about it is the purpose of many novelists whose books would like implausible tall stories if they did not dramatize possibilities be probable. One specialist

runaround showing bad wordspacing

Dummying

The layout of pages in a paper dummy is no different than the computer page-makeup. Indeed, the dummy layout is followed in the page-makeup. Making a dummy is simply a way of enabling the designer to do the layouts with more control over the design by having all the pages readily available for comparison and coordination. Of course, it's possible to achieve this also by doing the layouts on the computer and printing out the pages (thereby creating an electronic dummy), but some designers will find it more satisfactory to solve complex layout problems in heavily illustrated books by moving pieces of paper back and forth among several affected pages than making changes one page at a time on the computer. For whatever use dummying may be to you, here's how it's done.

A blank dummy is made, and the pages numbered. The most practical dummy is a Smyth-sewn, unbacked, uncovered book of about 70 lb. plain vellum paper. This will open flat, yet stay together, and the paper is tough enough to take a lot of handling.

The pages estimated for the frontmatter and backmatter are clipped together. The text and illustrations must fit into the pages remaining. Print out a set of galleys (unpaged proofs of text) (CH. 20) to be cut up and pasted or taped into place on the pages. The illustrations are scanned in low-res and numbered.

The number of each illustration must be written in the margin of the galley next to the line of text to which it relates. Each galley proof must be numbered and its number written about an inch apart all through the proof. This is so that any piece can be identified when the proofs are cut up.

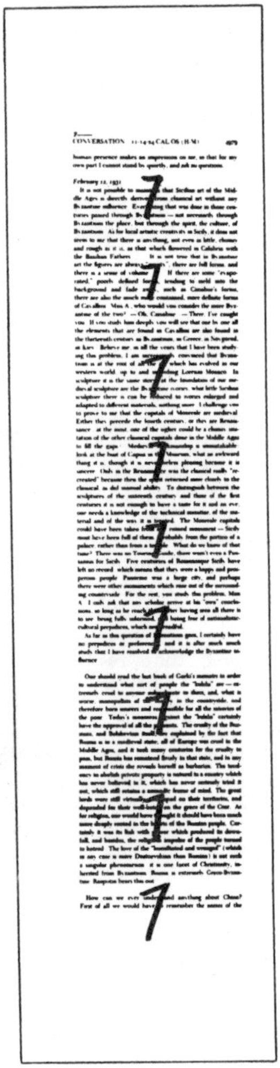

galley proof marked with galley number

Exactly how the layout is made depends on the nature of the book. If it's editorially sufficient that the illustrations appear within a few pages of the text reference, the problem is fairly simple. Examining a galley or two at a time, the designer can see how many of what size pictures will be needed, and the layouts may be made according to the general scheme visualized at the beginning. It's better to have pictures occur after the reference rather than before it, but, except for this requirement, it should be possible to make each illustration about the size allocated in the analysis (CH. 21).

Go through the entire dummy, indicating with pencil the amount of text and the size, shape, and position of each illustration. Before cutting up the galleys, mark them off with the appropriate page numbers written in the margin. If at the end you find that you have pages left over, or not enough pages, it may be possible to change the frontmatter and/or backmatter specs enough to reach the desired number of pages. If not, you can easily make changes in the page allocations of the text, since the galleys haven't been cut up. In this way you can be sure you'll have the right total number of pages before working out the detailed layouts. This is one of the advantages of dummying.

The same layout procedure may be used when the illustrations and text references must appear on the same spread, but only if there are not too many pictures in proportion to text. When there are three or four illustrations for each page, the problem of layout becomes so complex it's necessary to proceed spread by spread—working out each one in considerable detail—with no anticipation of a definite total number of pages. This situation prevails often in textbooks; the layout is completed to editorial requirements, and the frontmatter and backmatter are adjusted to make an even form—even if it's a small one.

Once the dummy is made, the illustrations can be scanned to final size and positioned with the text and captions in the computer page-makeup according to the layouts. The makeup may be done by the designer or a service bureau. This will go quickly since all the layout problems have been solved.

Captions & credits

■ **Captions**—These are elements of the page design just as much as pictures or text. If they're just a line or two, they may be used to contrast with a block of text or a picture. When they're extensive, they become blocks of type to be given the same graphic consideration as text.

Captions must be readable but must contrast with the text sufficiently to avoid confusion. They are usually brief, so they may be set one, two, or even three sizes smaller than text and still be readable. It helps to set them in italics or in another face. In crowded layouts, there's often a need to set captions in narrow measures, but when they're justified there's a limit to how short the line can be without running into wordspacing trouble (CHs. 5, 6).

When placing captions above and below illustrations, particularly rectangles, remember that there are usually more ascenders and caps than descenders. This means that there's optically more space below a line than above, so it's necessary to provide a little more space (perhaps 2 pts.) between pictures and captions placed below than those placed above. The closer the captions to the illustrations and the larger the type, the more significant this factor becomes.

■ **Credit lines**—Especially when the acknowledgment is to an institution, credits need be only legible. This satisfies the requirement to identify the source of a picture. In many cases, the credit line is an advertisement for the supplier of the picture and is disproportionate to the picture's contribution to the book—particularly when a fee has been paid. For such pictures, the credit may be made as inconspicuous as feasible; 4 or 5 pt. type is sufficient. Any position is valid that's visible, clearly associated with the relevant picture, and graphically useful.

Where an individual artist or photographer is credited for a substantial contribution, it's customary to include the credit in the frontmatter. In many books, the photo credits are put in the backmatter as a list or paragraph. Artists and photographers tend to prefer having the credit with the picture.

27. Frontmatter, part-titles, & backmatter

Frontmatter The frontmatter is the entrance to the book and so it should be revealing and interesting. It should invite readers and give them confidence that the book will be esthetically and practically satisfying. The front pages should be at least as excellent in every way as any part of the book. In books that have no chapter display type or illustrations, the frontmatter is the only place to provide visual interest and variety. This opportunity shouldn't be lost.

Frontmatter pages should follow the design of the rest of the book, where layout, typography, and feeling have been established. The problem is to design the frontmatter pages so that each will be entirely suited to its purpose and yet fit into the established patterns. Each page must be given careful consideration, no matter how unimportant it may seem to be.

Generally, the display type and layout style on frontmatter pages is the same as those of chapter openings, but not always. Some pages may be given subordinate headings that don't appear elsewhere in the book, or entirely different display type may be used.

The sequence of frontmatter pages is a matter of some dispute. Various arrangements are suggested by different authorities, and a case can be made for an order different from any of those. Below is a sequence widely accepted:

(1) half-title
(2) *ad card* (a list of other books by the author)
(3) title
(4) copyright
(5) dedication
(6) acknowledgments
(7) preface (and/or foreword)
(8) contents
(9) list of illustrations
(10) introduction
(11) second half-title (or first part-title)

These elements are discussed in the order listed above.

HALF-TITLE

The half-title before the title is an anachronism. It originated when books were stored and sold without covers, to be bound individually for the purchaser. The title page was printed on page 3 to protect it, and the book was not yet trimmed, so the folds were still closed, which made it necessary to repeat the title on the first page for outer identification. This requirement hasn't existed on any large scale for generations, but the custom hangs on.

The first half-title may be eliminated entirely and the page left blank, or it may be used for some other purpose. An inscription and/or autograph by the author is often written on this page (or the *flyleaf* of the endpaper). Much can be said for putting the dedication at the very beginning of the book rather than several pages back.

Page 1 may be used for a symbol or other element that sets the tone of the book. This might be an epigraph (a quotation supplied by the author), an illustration suggestive of the whole book, an element of the title page (such as a subtitle or a series title), or it could be the author's initials. This is your opportunity to set the stage or play an overture.

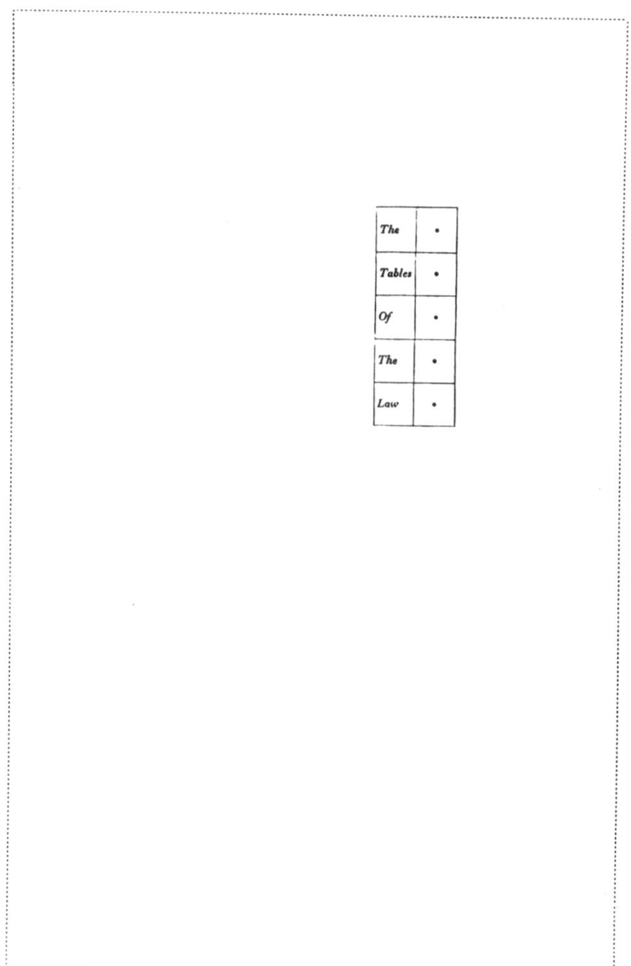

Although Paul Rand used the half-title, it's incorporated in a strongly suggestive design element.

One possibility is to use page 1 for a blurb about the book. This is a logical substitute for the jacket flap copy in paperbacks or other cases when there'll be no jacket (CH. 29). If the title *must* be repeated here, it should be made as inconspicuous as possible. Bear in mind that it appears on the jacket, binding, title page, and (sometimes) the second half-title as well. The repetition is particularly irritating if there's little frontmatter, when the title page is preceded and followed by half-titles almost immediately.

In designing page 1, remember that it's part of a spread, of which the other part is the endpaper or the inside of the paper cover. Also, consider what will happen to page 2 when the material on page 1 shows through, especially when 2 is part of the title spread. Try to back up all elements, particularly if the book uses lightweight paper.

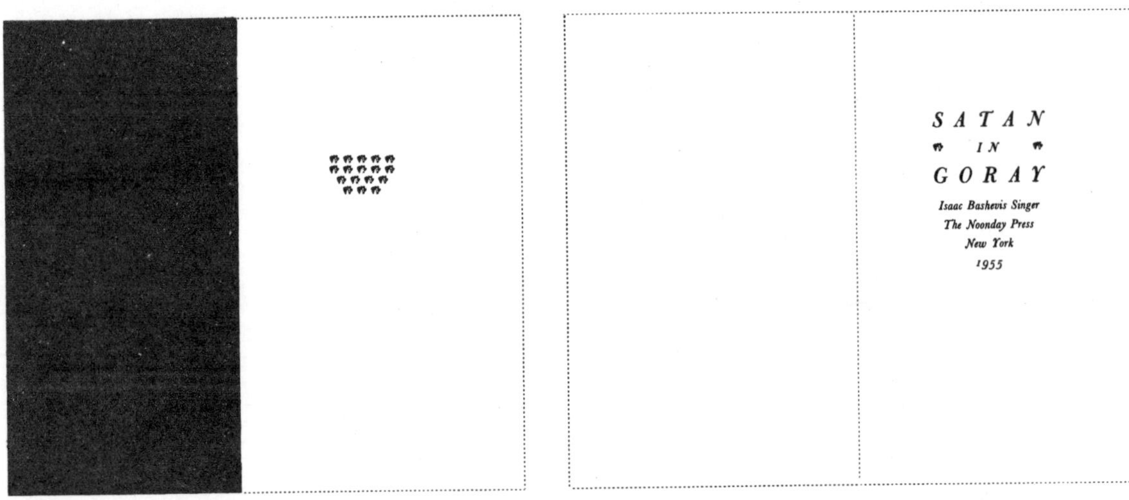

In this book designed by the author, a pattern of type ornaments is used on page 1 to prefigure the title page.

AD CARD The ad card is generally on the title-page spread, but it can go on another page except where it's important to call attention to a successful previous work by a little-known author. In this case, the older form of ad is sometimes used, i.e., "author of . . ." is placed beneath the author's name on the title page. Otherwise, the titles are listed under a separate heading (for example, "other books by . . .", etc.), which may be quite small. When the ad card isn't on the title spread, it's usually placed ahead of it on page 3, making the title spread pages 4 and 5.

TITLE PAGE The dominant feature of the frontmatter is the title page. To express its relationship to the book we might compare a book to the human body, and say that the text is the torso, the frontmatter the head, and the title page the face.

It's best to design the title page before the rest of the frontmatter. There should be perfect harmony among all the front pages, and it's better to coordinate the other pages with the title than to compromise the design of this key element to fit the others. However, the title page must be in complete harmony with the text that's already designed. The title page provides an outstanding opportunity to express the book's character and make an effective display, but it must never fail to be an integral part of the whole book—no matter how excellent it may be as an individual unit. It's sad to see a well-designed text and a handsome title page that don't go together. Although the parts are good, the total is a failure.

The tendency to produce unrelated title pages is very common. Designers frequently become engrossed in these attractive creations and begin moving things about without regard for what already exists. To avoid this, it's a good idea to work on the title page with a sample page in full view—to fill the eye with the spirit and character of the text.

■ **Position**—The title page is conventionally thought of as a right-hand page, but, as elsewhere, both sides of the spread are simultaneously visible and thus both are part of the title-page design. This doesn't mean that type or illustration must appear on both sides. It *does* mean that the design must reckon with the whole spread—even if there's nothing but space on half of it. Space is as much part of a design as the type and illustrations that form and divide it (CHs. 5, 22).

The right side of the spread is certainly the more prominent one. Where a conventional arrangement is in order, and there's no special consideration to indicate otherwise, the title-page type is just as well placed on the right-hand page—and so it is in most books. It has been customary, also, to confine the title-page type to the text-page area. This practice tends toward simplicity and unity—two highly desirable attributes—but there's no reason to be limited to it if your design objective can be realized in other ways.

Indeed, not only need the title not be confined to the text area

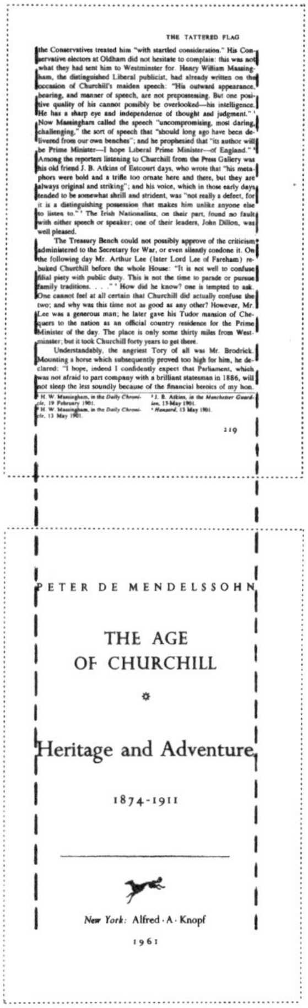
THE TATTERED FLAG

219

PETER DE MENDELSSOHN

THE AGE
OF CHURCHILL

Heritage and Adventure

1874-1911

New York: Alfred · A · Knopf
1961

a title page confined to the text page dimensions

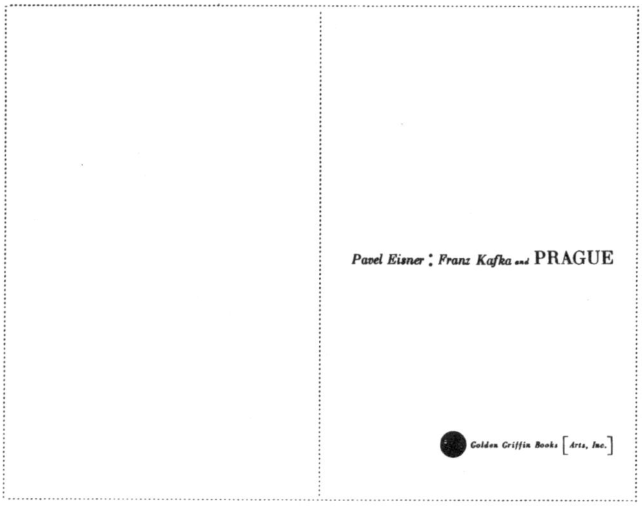
Pavel Eisner : *Franz Kafka* and PRAGUE

Golden Griffin Books [Arts, Inc.]

In this title spread with all type on one side, the left side space is part of the design.

a successful six-page title page by Merle Armitage

or the right-hand page, it doesn't necessarily have to appear entirely on one spread. If the problem calls for such treatment, the copy and illustrations may be extended over four, six, or more pages. Just as in a movie—which exists through successive frames as the book exists through successive pages—the title and credits may appear in sequence rather than on one page. Used inappropriately or ineptly this device could be irritating. Well handled, it can serve several useful purposes: (a) it may be used to build suspense, (b) it can be an effective way to deal with complicated and/or extensive copy, (c) it can be a means of creating atmosphere, and (d) it can help fill out a short book, provided the device is justified by a valid editorial purpose. But bear in mind that the title page isn't a poster that must catch the eye of a passing shopper—that's the role of the jacket or cover—it's for the use of those already aware of the title and interested in it enough to have opened the book.

■ **Elements**—The title page may contain all or some of the following elements:

(a) title
(b) author
(c) subtitle
(d) credits (translator, editor, illustrator, author of introduction and/or foreword and/or preface)
(e) imprint (the publisher's name)
(f) *colophon* (the publisher's trademark)
(g) date
(h) copyright notice
(i) quotation
(j) illustration
(k) ad card

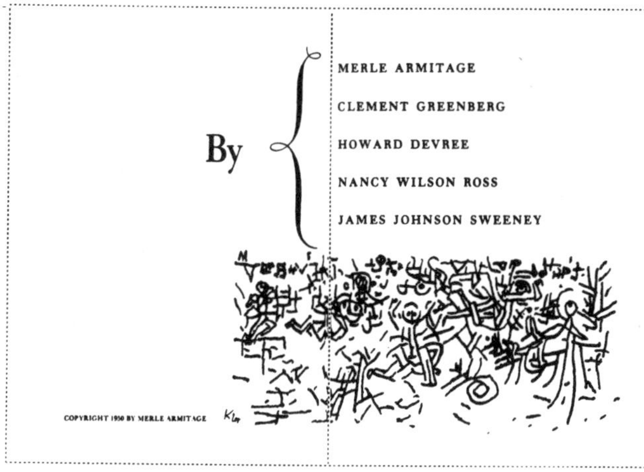
By
MERLE ARMITAGE
CLEMENT GREENBERG
HOWARD DEVREE
NANCY WILSON ROSS
JAMES JOHNSON SWEENEY

COPYRIGHT 1950 BY MERLE ARMITAGE

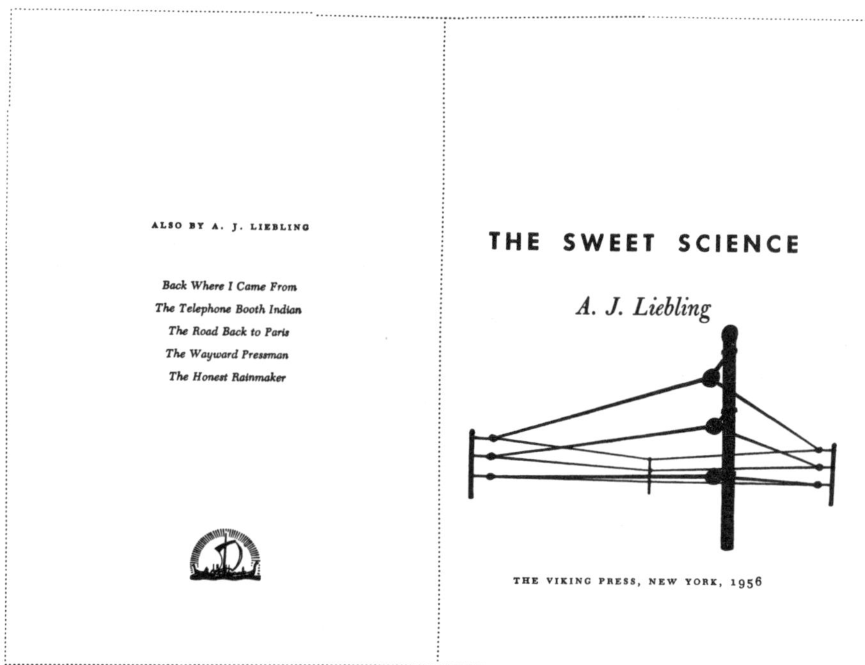
ALSO BY A. J. LIEBLING

Back Where I Came From
The Telephone Booth Indian
The Road Back to Paris
The Wayward Pressman
The Honest Rainmaker

THE SWEET SCIENCE

A. J. Liebling

THE VIKING PRESS, NEW YORK, 1956

the title page of a book on boxing, with an illuminating illustration by the designer

The designer's first job is to establish and maintain the proper degree of emphasis among these elements. Ordinarily, the order of importance would be roughly as listed above, but circumstances might suggest an entirely different one. A well-known author's name might be more important than the title. When the title is "literary" and the subtitle descriptive, it might be best to emphasize the latter. In extensively illustrated books it may be appropriate to give the illustrator billing equal to the author's, and so on. Discuss these questions with the editor before making a design.

■ **Illustration**—If illustration is used, some should appear on the title page, where it's likely to be most effective. Especially in books with titles that fail to reveal the nature of the text, illustration can serve a function in suggesting the subject. It's almost always possible to manage something, even on a small budget (CH. 7).

Sometimes a *"frontispiece"* is supplied with the ms. The term is misleading because it implies that this picture is something separate from the rest of the book. But the "frontispiece" is actually an illustration meant to appear on the title-page spread, and it should be treated as an element of the title page. This is true even if it's printed on different paper from the text—such as a halftone or color illustration on coated stock tipped into a book printed on antique paper. The variation in paper then becomes an element in the design to be used.

■ **Layout and typography**—The popular concept of a "frontispiece" is that of a picture alone on the left-hand page with all the type on the right. But, treating it as a title-page illustration, don't hesitate to move it to the right side of the spread, or to place some

Two spreads in which a "frontispiece" (not an illustration made for the title page) is made an integral part of the design. Left: design by Alvin Lustig. Below: design by Albert Cetta.

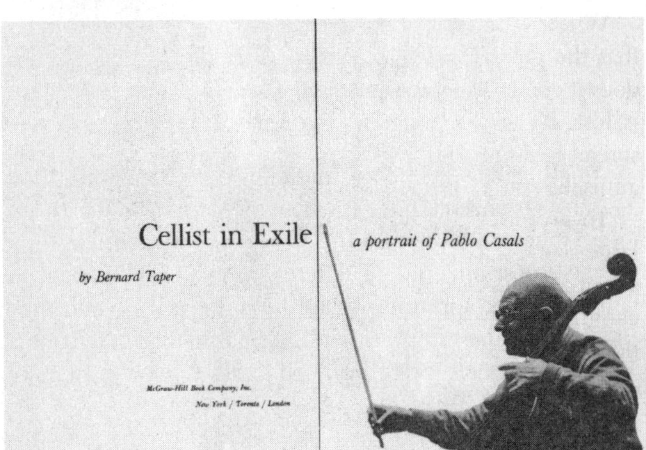

A title page design in perfect harmony with the text. Design by Joseph Blumenthal.

of the type on the left with the picture. It's most important to integrate the picture into the spread.

The title-page arrangement—whether symmetrical or asymmetrical—should be consistent with the design of the text (CHs. 24, 25). Not that blind consistency is necessary, but the ms. characteristics that suggested the chapter-opening arrangement would also indicate how to handle the title page. In both (and all) cases, the nature of the text is the key.

Nor is it necessary that the same type be used for the title page as for the other parts of the book. What is essential is unity and harmony. It doesn't matter whether these are achieved by using a close match or strong contrast. Sometimes a combination of both is most effective. Quite often, a good result is achieved by setting everything on the title page in the same face as the other type, except for the title itself—which may be set in a distinctly contrasting face. The same principles apply to the other aspects of typography (CH. 5).

Where type runs across the spread, it's important to recognize that the gutter does exist and is a substantial obstacle. Not only does it create a physical break in which a certain amount of space is lost, it's also a psychological barrier. Further, unless the title spread is in the middle of a signature, irregular folding may cause a misalignment of the two sides (CHs. 13, 29).

To avoid the worst effects of crossing the gutter, use a fairly large size of type. The gutter in a Smyth-sewn book requires that about 2½ picas of space be kept clear, to be sure that nothing gets caught in the fold. In order that this space doesn't make too noticeable a break in the line of type, it should be not very much greater than the normal space between words or letters—whichever falls at the *gutter*. For example, if the normal word-spacing is 1½ picas, a space of 2½ picas between words at the gutter won't be too disturbing, because almost 1 pica will disappear into the fold, so the optical space will be just about 1½ picas. However, a word space of 1½ picas would be normal for only quite a large size of type—perhaps 36 pt.—or for a widely letter-spaced line of somewhat smaller type. Since the space needed at the gutter is constant, it's obvious that the smaller the type, the more excessive that space will seem. Also, if the pages don't align, the fault is less noticeable when the type is larger.

In both examples the space between BOOK and MAKING is the same, and in both the pages are out of vertical alignment by the same amount.

In a perfect-bound book, add 1½ picas (before trim) to the gutter space, and in side-stitched books, add 3 picas. In both cases, the optical space remaining will be about 1½ picas, as in Smyth-sewn books (CHs. 13, 29).

■ **Color**—When a second color is used on a title page, it should be used as part of the design, rather than merely adding an element of gaud to the page. It should serve an editorial and graphic purpose (CH. 22).

Color can be used to establish emphasis, to create atmosphere, or to make graphic distinctions not otherwise possible. The conventional use of a second color is to print the title or a small illustration, but there are many other possibilities. Graphic elements in color may overprint the type successfully if they're light enough. Another possibility is to print a pattern or a solid panel with some or all type elements dropped out. Color borders have always been used, but there are certainly new ways to use them. When appropriate, a ghost effect may be obtained by printing a color in a very light value.

When using color on the title page, consider using it also on other pages on the same side of the sheet, at virtually no additional cost. Be sure, though, that the color makes sense wherever used. It's better not to use it at all than to throw it in simply because it's available.

The effect of a second color may be lost to a large degree if it's too dark. The color is affected by its contrast in value with the paper, particularly where it appears in small areas. When this contrast is almost as great as that of the black, the color (hue) itself becomes relatively unnoticeable. Second colors that are not more than 50% of the value of the black ink are most effective. The intensity of the color has some effect here, but not as much as the value, except in extreme cases.

In choosing a swatch of color to be matched, remember that color looks lighter in value and more intense in large areas than in small ones. When the color will be used for type or fairly narrow lines, the printed color will look considerably darker than on the swatch, even if the ink is an exact match. To avoid this, choose a swatch a bit lighter than the color you want.

COPYRIGHT NOTICE

The copyright notice customarily appears on the page backing the right side of the title spread or, occasionally, on the title page itself. The 1976 copyright law requires only that the notice be put in a "reasonable" place. This is taken to mean a place where it's easily found.

Usually, other material appears with the notice. The Library of Congress Control Number is almost always on the copyright page, where it's usually incorporated in the *CIP* (*Cataloging in Publication*) data (a reproduction of the reference card used by libraries) that many publishers print in their books to facilitate cataloging. The CIP card is one of the rare designs that's both functional and homely. It's convenient for librarians to have it on the copyright page, but it's a typographic blight and is probably just as useful at the back of the book where it won't offend. Another reference aid is the *ISBN* (*International Standard Book Number*), which provides a unique identification for every title to which such a number is assigned. This is a valuable tool for book distribution.

The country in which the book was printed is almost always indicated on the copyright page, particularly if it's the United States of America. Under both the old and new (1976) copyright laws, the copyright of a work by a U.S. citizen is affected by the place of printing. In many countries, this information is required by the customs service. The printer's name is often added, as well as a credit for the designer and others involved in the production of the book. Acknowledgments that involve copyrights (as in anthologies) should appear on the copyright page. If there are too many to fit on this page, they should begin on it and run over to the next page, or a notice is given that this material appears in the backmatter. (There is a divergence of legal opinion in this matter.)

The copyright notice isn't meant for the reader and may be set very small. As in credits on pictures, legibility is all that's required. If especially important credits are included, they're set larger. However, while the copyright-page content is usually of little interest, the type on it is a graphic element of the book no less important than any other. (In design, there are no unimportant parts. Everything must be on the same level of quality or the design loses its wholeness.) The copyright notice may be greatly subordinated in emphasis, but it must be entirely consistent in style with the rest of the book. It's necessary to stress this point because it's so common to see copyright pages that are badly at odds with the general scheme. Even in many otherwise well-designed books, one sees the copyright notice set as though it had not been given a thought. The most frequent fault is the use of a centered

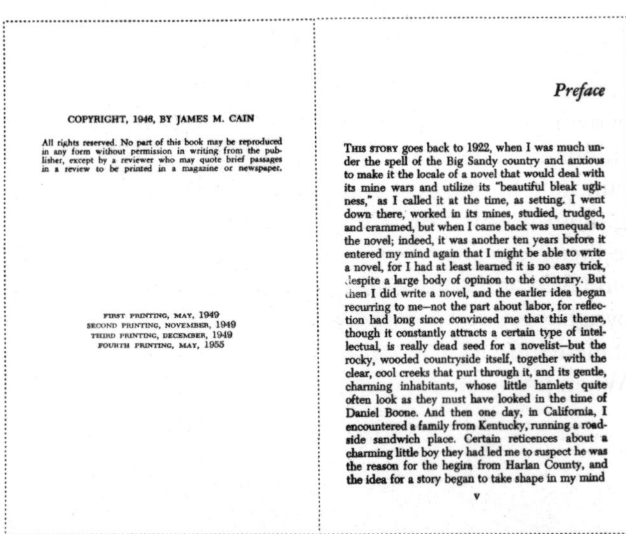
COPYRIGHT, 1946, BY JAMES M. CAIN

All rights reserved. No part of this book may be reproduced in any form without permission in writing from the publisher, except by a reviewer who may quote brief passages in a review to be printed in a magazine or newspaper.

FIRST PRINTING, MAY, 1949
SECOND PRINTING, NOVEMBER, 1949
THIRD PRINTING, DECEMBER, 1949
FOURTH PRINTING, MAY, 1955

Preface

THIS STORY goes back to 1922, when I was much under the spell of the Big Sandy country and anxious to make it the locale of a novel that would deal with its mine wars and utilize its "beautiful bleak ugliness," as I called it at the time, as setting. I went down there, worked in its mines, studied, trudged, and crammed, but when I came back was unequal to the novel; indeed, it was another ten years before it entered my mind again that I might be able to write a novel, for I had at least learned it is no easy trick, despite a large body of opinion to the contrary. But then I did write a novel, and the earlier idea began recurring to me—not the part about labor, for reflection had long since convinced me that this theme, though it constantly attracts a certain type of intellectual, is really dead seed for a novelist—but the rocky, wooded countryside itself, together with the clear, cool creeks that purl through it, and its gentle, charming inhabitants, whose little hamlets quite often look as they must have looked in the time of Daniel Boone. And then one day, in California, I encountered a family from Kentucky, running a roadside sandwich place. Certain reticences about a charming little boy they had led me to suspect he was the reason for the hegira from Harlan County, and the idea for a story began to take shape in my mind

v

a spread with copyright notice poorly related to the facing page arrangement in a book that has an asymmetrical pattern, or vice versa. The effect is jarring.

The copyright page is part of a spread that includes the facing page, and should be designed as such. But it's important that the copyright-page copy backs up elements of the title page to avoid showing through in open areas. To accomplish this, set the copy utilizing any of the available layout devices—line for line, centered, flush left or right, run-in in a block, all together, or in two or more parts—as long as the result is consistent with the general pattern.

a well-designed copyright/dedication spread

Library of Congress Catalog No. 63–13496
Copyright © The Joseph H. Hirshhorn Foundation

All rights reserved. No part of this book
may be reproduced in any form without
permission in writing from The Joseph H. Hirshhorn
Foundation, except by a reviewer who
may quote brief passages in a review to be
printed in a magazine or newspaper.

Distributed simultaneously in Canada by
McClelland and Stewart, Ltd.
Manufactured in the United States of America
by H. Wolff, New York

The pine tree, used on flags
during the American Revolution, was
the official emblem of the Armory Show.
The lettering used for the title on
the title-page and the initials at the
beginning of each chapter
is adapted from the cover of
the March, 1913 issue of Arts and Decoration
that featured the original Armory Show.

To
The members of the
Association of American Painters and Sculptors,
in memory.

DEDICATION

If there's a dedication, it usually appears on the page facing the copyright. The dedication should dominate the spread, but it shouldn't be too large. Text type size is about right under most circumstances. Names can be given added importance by setting them in small caps with letterspacing. Authors sometimes type their dedications in definite patterns, but the arrangement should be made to follow the typographic style of the book. After copyright notices, dedications are the most commonly inconsistent elements.

When frontmatter is being compressed to save pages, the dedication is sometimes placed on the copyright page itself. Actually, page 1 seems the most logical position, since the entire book is being dedicated, and this is where the author generally writes a signed inscription.

ACKNOWLEDGMENTS How acknowledgments are set will depend on their nature and importance. They may range from routine (such as the anthology credits mentioned in connection with copyrights) to virtual recognition of co-authorship. In many cases, the acknowledgments are not as important to the book as they are to the author, who may use them to gain goodwill or repay obligations. At other times, an acknowledgment may be so sincerely felt as to constitute almost a dedication. The type may range from the copyright notice size to text size; one size smaller than text is usually appropriate. On lengthy acknowledgments, the heading may be set in chapter-opening style; on brief copy, a subhead style will do. When only a few lines are involved, the heading may be omitted. Acknowledgments of minor importance may sometimes go in the backmatter.

PREFACE & FOREWORD There is some confusion about the terms "preface:", "foreword", and "introduction". They are often incorrectly interchanged. To some degree, the confusion is justified, because most dictionaries give about the same definition for all three, but there are real distinctions. A *preface* is written by the author and is generally about the writing of the book. A *foreword* is a comment on the book and/or the author by another person. An *introduction*, which may be by the author or another, may contain such matter, but it's primarily a preparation for, or explanation of, the content. These distinctions are editorial matters, but are of concern to the designer because they affect the position of the copy in the frontmatter.

It's logical to put prefaces and forewords *before* the contents because they're not part of the text. (Also, when a foreword is written by a prominent person, commercial considerations indicate a position up front.) Sometimes an exception is made when the preface and/or foreword run so long they push the contents page too far into the book.

In most cases, prefaces and forewords are set in text size, with the heading treated as a chapter opening. An exception is made occasionally when a very important and brief foreword is set more prominently than the text, or one is set in another size in order to adjust the length of the book.

CONTENTS The contents page has been the least satisfactorily solved problem in book design from the beginning. The early printers got off on the wrong foot and stayed there. In this matter, convention and tradition are of no help and are best disregarded. Logic and instinct must be the guides.

Especially in a complex book, the contents page is a major typographic design problem. A good contents page is an efficient and valuable tool, but it must also be closely integrated with the typographic scheme of the book. In addition, the contents page often has a role in selling the book, and this must be played well too. Primarily, the contents is an aid in using the book. Its function is to clarify the organization and simplify finding material.

When the contents won't fit on one page but will fit on two, it's better to run it on facing pages rather than on a right-hand page and its back-up, where there's always the danger that a browser will think the book contains only what is on the first page of contents. Putting the two pages on a spread also eliminates the inconvenience of turning the page, and enables both reader and buyer to see all of the contents in a glance.

Since the main purpose of a list of contents is to show on which page each item may be found, the most practical place for the page numbers is *directly following* the item titles. In the past, it was customary to place the titles flush left and the numbers flush right, with a row of dots (*leader*) connecting one to the other. Some years ago it was recognized that leaders look awful, but, instead of eliminating the need for them by moving the numbers close to the titles, the leaders were just eliminated, thus making it more difficult to find the page numbers; in books with a wide text page and short chapter titles, it's almost impossible to tell which number belongs to each title without using a ruler to align them. This arrangement is still used in some books, although it would appear to have no advantage except in making it convenient to add up the numbers, if anyone should care to do

a two-page contents on facing pages

Contents

preface viii
New York 3
Washington 81
Niagara 93
Chicago 103
Los Angeles 117
California 135
San Francisco 148
journey to Reno 158
on to Las Vegas 165
Los Angeles again 171

Grand Canyon 176
Santa Fé 182
Texas 198
New Orleans 211
the South 223
back to New York 230
North 249
at home in New York 276
Chicago revisited 302
adieu 327

so. The practice *can* be used successfully if the titles are all about the same length, and the line of numbers is moved so it's no more than about an em to the right of the longest title.

When the page number immediately follows the title, in most cases it's sufficient to separate title and number with an em space, although a punctuation mark or ornament may be preferable when the items are crowded or, as sometimes happens, the titles end with figures (for instance, dates). The page numbers may be placed before (to the left of) the titles if there are no

an impractical contents page

CONTENTS

CHAPTER		PAGE
I	Mr. O'Brien	1
II	Mr. Tibby	14
III	Mr. Cole	30
IV	Mr. Hockin	44
V	Carlota	64
VI	Nancy Nodden	79
VII	Taste	99
VIII	Conflict	108
IX	Love	123
X	A Wedding and After	136
XI	Art	153
XII	Encounters	163
XIII	Experience	179
XIV	Crime	193
XV	Devotion	212
XVI	Punishment	231
XVII	Despair	245
XVIII	Settlement	263
XIX	Home	280
XX	The Marvel	292
XXI	Departure	301
XXII	Masterpieces	313
XXIII	Happiness	317

chapter numerals. In a centered arrangement with not too many items, the numbers can function well placed immediately *below* the titles. The important point is that the numbers should be adjacent to the titles.

CONTENTS.

CONTENTS

left: a contents page with leaders; right: folios aligned but sufficiently close to titles

Contents

left: folios adjacent to titles; right: folios centered under titles

The contents should be extremely legible—which requires careful spacing as well as proper choice of type face and size. Type size alone doesn't ensure legibility. A judicious use of leading and indentions can set off a line of quite small type so that it's clearly visible, whereas a crowded page of larger type may be more difficult to read. In a complicated contents, a variety of sizes, italics, caps, small caps, boldface, and even other faces should be used as necessary to make a clear and useful page.

There's no need to set the word "chapter" above the chapter numbers, or to set the word "page" above a column of page numbers, if there is one. It's perfectly obvious what these numbers are. Also, it's usually not helpful to put running heads and folios on contents pages, as these only add to the problem of simplifying and clarifying. Occasionally, a contents running head is desirable in a book that contains material resembling a contents, and folios might be called for on a long contents preceded by a long, folioed preface.

Since it may be assumed that the book will be read from front to back, there's no need to make reference on the contents page to items that precede it. However, if there's a foreword by a prominent person, for sales purposes it may be a good idea to list it, with the writer's name.

☞ **CONTENTS**

Ideas About Ideas

11 HOW THEY ARE CHOSEN
12 CHOOSING ONE FOR YOURSELF
13 BEING IN BUSINESS
13 SOME THINGS TO THINK ABOUT

In Business

17 SETTING UP
19 SELLING
21 MANAGING
23 FINANCES

The Ideas

A. MAKING & SELLING

☞ Kitchen products 25

BAKED GOODS 26
26 BREAD
27 ROLLS
27 COOKIES
27 PETIT FOURS
27 BIRTHDAY CAKES
27 *Other baked goods*

CONFECTIONS 27
27 CANDY
28 FRUIT CONFECTIONS
28 CANDIED MINT LEAVES
28 NUTS

PICKLING AND PRESERVING 28
28 PICKLES
28 PRESERVES

DRINKS 29
29 MEAD
29 PEACHY
29 *Other drinks*

Other kitchen products 29
29 CANAPÉS AND HORS D'OEUVRES
29 SAUCES AND DRESSINGS

☞ Metalcraft 29

JEWELRY 30
WIRE WORK 31
SHEET WORK 31
ENGRAVING AND ETCHING 31

☞ Ceramics 31

33 DINNERWARE
33 JEWELRY
33 BUTTONS
33 SCULPTURE
34 GARDEN POTTERY
34 TILES
34 HOUSEHOLD POTTERY
Other ceramic products 34

☞ Enameling 34

35 RINGS
35 NECKLACES
35 EARRINGS
36 BUTTONS
36 NAME PLATES
36 COMPANY GIFTS
Other enameled products 36

a complicated contents

LIST OF ILLUSTRATIONS

The functional problem of a list of illustrations is about the same as that of a contents. The titles should be legible and the page numbers should be adjacent to them.

One special problem is how to give page references to illustrations on unfolioed inserts and wraps. The only practical solution is to use the term "facing page oo" for single pages, and "following page oo" where a group of such pages occurs together. Readers are thus directed to the group of illustration pages containing the picture they want to find, and they find the picture itself by using the sequence in the list.

INTRODUCTION

An introduction is almost always set like the text and its opening is in the style of the chapters. When it's considered part of the frontmatter, it may be set differently from the text in order to adjust the length of the book. When it's part of the text, it would be rather awkward to set it differently, but this may be done in some circumstances. For example, if the introduction is by a different writer than the text (as in anthologies) it may be set it in another style to emphasize this fact.

A question of style arises when the introduction (or preface or foreword) is signed by its author. If it's by the author of the text, no signature is really needed, but it's not uncommon to use initials at the end, often with a dateline, which is usually set on the left in a small size. If the introduction isn't by the author of the text, the name of the writer is better placed at the beginning, particularly if it's a prominent person whose name adds value to the book. More often, however, the name appears at the end.

In this connection, it's worth mentioning an odd and unexplained phenomenon. Almost invariably, and even though there may not be another style indication anywhere in the ms., the signature on the preface, foreword, or introduction will be marked for cap and small cap. It's never marked for even small caps, all caps, or italics, and it's rarely unmarked. The mystery is double—what fascination causes this particular item to be singled out for marking? and what universal force impels every author and/or editor to choose this particular style? The answer would be simple if we had one school in which all editors were trained uniformly, but alas, this isn't so—and the mystery remains.

SECOND HALF-TITLE

The second half-title, unlike the first, has a real function—to mark the end of the frontmatter and the beginning of the text, it being considered part of the text. Usually, the frontmatter pages are numbered in a sequence of Roman numerals (i, ii, iii, etc.), enabling the text to be made up into pages independently of the frontmatter, which is more subject to last-minute changes in copy and length. When this is the case, the second half-title is usually considered arabic 1. Some books are folioed all through in arabic numerals.

If a first half-title was set, the second may be an exact duplicate of it. If there's no first half-title, the second may be the book title, or some other material may be used on this page, such as was suggested for page 1.

When the book is divided into parts or books, it isn't necessary to have a second half-title, as its function is performed by the first part-title or book-title. However, when the introduction is considered part of the text, it comes after a second half-title and is folioed in the sequence of arabic numerals. The first part-title, if any, follows.

Part-titles Part-titles fall between chapter opening and title page in emphasis. It's important to keep this order of interest in mind while working on each one. You may prefer to design the part-titles before the title page, but if you do, don't make them so much more emphatic than the chapter openings that there's no room for a still more important treatment of the title. If the title page is done first, it should be enough stronger than the chapter openings to allow for the part-titles to fall in between.

The part-titles may include echoes or reiterations of a title-page motif. This tends to unify the design and enhance the effect of the title page. When appropriate, part-titles may vary considerably to reflect the nature of differing parts. For example, if the parts each deal with a different era, the titles might be designed in the styles of each period. If you do this, the part-titles must nevertheless preserve the unity and identity of the book, even though they're entirely unlike each other. (This is difficult, but not impossible.) Don't overlook the value of part-titles as opportunities to introduce

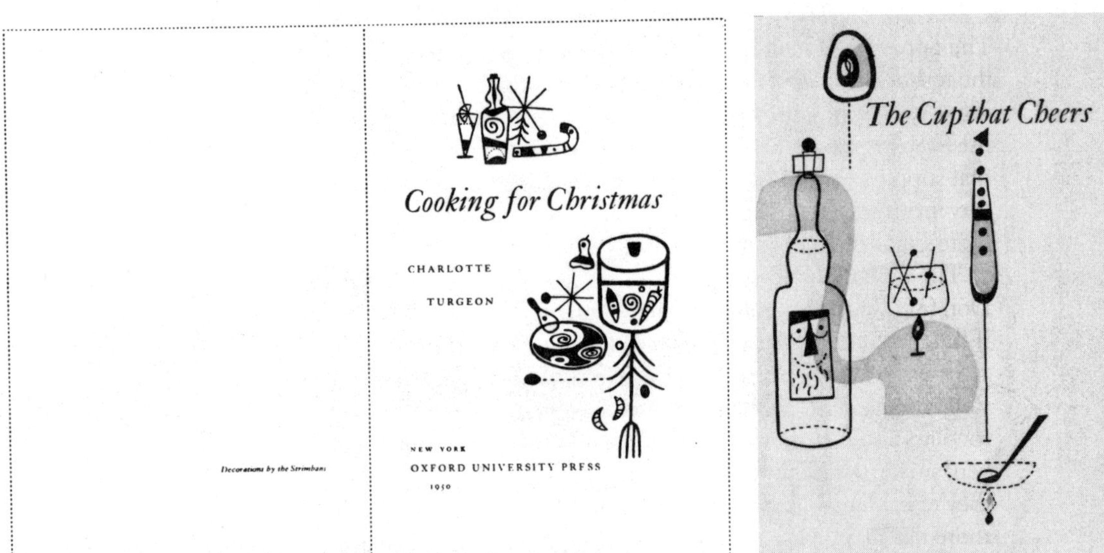

This design by John Begg carries the title-page feeling through the book by using the same type face and size for the title and part titles.

white space when the text is crowded and there's not much space around chapter openings and subheads.

There are usually few practical demands on part-title pages, so they offer great possibilities for the use of imagination in their treatment. In general, the considerations of typography, layout, illustration, etc. that apply to title pages are valid for part-titles as well.

Backmatter

Generally, part-titles are used to separate the parts of the backmatter that are reasonably long—say, six pages or more. Such part-titles may be omitted to save space, but then, if possible, begin each part of the backmatter on a right-hand page. The backmatter, though not part of the text, continues in the sequence of arabic folios.

Backmatter may contain almost any kind of material, but it can usually be encompassed under the following headings, which are listed in the order generally followed:

(1) appendix
(2) notes
(3) bibliography
(4) glossary
(5) index
(6) colophon

The sequence isn't very important. In general, material to which the reader may want to refer should be put at the end, where it's most accessible. If there's an index, it's invariably the last item except for the colophon or a note about the author, if there is one. Sometimes there's a glossary or a list of abbreviations that's used while reading. If these can't be placed at the end, it may be possible to print them on the endpapers.

APPENDIX

The appendix is really a catchall for any material that isn't part of the text or that doesn't fall under one of the other backmatter headings. Appendixes (or appendices, take your choice) may be letters, lists, tables, documents, charts, forms, speeches, etc.—anything that supplements or supports the text. The nature of the copy may vary from straight text to very complicated tabular material, so there's no way to indicate how it should be set.

The design of appendixes must, however, be based on their use. Don't set them very small just because they're not very important. If they're expecıed to be read, make them readable.

NOTES

Reference notes in the backmatter are likely to be of interest to scholars and researchers rather than the reader. They may be set in very small type, since they're not meant for continuous reading. If they're explanatory in nature, they should be set larger and made more readable. Reference notes should be made easy to use, so the subheads and running heads on these pages should be treated as they would be in reference books (CH. 28).

BIBLIOGRAPHY There are some variations in bibliography style, but generally the author's name comes first (last name, first name, middle name or initial), then the book title, publisher's address (city), publisher's name, year of publication. Often, one or more of the last three items is omitted. Sometimes, especially when the bibliography is divided by subject, as in this book, the book title may come first. The first items, whether title or author, go in alphabetical order.

Since there isn't much need for rapid reference in a bibliography, it isn't very important to use a distinctive way of setting the first items. They may be set in small caps, or simply in upper and lower case, with the book titles in italics. It helps to use a deep indent (usually 3 ems) for turnovers.

Bibliographies may be set quite small if necessary, but if the list of books isn't very long, it's just as well to set it in text size, or any other size that's being used elsewhere in the backmatter. Sometimes there's a paragraph of description for each title; these are usually set in a smaller size.

GLOSSARY A glossary is essentially a dictionary. The items should be set so as to stand out from the definitions. Caps can work well, but if the definition lines don't turn over, the caps may look too crowded one under the other. Small caps work better in this case; they're just as distinctive, but have more space around them. Boldface upper and lower case is also satisfactory. Most italics don't make sufficient contrast, and they can become confused with italicized words in the definitions. A colon or dash after the items helps set them off. If the definitions are long, the turnovers may be indented (hanging indent) to help the items stand out. Use a generous indent—at least 2 ems.

There's no need to capitalize the items unless they would ordinarily begin with a capital. To cap all the words eliminates the distinction between proper nouns and others.

INDEX The index is a unique typographic problem because the copy doesn't arrive until after pages have been made up (except when the book is being reset from another edition). Its length must be a guess unless, after makeup, you calculate how many lines will fit in the space available and tell the indexer how many items may be used.

To make this calculation, allow for sinkage on the first page and make a liberal allowance for turnovers (25% should be enough). Thus, if you have eight pages, and there's room for 50 lines per column, with two columns per page you'll have 100 lines per page or a total of 800 lines, less whatever is used for sinkage. If sinkage takes 70 lines (35 lines x 2 columns), there will be 730 lines avail-

abhyāntara vṛitti—that variety of ***prāṇāyāma*** in which the inhaled breath is held at maximal or near maximal lung capacity for as long as possible.

Aham Brahmāsmi—one of the great Vedic utterances used by a meditator as an aid in reaching the supreme state. It means "I am *Brahman.*"

ahaṃkāra—universal ego, of which the individual sense of "I-ness" is a manifestation.

ahiṃsā—noninjury by body, speech, and mind, and the general attitude of welfare for the entire world. It is one of the yamas.

ājñā cakra(m)—the sixth of the seven ***cakras***. It is located in the midbrain and is represented by the thalamus, which is the center of individual consciousness.

a glossary

able. To leave some room for error, drop half of the last page (50 lines), leaving 680. If 25% of the lines are turnovers, there'll be room for 510 items. This might work.

The index doesn't have to be set in large type, but the more legible it is, the better. If necessary, the type size may go down to 7 or even 6 pt., with no leading. If the trim-size is large enough to take three columns of 9 or 10 picas in width, plus about 9 pts. of space between columns, this may be a better solution for a long index. If the index is too short, it may be padded out by using a type almost as large as the text size, with 2 or 3 pts. of leading. Another method is to insert space between the alphabetical breaks. This may be justified somewhat by using large initial letters in the spaces. Rather than making a ridiculously inflated index, it might be better to add a part-title, or find another means of using the extra pages (CH. 24).

The organization of index copy is quite standardized, as there's not much choice. The problem is how to indicate the relative value of sub-items, sub-sub-items, etc. by indention, without getting them confused with turnover lines. In a simple index having only one class of sub-items, the main items are flush, the sub-items are indented one em, and the turnovers of both are indented 2 ems. When there are three or four classes of sub-items, each with turnovers, matters become more difficult. However, the problem is purely mechanical and will submit to a little thought aided by some rough diagrams and test settings.

There is a matter of choice in the use of "continued" lines. When sub-items or turnovers fall at the top of a column, some prefer to reset the main item, followed by "(continued)" or "(cont.)" above the first line. This is done mainly when the break comes at the top of the first column on a left-hand page, less often where the break is from a left-hand to a right-hand page (facing pages). The use of "continued" lines isn't vital, and may be decided on the basis of available space.

COLOPHON

In the early days of printing, the colophon was the printer-publisher's signature, usually consisting of a trademark and some information—his name, address, patron, date, etc. This material became separated when the functions of printer and publisher divided. Today, the publisher's name and address are called the imprint, the logo or trademark is often called the colophon, and sometimes a paragraph of information about the book's design and manufacture is called a colophon also. The imprint and logo now appear on the title page, while the descriptive colophon—which contains the name of the designer, printer, etc.—is usually put on the last page, although it sometimes appears on the copyright page. In most books there's no descriptive colophon at all. In some, it appears as a rather precious survival. There is, however, a proper place for a straightforward colophon in books of such quality as to justify pride on the part of all concerned with their making.

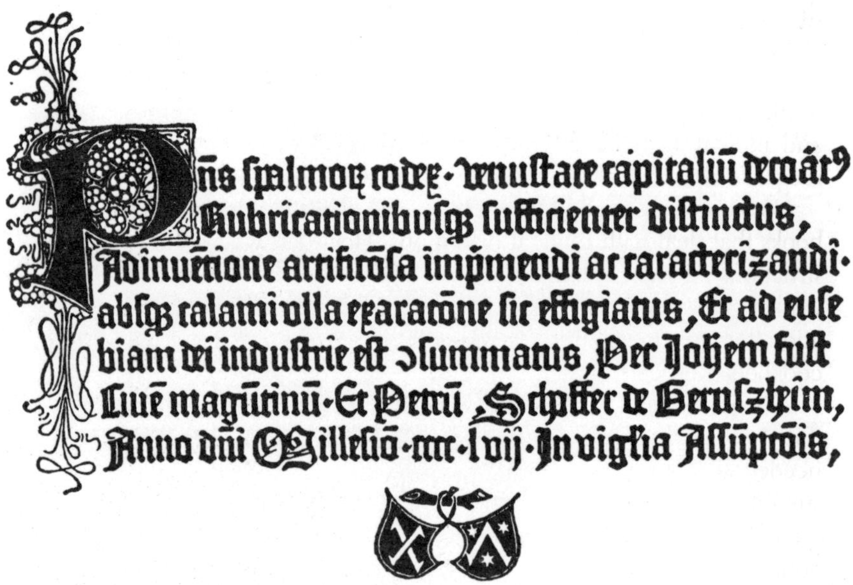
Pn̄s spalmorꝝ codex · venustate capitaliū decoratꝰ
Rubricationibusqȝ sufficienter distinctus,
Adinuētione artificiosa imprimendi ac caracterizandi·
absqȝ calami ulla exaracōne sic effigiatus, Et ad euse
biam dei industrie est ꝯsummatus, Per Johem fust
Ciuē maguntinū · Et Petrū Schoffer de Gernszheim,
Anno dni Millesiō · cccc · lvij · In vigilia Assūpcōis,

The colophon in Fust and Schoeffer's Psalter of 1457.

28. Special design problems

Discussions of design so far have been, with a few exceptions, about books in general, but there are categories of books with specific and unique problems that need to be discussed. Some of the most commonly encountered categories are dealt with in this chapter.

Cookbooks

Some of the cookbooks published each year are narrative in form and present no special problem. We are concerned here with recipe books, which have design problems unlike any other.

Cookbooks are used in basically the same way as other "how-to" books that deal with manual operations. However, where the instructions in most manuals are referred to less and less as the worker gains experience, in cooking, each recipe is a unique operation that must be followed step by step. It's this feature that makes cookbooks a special design problem.

As workshop guides, cookbooks require: (a) a high degree of legibility, (b) an arrangement that minimizes the amount of handling needed, (c) resistance to soiling, and (d) a format and construction suitable to the book's use. Legibility here means using type large enough to make reading possible while the book lies on a table or counter and the cook stands. This requires 12 pt. or even 14 pt. type in most faces. The leading should be at least 2 pts. and preferably 3 or more. This ideal often conflicts with a need to hold down the number of pages, but it's an important ideal. A large type size suggests a large page size also. True, a large book is less practical where work space is limited, but it's probably better to sacrifice a small amount of space than to require the bending, squinting, and handling caused by small type.

The handling a cookbook gets in use can be reduced by putting the complete instructions for each recipe on a single spread. (The book isn't doing a good job if, in the middle of a crucial sentence, the cook must turn the page with greasy or floury fingers or else suffer a culinary disaster.) It's difficult to achieve such an arrangement, especially if the text is crowded. It's almost impossible to manage without shifting recipes around. Such shifts are easiest to make in the ms., so the ideal situation is a page-for-page arrangement by the author that provides practical breaks. But this may not always be the answer; shifting the sequence of recipes is impossible when they're in alphabetical order, and sometimes extremely awkward when they're arranged by subject. Also, with such an arrangement it's usually difficult to avoid wide variations in spacing to achieve pages of uniform depth. However, there's really no reason why the pages *must be* uniform in depth, so this isn't a problem.

To avoid having to flatten the pages while the book is lying open on a table, the text should be kept well out of the gutter. A gutter margin of ⅞" (2.22 cm) is the minimum, and more is better. A mechanical binding enables the book to lie perfectly flat, which eliminates this problem, and, since the book can also be folded back all the way, this saves space too.

The text paper for cookbooks should be as dark as possible, consistent with readability, to minimize the effects of soiling. The standard buff or tan available in many lines is satisfactory, although any other color of suitable value and intensity (low) may be used. When using tinted stock, remember that the type must be chosen with consideration for the lower contrast between ink and paper. Lighter colors, even the regular off-whites, are satisfactory if the paper is waterproof or water-resistant so that it can be cleaned. Truly washable paper is too expensive for most cookbooks, but some water resistance is found in all plain papers, even the least expensive (CH. 11). Materials used on the covers of cookbooks should and can be washable (most washable materials are relatively soil resistant anyway, which is good, since few people take the trouble to wash them). The cost of plastic- or resin-impregnated materials is often not significantly greater than others, and pure vinyl, which is impervious to water and most other liquids (CH. 13), is in the medium range of binding material prices. Lacquer coating and plastic lamination—both liquid and sheet—protect pre-printed covers, although they're not always entirely satisfactory (CHs. 13, 29).

There are other important special factors in the design of cookbooks, such as the need for structural strength, ease of reference, etc., but they're not peculiar to cookbooks, being considerations in all instructional manuals (see "Reference books" below).

Art books The challenge in art books is to present the pictures in the best possible way without sacrificing too much in the layout and typography. In some books, however, the text is primary and the illustrations are merely adjuncts, as in many histories of art. These illustrations are informative rather than representative (CH. 7), and such books are not art books but books about art.

Where the purpose of the illustration is clearly representative, the closer to actual size (of the original picture) the reproduction can be made, the better—so, in principle, the larger the book the better. However, there's a point of diminishing returns in making books larger, in relation to reading convenience, shelf space, and manufacturing economy. The practical limit is about 10 x 13" (25.4 x 33 cm). Art books can be, and are, made larger, but to warrant that, the disadvantages of such size must be outweighed by some vital consideration. Usually, the consideration is a desire to make a big splash. That's a good enough reason if: (a) the retail price can stand the much higher manufacturing cost (in large sizes, many bindery operations no longer fit on machines and must be done by hand), and (b) the book consists almost entirely of reproductions, so that reading inconvenience is a minor factor. (There are cynics who doubt that the texts in art books are read at all.)

The large size of even an average art book page creates typographic difficulties. A 36-pica line of 11 or 12 pt. type has about 85 characters—which is more than enough (CH. 5). On the other hand, 36 picas isn't much on a page of, say, 9" (22.9 cm) width. Esthetically it can be made to work, especially if the arrangement is asymmetrical, but it may not provide enough text on the page. One alternative is double (or triple) column makeup

Books in which full-page pictures are faced by a descriptive text present a problem when there's a large variation in the amount of text. If most units of text are short but some are long, the typography must accommodate the large units and will look awkward with the small ones. Rather than using very small type to get the large units on one page, it might be better to run the text over at the back of the book (as in magazines) or to the following page. The latter will work only when the text will make an odd number of pages. Another possible solution is to continue the runover text at the bottom (or top) of the new text that follows. This can be done only where the next unit of text is short enough to fit on the page with the runover material. Otherwise, the new text will have to run over, and so on and on.

Putting all the text in one section and all the pictures in another has two advantages: (a) each section may be printed with the process and paper most suited to it, and (b) the pictures may be arranged without having to fit them to a text. From an editorial standpoint, this arrangement isn't very satisfactory, as the reader can't conveniently see the pictures while reading the relevant text. However, this is a very economical arrangement for coproductions (CH. 36).

A basic creative problem in art books is the relationship of the style of design to the style of the art in the book. There are three alternatives: the design may be: (a) unrelated to the art, (b) related to the period of the art, or (c) related to the spirit of the art. Period design is probably the least valid solution, except where the subject *is* a period or style of art. In books on the work of a particular artist or school, it's more reasonable to reflect the spirit and character of *the work* than the time in which the work was done. A dynamic and radical artist who lived during a conventional era would be badly served by a period treatment, just as a traditional artist living today would be misrepresented by a radical design. Something can be said for using a moderate contemporary style for all art books, thereby avoiding the hazards of choosing an appropriate expression in each case. Such a solution is definitely indicated in omnibus works, such as a museum or private collection, in which there's no single style or character.

Poetry The problem of style in the design of poetry books is very much the same as for art books—only more so. Again, unless the book is an anthology with no single style, the significant feature to which the design should relate is *the essence* of the poet's work. The need for harmony between the design and the character of the content is especially vital here because poems aim for direct communication between the psyches of poet and reader, so the designer must be very careful to avoid a false note that might break the spell. An entirely neutral design is virtually impossible, as *some* character will become evident in any work in which so many choices are made, so it's better to try to make appropriate choices, and fail somewhat, than to try to be neutral and arrive accidentally at something unsuitable. Here too, it's the nature of the work that's important, not the period in which it was done. This doesn't mean that place or period style elements shouldn't be used, only that such features are secondary to the main one—the spirit of the individual work.

As a practical typographic problem, poetry is unique, but there are several variations, depending on the form of the poems and the organization of the book. The latter is largely a question of whether the poems run in or begin on new pages. If there are so many poems that they must run in, the only associated problem is how to break stanzas at the end of a page. It's best not to break them at all, and full advantage of the available space should be taken to avoid such breaks. If this fails, keep a minimum of two lines on both pages. Beyond this point, breaking is a matter of judgment in individual cases. Each poem is a unique problem—especially the less formal modern poetry. However, formal or not, a poem is a delicately balanced work, and its physical arrangement is very important.

When the poems begin on new pages, breaking at the end of the page can be controlled somewhat. Make a line count of each poem, estimating turnovers as accurately as possible (CH. 21), and tabulate the counts. Choose as a maximum number of lines per page a figure that won't frequently result in breaks two or three lines from the ends of poems. For example, if most poems have fewer than 36 lines, only a few have between 37 and 40, and the remainder have well over 40 lines, then a 36-line page will create very few problems. On the other hand, a page of 34 or 35 lines might create many. A similar procedure is useful in avoiding turnovers on the width. Ideally, all lines in poetry should be printed exactly as written, with no turnovers due to accident of page size. This isn't always possible, but it should be attempted by making the text page the maximum feasible width. There is no excuse for using a measure too narrow to accommodate the longest lines of poetry until the margins have been reduced to the limit. This limit will depend partly on the nature of the poems. Where they consist mainly of long lines, the right-hand margin should be somewhat larger than is necessary for poems with only occasional long lines. The latter require no more than about ¼" (.64 cm) on right-hand pages and about 9⁄16" (1.43 cm) on left-hand pages. For poems with mostly short lines, a small outside margin and a fairly large inside margin on right-hand pages are necessary to bring the main body of type out of the gutter toward the middle of the page. On left-hand pages there's no such problem, as the short lines will fall naturally on the outer part.

To determine the most suitable measure, calculate the width of the longest lines and the shorter long lines to arrive at the number of characters in the average long line. Ideally, the measure should accommodate the average long lines, leaving only the longest to turn over. If all lines will fit, so much the better, but try to avoid a measure that will result in frequent one- or two-word turnovers.

Poetry is by nature aligned at the left, so it doesn't lend itself to centering. The only way it can be centered is optically, which is very awkward if there are any long lines. Such a situation presents two alternatives: (a) breaking the long lines, which isn't acceptable merely to achieve centering, or (b) moving the type mass to the left to accommodate the long lines, which is no longer centering. Good design respects the essential form of the material rather than forcing it into an unnatural arrangement. For most poetry, this means alignment at the left.

Some poets use typography to convey meaning. In typescripts, it's important to watch for indentions, groupings, or other arrangements that are meant to be followed exactly in setting and makeup. These are sometimes indistinguishable from vagaries due to irregular typing, so it's a good idea to check with the editor where special requirements are suspected. In some cases, the words may be arranged in curved forms, etc. (this has been done by Apollinaire, e. e. cummings, Norman Mailer, and others). Such graphic forms can be achieved readily with electronic layout programs.

In books of poems that don't run in, the type area varies in shape,

I had read and thrown.
Oh, but not to boast,
Ever since Nag's Head
Had my heart been great,
Not to claim elate,
With a need the gale
Filled me with to shout
Summary riposte
To the dreary wail
There's no knowing what
Love is all about.
Poets know a lot.
Never did I fail
Of an answer back
To the zodiac
When in heartless chorus
Aries and Taurus,
Gemini and Cancer
Mocked me for an answer.
It was on my tongue
To have up and sung
The initial flight
I can see now might –
Should have been my own –
Into the unknown,
Into the sublime
Off these sands of Time
Time had seen amass
From his hourglass.

42

10

THE QUESTIONER

WHEN EVENING bows its head so does the farmer,
I have seen him do it, haggard with sweat and fatigue
As he limps his way home to the daily chores,
I have been the man myself.

I have come to the lane that leads off toward the barns
And leaves the fields, and the streams of growing,
If one can think of earth as a moving tide
Where the flow is vertical.

I have stopped at the gates where maples lean on my shoulder
As confidential friends with nothing to say,
Staying to keep me company while the sunset
Squats on a burning hill.

Is this really the way it looks or is it seeming,
A distortion of the eye to fool the heart,
Collector of imitations, but still believing
It does not beat for nothing?

This is what I ask myself, is there a ledger
That adds this work and sweat to my account?
I know I do not fill my barns with dreaming,
But what's the accounting for?

visually centered poetry—short and long lines

poetry pages with structural order

96

LITTLE OLD LETTER

It was yesterday morning
I looked in my box for mail.
The letter that I found there
Made me turn right pale.

Just a little old letter,
Wasn't even one page long—
But it made me wish
I was in my grave and gone.

I turned it over,
Not a word writ on the back.
I never felt so lonesome
Since I was born black.

Just a pencil and paper,
You don't need no gun nor knife—
A little old letter
Can take a person's life.

97

CURIOUS

I can see your house, babe,
But I can't see you.
I can see your house,
But I can't see you.
When you're in your house, baby
Tell me, what do you do?

width, and depth on each page, so the problem is to achieve a sense of order and continuity. For this purpose, it's important to establish some constant relationships. Aligning the poems flush left helps by creating a uniform left-hand margin. Placement of poem titles and folios in a fixed relationship to the beginning of the poems is effective. By setting these units flush left or slightly indented from the left, a structural order is created in the upper left corner of each page. The poems then become variations on this order, rather than a chaotic succession of unrelated forms. Order can be achieved also by the use of recurring devices, such as rules, ornaments, etc., and it helps to use strongly positive typography—large or bold titles and/or numbers.

Plays

The question of style in designing books of plays, as in poetry and art books, is better resolved in favor of the spirit and essence of the work than its period. This approach has been used in stage productions with some notable successes, such as modern-dress versions of old plays, although indiscriminate use of contemporary style and dynamics is just as bad as blind use of period trappings based on date of composition.

Typographic considerations in play composition begin with the question: For what use is the volume primarily intended—for reading or for performance? When the book is to be used by actors, the text should have a greater degree of legibility than is otherwise necessary. The performers should be freed as much as possible from the need for close attention to the type, so that they may use their minds and bodies for acting. For example, consider the type used in television prompting. If half the size were used, the effort required to read it would distract the performers and diminish their effectiveness. The same principle holds for a performing copy of a play. True, the book isn't used during a public performance, but it *is* used for tryouts and other occasions during which the actors should be at their best.

Not only must the text be very legible in a performing edition, but there should be more emphasis on the names of the characters, as it's important that the actors quickly find their own lines. This means that the names of speakers should stand out clearly, with both typographic style and position contributing. It makes little difference whether the speaker's name is abbreviated or spelled out. The performers will identify their parts with whatever is used, once they have seen it. Indeed, an abstract symbol for each character might be less distracting and more readily recognized than a name. Particularly on a first reading, actors might have an easier time if they knew that their lines were preceded by a triangle or a circle rather than an unfamiliar name.

Where the conventional identification is used, there are several alternatives. If all the speeches are long, centering the speakers' names may work. However, if there are some short speeches (less than half a line), centered names are very awkward—practically, because the eye must shift repeatedly from center to left and back again; visually, because the centered names frequently will hang out in space with no type directly under them. Also, where the speeches are brief, the lines occupied by the speakers' names become a very large percentage of the total, and add substantially to the length of the book. This is true even when the names are flush or slightly indented from the left on separate lines. The most satisfactory solution then is to place the names at the beginning of each speech.

With the name on the first line of the speech, it's important to make it visually distinctive. The usual method is to use caps, small caps, or caps and small caps. Boldface is effective also. In performing editions, it's helpful to further set off the speakers' names by adding a colon, dash, or space at the end. In reading editions, a period is sufficient. Italics are not a good choice, as there's often italic within speeches (sometimes at the beginning). Then too, italics are generally used for stage directions. It's helpful to indent turnover lines, but this device can't do the whole job because it's not available where a succession of single-line speeches occurs.

Sometimes a distinction must be made between: (a) stage directions for the actors (*enters left*, *laughs*, etc.) and (b) information for the reader (setting, time, background of action, etc.). The relative emphasis will depend on whether the edition is for performance or reading.

Anthologies

The special problem in anthology design is that there's usually very diverse material to be set in a single typographic style. It's often quite difficult to devise a heading arrangement that will suit all the selections. The style chosen must create unity, yet it must be flexible.

A practical procedure is to set a sample page using the most complicated selection heading, and then have the editor mark up the rest of the headings, keying each element to one of those in the sample. When the headings of the selections vary drastically, it may be necessary to make an individual layout for each one.

Reference books

To a certain extent, all books are tools, but a reference book is entirely a practical instrument and its design is concerned with the problem of use almost to the exclusion of anything else. This doesn't mean that reference books can't be handsome. On the contrary, a particularly well-thought-out reference work is likely to have a distinct functional beauty, even if no conscious effort was made toward that end.

There are basically two kinds of reference books: (a) those that give facts and (b) those that give instructions.

■ **Fact books**—The main consideration is ease of locating items, so running heads and/or folios are of primary importance (CHs. 24, 25). Some readers are not inclined to use running heads or folios, so subheads and alphabetical indicators should be made prominent also. In directories, encyclopedias, and other reference books in which the user will be reading brief passages, the text type may be quite small, particularly where two-, three-, or four-column composition results in a narrow measure (CH. 5).

■ **Instruction books**—These are essentially the how-to books. In design, they follow most of the principles applicable to cookbooks, combined with those indicated above for other reference works. Learning requires effort, which most people tend to avoid, so the instructional book should be designed to *appear* simple in organization even if it's not. The designer should study the ms. until its organization is thoroughly understood. Only then is it likely that it can be made understandable to the reader.

It's particularly useful to give the various classes of headings and subheads contrasting treatment. The more nearly similar they are, the more confusion arises. Distinctly different treatments in typeface, size, space, position, and/or weight create a reassuring sense of order. Ample space around subheads, charts, etc. reduces the forbidding aspect of a page of difficult text. Don't design professional-level technical books without consideration for the readers' comfort, on the premise that since they *must* read the book, why bother to make it easy. This is unfair and, in the long run, impractical.

Textbooks

Textbooks are one of the major subdivisions of book publishing, but they're not really a separate category of book design, although, as close collaborations of author, editor, designer, and illustrator, they're unusual in the method by which they're created. It's true also that schoolbooks sometimes have features not often found in other books, such as tests, summaries, explanatory notes, etc., but these are typographically not much different from similar material used elsewhere. Essentially, textbooks are functionally reference books, and their editorial and mechanical problems may be approached accordingly.

The schoolbooks with the most special character are those for the elementary grades, especially the earlier ones. The design problems in these books are not so much different from instructional material for adults as they are more acute. A greater effort must be made to simplify and present material effectively. Illustration, color, particularly legible typography, and careful layout are required. These devices are just as useful in adult books of instruction, but they're not often used because they're thought to be unnecessary. In any case, the principles are the same: all available graphic devices must be used to achieve maximum clarity and arouse maximum interest. The latter is thought to be more important in books for children, because motivation is weaker, but this is true only in the sense that schoolchildren are *required* to learn what is in their books, whereas the adults who use instructional material are only those who have decided that they *want* to learn the subject. However, learning is a chore at any age and at any level of motivation, so textbooks should always be made as interesting as possible.

The specific design problems for the various kinds of textbooks can't be covered in detail here. In many respects, the material encountered will be similar to the various kinds discussed in CHs. 24, 25, but some situations will be so unique that their solution must be devised without the aid of anything but previous experience with the same or similar matter, if you have had any such. Always, the basic principles of design apply—analyze the problem, consider possible solutions, select the best one.

29. Binding design

In bookmaking practice, the binding design is customarily dealt with while the rest of the work is in progress, but it hasn't been mentioned until now to avoid interrupting the discussions of text and illustration.

Binding is given attention first in the creative visualization (CH. 22). Then some specifications on which to base a cost estimate are provided, probably at the time of making the basic decisions (CH. 23). Ideally, the actual binding design is made immediately after the sample pages, title page, etc. are designed, so that the entire book will be planned in one period without interruption or lapse of time. Unfortunately, it's rarely possible to work this way, but the main benefit of the procedure—a unity of concept—can be realized through the initial visualization. In any case, the general outlines of the binding design should be established by the present stage.

To understand the problem of binding design (which refers to all features of the book other than the planning and printing of its pages) it's necessary to realize that a book's binding has several functions.

The functions

Originally, the only purposes of a binding were to hold the pages together and protect them. The sheets were sewn together along the folded edge, and wooden boards at the beginning and end of the book were held in place by leather thongs joined to the threads holding the pages together. Later, the boards were covered with leather or vellum, which extended around the spine to conceal the threads.

Books were handwritten and were precious objects at that time (about the 9th century in the Middle East and parts of Europe), so they were decorated—usually with gold tooling, sometimes with inlays of semiprecious or precious stones. The decoration served only an esthetic or devotional purpose, except for its possible value in the marketing of a particularly handsome volume to a prince or merchant. The books were generally religious in nature and the binding designs, as well as the illuminated pages, were acts of glorification. (If they were sometimes acts of vanity we shouldn't object, since the results are so glorious.) However, if binding decoration was not at first of practical value, the techniques developed then were useful when they became needed a thousand years later.

highly decorated medieval manuscript book cover

Until printing spread through Europe in the 15th century, books were so few in number it was unnecessary to have titles on their covers for identification. The contents of manuscripts were well known to their proud owners or custodians. When books became numerous, the binding acquired an additional function—identification of the content. By the 19th century, competition among publishers resulted in the decoration of book bindings to attract buyers, so the binding then had four distinct purposes:

(a) construction,
(b) protection,
(c) identification, and
(d) attraction.

Now there's a fifth function. The binding must be *expressive* of the content. With the technical facilities available today, it's possible to create virtually any graphic effect on a book binding, so the binding design can be integrated with the design of the text to produce an expressively unified work. It's now possible to raise book design to a level of expression comparable to other ancillary arts, such as stage design and theater music.

VARIATIONS

The functions of binding apply not only to the casebound book, but to paperbacks and mechanical binding, although not in exactly the same way. To these variations must be added the matter of the jacket.

■ **Jackets**—The introduction of book jackets has complicated development of binding design in particular and book design in general. In a sense, the jacket is a superfluous cover, performing some of the functions which should, and could, be performed by the real cover of the book.

Having begun life as a plain paper wrapper meant only to prevent soiling (it was called the "dust jacket"), the jacket was given a sales role in the 1890s when the marketing of books became more aggressive. Publishers wanted to apply the then new techniques of advertising design to their books, but it was not technically possible to achieve the desired effects on book covers, nor were there many artists capable of such design working in the book field. The solution was to use the wrappers as posters, and call in advertising artists to design them.

jacket of 1897

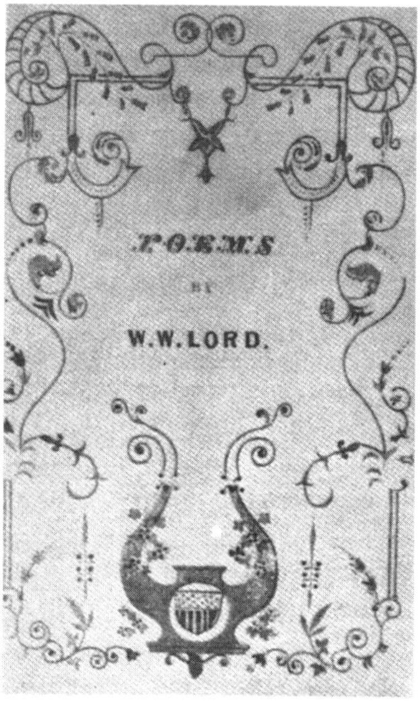

book jacket of 1845

Today, the wrapper isn't needed for its original protective purpose. The application of plastics to binding can provide adequate resistance to soiling and abrasion. Indeed, schoolbooks have preprinted covers and no jackets. The jacket's role in identification and attraction, and its ability to be expressive, are now well within the technical possibilities of the book cover. In fact, a book with a jacket actually has two covers. That this is unnecessary is demonstrated by the paperbacks. These have no jackets, sell to a considerable extent on the attractiveness of their cover designs, and provide less protection for their pages than any unjacketed hardbound book. Even though there are no flaps, a place is found in paperbacks for advertising copy.

Why then do jackets continue to be used? For one thing, by the time they became unnecessary they were a "tradition"—and traditions die hard. More significant is the legitimate doubt that covers can succeed in serving the poster requirements of a jacket and also be consistent with the character of the book. Certainly it's easier to design a jacket or a paper cover for maximum display effect if there's no need to integrate it with the design of the text. This fact, combined with a few relatively minor advantages, such as their value in library display and their usefulness in showing favorable comments, etc., will probably keep jackets in use for a long time to come, despite their anomalous role. Ironically, it seems that few people remove them after purchase. Coincidentally, the design of jackets has improved greatly since its early days, so keeping them on the books is less unreasonable than it was. (Here's a useful tip: used books by famous authors—particularly first editions—may bring high prices with their jackets and almost nothing without them.)

■ **Paperbacks**—For paperback binding, the standards of construction and protection are somewhat lower. For the other three functions—identification, attraction, and expression—paperback covers can, and often do, perform superlatively, although, as on jackets, the expressive function is sometimes slighted.

■ **Mechanical binding**—Mechanical binding is used when its particular structural features are required. As for identification, attraction, and expression, it functions the same as any external cover or jacket (mechanical bindings rarely have jackets).

Functional factors

Each decision in binding design must take into account all the functional factors. However, it's useful to think of the binding design elements in terms of the individual functional problems for which they're the solutions.

The manufacturing processes and materials are described in CH. 13. Binding costs in general are discussed in CHs. 13, 14. Here we deal only with the influence of these factors on binding design decisions.

For visual purposes, the design of jackets, paper covers, and hard covers will be considered different aspects of one problem—cover design. Distinctions are made only when a point peculiar to one aspect is discussed. And, of course, cover design is only one of the visual factors in binding.

CONSTRUCTION

The aspects of construction that most affect binding design are: (a) the method of holding the pages together and (b) the endpapers.

■ **Method of holding pages**—The choice of method—sewing, stapling, gluing (adhesive-binding), or mechanical binding—depends on the nature of the book and costs. NASTA textbook specs require thread or wire stitching for books under ¼" (.64 cm) bulk, those with bulk over ¼" may be adhesive-bound, and over ½" (1.27 cm) books may be Smyth sewn, adhesive-bound, or side thread stitched.

If sewing is used, the choice between Smyth and side stitching will probably be made for you. Side stitching holds the pages together so well that it tends to be difficult to keep the book open, so it's used only where utility and appearance must be sacrificed to strength. Saddle-wire stitching is used mainly for pamphlets, where there's only one signature and a paper cover. Side-wire stitching is probably the strongest and cheapest method of holding pages together, but it's less attractive even than side sewing with thread.

There are several economic advantages in adhesive-binding. No sewing or other considerations prevent folding larger (and thus fewer) signatures. Single leaves may be inserted without the cost of tipping, and the book is ready to be joined to its cover with fewer operations than a sewn book.

It's not price but function that indicates the use of a mechanical binding. With some of these, a book can be made to lie perfectly flat when open, stand up like an easel, or fold back on itself so that it's no larger when open than closed. Others enable pages to be removed, inserted, or changed around. The spiral wire or plastic comb kinds are relatively inexpensive, while the loose-leaf ring or post bindings can cost a lot. In general, mechanical bindings cost more than case binding.

Although function dictates the decision to use mechanical binding, the cost of materials for it is more significant than in other binding methods. This cost varies not only with the trim-size of the book and the kind of apparatus used, but with the book's thickness. For spiral wire and plastic comb bindings, as the bulk increases, the strength—and therefore the weight—of the wire or plastic used must increase also. In fact, it's not generally feasible to use this kind of binding on books over about 1" (2.54 cm) in bulk.

The kind of text and illustration paper used also has a bearing on the choice of binding method (CHs. 8, 11).

■ **Endpapers**—The choice of endpaper from the structural

standpoint depends on the book's characteristics. A book with many pages of heavy coated paper needs a stronger endpaper than another of the same trim-size printed on a bulking antique. A heavy book needs an endpaper of good edge and tensile strength, whereas a reference book needs one with good folding or flexing strength.

These varied considerations could cause problems, but fortunately, all papers sold specifically for endleaves are made strong enough to meet the NASTA standards for textbooks, and very few books require stronger paper. Actually, most 80 lb. (118 gsm), and even some of the 70 lb. (104 gsm), text papers are perfectly safe to use for endpapers in tradebooks of average size where no strenuous use is involved.

The regular white endpaper stocked by the binder is about the same quality as the colored endpapers available, but its price is slightly lower. On an average-sized book, however, the difference is only a few cents per copy. If one of the finer text papers is used, the price difference is greater (if the paper cuts out badly for the trim-size, the difference may be almost double).

Self-lining (pasting the first and last leaves of the text to the boards to perform the function of endpapers) is a relatively weak construction, suitable only for small to average-sized books of which repeated use is unlikely. The advantages are a substantial cost saving and the opportunity to print on all parts of the endleaves at no cost, since these are part of the text sheets themselves. In self-lined books the first four and last four pages are not counted in the pagination.

PROTECTION To protect a book effectively, the binding must be resistant to the ill effects of flexing, abrasion, soiling, tearing, impact, etc. The burden of providing such protection is shared by various features of the bound book: (a) cover material, (b) board, (c) headbands, (d) edge stain, and (e) the jacket.

■ **Cover material**—The most important protective feature of the cover material on a case binding is resistance to flexing and tearing. In both cases, the strength is needed at the joint (or hinge).

Flexing results from the opening and closing of the book. Since the cover material bends each time this occurs, it's necessary to use a material that can stand the probable number of flexings required by the particular book. Certainly a reference book will receive more flexings in its life than a topical work, so the former will require a stronger hinge; but the question of use is somewhat complicated by library practices. A title that might be expected to get no more than one or two readings (say, a novel) may get many times that number in a library—and some libraries will rebind a book upon purchase with a strong "library binding" while others may not.

NASTA specifications settle the question of strength for textbooks. Children's books meant for library use are often given special bindings by the publisher. They are often side stitched and frequently are bound in a cloth up to NASTA specs or better. The problem of hinge strength is given special consideration for reference books, manuals, etc., but for most general books the cover material is selected on the theory that it will be strong enough for normal use, and that libraries will rebind.

Tearing at the hinge generally occurs in the same kinds of books (particularly elementary textbooks) that can expect much flexing. There is little choice of material when NASTA standards are required, but there may be a question when using some papers and plastics. Many of these materials are likely to have relatively better flexing qualities than tearing strength.

Abrasion and soiling are hazards to which all books are subject to some degree. Again, school and library books are most vulnerable, so the materials required for them are made to take considerable abuse. On most books, abrasion is a problem mainly on the bottom edges of the cover, although reference books can expect exceptionally heavy wear on the sides. Any material used for cases should be either dyed-through, to avoid having another color show as the material wears thin, or heavily coated, or both. Soiling is an important consideration in cookbooks and other manuals whose users may have dirty hands (CH. 28). To prevent soiling, materials should be coated or impregnated with a resistant compound such as pyroxylin.

Since (a) the strains of flexing and tearing are only at the hinge and (b) there are relatively inexpensive materials that provide adequate protection for the sides of most tradebooks, it's a common practice to use three-piece covers on such books. A strong, flexible material—usually cloth or plastic—is used for the spine and hinges while a weaker but abrasion-resistant material—usually paper—is used on the sides. A soil-resistant paper can be used at a little higher cost.

If a three-piece cover is made on an end-feed, webfed casemaker in one operation in a quantity large enough to absorb the longer setting-up time (5000 is about the minimum), and there are no special running problems, the cost is about the same as making a one-piece cover. If, for example, a cloth is used for the spine and hinges and it extends the minimum amount onto the side boards (about ⅜"), the cost of the cloth plus a less expensive material on the sides will be less than using the cloth all over. The higher cost of the casemaking will probably not outweigh the cost advantage in materials. If the run is too short to warrant setting up a webfed machine, the three-piece cover can be made in two operations and may still be somewhat cheaper than the one-piece cover, but the cost difference will probably be so small that the loss of time and efficiency might not be justified.

The protective aspects of mechanical-binding cover materials involve only the resistance to abrasion and soiling needed for sides, as the flexing and tearing strains are borne by the mechanical device.

In general, the qualities of book-covering material can be determined by reference to the grade or price range. The decision to use a particular quality for a book should be taken in consultation with the binder or an experienced supplier.

For paperback covers, almost any stock may be used, provided it has sufficient folding strength, tear strength, rigidity, and abrasion resistance. How much is sufficient? This depends on what is expected of the book. If maximum protection is required, a hard cover is the answer. If maximum protection for the price is the object, the answer is the regular 10 pt. or 12 pt. coated-one-side stock usually used, with a plastic coating for extra abrasion and soil resistance.

■ **Boards**—Damage from impact, usually in dropping the book (or in using it as a missile in school), is borne mainly by the boards. If a good-quality and heavy-enough board is used, the book will ordinarily suffer not too badly, but a light board may crumple and the book will probably be ruined. Remember that the heavier the book the harder it falls, so a heavier, tougher board is needed. No material short of textbook specifications is likely to fare well under the stress of severe impact, but few books used outside the elementary schools are likely to receive such blows. *Warping* is a major problem if boards are not rigid enough.

■ **Headbands**—Headbands have no structural value, but they do provide a bit of protection for the spine. In pulling a book off a full shelf, the common practice is to apply pressure at the top of the book near the spine and pull down and out. The headband takes some of this strain, which might otherwise rip the spine.

■ **Edge stain**—The edge stain protects the edges from soiling caused by handling or the accumulation of dust and soot. This concerns mostly the top edge, and it's the top that's generally stained. The other edges *can* be stained, but this would be more for esthetic reasons. An interesting effect is obtained by staining the top and the fore-edge different colors, but this is a relatively expensive operation. Another idea is to color only the fore-edge, but this also costs more than staining the top.

■ **Jacket**—The protective factor in choosing jacket material is important because jackets do get relatively hard use. For most tradebooks, a 70 lb. (104 gsm) text stock is sufficient, although 80 lb. (118 gsm) is better. In coated papers, 80 lb. is the minimum. Heavier books and those that get exceptionally hard use, such as dictionaries, cookbooks, etc., usually get 100 lb. (148 gsm) coated stock. As on paperback covers, a plastic lamination is often added for its glossy appearance as well as its considerable contribution to the jacket's resistance to tearing, soiling, and wrinkling. Even more tear-strength can be added by folding over an extra 2 or 3" of paper at the top and bottom (*French fold*), but this adds substantial expense.

Protection of the book has two aspects: (a) structural—keeping the book intact during use—and (b) preservation of the book's bindery-fresh appearance in the bookstore and warehouse. The jacket isn't adequate for the former but it's of great help in the latter, so its material should be chosen with that function in mind.

A clear jacket of acetate or similar plastic material provides good protection and gives a luxurious, glossy finish to a book, like the cellophane wrapping on a perfume package, but it's not inexpensive. The cost is usually more than that of a four-color process jacket for an average-size book. The cost goes higher as the trim-size gets larger, but goes down for larger quantities. Wrapping books with plastic jackets is somewhat slower than with paper jackets, which adds to the cost. Here the thickness of the plastic is a factor (CH. 13). Also, these jackets have a tendency to become cloudy from the abrasion of normal use and sometimes crack or tear. Despite these drawbacks, a clear plastic jacket is effective packaging, usually worth its cost for books expected to sell on visual appeal—provided there's a really good cover design.

IDENTIFICATION

The strongest visual necessity in cover design is identification. The title, author's name (last name, at least), and publisher's imprint should appear on the spine in any case. Inclusion of the author's first name is preferred by some publishers.

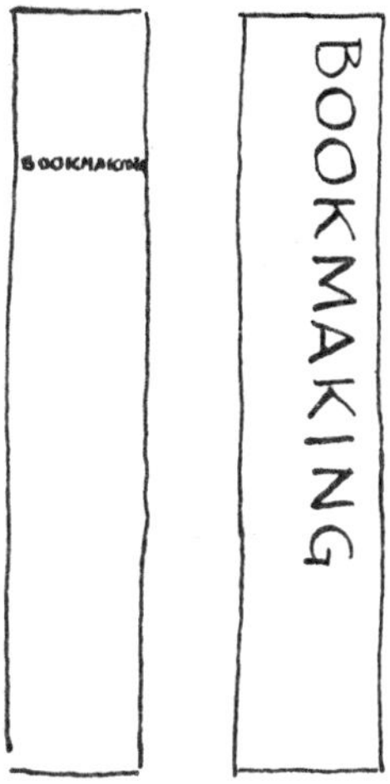

There's considerable disagreement about the title's position on the spine. Some insist that the title read horizontally on all but the narrowest spines. When it must be vertical, the convention in the U.S. is that it read from top to bottom. In England, they prefer the title running from bottom to top. The choice in each case is presumably based on legibility, but several factors affect the legibility of titles on spines, so no one position is best in all circumstances.

All other things being equal, a horizontal line is certainly easiest to read. However, a word that won't fit across the spine in larger than 12 pt. type would be much more legible set vertically in 48 pt. type. This is true of thick books as well as thin ones. Legibility is affected also by the contrast and clarity of the type. A poorly chosen color combination or typeface can kill the legibility of *any* arrangement. Conversely, a change in color can make an otherwise unsatisfactory arrangement work quite well.

Whatever may be said about the relative merits of bottom-to-top vs. top-to-bottom titles, it's a fact that italics and cursives are much more easily read from bottom to top. Roman type run this way is perpendicular to the horizontal, whereas italics are turned considerably less than 90°. When italics run down the spine, they're much more than 90° from the horizontal and require a twist of the neck to be read. Whether this disadvantage is worse than the inconvenience of reading an up title on a shelf of down titles is a matter of choice. The problem can be avoided by not using italics vertically on spines at all.

The need for putting the title and author's name on the front of the book varies with circumstances. They are of prime importance when the book is to be displayed and sold in stores—but this applies only to jackets, paperback covers, and hard covers of books having no printed jackets. When the book has a printed jacket, there's usually no reason to put the title on the front of the cover. The title is considered essential on the front cover of textbooks, not for the ultimate user, but for display at places where such books are offered for sale to school officials.

ATTRACTION For display in bookstores, the cover/jacket design must attract attention and hold it long enough for the title and author to be read. It isn't necessary that the title be the attracting element. A striking illustration or even an effective abstract pattern may be used to catch the eye, while the title itself may be quite small and/or reserved. In such cases, the design must be sufficiently intriguing to lure the shopper close enough to read the title. Occasionally, the title has been omitted entirely, with a very familiar illustration (usually the face of a well-known personality) carrying the entire burden of identification.

jacket designs that depend on illustrations for effectiveness

The competition for attention in bookstores is fierce. Not simply because of the huge number of titles published, but because the percentage of effective cover/jacket designs is increasing. Before the 1970s, outstanding jacket designs stood out in a desert of mediocrity. Today, they're the norm. This is good. It puts publishers under constant pressure to improve the quality of their design.

All this points to two principles: First, the effectiveness of a design is relative to its surroundings—"effectiveness" meaning, primarily, the ability to be noticed, which implies being different from the others. A red cover may be successful if no others are red, but probably not if surrounded by red ones. A photographic design may stand out on a shelf of typographic jackets, but might become lost in a display with all photographic designs. This isn't to say that the designer should strive only to be "different", but design trends should be taken into account, if only to avoid repeating the current fads.

The second principle is that use of the title as the attracting device, while not necessary, is probably best. The title is *the* identifying element—it often has overtones of meaning and association more specific than any illustration or pattern can have. Particularly when it's brief and descriptive (*"Horses"*, *"Play Ball!"*, etc.) it offers graphic opportunities which, combined with its literal meaning, make possible powerful effects. The poster value of the title tends to diminish as it becomes longer and less descriptive (unless it's really odd). On the other hand, when the book is by a very popular author it may be best to emphasize his or her name, and give the

effective use of title

emphasis on name recognition

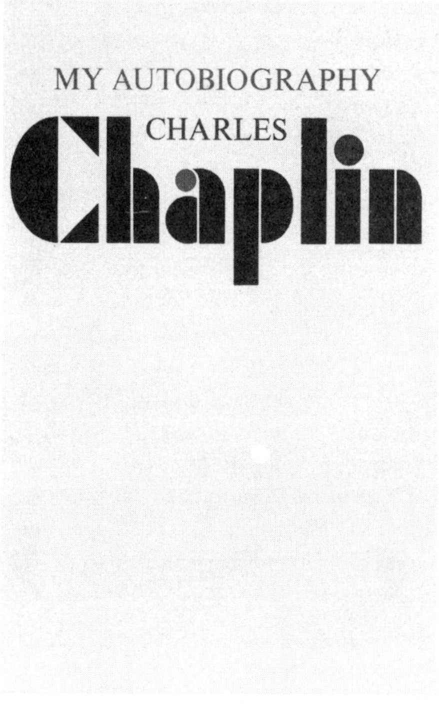

a dramatic use of subject interest

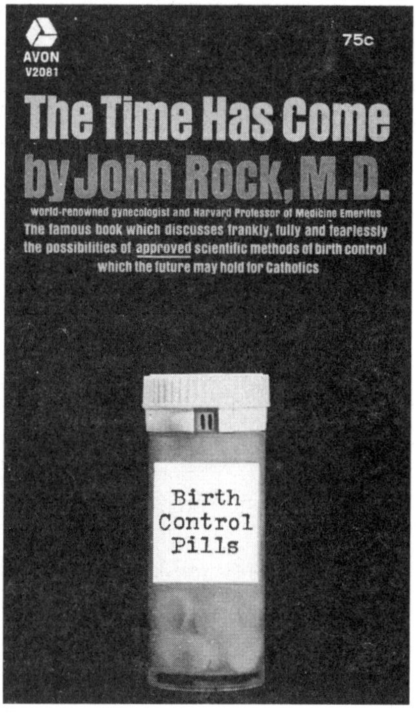

title a secondary, or equal, place. This choice must be made in consultation with the sales and editorial departments.

Don't overlook the element of attraction in designing the spine of a jacket or paperback cover. Most books eventually end up on shelves with only their spines showing—many spend their entire, brief, bookstore lives spine-out—so it's important to make the most of the small space on the spine to catch the browser's attention.

Not to be overlooked either is the large array of dramatic decorative effects used in jacket/cover design—foil stamping, embossing, debossing, *die cutting, spot laminations, holographic images*, and the many variations and combinations of these. They add substantially to cost, but are effective attention grabbers and can be worth the expense. Visit a finishing plant to learn about these techniques.

EXPRESSION Putting the title on the cover is sufficient for selling some books. Titles like *Algebra for Beginners* or *Operating a Drill Press* reveal enough about the book for prospective buyers to decide if they should look into it. On the other hand, a title such as *Out of the Blue* may be about aviation, meteorology, psychology, music, fishing, an unexpected visit, romance, retirement from the Navy, an invasion from another planet, or any number of other subjects, so it's necessary for the cover design to indicate what the book is about.

The cover, as well as the rest of the book, must be a reflection of the text. The degree of literalness or subtlety appropriate is discussed in CH. 22, but it's obvious that the cover design—if it has a sales role—is the place for direct expression. If it has no poster requirement, the principles of expression are the same as for the book as a whole. The elements of a cover involved in expression are: (a) subject, (b) illustration, (c) typography, (d) material, and (e) color.

■ **Subject**—When the cover is used for display, it must not hold the viewer's attention too long. If a browser becomes too intrigued with an intricate design, the time spent in this examination will be taken from the precious few seconds allotted to the book—seconds that could otherwise be spent reading the flap copy or perusing the content. Designs should be general as to the content of the book, but very specific about the subject. For example, a book about exploration of the Pacific Northwest isn't just about exploration, or about exploration of a wilderness in America, but about an expedition by a particular group of people to an area with specific characteristics in a certain period of American history. All these and other salient features of the book's subject should be evident in the design because they give the book its unique character. On the other hand, it's not especially desirable to illustrate an actual incident from the text. This wouldn't reveal any more about the nature of the book, and it might divert attention from further examination. Sometimes, of course, an incident in the book is so graphically dramatic it can be illustrated on the cover with good effect, but even then it should be a simple occurrence that can be grasped in an instant.

■ **Illustration**—If, despite the reservations noted above, you decide to use an illustration on a cover, it may be taken from inside the book or elsewhere. In any case, illustration use follows the principles discussed in CHs. 7, 8, 21, 22. On covers, the purpose is likely to be entirely suggestive, although it may be partly reproductive in the case of art books. The display consideration may affect an illustration's treatment. Indeed, the poster needs of cover design tend to separate the display cover esthetically from the rest of the book, making it difficult to maintain a feeling of unity.

■ **Typography**—Unity is a problem also in the choice of lettering or typography on the cover. A single style should prevail, but the needs of display may indicate a different kind, weight, or size of letter from that inside the book. However, remember that not only harmony but also contrast can create unity (CH. 5).

■ **Material**—The cover and the endpaper materials will be chosen partly on the basis of technical and economic considerations discussed earlier. The visual factors follow the principles indicated in CH. 22 and the visualized conception. Color and texture are the esthetic components of this choice. These may be selected tentatively for their desirability, but the final decisions must take the practical factors into account.

■ **Color**—On paperbacks and hardcover books with no printed jacket, if there's no color in the text, color choice for the cover is entirely open. Where there's color in the text, cover colors should be well related to those already used. Otherwise, any suitable colors can be chosen.

Besides the cover, there are four other binding elements that involve color: endpapers, ink or leaf, edge color, and headbands. These may be used to bridge over a poorly related combination of jacket and binding colors, but in any case, they provide an opportunity to use color for both attraction and expression.

Cover graphics

Production of jackets and paper covers requires no special techniques, but making designs on cloth or other binding materials presents some unique problems.

PREPRINTED COVERS

Printing on cloth, plastic, or nonwoven cover materials is almost always done by offset lithography, so the material must have a surface suitable for lithographic printing. Because of the wear to which book covers are subject, the printing usually gets a transparent coating to protect it from abrasion.

The cost of printing on binding materials is generally more

than printing on paper. Except where very long runs make coordinated webfed printing and webfed casemaking feasible, the high cost of preprinting covers is made higher by the necessity of making the cases on a sheetfed machine. However, no stamping is needed, and, if no jacket is needed, the cost becomes comparable to that of a stamped cover with a printed jacket.

Preprinted covers are relatively economical for short-run titles that would require sheetfed casemaking anyway. The ideal situation might be an edition of fewer than 3000 copies of a fairly small book. The saving in stamping dies would be relatively high per unit and the size of the book would permit the use of paper cover material, thus simplifying the printing (CH. 13). And, if a soft-finish paper were used, a coating wouldn't be needed.

It may be even more practical sometimes to preprint the covers by silk screen (CH. 12), which is suited to short runs and can produce excellent results if suitable copy is used. Also, silk screen ink is wear resistant enough so that no other finish is necessary, and the process can be used on the roughest materials.

This way to bind a small edition of a hardbound book is not much more expensive than a paperback binding. The economic advantages diminish as the quantity increases enough to make webfed casemaking feasible.

A variation of the preprinted cover is a three-piece binding on which a cloth spine is stamped and the sides are preprinted. There is no economic advantage here unless the design permits omitting a printed jacket. However, if the sides are printed in rolls and run with the cloth spine on a web-fed casemaker, this may cost no more than a sheet-fed one-piece preprinted cover.

STAMPED COVERS The stamping processes are described in CH. 13. The cost of stamping depends on the combination of labor and materials used. With several factors to juggle, it's possible to spend a little for a lot, or vice versa.

The labor cost of stamping is relatively uniform per impression. Price differences are in the kind and size of die, and the amount of ink or leaf used. Ink is a negligible cost factor unless an unusually large amount is required. Leaf varies somewhat according to color, but the main difference is between the cost of pigment or metallic leaf and genuine gold.

Labor costs can be held down by reducing the number of impressions. This can sometimes be done by using the stamping press's ability to run more than one roll of leaf at a time. There is room for considerable ingenuity in this area, but there are also mechanical limitations (CH. 13). Before planning this kind of operation, check with the bindery.

Economies in the amount of leaf used can be realized by careful placement of the elements to be stamped. For example, if two small elements in the same color are placed far enough apart so that the leaf can be "*jumped*" between them, you'll pay for only the amount of leaf they use. If they're a little too close, you may have to pay for the leaf covering all the space between—even though it's not used. This could easily be twice as much as the amount actually needed. In fact, if you stamp a border of leaf around the edge of the cover, you must expect to pay for all the leaf in the middle. Again, until you are experienced enough, check with the bindery.

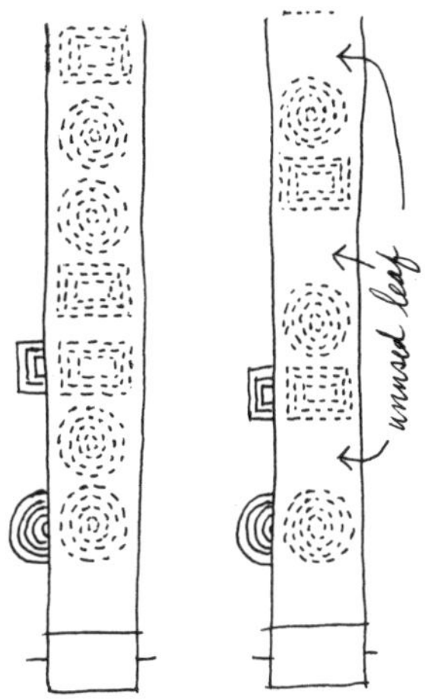

"*jumping*" *leaf*

Don't overlook the value of *blind stamping*. There is no cost at all for materials, and some very handsome effects are possible. True embossing requires expensive dies, but the effect of embossing can be obtained by the use of reverse (negative image) dies (CH. 13). This requires a design that includes the necessary background in a logical way.

In planning designs with leaf, remember that colors are not entirely dependable from one run to another, nor are paper or cloth colors. For this reason, it's not wise to use color combinations of such subtlety that a small color variation will spoil them.

Sketches

There are two reasons why it's important to make very comprehensive sketches for hardcover binding designs. First, these arrangements involve distinctive textures and colors that are usually not subject to adjustment. That is, having decided on a particular cloth, leaf, etc., the designer can rarely make small corrections of color and texture in the proof stage, as there are relatively few choices in these lines. Therefore, it's important to see in the sketch exactly how the end result will look. Second, once a sketch has been approved, the commitment of time and money needed to see a proof is usually so large that a major change due to dissatisfaction with the proof may be impossible, and will certainly be awkward.

The same principles apply to the preparation of sketches for jackets, paper covers, preprinted covers, etc., but with a lesser degree of necessity. The materials are rarely as significant in terms of color and texture as cloth is, and it's usually possible to modify colors without too much difficulty. However, changes are not desirable, and the best practice is to make all sketches as near as possible to the finished appearance. Here it's feasible to make comprehensive sketches by computer, where no special materials, such as cloth, are involved.

■ **Material**—Hardcover sketches should be made the actual size of the book on the actual material being proposed. The suppliers will be pleased to provide sample sheets for this purpose. It isn't necessary to make a cover with boards, etc., as you'll probably have sample covers made later. It's sufficient to trim the material to the size of the front cover plus the spine (see "Camera copy preparation" below). Bear in mind that it's not feasible to stamp in the ¼" (.64 cm) alongside the spine, since this is the hinge (or joint) and there's no board there.

■ **Layout**—The type, illustration, etc. to be stamped should be carefully arranged on paper in position on a same-size outline of the spine and side of the cover. Care must be taken to make certain that the type will fit on the spine. (By this time, the bulk of the book should have been definitely established.) If the sketch is approved, the copy for dies and plates will follow the layout exactly, so it's important to place everything properly.

■ **Transferring the design**—The means of transferring the layout to the cover material will depend on whether leaf or ink is to be used. For ink stampings, rub the back of the layout with a pencil or chalk similar in color to that desired, tape the layout in position on the material, and go over the letters or illustration with firm pressure of a fairly hard pencil. This will transfer a reasonably accurate facsimile. Note that wax-base pencils or crayons won't transfer.

The ink can be made to match the color in your sketch, but the leaf you specify can't be modified, so it's best to use the actual leaf in making the sketch. Samples of leaf may be obtained from the suppliers. To transfer gold leaf, you can use the pressure-sensitive leaf sold in stationery stores. This is genuine gold and is quite expensive but it's very simple to use. Place the sheet of gold underneath the layout face down on the cloth and apply fairly strong pressure with a very hard pencil or stylus on the type or (line) illustration. To apply pigment leaf, or other metallic leaf, heat is required. For this, obtain a tool sold in art supply and hobby shops for burning designs in wood and leather. This is an electric pencil-like device. Place a piece of the leaf face down under the layout and, when the tool has heated to the proper degree, apply light pressure with the point. Until the point is hot enough, it won't release the pigment; when it's too hot, it will burn through the paper. It takes a bit of practice to use this instrument well, but anyone can do it. (Warning: the point of that tool gets *very* hot, so don't leave it plugged in or forget where you put it.) There is another way to apply metallic leaf very easily and accurately provided the cover material isn't too rough. This is done with strips of heat-transferrable leaf available in art supply stores in gold and many colors. The leaf is placed face down on a xerographic copy of the type, and the color is transferred to the copy by ironing the leaf at the proper temperature. To use this for a cover sketch it must be possible to make the photocopy on the cloth—which may not be possible with the material you are using. (The leaf adheres *only* to xerographic copies.)

Blind stamping can be indicated by tracing the design with the burner without any leaf. For larger areas this isn't too satisfactory, and sometimes a better effect is obtained by using a leaf slightly

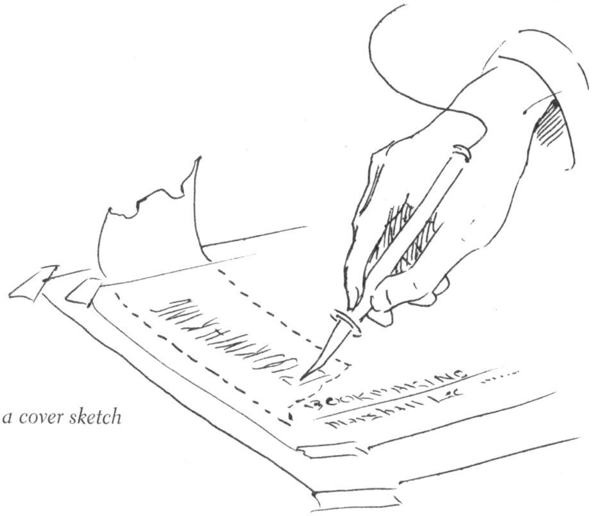

applying leaf on a cover sketch

darker than the material. To indicate colored panels on large areas, find a piece of cloth or paper of the proper color, cut it, and glue it down.

■ **Endpapers**—When colored endpapers are being suggested, get a sheet of the actual paper, fold it, trim it to the trim-size, and glue one page to the inside of the cover sketch. This will leave the ⅛" (.32 cm) borders (*squares*) around the edges of the glued-down half, and will leave the other half free, as it would be in the book.

■ **Edge stain**—This can be indicated by cutting a piece of colored paper the proper size (width of trim-size x paper bulk) and taping it to the back of the free leaf of endpaper at the top. One edge of the "topstain" will then be hinged to the top of the endsheet, so it can be bent over at right angles to it.

When the spine of the cover is folded back at the hinge, a three-sided box will be formed, showing the parts of the binding design in their correct relationship to each other. (The design is actually three-dimensional and shouldn't be judged in only two dimensions.) A length of headband cut to the paper bulk may be taped to the back edge of the "topstain" to complete the sketch.

a cover sketch

Camera copy preparation

PREPRINTED HARD COVERS

The only difference in copy preparation between preprinted hard covers and other kinds of printing is in positioning the copy on the material. For the dimensions of cover material, see CH. 13. About ⅛" (.32 cm) of the ⅝" (1.6 cm) allowed for turn-in, goes around the thickness of the board and the rest is on the inside of the cover. Copy that's meant to bleed at the edge of the cover should extend to ¼" (.64 cm) from the edge of the sheet. This will mean that about ⅛" of the copy will be covered by the endpaper.

PAPERBACK COVERS

The width of the trimmed cover for a flush-trimmed paperback (CH. 13) is the trim-size of the book doubled, plus the paper bulk and the thickness of the covers. Some people add 1/16" (.16 cm) to this to allow for some loss in going around the corners at the spine. The trimmed cover height is the same as the trimmed page size. The untrimmed cover has 1/8" (.32 cm) more on all four sides because it's put on the book before the pages are trimmed. If there are any bleeds, an additional 1/8" must be added to the copy on the bleed side. Be sure that the proper placement of the cover on the book is made clear to the bindery, if the design doesn't do so itself. This is particularly important for the spine.

JACKETS Copy for jackets needs 1/8" (.32 cm) more on top and bottom than paperback covers, because of the overhang of the boards. On the front edge, bleeds should extend at least 1/4" (.64 cm) past the edge, as the bleed should go around the thickness of the cover so that no white paper shows if the jacket isn't accurately wrapped on the book. Copy that bleeds on the back edge of the spine should extend 1/8" past the spine onto the back cover for the same reason. Jacket dimensions for a book of 7 x 10" (17.8 x 25.4 cm) trim-size, 7/8" (2.2 cm) paper bulk, and round back would be as shown in the illustration. See also discussion of cover dimensions under "Casemaking" in CH. 13.

The position of flap and back-cover copy is indicated relative to the front cover and spine. Again, if the position of the spine on the book isn't perfectly obvious, have a proper indication printed on the jacket. Be sure to provide enough space around the title to allow for misalignment in the wrapping. And note that the jacket spine for a round-backed book should be 3/16" (.48 cm) wider than for a flat back. However, it's safest to get a bound dummy to measure, since most books now aren't well rounded.

For both paperback covers and jackets be sure to get a correct layout from the binder and provide a copy for the printshop, so that all parties concerned will be working with the same dimensions. Most printshops that print covers and jackets supply templates that show the dimensions to be added to the trim-size.

CASES Layouts for cover stamping are much the same as layouts for jacket printing, except that only the front cover and spine (usually) are shown, and the layout isn't a computer "mechanical" but only an indication of position on paper. Proofs of the dies are positioned in a layout showing the edges of the front cover and spine, including any division of cover material (CH. 13). The dimensions are as indicated above for preprinted covers, except that there are no turn-ins here. Remember that there's a space of 1/4" (.64 cm) between the spine and the front and back cover boards (the hinge, or joint), in which no stamping can be done.

Making stamping dies is a photomechanical process, so the procedures for preparing camera copy apply (CH. 10). Since dies can be etched to various depths, it's sometimes necessary to indicate the depth desired.

The position of each die is indicated by measurements in inches from an outer edge of the cover and/or an edge of the spine. Where there's more than one impression, use overlays, as in multicolor printing. Dies should be kept at least 1⁄16" (.16 cm), and preferably more, from the edges of the spine. The stamping operation isn't as accurate as printing, and the inaccuracies of casemaking sometimes add to the error. The stamping layout for this book is shown.

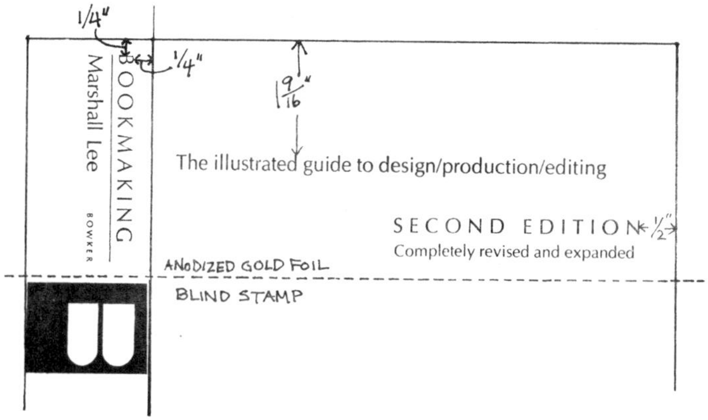

a stamping layout for Bookmaking Second Edition

SAMPLE COVERS

When the binding design has been approved, it's usually important to have the bindery make *sample covers*—which are the equivalent of proofs. Sample covers are made by hand, using the actual materials specified, and are stamped with the dies to be used for the edition. Besides providing a final opportunity to approve or modify the design, they reveal any problems in stamping and materials. If a particular leaf or ink doesn't show up sufficiently or won't take well on the cover material, it's better to find out on sample covers than when the edition is being run. However, sample covers are rather costly to make and they may be omitted when the design is very simple—for example, if the dies are being stamped in gold foil on a smooth black cloth.

Sometimes, alternative colors of leaf or material may be tried in sample covers, but in general, the design decisions should have been made in the sketch stage. Trial and error is uneconomical and, except in unusual circumstances, unprofessional. Besides its value for the publisher, the sample cover is a useful guide for the binder, who uses it as a model for stamping. An okayed cover with any corrections noted serves as the binder's "Master Proof". It should be sent to the bindery with the binding order or earlier.

Production

30. Ordering composition

There are basically two different circumstances in which composition is ordered: (1) a designer, either freelance or in-house, does the composition in the course of doing the design, or (2) the publisher orders the composition from a service bureau or typesetter. Obviously, designers don't "order" composition from themselves, but they do get approval to go ahead with the typesetting only after the publisher's various departments—editorial, production, marketing—are satisfied with the designer's specifications. This isn't really different when the composition is sent outside, except that the specifications are presented to the typesetter as a formal order, whereas the designer already has the specs in the style sheet. However the composition is ordered, the steps leading to the order are the same.

Estimates The sample pages usually contain enough information to enable an estimate of the cost of composition to be made and, with a few additional specifications, an estimate of the printing and binding costs. In most cases, such estimates are required before production of the book may begin.

The style sheet in the layout program contains the essential specifications for the estimator's use. It also provides a record of the specifications and enables the estimator to work while the layouts are being used for composition of the sample pages. When the sample pages are unusually complex, the estimator may need a copy of the layouts in addition to the specifications.

For a discussion of cost estimating, see CH. 14.

SPECIFICATIONS FOR ESTIMATE

Title: ______________________________ Author: ______________ Date: ________

Trim size: _____x _____" Designed for ________pages by ______________________ tel ______________

COMPOSITION

Text type: ____________________ size _______on ______ width _________ lines: full page _____ chap. op ______

Chapters begin: Left or right ____right only ____ runin ______ lines Part titles: backed ____backed blank ____

Part titles: type ______________________________ size _______on ______position ______________

Chapter heads (nos.): type ________________________ size _______on ______position ______________

Chapter titles: type ___________________________ size _______on ______position ______________

Initials: type ______________________________ stickup _____dropped _____ flush_____indented_________

Subheads:

A: type____________________ size:_____on ____ position _______________ pts above _______below ______

B: type____________________ size:_____on ____ position _______________ pts above _______below ______

C: type____________________ size:_____on_____position _______________ pts above _______below ______

D: type ____________________ size:_____on_____position _______________ pts above _______below ______

E: type____________________ size:_____on_____position _______________ pts above _______below ______

Special matter:

Extract: size ______on _____indent_____________ Tables: size ______on _______ ____________________

Lists: size ______on _____indent _____________ Poetry: size ______on _______ indent ______________

Footnotes: size ______on _____indent_____________ Index: size ______on _______ columns _______________

Other ____

Illustrations:

line _____@ _____pp halftone _____@ _____pp duotone _____@ _____pp simple color_____@ ____pp

process color _____@ _____pp ____

Captions: type____________________ size____on _____ position ______________________________

Credits: type____________________ size____on _____ position ______________________________

PRINTING

Offset ____POD ____ Bleeds: yes ____no ____ Color(s)______________________________________

Pages ________Print as ________________________ Print from ______________________________

Quantity ____________ Paper ____________________________________ supplied by: us______ printer_____

BINDING

Quantity ____________Inserts __________Wraps___________Sewing ___________Adhesive __________Endpapers__________

Headbands ____________Stain __________Back ______ Cover: Soft ___Hard ___board _________material _______________

___________________________________ ____Stamping: _______imp. leaf _______sq. in/imp. Ink ________

Jacket: supplied Cover–Soft: supplied Delivery: FOB bindery

Copyediting & keying

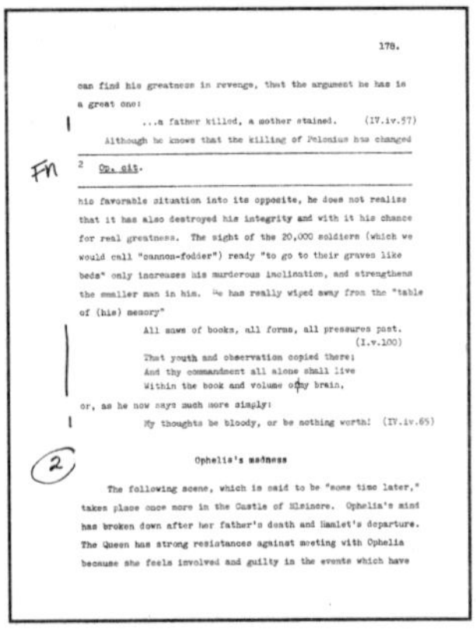
178.

can find his greatness in revenge, that the argument he has is a great one:

...a father killed, a mother stained. (IV.iv.57)

Although he knows that the killing of Polonius has changed

Fn [2] Op. cit.

his favorable situation into its opposite, he does not realise that it has also destroyed his integrity and with it his chance for real greatness. The sight of the 20,000 soldiers (which we would call "cannon-fodder") ready "to go to their graves like beds" only increases his murderous inclination, and strengthens the smaller man in him. He has really wiped away from the "table of (his) memory"

All saws of books, all forms, all pressures past. (I.v.100)
That youth and observation copied there;
And thy commandment all alone shall live
Within the book and volume of my brain,

or, as he now says much more simply:

My thoughts be bloody, or be nothing worth! (IV.iv.65)

(2) Ophelia's madness

The following scene, which is said to be "some time later," takes place once more in the Castle of Elsinore. Ophelia's mind has broken down after her father's death and Hamlet's departure. The Queen has strong resistances against meeting with Ophelia because she feels involved and guilty in the events which have

a keyed ms. page

When the sample pages have been approved by all concerned, the ms. is, presumably, ready for composition, but it it's *not* ready if it hasn't been completely copyedited to correct errors of fact, grammar, and spelling. Such corrections are just as easy to make in the ms. as in proof, where they're expensive to make (CHs. 6, 9, 20).

The copyeditor should also *key* the ms. to the sample pages where this is necessary. The sample will indicate *how* a number 2 subhead is to be set, but it can't tell the compositor *which* heads are number 2, which are number 1, etc. Sometimes the ms. is typed so well that these distinctions are perfectly clear, but that's rare. The best practice is to have every subhead keyed with a number (or letter) in a circle. Extract is ususally indicated by a vertical line in the margin, and any other special material should be identified in the margin by some clearly understood symbol. All markings should be made with a colored pencil. When the copy is very complex, several colors may be used (CH. 19).

Composition orders

No matter how complete the sample page specifications, no matter how well edited and keyed the ms., a written and signed composition order is essential. Compositors are entitled to a formal set of instructions to use in the event there's any misunderstanding—and a misunderstanding is far less likely to occur when there's a formal order. Also, neither the sample page specifications nor the estimate form answer all the questions. When a designer provides the composition, a formal order is just as important. While the designer has all the specs in the computer style sheet, these specs should be made part of the order to make sure that publisher and designer are thinking in terms of the same specifications.

The composition order should note proof requirements, at least for galley proofs (CHs. 6, 24, 25) if any. It should name the authority to be consulted on questions of style, grammar, and spelling—usually one of the major dictionaries (CH. 4)—although a properly edited ms. won't raise any questions other than the manner of breaking words at the end of a line. In this case, the instruction for punctuation, spelling, and other matters of style should be: Follow copy.

All the other information required should appear in the specifications set with the sample pages, except for certain questions of choice in connection with page-makeup which are not included in the composition order because they're subject to change after the castoff (CH. 31). These are discussed in CHs. 9, 32.

In most mss., particularly nonfiction, there are minor composition problems that are not covered by the sample pages, nor is it practicable to give such detailed instructions in the composition order. Also, on initial examination, some points may be missed by an inexperienced designer. The designer should go through the ms. thoroughly before typesetting, to find and dispose of any typographic problems not covered by the sample page or general instructions. Each instance should be marked for style where it occurs. Even where the general style has been established and shown in the sample—say, for tables—there may be unique headings or other material within some of the tables and these must be marked. No detail may be omitted, because *some* style must be used, and there may be a delay if you haven't made a decision before composition begins. Unfortunately, the rapid pace of most book publishing provides too little time for such careful attention, but the best effort must be made.

On the following page is a typical composition order form.

COMPOSITION ORDER

To:__________________________________**No.**____________**Date**__________

Designer__________________________**Tel**______________**email**__________

Title______________________________**Author**_____________**ISBN**__________

Trim size___x___**Est. pages**_____**Margins:** head____inside____**Lines:** full page____chap. op____

Text type__________________ __on___x___picas **Paragraph indent**_____ **Figs:** lining/o.s.

Running heads: left_______________________right__________________________

Folios__________________________**Space breaks**__________________________

Chapters begin: Left or right ❑ right only ❑ **Part titles:** backed ❑ backed blank ❑

Part titles: type___________________________position_______________________

Chapter heads (nos.): type____________________position_______________________

Chapter titles: type_________________________position_______________________

Initials: type______________________________ stickup/dropped flush/indented____

Subheads:

A: type______________________position___________________pts above___below___

B: type______________________position___________________pts above___below___

C: type______________________position___________________pts above___below___

D: type______________________position___________________pts above___below___

E: type______________________position___________________pts above___below___

Special matter:

Extract____

Tables____

Lists____

Poetry____

Footnotes____

Index:____

Other____

Illustrations:

No. line________halftone________duotone________simple color________process color_______

Captions: type____________________________position___________________________

Credits: type____________________________position____________________________

No. Proofs wanted:

Galleys ____pages: !st pass___2nd pass___3rd pass___final file___blues___other_____________

Pagination:

Frontmatter: Text: Backmatter:

Signed__________________

31. Castoff & makeup

Procedure at this point varies with the kind of book, the schedule, and circumstances. It's certainly most desirable to design the entire book—title page, frontmatter, backmatter, binding, and sample pages—at one time and have the maximum opportunity to achieve unity. In practice, however, this isn't always possible. Very often the title isn't yet definite or some part of the copy is incomplete. Pressures may require turning attention to other urgent work. Also, where there are many illustrations in text it's necessary to first determine the exact length of the text—because this will affect the treatment of illustrations and perhaps frontmatter and backmatter as well. This requires waiting until the complete and copyedited text document is available so that a castoff can be made.

The castoff

Since printing and binding efficiency requires having a practical number of pages in a book, which means a number divisible into the number of pages in the forms to be printed (CH. 12), it's necessary to calculate the total number of pages the book will run if set and pages are made-up according to the specifications in the sample pages. If this number shouldn't be a practical one, then adjustments in the layout and/or the specifications must be made.

An accurate castoff can be made on the computer, and that's the customary and probably the quickest method, but it's possible also to make an accurate castoff in the traditional way on paper. This solution is sometimes used for exceptionally complicated books with many illustrations integrated into a text having a lot of subheads and special matter. Designers who undertake the castoff and makeup of such a book on the computer should have an intimate knowledge of, and experience with, the capabilities and requirements of the layout program being used. Otherwise, it might be better to do the castoff on paper and then send the specs to a specialized composition house for the page-makeup to be executed on the computer. Since both methods are available, both are described below.

COMPUTER CASTOFF The author's text document is first edited and corrected, then copyedited and corrected, so that there should be no text changes once production begins. The copyeditor then keys the ms. (CH. 30), assigning code letters or numbers (*tags*) to the various elements of the text, such as heads, subheads, extracts, etc. The tags are given names (e.g., B head) and type specifications, which are entered in the style sheet (CH. 25) prepared when the sample pages were approved. The tags are then entered in the text document in the appropriate places so that the text can be made up into pages automatically.

The designer then refines the specifications for every element of text, deciding the way each situation in the page-makeup will be handled. This means, for example, indicating not only how much space there will be above and below a particular class of subhead, but what should be the minimum number of lines of text following those subheads and what should be done if there isn't room for that number of lines. (See the description of a paper castoff below for a detailed discussion of makeup problems.) When all the makeup specifications are entered in the style sheet, the computer is instructed to do the makeup accordingly (CH. 9).

For a book without illustrations, the page-makeup resulting from this procedure will give an accurate count of the number of pages the text will make if set according to the style sheet (CH. 21). If the book has illustrations, the castoff may be done in one of two ways. (1) The text can be made up without the illustrations, which will give you the number of pages the text alone will make, not the total number. Then a calculation of the space needed for the illustrations—using the sizes allocated in the analysis (CH. 21)—is added to give you an estimated total number of pages. A true count is obtained only when the illustrations are inserted in the makeup. (2) The illustrations, or boxes representing them, are included in the initial makeup. Obviously, this is the more satisfactory method, but it may not be possible if the illustrations are late in coming.

Even with a relatively simple unillustrated book, and almost certainly with an illustrated one, the makeup is likely to encounter unanticipated problems (CH. 9) that will need the designer's judgment to resolve, so the pagination will probably not be entirely accurate on the first pass. Once these problems are fixed, the makeup is rerun and should produce a correct total number of pages.

If this isn't the number wanted, there are a fair number of remedies available. These are discussed in the following description of paper castoffs.

The big advantage of a computer castoff is that when it's completed, so is the page-makeup.

PAPER CASTOFF

If a traditional castoff on paper is to be made, a set of galley proofs is printed. This should be done only when the text document has been fully corrected as described above. To make a castoff of a book of straight narrative text, measure off on the galleys the number of lines to go on each page (or column). First cut a strip of tough paper about 1" wide and a little deeper than the full text page. Lay it down on a galley proof or sample page, and along one edge make a ¼" mark at the base of each text line, up to the estimated number of lines on the text page. Number each mark consecutively, from one at the top, and make a wider mark every five lines. (It's useful to make a special mark indicating the number of lines on chapter-opening pages or any other frequently used measurement.) Using this scale, measure off the pages on the galleys, making a mark where each page ends (see illustration on next page). At the end of each galley, count how many lines remain from the end of the last full page and carry this number over to the next galley. When finished, go back to the first galley and number the pages straight through to the end. (Recheck this numbering carefully, as it's the most frequent cause of castoff error.)

Making an accurate castoff of a book containing many subheads, special matter, and illustrations is similar in procedure, but requires a great deal of care and good judgment. The simple job may be left to an intelligent assistant, but a difficult one is best done by the designer, as many decisions are involved which affect the layout of pages and other significant matters. With a particularly complicated book, it may be necessary to make a dummy (CHs. 10, 26), since a castoff would be too difficult.

KINDS OF CASTOFFS

There are two kinds of castoffs: unjustified and justified.

■ **Unjustified castoff**—This is simply a linear measurement without allowance for makeup problems such as alignment of short or long pages due to widows (CH. 9). However, an unlucky sequence of widows can throw a chapter over to another page by adding several lines, and, if there are part-titles or chapters beginning on right-hand pages, this can materially affect the overall length. An unjustified castoff has value only for a preliminary rough estimation of length.

■ **Justified castoff**—In a justified castoff, the makeup should come out exactly as calculated, which means that all problems must be solved in detail. These include: (a) final determination of the space to be used for illustrations, (b) disposition of odd amounts of space resulting from matter set in lines of various depths, (c) provisions for widows, and (d) disposition of the various problems caused by run-in breaks that fall at the ends of pages. Note that all items, including illustrations, are to be measured vertically in terms of text lines rather than inches or picas or other units of measurement.

the end. (Recheck this numbering carefully, it is the most frequent cause of castoff error.)

Casting-off a book of straight narrative text is fairly simple. Making an accurate castoff of a book containing many subheads, special matter, and illustrations is not very different in procedure, but requires a great deal of care and good judgment. The simple job may

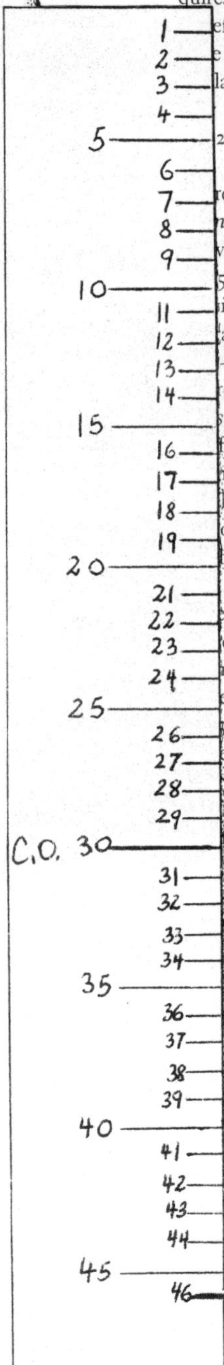

eft to a reasonably intelligent clerk, but a difficult one is best e by the designer, as many decisions are involved which affect layout of pages and other significant matters. With a particu- complicated book, it may be necessary to make a dummy 21) since a castoff would be too difficult.

e are 2 kinds of castoff: justified and unjustified.

njustified castoff—This is simply a linear measurement without vance for alignment of short or long pages due to widows 5) or other makeup problems. However, an unlucky sequence idows can throw a chapter over to another page by adding al lines and, if there are part-titles or chapters beginning on -hand pages, this can materially affect the overall length. For eason, an unjustified castoff has limited value.

stified castoff—To make a justified castoff, use revised galley fs if possible. Unrevised proofs may be used if the corrections ninor and the Author's Proofs are at hand, so that the effect of hanges can be taken into account. A difference of a line or two ome cases a word or two!) may have a serious effect when the ber of pages is very close to the limit.

a justified castoff, the pages should come out exactly as in eup, which means that all problems must be solved in detail. e include: (a) final determination of the space to be used for rations, (b) disposition of odd amounts of space resulting from er set in lines of various depths, (c) provisions for widows), and (d) disposition of the various problems caused by run- eaks that fall at the ends of pages.

treatment of spacebreaks, run-in chapter titles, and subheads fall at the bottoms of pages is a major problem of the castoff. osing, for example, that a number 1 subhead is normally in a space, but the preceding text ends only 4 lines from the m of the page. There are 2 alternatives: either the space d the subhead is reduced so that it, and a minimum number t lines below it, will fit, or the page will be kept short (like nd of a chapter) and the subhead will go at the top of the page. This choice requires policy decisions as to:

How many lines of space may be "stolen" from around the (The space may be reduced to the minimum acceptable visu- ut not less than that of an inferior class of head.)

What is the minimum acceptable number of text lines be- he head? (For most subheads, 2 lines are sufficient, for major ads or chapter openings 3 or 4 may be appropriate.)

If the head goes to the next page, how many lines of space d be left above it? (This is measured in *lines of text*, exclusive running head.)

e same procedure is followed whether the break is a minor d or a run-in chapter. In all cases, the relative value of the must be preserved.

One-line spacebreaks present a special problem when they fall at the bottom or top of the page. Some people prefer simply to omit the space. This solution does eliminate the graphic problem, but it is editorially unsound. The author puts in the line space because he *wants* a break in the text—inferior to a chapter or subhead to be sure, but presumably of some editorial value—and it should be maintained in all cases.

None of the alternate solutions is ideal, and each should be

CASTOFF PROBLEMS

The treatment of spacebreaks, run-in chapter titles, and subheads that fall at the bottoms of pages are major problems of the castoff. Suppose, for example, that a B subhead is normally in a five-line space, but the preceding text ends only four lines from the bottom of the page. There are two alternatives: either the space around the subhead is reduced so that it, with a minimum number of text lines below it, will fit, or the page will be kept short (like the end of the chapter) and the subhead will go at the top of the next page. This choice requires the following decisions:

(a) How many lines of space may be "stolen" from around the head? (The space may be reduced to the minimum acceptable visually, but not less than that of an inferior class of head.)

(b) What is the minimum acceptable number of text lines below the head? (For most subheads, two lines are sufficient: for major subheads or chapter openings, three or four may be appropriate.)

(c) If the head goes to the next page, how many lines of space should be left above it? (This is measured in *lines of text*, exclusive of the running head.)

The same procedure is followed whether the break is a minor subhead or a run-in chapter. In all cases, the relative value of the heads must be preserved.

One-line spacebreaks present a special problem when they fall at the bottom or top of the page. Some people prefer simply to omit the space. This solution does eliminate the graphic problem, but it's editorially unsound. The author puts in the line space because a break in the text is *wanted*—a break inferior to a chapter or subhead to be sure, but presumably of some editorial significance—so it should be maintained.

None of the alternative solutions is ideal, and each should be considered in relation to the running heads, if any. The simplest practice is to retain the one-line space at bottom or top as it falls, but this creates an ambiguous effect. The reader is usually less aware that there's a line space than that the text isn't aligned on the facing pages. When the space falls at the top, it's apparent enough only when there's a substantial running head on both pages. A two-line space may be used at the top, but when there's no running head, even this isn't really enough, particularly if the folding is inaccurate. One solution is to make top or bottom breaks more definite by introducing into the line space some unobtrusive typographic device such as an asterisk, colon, dash, or ellipse. Although this makes these breaks a little more prominent than the others, it's probably better to emphasize them somewhat than to omit them entirely. It might be even better to use a device in *all* spacebreaks, and thus eliminate the problem.

Where illustrations in the text are involved, the allowance of space must include the picture itself, the caption (if any), the space between picture and caption, and the space separating the illustration from the text.

Adjustments for length

When the castoff is completed, you'll know whether there are too few pages, too many, or—with luck—exactly the right number. There are many possible ways of coping with the problems.

■ **Too few pages**—If circumstances permit, pages can be added by: (a) stretching out the frontmatter and/or backmatter, (b) starting chapters on right-hand pages if they began left or right, or (c) making full-page titles (backed blank or not) of the chapter breaks. (This means upgrading the chapter break, and should have the editor's approval.) None of these measures requires a new castoff. Simply renumber the pages.

When none of the foregoing solutions is feasible or sufficient, it may be possible to: (a) reduce the number of lines on the text page (perhaps while increasing leading); (b) reduce the width of the text; (c) reduce the number of characters per line (either by using a different typeface or modifying the word or letterspacing—a change of less than four units is imperceptible but can make a difference in the length of the book); (d) increase the amount of space around heads, illustrations, etc.; or (e) increase the size of the illustrations themselves. In such cases, a new castoff should be made, using a set of revised galleys.

If only a few pages are left over, there's no harm in having a blank leaf or two at the front and/or back of the book. Where the number of blanks is large—say, eight or more—it is usually better to *cancel* them (cut them off the sheet).

■ **Too many pages**—The reverse of most of the above measures may be applied. In some cases, frontmatter can be telescoped by combining copyright notice and dedication, starting a foreword on the back of the contents instead of on the next right-hand page, etc. If chapters begin on right-hand pages, save the preceding blank pages (CHs. 9, 24) by allowing all chapters to begin left or right. Blanks backing part-titles can be saved by beginning the text on those pages. The entire two pages for each part-title can be saved by putting the part-title on the opening of the first chapter. Again, no new castoff is needed.

If these measures are not sufficient or practicable, it may be necessary to: (a) add one or more lines to the text page (perhaps while reducing leading), (b) increase the width of the text, (c) increase the number of characters per line, (d) decrease the space around heads (or even run in the chapters), or (e) decrease the size of illustrations. In most cases, it would be desirable to make a new castoff on a set of revised galleys.

If all the available measures are used and there are still too many pages, it may be necessary to print an additional four, eight, or sixteen pages—an expensive solution, to be avoided if possible.

Page-makeup problems

Most problems have been solved in a justified paper castoff, but there's one remaining—the handling of running heads. The questions are: (a) Should running heads appear on pages that have run-in chapters or subheads at the top? (b) What copy shall be used for running heads? (c) How shall the copy be cut if it won't fit in the space and style provided?

■ **Run-in subheads at top of page**—This issue is largely esthetic. An important factor is the amount of contrast between the running head and the subhead. If they're at all similar in style, they're less acceptable together than if they're very different. Usually, the running head is retained over subheads, but is omitted over chapter titles. Another consideration is the copy. When the running head repeats the title immediately beneath it, the repetition seems needless.

■ **Running-head copy**—The sample pages establish a general pattern, but many books have elements that don't conform. The scheme may call for part-title on the left and chapter title on the right, but what if there should be an untitled introduction after a part-title, or an epilogue after the last part, or some other such problem? There is no stock answer. In each case, the answer must fit the circumstances. Sometimes, the solution may be elimination of one running head; at other times, repetition of the same head on both sides. If the latter is chosen, and the left- and right-hand running heads are set in different styles, which style will be used?

■ **Cutting running-head copy**—This is an editorial function, but the designer should minimize the necessity for such cutting by choosing a style that provides for a large number of characters. In a book with long chapter titles, don't set them in letterspaced caps. If titles *must* be cut, tell the editor the maximum number of characters available.

The solution of makeup problems is helped by printing out the page or pages involved as you go along, in order to easily compare and relate them. This provides some of the layout advantages of a dummy. Where a dummy has been made, makeup is a routine matter of following instructions (CH. 9)—assuming the dummy has been properly marked (CH. 26).

Page proofs

In books of mainly text, there'll be little to check in page proofs other than running heads, the handling of run-in breaks, folios, and the makeup of chapter-opening pages. The latter can be a problem when uniform sinkage is desired. The number of text lines on the opening pages may vary because of run-in breaks or widows. It's important that instructions are provided for the disposition of space in such cases. It's usually best to maintain the sinkage and the space between items of display, letting the space between the display and text vary as necessary. Where chapters begin on right-hand pages only, it's possible to maintain all of the spacing, letting the foot margin vary. This won't be noticed since there's no facing full page.

Design changes Design changes in pages (other than changes needed to adjust length) should involve no more than minor adjustments of space, improvements in letterspacing of display lines, and occasional refinement of layout. Drastic changes are not to be taken lightly. Any major changes should have been made in sample pages. Indeed, one of the marks of a competent designer is the ability to achieve the objective in one try. Extensive and/or numerous changes in proof indicate that the designer is unable to visualize clearly or is unable to translate the visualization into effective specifications. The economics of book publishing are not suited to such deficiencies. True, first-rate work requires more care and effort than the ordinary product, and truly great work often needs to be fussed over and refined repeatedly, but few books that are published can support this kind of treatment. Generally, the designer must utilize the available time and energy to develop a concept of the book and improve its preparation. Once production is under way it must continue without major change, or the book will suffer serious consequences in cost and schedule.

32. Ordering prepress

There is no substitute for personal contact with the person(s) responsible for your job at the service bureau or prepress house. Establish communication with someone who will answer to you throughout the job. Observe the following procedures and practices:

(a) Before submitting the artwork or files, discuss your goals and describe unusual aspects of the job, technical specifications, and proof and final output requirements.

(b) Be absolutely sure that your specifications for proofs and output accord with the needs of the printshop to which the work will be going.

(c) Ask questions.

(d) Anticipate problems and correct them in advance.

(e) Keep on top of the job.

Selecting a service bureau or prepress service

Your selection should satisfy three criteria: quality, service, and economy. Comparison shopping can turn up differences that will help you make a selection. It may be most efficient (in both cost and effort) to work with two different specialized bureaus—one for black & white, another for color. To help determine if a service bureau is appropriate for your needs, ask these questions:

(a) Is the equipment (scanner, imagesetter, etc.) it uses right for the kind of output you need? Ask for a few test pages from your files to check for compatibility problems.

(b) Is it accustomed to working with the type of documents you have? It may be great at high-resolution color output but not experienced with complex impositions. Some shops are not as comfortable working with Windows files as with Mac (or vice versa).

(c) What kinds of clients does it have? If its business is mainly with advertising agencies, for example, it may not be used to book work. It may be generally efficient, but a service bureau with steady book business will have developed procedures to facilitate the processes you need.

(d) Is it able to handle the programs used in your files? Some service bureaus may not be able to use files from certain drawing or layout programs.

(e) Does it have the fonts you used, or will you have to provide copies of them? Samples of test pages should reveal such problems.

(f) What kind of removable storage media does it support? All service bureaus work with Zip and Jaz disks; inquire about the portable drive cartridges or other media you may have.

(g) What are its quality-control procedures in terms of chemical replenishment, equipment calibration, film density, etc.? Maintenance of high technical standards is essential for consistency throughout a job.

(h) How much responsibility will it assume for problems that may be inherent in your file, or for hardware/software conflicts?

(i) Are its scheduling procedures acceptable? What is normal turnaround compared to rush service? Describe your job and ask for a complete schedule.

(j) How does it charge? Services have different billing systems. Some bill by the hour (or minute), others per page. Ask about billing for situations like troubleshooting and file repair. Ask about a cutoff limit on time-charged jobs when you would be called for further instructions.

(k) Will it provide references to clients with jobs similar to yours?

Submitting files for prepress

Your order should have at least the following information:

(a) name and version of the program in which the files are prepared;
(b) names and formats of the files you want to have output;
(c) fonts used (supply copies on disk);
(d) size, line screen, and resolution of images to be scanned;
(e) kind of color for separation: process or spot;
(f) resolution, size, and kind of output: paper or film (positive/negative);
(g) proofs required: blueprints, Matchprint, Chromalin, color keys, etc.

Most printshops require an electronic data form that includes the above information. See sample form opposite.

It's important to provide a dummy or printout with the disk submitted (CH. 10). If mechanicals instead of digital files are submitted (CH. 10), the first three items listed above will, of course, be omitted from the order. Include in the order any specific instructions needed to facilitate accurate translation to film or plates.

Before the final files are sent to the prepress house or printshop they should be carefully checked in detail (*preflighting*). This is customarily done by whoever prepared the file—the designer or compositor. If preflighting is left to the prepress shop to perform, the responsibility for error nevertheless remains with the preparer. There are several preflighting programs available, but preflighting isn't easy to do properly. It shouldn't be undertaken by someone inexperienced.

Prepress houses and printshops generally convert final files they receive to PDF format (CH. 6), but many shops expect to get the files already converted, thus reducing not only their costs but their risk of responsibility for error. If you refuse to do the conversion (which isn't simple), they will do it, but charge for their service.

ELECTRONIC OUTPUT REQUEST

DOCUMENT

Filename: Last modified:
Document Size: Kb QuarkXPress versions:
Total Pages: Page Width: Page Height:

REQUIRED XTENSIONS:

ACTIVE XTENSIONS:

DOCUMENT FONTS:

EXTERNAL NAME INTERNAL NAME PRINTER FONT FILENAME

PICTURE FONTS

PICTURE EXTERNAL NAME

GRAPHICS (EDGE VALUES MEASURED FROM TOP-LEFT OF PAGE.)

NAME

TYPE PAGE SIZE BOX ANGLE PIC ANGLE SKEW XSCALE YSCALE TOP EDGE LEFT EDGE DPI TYPE

PARAGRAPH STYLE SHEETS

H&JS

COLORS

TRAPPING (UNLESS NOTED, COLORS ARE TRAPPED AUTOMATICALLY)

Trapping Preferences Information:
Trapping Method: Absolute
Process Trapping: On/Off
Auto Amount: pt

Indeterminate: pt
Knockout Limit: %
Overprint Limit: %
Ignore White: On/Off

COLOR PLATES

33. Ordering paper

Choice of paper should be made in consultation with both paper supplier and printshop; many judgments are involved and the specialists can be of great help. In ordering paper, knowledge of the factors should be sufficient, but it's such a complex system that it pays to check your calculations with the paper supplier, even if you think you have the right answer.

Papermaking is no longer the art it was when it was done by hand, but neither is the manufacture so precise that it can be depended upon for perfect uniformity. Some variations of color, finish, weight, etc. may occur from lot to lot—or even in different parts of one lot—and cause trouble. To a certain extent this must be expected and accepted, but when the acceptable limits are exceeded, a complaint is in order. At such times (and many others), it's very important to be dealing with a reliable merchant. But always consider that difficulties with the paper may be due to faults in the pressroom as well as in the mill or warehouse.

Calculating quantities

When buying book paper in sheets, determine how many pages will *cut out* of (divide into) each sheet (a sheet has double the number of pages in each form) and divide this into the total number of pages in the book to get the number of sheets needed per book. Multiply this figure by the number of books to be printed and add a certain percentage of the total for *spoilage*. This percentage varies according to the number of colors, difficulties of printing, and length of run. Most of the spoilage occurs during the trial and error of makeready. On short runs (3000 to 5000), this may be 5 to 7% per color, on long runs perhaps 3 to 5%, depending on the printing problem. The extra paper provided should allow for some spoilage in binding too, usually about 3%. The printshop and bindery should be asked what they require for spoilage in each case.

Example: An edition of 5000 copies of a 256-page book, trim-size

5⅜ x 8" (13.7 x 20.32 cm) being printed in 64-page forms, with two colors on each form.

(a) To print 64-page forms of 5⅜ x 8" requires a sheet size of 44 x 66" (111.8 x 167.6 cm).

(b) One form of 64 pages on each side of sheet = 128 pages per sheet.

(c) 128 pages per sheet requires 2 sheets for a 256-page book.

(d) 2 sheets per book x 5000 books = 10,000 sheets.

(e) Printer's spoilage @ 5% per color x 2 colors = 10%, plus binder's spoilage of 3% totals 13%.

(f) 10,000 sheets plus 13% (1300) = 11,300 sheets to be ordered.

The same method applies when ordering paper for jackets or for any other purpose.

The size of the sheet required should always be discussed with the printshop because the sheet must fit one of their presses, with allowances made for grippers, bleeds, guides, etc. Also, they may be planning to print 2-up and will need a correspondingly larger sheet.

The procedure for ordering paper in rolls for webfed printing or binding machines isn't very different. The size of the form is determined from the size of each page or unit, and this decides the width of the roll. Either dimension of the form may be used for roll width, depending on which way the grain is to run on the page. The other dimension of the form is multiplied by the number of impressions to be printed and doubled (each form is backed up) to get the length of the roll needed. To this amount is added spoilage.

Thus, if the book used in the preceding example were being printed on a webfed press in a quantity of 50,000 copies, it would probably be printed with two 22" (55.9 cm)-wide webs running together, each with an 8-page form on both sides, or 16 pages per web. Here is how the paper needed is calculated:

(a) To fold properly, the grain must run the long way of the page, so the 8¼" (untrimmed) would run the length of the roll.

(b) Each web has sixteen forms of 8 pages, backed by 8, with 2 pages per form along the roll length. Thus, every 16½" (41.9 cm) of length of the two rolls will contain 32 pages. 50,000 x 16½" = 825,000" (209.6 m).

(c) So, each 32 pages requires 825,000" of paper 44" wide. For 256 pages, multiply 825,000" by 8 to get 6,600,000" or 550,000' (167,640 m).

(d) Spoilage of 10% (web spoilage generally runs higher) makes a total of 605,000' (184,451 m) of paper x 44" needed.

Actually, except for lightweight papers, rolls are usually ordered by weight rather than length. To calculate the weight needed, simply find the sheet size and figure as though ordering sheets (but add the extra web spoilage).

When paper is ordered from stock, the exact amount required

will be delivered. When the paper is made to order, it's not possible to be sure of the quantity because the paper machine runs so fast it can't always be stopped at precisely the point desired, and spoilages in the various papermaking operations are unpredictable. The smaller the amount made, the larger will be the percentage of variation. Paper trade customs provide that the customer must accept and pay for a certain percentage more or less than the amount ordered, or elect to specify "not more than" or "not less than" a certain quantity. In such cases, the percentage of variation one must accept is considerably larger than otherwise. In large quantities, the percentage of variation (*overrun* or *underrun*) isn't likely to be serious—perhaps 1 or 2%. On very small orders, say 1000 lbs., the amount delivered may be as much as 20% more or less than was ordered. (Only a few mills will even make orders so small.)

It's easy to make a serious arithmetical error in calculating paper quantities, and even the most experienced people get a trifle nervous about ordering large amounts. Although the paper suppliers check your figures, they may make the same mistake you made (and the responsibility is yours), so use this simple practical test: Take a book of about the same size and kind as yours will be and weigh it. If it weighs 1 lb. and you are making 5000 books, you know that you should be ordering about 5000 lbs. of paper. (The hard cover on the book will account for spoilage and then some. For a more accurate result use a paperback.) This won't show up a minor mistake, but you'll certainly know that you shouldn't be ordering 500 or 50,000 lbs.

Calculating cost The price of book and cover paper is based on weight. For each brand and grade of paper there's a sliding scale of prices per pound according to the amount ordered, with the lowest prices for the largest quantities. The range is considerable, the highest prices being two or three times as much as the lowest, so it's vital to know the exact amount of paper needed. A small difference in quantity can shift the price into another bracket and make a difference of 15% or more. Because of this, it's quite possible for a larger amount of paper to cost less than a smaller amount.

The price brackets vary somewhat according to the item, but the most commonly used are: 1 carton, 4 cartons, 16 cartons, 5M lbs. (2268 kg), 10M lbs. (4536 kg), 40M lbs. (18,144 kg) (*carload*). (M= 1000.) The amount of paper in a carton varies according to the size and weight of the sheet, but it's usually about 150 lbs. (68 kg). Large quantities may be bought on skids or may be packed in cartons at a slightly higher price.

A price list will give prices for each bracket and show the M weight and number of sheets per carton for each size of sheet in stock. Thus, if we are buying paper for the book described in the above example, the table will show that there are 500 sheets per carton for the 44 x 66", 306M, 50 lb. basis (CH. 11). We had calculated that we should be ordering 11,300 sheets, which divided by 500 is 22.6 cartons. This puts us in the 16-carton bracket (16 cartons to 5000 lbs.). If the price per pound is $.3160 (the price is usually given per 100 lbs., but it's easy to move the decimal point), to know the total cost it's necessary to know how many pounds are needed. So, if 1000 sheets weigh 306 lbs. (138.80 kg), then 11,300 will weigh 11.3 x 306 or 3458 lbs. (1609.37 kg). Multiply this by the cost per pound, $.3160, and you have the cost of the paper—$1092.73. If a making-order is involved, there could be additional charges for special size, finish, grain, or color, or a variation due to an underrun or overrun. (Very lightweight papers also carry a price penalty because of the extra fillers needed for opacity.)

While the base price of paper made to order is no higher than stock paper (if the quantity is sufficient), remember that the color or finish may not come out exactly as hoped for, there may be an overrun to pay for, or the delivery time may be a problem. Worse yet, a strike or accident may make it impossible to deliver the order at all. Also, there could be a problem if a reprint is needed in a quantity too small to warrant a making-order. If the printing is sheetfed and there's a stock size larger than the sheet required, there's only the cost of extra paper and cutting it but the problem could be serious if no larger size is made. The same would be true of a roll order.

Against these considerations may be weighed the advantage of having a special color or finish, and the money saved when a made-to-order size prevents waste that would occur if a stock sheet were used. For example, if the page size of a book is 5¾ x 9¼" (14.61 x 23.5 cm), and a standard 38 x 50" (96.52 x 127 cm) sheet is used, a strip 3"x 38" (7.62 x 96.52 cm)—and 8% of the paper cost—would be wasted. This can be saved by having the paper made 35 x 50" (88.9 x 127 cm).

Selecting paper

It might seem more logical to put "selecting paper" ahead of "ordering paper", but to make practical selections it's necessary to know the problems of paper buying. For example, unless a making-order is feasible, availability may have as much effect on paper choice as price and preference. Where price is a consideration (and it usually is), it's much easier to choose between a half-dozen possibilities if you can roughly calculate the prices yourself.

The selection of paper involves esthetic factors (color, texture, etc.) (CHs. 22, 23), but the first consideration must be suitability to the technical requirements of the printing process being used.

■ **Offset lithography**—For process color or halftone printing it's best to have maximum contrast between the color of paper and ink. Most papers are made with halftone printing in mind, so they tend to be relatively hard of surface and bright white. In some lines, fluorescent dyes are used to increase the brightness. For books in which the halftones need not dazzle, there are off-white papers available (such as this one).

Any standard paper will take 133-line screen, and most sheets will handle 150 well. For 175-line and finer screens, a matte-coated stock is best. Perfectly good halftones—and even process color—can be printed on papers with embossed (raised) textures.

Most books are printed on 50 to 70 lb. paper, with 50 lb. (and occasionally 45 lb.) antique used for books with very many pages, and 70 lb. (and occasionally 80 lb.) for those with few. In general, trade publishers like as thick a book as possible (CHs. 2, 23) up to the point where there's no longer much sales advantage and it becomes desirable to keep the paper cost down. However, if the use of bulky paper fails to produce the thickness wanted, it may be necessary to increase the weight. Some illustrated books with a high retail price may use 100 lb. or heavier paper to get enough bulk, since they need a matte-coated or full-coated stock for reproduction quality. In books of very many pages, the lighter weights of paper are used, but it's best to use a more calendered finish to reduce bulk rather than extremely light weights. The latter are not only expensive, but they cause difficulty in printing, especially in large sheets, so many printers charge a penalty for handling paper below about 40 lb. basis weight.

Opacity is related to weight and is usually affected by bulk. Bulking antiques have good opacity, because the light is scattered by the loose construction, and heavier weights have better opacity due to more fiber and/or filler, although a heavily calendered 60 lb. stock may be less opaque than a bulky, loose-fibered 50 lb. sheet. Two sheets of the same weight and finish may vary in opacity if their ingredients differ. Papers coated on both sides are very opaque because of the density of the two layers of clay. Coated-one-side stock, which is usually used over an opaque surface (labels, jackets, etc.), tends to poor opacity because the base stock has very little. Opacity is important in books with halftones or with pages of irregular layout in which type or illustrations back up areas of open space.

■ **Xerography**—Although some copying machines that use xerography require paper coated with a zinc oxide compound, others can use plain papers. The sophisticated xerographic printing machines used for ultra-short-run book printing (i.e., print-on-demand) use standard book papers, although with some limitations of weight and sheet size. These limitations are subject to change as the machines are developed, but at this writing weights are generally limited to 50 and 60 lb., and sizes range between 5 x 8" (12.7 x 20.32 cm) and 8½ x 11" (21.6 x 27.9 cm). The choice of papers is limited to the few items stocked by paper suppliers for the POD printshops.

■ **Silk screen**—Any paper can be printed.

34. Ordering printing

The book is ready to go to press when: (a) all proofs have been finally corrected and approved; (b) the plates, if any, have been made and checked for quality, errors, and damage; (c) the paper is on hand; and (d) the printshop is in possession of complete instructions and a written, signed order to proceed. To arrive at this point, it's necessary to select a printshop. (Note that in the U.S., almost all specialized book printers are also binders, but this is less so abroad.)

Selecting a printshop

In choosing a plumber or shoemaker, the only considerations are competence, reliability, and prices, plus your personal convenience and preference. Presumably, any one of many plumbers or shoemakers can do what you require. When selecting a printshop, all of these considerations apply, but in addition you must find a shop equipped with the plant and experience to match the specific job in question. Printshops vary tremendously in the kind of work they can do—and do well.

A place with one desktop laser printer is a printshop and so is one with a dozen four-color web-offset presses with synchronized folders. If you need 300 letterheads, the first place is the best one for you. Should you want 100,000 copies of a book illustrated with color photography, it's strongly recommended that you select the second place. The economical printing of any job requires selection of a printshop specializing in that kind of work. The laser printer shop *could* print your book, and the shop with the web presses *could* print your letterheads—but in both cases the cost would be astronomically higher.

Until you've had enough experience to find the right printshop yourself, it's best to ask the advice of an expert. A direct approach to a shop may be successful—if that one happens to be right for your job or refers you to a suitable one. However, there's always the chance that the shop will take on the job even though it's not a good choice for it; they may need the work badly or may not know enough to realize that another shop could do the job better.

There are many considerations involved in matching printshop to job. The main ones are:

(a) the *kind* of presses (offset lithography, xerographic),
(b) the *size* of presses,
(c) the *number* of presses (capacity to produce),
(d) the kind of work done,
(e) the quality of work,
(f) the quality of the plant and equipment,
(g) the schedule, and
(h) the prices.

The printing order

All the information needed by the printshop should appear on the printing order except for details relating to individual pages, and at least a reference to those details should be included. For example, if it's necessary to provide a dummy giving individual margins for each page, the printing order should have a note indicating that such a dummy is being supplied. This ensures that no directions will be overlooked because they're separate from the order.

The printing order should constitute both the official instructions and the official authorization for doing the job. The latter requires only: (a) a statement to the effect that the job is to be done according to the instructions therein, (b) the number of copies to be printed, (c) the place to which the printed sheets are to be delivered, and (d) the buyer's signature with the date.

The instructions should be complete, and it's best to use a printed form, if only to be sure that nothing is overlooked. On page 442 is a sample form that could be used for any kind of printing. Bear in mind that the printing order is a purchasing order; it should have a number and be treated in the same manner as other financial records. It should be accompanied by a copy of the cost estimate.

DIFFERENT KINDS OF PRINTING

There are basic differences between ordering offset lithography and xerography. When ordering offset, the job is ordinarily ready to go on press using plates produced in a prepress or print shop. In xerography, there are no plates (CH. 12), but the final file must be sent to the printshop with the order.

In both cases, send with the order—for general information and, where necessary, matching—a set of final page proofs and okayed proofs of any illustrations. If there's a dummy, that should be delivered also, to give the shop an idea of what the finished job is supposed to be like.

In ordering the printing of jackets or paperback covers, a proof should be provided with marks indicating where the printed sheets are to be trimmed.

INFORMATION REQUIRED

Regardless of the method of printing, the dimensions of the job—trim-size, basic margins, total number of pages—must be clearly indicated. For offset printing, add any pertinent information about binding, such as the placement of wraps and inserts. Although the printshop will get the imposition from the binder, providing the primary information is extra insurance against error. In xerographic printing, since all pages are printed on single sheets, there are no wraps or inserts.

Unless the printshop is supplying the paper, information about the paper to be provided should include its name, size, weight, quantity, source, and delivery date. This enables the printshop to make direct contact with the supplier in case of any trouble with the stock while on press. Although the paper for sheetfed printing is ordered by weight and number of sheets (CH. 11), the printshop's records are usually kept in *reams*, so it's best to indicate the quantity that way on the printing order. Parts of reams are expressed in fractions, using twentieths as the unit (1 ream = 500 sheets, 200 sheets = 8/20 ream).

Ordinarily, the choice of kind of plates to be used (CH. 12) is left to the printshop, unless special publication plans might affect the decision. If possible, the printing of separate sections of illustrations should be done after the text is off press. This enables adjusting the illustration run to the actual net number of text sheets—which may be somewhat more or less than the quantity ordered.

INK COLORS

On printing orders, specify the color(s) of ink to be used. If there's to be a color other than black, provide a PMS number (CH. 8), or a substantial swatch to match, or specify a standard ink that can be ordered by the manufacturer's number. Swatches should be at least two square inches and solid in tone. Watercolor or pencil swatches that vary in color are difficult to match. The ink should be specified as transparent or opaque, and, where appropriate, the sequence in which the colors are to be printed should be indicated (CH. 8).

ARCHIVING FILES

The files from which a book is made are a valuable asset for a publisher. The printshop may accept responsibility for archiving the final files supplied to them for producing the book, but it's wise for the publisher to maintain an archive with copies of these files, as well as any supporting files needed to create and/or modify them. Most often, the printshop is supplied with PDF or PostScript files. These are adequate for producing an exact reprint, but since they can't be easily edited, the publisher should keep copies of the document and image files from which they were made, so that the book can be easily updated or modified for other uses. There are several *Digital Asset Management* (DAM) software systems for organizing, indexing, and storing files. These large and expensive systems are common in the larger publishing houses but are generally beyond the means of the smaller ones. Smaller publishers can create their archive by recording the files on CDs or other stable media or by arranging storage with their printshop. Failure to archive these files in *some* way wastes a valuable asset.

PRINT ORDER

To: ______________________ No. ____ Date:__________
Title: ______________________________________
Author: ___________________________ISBN__________

TEXT:
Trim size: ___ x ___" Pages: _____ to print as: __________
Print from: ______________________________________
which you'll receive from:__________________________
Contact: ___________________________Tel: ___________
Margins: inside ____ head (after trim) ___Quantity:__________
Get folding imposition from:_________________________
Bleeds: yes/no Color(s): ____________________________
Paper:________________ size _______ weight _______
qty____________ from________________ due _______

ILLUSTRATION INSERTS
No. pages: ______ as ______________________________
Placement: _______________________________________
Color(s): ____
Paper:________________ size _______ weight _______
qty____________ from ________________ due _______

Show book blues for OK before printing to:
_________________________Tel:__________________
e-mail:____
Send _____ sets F & Gs when ready to:_________________
Deliver sheets to: _________________________________
to be at destination by: ____________________________

PAGINATION*
page
( ) ______________________
( ) ______________________
( ) ______________________
( ) ______________________
( ) ______________________
( ) ______________________
( ) ______________________
( ) ______________________
( ) ______________________
( ) ______________________
( ) ______________________
( ) ______________________
( ) ______________________
( ) ______________________
( ) ______________________
( ) ______________________
( ) ______________________
( ) ______________________

*Order of parts of book by page

ARCHIVING
Return all disks with blues to:

____

Signed: ______________________________

A sample print order form.

35. Ordering binding

The binding order

Like composition and printing orders, the binding order is both instruction and authorization. The order sometimes indicates that only part of the printed edition is to be completely bound. If so, specify what is to be done with the sheets being held. Most binders prefer to hold sheets in the form of folded, gathered, and sewn books, partly because it's more economical to do these procedures for the whole edition at the same time, and partly because it's more convenient to store the unbound books that way than as flat sheets.

The order should contain instructions for the disposition of the bound copies—how they're to be packed, whether they're to be held at the bindery or shipped, and if shipped, to where. Here, too, a printed binding order form saves time and reduces the likelihood of important omissions. A typical order form appears on the following page. Don't forget to provide an authorized signature with a date.

Unless the bindery and printshop are parts of one company, to prevent a mix-up, indicate on the binding order where the printed sheets and jackets or covers are coming from. This enables the binder to act directly when there's a delay or discrepancy in shipment.

The items listed on the sample order form are generally self-explanatory, but there are a few points worth mentioning:

(a) Where illustration inserts, wraps, and/or tips are not clearly identified by captions or folios, it's best to order a set of folded and gathered sheets for checking and then give instructions for their placement.

(b) Presumably, your dies and jacket or cover were made to fit a bulk calculated from the paper bulking tables or derived from a dummy. As there's considerable latitude in smashing (CH. 13) antique book papers, if you specify on the binding order the bulk you want, the smash can be adjusted accordingly.

(c) Provide a color swatch to match for the edge stain, if any.

(d) Attach a printed copy of the jacket indicating how it's to be placed on the book. This is best done by marking the point on the jacket that's to fall at the front joint.

Schedule Space is usually a problem in a bindery so it's very awkward if a partly finished job must be stored because something is missing. For this reason, few binders will schedule a job unless everything—text sheets, illustrations, dies, cover materials, and jackets—is on hand. Binderies are likely to make charges for storage of materials held while waiting, or for completed books held for later delivery.

The binding order may have to be delayed for some reason—perhaps because of an uncertainty concerning the jacket or illustrations—that doesn't affect the cover materials or stamping. If the schedule is tight (as it usually is by binding time), return the approved sample cover to the binder with instructions to go ahead with ordering the materials and leaf. If these orders are delayed until the binding order is ready, it may turn out that a needed item isn't in stock and there isn't time enough to wait for it.

Binding Order

Date__________

Title__________

Author__________

PLEASE BIND __________ (Quantity)

FROM __________ PRINTING OF __________ HOLD BALANCE OF SHEETS __________

SHEET SIZE __________ FROM

TRIMMED SIZE __________ wide __________ high FULL TRIM ☐ SMOOTH TOP, ROUGH SIDE & FOOT ☐

MARGINS FOR TEXT: Gutter __________ Head __________ TOTAL PAGES __________

PRINT AS __________ FOLD AS __________ SEWING __________ ADHESIVE __________

BULK __________ ENDPAPERS:

LINING: super & paper ☐ other __________ STAIN __________

HEADBANDS __________ REINFORCEMENTS __________

INSERTS/ILLUSTRATIONS: ____ pp. TO BIND AS __________

BACK: ROUND ☐ other __________ BOARDS __________

COVERS __________

STAMPING: Spine __________ FRONT __________

Verso __________ DIES FROM __________

JACKETS FROM __________

SPECIAL INSTRUCTIONS:

PACKING __________

BOUND STOCK READY __________ *Signed* __________

A sample binding order form.

36. Co-productions

A co-production is a book produced at one time for two or more publishers. The participating publishers may be of the same country—e.g., a trade publisher and a book club—or of different countries. The purpose of a co-production is to save money by sharing costs and benefiting from the economies of large quantities.

The economics

There are two kinds of costs in book production: (a) *plant costs*—one-time expenses that are not affected by the length of the run—and (b) manufacturing costs—the costs of labor and materials, which vary according to the number of copies printed and bound. The main economies in co-productions are found in sharing plant costs. Some books with high plant costs are prohibitively expensive in the quantities that one publisher can sell, and the only way they can be economically published is by arranging a co-production. For example, a book with a large number of color illustrations (CH. 21) might have a plant cost of $50,000; for an edition of 5000 copies this means $10 per copy. By the usual publishing calculations (CH. 2) this alone would require about $50 in the projected retail price. Adding manufacturing and the other publishing costs, the retail price would come to about $100, which would price the project out of its market. However, if publishers in four other countries were each able to sell 5000 copies, the total printing would be 25,000 copies and the plant cost would come down to $2 per book—only about $10 of retail price. This would enable a retail price of about $60, a practical amount for the book.

There are some fixed costs in the manufacturing processes also that can be divided among participants in a co-production. These are the setting-up or *makeready* costs in printing and binding (CHs. 12, 13). Again, for a short run the makeready costs loom large; divided among a large number of copies they can be almost negligible.

Another possible saving in the manufacturing costs of a co-production is in lower prices for larger quantities of materials. Book cloth and paper are sold by the yard and pound at prices that decrease as the size of the order increases. These decreases are not gradual but occur at widely spread breaks in quantity. In paper, for example, the pound price in the United States is usually the same from 5000 lbs. (2268 kg) to 10,000 lbs. (4536 kg) (CH. 11), but over 10,000 lbs. it drops substantially. Thus, the unit cost of paper for an edition of 5000 that requires 7500 lbs. (3402 kg) would be lowered if another edition of only 2000 copies—requiring about 3000 lbs. (1361 kg) of paper—were added to the run. There would also be a reduction in the amount of paper used per copy, since the spoilage in makeready would be the same for 5000 copies as for 7000, and the cost of the spoiled paper would be shared.

It's customary for foreign-language participants in a co-production to translate the text and set their type at their own expense. Traditionally, they supply the originating publisher or producer with films of the text in their language. Increasingly, however, the originating publisher provides each foreign-language partner with a duplicate final page file, in which the foreign-language text replaces the original one, leaving the graphic elements in place. The foreign publishers also pay for the cost of their text plates, for changing the text plates during the press run, and, usually, for shipping their books. In compensation for these extra costs, they generally pay a smaller royalty than English-language publishers.

Co-productions with book clubs usually don't involve sharing plant costs, and sometimes not even the makeready costs. When a book club is sold books at the run-on price, the only possible saving is in materials, and often even this doesn't occur, because the additional quantity isn't enough to lower the price.

Procedures

PREPARATION

In a co-production originating with a U.S. publisher, the costs of typesetting and prepress are shared equally among English-language publishers, except for a very minor additional cost to the co-publishers for making their changes on the title page, copyright page, and jacket or cover. When a foreign-language publisher is involved, the cost of English-language composition is shared only by the English-language publishers, since the text must be set again in the foreign language at the expense of the foreign publisher.

In scheduling, it's important to leave enough time for the translation, typesetting, proofreading, and preparation of films for the foreign-language text(s). The most common and difficult problem in co-productions is getting the foreign-language files or text films in time to keep the press schedule.

Since it's necessary to make a complete set of plates to print the black type for each foreign-language publisher, if they're supplying film they should send their text with a complete page on each single piece of film—with register marks to enable the printshop to position the pages properly on the flats.

Rather than combine the film for the black plate of the color illustrations with the text film, it's better to leave them separate so that a single set of illustration film may be used for making the black plates for all languages. When this is done, the black illustration film and the text film are exposed separately onto a plate to make a single plate that includes both. If CTP production (CH. 10) is used, separate black plates are produced for each edition using the composed files.

Be aware that U.S. printshops make plates from negative film, while in most other countries positive film is used. Also, when ordering film it's necessary to indicate if it's *right-reading* with the emulsion down or up. Since printshops have different preferences, be sure to coordinate your specs when doing a co-production

PRINTING & PAPER

While the largest economy in co-productions is in plant and prepress, the worst complications are in printing, where the main difficulty is coordination.

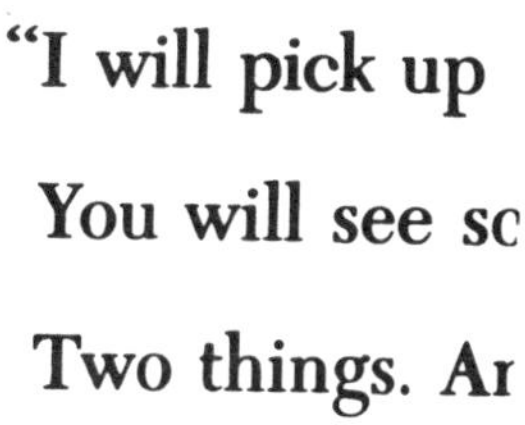

right reading

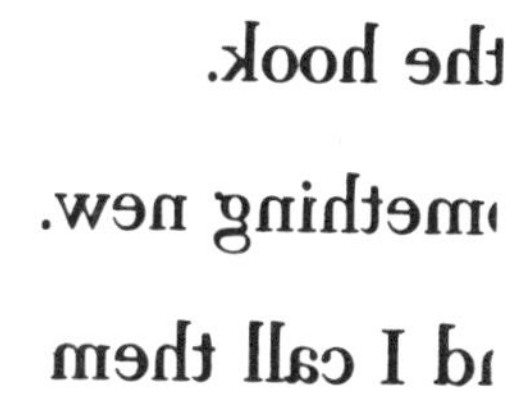

wrong reading

In a co-production, it isn't acceptable to delay delivery to the other participants because of the failure of one or two publishers to send films or files as promised, so it's necessary to plan an alternative procedure. If the printing is sheetfed, this usually means making a set of black plates with the illustrations but without text so that the color printing can be done in one run, even if the text for late participants must be printed separately later. Since the cost of color makeready is much higher than that for black only, the late publishers get most, but not all, of the benefit of the combined printing. For web printing with in-line folding, there's no alternative but to wait for the late publishers or run without them, in which case they must bear the expense of printing alone. Provision for this possibility should be included in the contracts.

Another complication is the difficulty of getting the right quantities for each participant. When only one edition is being printed, with only one makeready for each form, the paper allocation can usually be worked out pretty well. With a co-production, there are several changes of black plates, with a makeready for each, and paper is spoiled each time—multiplying the uncertainty factor. This makes it hard to come out with the desired quantity for each publisher—especially the last one, who may come up short if the paper runs out because spoilage for the others ran higher than expected.

Then there's the problem of quality control, which is in the hands of the originating publisher. There should be no trouble if the results are excellent, but no matter how good it is, it may not satisfy everyone, since publishers in each country tend to have a national sense of color. Some like it more intense, others prefer softer effects. Some lean towards reddish color, others like yellower tints. It's a good idea to check these preferences with the participants before printing.

It doesn't happen often, but it's not unknown for a printshop to mix up the plates and/or the quantities in co-productions. Sometimes the plate with the British copyright is put on press to back up the U.S. title page or vice versa. Sometimes the quantity for the French edition is run for the German or vice versa. If you are at the press, you should be able to catch such gaffes before they go too far. If not, the results can be disastrous.

It makes little difference where the prepress work is done, since proofs, film, etc. can be easily and inexpensively sent by air. However, the cost and time involved in getting printed sheets or bound books to the participating publishers is an important element in deciding where to print. The cost of transporting a book of, say, 7 x 10" (17.8 x 25.4 cm) across an ocean might be 30¢ to 35¢, depending on its thickness and the number shipped (the cost is based on volume), so it's usually best to print on the continent where most of the books will be delivered. But there are other elements to consider: (a) the relative costs of printing in each country—which are affected by currency exchange rates and inflation as well as the national economies, (b) convenience of access (watching the printing when the press is thousands of miles from home is a lot more time-consuming and expensive than when it's nearby), (c) language differences, and (d) shipping time. All these considerations, plus the relative merits of individual printshops, must be weighed carefully—and remember that the work will be done perhaps six, eight, or more months after the decision is made, when conditions may be different.

The *plate change* problems for jackets and paperback covers are about the same as for the text. If possible, make these designs for co-productions so that the minimum number of colors will be affected by plate changes. The ideal design has all type in black, so that only the black plate need be changed.

The paper for a co-production is ordered just as though there was to be only one edition printed, except for the additional spoilage allowance for the black plate changes. It's best to ask the printshop to calculate these quantities. In webfed printing, paper spoilage is relatively high at best, and the spoilage for these plate changes can be considerable. If expensive paper is used, the extra spoilage can wipe out the web-printing cost advantage, so it's wise to get prices for sheetfed printing as well. This becomes an especially important consideration for reprinting, when the quantities are likely to be smaller than those of the first run, and less economical for web presses.

If a co-production is to be printed abroad, it's important to see samples of the paper the printshop intends to use. Paper in one country doesn't necessarily match the grades that are made in other countries.

In times of paper shortages there can be long waits for deliveries, so try to get quantity commitments from participating publishers well in advance of printing, to ensure that the paper can be ordered in good time.

BINDING

There are few special problems in binding co-productions. All binding operations except stamping can be run with a single makeready for all editions, since the language differences don't affect these procedures. In stamping, or in preprinting covers, there's a change of imprint for the English-language publishers and a complete change of dies for the foreign-language participants. The number of plate changes in preprinting covers, as for jackets and paperback covers, depends on the design.

Keeping the various editions separated—and making certain that the Italian covers are not put on the Spanish books or the French jackets put on the Italian books, etc.—isn't a difficult matter for a well-run bindery, but mistakes do happen. To prevent such disasters, alert the binder to this problem just before the work begins.

For overseas shipment, books are normally shipped in *containers*. These are huge watertight metal boxes 20' or 40' (6.15 m or 12.3 m) long. They are loaded at the warehouse or bindery, sealed shut, and put on ships. Containers provide complete protection in transit (unless the ship sinks), so normal packing for books is sufficient. Nevertheless, all the publishers in a co-production should be asked to provide packing and shipping instructions, since they usually have definite preferences about the handling of their books. For any situation where containers are not used, books should be packed in waterproof cartons and loaded on skids that are shrinkwrapped in plastic.

In conclusion

This discussion of co-productions may or may not make the operation seem terribly difficult. In case you have any doubt, it *is*. The difficulty multiplies when there are five or six participants—but it's bad enough with only three. Getting all parties to agree to a single plan and schedule is hard, but the big trouble comes when one or more publishers fail to keep their schedules, send the wrong material, or make changes at the last minute. Inevitably, some of these things *always* happen. The economic advantages of co-productions are real, and can be decisive for a publishing project, but any decision to try one must be taken with the full knowledge that they're not easy to do well, and lots of experience, as well as good luck, are necessary.

APPENDIX

Sources of information

Some of the titles listed below are long out of print, but they're too interesting and/or useful not to be included. They should be available in some libraries and from used-book sources.

BOOKS

General

The Business of Books: How International Conglomerates Took over Publishing and Changed the Way We Read—André Schiffrin. Verso. 2000. (Discusses loss of standards in contemporary publishing.)

The Complete Index to Fine Print—Sandra Kirshenbaum. Oak Knoll Press. 2003. (Final issue of *Fine Print Magazine*, providing descriptions of fine letterpress books, articles on binding, papermaking, and calligraphy.)

How a Book Is Made—Aliki. HarperCollins. 1987.

How to Be Your Own Literary Agent: The Business of Getting a Book Published—Richard Curtis. Mariner Books. 2003. (A full account of the process, from submissions to contract negotiations.)

How to Get Happily Published—Judith Appelbaum. HarperCollins. 5th ed. 1998. (An informative source for writers.)

Literary Agents: A Complete Guide—Judith Johnson Sherwin. New York. Poets & Writers. 1978. (How literary agencies work; relations with writers and publishers.)

Professional Prepress, Printing and Publishing—Frank J. Romano. Prentice Hall. 1999.

A Writer's Guide to Book Publishing—Richard Balkin. Plume. 3rd ed. 1994. (Describes the needs, wants, and ways of publishers.)

Writing, Illustrating, and Editing Children's Books—Jean Poindexter Colby. Hastings House. 1970. (Standard how-to account.)

HISTORY

The Book in America—Hellmut Lehmann-Haupt, Lawrence C. Wroth, and Rollo G. Silver. R. R. Bowker. Revised ed. 1951. (Comprehensive one-volume history, 1630–1950; original edition, 1939.)

Book Publishing in America—Charles A. Madison. R. R. Bowker. 1966. (Highlights of 300 years of history.)

Five Hundred Years of Printing—John Trevitt and Sigfrid H. Steinberg. Oak Knoll Press. 4th ed. 1996.

A History of the Book in America—Hugh Amory and David D. Hall, eds. University Press. 1999. (Five-volume series covering history from colonial times to present.)

A History of Book Publishing in the United States—Vol. 1, 1630–1865; Vol. 2, 1865–1919; Vol. 3, 1919–1940; Vol. 4, 1940–1980—John A. Tebbel. R. R. Bowker. 1972, 1975, 1978, 1981. (The most comprehensive history.)

The House of Harper—Eugene Exman. Harper & Row. 1967. (Lively, surprisingly unbiased account of the firm's first 150 years.)

Perspectives on American Book History: Artifacts and Commentary (Studies in print culture and the history of the book)—Scott E. Casper, Joanne D. Chaison, and Jeffrey D. Groves, eds. University of Massachusetts Press. 2002. (A collection of primary source materials and essays on American print culture.)

MEMOIRS

At Random: The Reminiscences of Bennett Cerf—Bennett and Christopher Cerf. Random House. 2002. (Edited oral reminiscences of the co-founder of Random House.)

The Bowker Lectures on Book Publishing—R. R. Bowker. 1957. (The first 17 Bowker Memorial Lectures.)

Portrait of a Publisher—Alfred A. Knopf. A. A. Knopf. 1965. (Reminiscences of one of the world's great publishers.)

Publishers on Publishing—Gerald Gross, ed. Grosset & Dunlap (paperback). 1961. (Anthology of publishers' writings; enlightening, amusing.)

The Truth about Publishing—Sir Stanley Unwin. Academy Chicago Publishing. 8th ed. 2001. (Reprint of the revised 7th edition, 1960, of Sir Stanley's classic treatise.)

OPERATIONS

The Art and Science of Book Publishing—Herbert S. Bailey Jr. Ohio University Press. 3rd ed. 1990. (Examines the fiscal responsibilities of publishers.)

The Art of Literary Publishing: Editors on Their Craft—Bill Henderson. Pushcart Press. 1995.

Beyond the Bestseller: A Literary Agent Takes You inside the Book Business—Richard Curtis. New American Library. 1989.

Book Business: Publishing Past, Present, and Future—Jason Epstein. W. W. Norton. 2002. (A valuable survey by the long-time Random House editor.)

Book Publishing: The Basic Introduction—John P. Dessauer. Continuum Publishing. Expanded ed. 1998.

A Candid Critique of Book Publishing—Curtis G. Benjamin. R. R. Bowker. 1977. (A top executive's views on publishing operations.)

Opportunities in Publishing Careers—Robert A. Carter, S. William Pattis, and Blythe Camenson. McGraw-Hill. 2000.

Who Does What and Why in Book Publishing—Clarkson N. Potter. Carol Publishing. Group. 1990. (Illuminates the roles of editors and publishers.)

Editing

GENERAL

The Careful Writer: A Modern Guide to English Usage—Theodore M. Bernstein. Free Press. 5th ed. 1995. (Author was for many years the *New York Times* copy chief.)

Copyediting: A Practical Guide—Karen Judd. Crisp Publications. 3rd ed. 2001. (Advice on how to be a copyeditor.)

Editor to Author: The Letters of Maxwell E. Perkins—Maxwell E. Perkins. Cherokee Publishing. 1997. (Correspondence with Hemingway, Wolfe, Fitzgerald, Galsworthy, and others.)

Editors on Editing: What Writers Need to Know about What Editors Do—Gerald Gross, ed. Grove Press. 3rd ed. 1993. (Writings by various editors; good source of information on editorial functions.)

Handbook for Scholars—Mary-Claire Van Leunen. Oxford University Press. Revised ed. 1992. (A manual of information dealing with authorship.)

Mark My Words: Instruction and Practice in Proofreading—Peggy Smith. Editorial Experts. 3rd ed. 1993.

Max Perkins, Editor of Genius—Scott A. Berg. Riverhead Books. 1997. (Biography of the great Scribner editor.)

What Is an Editor? Saxe Commins at Work—Dorothy Commins. University of Chicago Press. 1981. (A top editor's reports, correspondence, and notebooks.)

STYLE

American Medical Association Manual of Style: A Guide for Authors and Editors—Cheryl Iverson, ed. Williams & Wilkins. 9th ed. 1998. (A specialized style manual for medical writing.)

The Art of Editing—Brian S. Brooks, Jack Sissors, and Floyd K. Baskette. Allyn & Bacon. 7th ed. 2000. (A leading book in the field.)

Britannica Book of English Usage—Christine Timmons and Frank Gibney, eds. Doubleday/Britannica Books. 1st ed. 1980.

Chicago Manual of Style—University of Chicago Press. 15th ed. 2003. (The leading authority used in book publishing.)

Copyediting: The Cambridge Handbook—Judith Butcher. Cambridge University Press. 3rd ed. 1992. (British, scholarly.)

A Deskbook of American Spelling and Style—Rudolf Franz Flesch. HarperCollins. 1981.

The Elements of Style—William Strunk Jr., E.B. White, Charles Osgood, and Roger Angell. Allyn & Bacon. 4th ed. 2000. (The widely respected guide to precision and clarity in English writing.)

English Grammar: HarperCollins College Outline Series—David I. and Barbara J. Daniels. HarperCollins. 1991.

Miss Thistlebottom's Hobgoblins: The Careful Writer's Guide to the Taboos, Bugbears, and Outmoded Rules of English Usage—Theodore M. Bernstein. Noonday Press. Reissue ed. 1991.

The New York Public Library Writer's Guide to Style and Usage—Andrea Sutcliffe. HarperCollins. 1st ed. 1994.

New York Times Manual of Style and Usage: The Official Style Guide Used by the Writers and Editors of the World's Most Authoritative Newspaper—Lewis Jordan, ed. Quadrangle/New York Times Books. 2002.

On Writing Well—William Zinsser. HarperCollins. 2001.

Proofreading and Copy Preparation: A Textbook for the Graphic Arts Industry—Joseph Lasky. Agathon Press. 1971. (An oldie, but still useful.)

Punctuate It Right!—Harry Shaw. Harper Perennial. 2nd ed. 1993.

Schaum's Outline of Punctuation, Capitalization, and Spelling—Eugene Ehrlich. McGraw-Hill. 2nd ed. 1992.

Scientific Style and Format: The CBE Manual for Authors, Editors, and Publishers—Style Manual Committee and Council of Biology Editors. Cambridge University Press. 6th ed. 1994. (A specialized manual, but includes general style conventions.)

Spell It Right!—Harry Shaw. Harper Perennial. 4th ed. 1993.

United States Government Printing Office Style Manual—GPO. 2001. (Order from Supt. of Documents.)

Woe Is I—Patricia T. O'Conner. Riverhead. 1996. (Subtitled: "The Grammarphobe's Guide to Better English in Plain English". Helpful and amusing.)

Words Fail Me—Patricia T. O'Conner. Harvest/Harcourt. 1999. (Subtitled: "What Everyone Who Writes Should Know about Writing".)

REFERENCE

Dictionary of Modern English Usage—H. W. Fowler and Ernest Gowers, eds. Oxford University Press. 2nd ed. 1985.

Editing Fact and Fiction: A Concise Guide to Book Editing—Leslie T. Sharpe and Irene Gunther. Cambridge University Press. 1994.

Electronic Manuscript Preparation and Markup: American National Standard for Electronic Manuscript Preparation and Markup—Published for the National Information Standards Organization by Transaction Publishers. 1991.

Harbrace College Handbook—John C. Hodges, Winfred Bryan Horner, Suzanne Strobeck Webb, and Robert Keith Miller. International Thomson Publishing. 13th ed. 1998. (Manual for grammar and rhetoric.)

The Little Brown Handbook—H. Ramsey Fowler and Jane Aaron. Longman. 8th ed. 2002. (Compilation of writing and grammar usage.)

Roget's International Thesaurus—Barbara Ann Kipfer, ed. Harper-

Collins. 6th ed. 2001. (Topical arrangement, following principles of the original work, but thoroughly updated; widely recommended.)

Technical Editing—Carolyn D. Rude, David Dayton, and Bruce Maylath. Longman. 3rd ed. 2001. (Provides information on electronic editing, and legal issues in publishing.)

Webster's New World Speller-Divider—Shirley M. Miller. Word Publishing. 2nd ed. 1992. (Based upon *Webster's New World Dictionary of the American Language*, college edition.)

Words into Type—Marjorie E. Skillen and Robert Malcolm Gay. Pearson PTP. 3rd ed. 1974. (Classic guide to grammar, style, usage, and manuscript protocol. Still good.)

Design & typography

GENERAL

American Typography Today—Rob Carter. John Wiley & Sons. 1997. (Critical analysis of 24 modern typographic designers.)

Big Type—Roger Walton. HBI. 2002. (Examples of work with designers' comments and analysis.)

Books and Printing—Paul A. Bennett, ed. Frederic C. Beil. 1991. (Reprint of 1951 collection of essays by typographers and designers.)

Books for Our Time—Marshall Lee, ed. Oxford University Press. 1951. (Essays and specimens by leading innovative designers; 150 books illustrated.)

Contemporary American Bookbinding—The Grolier Club. Grolier Club. 1990.

Digital Book Design and Publishing—Douglas Holleley. Cary Graphic Press. 2001.

Dramatic Color by Overprinting—Donald E. Cooke. North American Publishing, 2nd ed. 1974. Original ed., Winston, 1955. (A useful tool.)

The Elements of Graphic Design: Space, Unity, Page Architecture, and Type—Alex W. White. Allworth Press. 2002.

An Essay on Typography—Eric Gill. David R. Godine. Reissued 1993. (A classic.)

Fine Print on Type: The Best Fine Print Magazine on Type—Charles Bigelow, Paul Hayden Duensing, and Linnea Gentry, eds. Bedford Arts. 1989. (Essays on typography and design by distinguished designers.)

The Form of the Book: Essays on the Morality of Good Design—Jan Tschichold and Robert Bringhurst, eds. Hartley & Marks. 1997. (An important book by a master.)

Graphic Design Sources—Kenneth J. Hiebert and Armin Hofmann. Yale University Press. 1998. (Discusses techniques in graphic design and typography.)

Graphic Forms—György Kepes, and others. Harvard University Press. 1949. (Top graphic artists of the era discuss the arts as related to the book.)

How Typography Happens—Ruari McLean. Oak Knoll Press. 2000. (A study of the evolution of typography as an art form.)

Illuminating Letters: Typography and Literary Interpretation—Megan L. Benton and Paul C. Gutjahr, eds. University of Massachusetts Press. 2001. (Considers the relationship between typography and literary interpretation in old and new forms of communication.)

Into Print: Selected Writings on Printing History, Typography, and Book Production—John Dreyfus. British Library. 1994. (Comprehensive view of printing history and 20th century typography.)

An Introduction to Color—R. M. Evans. John Wiley & Sons. 1970. (Properties: physical, psychological.)

The New Typography—Jan Tschichold and Ruari McLean, trans. University of California Press. 1998. (A highly regarded source of modern typographical design, providing theories, history, and guidelines for design and print.)

On Book Design—Richard Hendel. Yale University Press. 1998.

Rudolf Koch: Letterer, Type Designer, Teacher—Gerald Cinamon. Oak Knoll Press. 2000. (Biography of a leading German typographer.)

Texts on Type: Critical Writings on Typography—Steven Heller and Philip B. Meggs. Allworth Press. 2001. (A compilation of 50 essays.)

True to Type—Ruari McLean. Oak Knoll Press. 2000. (Autobiography of the well-known British book designer and typographer.)

Twentieth Century Type Designers—Sebastian Carter. W. W. Norton. New edition. 1995

HISTORY

American Book Design and William Morris—Susan Otis Thompson. Oak Knoll Press. 2nd ed. 1997. (Reprint of first edition, with a foreword by Jean-Francois Vilain.)

The Art of the Printed Book, 1455–1955—Joseph Blumenthal and Pierpont Morgan Library. David R. Godine. 1994. (Essays and 125 reproductions from a Morgan Library exhibition.)

The Book: The Story of Printing & Bookmaking—Douglas C. McMurtrie. Oxford University Press. 3rd ed. 1997. (The classic tradition.)

Book Typography, 1815–1965—Kenneth Day, ed. University of Chicago Press. 1966.

A Century for the Century: Fine Printed Books 1900–1999—Martin Hutner and Jerome Kelly. Grolier Club. 1999. (Survey of excellence in book production in the 20th century.)

Five Hundred Years of Book Design—Alan Bartram. Yale University Press. 2001.

Five Hundred Years of Printing—S. H. Steinberg and John Trevitt.

British Library Publications. 4th ed. 1996.

Four Centuries of Fine Printing—Stanley Morison. Barnes & Noble. Revised ed. 1960. (Essay by the outstanding early 20th century English typographer and historian; 192 reproductions of book pages from 1465 to 1924.)

Front Cover: Great Book Jacket and Cover Design—Alan Powers. Mitchell Beazley. 2001.

Graphic Design History—Steven Heller and Georgette Ballance, eds. Allworth Press. 2001. (The evolution of design and typography in America.)

A History of Graphic Design—Philp B. Meggs. John Wiley & Sons. 3rd ed. 1998. (A reference book for graphic designers.)

History of Printing in America—Isaiah Thomas. Outlet. Reprint ed. 1983. (Originally published in 1810 by the prominent Revolutionary-era printer.)

A History of the Printed Book—Lawrence C. Wroth, ed. Limited Editions Club (*The Dolphin, vol. 3*). 1938. (Large, well-illustrated study by experts on various aspects.)

Letter Perfect: The Art of Modernist Typography, 1896–1953—David Ryan. Pomegranate. 2001.

Printing and the Mind of Man: The Impact of Print on Five Centuries of Western Civilization—John Carter and Percy H. Muir, eds. K. Pressler. 2nd ed. 1983.

Printing Types: Their History Forms and Use—Daniel Berkeley Updike. Oak Knoll Press. 3rd ed. 2001. (An essential classic; original edition 1922.)

The Shaping of Our Alphabet—Frank Denman. Knopf. 1955. (Interesting, well-illustrated history of letters and type.)

A Short History of the Printed Word—Warren Chappell and Robert Bringhurst. Hartley & Marks. 2nd ed. 2000. (Handsomely illustrated account by a famous illustrator and designer.)

The 26 Letters—Oscar Ogg. Crowell. Revised ed. 1971. (Development of the Roman alphabet; extensively and charmingly illustrated by the author-designer.)

The Typographic Book, 1450–1935—Stanley Morison and Kenneth Day. University of Chicago Press. 1964. (Illustrated study.)

PRACTICE

About Face: Reviving the Rules of Typography—David Jury. Rotovision. 2002.

Asymmetrical Typography—Jan Tschichold. Van Nostrand Reinhold. 1967. (Brilliant statement of "modern" typography.)

Creative Typography—Marion March. North Light Books. 1988. (A survey of typography examining the use of space, format, and color.)

Design Basics: Ideas and Inspiration for Working with Layout, Type and Color in Graphic Design—Joyce Rutter Kaye. Rockport. 2002.

Designing Books—Jan Tschichold. Wittenborn. 1951. (Rules for conventional typography; written after the author of *Asymmetrical Typography* changed his views.)

Designing Books: Practice and Theory—Jost Hochuli and Robin Kinross. Hyphen. 1996.

Designing with Type: A Basic Course in Typography—James Craig, William Bevington, and Susan E. Meyer, eds. Watson-Guptill Publications. 4th ed. 1999. (Widely used typography textbook updated with information on digital typesetting.)

Editing by Design: A Guide to Effective Word-and-Picture Communication for Editors and Designers—Jan White. R. R. Bowker. 2nd ed. 1982.

The Elements of Typographic Style—Robert Bringhurst. Hartley & Marks. 2nd ed. 1997. (Includes history and a glossary of typography terms.)

Graphic Design Manual: Principles and Practice—Armin Hoffman. Arthur Niggli Verlag. 2001.

Introduction to Typography—Oliver Simon. Faber & Faber. 1969. (Reprint of 1949 original.)

Making Digital Type Look Good—Bob Gordon. Watson-Guptill Publications. 2001.

The Non-Designer's Design Book—Robin Williams. Peachpit Press. 1994. (Discusses general design principles.)

Structure of the Visual Book—Keith A. Smith. Keith Smith Books. 3rd ed. 1995. (Discusses how to make an expressive design.)

Typographic Design: Form and Communication—Rob Carter, Ben Day, and Philip Meggs. John Wiley & Sons. 3rd ed. 2002. (Examines color in typographic design.)

Using Type Right—Philip Brady. North Light Books. 1988. (Basic rules for working with type.)

TYPE *About Alphabets*—Hermann Zapf. MIT Press. 1970. (Comment by a leading type designer.)

The Alphabet and Elements of Lettering—Frederic W. Goudy. Fromm International. 1989. (Reprint of 1918 and 1922 essays, revised and enlarged for 1942 book published by the University of California Press.)

American Metal Typefaces of the Twentieth Century—Mac McGrew. Oak Knoll Press. 1993. (Discusses 1600 classical and unique typefaces.)

Manuale Typographicum—Hermann Zapf. MIT Press. 1970. (100 pages by the famous type designer.)

Name This Font: A Practical Encyclopedia of Letter Forms—Thomas V. Skrivan. GraphicPage. 2001.

Revival of the Fittest: Digital Versions of Classic Typefaces—Philip B. Meggs, Roy McKelvey, and Ben Day. RC Publications. 2000.

Treasury of Alphabets and Lettering—Jan Tschichold. W. W. Norton. 1995. (150 fine alphabets, with comment by a master typographer.)

Typographic Variations—Hermann Zapf. Myriade Press. New edition. 1978.

Typologia—Frederic W. Goudy. University of California Press. 1978. (Collection of studies and comments on the design of typefaces.)

Illustration

American Picturebooks from 'Noah's Ark' to 'The Beast Within'—Barbara Bader. Macmillan. 1976. (Definitive history of the illustrating of picture-books for children from mid-19th century to 1976.)

The Art of Art for Children's Books—Diana Klemin. Murton Press. 1982.

The Art of the Book: From Medieval Manuscript to Graphic Novel—James Bettley, ed. H. N. Abrams. 2001.

The Artist and the Book, 1860–1960—Boston Museum of Fine Arts. 1961. (Excellent survey of book illustration.)

Children's Book Illustration and Design—Julie Cummins, ed. PBC International. 1997. (Demonstrates styles of various picture-book artists.)

Children's Book Illustration: Step by Step Techniques; A Unique Guide from the Masters—Jill Bossert. Watson-Guptill Publications. 1998.

Five Hundred Years of Art in Illustration—Howard Simon. Hacker. 1977.

A History of Book Illustration: The Illuminated Manuscript and the Printed Book—David Bland. University of California Press. Revised 2nd ed. 1969. (Comprehensive, extensively illustrated; a major work.)

The Illustrated Book—Frank Weitenkampf. Harvard University Press. 1938. (Thorough, scholarly history.)

Illustrating Children's Books—Children's Book Council (brochures). 2003. (Brief outlines; includes lists for further reading.)

Myth, Magic, and Mystery: One Hundred Years of American Children's Book Illustration—Robert Rinehart Publishers in cooperation with the Chrysler Museum of Art. 1996.

Oscar Wilde's Decorated Books—Nicholas Raymond Frankel. University of Michigan Press. 2000. (Analyzes Wilde's contributions to book design.)

The Very Best of Children's Book Illustration—The Society of Illustrators. North Light Books. 1993. (The work of 160 artists from the 1992 Society of Illustrators exhibition.)

What Do Illustrators Do?—Eileen Christelow. Clarion Books. 1999. (All the steps in creating picture-books.)

Book Production Procedures for Today's Technology—Fred Dahl. Inkwell Publishing. 2001.

Production

GENERAL

Graphics Master 7: Workbook of Reference Guides & Graphic Tools for the Design, Preparation, and Production of Print and Internet Publishing—Dean Phillip Lem. Dean Lem Associates. 2000.

Great Production by Design—Constance J. Sidles. North Light Books. 1998. (A print production guide with reference to prepress, paper, color, and binding.)

Handbook of Print Media—Helmut Kipphan, ed. Springer. 2001. (A contemporary manual describing printing techniques and processes.)

Pocket Pal: A Graphic Arts Production Handbook—International Paper. 2000. (A well-established practical guide.)

Production for Graphic Designers—Alan Pipes. Prentice Hall. 3rd ed. 2002.

Production for the Graphic Designer—James Craig. Watson-Guptill Publications. 2nd ed. 1990.

COMPOSITION

Book Manufacturing—Richard Hollick. Cambridge University Press. 1986. (Fifth volume in a series of practical guides. About the preparation and handling of manuscript.)

Chicago Guide to Preparing Electronic Manuscripts: For Authors and Publishers–University of Chicago Press. 1987. (This supplement to the 13th edition of *The Chicago Manual of Style* offers practical guidelines for preparing authors' disks for typesetting.)

PREPRESS

Designer's Prepress Companion—Jessica Berlin. National Association for Printing Leadership. 2002.

Digital Prepress Technologies—Geoffrey Brett. Pira International. 2000.

Pocket Guide to Digital Prepress—Frank J. Romano. Delmar Learning. 1995.

Prepress: Building Innovative Design through Creative Prepress Techniques–Constance J. Sidles. Rockport Publishers. 2000. (Explains prepress techniques as well as scheduling and budgeting.)

Print Publishing: A Hayden Shop Manual—Donnie O'Quinn. Hayden Books. 2000. (A guide to prepress production and frequent errors.)

PRINTING

Color in the 21st Century: A Practical Guide for Graphic Designers, Photographers, Printers, Separators, and Anyone Involved in Color Printing—Helene W. Eckstein. Watson-Guptill Publications. 1991.

Getting It Printed: How to Work with Printers and Graphic Imaging

Services to Assure Quality, Stay on Schedule, and Control Costs—Mark Beach and Eric Kenly. North Light Books. 1999.

How to Check and Correct Color Proofs: Everything You Need to Know to Guarantee a Great Printed Piece—David Bann and John Gargan. North Light Books. 1990.

The Lithographer's Manual—Raymond N. Blair and Thomas M. Destree, eds. The Graphic Arts Technical Foundation. 9th ed. 1994. (Covers every aspect of production practice and theory.)

Pocket Guide to Digital Printing—Frank Cost. Delmar Learning. 1996.

BINDING

Bookbinding in America—Hellmut Lehmann-Haupt and others. R. R. Bowker. 1967. (Reprint of 1941 edition; bookbinding in both aspects, commercial and handcraft.)

Bookbinding: Its Background and Techniques—Edith Diehl. Dover. 1985. (Originally Rinehart, 1946; definitive.)

Paper

A Brief History of Paper—Carol Schwartzott. C. Schwartzott. 1993.

Handbook of Pulp and Paper Technology—Kenneth W. Britt. Van Nostrand Reinhold. 2nd ed. 1975.

The History and Technique of an Ancient Craft—Dard Hunter. Dover. 1978. (Classic in its field.)

Papermaking—Jules Heller. Watson-Guptill Publications. 1997.

The Story of Papermaking—Edwin Sutermeister. R. R. Bowker. 1954. (Technical but readable review of the process.)

Working with Papers: A Guide for Printers—Michael Bruno and Leonard Schlosser. National Association of Printers and Lithographers (pamphlet). 1977. (Useful also for publishers.)

Reference

GENERAL

Books in Print—R. R. Bowker. (Annual compendium of information on books and authors.)

Bowker Annual of Library and Book Trade Information—David Bogart, ed. R. R. Bowker.

Business and Legal Forms for Authors and Self-Publishers—Tad Crawford. Allworth Press. 1996. (A helpful compilation of basic forms and tear-out forms for actual use, including sample contracts.)

Children's, Writer's & Illustrator's Market—Alice Pope and Mona Michael, eds. Writer's Digest Books. 2003. (Includes agent, publisher, and conference listings as well as interviews with authors, magazine editors, and book publishers.)

The Designer's Lexicon: The Illustrated Dictionary of Design, Printing and Computer Terms—Alastair Campbell. Chronicle Books. 2000. (Cross-disciplinary technical dictionary including over 4000 terms supplemented by 400 color diagrams and illustrations.)

Glossary of Graphic Communications—Pamela J. Groff. Graphic Arts Technical Foundation. 3rd ed. 1997.

Guide to Reference Books—Robert Balay, ed. American Library Association. 11th ed. 1996. (Librarians call it the bible of reference to references.)

Information Please Almanac—Information Please. (Published annually.)

Literary Market Place—Information Today. (Annual directory to publishers, agencies, associations, suppliers, manufacturers, book trade services, review media, etc.)

Manufacturing Standards and Specifications for Textbooks—Advisory Commission on Textbook Specifications. 2003. (Published by the Book Manufacturers' Institute, the Association of American Publishers, and the National Association of State Textbook Administrators.)

World Almanac and Book of Facts—Press Publishing. (The New York World). (An annual reference book from 1923 to the present.)

COPYRIGHT

Copyright Handbook—Donald Johnston. R. R. Bowker. 2nd ed. 1982. (Detailed guide to the 1976 copyright law.)

Copyright, Its History and Its Laws: A Summary of the Principles and Law of Copyright, with Especial Reference to Books—R. R. Bowker. 1986.

Copyright Law of the United States of America and Related Laws—U. S. Copyright Office, Library of Congress. 2000. (The official texts.)

Dealing with Copyrights—Richard Wincor. Oceana Publications. 2000. (A comprehensive introduction to copyright, focusing on how copyright is applied.)

Digital Copyright: Protecting Intellectual Property on the Internet—Jessica Litman. Prometheus Books. 2001. (Demonstrates how the World Wide Web has the potential to restructure copyright laws in the U.S.)

The Future of Ideas: The Fate of the Commons in a Connected World—Lawrence Lessig. Random House. 2001. (Analyzes the current trend to extend copyrights and the impact this has on publicly held material.)

The New and Updated Copyright Primer—Association of American Publishers and Permission Advisory Committee (manual). 2000.

Visual Artist's Guide to the New Copyright Law—Tad Crawford. Graphic Artists Guild. 1978.

The Writer's Legal Guide: An Author's Guild Desk Reference—Tad Crawford and Kay Murray. Allworth Press. 3rd ed. 2002. (Provides writers with legal information on copyright and First Amendment law.)

DICTIONARIES

The American Heritage Dictionary of the English Language—Houghton Mifflin. 4th ed. 2001. (Comprehensive dictionary; includes color photos, illustrations, maps, and a CD-ROM.)

Harper Dictionary of Contemporary Usage—William Morris, ed. Harper & Row. 2nd ed. 1985. (Created with the assistance of a panel of 165 distinguished consultants on usage.)

Merriam Webster's Collegiate Dictionary—Merriam-Webster. 11th ed. 2003.

Merriam-Webster's New International Unabridged Dictionary, Second Edition—(The unequalled standard dictionary for words existing before 1934.)

Oxford Dictionary of American Usage and Style—Bryan A. Garner. Berkeley Publishing Group. 2000.

Random House Dictionary of the English Language—Stuart Berg Flexner and Leonore Crary Hauck, eds. Random House. 2nd ed. 1993. (An unabridged dictionary.)

Webster's New World Dictionary of American English—Victoria Neufeldt and David B. Guralnik, eds. Webster's New World. 3rd ed. 1991.

ENCYCLOPEDIAS

Concise Columbia Encyclopedia—Paul Lagasse, ed. Houghton Mifflin. 3rd ed. 1995.

Encylopedia of the Book—Geoffrey Ashall Glaister. Oak Knoll Press. 2nd ed. 2001. (Definitions of terms used in bookmaking, printing, papermaking, and the book industry.)

Typography: An Encyclopedic Survey of Type Design and Techniques throughout History—Friedrich Friedl, Nicolaus Ott, and Bernard Stein. Black Dog & Leventhal Publishers. 1998. (Compilation of designers' biographies and information on type in English, German, and French.)

Writer's Encyclopedia—Amanda Boyd, ed. Writer's Digest Books. 3rd ed. 1996. (A writer's reference with more than 1300 items.)

OTHER SOURCES

The internet

American Institute of Graphic Arts (www.aiga.org)—A forum for design professionals to exchange ideas and information about design.

Book Manufacturers' Institute (www.bmibook.com)—The well-respected trade association of the book manufacturing industry.

Books in Print (www.booksinprint.com)—Provides bibliographic information, book reviews, and author biographies for over 3.5 million titles.

Bookbuilders of Boston (www.bbboston.org)—An organization for people in book publishing and manufacturing in New England.

Bookwire (www.bookwire.com)—Provides an index to book resources on the Internet.

Color Marketing Group (www.colormarketing.org)—An international association of color design professionals.

Digital Printing and Imaging Association (www.dpi.org)—Provides information on products and technology.

Graphic Artists Guild (www.gag.org)—A union of designers, illustrators, web page creators, and production artists in America.

Identifont® (www.identifont.com)—Enables the user to identify a font from a sample by answering a series of questions. The site includes information about fonts from the main type libraries.

International Pre-press Association (www.ipa.org)—Explores the newest forms of graphic communication.

PC Magazine (www.pcmag.com)—A leading publication that reviews computer and Internet products.

Pira International (www.pira.co.uk)—The prime business resource for printing, packaging, publishing, and paper industries.

Publist.com (www.publist.com)—Provides free information on familiar and hard-to-find publications throughout the world.

Type Directors Club (www.tdc.org)—An international organization for people interested in contemporary design and typography.

Ulrich's Periodicals Directory (www.ulrichsweb.com)—A resource for information on magazines, journals, newspapers, etc.

WritersNet (www.writers.net)—An Internet directory of writers, publishers, editors, and literary agents.

Periodicals

American Printer Magazine—29 N. Wacker Street, Chicago, IL 60606. (Monthly trade magazine for printers and graphic artists.) (http://americanprinter.com)

Communication Arts—110 Constitution Drive, Menlo Park, CA 94025. (Largest design magazine in the world; eight issues a year.) (www.commarts.com)

Printing Impressions—North American Publishing. 401 N. Broad Street, Philadelphia, PA 19108. (Monthly on printing practice, equipment, methods, trends.) (www.piworld.com)

Publishers Weekly—360 Park Avenue South, New York, NY 10010. (News and trends of the book industry, people, forecasts of new books.) (www.publishersweekly.com)

Quill & Quire—70 The Esplanade, Suite 210, Toronto, Canada M4M-2L9. (Monthly magazine of the Canadian book industry.) (www.quillandquire.com)

U & l c (Uppercase & Lowercase Magazine)—International Typeface Corp., 200 Ballardvale Street, Wilmington, MA 01887. (Monthly journal of graphic design.) (www.itcfonts.com)

Associations

The organizations listed below are some of the more important business or professional groups active in the book industry. Details about these organizations, and about many others, including specialized and local groups, are given in the annual *Literary Market Place* (Bowker).

Organizations concerned largely with standards and appreciation of the book arts.

American Institute of Graphic Arts (AIGA)(www.aiga.org)
American Printing History Association (APHA) (www.printinghistory.org)
Bookbuilders of Boston (www.bbboston.org)
Bookbuilders West—San Francisco (www.bookbuilders.org)
Chicago Book Clinic (www.chicagobookclinic.org)
The Typophiles (www.typophiles.org)

Business and technical associations

American Booksellers Association (www.bookweb.org)
American Paper Institute (www.api.org)
American Society of Media Photographers (ASMP) (www.asmp.org)
Association of American Publishers (www.publishers.org)
Association of American University Presses (www.aaupnet.org)
Association of Canadian Publishers—Toronto (www.publishers.ca)
Book Industry Study Group, Inc. (www.bisg.org)
Book Manufacturers' Institute (www.bmibooks.com)
Canadian Book Publishers Council—Toronto (www.pubcouncil.ca)
The Graphic Arts Information Network (www.gain.net)
Graphic Arts Technical Foundation (www.gatf.org)
Research and Engineering Council of Graphic Arts Industries (NAPL) (www.recouncil.org)
Technical Association of the Pulp and Paper Industry (www.tappi.org)
The World Paper Center (www.worldpapercenter.org)

Professional and craft associations

The Authors Guild (www.authorsguild.org)
Bookbinders Guild of New York (www.bbgny.org)
Copyright Society of the USA (www.csusa.org)
International Association of Printing House Craftsmen, Inc. (www.iaphc.org)
PEN American Center (www.pen.org)

Libraries

Any major library contains items of bookmaking interest. The following are some that have important specialized collections and/or exhibitions on the subject.

Book Club of California—San Francisco (www.bccbooks.org)
Borough of Manhattan Community College (www.bmcc.cuny.edu)
Brown University—Providence, RI (www.brown.edu)
Carnegie Mellon University—Pittsburgh (www.cmu.edu)
Columbia University—New York City (www.columbia.edu)
Dartmouth College—Hanover, NH (www.dartmouth.edu)
R. R. Donnelley & Sons Co.—Chicago (www.rrdonnelley.com)
Grolier Club—New York City (www.grolierclub.org)
Harvard University—Cambridge, MA (www.harvard.edu)
Henry E. Huntington Library—San Marino, CA (www.huntington.org)
Hunter College—New York City (www.library.hunter.cuny.edu)
Kansas State University—Emporia (www.ksu.edu)
Library of Congress—Washington, D.C. (www.loc.gov)
Museum of Fine Arts—Boston (www.mfa.org)
Newberry Library—Chicago (www.newberry.org)
The Pierpont Morgan Library—New York City (www.morganlibrary.org)
Princeton University Library—Princeton, NJ (www.princeton.edu)
Rochester Institute of Technology—Rochester, NY (www.rit.edu)
Smithsonian Institution—Washington, D.C. (www.si.edu)
Syracuse University—Syracuse, NY (www.syracuse.edu)
University of California—Berkeley (www.berkeley.edu)
University of California—Los Angeles (www.ucla.edu)
University of Indiana—Bloomington (www.indiana.edu)
University of Kentucky—Lexington (www.uky.edu)
University of Texas—Austin (www.utexas.edu)
University of Wyoming—Laramie (www.uwyo.edu)
Williams College—Williamstown, MA (www.williams.edu)
Yale University—New Haven, CT (www.yale.edu)

Publishing courses

Carnegie Mellon School of Design—Undergraduate Program in Communication Design (www.cmu.edu)
City College of New York—Certificate Program (www.ccny.cuny.edu)
Columbia University—Publishing Courses (www.columbia.edu)
George Washington University
Hofstra University—Undergraduate Program (www.hofstra.edu)
Hunter College
New School for Social Research
New York University—Graduate Program (Master of Science in

Publishing), Certificate Program, and Summer Institute (www.nyu.edu)

Pace University—Graduate Program (Master of Science in Publishing), Combined B.A. English/M.S. Publishing (5 year program), Certificate Program, and On-Line Certificate Program (www.pace.edu)

Parson's School of Design—Undergraduate Program in Communication Design (www.parsons.edu)

Printing Industries of Metropolitan New York

Rice University

Rochester Institute of Technology—The Digital Imaging & Publishing Technology Undergraduate Programs (www.rit.edu)

School of Visual Arts—Undergraduate Program in Graphic Design and Illustration (www.schoolofvisualarts.edu)

Simmons College

Stanford University—Professional Publishing Course (www.stanford.edu)

University of Chicago—Open Enrollment Seminars and Courses (www.uchicago.edu)

University of Denver—Summer Publishing Institute (www.du.edu)

University of Virginia—Certificate Program (www.virginia.edu)

Metric system conversion tables

Inch/centimeter conversion table

Inches		Centimeters	Inches		Centimeters
1/16	=	.1588	(1 *Foot*) 12	=	30.48
1/8	=	.3175	13	=	33.02
3/16	=	.4763	14	=	35.56
1/4	=	.635	15	=	38.10
5/16	=	.7938	16	=	40.64
3/8	=	.9525	17	=	43.18
7/16	=	1.1113	18	=	45.72
1/2	=	1.27	19	=	48.26
9/16	=	1.4288	20	=	50.80
5/8	=	1.5875	21	=	53.34
11/16	=	1.7463	22	=	55.88
3/4	=	1.905	23	=	58.42
13/16	=	2.0638	(2 *Feet*) 24	=	60.96
7/8	=	2.2225	25	=	63.50
15/16	=	2.3815	26	=	66.04
1	=	2.54	27	=	68.58
2	=	5.08	28	=	71.12
3	=	7.62	29	=	73.66
4	=	10.16	30	=	76.20
5	=	12.70	31	=	78.74
6	=	15.24	32	=	81.28
7	=	17.78	33	=	83.82
8	=	20.32	34	=	86.36
9	=	22.86	35	=	88.9
10	=	25.40	(1 *Yard*) 36	=	91.44
11	=	27.94	39.37	=	100.0 (1 *Meter*)

NB: Metric dimensions in the text are carried to a maximum of two digits following the decimal point.

Frequently used inch dimensions and sizes converted into centimeters

PAGE SIZES

Inches		*Centimeters*
5⅜ × 8	=	13.65 × 20.32
5⅝ × 8⅜	=	14.29 × 21.27
5½ × 8¼	=	13.97 × 20.96
6⅛ × 9¼	=	15.56 × 23.5
8½ × 11	=	21.59 × 27.94
9 × 12	=	22.86 × 30.48
12 × 18	=	30.48 × 45.72

SHEET SIZES

Inches		*Centimeters*
17½ × 22½	=	44.45 × 57.15
19 × 25	=	48.26 × 66.04
20 × 26	=	50.8 × 66.04
22½ × 35	=	57.15 × 88.9
25 × 38	=	63.5 × 96.52
30 × 44	=	76.20 × 111.76
35 × 45	=	88.9 × 114.3
38 × 50	=	96.52 × 127
41 × 61	=	104.14 × 154.94
44 × 66	=	111.76 × 167.64
50 × 76	=	127 × 193.04

Metric weight conversion and equivalents

Pounds	*Kilograms*	*Equivalents in grams for text paper weights*
1	.4536	
30	13.61	44.4
40	18.14	59.1
45	20.41	66.5
50	22.68	73.9
60	27.22	88.7
70	31.75	103.5
80	36.29	118.3
90	40.82	133.1
100	45.36	147.9
120	54.43	177.4
150	68.04	
300	136.08	

The column headed "kilograms" gives the actual *conversion* of avoirdupois weight to metric measure. (To convert kilograms to grams, move the decimal point three places to the right, i.e., 1 kilogram = 1000 grams.) The right-hand column gives the *equivalent* gram weights of paper measured by the metric system. These weights are based on one sheet one square meter in size (expressed as "gsm"). The pound weights in the left-hand column are U.S. basis weights for text papers (500 sheets of 25 x 38").

To convert U.S. text weight to gsm weight, multiply by 1.479
To convert U.S. cover weight to text weight, multiply by 1.827

U.S*/ Didot point equivalent table

U.S.		DIDOT	U.S.		DIDOT
1	=	.935	18	=	16.823
2	=	1.869	19	=	17.757
3	=	2.804	20	=	18.692
4	=	3.738	21	=	19.627
5	=	4.673	22	=	20.561
6	=	5.608	23	=	21.496
7	=	6.542	24	=	22.430
8	=	7.477	30	=	28.038
9	=	8.411	36	=	33.646
10	=	9.346	42	=	39.253
11	=	10.281	48	=	44.861
12	=	11.215	54	=	50.468
13	=	12.150	60	=	56.074
14	=	13.084	66	=	61.684
15	=	14.019	72	=	67.291
16	=	14.954	84	=	78.506
17	=	15.888	96	=	89.722

*The same point system is used by the United States and Great Britain.

Index

When technical terms first appear in the text they are italicized and are either defined or their meaning is made clear by the context.

C

J

U

V

W

BOOKMAKING: Editing/design/production

This book was designed by the author and
produced by Balance House, Ltd., Schuylerville, NY
Composition by Mulberry Tree Press, Inc., Northport NY
(www.mulberrytreepress.com) performed in QuarkXPress
The text type is 11 on 13 Electra x 24 picas
The display type is Electra and Arial Black
Printing and binding by QuebecorWorld Versailles, KY
The text paper is Frazier Q Liberty F cream vellum 60 lb.
Cover material: 12 Pt. Cover Stock
Back endpaper: Multicolor Antique Oriental Gold